STRATEGIC MANAGEMENT

CREATING COMPETITIVE ADVANTAGES

FIFTH CANADIAN EDITION

Gregory G. Dess
University of Texas at Dallas

Alan B. Eisner
Pace University

Gerry McNamara
Michigan State University

and

Theodore Peridis
Schulich School of Business, York University

David Weitzner
Schulich School of Business, York University

Mc
Graw
Hill
Education

Strategic Management: Creating Competitive Advantages
Fifth Canadian Edition

The Internet addresses listed in the text were accurate at the time of publication. The inclusion of a website does not indicate an endorsement by the authors or McGraw-Hill Ryerson, and McGraw-Hill Ryerson does not guarantee the accuracy of information presented at these sites.

ISBN-13: 978-1-25-927584-5
ISBN-10: 1-25-927584-1

1 2 3 4 5 6 7 8 9 0   WEB   20 19 18

Printed and bound in Canada.

Care has been taken to trace ownership of copyright material contained in this text; however, the publisher will welcome any information that enables it to rectify any reference or credit for subsequent editions.

Portfolio Director: *Nicole Meehan*
Portfolio Managers: *Kim Brewster and Kevin O'Hearn*
Senior Marketing Manager: *Cathie Lefebvre*
Content Developer: *Brianna McIlwain*
Senior Portfolio Associate: *Stephanie Giles*
Supervising Editor: *Jessica Barnoski*
Photo/Permissions Researcher: *Indu Arora*
Copy Editor: *Sarah Fulton*
Plant Production Coordinator: *Sarah Strynatka*
Manufacturing Production Coordinator: *Sheryl MacAdam*
Cover Design: *Lightbox Visual Communications, Inc.*
Interior Design: *Lightbox Visual Communications, Inc.*
Composition: *SPi Global*
Cover Image: *Board © Everythingpossible | Dreamstime.com; Tablet VICTOR DE SCHWANBERG*
Printer: *Webcom Ltd.*

Dedication

To my family, Margie and Taylor; my parents, Bill and Mary Dess; and Glenn F. Kirk.
–Greg

To my family, Helaine, Rachel, and Jacob.
–Alan

To my wonderful wife, Gaelen; my children, Megan and AJ; and my parents, Gene and Jane.
–Gerry

To all those that teach me something new every day. Thank you.
–Theo

To my family, Alana, Moishe, Shaindy, and Leah.
–David

About the Authors

Theodore Peridis is Professor and past Chair of the Policy and Strategic Management Area at the Schulich School of Business, York University; the Director of the Global Leadership Program; a Visiting Professor at IMD in Lausanne, Switzerland; and he spearheads Schulich's MBA program in India. His research and teaching interests lie in the areas of strategic management, strategic alliances, and mergers and acquisitions. He has published numerous articles in academic and practitioner journals, books, and book chapters and is frequently quoted in the business sections of the *Globe and Mail,* the *National Post,* the *Toronto Star,* on CBC television, and Global television, as well as in *Bloomberg* and *Executive.* He received his PhD from the Stern School of Business at New York University and has taught in Europe, North and South America, the Middle East, and Asia. Professor Peridis has received many academic and teaching awards and recognition for his work. Among them, he was named Schulich's "Best in Class" by *Canadian Business* magazine and "Professor of the Year" for the Kellogg-Schulich Executive MBA program.

David Weitzner is an Assistant Professor of Strategy at the Schulich School of Business, York University, where he is also the coordinator of the undergraduate Integrative Business Simulation program. His research and teaching interests are in strategic management, stakeholder theory, business ethics, and decision making under uncertainty. He has published numerous articles on these subjects in both academic journals and book chapters. He is an accomplished lecturer who has been nominated for the "Seymour Schulich Award for Teaching Excellence" in both the MBA and BBA programs every year he has taught, as well as for the 2010 "Best Lecturer in Ontario" award, sponsored by TVOntario. His research has been covered by the *Big Ideas* television program, as well as in the pages of the *National Post,* and the *Financial Post Business Magazine.* He received his PhD in Strategy, as well as his MBA, from the Schulich School of Business, and has an Honours BA in Philosophy from the University of Western Ontario.

Gregory G. Dess is the Andrew R. Cecil Endowed Chair in Management at the University of Texas at Dallas. His primary research interests are in strategic management, organization–environment relationships, and knowledge management. He has published numerous articles on these subjects in both academic and practitioner-oriented journals. He also serves on the editorial boards of a wide range of practitioner-oriented and academic journals. In August 2000, he was inducted into the *Academy of Management Journal*'s Hall of Fame as one of its charter members. Professor Dess has conducted executive programs in the United States, Europe, Africa, Hong Kong, and Australia. During 1994, he was a Fulbright Scholar in Oporto, Portugal. In 2009, he was the recipient of an honorary doctorate from the University of Bern (Switzerland). He received his PhD in Business Administration from the University of Washington (Seattle) and a BIE degree from Georgia Tech.

Alan B. Eisner is the Professor of Management and Graduate Management Program Chair at the Lubin School of Business, Pace University. He received his PhD in management from the Stern School of Business, New York University. His primary research interests are in strategic management, technology management, organizational learning, and managerial decision making. He has published research articles and cases in journals, including *Advances in Strategic Management, International Journal of Electronic Commerce, International Journal of Technology Management, American Business Review, Journal of Behavioral and Applied Management,* and *Journal of the International Academy for Case Studies.* He is the Associate Editor of the Case Association's peer reviewed journal, *The CASE Journal.*

Gerry McNamara is a Professor of Management at Michigan State University. He received his PhD from the Carlson School of Management at the University of Minnesota. His research focuses on strategic decision making, organizational risk taking, and mergers and acquisitions. His research has been published in numerous journals, including the *Academy of Management Journal, Strategic Management Journal, Organization Science, Organizational Behavior and Human Decision Processes, Journal of Management,* and *Journal of International Business Studies.* His research on mergers and acquisitions has been abstracted in the *New York Times, Bloomberg BusinessWeek, The Economist,* and *Financial Week.* He is currently an Associate Editor for the *Academy of Management Journal.*

Brief Contents

Contents

Preface

Introduction to the Fifth Canadian Edition

Welcome to the fifth Canadian edition of *Strategic Management: Creating Competitive Advantages*. We are pleased to further build on the overwhelmingly positive response to the previous editions, and we are most grateful for the constructive and extensive feedback we have received from the many instructors who took the time to review and comment on our work. Their input has been invaluable and has led to improvements that make this fifth edition even more relevant, comprehensive, and student-friendly, while retaining all the valuable elements of the previous editions.

The last few years have seen tremendous changes in the world of business, society, and economy with technology becoming even more ubiquitous in our lives, the developing world taking a central stage in global affairs, and the rebalancing of priorities in many countries of the old world across Europe and North America. Some companies have struggled to respond to these developments, and many others have thrived by harnessing the immense capabilities of technology and the people in their organization.

This textbook reflects the state-of-the-art thinking in the field of strategic management and brings into focus the Canadian business landscape and the uniqueness of our country's economic, political, historical, and social evolution. We strive to preserve tradition while introducing the topics that concern practicing managers today: shared value creation, globalization, disruptive technology, digital transformations, rapid innovation, ethics, corporate social responsibility, governance, and entrepreneurship.

Let us consider the obvious question: Why did we want to write this book? Why did we want to continue bringing it up to date and creating new editions? After all, there are already some good strategy textbooks on the market. Our personal reflections though, from our own classrooms continue to convince us that there is still a need for a book that students will find highly relevant and readable as well as rigorous. To this end, we endeavour both to cover all the traditional bases and to integrate throughout the book key themes that are vital to an understanding of strategic management.

To bring strategy concepts to life, we have incorporated hundreds of short examples from business practices to illustrate virtually every concept in the book, and we have provided dozens of "Strategy Spotlights"—more detailed examples of actual situations—to drive home the key points. We have also developed three separate chapters addressing timely subjects about which all business students should have a solid understanding: the role of intellectual assets and knowledge in value creation; the importance of disruptive technologies and the resulting digital business strategies that can create competitive advantages in the twenty-first century; and the value of fostering entrepreneurship in established organizations and new venture startups.

Most importantly, we consider and reflect on both the traditional bases and the key themes from a uniquely Canadian perspective. Because Canada is so close to the United States—geographically, economically, and technologically—we often forget how our own values and institutions give rise to very distinct and different organizations in the private, public, and not-for-profit sectors. We highlight such uniqueness by incorporating Canadian introductory cases in all chapters of the book, by emphasizing Canadian-centred Strategy Spotlights, and more than 120 Canadian examples throughout the text. Every page in this book celebrates Canadian management achievements, although, whenever appropriate, we also recognize weaknesses and situations where Canadian managers have fallen short of strategic management success.

On the basis of the many useful insights from our reviewers as well as reflection on the changes that have occurred in the field of strategic management and the "real world," we have introduced several improvements to the fifth Canadian edition. The book incorporates the uniqueness of Canada as a country and as a place where many diverse organizations operate and thrive, but it still retains all the elements that thousands of instructors and students of numerous strategic management courses found attractive in previous editions.

Superior Learning Solutions and Support

The McGraw-Hill Education team is ready to help you assess and integrate any of our products, technology, and services into your course for optimal teaching and learning performance. Whether it's helping your students improve their grades or putting your entire course online, the McGraw-Hill Education team is here to help you do it. Contact your Learning Solutions Consultant today to learn how to maximize all of McGraw-Hill Education's resources.

For more information, please visit us online: http://www.mheducation.ca/he/solutions.

Key Features of *Strategic Management,* Fifth Canadian Edition

Among the many exciting features the fifth Canadian edition offers, we highlight the following:

- Compelling chapters that cover all of the strategy bases and address contemporary topics. We divide the chapters logically into the traditional sequence: **strategic analysis, strategic formulation,** and **strategic implementation.** In addition, we provide chapters on timely topics, such as digital strategies, intellectual capital, knowledge management, and entrepreneurship. A supplementary appendix on **Analyzing Strategic Management Cases** is included for instructors and students who wish to cover this relevant material that provides insights on how to tackle a case and get the most out of this unique pedagogical opportunity. It not only contains the traditional treatment of the subject and instructions about analyzing cases, but it also offers suggestions on how to manage case analysis meetings and avoid distractions and time-wasting activities. Moreover, the section is augmented by two sub-appendices that include a comprehensive overview of financial ratio analysis that should be used in analyzing strategy cases, as well as a very informative source of databases, websites, and publications wherein students can find invaluable information about companies, industries, and the business environment. This last section covers both global and uniquely Canadian sources, and it represents a very comprehensive guide to a virtual library that students would find useful, not just for their strategy course but for all their academic courses, as well as in their subsequent work environment.

- We devote **equal attention to each of the three processes of strategic management.** Strategic analysis commonly receives the most exposure, reflecting on the traditional industrial organization roots of the field. Yet observing managers in real time and analyzing their ultimate successes has clearly demonstrated that more rests on how decisions are made and executed than on which models are employed in gathering and making sense of the pertinent information. We have striven to balance the coverage of strategic analysis and to give the same emphasis to strategic formulation and strategic implementation, allocating the 12 chapters of the textbook equally among the three strategic management processes.

- **Key strategic concepts** are introduced in a clear and concise manner and are followed by timely and interesting examples from management practice. These concepts include shared-value creation, SWOT analysis, five-forces analysis, the resource-based view of the firm, value-chain analysis, dynamic capabilities, competitive advantage, social network analysis, stakeholder theory, disruptive innovation, diversification and portfolio analysis, boundaryless and ambidextrous organizations, culture, leadership, ethical decision making, sustainability, creative intelligence, and corporate governance.

- Extensive use of **Strategy Spotlights** throughout the book provides relevant, interesting illustrations of actual management practices, boosts student interest, and reinforces student learning. We have provided a balance of Canadian and international spotlights to encourage students to think both locally and globally.

- The text provides a thorough grounding in ethical decision-making, shared-value creation, globalization, and disruptive technology. These concepts are central themes throughout the book and form the basis for many of the Strategy Spotlights in the chapters. We explore in detail the challenges associated with the new paradigms of managing for shared-value creation and multiple stakeholders, and how these approaches relate to classic analytical tools, such as value-chain analysis. We present an analytical model of disruptive innovation, the utility–identity curve that helps predict vulnerability to disruptive technologies, as well as a discussion on the threats to sustainability. We offer a model of four approaches to integrating ethics into strategic postures, as well as a detailed discussion on the role of the board in supporting an ethical orientation. In short, our textbook does not pay lip service to the emerging issues that are shaping the contemporary field of strategy but integrates these topics fully and with the same amount of rigour with which classic themes have been treated.

- Many of the key concepts are applied to startup firms and **smaller businesses.** This is particularly important, since many students plan to work in small and medium-sized enterprises (SMEs).

- Consistent chapter format and features **reinforce learning.** Each chapter begins with a list of the key learning objectives. The opening case describes a situation in which a company's performance was critically affected by specific strategy concepts and provides the foundation for the ensuing discussion. The learning objectives (LO) are identified throughout the text as they are developed and elaborated upon.

- At the end of each chapter, there are four different types of **questions and exercises** that help students assess their understanding and application of the material: summary review questions, experiential exercises, application questions and exercises, and ethics questions. We have also developed a feature that encourages students to reflect on their professional careers utilizing the concepts presented in each chapter.

- *Strategic Management* features the best chapter **teaching notes** available today. Rather than just summarize key points, we focus on "value-added" material to enhance the teaching and learning experiences. Each chapter includes literally dozens of questions to spur discussion as well as many examples from management practice to provide further illustrations of key points. We have worked hard to provide a complete package that will make classes relevant, rigorous, and rewarding for the instructors and the students.

- The fifth Canadian edition further builds on these features to enhance the value of our book for both instructors and students. The **opening cases** that lead off each of the chapters discuss well known Canadian organizations, such as Bell Media, the Hudson's Bay Company and the Canadian Broadcasting Corporation, as well as the inroads of American firms such as Target and Uber into the Canadian marketplace. We have also included as lead cases lesser known but equally impressive Canadian enterprises, such as Stantec, or smaller firms such as JoieFarm and Canopy Growth, and have discussed all cases within a Canadian and international context. Canadian organizations face unique challenges, operate within distinct structures and institutions, and employ management practices that reflect our unique history and vast geography. We feel it is often more instructive to analyze things that can go wrong when strategy concepts are not followed than to observe and exalt perfection; therefore, many of these mini-cases address flawed decisions and bad situations that have led to significant erosion of value and destruction of competitiveness.

- We incorporate the key role of **corporate governance** in the strategic management process, reflecting on the most controversial topic and stepping into the very heated debate regarding today's business organizations. Corporate governance issues manifest themselves very differently within the Canadian context due to our unique regulatory environment and the concentration of corporate ownership. Our discussion takes such uniqueness into consideration and highlights its advantages and disadvantages.

Acknowledgements

Strategic Management, Fifth Canadian Edition, represents far more than just the joint efforts of the six authors. Rather, it is the product of the collaborative inputs and contributions of many individuals. Moreover, it reflects the accumulated outcome of additions, developments, and improvements of the four prior editions.

During the preparation of the first Canadian edition, Neeraj Julka provided extensive research and spent hundreds of hours compiling the information for the Canadian examples, and JoAnne Stein and Clara Kan, administrative assistants at Schulich, worked diligently to make up for many missed deadlines and last-minute changes. The students of an experimental section of a strategic management course generated many suggestions for the second edition. Lindsay Hillcoat and Patricia Schindelheim did a splendid job in creating some of the most insightful and well-researched material for a number of introductory cases that enriched the third Canadian edition. Kelly Whitehead did an incredible job—going above and beyond the call of duty—compiling research and data for the introductory cases that made up the heart of the fourth Canadian edition. We were fortunate to have Kelly's involvement in the fifth edition as well and we benefited from her research skills and teaching experience to rebalance the coverage of a number of topics throughout the text and develop a brand new set of introductory cases.

We would be remiss if we did not acknowledge the ongoing and generous support of all our colleagues at the Schulich School of Business, whose encouragement and patience created an environment that allowed us to undertake and complete this project and, at the same time, protected us from the many distractions that crept up daily to derail the completion of each edition of the book.

The team at McGraw-Hill Ryerson, consisting of Human-Centered Design Manager Kim Brewster Kapp, Portfolio Manager Kevin O'Hearn, Content Developer Brianna McIlwain, Supervising Editor Jessica Barnoski, Permissions Researcher Indu Arora and the exceptional Copy Editor Sarah Fulton, should rightly be part of the author list, since they did some of the real work to bring this effort to fruition. Throughout the process they skillfully coached, motivated, guided, and, most of all, put up for much too long with not-so-reliable and quite mercurial authors, and made them look good.

Most importantly, we want to acknowledge our families. So frequently throughout this project, they had to be disappointed when yet one more weekend was taken from personal time together and given instead to pushing forward with the writing of "the book." To all, we are truly grateful.

Theo Peridis
David Weitzner
Toronto

A Guided Tour

Strategic Management: Creating Competitive Advantages, Fifth Canadian Edition, has been organized around the traditional sequence of topics and concepts in strategy, while bringing into focus the Canadian business landscape and the uniqueness of our country's economic, political, historical, and social evolution. We have also introduced timely topics that concern managers today, such as globalization, technology and innovation, ethics, corporate governance, and entrepreneurship.

Please take a moment to look through the elements below and better acquaint yourself with this text and its pedagogical features.

Chapter Map

The Chapter Map at the beginning of each section guides instructors and students through the organizational structure of the text.

Part One	STRATEGIC ANALYSIS

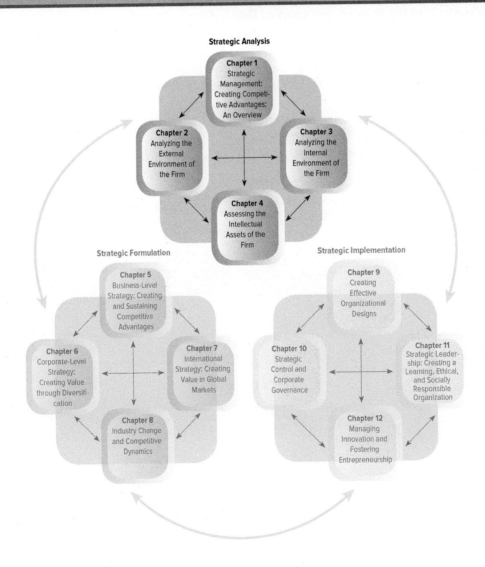

Learning Objectives

Each chapter begins with a set of Learning Objectives—key learning objectives inform students about what should be understood after reading the chapter. In addition, these Learning Objectives (LOs) are identified throughout the chapter as they are developed and elaborated on.

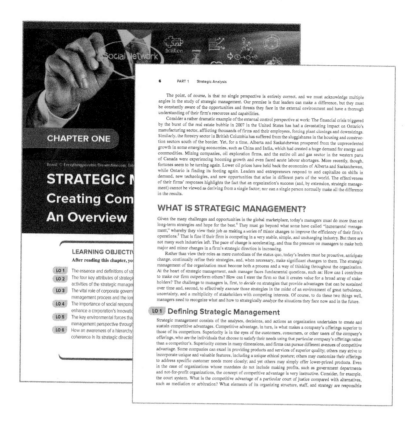

Chapter-Opening Cases

The opening case of each chapter describes a situation in which a company's performance was critically affected by specific strategy concepts and when appropriate, it asks "What went wrong?"

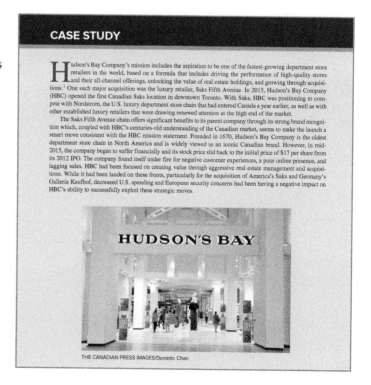

Strategy Spotlights

These detailed and varied examples provide relevant, interesting illustrations of actual management practices that help boost student interest and reinforce learning. Many of these Spotlights are new to the fifth Canadian edition and illustrate Canada's varied companies.

2.2 STRATEGY SPOTLIGHT

Spies in the Skies

"There is nothing new in companies spying on each other," according to Norman Inkster, a Royal Canadian Mounted Police (RCMP) chief from 1987 to 1994, who now runs a private investiga... today, it's about h... difficult to detect an...

A few years ago, the massive civil lawsuit over c... resort to in the name of c... opinion: Air Canada, long th... years the darling of investo...

In its statement of clai... Canada claimed that WestJ... "screen scraper," a progran... A standard airline perk allo... a personal code which allo... one (or something) had use... between May 2003 and M... the site was tapped 4,973... Airlines International emplo... was taken over by Air Car... Lafond admitted providing... but said that he did not thin... its own profits using the ille... in damages.

In response, WestJet... counter-suit, accused Air C... sent investigators to rifle th...

Eventually, the two si... unethical and unacceptabl... Air Canada's choice of char...

Sources: K. Macklem, "Spies Ir... 5/30/2006; *Financial Times*, J...

6.2 STRATEGY SPOTLIGHT

Canadian Tire: Growing to Stay on Top

Canadian Tire has expanded from its origins as a well-known retailer of automotive supplies to a broadly diversified mix of businesses under three very distinct subsidiaries: FGL Sports Ltd, Mark's, and Canadian Tire Financial Services. FGL Sports Ltd. owns brands such as Sport Chek, a chain of reputable sporting goods stores; Mark's sells fashionable clothing, uniforms, and work attire in some 380 stores across the country; and Canadian Tire Financial Services offers branded credit cards as well as lines of credit and personal loans. The activities of the three subsidiaries complement the flagship retail operations.

Ninety percent of Canadians are said to live within 15 minutes of one of Canadian Tire's 490 stores. Each store is independently owned by an associate dealer in an arrangement that requires commitment from dealers and gives them the autonomy to run their own stores the best they can and the right to veto decisions made by the centre that would not work in their local community.

While Canadian Tire enjoys enviable brand recognition and is considered a Canadian retail icon, it has also been under enormous pressure to remain competitive in the new retail environment. The company is struggling to figure out what it needs to do to remain an industry leader. In response to Amazon and other online retailers, Canadian Tire has been slow to roll out a new e-commerce website and to support the development of a stand-out digital retail strategy. Up against stiff competition in Home Depot and Walmart, the company still prides itself on its 30-million square feet of retail space and the fact that its printed flyers are the most read in Canada. These are laudable points of differentiation in the old competitive landscape, yet the two competitive giants continue to erode Canadian Tire's market share.

Without a doubt, Canadian Tire's diversification efforts have successfully strengthened the firm through a host of related business lines while reinforcing its core strategic strengths. But in the new retail landscape, will this be enough to assure that they continue to stay ahead of the competition?

Sources: Anonymous, Canada's Changing Retail Market, Industry Canada, 2 Aug 2013; Anonymous, Canadian Tire Corporation, Ltd, Reference for Business, 2014; Anonymous, Canadian Brands Top 40, Canadian Business, 2014; Nguyen, Linda, Canadian Tire to Launch E-Commerce Site, CTV News, 7 Nov. 2013; Offman, Craig, How to fix Canadian Tire, The Globe and Mail, 23 June 2011; the company's financial statements and website.

Chapter-Ending Material

The end-of-chapter material challenges students to apply the central strategy concepts emphasized in each chapter. This material includes **Summary Review Questions, Reflecting on Career Implications, Experiential Exercises, Application Questions and Exercises,** and **Ethics and Corporate Social Responsibility Questions.** Exercises blend online and reflective activities.

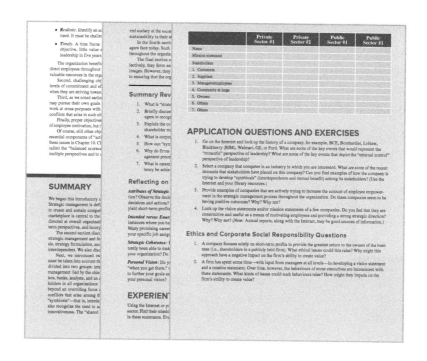

connect®2

Mc Graw Hill Education

The Complete Course Solution

We listened to educators from around the world, learned about their challenges, and created a whole new way to deliver a course.

Connect2 is a collaborative teaching and learning platform that includes an instructionally designed complete course framework of learning materials that is flexible and open for instructors to easily personalize, add their own content, or integrate with other tools and platforms.

- Save time and resources building and managing a course.
- Gain confidence knowing that each course framework is pedagogically sound.
- Help students master course content.
- Make smarter decisions by using real-time data to guide course design, content changes, and remediation.

MANAGE — Dynamic Curriculum Builder

Quickly and easily launch a complete course framework developed by instructional design experts. Each Connect2 course is a flexible foundation for instructors to build upon by adding their own content or drawing upon the wide repository of additional resources.

- Easily customize Connect2 by personalizing the course scope and sequence.
- Get access to a wide range of McGraw-Hill Education content within one powerful teaching and learning platform.
- Receive expert support and guidance on how best to utilize content to achieve a variety of teaching goals.

MASTER — Student Experience

Improve student performance with instructional alignment and leverage Connect2's carefully curated learning resources. Deliver required reading through Connect2's award-winning adaptive learning system.

- Teach at a higher level in class by helping students retain core concepts.
- Tailor in-class instruction based on student progress and engagement.
- Help focus students on the content they don't know so they can prioritize their study time.

MEASURE — Advanced Analytics

Collect, analyze and act upon class and individual student performance data. Make real-time course updates and teaching decisions backed by data.

- Visually explore class and student performance data.
- Easily identify key relationships between assignments and student performance.
- Maximize in-class time by using data to focus on areas where students need the most help.

Course Map
The flexible and customizable course map provides instructors full control over the pre-designed courses within Connect2. Instructors can easily add, delete, or rearrange content to adjust the course scope and sequence to their personal preferences.

Implementation Guide
Each Connect2 course includes a detailed implementation guide that provides guidance on what the course can do and how best to utilize course content based on individual teaching approaches.

Instructor Resources
A comprehensive collection of instructor resources are available within Connect2. Instructor Support and Seminar Materials provide additional exercises and activities to use for in-class discussion and teamwork.

For more information, please visit www.mheconnect2.com

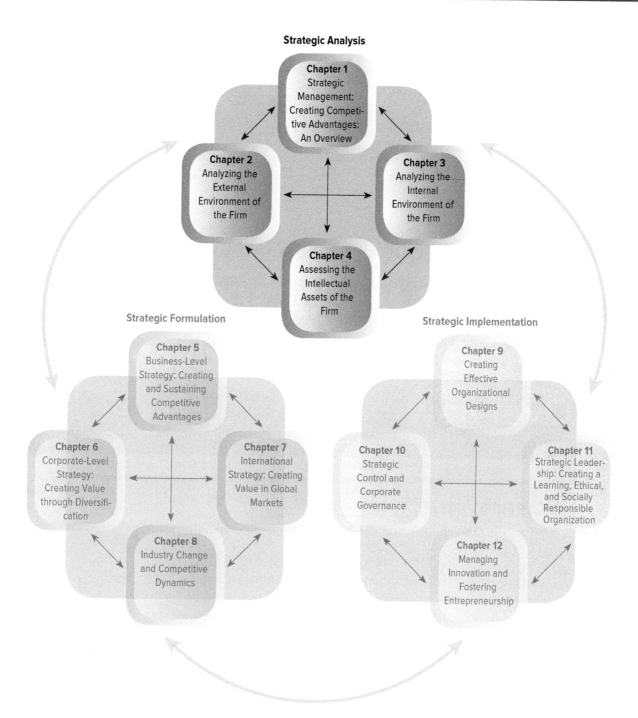

Strategic Analysis

Chapter 1
Strategic Management: Creating Competitive Advantages: An Overview

Chapter 2
Analyzing the External Environment of the Firm

Chapter 3
Analyzing the Internal Environment of the Firm

Chapter 4
Assessing the Intellectual Assets of the Firm

Strategic Formulation

Chapter 5
Business-Level Strategy: Creating and Sustaining Competitive Advantages

Chapter 6
Corporate-Level Strategy: Creating Value through Diversification

Chapter 7
International Strategy: Creating Value in Global Markets

Chapter 8
Industry Change and Competitive Dynamics

Strategic Implementation

Chapter 9
Creating Effective Organizational Designs

Chapter 10
Strategic Control and Corporate Governance

Chapter 11
Strategic Leadership: Creating a Learning, Ethical, and Socially Responsible Organization

Chapter 12
Managing Innovation and Fostering Entrepreneurship

CHAPTER ONE

STRATEGIC MANAGEMENT:
Creating Competitive Advantages:
An Overview

LEARNING OBJECTIVES

After reading this chapter, you should have a good understanding of:

LO 1 The essence and definitions of strategy, strategic management, and competitive advantage.

LO 2 The four key attributes of strategic management and the three principal and interrelated activities of the strategic management process.

LO 3 The vital role of corporate governance and stakeholder management in the strategic management process and the long-term success of all organizations.

LO 4 The importance of social responsibility, including environmental sustainability, and how it can enhance a corporation's innovation strategy.

LO 5 The key environmental forces that create unpredictable change and call for a greater strategic management perspective throughout the organization.

LO 6 How an awareness of a hierarchy of strategic goals can help an organization achieve coherence in its strategic direction.

Why do some firms outperform others? How is it that struggling firms can become stars while high flyers can become earthbound very rapidly? An organization's performance is directly linked to the choices its managers make about their strategy and to the organization's ability to execute this strategy successfully. Consider the following examples:

When Walmart announced its intentions to enter the Canadian retail scene in the late 1980s, most established companies—large and small alike—were justifiably concerned. Walmart, in a short 20 years, had risen to become the world's largest and most formidable retailer. Within a few years of entering the Canadian market, and as a direct result of Walmart's aggressive strategy, venerable Canadian retail icons, such as Eaton's, had disappeared. Some, such as Hudson's Bay Company, required extensive restructuring and, for a time, even fell onto the hands of foreign owners, whereas others, including Canadian Tire, were able to face the onslaught head-on and not only survived but thrived in the new competitive landscape. More recently, Target, Walmart's smaller and more nimble competitor in the U.S., failed miserably in its attempt to replicate its American success in the Canadian retail scene and had to beat a hasty and expensive retreat.

A second example, Bombardier, has been a Canadian success story of genius and serendipity. It was able to carve a unique place for itself in a range of industries, including aerospace, public transit, and outdoor recreational equipment. Across these industries, Bombardier has successfully competed against global powerhouses, such as Boeing, Airbus, Siemens, Honda, and Yamaha. Today, the firm enjoys enviable positions among the world's leaders in corporate and commercial jets, railroad equipment, automated people-movers, and regional transportation systems. Yet Bombardier is struggling to make inroads into the global market with its latest commercial jets, even though experts overwhelmingly endorse the technical and economic superiority of the C Series over the competing airliners, Boeing 737 and Airbus A320.

Let us look closer into the fortunes of one of Canada's corporate icons and how it is responding to the shifting competitive landscape.

CASE STUDY

Hudson's Bay Company's mission includes the aspiration to be one of the fastest-growing department store retailers in the world, based on a formula that includes driving the performance of high-quality stores and their all-channel offerings, unlocking the value of real estate holdings, and growing through acquisitions.[1] One such major acquisition was the luxury retailer, Saks Fifth Avenue. In 2015, Hudson's Bay Company (HBC) opened the first Canadian Saks location in downtown Toronto. With Saks, HBC was positioning to compete with Nordstrom, the U.S. luxury department store chain that had entered Canada a year earlier, as well as with other established luxury retailers that were drawing renewed attention at the high end of the market.

The Saks Fifth Avenue chain offers significant benefits to its parent company through its strong brand recognition which, coupled with HBC's centuries-old understanding of the Canadian market, seems to make the launch a smart move consistent with the HBC mission statement. Founded in 1670, Hudson's Bay Company is the oldest department store chain in North America and is widely viewed as an iconic Canadian brand. However, in mid-2015, the company began to suffer financially and its stock price slid back to the initial price of $17 per share from its 2012 IPO. The company found itself under fire for negative customer experiences, a poor online presence, and lagging sales. HBC had been focused on creating value through aggressive real estate management and acquisitions. While it had been lauded on these fronts, particularly for the acquisition of America's Saks and Germany's Galleria Kaufhof, decreased U.S. spending and European security concerns had been having a negative impact on HBC's ability to successfully exploit these strategic moves.

HBC needed to revisit their approach and recognize that appealing to a high-end market required a fresh, new look, strong e-commerce presence, and exceptional customer service. They continued to look to acquisitions

THE CANADIAN PRESS IMAGES/Dominic Chan

to solve these strategic challenges. In 2016, HBC acquired online shopping and lifestyle website Gilt in order to further build its growing digital business.

Meanwhile, the expanding presence in the Canadian market of luxury retail giant Nordstrom was creating some serious challenges for HBC. Nordstrom's goods are typically priced lower than those of Saks and other competitors in the luxury retail market and Nordstrom is renowned for its exemplary customer service. With the rising number of customer complaints at HBC due to poor in-store service and a floundering online presence, Nordstrom's strengths in these two arenas offers them a strong competitive advantage. In the luxury goods market, customers have grown to expect exceptional customer service and Nordstrom, unlike HBC, is well-positioned to meet those expectations. Furthermore, Nordstrom is praised for its digital strategy, having made significant investments to capture online sales through an easy-to-use platform.

Nordstrom's slow and steady expansion strategy, with no more than one store opening every six months, has allowed them to learn about and adapt to the Canadian market. Focused on providing the Nordstrom experience familiar to Canadian consumers who shop across the border, the chain learned from the mistakes of Target, which crashed and burned in the Canadian market after providing a sub-par customer experience and expanding too quickly on too grand of a scale.

Until recently, the Canadian luxury goods market was considered underserved, but in the past few years HBC and many of its major competitors have begun looking to expand. Holt Renfrew in 2014 committed to spending $300 million to open two new stores and revamp older locations. HBC announced plans to open up to seven Saks Fifth Avenue locations and up to 25 Saks Off Fifth locations. And with the expansion of Nordstrom there is no doubt that the market is becoming saturated and even more competitive. To stand out among rival firms, HBC needs to adapt its strategy to the changes in the market and to the threats posed by the expansion of Nordstrom. ■

Will HBC's unique history in Canada be sufficient to assure continued success in an increasingly competitive industry that is bound to continue getting disrupted? What steps should HBC take to better stand out and protect itself from the emerging threats of new players in the Canadian luxury retail industry? Are the pillars on which its mission currently rests robust enough to guide effective responses to new competitive challenges?

Answers to questions like these lie at the very heart of the discipline of strategic management and form the subject of this book. We define strategic management as the decisions and actions organizations undertake to create and sustain competitive advantages. It is these advantages over competitors that make firms unique and lead to organizational success over time. Senior management is at the centre of these decisions and actions; nonetheless, all managers in an organization contribute to the strategic management processes. Leaders, such as those at HBC, Bombardier, and Canadian Tire, face a large number of unusual challenges in today's global marketplace. In deciding how much credit (or blame) they deserve, one might consider the *romantic* view of leadership.[2] Here, the implicit assumption is that the leader is the key force in determining an organization's success—or the lack thereof. This view dominates business magazines such as *Fortune, Forbes, BusinessWeek,* and *Canadian Business,* in which the chief executive officer (CEO) is either lauded for his or her firm's success or chided for the organization's demise.

Consider, for example, the credit that has been bestowed on such leaders as Steve Jobs, Jack Welch, Andrew Grove, Isadore Sharpe, and Frank Stronach for the tremendous accomplishments of their firms Apple, General Electric, Intel, Four Seasons Hotels and Resorts, and Magna International, respectively. In the world of sports, managers and coaches, such as Scotty Bowman or Pat Quinn, get a lot of the credit for their teams' outstanding successes in the field and on the ice. Take, for example, Apple. Its phenomenal success has been attributed almost entirely to the late Steve Jobs, its legendary former CEO, who died in 2011. Apple's string of hit products, such as the iMac, iPhone, and iPad, are a testament to his genius for developing innovative, user-friendly, and aesthetically pleasing products. In addition to being a perfectionist in product design, Jobs was also a master showman with a cult following. During his tenure as CEO between 1997 and 2011, Apple's market value soared by over $300 billion. In the same vein, when in January 2009 he announced that he was taking a six-month medical leave, Apple's stock dropped 10 percent, wiping out approximately $5 billion in market value.

Conversely, when things do not go well, the failure of an organization can rightfully be attributed largely to its leader. After all, when Nortel, a telecommunications powerhouse that was at one point the most valuable public firm in Canada—worth over $400 billion and accounting for as much as 36 percent of the TSE 300—got into trouble, it was a series of senior management decisions that brought it close to bankruptcy and left it with few assets and a handful of employees.[3] In 1997, Nortel's CEO, John Roth, had embarked on an ambitious journey to transform the old telephone equipment manufacturer into an Internet powerhouse, producing fibre-optic networks and telecommunication systems for the digital age. In the process, Roth earned the "Outstanding CEO of the Year" award in 2000 and catapulted Nortel to the global stage alongside much larger competitors, such as Cisco, Siemens, and Alcatel. In his enthusiasm to pump up revenues, Roth aggressively courted huge contracts that left little margin for error. Such risks are generally inadvisable, especially when market and economic conditions get eroded. Nonetheless, Roth repeatedly ignored the warning signs and continued to make rosy forecasts. Profits and the firm's stock price eventually took a big hit when it became apparent that Nortel could not deliver on its promises. In the end, both Roth and his successor, Frank Dunn, a long-time Nortel employee and accountant who was brought in to clean up the mess, were disgraced. The Royal Canadian Mounted Police (RCMP) filed criminal charges against a number of senior management executives for manipulating the financial picture of the company to meet analysts' expectations and collect millions in bonuses. Nortel entered bankruptcy proceedings, sold most of its valuable assets, let go of thousands of employees, and recorded revenues of a meagre $28 million in 2010.

However, this is only part of the picture. Another perspective on leadership highlights *external control.* Here, rather than making the implicit assumption that the leader is the most important contributor in determining organizational performance, the focus is on external factors that may positively or negatively affect a firm's success. One does not have to look far to find support for this perspective. For example, IMAX rode the wave of digitization of a string of spectacular action movies coming out of Hollywood studios and the opening of the cinema market in China. Many others firms in this space, such as Sony and Dolby, have fared equally well. Nortel was negatively impacted by the worldwide recession that began in 2000, which drastically cut the demand for telecommunication equipment and services. Other rivals, such as Alcatel and Lucent Technologies, were also negatively affected. Furthermore, as we will see later on, other perspectives ascribe the success of an organization primarily to unique combinations of skills and resources that are rare and invaluable in creating the products and services offered to the market.

The point, of course, is that no single perspective is entirely correct, and we must acknowledge multiple angles in the study of strategic management. Our premise is that leaders can make a difference, but they must be constantly aware of the opportunities and threats they face in the external environment and have a thorough understanding of their firm's resources and capabilities.

Consider a rather dramatic example of the external control perspective at work: The financial crisis triggered by the burst of the real estate bubble in 2007 in the United States has had a devastating impact on Ontario's manufacturing sector, afflicting thousands of firms and their employees, forcing plant closings and downsizings. Similarly, the forestry sector in British Columbia has suffered from the sluggishness in the housing and construction sectors south of the border. Yet, for a time, Alberta and Saskatchewan prospered from the unprecedented growth in some emerging economies, such as China and India, which had created a huge demand for energy and commodities. Mining companies, oil exploration firms, and the entire oil and gas sector in the western parts of Canada were experiencing booming growth and even faced acute labour shortages. More recently, though, fortunes seem to be turning again. Lower oil prices have held back the economies of Alberta and Saskatchewan, while Ontario is finding its footing again. Leaders and entrepreneurs respond to and capitalize on shifts in demand, new technologies, and new opportunities that arise in different parts of the world. The effectiveness of their firms' responses highlights the fact that an organization's success (and, by extension, strategic management) cannot be viewed as deriving from a single factor; nor can a single person normally make all the difference in the results.

WHAT IS STRATEGIC MANAGEMENT?

Given the many challenges and opportunities in the global marketplace, today's managers must do more than set long-term strategies and hope for the best.[4] They must go beyond what some have called "incremental management," whereby they view their job as making a series of minor changes to improve the efficiency of their firm's operations.[5] That is fine if their firm is competing in a very stable, simple, and unchanging industry. But there are not many such industries left. The pace of change is accelerating, and thus the pressure on managers to make both major and minor changes in a firm's strategic direction is increasing.

Rather than view their roles as mere custodians of the status quo, today's leaders must be proactive, anticipate change, continually refine their strategies, and, when necessary, make significant changes to them. The strategic management of the organization must become both a process and a way of thinking throughout the organization. At the heart of strategic management, each manager faces fundamental questions, such as: How can I contribute to make our firm outperform others? How can I steer the firm so that it creates value for a broad array of stakeholders? The challenge to managers is, first, to *decide* on strategies that provide advantages that can be sustained over time and, second, to effectively *execute* those strategies in the midst of an environment of great turbulence, uncertainty, and a multiplicity of stakeholders with competing interests. Of course, to do these two things well, managers need to recognize what and how to strategically *analyze* the situations they face now and in the future.

LO 1 Defining Strategic Management

Strategic management consists of the analyses, decisions, and actions an organization undertakes to create and sustain competitive advantages. Competitive advantage, in turn, is what makes a company's offerings superior to those of its competitors. Superiority is in the eyes of the customers, consumers, or other users of the company's offerings, who are the individuals that choose to satisfy their needs using that particular company's offerings rather than a competitor's. Superiority comes in many dimensions, and firms can pursue different avenues of competitive advantage. Some companies can excel in providing products and services of superior quality; others may strive to incorporate unique and valuable features, including a unique ethical posture; others may customize their offerings to address specific customer needs more closely; and yet others may simply offer lower-priced products. Even in the case of organizations whose mandates do not include making profits, such as government departments and not-for-profit organizations, the concept of competitive advantage is very instructive. Consider, for example, the court system. What is the competitive advantage of a particular court of justice compared with alternatives, such as mediation or arbitration? What elements of its organizing structure, staff, and strategy are responsible for providing resolutions to disputes that are speedier, fairer, or perceived as more just than the alternatives? The answers are important because they can influence whether the populace will trust the court and whether government will then adequately fund it rather than divert resources to its "competitors."

The above definitions of strategic management and competitive advantage capture two main elements that go to the heart of the field of strategic management. First, the strategic management of an organization entails three ongoing processes: analysis, decisions, and actions. That is, strategic management is concerned with the analysis of strategic goals (vision, mission, and strategic objectives) along with the analysis of the internal and external environments of the organization. Next, leaders must make strategic decisions. These decisions, broadly speaking, address two basic questions: (1) Which industries should we compete in? and (2) How should we compete in those industries? These questions also often involve an organization's domestic operations as well as its international operations. And last are the actions that must be taken. Decisions, of course, are of little use unless they are acted on. Firms must take the necessary actions to implement their strategies. This requires leaders to allocate the necessary resources and to design the organization and align stakeholders to bring the intended strategies to reality. Strategic management is, therefore, a process and an evolving managerial responsibility that requires a great deal of interaction among these three subprocesses. It should be noted that although each of the three subprocesses can conceptually be viewed as occurring distinctly and in sequence, effective managers engage in all three, all the time. Their actions provide insights and experiences that further inform their understanding of what is going on in the marketplace as well as what their firm is capable of accomplishing. Such appreciation allows them to continuously refine or drastically change their adopted strategies.

Second, the essence of strategic management is the study of the reasons for some firms outperforming others.[6] Thus, managers need to determine how a firm is to compete so that it can obtain advantages that are sustainable over a long period. That means focusing on two fundamental questions:

1. *How should we compete to create competitive advantages in the marketplace?* Managers need to determine if their firm should position itself as the low-cost producer or develop products and services that are unique—which would enable the firm to charge premium prices—or some combination of both.

2. *How can we create competitive advantages in the marketplace that are unique and valuable but also difficult for competitors to copy or substitute?*[7] Managers need to make such advantages sustainable rather than temporary.[8]

Ideas that work are almost always immediately copied by rivals. In the 1980s, American Airlines tried to establish a competitive advantage by introducing the frequent flyer program. Within months, all major airlines in the United States, as well as in Canada and the rest of the world, had similar programs. Overnight, instead of being a competitive advantage, the frequent flyer program became a necessary tool for competitive parity. The challenge, therefore, is to create a competitive advantage that is sustainable.

Sustainable competitive advantage cannot be achieved through operational effectiveness alone.[9] Most of the popular management innovations of the last two decades—for example, total quality, just-in-time, benchmarking, business process re-engineering, and outsourcing—are about operational effectiveness. Operational effectiveness means performing similar activities better than rivals. Each of the management innovations just mentioned is important, but none leads to sustainable competitive advantage for the simple reason that competitors are also using them. Strategy is all about being different. Sustainable competitive advantage is possible only through performing different activities from rivals or performing similar activities in different ways. Some companies, such as Walmart, Canadian Tire, and IKEA have developed unique, internally consistent, and difficult-to-imitate activity systems that provide them with sustained competitive advantages. A company with a good strategy must make clear choices about what it wants to accomplish. Trying to copy what its rivals do eventually leads to mutually destructive price competition, not long-term advantage.

LO 2 The Four Key Attributes of Strategic Management

Four attributes distinguish strategic management from all other functions, such as accounting, finance, marketing, or operations, which are performed inside an organization.[10] Exhibit 1-1 states our definition of strategic management and identifies its four attributes.

> **EXHIBIT 1-1**   STRATEGIC MANAGEMENT CONCEPTS

Definition: Strategic management consists of the analysis, decisions, and actions an organization undertakes to create and sustain competitive advantages.

Key attributes of strategic management:

1. directs the organization toward overall goals and objectives
2. includes multiple stakeholders in decision making
3. incorporates short-term and long-term perspectives
4. recognizes trade-offs between efficiency and effectiveness

---

1. Strategic management is directed toward overall organizational goals and objectives. That is, effort must be directed at what is best for the total organization, not just a single functional area. Some authors have referred to this perspective as "organizational versus individual rationality."[11] In other words, what might look "rational" or most appropriate for one functional area may not be in the best interests of the entire firm. For example, operations may decide to schedule long production runs of similar products to lower unit costs. However, the standardized output may be counter to what the marketing department needs to appeal to a sophisticated and demanding target market. Similarly, research and development may "over engineer" a product to develop a far superior offering, but the design may make the product so expensive that market demand is minimal. In studying strategic management, we look at cases and strategic issues from the perspective of the whole organization rather than that of the functional areas in which students might have the most training and experience.

2. Strategic management includes multiple stakeholders in decision making. Managers must incorporate the often conflicting demands of a wide array of stakeholders when making decisions.[12] Stakeholders are individuals, groups, and organizations that have a "stake" in the success of the organization, including owners (shareholders in a publicly held corporation), employees, customers, suppliers, the community at large, and so on. Managers will not be successful if they continually focus on a single stakeholder. For example, if the overwhelming emphasis is on generating profits for the owners, employees may become alienated, customer service may suffer, and suppliers may become resentful of continual demands for pricing concessions. Many organizations have been able to satisfy multiple stakeholder needs simultaneously. In doing so, financial performance may actually increase because employees who are satisfied with their jobs make a greater effort to enhance customer satisfaction, leading to higher profits. Furthermore, effective stakeholder management can lead to new possibilities for innovation as a firm's stakeholders are more willing to share sensitive information when they perceive the firm as a trustworthy partner.

3. Strategic management incorporates both short-term and long-term perspectives. Peter Senge, a leading strategic management author at the Massachusetts Institute of Technology (MIT), has referred to this need as a "creative tension."[13] That is, managers must maintain a vision for the future of the organization as well as a focus on its present operating needs. However, financial markets can exert significant pressure on executives to meet short-term performance targets. Moreover, even though managers throughout the organization should maintain a strategic management perspective and assess how their actions impact the overall attainment of organizational objectives, lower-level management frequently has a narrow, "silo," short-term viewpoint. For example, laying off several valuable employees may help cut costs and improve profits in the short term, but the long-term implications for employee morale and customer relationships may suffer—leading to subsequent performance declines.[14]

4. Strategic management involves the recognition of trade-offs between effectiveness and efficiency. Closely related to the third point above, this recognition means awareness of the need to strive to act both effectively and efficiently as an organization. Some authors have referred to this as the difference between "doing the right thing" (effectiveness) and "doing things right" (efficiency).[15] Even though managers are required to allocate and use resources wisely, they must still direct their efforts toward the attainment of

overall organizational objectives. Managers who are totally focused on meeting short-term budgets and targets may fail to attain the broader goals of the organization. Consider the following anecdote told by Norman Augustine, formerly CEO of the defence industry giant Martin Marietta (now Lockheed Martin):

> I am reminded of an article I once read in a British newspaper, which described a problem with the local bus service between the towns of Bagnall and Greenfields. It seemed that, to the great annoyance of customers, drivers had been passing long queues of would-be passengers with a smile and a wave of the hand. This practice was, however, clarified by a bus company official who explained, "It is impossible for the drivers to keep their timetables if they must stop for passengers."[16]

Clearly, the drivers who were trying to stay on schedule had ignored the overall mission. As Augustine noted, "Impeccable logic, but something seems to be missing!"

Successful managers must make many trade-offs. It is central to the practice of strategic management. At times, managers must focus on the short term and efficiency; at other times, the emphasis is on the long term and expanding a firm's product-market scope to anticipate opportunities in the competitive environment. For example, consider Kevin Sharer's perspective. Sharer is the retired CEO of the giant $15 billion biotechnology firm, Amgen. In a 2004 interview he advised the following:

> A CEO must always be switching between different altitudes—tasks of different levels of abstraction and specificity. At the highest altitude, you're asking the big questions: What are the company's mission and strategy? Do people understand and believe in these aims? Are decisions consistent with them? At the lowest altitude, you're looking at on-the-ground operations: Did we make that sale? What was the yield on that last lot in the factory? How many days of inventory do we have for a particular drug? And then there's everything in between: How many chemists do we need to hire this quarter? What should we pay for a small biotech company that has a promising new drug? Is our production capacity adequate to roll out a product in a new market?[17]

Sharer's description of juggling tasks of different "altitudes" relates to **ambidexterity,** that is, a manager's capacity to both align resources to take advantage of existing product markets as well as proactively explore new opportunities; it is viewed as a critical managerial quality of success.[18]

THE STRATEGIC MANAGEMENT PROCESS

We have identified three ongoing processes—analysis, decisions, and actions—that are central to strategic management. In practice these three processes, often referred to as *strategy analysis, strategy formulation,* and *strategy implementation,* are highly interdependent. Moreover, these three processes do not take place in a sequential fashion.

Henry Mintzberg, an influential management scholar at McGill University, argues that the concept of strategic management as a process in which analysis is followed by optimal decisions and their subsequent meticulous implementation neither describes the strategic management process accurately nor prescribes ideal practice.[19] The business environment, he argues, is far from predictable, constraining the ability for analysis. Moreover, decisions in an organization are seldom based on optimal rationality alone, given the political processes that occur in all organizations.

Mintzberg proposed an alternative model of strategy development. As depicted in Exhibit 1-2, decisions deriving from analysis constitute the *intended* strategy of the firm. For a variety of reasons, the intended strategy rarely survives in its original form. On the one hand, unforeseen environmental developments, unanticipated resource constraints, or changes in managerial preferences may result in at least some parts of the intended strategy remaining *unrealized.* On the other hand, good managers will want to take advantage of a new opportunity presented by the environment, even if it was not part of the original set of intentions. New federal and provincial legislation promoting renewable energy has attracted many established corporations, such as Siemens, General Electric, and Suncor, as well as startups, to direct their attention and re-deploy their research and development (R&D) capabilities to develop new technologies and "green" solutions to environmental challenges. Such strategic moves do not necessarily constitute components of the original strategies of firms, and can be opportunistic responses to unfolding events, but they are certainly components of *emergent* strategies. The final *realized* strategy of any firm is a combination of deliberate and emergent strategies.

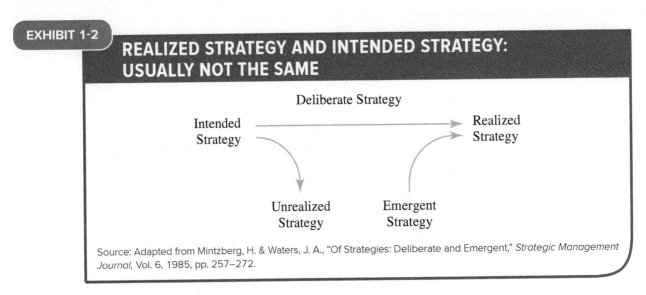

EXHIBIT 1-2

REALIZED STRATEGY AND INTENDED STRATEGY: USUALLY NOT THE SAME

Source: Adapted from Mintzberg, H. & Waters, J. A., "Of Strategies: Deliberate and Emergent," *Strategic Management Journal,* Vol. 6, 1985, pp. 257–272.

Addressing each of the three strategic management processes separately does, nevertheless, serve some useful pedagogical purposes. It allows us to develop a better appreciation of what each entails and to consider the concepts, frameworks, and tools that can be used by managers who engage in each. It serves to demonstrate that effective strategic management poses complex challenges and that sometimes things can go wrong.

Exhibit 1-3 depicts the strategic management process (or at least an unambiguous and systematic reflection of it) and indicates how it ties into the chapters in the book. Consistent with our discussion above, we use two-way arrows to convey the interactive nature of the processes. Next, we briefly elaborate on what each of the three strategic management processes entails.

Strategy Analysis

Strategy analysis may be considered the starting point of the strategic management process. It consists of the "advance work" that must be done to effectively formulate and implement strategies. Analysis is about understanding what is going on, why situations have unfolded in particular ways, what issues the organization faces at present and in the future, whether and why the organization has been successful, and what others may be doing and why. Most importantly, analysis is about making sense of the elements and the interactions that formed the organization's world in the past and will continue to be of importance in the future.

EXHIBIT 1-3

THE STRATEGIC MANAGEMENT PROCESS

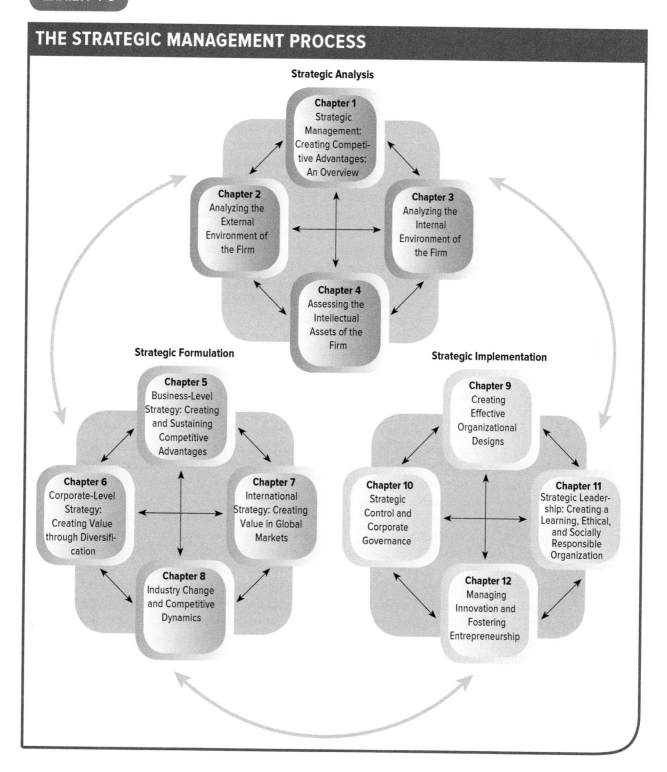

Strategic Analysis

Chapter 1
Strategic Management: Creating Competitive Advantages: An Overview

Chapter 2
Analyzing the External Environment of the Firm

Chapter 3
Analyzing the Internal Environment of the Firm

Chapter 4
Assessing the Intellectual Assets of the Firm

Strategic Formulation

Chapter 5
Business-Level Strategy: Creating and Sustaining Competitive Advantages

Chapter 6
Corporate-Level Strategy: Creating Value through Diversification

Chapter 7
International Strategy: Creating Value in Global Markets

Chapter 8
Industry Change and Competitive Dynamics

Strategic Implementation

Chapter 9
Creating Effective Organizational Designs

Chapter 10
Strategic Control and Corporate Governance

Chapter 11
Strategic Leadership: Creating a Learning, Ethical, and Socially Responsible Organization

Chapter 12
Managing Innovation and Fostering Entrepreneurship

Strategy analysis starts with an appreciation of the organization's goals and objectives. Various stakeholders have different expectations and aspirations with respect to what an organization should stand for and what it should strive to accomplish. Analysis of organizational goals and objectives (Chapter 1) addresses how organizations reconcile those divergent positions and why organizations must have clearly articulated goals and objectives if they are to channel the efforts of individuals throughout the organization toward common ends. Goals and objectives also provide a means of allocating resources effectively. A firm's vision, mission, and strategic objectives form a hierarchy of goals that range from broad statements of intent and bases for competitive advantage to specific, measurable strategic objectives.

Next, strategy analysis entails an in-depth understanding of the external environment (Chapter 2). Managers monitor and scan the environment and also analyze competitors. Such information is critical in determining the opportunities and threats in the external environment. Two complementary frameworks are typically employed to provide the structure for analysis of the external environment—one capturing the general environment and the other the industry environment, which encompasses competitors, suppliers, and customers. Strategy analysis of the external environment relies critically on extensive use of tools developed in diverse fields, such as macroeconomics and microeconomics, political science, marketing, consumer behaviour, operations management, international business, sociology, and psychology. These tools help managers make sense of the world that surrounds them.

In addition to the external environment, strategy analysis must focus on a firm's internal environment (Chapter 3). What does the firm do? How does it create the products and services it brings to the market? Why does it do things a certain way? Such analysis helps identify both strengths and weaknesses that can, in part, determine how well a firm will succeed in an industry. Analyzing the strengths and relationships among the activities that constitute a firm's value chain (such as operations, marketing and sales, and human resource management) can be a means of uncovering potential sources of competitive advantage for the firm.

Probably the most important elements within an organization that contribute vitally to its success are the knowledge and skills of its workers, as well as its intellectual assets, such as technology, patents, and trademarks (Chapter 4). In addition to human capital, we discuss how well the organization creates networks and relationships among its employees, customers, suppliers, and alliance partners.

Strategy Formulation

An organization makes decisions about the strategies it will pursue and the bases for the competitive advantage that it will attempt to build. Its overall strategy is developed at several levels. First, business-level strategy addresses the issue of how to compete in given business environments to attain competitive advantage (Chapter 5). How firms compete and outperform their rivals and how they achieve and sustain competitive advantages form the essence of strategic management. Successful firms strive to develop bases for competitive advantage. These can be achieved through cost leadership, by differentiation, and by focusing on a narrow or industry-wide market segment. Some advantages can be more sustainable over time, and a firm's business-level strategy changes with the industry life cycle—that is, the stages of introduction, growth, maturity, and decline.

Second, corporate-level strategy focuses on two issues: (1) which businesses to compete in and (2) how businesses can be managed to achieve synergy—the creation of more value by working together rather than operating as stand-alone businesses (Chapter 6). Firms consider the relative advantages and disadvantages of pursuing strategies of related or unrelated diversification and make choices regarding the various means they can employ to diversify—internal development, mergers and acquisitions, and joint ventures and strategic alliances.

Third, a firm must determine the best method for developing international strategies as it ventures beyond its national boundaries (Chapter 7). When firms expand their scope of operations to include foreign markets, they encounter many opportunities and potential pitfalls. They must decide not only on the most appropriate entry strategy but also how they will go about attaining competitive advantages in international markets. Many successful international firms have been able to attain both lower costs and higher levels of differentiated products and services through the successful implementation of a "transnational strategy."

Finally, entrepreneurship addresses how individuals recognize new business opportunities, create new business ventures, identify effective strategies, and develop entrepreneurial leadership skills to successfully launch and sustain these enterprises (Chapter 8). In the process, they frequently disrupt existing market structures and introduce new business models that better respond to market needs.

Strategy Implementation

Effective strategies are of no value if they are not properly executed. Managers are called to take action and coordinate the activities within their organization to help guide the implementation of the chosen strategies. Moreover, managers align their firm's activities with those of their suppliers, customers, and alliance partners in ways that will achieve desirable outcomes. Strategy implementation encompasses the systems, structures, attitudes, and behaviours that make things happen within organizations.

First, strategy implementation calls on firms to adopt organizational structures and designs that are consistent with their strategies (Chapter 9). Organizational structures define how the various units within an organization relate and interact and how information flows across them. In addition, they establish the appropriate organizational boundaries. These should be sufficiently flexible and permeable to incorporate alliance partners and capitalize on the capabilities of other organizations.

Firms, especially the modern complex public corporations of today, need to have in place an effective corporate governance structure that aligns the interests of managers with those of the owners of the firm as well as other stakeholders (Chapter 10). Corporate governance involves not only the board of directors and actively engaged shareholders but also proper managerial reward and incentive systems, along with the strategic control mechanisms that set boundaries on managers' behaviours.

Strategy implementation is, in large part, about leadership (Chapter 11). Today's managers are expected to do much more than manage their troops by telling them what to do. They are called to provide a vision, inspire, and lead ethically and with integrity. Moreover, they recognize that today's successes do not guarantee success in the future. Firms must continuously improve and find new ways to grow and renew (Chapter 12). Instilling an entrepreneurial attitude and fostering experimentation throughout the organization help to identify new opportunities even as specific strategies that will enhance the firm's innovative capacity are being formulated.

LO 3 THE ROLE OF CORPORATE GOVERNANCE AND STAKEHOLDER MANAGEMENT

Most business enterprises that employ more than a few dozen people are organized as corporations. According to financial theory, the overall purpose of a corporation is to maximize shareholder value, which is reflected in long-term returns to the owners or shareholders. When considering not-for-profit organizations, nongovernmental organizations (NGOs), and entities in the public sector, the absence of direct ownership might, on the surface, complicate things. Yet, even there, one may ask: Who is really responsible for defining and fulfilling the organization's purpose? Corporate governance is frequently seen as the vehicle to carry out this responsibility. Some have defined corporate governance as "the relationship among various participants in determining the direction and performance of corporations. The primary participants are (1) shareholders, (2) the management (led by the chief executive officer), and (3) the board of directors."[20]

The board of directors (BoD) consists of the elected representatives of shareholders. They are charged with overseeing management and ensuring that the interests and motives of management are aligned with those of the owners (i.e., shareholders). In many cases, the BoD is diligent in fulfilling its purpose. For example, Intel Corporation, the giant $36-billion maker of microprocessor chips, is widely recognized as an excellent example of sound governance practices. Its BoD has established guidelines to ensure that its members are independent of the executive management team, and it provides detailed procedures for formal evaluations of both directors and the firm's top officers.[21]

Recently, there has been much criticism, as well as cynicism, from both the general public and the business media about poor performance in management and the BoDs of large corporations. We only have to look at the scandals at firms such as Arthur Andersen, Best Buy, Olympus, Enron, Tyco, and ImClone Systems. Such malfeasance has led to an erosion of the public's trust in corporations. For example, according to the 2014 CNBC/Burson-Marsteller Corporation Perception Indicator, a global survey of 25,000 individuals, only 52 percent of the public in developed economies has a favourable view of corporations.[22] Forty-five percent feel corporations have "too much influence over the government." More than half of the U.S. public take the view that "strong and influential" corporations are "bad" even if they are promoting innovation and growth, and only 9 percent say corporate CEOs are "among the most respected" in society. Perhaps it will be a bit reassuring to big business that a 2013 poll revealed that the public's view of the U.S. Congress was significantly less positive than its view of root canals, NFL replacement referees, colonoscopies, France, and even cockroaches!

One area in which public anger is most pronounced is the excessive compensation paid to the top executives of well-known firms. It is now clear that much of the bonus pay awarded to executives on Wall Street in recent years was richly undeserved.[23] In the three years that led up to the collapse of seven big financial institutions in 2008, their chief executives received over $80 million in performance bonuses and raked in an additional $210 million by cashing in stock options and collecting on severance pay packages. And things did not stop there. In 2011, financial stocks at 35 of the 50 largest financial companies fell. The sector lost 17 percent—compared to flat performance for the Standard & Poor's 500. However, even as the sector struggled, the average pay of finance company CEOs rose 20.4 percent. For example, JPMorgan CEO Jamie Dimon was the highest-paid banker with $23.1 million in compensation—an 11 percent increase from the previous year. The firm's shareholders didn't do as well—JPMorgan stock fell 20 percent.[24]

Of course, excessive executive pay is not restricted to financial institutions. Consider Staples, whose earnings fell by 43 percent in the first quarter of 2014 after a rough 2013 during which operating income dropped by double digits. As expected, Staples' earnings weren't high enough for top executives to receive incentive pay. But the board decided to approve a "reinvention cash award" to motivate and retain the company's already well-paid executives. As a result, CEO Ron Sargent was given $300,000 in cash on top of his $10.8 million total compensation package—which had already increased 40 percent in 2013. (Shareholders, meanwhile, had lost 25 percent over the year.) As noted by Will Becker, an analyst with Behind the Numbers, "This is the worst kind of bonus, as the compensation committee essentially changed the rules of the game after the game had already been played."[25]

Despite the primacy of generating shareholder value, managers who focus solely on the interests of the owners of the business will often make poor decisions that lead to negative, unanticipated outcomes. For example, mass layoffs to increase profits, ignoring issues related to conservation of the natural environment in order to save money, and exerting undue pressure on suppliers to lower prices can certainly harm a firm in the long run by leading to negative outcomes, including alienated employees, increased governmental oversight and fines, and disloyal suppliers.

In addition to *shareholders*, there are other *stakeholders* that must be explicitly taken into account in the strategic management process.[26] A stakeholder can be defined as an individual or a group, inside or outside the company, that has an interest in an organization's actions and performance. Stakeholders are affected by what an organization does and can influence, to varying degrees, its performance. Although companies typically have different stakeholders, each generally has five prominent stakeholder groups: customers, employees, suppliers (of goods, services, and capital), the community at large, and, of course, the owners.[27]

In essence, stakeholders have a "stake" in how a company competes, how it conducts its affairs, how it uses its own as well as the public's resources, and how it performs. Some stakeholders may be able to exert direct influence on those decisions, whereas others may only be passive recipients of the consequences. Exhibit 1-4 provides a list of major stakeholder groups and their claims on a company.

EXHIBIT 1-4 AN ORGANIZATION'S KEY STAKEHOLDERS AND THEIR CLAIMS

Stakeholder Group	Nature of Claims
Shareholders	Returns, dividends, capital appreciation
Employees	Wages, benefits, job security, safe and healthy work environment, career opportunities
Suppliers	Payment on time, assurance of continuing relationship
Creditors	Payment of interest, repayment of capital
Customers	Value, warranties, honesty
Government	Taxes, compliance with regulations, employment opportunities for citizens
Community	Social involvement, financial contributions to the local economy and to charities, not polluting the environment, employment opportunities for the community's members

Consider, for example, the Canadian public health system and the organizations within it, such as hospitals, clinics, ethical and generic pharmaceutical manufacturers, pharmacies, individual doctors and their professional associations, insurance companies, patients and their families, patient advocacy groups, and the government and taxpayers who are paying for it all. Each one of those organizations has to consider multiple stakeholders in making critical decisions because each decision has the potential to seriously affect the well-being of a number of individuals and groups. In turn, each stakeholder will attempt to exert whatever degree of influence it can to direct the decisions to serve its own interests.

Alternative Perspectives of Stakeholder Management

The role of stakeholder management in the strategic management process can be considered under different perspectives.[28] In one view, the role of management is to consider various stakeholders to be competing for the attention and resources of the organization. The gain of one individual or group is the loss of another individual or group. That is, employees want higher wages (which drive down profits); suppliers want higher prices for their inputs and slower, more flexible delivery times (which drive up costs); customers want fast deliveries and higher quality (which drive up costs); the community at large wants charitable contributions (which take money away from profits or other uses); and so on. This zero-sum thinking is rooted, in part, in the traditional conflict between workers and management, limited resources, and competing priorities of diverse stakeholders. This thinking typically subscribes to the supremacy of shareholders as the residual claimants of a corporation's wealth. Arguably, all other stakeholders have explicit or implicit contracts that management is expected to fulfil, whether they are employment contracts, supplier contracts, community citizenship, tax obligations, or regulatory requirements.[29] Management's obligations to satisfy the demands that arise from these contracts constrain the firm's ability to deploy resources available to it in other ways; however, the cooperation of stakeholders is necessary for the firm to be able to undertake its business activities. In return for their cooperation, stakeholders receive payoffs, monetary or otherwise; a firm that is able to produce returns that exceed these payoffs would also be able to provide returns to its owners, the residual claimants. This perspective is clean in that each stakeholder has a simple objective function and a firm can view stakeholders as direct and independent contractors who control the resources the firm needs and are willing to make transactions in which resources are exchanged for specific returns. The complexity of enlisting and fulfilling all these contracts, however, should not be underestimated since, frequently, neither the demands nor the obligations are explicit, and nor do they necessarily line up in a neat sequence. Nonetheless, the residual claimants are the ones who matter most, whereas all other stakeholders are only entitled to what has been promised to them in their contracts.

Although some conflicting demands will always be placed on the organization by its various stakeholders, there is value in exploring how the organization can achieve better results through *stakeholder symbiosis,* a concept which recognizes that stakeholders are dependent on each other for their success and well-being.[30] That is, managers acknowledge the interdependence among employees, suppliers, customers, shareholders, and the community at large, and incorporate this understanding in their decisions. At one point, Sears, for example, had developed a sophisticated quantitative model that captured the concept of symbiosis. With this model, Sears could predict the relationship between employee satisfaction, customer satisfaction, and financial results.[31] The Sears model found that a 5-percent improvement in employee attitudes led to a 1.3-percent improvement in customer satisfaction, which, in turn, would drive a 0.5-percent improvement in revenue. Moreover, some would argue that shareholders of public corporations are investors, not owners—financiers who do assume risk but are no different from other stakeholders. Indeed, shareholders may lose their invested capital if things go bad with the firm; however, managers, employees, and the community assume even higher levels of risk, such as losing their only source of income, their well-being, their natural environment, and their safety and health.

Recently, we have also witnessed a new phenomenon, aptly labelled *crowd sourcing,* in which a firm finds ways for some of its stakeholders to depart from their traditional fixed roles and play multiple roles, further elevating their interdependence with the firm and other stakeholders.[32] Of course, many years ago customers unwittingly became their own tellers when banks introduced Automatic Teller Machines (ATMs). But with the power of the Internet, the phenomenon has proliferated. Amazon, for instance, has successfully convinced its customers to write online reviews to help it create additional value for other customers. Wikipedia is written and continuously updated by thousands of its own users. The Linux operating system is developed, fixed, and customized by an online open-source community. Intuit has created online customer support forums where customers soliciting advice and asking technical questions about Quicken, the leading personal finance software, receive responses from fellow customers, not from Intuit employees. Needless to say, the claims of such stakeholders do not fall neatly within the categories we have listed in Exhibit 1.4. Contributors to crowdsourcing, who might also be customers of the same firm, may have expectations of loyalty, acknowledgement of contribution, respect, or payoffs that go beyond simply receiving value for their purchases.

LO 4 Social Responsibility: Moving beyond the Immediate Stakeholders

Increasingly, organizations are expected to acknowledge and act on the interests and demands of stakeholders, such as citizens and society in general, which lie beyond their immediate constituencies—customers, owners, suppliers, and employees. *Corporate social responsibility (CSR)* calls on firms to consider the changing relationships among business, society, and government and to act in a socially responsible manner.[33]

Social responsibility is the expectation that businesses or individuals will strive to improve the overall welfare of society.[34] From the perspective of a business, this means that managers must take active steps to make society better by virtue of the business being in existence. As social norms and values change, a corporation's actions that constitute socially responsible behaviour tend to change as well. In the 1970s, affirmative action was a high priority, and firms responded. During the 1990s, the public became increasingly concerned about the quality of the physical environment. Many firms responded by engaging in recycling and reducing waste. Today, in the wake of heightened awareness about climate change, a new kind of priority has arisen: the need to be responsible about and protect the environment, reduce emissions, and battle global warming.

Demands for greater corporate social responsibility have accelerated. They rise from many quarters, including corporate critics, social investors, activists, and customers, who increasingly assess a firm's corporate responsibility when making purchasing decisions. Such demands go beyond product and service quality and embrace a focus on such issues as labour practices, environmental sustainability, financial and accounting reporting, procurement, and environmental practices.[35]

The Concept of "Shared Value"

Capitalism is typically viewed as an unparalleled vehicle for meeting human needs, improving efficiency, creating jobs, and building wealth.[36] However, a narrow conceptualization of capitalism has prevented business from harnessing its full potential to meet society's broader challenges. The opportunities have always been there but have been overlooked. It is increasingly acknowledged that businesses acting as businesses, not as charitable donors, are the most powerful force for addressing the pressing issues that we face. A new conception of capitalism redefines the purpose of the corporation as creating *shared value,* not just profit per se. This will drive the next wave of innovation and productivity growth in the global economy.

Shared value can be defined as policies and operating practices that enhance the competitiveness of a company and simultaneously advancing the economic and social conditions in which it operates. Shared value creation focuses on identifying and expanding the connections between societal and economic progress.

Shared value is not about personal values. Nor is it about "sharing" the value created by firms—a redistribution approach. Rather, it is about expanding the total pool of economic and social value. A good example of this difference can be seen in the fair trade movement. Fair trade aims to increase the proportion of revenue that goes to poor farmers by paying them higher prices for their crops. Although this may be motivated by a noble sentiment, fair trade mostly redistributes value rather than expanding the overall amount of value created.

A shared value perspective, however, would focus on improving growing techniques and strengthening the local cluster of supporting suppliers and other institutions to increase farmers' efficiency, yields, product quality, and sustainability. This leads to a bigger pie of revenue and profits that benefits both farmers and the companies that buy from them. Early studies of cocoa farmers in Ivory Coast, for example, suggest that while fair trade can increase farmers' incomes by 10 to 20 percent, shared value investments can raise their incomes by more than 300 percent! Initial investment and time may be required to implement new procurement practices and develop the cluster; however, the return will be greater economic value and broader strategic benefits for all participants.

A firm's value chain inevitably affects—and is affected by—numerous societal issues. Opportunities to create shared value arise because societal problems can create economic costs in the firm's value chain. Such external factors inflict internal costs to the firm, even in the absence of regulation or resource taxes. For example, excess product packaging and greenhouse gases are not just costly to the environment but also costly to businesses.

The shared value perspective acknowledges that the congruence between societal progress and value chain productivity is far greater than traditionally believed. The synergy increases when firms consider societal issues from a shared value perspective and invent new ways of operating to address them. So far, however, relatively few firms have reaped the full productivity benefits.

Let us look at what a few companies are doing to reap "win–win" benefits by addressing societal challenges and, in so doing, enjoying higher productivity and profitability:

- Hindustan Unilever has created a new direct-to-home distribution system. Under the name Project Shakti, it is operated by underprivileged female entrepreneurs in Indian villages. The firm provides microcredit and training and has more than 45,000 entrepreneurs covering about 100,000 villages across 15 Indian states. The initiative provides benefits to communities not only by giving women skills that often double their household income but also by reducing the spread of communicable diseases through increased access to hygiene products. The unique ability of business to market to hard-to-reach consumers can benefit society by getting life-altering products into the hands of people that need them. Project Shakti now accounts for 5 percent of Unilever's total revenues in India. It has also extended the company's reach into rural areas and built its brand in media-dark regions, creating major economic value for the company.

- Leading companies have learned that because of lost workdays and diminished employee productivity, poor health costs them far more than health benefits do. For example, Johnson & Johnson has helped employees stop smoking (a two-thirds reduction in 15 years) and has implemented many other new wellness programs. Such initiatives have saved the company $250 million on health care costs, a return of $2.71 for every dollar spent on wellness from 2002 to 2008. Further, Johnson & Johnson has benefited from a more present and productive workforce.

- Olam International, a leading cashew producer, traditionally shipped its nuts from Africa to Asia for processing. By opening local processing plants and training workers in Tanzania, Mozambique, Nigeria, and Ivory Coast, Olam cut its processing and shipping costs by as much as 25 percent and greatly reduced carbon emissions! Further, Olam built preferred relationships with local farmers. It has provided direct employment to 17,000 people—95 percent of whom are women—and indirect employment to an equal number of people in rural areas, where jobs were otherwise not available.

The Triple Bottom Line: Incorporating Financial as Well as Environmental and Social Costs

To remain viable in the long run, companies increasingly recognize the imperative of measuring their deployment and use of productive assets as well as their outcomes more comprehensively than what has been captured by traditional accounting methods. Economists have talked about "externalities" for years, but until recently, accounting did not have the means and governments did not require that firms measure their use and depletion of "free goods" or the ecological or social impact of their activities. However, a series of ecological problems and social challenges that have been directly linked to firms' activities have compelled them to recognize interdependencies, explicitly measure their impact, and adopt what is called a *triple bottom line,* a technique that involves assessing financial as well as environmental and social performance.[37] Shell, NEC, and Procter & Gamble, along with other corporations, have realized that failing to account for the environmental and social costs of doing business poses risks to the company and to the community in which it operates.

The first bottom line presents the financial measures that all leaders are familiar with.[38] The second bottom line assesses ecological and material capitals. And the third bottom line measures human and social capitals. For example, starting with its 1999 annual report, BP Amoco reports on such performance indicators as annual sales and operating costs (bottom line #1); levels of hydrocarbon emissions, greenhouse emissions, and oil spills compared with the prior year (bottom line #2); and its workforce safety record, employee training, and philanthropic contributions (bottom line #3).

Social responsibility for Suncor Energy of Calgary means accountability to employees and to the communities where they work. Suncor reports annually on environmental, social, and economic performances. Given the location of many of its operations, its commitment to be socially responsible means extensive consultations with Indigenous communities and substantial investments in community projects involving the Athabasca Tribal Council and Métis communities. Such activity helps ensure that those communities share the benefits of oil sands development and industry relations agreements with the Fort McKay, Athabasca Chipewyan, and Mikisew Cree First Nations.[39]

Environmental sustainability is now a value embraced by the most competitive and successful multinational companies. A McKinsey survey of more than 400 senior executives found that 92 percent view environmental challenges as one of the central issues in the twenty-first century. Virtually all executives acknowledged their firm's responsibility to control pollution, and 83 percent agreed that corporations have an environmental responsibility for their products even after they are sold.[40] For many successful firms, environmental values are becoming a central part of their cultures and management processes. According to a KPMG study of 350 firms, more multinationals are recognizing the benefits of improving their environmental performances, saving money, and boosting share performance by taking a close look at how their operations impact the environment.[41]

Many firms have profited by investing in socially responsible behaviour, including those activities that enhance environmental sustainability. However, how do such "socially responsible" companies fare in terms of shareholder returns compared to benchmarks such as the Standard & Poor's 500 Index? Let's look at some of the evidence.

Socially responsible investing (SRI) is a broad-based approach to investing that now encompasses an estimated $3.7 trillion, or $1 out of every $9 under professional management in the United States.[42] SRI recognizes that corporate responsibility and societal concerns are considerations in investment decisions. With SRI, investors have the opportunity to put their money to work in building a more sustainable world while earning competitive returns in the short and long terms.

And, as the saying goes, nice guys don't have to finish last. The ING SRI Index Fund, which tracks the stocks of 50 companies, enjoyed a 47.4 percent return in a recent year. That easily beat the 2.65 percent gain of the Standard & Poor's 500 stock index. Furthermore, a review of the 145 socially responsible equity mutual and exchange-traded funds tracked by Morningstar also showed that 65 percent of them outperformed the S&P 500.[43]

The ROIs on sustainability projects, however, are often very difficult to quantify for a number of reasons, including the following:

1. *The data necessary to calculate ROI accurately are often not available when it comes to sustainability projects.* However, sustainability programs may often find their success beyond company boundaries, so internal systems and process metrics can't capture all the relevant numbers.

2. *Many of the benefits from such projects are intangible.* Traditional financial models are built around relatively easy-to-measure, monetized results. Yet many of the benefits of sustainability projects involve fuzzy intangibles, such as the goodwill that can enhance a firm's brand equity.

3. *The payback period is on a different time frame.* Even when their future benefits can be forecast, sustainability projects often require longer-term payback windows.

Clearly, the case for sustainability projects needs to be made on the basis of a more holistic and comprehensive understanding of all the tangible and intangible benefits rather than whether or not they meet existing hurdle rates for traditional investment projects. For example, 3M uses a lower hurdle rate for pollution prevention projects. When it comes to environmental projects, IKEA allows a 10- to 15-year payback period, considerably longer than it allows for other types of investment. And Diversey, a cleaning products company, has employed a portfolio approach, establishing two hurdles for projects in its carbon reduction plan: a three-year payback and a cost per megaton of carbon avoided. Out of 120 possible projects ranging from lighting retrofits to solar photovoltaic systems, only 30 cleared both hurdles, although about 60 could reach one. An expanded 90-project portfolio, all added together, met the double hurdle. Subsequently, Diversey was able to increase its carbon reduction goal from 8 to 25 percent and generated a higher net present value.[44]

Such approaches are the result of the recognition that the intangible benefits of sustainability projects—such as reducing risks, staying ahead of regulations, pleasing communities, and enhancing employee morale—are substantial even when they are difficult to quantify. Just as companies spend large fortunes on launching advertising campaigns or initiating R&D projects without a clear quantification of financial returns, sustainability investments are necessary even when it is difficult to calculate the ROE of such investments. The alternative of not making these investments is often no longer feasible.

LO 5 THE STRATEGIC MANAGEMENT PERSPECTIVE: AN IMPERATIVE THROUGHOUT THE ORGANIZATION

Competing successfully in today's increasingly complex and interconnected world requires managers to take an integrative view of their organization and assess how all of the functional areas and activities fit together to help the organization achieve its goals and objectives. This cannot be accomplished if only the top managers in the organization take an integrative, strategic perspective of issues facing the firm with everyone else fending for themselves in their independent, isolated functional areas. When guided by a silo mentality, marketing and sales will tend to favour broad, tailor-made product lines; production will demand standardized products that are relatively easy to make so that manufacturing costs can be kept low; research and development will design products to demonstrate technical elegance; and so on. To succeed, a firm must align its workers throughout the organization to make decisions and strive toward overall goals.

As noted by Peter Senge of MIT, the days when Henry Ford, Alfred Sloan, and Tom Watson (top executives at Ford, General Motors, and IBM, respectively) "learned for the organization" are now over:

> In an increasingly dynamic, interdependent, and unpredictable world, it is simply no longer possible for anyone to "figure it all out at the top." The old model, "the top thinks and the local acts," must now give way to integrating thinking and acting at all levels. While the challenge is great, so is the potential payoff. "The person who figures out how to harness the collective genius of the people in his or her organization," according to former Citibank CEO Walter Wriston, "is going to blow the competition away."[45]

Many driving forces are increasing the need for a strategic perspective and greater involvement throughout the organization.[46] Among the most important of these are globalization, technology, and intellectual capital.[47] These forces are inherently interrelated; collectively, they are accelerating the rate of change and uncertainty that managers at all levels must deal with. Even though international trade has existed for centuries, the flow of capital, people, and information is today truly global, thanks to digital networks, global sourcing, free trade agreements, and interconnected systems. Competitive moves in one market can impact firms in other segments of the global economy, creating ripple effects and further challenging competitors to respond. Managers must address the paradoxical demand to think globally and act locally. They have to move resources and information rapidly around the world to meet local needs. They also face new challenges when formulating strategies: volatile political situations, difficult trade issues, ever-fluctuating exchange rates, unfamiliar cultures, and gut-wrenching social problems.[48] Today, managers must be more literate in the ways of foreign customers, commerce, and competition than ever before. Globalization requires that organizations increase their ability to learn and collaborate and to manage diversity, complexity, and ambiguity. The information needed to act effectively is dispersed around the world, and top-level managers cannot wait for it to reach them to make coordinated decisions.

Creating and applying knowledge to deliver differentiated products and services of superior value for customers requires the acquisition of superior talent as well as the ability to develop and retain that talent.[49] Successful firms create an environment with strong social and professional relationships, where people feel strong "ties" to their colleagues and their organization.

Technologies are used to leverage human capital and to facilitate collaboration among individuals.[50] The challenge for management is to instill human capital with a strategic perspective and use its talents to effectively help the organization attain its goals and objectives.

Strategy Spotlight 1.1 discusses the global market for talent. It illustrates how forces of globalization, technology, and intellectual capital can be related.

1.1 STRATEGY SPOTLIGHT

The Global Market for Talent

Globalization today involves the movement of people and information across borders, not just goods and investment. Many technology-strategy consultants operating in North America, making over $150,000 annually, are blissfully unaware of the challenges posed by the likes of Ganesh Narasimhaiya.

Ganesh is a 30-year-old Indian who enjoys cricket, R&B music, and bowling. He has a bachelor's degree in electronics and communications, and he can spin out code in a variety of languages: COBOL (Common Business-Oriented Language), Java, and UML (Unified Modelling Language), among others. Ganesh has worked on high-profile projects for Wipro, a $903-million Indian software giant, for companies all over the world. He helped GE Medical Systems roll out a logistics application throughout Southeast Asia. He proposed a plan to consolidate and synchronize security solutions across a British client's ebusiness applications. And he developed a strategy for transferring legacy system applications onto the Web for a company in Norway. He works 18 or 19 hours a day at a customer site, and for that he may earn as much as $7,000 a month. When he is home in Bangalore, India, his pay is about one-quarter of that—$21,000 a year. But by Indian salary standards, this is a small fortune.

Ganesh is part of Wipro's strategy of amassing a small force of high-level experts who are increasingly focused on specific industries and can compete with anyone for a given consulting project. Wipro's Trojan Horse is the incredibly cheap offshore outsourcing solution that it can provide. The rise of a globally integrated knowledge economy is a blessing for developing nations. What it means for the North American and Western European skilled labour forces is less clear. This is something that strategy consultants working for Accenture and EDS in the United States, Canada, or Germany need to think about. Why? In 2015, Forrester Research estimated that at least 3.3 million white-collar jobs and $136 billion in wages have shifted from the United States alone to countries with low-cost labour. With dramatically lower wage rates and the same level of service, how is the western technology professional going to compete with Ganesh and his colleagues?

Sources: K. H. Hammonds, "Smart, Determined, Ambitious, Cheap: The New Face of Global Competition," *Fast Company*, February 2003, pp. 91–97; P. Engardio, A. Bernstein; and M. Kripalani, "Is Your Job Next?" *BusinessWeek*, February 3, 2003, pp. 50–60.

To develop and mobilize people and other assets in the organization, leaders are needed throughout the organization.[51] No longer can organizations be effective if the top "does the thinking" and the rest of the organization "does the work." Everyone needs to be involved in the strategic management process. Peter Senge noted the critical need for three types of leaders:

1. Local line leaders, who have significant profit and loss responsibility.
2. Executive leaders who champion and guide ideas to create a learning infrastructure and establish a domain for taking action.
3. Internal networkers, who, although having little positional power and formal authority, generate their power through the conviction and clarity of their ideas.[52]

Sally Helgesen, author of *The Web of Inclusion: A New Architecture for Building Great Organizations,* made a similar point about the need for leaders throughout the organization. She asserted that many organizations "fall prey to the heroes-and-drones syndrome, exalting the value of those in powerful positions while implicitly demeaning the contributions of those who fail to achieve top rank."[53] Cultures and processes in which leaders emerge at all levels, both up and down as well as across the organization, typify today's high-performing firms.[54]

Top-level executives are essential for setting the tone and serve as catalysts for employees to take charge. Consider Richard Branson, founder of the Virgin Group, whose core businesses include retail operations, hotels, communications, and an airline. He is well known for creating a culture and an informal structure in which anybody in the organization can be involved in generating and acting on new business ideas. Here is what he said:

> [S]peed is something that we are better at than most companies. We don't have formal board meetings, committees, etc. If someone has an idea, they can pick up the phone and talk to me. I can vote "done, let's do it." Or, better still, they can just go ahead and do it. They know that they are not going to get a mouthful from me if they make a mistake. Rules and regulations are not our forte. Analyzing things to death is not our kind of thing. We very rarely sit back and analyze what we do.[55]

To inculcate a strategic management perspective throughout the organization, many large traditional organizations often require a major effort in transformational change. This involves extensive communication, training, and development to strengthen a strategic perspective within the organization. Ford Motor Company is one such example. Ford instituted a major cultural overhaul and embarked on a broad-based attempt to develop leaders throughout the organization. It wanted to build an army of "warrior entrepreneurs"—people who have the courage and skills to reject old ideas and who believe in change passionately enough to make it happen. To instill this new perspective within a single year, Ford sent about 2,500 managers to its Leadership Development Center to participate in one of four programs—Capstone, Experienced Leader Challenge, Ford Business Associates, and New Business Leader—infusing in them not just the mindset and vocabulary of a revolutionary but also the tools necessary to achieve a revolution. At the same time, through the Business Leaders Initiative, a further 100,000 salaried employees worldwide participated in business leadership "cascades," involving intense exercises that combined trickle-down communications with substantive team projects.[56] Similarly, Whirlpool, the world's largest producer of household appliances, brought about a significant shift in the firm's culture by encouraging innovation through a five-year initiative that included both financial investments in capital spending as well as a series of changes in management processes, including training innovation mentors, making innovation a significant component of leadership development programs, enrolling all its salaried employees in business innovation courses, and providing them with online access to multiple innovation tools and data.[57] The results have been impressive. Throughout the organization, innovative ideas from cross-functional teams have been responsible for new product designs, the firm's next-generation concept products have been featured in the Louvre and at the Smithsonian, and the firm's share price has doubled in value.

LO 6   ENSURING COHERENCE IN STRATEGIC DIRECTION

For a firm to be successful, employees and managers throughout the organization must strive for common goals and objectives. To be able to face today's competitive challenges, all elements of the organization must be pushing in the same direction rather than working at cross-purposes. When the desired results are clearly specified, it becomes much easier to move forward. Otherwise, without a clear vision of what the firm is striving to accomplish, no one really knows what to work toward.

Organizations best express priorities through stated goals and objectives that form a *hierarchy of goals*. The hierarchy of goals for an organization includes its vision, mission, and strategic objectives. Exhibit 1-5 depicts the hierarchy of goals and highlights how they serve to connect all parts of the organization both horizontally and vertically. On the one hand, what visions may lack in specificity, they make up for in their ability to evoke powerful and compelling mental images. On the other hand, strategic objectives tend to be more specific and provide a more direct means of determining if the organization is moving toward broader, overall goals.[58]

EXHIBIT 1-5

AN ORGANIZATION'S HIERARCHY OF GOALS

Vision

Mission

Objectives

Departmental objectives and goals

Organizational Vision

The starting point for articulating a firm's hierarchy of goals is the company vision. It is often described as a goal that is "massively inspiring, overarching, and long-term."[59] A vision represents a destination that is driven by, and evokes, passion. An effective vision conveys management's intent and articulates the desired future state of the company. In essence, a vision tells the world "what we want to be when we grow up, when we finally arrive at our destination." At the same time, it is a stretch that inspires employees to strive to achieve more and serves as a call to action.

Developing and implementing a vision is one of a leader's central roles. In a survey of 1,500 senior leaders, 870 of whom were CEOs (from 20 different countries), respondents were asked what they believed were the key traits that leaders must have. Ninety-eight percent responded that "a strong sense of vision" was the most important. Similarly, when asked about critical knowledge skills, the leaders cited "strategy formulation to achieve a vision" as the most important skill. Ninety percent also reported a lack of confidence in their own skills and ability to conceive a vision for their organization. For example, T. J. Rogers, CEO of Cypress Semiconductor, an electronic chipmaker that faced some difficulties in 1992, lamented that his own short-sightedness had caused the danger: "I did not have the 50,000-foot view and got caught."[60]

One of the most famous examples of a vision is Disneyland's: "To be the happiest place on earth." Other past and present examples include:

- "Restoring patients to full life" (Medtronic)
- "More! Providing Canadians with a one-stop destination in meeting their food and everyday household needs" (Loblaw)
- "Clear; Simple; First; True; Profitable; Proud" (Bell Canada Enterprises, BCE)
- "The elimination of all workplace fatalities, injuries, and illnesses" (Workplace Safety and Insurance Board, WSIB (Ontario))

- "Our vision is to be the world's best quick service restaurant experience" (McDonald's)
- "To be North America's leading energy delivery company" (Enbridge)

Although it is difficult to accurately measure how well such visions are being achieved, they do provide a fundamental statement of an organization's sense of its own *purpose* and reflect the collective *values* of its stakeholders, their aspirations, and their goals. A good vision statement tells everybody, both inside and outside the organization, what the organization stands for, what inspires its management and employees, and what gets them going and motivates them to strive to excel. Such visions go well beyond narrow financial objectives and strive to capture both the minds and hearts of employees. Another way to consider a vision is to ask such questions as, If we were immensely successful in what we do, how would that success look, say, 10 years from now? If someone was talking about our organization in glowing terms, what would we like them to be saying about us?

A vision statement may contain a slogan, a diagram, or a picture—whatever grabs the attention of those looking at it.[61] The aim of a slogan is to capture the essence of a more formal vision in a few words that are easily remembered and yet evoke the spirit of the entire vision. In its 20-year battle to dominate the photocopy equipment business, Canon's slogan was "Beat Xerox." Similarly, Motorola's slogan was "Total Customer Satisfaction," while BMW famously wants to be known as "The Ultimate Driving Machine," and Nike says "Just Do It."

Vision statements are not a cure-all. Sometimes they backfire and erode a company's credibility. A vision may or may not succeed; it depends on whether everything else happens according to the firm's strategy. Visions fail for many reasons, including those discussed in the following paragraphs.[62]

The Walk Does Not Match the Talk

An idealistic vision can arouse employee enthusiasm. However, that same enthusiasm can be quickly dashed if employees find that senior management's behaviour is not consistent with the vision. Often, the vision is a sloganeering campaign of new buzzwords and empty platitudes such as "devotion to the customer," "teamwork," or "total quality" that are not consistently backed by management's actions.

Irrelevance

A vision that is created in a vacuum—unrelated to environmental threats or opportunities or to an organization's resources and capabilities—often ignores the needs of those who are expected to buy into it. When the vision is not anchored in reality, employees will reject it.

Not the Holy Grail

Managers often search continually for the one elusive solution that will solve their firm's problems—that is, the next Holy Grail of management. They may have tried other management fads only to find that these fell short of their expectations. However, they remain convinced that one exists. Visions support sound management, but they require everyone to walk the talk and be accountable for their behaviour. A vision cannot simply be viewed as a magic cure for an organization's problems.

An Ideal Future Irreconciled with the Present

Although visions are not designed to mirror reality, they do need to be anchored in it somehow. People have difficulty identifying with a vision that paints a rosy picture of the future but either takes no account of the often hostile environment in which the firm competes or ignores some of the firm's weaknesses.

Tunnel Vision

Too much focus on a concrete vision, unwillingness to consider flexible avenues toward the destination, and reluctance to reconsider in light of new realities and new challenges can cause tunnel vision. Visions are not to be changed frequently or lightly, but there is a fine line between commitment and rigidity.

Mission Statements

A company's mission differs from its vision in that the mission encompasses both the purpose of the company and the basis of competition and competitive advantage.

For example, in Exhibit 1-6 you can review the vision and mission statements as they were articulated by the Workplace Safety and Insurance Board (WSIB) back in 2010. WSIB is a $3.5-billion entity mandated to administer Ontario's no-fault workplace insurance plan for workers and employers in the province and insuring over $150 billion in annual payroll. Note that the vision statement is broad, but the mission statement is more specific and focuses on the means by which the organization will achieve its vision. This includes providing specific avenues that will direct the organization's efforts, identifying key partners, markets, and services that will make it happen.

EXHIBIT 1-6   COMPARING THE WSIB'S VISION AND MISSION

Vision
The elimination of all workplace fatalities, injuries, and illnesses

Mission
"To lead, prevent, and preserve" • Lead and partner with others in the creation of healthy and safe workplaces. • Prevent and respond to fatalities, injuries, and illnesses and measurably lessen their impacts on workers, their families, and the workplaces of Ontario when they do occur. • Preserve a strong and sustainable workplace safety and insurance system that will continue to serve the people of Ontario.

Sources: WSIB Annual Report and publication.

Compare this to Starbucks's mission: *"to inspire and nurture the human spirit - one person, one cup, and one neighborhood at a time."* While very different from WSIB's, it does the job quite well. Effective mission statements incorporate the concept of stakeholder management, suggesting that organizations must respond to multiple constituencies if they are to survive and prosper. Customers, employees, suppliers, and owners are the primary stakeholders, but others may also play an important role in a particular corporation. Mission statements also have the greatest impact when they reflect an organization's enduring, overarching strategic priorities and competitive positioning. Mission statements can also vary in length and specificity. The two mission statements below illustrate these issues:

- "To produce superior financial returns for our shareholders as we serve our customers with the highest quality transportation, logistics, and ecommerce." (Federal Express)

- "To be the very best in the business. Our game plan is status go. . .we are constantly looking ahead, building on our strengths, and reaching for new goals. In our quest of these goals, we look at the three stars of the Brinker logo and are reminded of the basic values that are the strength of this company. . .People, Quality, and Profitability. Everything we do at Brinker must support these core values. We also look at the eight golden flames depicted in our logo and are reminded of the fire that ignites our mission and makes up the heart and soul of this incredible company. These flames are: Customers, Food, Team, Concepts, Culture, Partners, Community, and Shareholders. As keeper of these flames, we will continue to build on our strengths and work together to be the best in the business." (Brinker International, whose restaurant chains Chili's Bar & Grill and Maggiano's Little Italy operate across 31 countries ranging from the United States and Canada, to Australia, Japan, and Saudi Arabia)[63]

Few mission statements identify profit or any other financial indicator as the sole purpose of the firm. Indeed, most do not even mention profit or shareholder return.[64] Employees of organizations or departments are usually the mission's most important audience. For them, the mission should help build a common understanding and promote a nurturing of purpose and commitment.

Profit maximization not only fails to motivate people but also does not differentiate between organizations. Every corporation wants to maximize profits over the long term. A good mission statement, thus, must communicate why an organization is special and different. Studies that linked corporate values and mission statements with financial performance found that the most successful firms mentioned values other than profits. The less successful firms focused almost entirely on profitability.[65] In essence, profit is the metaphorical equivalent of oxygen, food, and water, which the body requires. They are not the purpose in life, but without them there is no life.

Vision statements tend to be quite broad and enduring and often represent an inspiring, overarching, and emotionally driven destination. A firm's mission, in contrast, tends to be more specific and to address questions concerning the organization's reason for being and the basis of its intended competitive advantage in the marketplace. It should change when competitive conditions change or the firm is faced with new threats or opportunities.

Strategic Objectives

Strategic objectives are used to operationalize the mission statement. That is, they help provide guidance on how the organization can fulfil or move toward the "higher goals" in the goal hierarchy—the mission and the vision. As a result, they tend be more specific and cover a more well-defined time frame. Objectives are specific and concrete yardsticks that measure the progress toward the organization's mission and vision.[66] If an objective lacks specificity or measurability, it is not very useful, simply because there is no way of determining whether it is helping the organization to move forward.

Exhibit 1-7 lists several strategic objectives of corporations, divided into financial and non-financial categories. Many strategic objectives aim toward generating greater profits and returns for the owners of the business, but some are directed at customers or society at large.

EXHIBIT 1-7 **STRATEGIC OBJECTIVES**

Strategic Objectives (Financial)

- Increase sales growth 6 percent to 8 percent and accelerate core net earnings growth to 13 percent to 15 percent per share in each of the next five years. (Procter & Gamble)
- Generate Internet-related revenue of $1.5 billion. (Automation)
- Increase the contribution of Banking Group earnings from investments, brokerage, and insurance from 16 percent to 25 percent. (Wells Fargo)
- Cut corporate overhead costs by $30 million per year. (Fortune Brands)

Strategic Objectives (Non-financial)

- Ensure that a majority of our customers, when surveyed, say they consider Wells Fargo the best financial institution in the community. (Wells Fargo)
- Operate 6,000 stores by 2010—up from 3,000 in the year 2000. (Walgreens)
- Develop a smart card strategy that will help us play a key role in shaping online payments. (American Express)
- Reduce greenhouse gases by 10 percent (from a 1990 base) by 2010. (BP Amoco)

Sources: Company documents and annual reports.

For an objective to be meaningful, it needs to satisfy several S.M.A.R.T. criteria. That is, it must be each of the following:

- *Specific.* Provide a clear message as to what needs to be accomplished (e.g., market share, new product introductions, and customer satisfaction scores).

- *Measurable.* Contain indicators that explicitly measure progress toward fulfilling the objective (e.g., 15-percent market share; 3 new product launches; 10-percent increase in customer retention).

- *Appropriate.* Connect and be consistent with the vision and mission of the organization.

- *Realistic.* Identify an achievable target, given the organization's capabilities and opportunities in the environment. It must be challenging but doable.

- *Timely.* A time frame for accomplishing the objective is important. Without a timeline for achieving the objective, little value exists in setting goals (e.g., three new product launches every six months, market leadership in five years, employee training goals in 12 months).

The organization benefits significantly when its objectives satisfy the above criteria. First, these criteria help direct employees throughout the organization toward common goals. This, in turn, helps concentrate and conserve valuable resources in the organization to work collectively in a timelier manner.

Second, challenging objectives can motivate and inspire employees throughout the organization to higher levels of commitment and effort. A great deal of research has supported the notion that individuals work harder when they are striving toward specific goals instead of being asked simply to do their best.

Third, as we noted earlier in the chapter, there is always the possibility that different parts of an organization may pursue their own goals rather than the overall company goals. Although well intentioned, these goals may work at cross-purposes with those of the organization as a whole. Meaningful objectives, thus, help resolve the conflicts that arise in such situations.

Finally, proper objectives provide a yardstick for rewards and incentives. Not only do they lead to higher levels of employee motivation, but they also help ensure a greater sense of equity and fairness when rewards are allocated.

Of course, still other objectives are even more specific. These are often referred to as *short-term objectives*—essential components of "action plans" that are critical in implementing a firm's chosen strategy. We will discuss these issues in Chapter 10. Chapter 3 presents a comprehensive approach to measuring the progress toward results, called the "balanced scorecard," which uses accounting and other metrics to monitor business activities from multiple perspectives and to align managerial decisions and actions with the organization's vision.

SUMMARY

We began this introductory chapter by defining strategic management and delineating some of its key attributes. Strategic management is defined as "consisting of the analysis, decisions, and actions an organization undertakes to create and sustain competitive advantages." The issue of how and why some firms outperform others in the marketplace is central to the study of strategic management. Strategic management has four key attributes: It is directed at overall organizational goals, includes multiple stakeholders, incorporates both short-term and long-term perspectives, and incorporates trade-offs between efficiency and effectiveness.

The second section discussed the strategic management process. Here, we adhered to the above definition of strategic management and focused on three core activities in the strategic management process—strategy analysis, strategy formulation, and strategy implementation. We noted how these activities are highly interrelated and interdependent. We also discussed how each of the 12 chapters in this text fits into the three core activities.

Next, we introduced two important concepts—corporate governance and stakeholder management—that must be taken into account throughout the strategic management process. Governance mechanisms can be broadly divided into two groups: internal and external. Internal governance mechanisms include shareholders (owners), management (led by the chief executive officer), and the board of directors. External control is exercised by auditors, banks, analysts, and an active business press, as well as the threat of takeovers. We identified five key stakeholders in all organizations: owners, customers, suppliers, employees, and society at large. Successful firms go beyond an overriding focus on solely satisfying the interests of the owners. Rather, they recognize the inherent conflicts that arise among the demands of the various stakeholders as well as the need to endeavour to attain "symbiosis"—that is, interdependence and mutual benefit among the various stakeholder groups. Managers must also recognize the need to act in a socially responsible manner which, if done effectively, can enhance a firm's innovativeness. The "shared value" approach represents an innovative perspective on creating value for the firm and society at the same time. The managers also should recognize and incorporate issues related to environmental sustainability in their strategic actions.

In the fourth section, we discussed factors that have accelerated the rate of unpredictable changes that managers face today. Such factors and the combination of them have increased the need for managers and employees throughout the organization to have a strategic management perspective and to become more empowered.

The final section addressed the need for consistency in a firm's vision, mission, and strategic objectives. Collectively, they form an organization's hierarchy of goals. Visions should evoke powerful and compelling mental images. However, they are not very specific. Strategic objectives, in contrast, are much more specific and are vital to ensuring that the organization is striving toward fulfilling its vision and mission.

Summary Review Questions

1. What is "strategic management"? What are its four key attributes?

2. Briefly discuss the three key activities in the strategic management process. Why is it important for managers to recognize the interdependent nature of these activities?

3. Explain the concept of "stakeholder management." Why shouldn't managers be solely interested in shareholder management—that is, maximizing the returns for owners of the firm (its shareholders)?

4. What is corporate governance? What are its three key elements, and how can it be improved?

5. How can "symbiosis" (interdependence, mutual benefit) be achieved among a firm's stakeholders?

6. Why do firms need to have a strategic management perspective and empowerment in the strategic management process throughout the firm?

7. What is meant by a "hierarchy of goals"? What are the main components of it, and why must consistency be achieved among them?

REFLECTING ON CAREER IMPLICATIONS

Attributes of Strategic Management: How do your activities and actions contribute to the goals of your organization? Observe the decisions you make on the job. What are the short-term and the long-term implications of your decisions and actions? For your organization? For you personally? Have you recently made a decision that might yield short-term profits but might negatively impact the long-term goals of the organization?

Intended versus Emergent Strategies: Have you been too inflexible in your career strategies? Identify specific instances where you have taken advantage of new opportunities as they arose, or where you could have but did not. Many promising career opportunities may "emerge," even though they were not part of your intended strategy or your specific job assignment.

Strategic Coherence: Have you focused your efforts on the "big picture" in your organization? Have you consistently been able to make connections among your work and the vision, the mission, and the strategic objectives of your organization? Do you know how your actions contribute to each one of the three?

Personal Vision: Do you have a sense of purpose and aspiration for yourself? Do you know what you want to be "when you get there," wherever your "there" is? Can you identify the specific steps you take in your everyday life to further your goals and achieve your vision? What about the decisions you make or fail to make that detract from your personal vision?

EXPERIENTIAL EXERCISE

Using the Internet or your library sources, select four organizations—two in the private sector and two in the public sector. Find their mission statements. Complete the following table by identifying the stakeholders that are mentioned in these statements. Evaluate the differences between the firms in the private sector and those in the public sector.

	Private Sector #1	Private Sector #2	Public Sector #1	Public Sector #1
Name				
Mission statement				
Stakeholders				
1. Customers				
2. Suppliers				
3. Managers/employees				
4. Community at large				
5. Owners				
6. Others				
7. Others				

APPLICATION QUESTIONS AND EXERCISES

1. Go on the Internet and look up the history of a company, for example, BCE, Bombardier, Loblaw, Blackberry (RIM), Walmart, GE, or Ford. What are some of the key events that would represent the "romantic" perspective of leadership? What are some of the key events that depict the "external control" perspective of leadership?

2. Select a company that competes in an industry in which you are interested. What are some of the recent demands that stakeholders have placed on this company? Can you find examples of how the company is trying to develop "symbiosis" (interdependence and mutual benefit) among its stakeholders? (Use the Internet and your library resources.)

3. Provide examples of companies that are actively trying to increase the amount of employee empowerment in the strategic management process throughout the organization. Do these companies seem to be having positive outcomes? Why? Why not?

4. Look up the vision statements and/or mission statements of a few companies. Do you feel that they are constructive and useful as a means of motivating employees and providing a strong strategic direction? Why? Why not? (*Note:* Annual reports, along with the Internet, may be good sources of information.)

ETHICS AND CORPORATE SOCIAL RESPONSIBILITY QUESTIONS

1. A company focuses solely on short-term profits to provide the greatest return to the owners of the business (i.e., shareholders in a publicly held firm). What ethical issues could this raise? Why might this approach have a negative impact on the firm's ability to create value?

2. A firm has spent some time—with input from managers at all levels—in developing a vision statement and a mission statement. Over time, however, the behaviours of some executives are inconsistent with these statements. What kinds of issues could such behaviours raise? How might they impede on the firm's ability to create value?

CHAPTER TWO

Analyzing the External Environment of the Firm

LEARNING OBJECTIVES

After reading this chapter, you should have a good understanding of:

LO 1 The elements that constitute a firm's general environment and their impact on the firm's strategies and performance.

LO 2 How to define the competitive environment and delineate industry boundaries.

LO 3 Why environmental scanning, environmental monitoring, and collecting competitive intelligence are critical inputs to developing forecasts of the business environment.

LO 4 Why scenario planning is a useful technique for firms competing in industries characterized by unpredictability and change.

LO 5 How trends and events in the general environment and forces in the competitive environment are interrelated and affect performance.

LO 6 How forces in the competitive environment can affect profitability and how a firm can improve its competitive position by increasing its power vis-à-vis those forces.

LO 7 The concept of strategic groups and their strategy and performance implications.

CASE STUDY

Shomi, a Canadian streaming service introduced in 2014, officially shut down operations on November 30, 2016.[1] After initially being available only to Internet and television subscribers of Rogers and Shaw Communications, Shomi was made available to the general public in August of 2015 and was expected to become a strong Canadian competitor to Netflix, alongside its domestic competition, Bell's CraveTV. Why, then, did Shomi throw in the towel only two years after its launch?

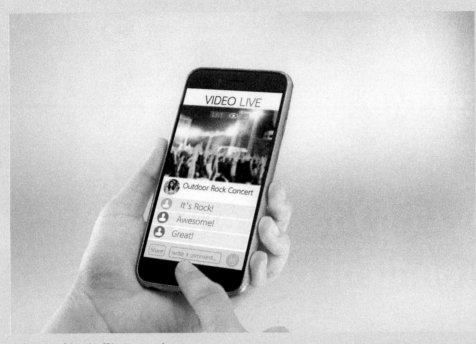

panuwat phimpha/Shutterstock.com

In a press release in late 2016, senior vice-president David Asch noted two main factors in Shomi's demise. "The business climate and online video marketplace have changed markedly in the last few years. Combined with the fact that the business is more challenging to operate than we expected, we've decided to wind down our operations." While we don't know all the difficulties Asch and his team faced in their efforts to successfully operate a streaming service, there is little doubt regarding the rapid changes in the business climate and their powerful impact on any organization.

In June 2016, a study from Solutions Research Group noted that Netflix had 5.2 million Canadian subscribers, while CraveTV and Shomi combined had fewer than 700,000. Three major aspects within the streaming business climate can help explain why: First-mover advantages turned Netflix into the 'Kleenex' of the industry; Netflix wasn't aligned with the incumbents in the Canadian market nor associated with their legacy costs or reputations, and could therefore turn its newness into a significant advantage over both CraveTV and Shomi; and, finally, Netflix's research and development budget far surpassed that of Shomi, directing the focus within the industry and the attention of customers to exclusive or original content.

Netflix, as the first mover in the streaming industry, shaped many of the key dimensions that defined competition in the marketplace. Firstly, Netflix was able to develop the expectations for standards in the industry. Pricing, features, and original content were all developed and set by Netflix long before Shomi entered the market. As a new entrant, Shomi had difficulties matching both the size and scope of Netflix's library while maintaining its low prices. Due to its domination of the streaming services industry, Netflix has been dubbed the 'Kleenex' of streaming services, a phenomenon in which the name of a brand becomes associated with the service or product itself (such as Google), providing an immeasurable advantage over Shomi.

Secondly, Shomi was offered by incumbent players in the Canadian telecommunications industry and, for the first year of its existence, this meant it was inextricably linked to either Rogers or Shaw Communications. In Canada, the 'cord cutters,' or people most interested in leaving traditional cable for a streaming service, are often the same people who are trying to leave either Bell or Rogers, the incumbent players in the telecommunications field. Instead of providing a benefit through access to Rogers' broad customer base, Shomi's association with the telecommunications giant became a detriment because the people most likely to purchase streaming services were also those more likely to reject incumbent players.

Finally, Netflix is spending upwards of $300 million USD annually on research and development. This extensive war chest is divided between three major expenditures: the development of advanced algorithms, intended to predict viewer patterns and desires; ensuring availability of Netflix on every possible device; and investing in original content. Shomi just couldn't match those numbers. Simply put, manually curated lists of content could not outperform advanced algorithms that can instantly detect and re-prioritize suggestions to viewers to increase viewership and perceived value. Shomi was also slow to add device availability. In addition, Netflix's investments in original content have paid off. Subscribers come for popular original shows such as *13 Reasons Why, Orange is the New Black, Stranger Things,* and *Narcos,* not for reruns of *Gilmore Girls* and *Modern Family.* Shomi, offering only reruns of popular shows, couldn't compete with Netflix's sustained competitive advantage, developed through their original content.

Shomi's exodus from the Canadian streaming industry highlights the critical need for companies to monitor the external environment, both at the firm and industry level. An analysis of the streaming industry would have shown Shomi to be at a disadvantage relative to Netflix. While Rogers and Shaw Communications were correct in noting the opportunities available in streaming services, they neglected to note the many threats present in the industry from Netflix and the bias against incumbent telecommunications players. Ultimately, poor reading of the external environment cost Rogers and Shaw Communications upwards of a $100 million loss. ▪

To be successful, managers must recognize both opportunities and threats in their firm's external environment. They have a wide array of external stakeholders who can affect, or are affected by, the value-creating activities of a firm. Successful managers must be aware of what is going on outside their company. If they focus exclusively on the efficiency of internal operations, their firm may degenerate into the world's most efficient producer of buggy whips or carbon paper. A firm's strategy can easily stray away and get out of touch with the evolving realities of the marketplace. Management's assumptions, premises, and beliefs can start diverging from or become inconsistent with the actual structure of the relevant industry, the competition, and the customers. Managers at Rogers and Shaw needed to figure out how to contend with the true competitive power of Netflix and the shifting dynamics in the streaming industry. Relying solely on the power of its backers was not sufficient.

LO 1

To understand the business environment of a particular firm, managers need to continuously analyze and stay abreast of both the *general environment* and the firm's *industry* and *competitive environment.* The general environment consists of myriad elements that an organization finds outside its own boundaries and which have some bearing on its ability to exist and thrive. Many factors shape the organization's general environment, and the interrelationships among those factors are typically beyond the control of the managers of any given organization. Such factors as government legislation, general economic trends, globalization, advances in technology, national cultural differences, the general level of education, and an aging population could potentially and critically affect the fortunes of a particular organization, yet its managers are largely powerless in any significant attempt to influence these factors.

Within this broad general environment, firms typically compete with other firms in the same industry. Industry, or a company's competitive environment, is composed of a set of firms that produce similar products or services, sell to similar customers, and use similar methods of production. An *industry* is commonly viewed from the suppliers' perspective and is defined as a collection of similar producers and firms that employ fairly similar production processes. The beer industry, for example, consists of all the firms that own and operate brewing facilities, whether large or small, with a national or local presence. Under this perspective, Molson, Labatt, Sleeman, Moosehead, and a host of microbrewers, such as Yukon, Big Rock, Great Western, Brasserie McAuslan, Nelson, Creemore Springs, Fireweed, Fort Garry, Storm Brewing in Newfoundland, and Wellington, constitute the beer industry in Canada. A manager defining the industry for a strategy analysis will look to the list of firms, their relative strategies, their product offerings, as well as the various markets and consumers served by those firms. Possible substitute products, such as wines and spirits, will also be considered.

LO 2

However, such a definition of an industry might not be complete. Until 2016, SABMiller, the world's second largest brewer, sold beer in Canada under licence but did not own any brewing capacity. Should an industry analyst consider their global strategic posture or that of their local licensees? In 2016, Anheuser-Bush InBev bought SABMiller. AB-InBev already owned Labatt. Who is now the competitor? What about some strong imports, such as Corona and Heineken? They ship their products into Canada from far-off locations. What about another global brewer, Sapporo, which owns a venerated Canadian brewer, Sleeman? What about the forays of some of the Canadian firms overseas, most notably Molson's merger with Coors or its acquisition of Kaiser in Brazil? Although questions about market share, market coverage, or competitive behaviour will clearly have to incorporate those additional players, they may have little relevance in discussions about suppliers, local production capacity or capacity utilization, or domestic distribution and regulations. To complicate matters further, Ontario's, The Beer Store, the province's legally sanctioned and, until recently, exclusive, retail distributor of beer, which was originally set up and owned by the three largest local brewers (Molson, 49 percent; Labatt, 49 percent; and Sleeman, 2 percent) is, as a result of those corporate marriages, today effectively controlled by foreign players.

An industry can also be viewed from the market's perspective. Consumers seek to satisfy their needs through the use of products and services. An industry consists of all those producers whose products can satisfy similar consumer needs. Thus, an opera company, the symphony, various theatres, and a professional sports franchise all compete for the entertainment dollars of a city's residents and could rightly belong in the same industry, even though their operations are drastically different. Similarly, fancy chocolates, good wines, and flowers are competing options for consumers looking to express gratitude for a dinner invitation.

Alternative definitions of an industry may arise from identical products offered by very different firms. Consider, for example, a firm that sources from China and supplies accessories for power tools, drill bits, and blades to retailers, such as Canadian Tire, Home Depot, and Rona. What is a meaningful definition of its industry? Does it consist of other producers of power tool accessories, such as Stanley or Black & Decker, which produce similar accessories in North America? Or does it consist of other wholesalers that source small parts and tools from China, Korea, or Vietnam? Should both types be included in the definition of the industry? How can one make comparisons? Understandably, the issues faced by each are drastically different though they depend on the same markets for their business. Consumers, furthermore, may not really know or care whether the accessories come from one place or another.

Time is another factor in defining the boundaries of an industry. When the time dimension of a specific issue under consideration is relatively short, direct competitors belong in the same industry, and firms that produce different products for different markets can safely be left out. But when the strategy analysis encompasses a longer timeline, the assumption of strategic distance is no longer safe. Distant firms can find themselves in direct competition in the long run. For example, foreign competitors can enter the market within a long enough time frame, and the adoption of new technology can allow firms to leapfrog the competition.

Technological developments also raise substantial issues about the boundaries of industries. Telephone companies used to be quite distinct from radio and television broadcasters, which again were separated from the cable companies. The three industries were populated by different players, had unfolded very differently, and faced unique competitive pressures. Today, convergence is the buzzword in the whole sector, and everybody accepts the direct competition among Bell Canada Enterprises (BCE), Rogers, Telus, and Shaw. Moreover, Apple, Google, Netflix, and Microsoft have entered the fray and have become fierce rivals, despite operating from distinct platforms with very different business models.

Gathering industry information and understanding the competitive dynamics among the different companies in the industry are keys to successful strategic management. The challenge for managers is to define the industry broadly enough to incorporate the relevant issues but not so broadly that their focus is rendered meaningless. In their award-winning book *Competing for the Future,* Gary Hamel and C. K. Prahalad suggest that "every manager carries around in his or her head a set of biases, assumptions, and presuppositions about the structure of the relevant 'industry,' about how one makes money in the industry, about who the competition is and isn't, about who the customers are and aren't, and so on."[2] Environmental analysis requires managers to continually question these assumptions. Peter Drucker labelled these interrelated sets of assumptions the "theory of the business."[3]

A firm's strategy may be good at one point in time, but it may go astray when management's frame of reference gets out of touch with the realities of the actual business situation. This happens when management's assumptions, premises, or beliefs are incorrect or when internal inconsistencies among them render the overall "theory of the business" invalid. The past may be instructive, but there are no guarantees that it will repeat itself in the future. As Warren Buffett, investor extraordinaire, colourfully notes, "Beware of past performance 'proofs.' If history books were the key to riches, the Forbes 400, the list of the world's wealthiest people, would consist of librarians."

CREATING THE ENVIRONMENTALLY AWARE ORGANIZATION

So how do managers become environmentally aware? Ram Charan, an adviser to many Fortune 500 CEOs, provides some useful insights with his concept of perceptual acuity.[4] He defines it as "the ability to sense what is coming before the fog clears." He draws on Ted Turner as an example: Turner saw the potential of 24-hour news before anyone else did. All the ingredients were there, but no one had connected them until he created CNN. Like Turner, the best CEOs are compulsively tuned to the external environment and seem to have a sixth sense that picks up anomalies and detects early warning signals that may represent key threats or opportunities.

How can perceptual acuity be improved? Although many CEOs may complain that the top job is a lonely one, they can't do it effectively if they are sitting alone in their office. Instead, high-performing CEOs are constantly meeting with people and searching out information.

Charan provides three examples:

- One CEO gets together with his critical people for half a day every eight weeks to discuss what's new and what's going on in the world. The setting is informal, and outsiders often attend. The participants look beyond the lens of their industry because some trends that affect one industry may impact others later on.

- Another CEO meets four times a year with about four other CEOs of large, but noncompeting, diverse global companies. Examining the world from multiple perspectives, they share their thinking about how different trends may develop. The CEO then goes back to his own weekly management meeting and throws out "a bunch of hand grenades to shake up people's thinking."

- Two other companies ask outsiders to critique strategy during their board's strategy sessions. Such input typically leads to spirited discussions that provide valued input on the hinge assumptions and options that are under consideration. One time, the focus was on pinpointing the risk inherent in a certain strategy. In another case, discussions led to finding that the company was missing a valuable opportunity.

Managers use three important processes—scanning, monitoring, and gathering competitive intelligence—to enhance their environmental awareness, better understand the environment that surrounds them, and develop forecasts about the future.[5] Exhibit 2-1 illustrates the relationship among these important activities. In addition to forecasts, when smart managers feel that the future is truly murky and they cannot confidently foresee what it may hold, they build scenarios—mental landscapes of how the world may unfold—and engage in scenario planning, which allows them to anticipate major future changes in the external environment.[6] Finally, managers frequently organize their analysis of and structure their conclusions about their outlook of the environment using the SWOT (Strengths, Weaknesses, Opportunities, and Threats) analysis framework. We review each of these tools below.

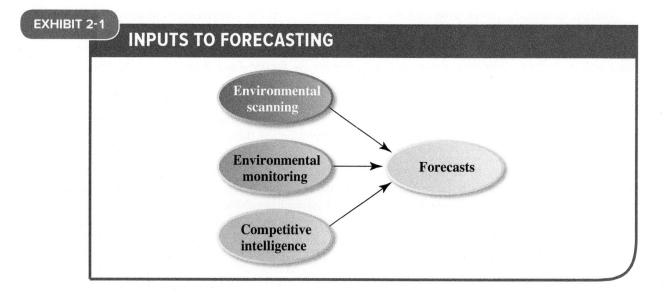

EXHIBIT 2-1

INPUTS TO FORECASTING

Environmental scanning

Environmental monitoring → Forecasts

Competitive intelligence

LO 3 # Scanning, Monitoring, Competitive Intelligence, Forecasting, and Scenario Analysis

Environmental Scanning

Environmental scanning involves surveillance of a firm's external environment to predict future environmental changes and detect changes already under way.[7] Successful environmental scanning alerts the organization to critical trends and events before the changes have developed a discernible pattern and before competitors recognize them.[8,9]

Spotting key trends requires a combination of knowledge and familiarity with the business and the customer, as well as keeping an eye on what is happening around us. Such big-picture/small-picture perspective enables us to better identify the emerging trends as they take shape. Exhibit 2-2 offers some suggestions on how to spot hot trends; specifically, it suggests listening, paying attention, and following trends both online and in more traditional formats.

EXHIBIT 2-2

HOW TO SPOT NEW TRENDS

- **Listen:** Ask your customers questions about your products and services. Ask what they are looking for next. Find out what media they are watching and what they think of current events.

- **Pay attention:** Read trade publications related to your industry to identify key issues. Watch industries that are always on the cutting edge, such as music, fashion, and design, to discover emerging trends that may affect your business.

- **Follow trends online:** Trend-monitoring websites, such as trendhunter.com and jwtintelligence. com, offer up the trends du jour. Add them to your regular Web-surfing itinerary. Participate in chat rooms, and find out what people are talking about. Organize online or in-person focus groups to learn what people are thinking. You can also launch social media groups or chat rooms to gather direct feedback from your customers.

Sources: suggestions inspired by Moran, G. 2008 "Be Your Own trendspotter" *Entrepreneur*, December 17, 2008.

Companies frequently seek insights from studies conducted by outside experts in a particular industry. For example, drawing on studies of the global automobile industry, one could identify several "key issues":[10]

- *Globalization.* Although not a new trend, globalization has significantly intensified, with enormous opportunities opening up in Asia, central and Eastern Europe, and Latin America. Moreover, new manufacturers from China and India are making their presence felt beyond their local markets.

- *Time to Market.* A gap still exists between product development cycles in the United States and Europe compared with those in Japan. This gap persists even though Japanese companies have been moving operations to other countries.

- *Shifting Roles and Responsibilities.* Design responsibility, purchasing, and even project management and systems engineering are shifting from the original equipment manufacturers to integrators and other suppliers.

All firms in the industry are affected by such developments, and executives are called to consider them in their strategic responses.

Strategy Spotlight 2.1 shows how Dell uses online media and crowdsourcing to help it keep abreast of trends and promising opportunities.

2.1 STRATEGY SPOTLIGHT

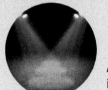

How Dell Enhances Its Environmental Awareness

As one of the largest technology companies in the world, Dell Inc. prides itself on its ability to innovate. In fact, the company has a unique platform for open innovation that allows it to connect with its customers and other stakeholders in an innovative way. IdeaStorm is an online interface which allows stakeholders to post their ideas or concerns and share them with the company. Since its inception, more than 16,000 ideas have been submitted, and more than 500 ideas have been implemented, such as Dell's Global Green Packaging Strategy, implemented in 2008 as a response to stakeholders wanting more environmentally friendly packaging.

To improve IdeaStorm to become even more efficient with stakeholder ideas, the company created the concept of "Storm Sessions," where a Dell representative can pose a question in order to have more directed replies from Dell stakeholders. Examples of session topics include discussions on how the Internet can drive innovation for sustainable business, as well as further opportunities for Dell to go green.

Sources: K, Vida, Storm Sessions Launch on IdeaStorm, *Dell,* 14 Dec 2009; Smith, Ian, Successful Crowdsourcing with Dell's Ideastorm, *Intelegia,* 11 Apr 2012; Israel, Shel, Dell Modernizes Ideastorm, *Forbes,* 27 Mar 2012, Huynh, Rene, New Storm Session: How can the internet drive innovation for sustainable business?, *Dell,* 3 Nov 2011, Mosmeyer, Michelle, Storm Sessions Go Green, *Dell,* 3 May 2010.

Environmental Monitoring

Environmental monitoring tracks the evolution of environmental trends, sequences of events, or streams of activities. The trends may be recognized by the firm by accident or brought to its attention through its environmental scanning or from outside the organization. Consider the automobile industry example mentioned above. Although environmental scanning may make the automobile industry executive aware of these trends, this is not sufficient. The ability to respond to those trends requires close monitoring, which involves closer ongoing scrutiny. For example, managers should closely monitor sales in Asia, Central and Eastern Europe, and Latin America. They should observe how fast Japanese companies and other competitors bring products to market compared with their own firm. What about escalating oil prices and their implications for consumer attitudes, let alone their wallets? Managers should also study trends with their own suppliers or integrators in purchasing, project management, and systems engineering. Monitoring enables firms to evaluate how dramatically environmental trends are changing the competitive landscape.

Other trends to monitor could be demographics and aging, as well as the percentage of gross domestic product (GDP) spent on health care (for a medical devices firm), shifts in insurance coverage and the balance between government dollars and privately covered expenses (for a pharmaceutical firm), new building permits (for an appliance manufacturer), or housing starts (for a furniture retailer).

Competitive Intelligence

Competitive intelligence (CI) helps firms better define and understand their industry as well as identify rivals' strengths and weaknesses.[11] It includes the intelligence gathering associated with the collection of data on competitors and the interpretation of such data for managerial decision making. Competitive intelligence helps a company avoid surprises by anticipating competitors' moves and decreasing its own response time.[12]

Examples of competitive analysis are evident in daily newspapers and periodicals, such as *The Globe and Mail* (Report on Business), *The Wall Street Journal, BusinessWeek,* and *Fortune.* For example, banks continually track home loan, auto loan, and Guaranteed Investment Certificates (GIC) interest rates charged by competitors in a given geographic region. Major airlines change hundreds of fares daily in response to competitors' tactics. Car manufacturers are keenly aware of announced cuts or increases in rivals' production volumes, sales, and sales incentives (e.g., rebates and low interest rates on financing). They use this information to plan their own marketing, pricing, and production strategies. Exhibit 2-3 provides some insights into what CI is (and what it is not).

EXHIBIT 2-3   **WHAT COMPETITIVE INTELLIGENCE IS AND IS NOT!**

Competitive Intelligence Is . . .	Competitive Intelligence Is Not . . .
1. **Information** that has been analyzed to the point where it is possible to make an appropriate decision.	1. **Spying.** Spying implies illegal or unethical activities. It rarely occurs because most corporations do not want to find themselves in court or upsetting shareholders.
2. **A tool** to alert management early to both threats and opportunities.	2. **A crystal ball.** CI gives corporations good approximations of reality, short term and long term. It does not predict the future.
3. **A means to deliver reasonable assessments.** CI offers approximations of the market and the competition. It is not a peek at a rival's financial books. Reasonable assessments are what modern entrepreneurs need and want on a regular basis.	3. **Database search.** Databases offer just that—data. They do not analyze the data in any way. They certainly do not replace human beings, who make decisions by examining the data and applying their common sense, experience, and intuition.
4. **A way of life, a process.** If a company uses CI the way it should be used, CI becomes everyone's job—not just the strategic planning or marketing staff's. It is a process by which critical information is available to those who need it.	4. **A job for one smart person.** A CEO may appoint one person as the CI ringmaster, but one person cannot do it all. At best, the ringmaster can keep management informed and ensure that others become trained to apply this tool within their business units.

Sources: G. Imperato, "Competitive Intelligence—Get Smart!" *Fast Company,* April 1998, p. 269; and F. M. Fuld, "What Competitive Intelligence Is and Is Not!" www.fuld.com/whatCI.html.

The Internet has dramatically accelerated the speed with which firms can acquire competitive intelligence. Creativity and effective information-gathering skills are critical for meaningful intelligence. Specialist firms have sprouted to assist with the process. For example, in one case, a client wanted to determine the size, strength, and technical capabilities of a privately held company. Initially, it was difficult to get detailed information.[13] Then one analyst used Deja News, a unit of Google, to tap into some online discussion groups. The analyst's research determined that the company being researched had posted 14 job openings on one Usenet group. That posting was a road map to the competitor's development strategy.

At times, a firm's aggressive efforts to gather competitive intelligence may lead to unethical or illegal behaviours.[14] Strategy Spotlight 2.2 tells the story of two well-known rivals, who probably crossed the line in their efforts to gather competitive intelligence. Strategy Spotlight 2.3 provides an example of a company, United Technologies (UT), which has set clear guidelines to prevent unethical behaviour.

A word of caution: Executives must be careful to avoid spending so much time and effort tracking the competitive actions of traditional competitors that they ignore new competitors. Further, broad changes and events in

2.2 STRATEGY SPOTLIGHT

Spies in the Skies

"There is nothing new in companies spying on each other," according to Norman Inkster, a Royal Canadian Mounted Police (RCMP) chief from 1987 to 1994, who now runs a private investigation firm. "In the old days, it usually meant breaking into rivals' offices; today, it's about hacking into websites and electronic files," tactics that Inkster says can be difficult to detect and hugely damaging.

A few years ago, the Air Canada–WestJet battle moved from the skies to the courtrooms. A massive civil lawsuit over corporate espionage provided a rare glimpse into the dirty tricks rivals may resort to in the name of competition. The critical battle was also playing out in the court of public opinion: Air Canada, long thought to be a corporate bully, appeared to be the victim, and WestJet, for years the darling of investors and the flying public, was cast as the bad guy.

In its statement of claim, which accused WestJet of "high-handed and malicious" conduct, Air Canada claimed that WestJet surreptitiously tapped into Air Canada's employee website and set up a "screen scraper," a program designed to automatically lift data off one site and dump it into another. A standard airline perk allows staff to travel almost free on flights with open seats. Employees receive a personal code which allows them to check which flights are available. Air Canada found that someone (or something) had used a single access code to enter the system an astounding 243,630 times between May 2003 and March 2004, for an average of 786 hits a day. On one extraordinary day, the site was tapped 4,973 times. The code allegedly belonged to Jeffrey Lafond, a former Canadian Airlines International employee, who had accepted a buyout package soon after Canadian Airlines was taken over by Air Canada—a package that included two staff tickets per year for five years. Lafond admitted providing his employee and personal ID numbers to WestJet co-founder Mark Hill but said that he did not think the load-factor information was relevant. Alleging that WestJet boosted its own profits using the illegally obtained information, Air Canada claimed a whopping $220 million in damages.

In response, WestJet claimed that the suit was an attempt at embarrassing a rival and, in a counter-suit, accused Air Canada of stealing WestJet's confidential information. Allegedly, Air Canada sent investigators to rifle through a WestJet executive's garbage to obtain data!

Eventually, the two sides settled their dispute when WestJet admitted that its conduct was unethical and unacceptable and agreed to a $15.5 million settlement and a substantial donation to Air Canada's choice of charities.

Sources: K. Macklem, "Spies in the Skies," *Maclean's,* September 20, 2004, pp. 20–24; Reuters, posting 5/30/2006; *Financial Times,* July 10, 2006, p.18.

2.3 STRATEGY SPOTLIGHT

Ethical Guidelines on Competitive Intelligence: United Technologies

United Technologies (UT) is a $56-billion global conglomerate composed of world-leading businesses with rich histories of technological pioneering, such as Otis Elevator, Carrier Air Conditioning, and Sikorsky (helicopters). It was founded in 1853 and has an impressive history of technological accomplishments. UT built the first working helicopter, developed the first commercially available hydrogen cells, and designed complete life support systems for space shuttles. UT believes strongly in a robust code of ethics. In the last decade, it has clearly articulated its principles governing business conduct. These include an antitrust guide, an ethics guide when contracting with the U.S. government as well as foreign governments, a policy on accepting gifts from suppliers, and guidelines for the proper use of email. One such document is the Code of Ethics Guide on Competitive Intelligence. This encourages managers and workers to ask themselves the following five questions whenever they have ethical concerns:

1. Have I done anything that coerced somebody to share this information? Have I, for example, threatened a supplier by indicating that future business opportunities will be influenced by the receipt of information with respect to a competitor?

2. Am I in a place where I should not be? If, for example, I am a field representative with privileges to move around in a customer's facility, have I gone outside the areas permitted? Have I misled anybody to gain access?

3. Is the contemplated technique for gathering information evasive? Does it involve sifting through trash or setting up an electronic "snooping" device directed at a competitor's facility from across the street?

4. Have I misled somebody in a way that the person believed sharing information with me was required or would be protected by a confidentiality agreement? Have I, for example, called and misrepresented myself as a government official who was seeking some information for some official purpose?

5. Have I done something to evade or circumvent a system intended to secure or protect information?

Sources: Nelson, B. 2003. The thinker. Forbes, March 3: 62–64; and The Fuld war room—Survival kit 010. Code of ethics (printed 2/26/01); and www.yahoo.com.

---

the larger environment may have a dramatic impact on a firm's viability. Peter Drucker, whom many consider the father of modern management, wrote:

> Increasingly, a winning strategy will require information about events and conditions outside the institution: noncustomers, technologies other than those currently used by the company and its present competitors, markets not currently served, and so on.[15]

Consider the fall of the mighty *Encyclopaedia Britannica,* once the global leader of printed information in the English speaking world.[16] Its demise was not caused by a traditional competitor in the encyclopedia industry. It was caused by new technology. CD-ROMs came out of nowhere and devastated the printed encyclopedia industry. Why? A full set of the *Encyclopaedia Britannica* sells for about $2,000, but an encyclopedia on CD-ROM, such as *Microsoft* Encarta®, sells for about $50. To make matters worse, many people receive Encarta free with their personal computers. Moreover, Wikipedia is freely available to everyone with access to the Internet, and it is constantly updated.

A manager typically has at his or her disposal a plethora of sources for information and insights. The Internet, online services such as D&B, Factiva, S&P, and Thomson Reuters, trade shows and conferences, professional networks, industry analysts' reports, and government publications are but a few of the many sources at hand, of which there are so many that the danger may rest less in not being able to find out what is going on around him or her and more in being overwhelmed by too much information and paralyzed by an inability to process all that seems pertinent. Nevertheless, managers must develop the habit of continuous awareness and curiosity and use judgment to sift through the mountains of accessible data and information to make sense of it all. Frameworks and tools, such as those presented in this chapter and the next chapter, are useful means to assist managers in putting that information to productive use.

Environmental Forecasting

Environmental scanning, monitoring, and competitive intelligence are important inputs for analyzing the external environment. However, they are of little use unless they provide raw material that is reliable enough to help managers make accurate forecasts. Environmental forecasting involves the development of plausible projections about the direction, scope, speed, and intensity of environmental change.[17] Its purpose is to predict change. It asks: How long will it take a new technology to reach the marketplace? Will the present social concern about an issue result in new legislation? Are current lifestyle trends likely to continue?

Some forecasting issues are much more specific to a particular firm and the industry in which it competes. Since the late 1990s, Bombardier had been contemplating future trends in people's travel patterns to help it decide whether to invest in a new-generation aircraft that can carry between 110 and 135 passengers. Eventually, it announced its plan for the new aircraft, but only five years after Embraer had introduced its own version, which helped the Brazilian firm move into the third spot in global rankings of aerospace manufacturers and displace its Canadian rival. Bombardier used high oil prices to emphasize the economics of its proposed design, claiming that state-of-the-art materials and a completely redesigned engine would make the aircraft 20 percent more efficient than anything else available in the market, thereby justifying its late entry and belated response. Within the same industry, Europe's Airbus bet its future on the A380, a giant airliner that can carry up to 800 passengers and aims to ease congestion in some of the world's busiest airports. By contrast, Boeing maintains that the future lies in smaller planes, such as its 787, which can quickly move in and out of busy airports. Each company has bet billions of dollars on its own belief about how the future will unfold in the airline industry.

A danger of forecasting is that managers may view uncertainty as black and white and ignore important grey areas. Either they assume that the world is certain and open to precise predictions, or they assume it is uncertain and completely unpredictable.[18] Underestimating uncertainty can lead to strategies that neither defend against looming threats nor take advantage of opportunities. In 1977, Kenneth H. Olsen, then president of Digital Equipment Corp., announced, "There is no reason for individuals to have a computer in their home," and directed all his firm's research efforts toward mainframe computers and workstations. The explosion in the personal computer market was not easy to detect in 1977, but it was clearly within the range of possibilities that industry experts were discussing at the time. Similarly, there have been numerous underestimates of the growth potential of new telecommunication services. The electric telegraph was derided by Ralph Waldo Emerson, and the telephone had its skeptics. Similarly, with the invention of television, "experts" could not imagine people sitting in front of these "boxes" for hours at a time instead of listening to the radio. In turn, radio was expected to disappear soon after the cassette and CD players were introduced. An "infamous" McKinsey study in the early 1980s predicted fewer than one million users of cellular phones in the United States by the year 2000.[19]

Obviously, poor predictions never go out of vogue. Consider some of the "gems" associated with the global financial crisis that began in 2008.[20]

- "Freddie Mac and Fannie Mae are fundamentally sound. . . . I think they are in good shape going forward."—Barney Frank (D-Mass.), House Financial Services Committee Chairman, July 14, 2008. *(Two months later, the government forced the mortgage giants into conservatorships.)*

- "Existing home sales to trend up in 2008"—Headline of a National Association of Realtors press release, December 9, 2007. *(On December 23, 2007, the group said November sales were down 11 percent from a year earlier in the worst housing slump since the Great Depression.)*

- "I think you'll see $150 a barrel [of oil] by the end of the year."—T. Boone Pickens, June 20, 2008. (Oil *was then around $135 a barrel. By late December, it was around $40.)*

- "I expect there will be some failures. . . . I don't anticipate any serious problems of that sort among the large internationally active banks."—Ben Bernanke, Federal Reserve Chairman, February 28, 2008. *(In September, Washington Mutual became the largest financial institution in U.S. history to fail. Citigroup needed an even bigger rescue in November.)*

- "In today's regulatory environment, it's virtually impossible to violate rules."— Bernard Madoff, money manager, October 20, 2007. (On *December 11, 2008, Madoff was arrested for allegedly running a Ponzi scheme that may have lost investors $50 billion. He was sentenced to 150 years in prison on July 29, 2009.)*

At the other extreme, if managers assume the world is unpredictable, they may abandon the analytical rigour of their traditional planning process and base their strategic decisions on gut instinct. Such a "just do it" approach has led many executives to place uninformed bets on emerging products or markets that have resulted in record write-offs.

LO 4 Scenario Analysis

A more in-depth approach to forecasting involves scenario analysis. It draws on a range of disciplines and interests, among them economics, psychology, sociology, and demographics. It usually begins with a discussion of participants' thoughts on ways in which societal trends, economics, politics, and technology may affect the issue under discussion.[21] Consider Lego, for example. The popular Danish toy manufacturer has a strong position in its market for "construction toys." However, what would happen if its market, broadly defined, changed dramatically? After all, Lego competes not only with producers of similar products, such as Mega Bloks, Canada's largest toy manufacturer, it also competes on a much broader canvas for a share of children's playtime. From this perspective, Lego products have numerous competitors, many of them computer based; still others have not yet been invented. Lego may end up with an increasing share of a narrow, shrinking market, much like IBM in the declining days of the mainframe computer. To avoid such a fate, Lego has been very proactive in re-branding itself and creating a popular entertainment subculture that includes successful movies, character tie-ins and amusement parks. In this spirit, managers must consider their future in a context wider than their present, traditional markets. They need to lay down guidelines for at least 10 years into the future in order to anticipate rapid changes. Scenarios represent one technique that can assist managers in coping with the uncertainty and unpredictability of today's rapidly changing world, where competition can appear from anywhere at any time and where the rules of the game can change with little warning.

Scenario analysis is different from other tools for strategic planning, such as trend analysis or high and low forecasts. The origins of scenario planning lie in the military, which used the technique during World War II to effectively cope with multiple challenges, limited resources, and great unpredictability in the unfolding of the war.[22] Strategy Spotlight 2.4 provides an example of scenario analysis at Shell Oil Company, one of the earliest adopters of this kind of analysis, which used it to prepare to cope with the uncertainty of extreme volatility in oil prices. Other practitioners of scenario planning include Levi Strauss, which uses it to consider potential impacts of everything from cotton deregulation to the unlikely occurrence of the total disappearance of cotton from the earth. Also, a German insurance company contemplated the fall of the Berlin Wall and made plans to expand in Central Europe. And in 1990, when Nelson Mandela was released from a South African prison, he met with a panel that helped him create scenarios to chart the country's possible futures. Scenario planning helps by considering not trends or forecasts but how these could be upset by unpredictable events.

SWOT Analysis

To understand the business environment of a particular firm, one needs to analyze both the general environment and the firm's industry and competitive environment. Generally, firms compete with other firms in the same industry. An industry is composed of a set of firms that produce similar products or services, sell to similar customers,

2.4 STRATEGY SPOTLIGHT

Scenario Planning at Shell Oil Company

In the 1960s and 1970s, Shell combined analytical tools with information to create scenarios of possible outcomes. The result of the 1973 oil embargo was a sharp increase in crude oil prices, short supplies of gasoline for consumers, and a depressed world economy. However, Shell's strategic planning, which included the use of scenarios, had strongly suggested that a more unstable environment was coming, with a resulting shift of power from oil companies to oil producers. As a result of the precautionary actions it took, Shell was in a better position than most oil companies when the 1973 embargo occurred. Shell also uses scenario planning to plan major new oil field investments. This is because elements of risk can be identified and explored over a considerable period of time.

The Shell process of scenario planning involves the following stages:

1. Interviews with people both inside and outside the business, using an open-ended questioning technique to encourage full and frank answers.

2. Analysis of interviews by issue to build a "natural agenda" for further processing.

3. Synthesis of each agenda so as to draw out underlying areas of uncertainty or dispute and possible interrelationships among issues.

4. A small number of "issues workshops" to explore key issues to improve understanding and identify gaps for further research (these generate a wide range of options for strategy).

5. A scenario workshop to identify and build a small number of scenarios, which may occur in some 10 to 15 years' time or even later.

6. A testing of strategy options against the scenarios to assess robustness (i.e., whether or not a given strategy is effective under more than one scenario).

Sources: R. Martin, "The Oracles of Oil," *Business 2.0,* January 2002, pp. 35–39; J. Epstein, "Scenario Planning: An Introduction," *The Futurist,* September 1998, pp. 50–52; and Touchstone Renard Management Consultants website: www.touchstonerenard.co.uk.

and use similar methods of production. Gathering industry information and understanding competitive dynamics among the different companies in an industry is key to successful strategic management.

One of the most basic techniques for analyzing firm and industry conditions is **SWOT analysis.** SWOT stands for strengths, weaknesses, opportunities, and threats. It provides "raw material"—a basic listing of conditions both inside and surrounding the company.

The general idea of SWOT analysis is that a firm's strategy must include the following:

- Build on the firm's strengths
- Remedy its weaknesses or work around them
- Take advantage of the opportunities presented by the environment
- Protect the firm from the threats

Despite its apparent simplicity, the SWOT approach has been very popular. First, it forces managers to consider both internal and external factors simultaneously. Second, its emphasis on identifying opportunities and threats makes firms act proactively rather than reactively. Third, it raises awareness about the role of strategy in creating a match between the environmental conditions and the firm's internal strengths and weaknesses. Finally, its conceptual simplicity is achieved without sacrificing analytical rigour.

The "strengths and weaknesses" portion of SWOT refers to the areas within the firm where it excels, where its traditional points of power, ability, and capacity lie (strengths), and, conversely, where there may be disadvantages and where it may be lacking relative to its competitors (weaknesses). Examples of strengths may be superior knowledge, strong brands, state-of-the-art facilities, unique access to certain markets, highly motivated workforce, extensive distribution networks, deep financial pockets, and strong leadership. In contrast, weaknesses can be found in difficulties in accessing raw materials, wounded brands, high financial leverage, and pending lawsuits. Strengths and weaknesses are addressed more extensively in Chapter 3, through our discussion of an organization's value chain and the resource-based view of the firm.

Opportunities and threats are environmental conditions external to the firm. These could be factors in the general environment, such as improving economic conditions that cause lower borrowing costs or an aging population that demands new services for leisure and convenience. Opportunities can arise from technological developments, such as the Internet and telecommunications or advances in biotechnology. One can find opportunities almost everywhere, in identifying new market needs, new and better ways to respond to existing needs, new ways of delivering products and services, new applications of technology, easing regulatory conditions, industry consolidation, or technology convergence. Threats can arise from formidable competitors, new legislation, an aging population, shifts in the tastes and values of consumers, protectionism, terrorism, an oil crisis, increasing commodity prices, or a new technology that threatens to make the firm's products obsolete.

Although opportunities and threats are rather subjective interpretations of what is unfolding in a firm's external environment, and two informed individuals can easily come up with two different lists, it is important that managers systematically consider each area of their general and competitive environments for specific opportunities as well as for looming threats. It is also important not to cast the net too narrow. Strategists who rely on traditional definitions of their industry and competitive environment often focus their sights too narrowly on current customers, technologies, and competitors. Hence, they fail to notice important changes in the periphery of their environment— changes that may trigger the need to redefine industry boundaries and identify a whole new set of competitive relationships. It is also important not to focus too much on one moment in time. Strategy and competition unfold over time. As circumstances change, a static analysis cannot capture the dynamics of the competitive environment; managers risk missing the changing impact on their strategies and competitiveness.

Not all trends, opportunities, and threats apply equally to all companies within an industry, and one firm's SWOT analysis is not applicable to another. Specific trends may benefit some companies but harm others. Consider, for example, the heightened awareness about health and fitness, which presents an opportunity to some companies (e.g., health clubs and diet food producers), but represents a clear threat to others (e.g., tobacco firms and breweries).

It is also worth noting that SWOT analysis is not the perfect solution to strategic planning and should not be seen as an end in itself. It is a framework that allows a manager to classify issues and observations in a meaningful and useful way. It does, however, have its limitations. It is simply a starting point for discussion. By listing the firm's attributes, managers identify the raw material needed to perform more in-depth strategic analysis. SWOT analysis cannot, however, yield environmental forecasts; nor can it show managers how to achieve a competitive advantage. SWOT's value lies in providing a systematic framework to initiate discussion among thoughtful managers who are contemplating the challenges and opportunities facing their firm.

LO 5 THE GENERAL ENVIRONMENT

The general environment is composed of stakeholders and factors that can have dramatic effects on a firm's strategy and critically affect its performance. Yet, typically, a firm has little ability to predict the trends and events in the general environment and even less ability to control them. It is difficult to predict future political events, such as the ongoing Middle East unrest and tensions on the Korean peninsula. It is not easy to anticipate and be prepared for shocks, such as skyrocketing oil and other commodity prices, the SARS (severe acute respiratory syndrome) crisis, "mad cow" disease outbreak, terrorism, and others; nor is it easy to fathom their financial, social, and economic impacts. Who would have guessed that the Internet would impact national and global economies as it has done over the past two decades? In the 1980s, the Internet was little more than a tool for academic researchers to exchange computer files. In less than 20 short years, dramatic innovations in information technology, along with many other factors, helped keep inflation in check across the world by lowering the cost of doing business and bringing the world closer together.

We divide the general environment into six segments: (1) demographic/psychographic, (2) sociocultural, (3) political/legal, (4) technological, (5) economic, and (6) global. First, we discuss each segment and provide a summary of the segment and examples of how events and trends in each segment can impact industries. Then, we address relationships among the general environment segments and consider how similar trends and events can have varying impacts across industries. Exhibit 2-4 provides examples of key trends and events in each of the six segments of the general environment.

EXHIBIT 2-4 GENERAL ENVIRONMENT: KEY TRENDS AND EVENTS

Demographic/Psychographic
- Aging population
- Rising affluence
- Changes in ethnic composition
- Geographic distribution of population
- Greater disparities in income levels
- Education
- Diminishing sense of loyalty to corporations among urban professionals

Sociocultural
- More women in the workforce
- Increase in the number of temporary workers
- Greater concern for fitness
- Greater concern for the environment
- Postponement of family formation

Political/Legal
- Protection of cultural industries (e.g., CRTC[1])
- Indigenous land claim settlements
- Deregulation of utility and other industries
- Increases in provincially mandated minimum wages
- Taxation at provincial and federal levels
- Legislation on corporate governance reforms in bookkeeping, stock options, etc.

Technological
- Genetic engineering
- Emergence of Internet technology
- Computer-aided design/computer-aided manufacturing (CAD/CAM) systems
- Research in synthetic and exotic materials
- Pollution/global warming
- Miniaturization of computing technologies
- Wireless communications
- Nanotechnology

Economic
- Interest rates
- Unemployment
- Consumer Price Index
- Trends in GDP[2]
- Changes in stock market valuations

Global
- Increasing global trade
- Currency exchange rates
- Emergence of China and India as economic powers
- Trade agreements among regional blocs (e.g., NAFTA,[3] EU,[4] ASEAN[5])
- More countries entering the WTO[6] (leading to decreasing tariffs/free trade in services)

[1] CRTC, Canadian Radio-Television Telecommunications Commission
[2] GDP, gross domestic product
[3] NAFTA, North American Free Trade Agreement
[4] EU, European Union
[5] ASEAN, Association of the South East Asian Nations
[6] WTO, World Trade Organization

The Demographic/Psychographic Segment

Demographics are the most easily understood and quantifiable elements of the general environment. They are at the root of many changes in society. Demographics include elements such as an aging population,[23] rising or declining affluence, changes in ethnic composition, geographic distribution of the population, and disparities in income level. Psychographics reflect the various attitudes and interests among individuals and complement the demographic characteristics of the population. Psychographics capture the differences among individuals who may belong to a particular group, such as urban professionals, college students, and stay-at-home fathers, but vary widely in their perceptions, priorities, and the ways they interpret and react to external events.

The impact of a demographic trend, like trends in all segments of the general environment, varies across industries. The aging of the Canadian population might have a positive effect on the real estate and consumer industries but a negative impact on manufacturers of diapers and baby food. Rising levels of affluence in many developed countries bode well for such industries as brokerage services and upscale pets and supplies. However, these same trends may have an adverse effect on fast-food chains because people can afford and prefer to dine at higher-priced restaurants. Fast-food restaurants depend on minimum-wage employees for efficient operation, but the competition for labour intensifies as more attractive employment opportunities become prevalent, thus threatening the employment base for restaurants. Let us look at the details of some of these trends.

The aging of the population in Canada and in other developed countries has important implications. Many of the aging "baby boomers" (those born between 1945 and 1964), who control an estimated 80 percent of the wealth in Canada, are now retired or approaching retirement.[24] By 2025, nearly one-fifth of Canadians will be over 65 years old. This may be good news for drugstores, which see older patients seven times more often than younger ones.[25] The life insurance industry also benefits from increasing life expectancies, but hospitals find their budgets strained by the more expensive and more intensive health-related needs of the aging population.

Another demographic trend is the shift toward smaller households. In 2016, one-person households became the most common type of household in Canada, accounting for 28.2 percent of all households. This surpassed for the first time the number of households comprised of couples with children, which itself accounted for only 26.5 percent of all households. Smaller family sizes are due, in part, to decreasing fertility rates, but there has also been an increase in the number of childless couples and "empty nesters" (parents whose children have moved out). At the same time, more young adults, aged 20 to 34 years, are continuing to live with their parents. Between 2001 and 2016, the number of young adults living with their parents rose from 24.6 percent to 35 percent. The reasons behind such demographic shifts can be complex, but understanding those reasons can help firms to capitalize on the opportunities they offer.

The Sociocultural Segment

Sociocultural forces influence the values, beliefs, and lifestyles of a society. Examples include a higher percentage of women in the workforce, more dual-income families, increases in the number of temporary workers, greater concern for healthy diets and physical fitness, greater interest in the environment, and more and more people choosing to postpone having children. Such forces enhance sales of products and services in many industries but depress sales in others. The increased numbers of women in the workforce and dual-income families have, in turn, increased the need for business clothing merchandise but decreased the demand for baking product staples. A greater concern for health and fitness has helped industries that manufacture exercise equipment and healthful foods but has negatively impacted industries that produce snack foods and candy.

Sociocultural norms impact attitudes about entrepreneurship and the startup activities of firms. Canada, together with the United States and Israel, scored the highest among respondents in terms of their propensity to start a business and the general view that starting a new business was a "respected occupation."[26] Such attitudes have traditionally served countries well by encouraging individuals to take risks and to venture on their own, both of which bode well for the economic prosperity of the country.

The trend toward higher educational attainment among women has led to the increased participation of women in upper management positions. While many would argue that there is still sexism rooted in the workplace and that the existence of a "glass ceiling" prevents women from professional advancement, undisputed statistics also show that more women in Canada have postsecondary degrees compared with men. Recent Statistics Canada figures show women representing 57.7 percent of graduates. Furthermore, during the first fifteen years of this century, the number of women earning MBAs increased by 29 percent compared with only a 15 percent increase for men.[27] Given these educational attainments, it is hardly surprising that companies owned by women have been one of the key drivers of the economy. Canada boasts one of the highest rates of female employers and persons heading their own business, at over 40 percent, compared with 35 percent in the United States and fewer than 30 percent in most of Europe.[28]

The Political/Legal Segment

Political processes and legislation define the regulations that industries must comply with.[29] Key elements of the political/legal arena include environmental regulation, occupational health and safety legislation, immigration policies, deregulation of utilities and other industries, and increases in provincially mandated minimum wages.

Government legislation has a significant impact on corporations. The U.S. Congress passed the Sarbanes–Oxley Act in 2002, and Canada followed soon after with similar provisions which greatly increased the accountability of auditors, executives, members of boards of directors, and corporate lawyers. Those provisions were introduced in response to the widespread perception that existing governance mechanisms had failed to protect the interests of shareholders, employees, and creditors, brought about by the embarrassing revelations and criminal activities associated with executives within Enron, Tyco, WorldCom, and Hollinger International. The provisions have significant ramifications for all public and private corporations on both sides of the border as well as for numerous European and Asian companies that trade and have transactions with the North American financial markets.

As with many factors in the general environment, changes that benefit one industry may adversely affect others. Following the terrorist attacks of September 11, 2001, and the precipitous drop in air travel, the U.S. government announced financial assistance to the ailing airline industry to the tune of $5 billion cash and a further $10 billion in loan guarantees. Of course, the hotel and hospitality industries demanded similar assistance but received nothing. Opponents have argued that such schemes only enrich the shareholders of airline stocks at the expense of taxpayers. Related arguments have been raised in Canada with regard to financial assistance that has frequently been extended to Bombardier Inc. in order to enable it to continue assembling planes in Quebec and Ontario. In fact, in the last few years, the government of Quebec has extended loan guarantees exceeding $2.3 billion to Bombardier in an effort to retain its high-paying jobs in the province.

Since Confederation, subsequent Canadian governments have adopted industrial policies that have been both interventionist and protectionist.[30] As a result, every facet of the Canadian economy operates within a framework of thousands of regulations, and more than 700 Crown corporations have been involved in everything from selling liquor to producing nuclear reactors. Although the rationale has always been a desire to maintain economic and cultural independence from the United States, critics argue that such regulations were also responsible for the relative underperformance of the Canadian economy in the latter part of the twentieth century compared with most of the other industrialized nations.

The Technological Segment

Developments in technology lead to new products and services and improve how they are produced and delivered to the end user. Innovations can create entirely new industries and alter the boundaries of existing industries.[31] Notable technological developments and trends include genetic engineering, nanotechnology, and research in artificial and exotic materials.

Likely the most significant technological development of our time is the combination of information technology (IT) and the Internet. The Internet has reduced the cost of getting information and increased its availability in impressive ways. For example, Fidelity Investments has found that it costs $15 to handle a transaction over the phone but less than a cent to perform that same transaction on the Web.[32] Airlines have saved billions of dollars by diverting passengers away from commissioned travel agents and their own telephone operators, which traditionally cost in excess of 5 percent of the price of a ticket; purchases on the airlines' own websites cost pennies and, as an added benefit, decrease errors and increase loyalty among their customers.

However, there are some downsides to technology development. In addition to ethical issues raised by advances in biotechnology, there are threats to the earth's environment associated with the emission of greenhouse gases, pollution, and global warming. To combat such problems, some firms in the petroleum industry are taking creative and proactive steps. BP Amoco, for example, is carrying out a plan to decrease its greenhouse gas emissions by giving each of its 150 business units a quota of emission permits and encouraging the units to trade among themselves. If a unit cuts emissions and has leftover permits, it can sell them to other units that are having difficulty meeting their goals.[33]

The Economic Segment

The economy affects all industries, from suppliers of raw materials to manufacturers of finished goods and services, as well as all organizations in the service, wholesale, retail, government, and nonprofit sectors. Key economic indicators include interest rates, unemployment rates, the consumer price index, the GDP, and net disposable income. Interest rate increases have a negative impact on the residential home construction industry but a negligible (or neutral) effect on industries that produce essential consumer products, such as prescription drugs or common grocery items.

Other economic indicators are associated with equity markets. Perhaps the most watched is the Dow Jones Industrial Average (DJIA), which is composed of 30 large industrial firms. When stock market indexes increase, consumers' confidence and spending increase, and there is often an increased demand for luxury items, such as jewellery and automobiles. But when stock valuations decrease, demand for these items shrinks. Until recently, the energy boom had pushed real estate prices in Calgary to new highs; the stratospheric Toronto and Vancouver real estate markets have been attributed to the cities' appeal to Canadians and new immigrants as places of employment opportunity and a desired quality of life. In addition, these cities have appeal to jittery foreign buyers looking for a safe place to park their wealth.

The Global Segment

More and more firms have been expanding their operations and market reach beyond the borders of their "home" countries. Globalization provides opportunities to reach much larger potential markets as well as access a broader base of factors of production, such as raw materials, labour, skilled managers, and technical professionals.

Examples of important elements in the global segment include exchange rates, global trade, the fastgrowing economies of China and India, trade agreements among regional blocs (e.g., North American Free Trade Agreement (NAFTA), European Union (EU), Association of Southeast Asian Nations (ASEAN), and the General Agreement on Tariffs and Trade (GATT). Increases in trade across national boundaries provide benefits to the cargo and shipping industries but have a minimal impact on service industries, such as bookkeeping and medical services. The emergence of China as an economic power has benefited many industries and sectors, including steel, construction, and computers, as well as consumer goods. Nonetheless, it has had a negative impact on the clothing sector in North America and has posed serious challenges to many manufacturers.

Few industries are as global as the automobile industry. Consider just a few examples of how some of the key players expanded their reach into Latin America during the 1990s. Fiat built a new plant in Argentina; Volkswagen retooled a plant in Mexico to launch the new Beetle; DaimlerChrysler built a new plant as a joint venture with BMW to produce engines in Brazil; and General Motors built a new car factory in Brazil. Suppliers to the industry have followed suit. Magna and Dofasco have built facilities in the region to supply components on a just-in-time basis to those plants. Why the interest in this region? In addition to the region's low wage rates and declining trade barriers, its population of 400 million is very attractive. But the real bonus lies in the 9-to-1 people-to-cars ratio in the region compared with a 2-to-1 ratio in developed countries. With this region's growth expected to be in the 3- to 4-percent range in the first part of the twenty-first century, sales should increase at a healthy rate.[34]

Similarly, consider the extent of globalization in the Norwegian shipping industry. Despite a small population of only 4.5 million, Norway developed the world's third largest merchant fleet. And as the world's second largest oil exporter, it has the vessels and equipment needed to service oil fields off its storm-prone coasts. When the warship *USS Cole* was severely damaged by terrorists on October 12, 2000, it was returned to the United States from Yemen aboard a giant Norwegian-owned transport ship, the *Blue Marlin*. Frederik Steenbuch, manager of

Oslo-based Offshore Heavy Transport, which owns the *Blue Marlin,* stated: "This has nothing to do with Norway. It is purely international. The Blue Marlin was built in Taiwan, flies a Panamanian flag, and has a crew from Latvia. The key machinery on board was built in Korea under a Danish licence."[35]

Relationships among the Elements of the General Environment

In our discussion of the general environment, we see many relationships among the various elements.[36] For example, two demographic trends—the aging of the population and regional population shifts—have important implications for the economic segment (in terms of tax policies to provide benefits to increasing numbers of older citizens) and the political segment (in terms of the relative priorities set on the government's agenda). Another example is the emergence of IT as a means to increase the rate of productivity gains across many developed countries. Such use of IT results in lower inflation (an important element of the economic segment) and helps offset costs associated with higher labour rates.

The effects of a trend or event in the general environment vary across industries. When commodity prices increased, especially for oil and gas, they boosted the economies of Alberta, Saskatchewan, and Newfoundland, generated economic prosperity and high employment, and put upward pressure on housing prices across the region. Yet the same commodity boom also increased the value of the Canadian dollar by some 50 percent against the U.S. dollar. This, in turn, had devastating effects on the manufacturing sector in Ontario and Quebec, whose exports to the United States were hammered by the increasing value of the loonie. More recent depressed energy prices have had the opposite effects across the country. When the housing and financial crises of 2007/2008 hit the United States they also crippled the Canadian automotive industry, which had traditionally relied on a healthy American market for its products. Similarly, governmental legislation that permits the importation of prescription drugs from Canada into the United States is a very positive development for Canadian drugstores but has a negative effect on drug manufacturers in the United States. Exhibit 2-5 provides other examples of how the impact of trends or events in the general environment can vary across industries.

EXHIBIT 2-5 THE IMPACT OF GENERAL ENVIRONMENTAL TRENDS AND EVENTS ON VARIOUS INDUSTRIES

Segment/Trends and Events	Industry	Positive	Neutral	Negative
Demographic/Psychographic				
Aging population	Health care	✓		
	Baby products			✓
Rising affluence	Brokerage services	✓		
	Fast foods			✓
	Upscale pets and supplies	✓		
Sociocultural				
More women in the workforce	Clothing	✓		
	Baking products (staples)			✓
Greater concern for health and fitness	Home exercise equipment	✓		
	Meat products			✓
Political/Legal				
Environmental legislation	Heavy manufacturing			✓
	Environmental consulting	✓		
	Plastics, chemicals			✓

(Continued)

Segment/Trends and Events	Industry	Positive	Neutral	Negative
Technological				
Genetic engineering	Pharmaceutical	✓		
	Publishing		✓	
Pollution/global warming	Engineering services	✓		
	Petroleum			✓
Economic				
Interest rate increases	Residential construction			✓
	Most common grocery products		✓	
Global				
Increasing global trade	Shipping	✓		
	Personal service		✓	
Emergence of China as an economic power	Soft drinks	✓		
	Defense			✓

Crowdsourcing: A Technology That Affects Multiple Segments of the General Environment

Before moving on, let's consider the Internet. The Internet has been a leading and highly visible component of a broader technological phenomenon—the emergence of digital technology. These technologies are altering the way business is conducted and having an effect on nearly every business domain. One application of digital technology is crowdsourcing, which we will encounter as a theme throughout the text. It has affected multiple elements of the general environment, such as technology, globalization, and economics. When and where did the term "crowdsourcing" originate?[37] In January 2006, open sourcing—software developed as a public collaboration—was, for most businesspeople, little more than an online curiosity. At that time, Jeff Howe of *Wired* magazine began to write an article about the phenomenon. However, he soon discovered a far more important story to be told: Large—and small—companies in a wide variety of industries had begun farming out serious tasks to individuals and groups on the Internet. Together with his editor, Mark Robinson, they coined a new term to describe the phenomenon: crowdsourcing. In June 2006, Howe's article appeared. In it, crowdsourcing was defined as the tapping of the "latent talent of the (online) crowd." It has become the term of choice for a process that is infiltrating many aspects of business life.

Since its early beginnings, crowdsourcing has claimed some well-known successes, particularly on the product-development front. Consider:

- The Linux operating system, created as an open-source alternative to Windows and UNIX, can be downloaded for free and altered to suit any user's needs. And with all the firepower brought to bear by the online open-source community, bugs in the system get fixed in a matter of hours.

- One of Amazon's smartest moves was to invite its customers to write online reviews. The customers are neither paid nor controlled by the company, but the content that they create adds enormous value to other customers and, therefore, to Amazon.

- Roughly five million users per month swear by Wikipedia. The free online encyclopedia is created and updated by Internet volunteers to the tune of roughly two million articles and counting.

Throughout this book, we introduce examples of crowdsourcing and show its relevance to key strategy concepts. For example, in Chapter 3, we discuss how Procter & Gamble used it to develop social connections through digital media that enable the firm to co-design and co-engineer new innovations with buyers. In Chapter 4, we discuss how SAP, the giant software company, uses crowdsourcing to tap knowledge well beyond its own boundaries through nearly three million participants in its Community Network. In Chapter 5, we explain how Unilever is using crowdsourcing to advance its sustainability initiatives. And in Chapter 12, we discuss how NASA is working with Innocentive to overcome some of the technology challenges associated with deep-space missions.

Strategy Spotlight 2.5 explains how Lego has used crowdsourcing to help the toy maker strengthen its ties to customers and increase revenues.

2.5 STRATEGY SPOTLIGHT

Lego's Effective Use of Crowdsourcing

Lego runs its crowdsourcing program with Cuusoo System, a Japanese company. "Both children and adults these days are used to being, and expect to be, more involved," says Mads Nipper, chief marketing officer at Lego's headquarters in Billund, Denmark. Through their site, Lego Cuusoo—which translates roughly to "my Lego wish" in Japanese—helps the company develop ideas that its 180 designers might not come up with on their own.

How does it work? People create a model, take photos, write a project description, and submit their idea on the Lego website (ideas.lego.com). Projects that garner more than 10,000 votes from site visitors are evaluated by designers and executives to ensure they meet such requirements as safety and playability and fit with the Lego brand. Those whose models are chosen get 1 percent of their toy's net revenue. Plus, the Lego website asserts, "You're featured in the set materials, receive a royalty on sales, and are recognized as the product creator." Projects are reviewed about three times a year. As of this writing, toys scheduled for the next round of review include a bird, an Apple store, and a train inspired by writer Jules Verne.

A recent winner was Brent Waller, a 35-year-old video game developer who spent his childhood crafting plastic brick versions of characters from such television movies as *Teenage Mutant Turtles* and *Batman*. Waller's persistence paid off! His miniature version of the Cadillac ambulance from Bill Murray's 1984 comedy *Ghostbusters* went into production in June 2014. Claims Waller: "It's any Lego fan's dream to have an official set they created." He had struck out a few times before his big hit when his previous designs of houses, robots, and the Batmobile weren't chosen.

Sources: Gustafsson, K. 2014. Who ya gonna call? Lego dials fans. Bloomberg Businessweek, March 19: 27–28; and https://ideas.lego.com/dashboard.

LO 6 THE COMPETITIVE ENVIRONMENT

In addition to the general environment, managers must consider the *competitive environment* (also sometimes referred to as the *task* or *industry environment*). The nature of competition in an industry and the profitability of a particular firm are more directly influenced by developments in the competitive environment than the general environment.

The competitive environment consists of many factors that are highly relevant to a firm's strategy. These include existing or potential competitors, customers, and suppliers. Potential competitors may include a supplier considering forward integration, such as an automobile manufacturer acquiring a rental car company, or a firm in an entirely new industry introducing a similar product that uses a more efficient technology.

In the following sections, we discuss key concepts and analytical techniques that managers should use to assess their competitive environments. First, we examine Michael Porter's five-forces model that illustrates how these forces can be used to explain individual firms' profitability in an industry.[38] Then, we address the concept of strategic groups, which demonstrates that even within an industry, it is often useful to group firms on the basis of similarities in their strategies. Firms within a strategic group tend to react similarly to external events, and competition tends to be more intense among firms within a strategic group than among strategic groups.

Porter's Five-Forces Model of Industry Competition

The "five forces" model developed by Michael E. Porter has been the most commonly used analytical tool for examining the competitive environment.[39] It describes the competitive environment in terms of five basic competitive forces:

1. The threat of new entrants
2. The bargaining power of buyers
3. The bargaining power of suppliers
4. The threat of substitute products and services
5. The intensity of the rivalry among competitors in an industry

Each of these forces affects a firm's ability to compete in a given market. Together, they determine the profit potential for a particular industry. The model is shown in Exhibit 2-6. Managers should be familiar with the five-forces model for several reasons. It helps them assess the overall attractiveness of an industry and decide whether their firm should remain in or exit that industry. It provides the rationale for increasing or decreasing resource commitments. The model helps assess how to improve a firm's competitive position with regard to each of the five forces. For example, managers can use insights provided by the five-forces model to create higher entry barriers that discourage new rivals from competing with their firm.[40] Or they may develop strong relationships with their distribution channels to better balance the bargaining power of their buyers.

The Threat of New Entrants

The threat of new entrants refers to the possibility that the profits of established firms in the industry may be eroded by new competitors. The extent of the threat depends on existing barriers to entry and the combined reactions

EXHIBIT 2-6

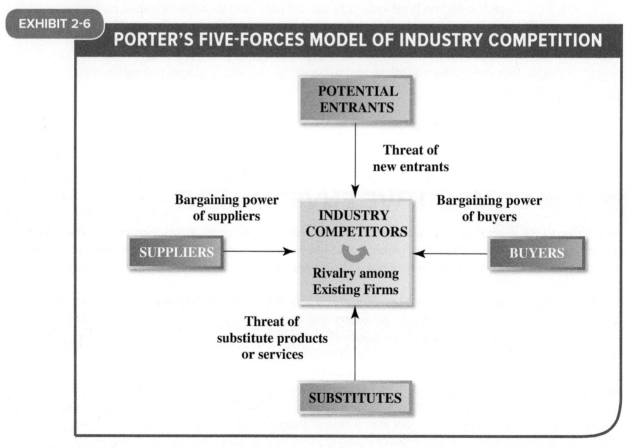

PORTER'S FIVE-FORCES MODEL OF INDUSTRY COMPETITION

from existing competitors. If entry barriers are high and/or the newcomer can anticipate a sharp retaliation from established competitors, the threat of entry is low. These circumstances discourage new competitors. There are six major sources of entry barriers:

- *Economies of scale.* Economies of scale refer to spreading the costs of production and other business activities over a large number of units produced. The per-unit cost of a product typically decreases as the absolute volume produced within a period increases. Larger facilities, automation, fixed overhead costs, and advertising expenses can be some of the typical sources of economies of scale for a traditional manufacturer. For example, research and development (R&D) costs, commercialization expenses, and legal and regulatory compliance give significant rise to economies of scale in the pharmaceutical industry. The presence of such economies of scale in an industry deters entry by forcing the firm contemplating entry to come in on a large scale and risk strong reaction from existing firms or come in on a small scale and accept a cost disadvantage.

- *Product differentiation.* When existing competitors have strong brand identification and customer loyalty, differentiation creates a barrier to entry by forcing entrants to spend heavily to overcome existing customer loyalties. Building a brand requires enormous investment, takes time, and is, of course, fraught with risk.

- *Capital requirements.* The need to invest large financial resources to compete creates a barrier to entry, especially if the capital is required for risky or unrecoverable upfront advertising or R&D.

- *Switching costs.* A barrier to entry is created by the existence of one-time costs that the buyer faces when switching from one supplier's product or service to another. Specialized equipment, non-standardized technologies, and unique inputs to a specific production process are some of the elements that generate switching costs and make it harder for customers to move away from an established firm to a new entrant.

- *Access to distribution channels.* The new entrant's need to secure distribution for its product can create a barrier to entry. Exclusive agreements, restrictive practices, and franchise networks provide preferential access to an incumbent and preclude newcomers from establishing a foothold in a market.

- *Cost disadvantages independent of scale.* Some existing competitors may have advantages that are independent of size or economies of scale. These derive from the following:

  - Proprietary product

  - Favourable access to raw materials

  - Government subsidies

  - Favourable government policies

In an industry where few, or none, of these entry barriers are present, the threat of new entry is high. If a new firm can launch its business with little capital investment or can operate efficiently despite its small scale of operation, it is likely to be a serious threat, as new competitors can easily erode the profits of established firms. Such industries as dry cleaning, craft brewing, consulting, and much of retailing present few barriers and experience a constant entry and exit of players as, in these industries, firms can set up operations very easily and compete locally without much regard for global brands or large scale.

The Bargaining Power of Buyers

Buyers threaten an industry by forcing down prices, bargaining for higher quality or more services, and playing competitors against each other. These actions erode industry profitability.[41] The power of each large buyer or buyer group depends on the attributes of the market situation and the importance of that group's purchases to the industry's overall business.

Loblaw's President's Choice line of products demonstrates how a buyer can exert power over its suppliers by creating conditions to its advantage. Since the President's Choice brand belongs to Loblaw, the producers have little influence on product design, features, or placement, and they must compete on price to attract the business from the powerful supermarket chain. Margins have decreased across the board among major producers in the food industry since Loblaw introduced its private label. Things deteriorated further for producers when the success of

Loblaw was followed by many other food retailers' own private labels. Similarly, Walmart absorbs 30 percent of Procter & Gamble's global production and critically affects the performance of one of the world's largest consumer goods corporations. A buyer is potentially more powerful under the following conditions:

- *It purchases large volumes relative to a seller's total sales.* If a large percentage of a supplier's sales are purchased by a single buyer, the importance of the buyer's business to the supplier increases. Large-volume buyers are particularly powerful in industries with high fixed costs (e.g., automobile manufacturers to the steel industry).

- *The products it purchases from the industry are standard or undifferentiated.* Confident that they can always find alternative suppliers, buyers play one company against the other, as in commodity grain products.

- *The buyer faces few switching costs.* Switching costs lock the buyer to particular sellers. Specialized components force buyers to deal with specific suppliers and largely accept their terms. Conversely, when buyers can easily switch between suppliers for their needs, they can play one supplier against another. The buyer's power is further enhanced if the seller faces high switching costs—if, for example, it has to commit substantial resources upfront for equipment or product design to earn the buyer's business.

- *It earns low profits.* Low profits create incentives to lower purchasing costs. However, highly profitable buyers are generally less price sensitive.

- *The buyers pose a credible threat of backward integration.* If buyers are either partially integrated or pose a credible threat of backward integration, they are typically able to secure concessions.

- *The industry's product is unimportant to the quality of the buyer's products or services.* When the quality of the buyer's products is not affected by the industry's product, the buyer is more indifferent to the input's features and concentrates, instead, on negotiating the lowest price.

At times, a firm or set of firms in an industry may increase its buyer power by using the services of a third party. FreeMarkets Online is one such third party.[42] Pittsburgh-based FreeMarkets has developed software that enables large industrial buyers to organize online auctions for qualified suppliers of semi-standard parts, such as fabricated components, packaging materials, metal stampings, and services. By aggregating buyers, FreeMarkets increases the buyers' bargaining power. The results are impressive. In its first 48 auctions, most participating companies saved over 15 percent; some saved as much as 50 percent.

The Bargaining Power of Suppliers

Suppliers can exert bargaining power over participants in an industry by threatening to raise prices, alter the terms of supply, or even lower the number of features and reduce the quality of goods and services they provide to the industry. Powerful suppliers can squeeze the profitability of firms in an industry to the point of taking away all the profits.[43] The factors that make suppliers powerful tend to be mirror opposites of those that make buyers powerful. A supplier will be potentially more powerful in the following circumstances:

- *The supplier industry is dominated by a few companies and is more concentrated (few firms dominate the industry) than the industry it sells to.* Suppliers selling to fragmented industries exert influence over prices, quality, and terms.

- *The industry is not an important customer of the supplier.* When suppliers sell to several industries and a particular industry does not represent a significant fraction of their sales, suppliers are able to exert power.

- *The supplier's product is an important input to the buyer's business.* When such inputs are important to the success of the buyer's manufacturing process or product quality, the bargaining power of suppliers is high.

- *The supplier's products are differentiated, or it has built up switching costs for the buyer.* Differentiation or switching costs facing the buyers cut off their options to play one supplier against another. When buyers are unable to substitute among different inputs, their suppliers can exert substantial power in determining prices and terms. (Conversely, even large suppliers can be affected if they have to compete with substitutes.)

- *The supplier group poses a credible threat of forward integration.* This provides a check against the industry's ability to improve the terms by which it purchases.

When considering supplier power, we typically focus on companies that supply raw materials, equipment, machinery, and associated services. But the supply of labour is also an important input to businesses, and labour's power varies over time and across occupations and industries. Currently, the outlook is not very good for semi-skilled and unskilled labourers who face numerous substitutes, most notably, technology. Correspondingly, their wages have barely kept up with inflation. Immigration, de-unionization, and globalization have also diminished the relative bargaining power of those sectors of the labour market. In contrast, workers with the right skills and jobs have enjoyed the spoils of the New Economy and will likely continue to do so in the foreseeable future. Knowledge workers with specialized training and expertise are highly desirable and can command high compensation for their contributions; few viable substitutes currently exist to threaten their clout in the labour market.

The Threat of Substitute Products and Services

All firms within an industry compete with other industries producing substitute products and services. Substitutes limit the potential returns of an industry by placing a ceiling on the prices that firms in that industry can charge. The more attractive the price-to-performance ratio of substitute products, the tighter is the lid on an industry's profits.

Identifying substitute products involves searching for other products or services that can perform the same function as the industry's offerings or satisfy the same needs of its customers. Flowers, greeting cards, and a box of chocolates have few physical characteristics in common, but they are easy substitutes in the eyes of well-wishing consumers. Identifying substitute products is not always easy; it is a subtle task that can lead a manager into businesses seemingly far removed from the industry. For example, the airline industry might not consider video camera technology much of a threat. But as digital technology has improved and wireless and other forms of telecommunication have become more efficient, teleconferencing has become a viable substitute for business travel for many executives. Strategy Spotlight 2.6 describes IBM's uses of teleconferencing as an alternative to business travel. Similarly, Hewlett-Packard Company (HP) with some 320,000 employees and offices worldwide uses technology to coordinate virtual teams involved in a multitude of projects and has installed, in most of its locations, virtual conference rooms that can instantly bring people together to a meeting without anyone ever having to step inside an airport.[44] The Halo system uses high-definition cameras and monitors to enable participants to see each other in life-size images. They can speak in real time while sharing documents and video and slide presentations. More importantly, HP has partnered with the Marriott Hotels chain to build facilities in multiple locations and make these services available to corporate customers around the world. While Marriott may get some of the old business travel dollars that are going to substitute products, the airlines are certainly left out in the cold.

2.6 STRATEGY SPOTLIGHT

Substituting Business Travel with Technology: IBM

Teleconferencing can save both time and money, as IBM found out with its "Manager Jam" idea. With over 350,000 employees, including 30,000 managers scattered around six continents, IBM is one of the world's largest businesses. The shift to an increasingly mobile workplace means many managers supervise employees they rarely see face to face. To enhance coordination, Samuel Palmisano, IBM's CEO, launched a program exploring the role of the manager in the twenty-first century. Manager Jam, as the project was nicknamed, was a 48-hour real-time Web event, in which managers from 50 different countries swapped ideas and strategies for dealing with problems shared by all of them, regardless of geography. Some 8,100 managers logged on to the company's intranet to participate in the discussion forums— without having to leave their offices for a single moment.

Sources: Based on Tischler, L., 2002. IBM: Manager Jam, *Fast Company,* October: 48.

The Intensity of Rivalry among Competitors in an Industry

Firms use certain tactics, such as price competition, advertising battles, product introductions, and improved customer service or better warranties to win over customers and build their businesses. Some forms of competition, such as price competition, are typically quite destabilizing and are likely to erode the average level of profitability in an industry. Rivals typically match price cuts, an action that lowers profits for all firms. In contrast, advertising battles expand overall demand or enhance the level of product differentiation for the benefit of all firms in the industry. Rivalry, of course, differs across industries. In some instances, it is characterized as being warlike, bitter, or cut-throat, whereas in other industries it is described as being polite and mannerly. Intense rivalry is the result of several interacting factors, including the following:

- *Numerous or equally balanced competitors.* When there are many firms in an industry, the likelihood of mavericks is great. Some firms believe they can make moves without being noticed. Even when there are relatively few firms, and they are nearly equal in size and resources, instability results from fighting among companies that have the resources for sustained and vigorous retaliation.

- *Slow industry growth.* Slow industry growth turns competition into a fight for market share, since firms seeking to expand their sales have to earn those new sales away from their competitors.

- *High fixed costs.* High fixed costs create strong pressures for all firms to increase capacity. Excess capacity often leads to escalating price cutting.

- *Lack of differentiation or switching costs.* Where the product or service is perceived as a commodity or near commodity, the buyer's choice is typically based on price, service, and well-defined features, resulting in pressures from intense price and service competition. Lack of switching costs has the same effect, as competitors can easily replace each other's product offerings.

- *Capacity augmented in large increments.* Where economies of scale require that capacity be added in large increments, capacity additions can be very disruptive to the industry supply–demand balance.

- *High exit barriers.* Exit barriers are economic, strategic, and emotional factors that keep firms competing, even though they may be earning low or negative returns on their investments. Some exit barriers take the form of specialized assets, fixed costs of exit, strategic interrelationships (e.g., relationships between the business units and others within a company in terms of image, marketing, shared facilities, and so on), emotional barriers, and government and social pressures (e.g., governmental discouragement of exit because of concern about job losses).

Rivalry between firms is often based solely on price, but it can involve other factors. Strategy Spotlight 2.7 discusses the intense rivalry among Canada's airlines and the many elements that resulted in a rather distracting competition wherein the players had difficulty understanding each other's competitive moves.

2.7 STRATEGY SPOTLIGHT

Rivalry in the Canadian Skies

In 2005, the Canadian domestic airline industry was in a state of flux. Air Canada had just come out of a bankruptcy reorganization that effectively wiped out all shareholders' investments in the company. When the reorganization was approved, Air Canada's shares were charitably valued at $0.02 per share. After the reorganization, the original bondholders of its debt became the owners of its parent, ACE Aviation Holdings. Air Canada had been able to shed a substantial portion of its debt burden and was in a better position to face the high fuel costs plaguing the industry and to handle heavy labour costs—the legacy of its prosperous past. Air Canada had come out of the reorganization with all of its route network and fleet intact. It still operated extensively across the U.S. border, to the Caribbean, Mexico, Central America, the five main European capitals and, increasingly, to Asia.

Yet the big competitive battle was still within Canada's borders. Its major competitor, WestJet of Calgary had a fleet of very efficient workhorses in its Boeing 737s and was flying point to point within Canada and a limited number of routes to the U.S. The competition was intense, even though Air Canada held 62 percent of the domestic market and WestJet only 28 percent. Two smaller players, Jetsgo of Montreal and CanJet Airlines of Halifax, had 8 and 2 percent, respectively. The presence of Jetsgo seemed to be clouding the competitive dynamics. Jetsgo was fighting for its life with load factors that industry analysts speculated were below break-even. It was continuously underpricing the two larger carriers in an effort to attract new customers and was making headlines with "One Dollar" fares. CanJet followed suit, reducing fares for all overlapping routes. Although these two smaller airlines represented a very small slice of the market, they were forcing lower ticket prices on everybody.

To complicate matters further, Fidelity Investments, the largest mutual fund company in the U.S., owned shares, through its various holdings, in Air Canada and WestJet, and it had also invested in Jetsgo. Analysts had been questioning the motives of Fidelity and had estimated that the existing state of affairs primarily hurt WestJet shares. If Jetsgo were to disappear, the big beneficiaries would not be the flying public or the employees but, rather, WestJet owners whose shares would appreciate by some 40 percent. A rational, wealth-maximizing shareholder would be expected to dump Jetsgo and watch his or her holdings in WestJet appreciate overnight. The rivalry among competitors in the domestic airline industry was extremely intense, and the competitive avenues readily expanded beyond the traditional dimensions.

As a postscript, Jetsgo filed for bankruptcy in March 2005. Overnight, ACE and WestJet shares went up by 15 and 50 percent, respectively. Consumers complained that within a day or so, fares also increased by 10 to 20 percent on various domestic routes, although both airlines fervently denied that specific increases had anything to do with the disappearance of a nuisance competitor.

How the Internet and Digital Technologies Are Affecting the Five Competitive Forces

The Internet and other digital technologies are having a significant impact on nearly every industry. These technologies have fundamentally changed the ways businesses interact with each other and with customers. In most cases, these changes have affected industry forces in ways that have created many new strategic challenges. For example, the threat of new entrants has increased because digital and Internet-based technologies lower barriers to entry. Businesses that reach customers primarily through the Internet may enjoy savings on traditional expenses, such as office and retail space rent, sales force salaries, printing, and postage. This encourages more entrants who, because of the lower startup expenses, see an opportunity to capture market share by offering a product or performing a service more efficiently than existing competitors do. Similarly, competitors from other countries and distant locations can use their presence on the Internet to compete with local businesses without the need to establish a physical presence and incur the costs of setting up a local office. Young firms can provide services that cater to a niche and do so more effectively by attracting customers from a much broader geographic range who are still part of that narrow niche and who perceive the superior value of the specialized service.

Buyers' bargaining power may increase as consumers can access more information faster and more efficiently with a click of the mouse. The Internet allows consumers to shop for the features they want and compare similar offerings, even if these offerings are physically half a world apart. Moreover, businesses can access consumers directly, bypassing intermediaries, such as wholesalers, distributors, and retailers, and share some of the savings in the form of lower prices. Consumers can co-create products and personalize their purchases to fit more closely with their particular needs. Whether these are custom-fitting jeans, automobile features, or computer components, consumers can use the Internet and digital technologies to design individualized products and purchase them online.

Already, the Internet and digital technologies have drastically accelerated and streamlined the process of acquiring supplies, procurement, ordering, and re-ordering of raw materials, parts, and components. Just-in-time processes rely on information systems to tightly coordinate activities and the flow of goods within the value chain and across suppliers and their customers. At the same time, procurement technologies can be imitated by competing suppliers, and technologies that make it possible to design and customize new products are rapidly being used by all competitors.

Because the Internet creates more tools and means for competing, rivalry among firms is likely to be more intense. Only those competing firms that can use digital technologies to give themselves a distinct image, create unique product offerings, or provide, faster, cheaper, and smarter services are likely to capture greater value with the new technology. Yet such gains are hard to sustain because, in most cases, the new technology can be imitated quickly. The Internet tends to increase rivalry by making it difficult for firms to differentiate themselves and by lowering switching costs; customers can easily "shop around" for the best offering at the lowest price and readily compare products that technology displays virtually side by side. The Internet and digital technologies drastically influence industry structures by affecting each one of the five forces in unique and different ways. These influences also change how companies develop and deploy strategies to create and sustain competitive advantages.

Using Industry Analysis: A Few Caveats

For industry analysis to be valuable, a company must collect and evaluate a wide variety of information from many sources. As the trend toward globalization accelerates, information on foreign markets as well as on a wider variety of competitors, suppliers, customers, substitutes, and potential new entrants becomes more critical. Industry analysis helps a firm not only to evaluate the profit potential of an industry but also to consider various ways to strengthen its position vis-à-vis the five forces.

First, managers should not necessarily always avoid low-profit industries (or low-profit segments in profitable industries). Such industries can still yield high returns for some players who pursue sound strategies. As examples, consider Paychex, a payroll-processing company, and WellPoint Health Network, a huge health care insurer:[45]

> Paychex, with $2 billion in revenues, became successful by serving small businesses. Existing firms had ignored them because they assumed that such businesses could not afford the service. When Paychex's founder, Tom Golisano, failed to convince his bosses at Electronic Accounting Systems that they were missing a great opportunity, he launched the firm. It now serves nearly 600,000 clients in the United States and Germany. Paychex's after-tax-return on sales is a stunning 24 percent.
>
> In 1986, WellPoint Health Network (when it was known as Blue Cross of California) suffered a loss of $160 million. That year, Leonard Schaeffer became CEO and challenged the conventional wisdom that individuals and small firms were money losers. (This was certainly "heresy" at the time—the firm was losing $5 million a year insuring 65,000 individuals!) However, by the early 1990s, the health insurer was leading the industry in profitability. The firm has continued to grow and outperform its rivals even during economic downturns. By 2010, its revenues and profits were $65 billion and $4.8 billion, respectively—each figure representing an *annual* increase of over 18 percent for the most recent four-year period.

The five-forces analysis implicitly assumes a zero-sum game, determining how a firm can enhance its position relative to the forces. Yet such an approach can often be short-sighted; that is, it can overlook the many potential benefits of developing constructive win–win relationships with suppliers and customers. Establishing long-term mutually beneficial relationships with suppliers improves a firm's ability to implement just-in-time inventory systems, which allow it to manage inventories better and respond faster to market demands. Conversely, a company that exploits its powerful position against a supplier will likely face reprisal when the balance of power shifts.[46] By working together as partners, suppliers and manufacturers can provide the greatest value at the lowest possible cost. Later chapters address such collaborative relationships and how they can be made most effective.

The five-forces analysis has also been criticized for being essentially a static analysis. However, this position rather reflects the way the analysis is typically used, and it misses two critical points that are reflective of the dynamic nature of the five-forces model.[47] First, the model should not be used to describe the structure of an industry at a single moment in time. It might represent how various elements align in a single instant, but it does not convey how they got there or the direction in which they are heading. Similarly, the five-forces analysis depicts an industry that might be converging or diverging, where firms are increasing or withdrawing from their involvement in various activities, and where developments are continuous or discontinuous. The analysis requires that managers elaborate on those issues before conclusions can be drawn.

Moreover, both scholars and practitioners recognize that external forces as well as strategies of individual firms are continually changing the structure of all industries. The search for a dynamic theory of strategy has led to greater use of game theory in industrial organization economics research and strategy research. On the basis of game theory considerations, Brandenburger and Nalebuff introduced the concept of the *value net*,[48] which, in many ways, is an extension of the five-forces analysis (Exhibit 2-7). The value net represents all the players in the game and analyzes how their interactions affect a firm's ability to generate and appropriate value. The vertical dimension of the net includes suppliers and customers. The firm has direct transactions with them. On the horizontal dimension are substitutes and complementors, players with whom a firm interacts but may not necessarily transact. The concept of complementors is perhaps the single most important contribution of value net analysis and hence is explained in more detail in the next paragraph.

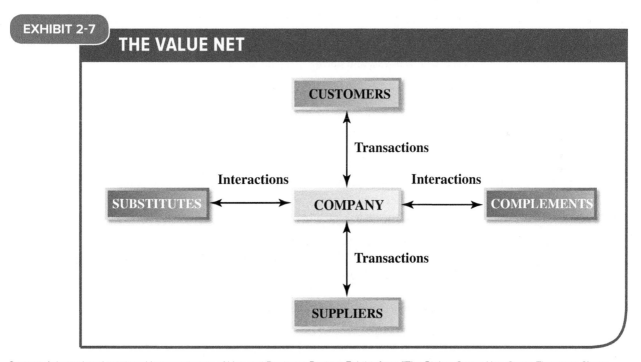

EXHIBIT 2-7   **THE VALUE NET**

CUSTOMERS

Transactions

Interactions — SUBSTITUTES — Interactions

COMPANY

COMPLEMENTS

Transactions

SUPPLIERS

Complements typically are products or services that have possible impact on the value of a firm's own products or services. Those who produce complements are usually referred to as *complementors*. Powerful computers are of no value to a user without the necessary software. Similarly, new and better software can be useful only with the hardware needed to run it. This is equally true in the video game industry, where the game consoles and video games complement each other. Nintendo's success in the early 1990s was a result of its ability to manage its relationship with its complementors. It built a security chip into the hardware and then licensed the right to develop games to external firms. These firms paid a royalty to Nintendo for each copy of the game sold. The royalty revenue enabled Nintendo to sell game consoles at close to their cost, thereby increasing their market share; this, in turn, caused more games to be sold and more royalties to be generated. Yet complementors have their own interests. It would be naive to assume that they would always sacrifice their own interests for the good of the partnership. Strategy Spotlight 2.8 shows how Apple's relationship with its complementors evolved during the early years of the introduction of the iPod.

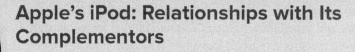

2.8 STRATEGY SPOTLIGHT

Apple's iPod: Relationships with Its Complementors

In 2002, Steve Jobs began his campaign to cajole the major music companies into selling tracks to iPod users through the iTunes Music Store. The music industry had been burned by illegal file-sharing services, such as Napster and Kazaa, and wanted nothing to do with digital music. Still, Jobs' vision and commitment to safeguard against piracy persuaded them reluctantly to climb on board. The iPod was a phenomenal success, and both sides made a killing. The music companies received between 60 and 70 cents from each download, and the iTunes Music Store became a $4-billion business capturing 80 percent of the market for legal downloads.

By 2005, though, when the contracts came up for renewal, the relative power of the two sides had shifted. iTune's market dominance was instrumental in Apple's meteoric success in the sales of iPods, and the firm had little interest in seeing these sales jeopardized by a price increase in the music download tracks. Apple was adamant about keeping the price of a download at 99 cents, although the music companies wanted to charge $1.50 or $2 for some of the more popular tracks. Negotiations were less than win–win, and Apple's complementors had no choice but to relent.

Sources: Reisinger, D. 2012. Why the iPod (yes, the iPod) still matters. Fortune, October 8: 79; Hesseldahl, A. 2008. Now that we all have iPods. *BusinessWeek,* December 15: 36; Apple Computer Inc. 10-K, 2010; 2012 Apple, Inc. Annual Report; and, Yoffie, D. B. & Kwak, M. 2006. With friends like these: The art of managing complementors. *Harvard Business Review,* 84(9): 88–98.

The opposite dynamics can be seen from the challenges faced by another successful company, Canada Goose, known for its premium quality winter outerwear. Strategy Spotlight 2.9 explores how the company is trying to dwarf counterfeit jackets coming out of China and Vietnam, even Sweden.

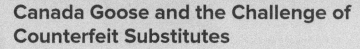

2.9 STRATEGY SPOTLIGHT

Canada Goose and the Challenge of Counterfeit Substitutes

Canada Goose (CG) is viewed by its loyal customers as a premium brand, widely sought after for the high quality, functionality, and iconic style of its products. Consumers across the globe have come to rely on Canada Goose jackets to survive freezing winters and its sought after outerwear can be found in cities as diverse as Tokyo, New York, Toronto, Milan, and Stockholm and in some forty countries around the world.

With this success, though, there come competitors with cheap replicas using inferior components and producing in countries with lower manufacturing costs. During the last few years, CG has pursued numerous lawsuits against the unlawful replication of its designs. In a late 2013 court case it sued Sears for selling look-alike CG parkas. Earlier in that year, CG sued International Clothiers Inc. for designing a logo and positioning it on jackets to mimic the Canada Goose Arctic Program trademark. In another successful lawsuit, CG pursued Swedish counterfeiters selling a poor replica of the iconic jacket that used raccoon and dog fur around the hood, as compared to the traditional and more expensive coyote fur. CG ascertained on the basis of its own and independent lab tests that the replicas contained inferior fillings did not contain real goose down feathers.

Pursuing such cases, CG is sending a strong message to its competitors and replicators as much as to its loyal customers: it has absolutely no tolerance for copycats and imitators. CG gained its competitive edge through manufacturing its products in Canada. Preserving an image of the ultimate high-quality Canadian brand justifies the premium price CG charges for its products and is essential to CG's continued success in building a global presence.

Sources: Anonymous, 2013, Canada Goose wins $105K in Swedish counterfeit case, CBC News, October 23; Anonymous, 2013, Canada Goose sues Sears Canada over look-alike parka, *Financial Post,* August 11; Jones, A, 2012, Rivals logo ruffles Canada Goose feathers, Global Advisor, February 23; Anonymous, 2011, Canada Goose vs. counterfeiters, *National Post,* July 19; Schmidt, S., 2012, Canada Goose executive urges MPs to crack down on counterfeit goods, O.Canada, October 24.

LO 7 Strategic Groups within Industries

In an industry analysis, two assumptions are unassailable: (1) No two firms are totally different; and (2) no two firms are exactly the same. The analysis can be enhanced by identifying groups of firms that are mostly similar to each other, which are known as *strategic groups.*[49] This is important because rivalry tends to be greater among firms that are alike. Canadian Tire, for instance, is more concerned about Walmart than about Holt Renfrew, and Mercedes is more concerned about BMW than about Hyundai.[50]

The concept of strategic groups is, however, more complex than these examples may convey. Classifying an industry into strategic groups involves judgment. If classification is to be useful as an analytical tool, one must exercise caution in deciding what dimensions to use to map the firms. Dimensions include breadth of product and geographic scope, price or quality, degree of vertical integration, type of distribution (e.g., dealers, mass merchandisers, private label), and so on. Dimensions should also be selected to reflect the variety of strategic combinations in an industry. For example, if all firms in an industry have roughly the same level of product differentiation (or R&D intensity), this would not be a good dimension to select.

What is the value of the concept of strategic groups as an analytical tool? First, strategic groupings help a firm identify barriers to mobility, which protect a group from attacks by other groups.[51] Mobility barriers are factors that deter the movement of firms from one strategic position to another. For example, in the chainsaw industry, the major barriers protecting the high-quality or dealer-oriented group are technology, brand image, and an established network of servicing dealers.

The second value of strategic grouping is that it helps a firm identify groups whose competitive position may be marginal or tenuous. One may anticipate that these competitors might exit the industry or try to move into another group. This has been the case in recent years in the retail department store industry, where firms such as Sears and the Hudson's Bay Company have experienced extremely difficult times because they were stuck in the middle—neither an aggressive discount player, such as Walmart, nor a prestigious upscale player, such as Holt Renfrew.

Third, strategic groupings help chart the future directions of firms' strategies. Arrows emanating from each strategic group can represent the direction in which the group (or a firm within the group) seems to be moving. If all strategic groups are moving in a similar direction, this could indicate a high degree of future volatility and intensity of competition. In the automobile industry, for example, the competition in the minivan and sport utility segments has intensified in recent years, as many firms have entered those product segments.

Fourth, strategic groups are helpful in thinking through the implications of each industry trend. Is the trend decreasing the viability of a group? If so, in what direction should the strategic group move? Is the trend increasing or decreasing entry barriers in a given group? Will the trend decrease the ability of one group to separate itself from other groups? Such analysis can help in making predictions about industry evolution. A sharp increase in interest rates, for example, would tend to have less impact on providers of higher-priced goods (e.g., Porsche) than on providers of lower-priced goods (e.g., Hyundai's Accent or Elantra). The Accent customer base is much more price sensitive.

Exhibit 2-8 provides a strategic grouping of the worldwide automobile industry.[52] In this case, we have identified four strategic groups. In the top left-hand corner are high-end luxury automakers, which focus on a very narrow product market. Most of the cars produced by the members of this group cost well over $1,000,000. Some cost many times that amount. The Ferrari F60 costs roughly $2,500,000 and the Lamborghini Veneno $4,500,000.[53] Players in this market have a very exclusive clientele and face little rivalry from other strategic groups. At the other extreme, in the lower left-hand corner, is a strategic group that identifies with low-price and simple features, but still has a narrow product range and targets a narrow market. These players, Hyundai and Kia, limit competition from other strategic groups by pricing their products as low as possible. Another group, near the middle, consists of firms high in product pricing and quality and average in their product-line breadth. The final group, at the far right, consists of firms with a broad range of products and multiple price points. These firms have entries that compete at both the lower end of the market (e.g., Ford Focus) and the higher end (e.g., Chevrolet Corvette). Of course, the recent introduction of electric cars and the "soon to come to a road near you" driverless cars are likely to rejig this mapping of the global automobile manufacturing industry.

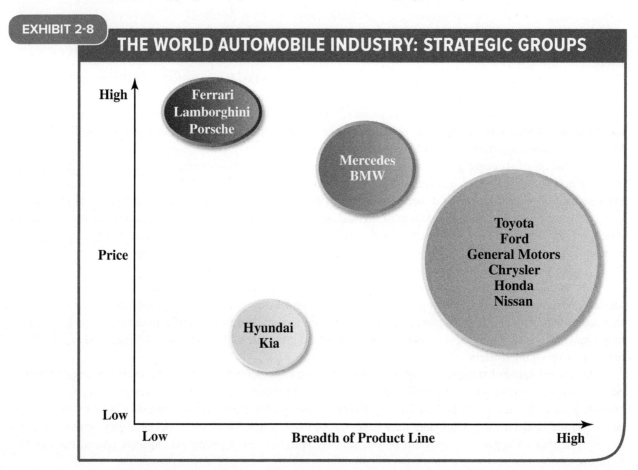

EXHIBIT 2-8

THE WORLD AUTOMOBILE INDUSTRY: STRATEGIC GROUPS

Note: The firms in each group are only representative; not all firms are included in the mapping.

It is true that the auto market has been very dynamic and that competition has intensified in recent years. Firms from different groups have come to compete in the same product markets, such as minivans and sport utility vehicles. Against GM's and Toyota's very successful SUVs, Mercedes entered the fray with the M series at the same time that BMW introduced the X5. Porsche also made an entry with Cayenne. In another series of moves, Toyota, Nissan, and Honda have successfully introduced Lexus, Infiniti, and Acura, respectively, to compete for the same upscale market. Some may interpret these moves as retaliatory intrusions in each other's territory. Finally, a series of more recent entries are likely to intensify the situation further in the foreseeable future; China's

Zhejiang Geely Holding Company, China's Chery Automobile Company, and India's Tata Motors are three firms from emerging markets. Each has introduced models and is looking to carve a niche in the market at an even lower price point with new subcompacts that are even smaller than what the market has been accustomed to. Chery's QQ model sells for between $4,000 and $6,000 in the Chinese market and has horsepower in the range of 51 to 74. Geely's best-selling four-door sedan retails around $6,500; to complicate things further, Geely also acquired Volvo, the venerable Swedish nameplate renowned for its quality, in 2010. Finally, Tata unveiled the Nano with an astonishing retail price of only $2,500 for a four-door, five-seat hatchback that gets 22 kilometres per litre.

SUMMARY

Managers must continuously analyze the external environment to minimize or eliminate threats and exploit opportunities. This involves a continuous process of environmental scanning and monitoring as well as obtaining competitive intelligence on present and potential rivals. These activities provide valuable inputs for developing forecasts. In addition, many firms use scenario planning to anticipate and respond to volatile and disruptive environmental changes.

We identified two types of environment: the general environment and the competitive environment. The six segments of the general environment are demographic/psychographic, sociocultural, political/legal, technological, economic, and global. Trends and events occurring in these segments, such as the aging of the population, higher percentages of women in the workplace, governmental legislation, and increasing (or decreasing) interest rates, can have a dramatic effect on a firm. A given trend or event may have a positive impact on some industries and a negative or neutral impact on others. We also considered the role of the Internet and in particular crowdsourcing as forces shaping the general environment through advances in technology and changes to the ways in which business is conducted.

The competitive environment consists of industry-related factors and has a more direct impact than does the general environment. Porter's five-forces model of industry analysis includes the threat of new entrants, buyer power, supplier power, threat of substitutes, and rivalry among competitors. The intensity of these factors determines, in large part, the average expected level of profitability in an industry. A sound awareness of such factors—in isolation and in combination—is beneficial not only for deciding what industries to enter but also for assessing how a firm can improve its competitive position. In employing the five-forces analysis, one should remember that it should not be viewed as a static model, recognize that it is based on an antagonistic view of the world, and find ways to consider complex interrelationships among a firm's web of interactions and transactions. The general environment and the competitive environment are quite interdependent, and changes in one segment can greatly affect factors in another segment.

The concept of strategic groups is also important in analyzing the external environment of a firm. No two organizations are exactly the same; nor are they completely different. Firms can be placed in strategic groups on the basis of similarities in their resources and strategies. The concept of strategic groups is valuable for determining mobility barriers across groups, identifying groups with marginal competitive positions, charting the future directions of firm strategies, and assessing the implications of industry trends for the strategic group as a whole.

Summary Review Questions

1. Why must managers be aware of a firm's external environment?
2. What is gathering and analyzing competitive intelligence, and why is it important for firms to engage in it?
3. Discuss and describe the six elements of the external environment.
4. Select one of these elements, and describe some changes relating to it in an industry that interests you.
5. Discuss implications of crowdsourcing on the ways business is conducted in the Internet age.
6. Describe how the five-forces analysis can be used to determine the average expected profitability in an industry.
7. What are some of the limitations (or caveats) in using the five-forces analysis?
8. Explain how the general environment and competitive environment are highly related. How can such interrelationships affect the profitability of a firm or industry?
9. Explain the concept of strategic groups. What are the performance implications?

REFLECTING ON CAREER IMPLICATIONS

Creating the Environmentally Aware Organization: What are some ways in which you can engage in scanning, monitoring, and intelligence gathering for future job opportunities? Consider, for example, subscribing to your field's professional publications and becoming actively involved in relevant professional organizations. Participate in online discussion groups relating to your work. What are the themes that seem to come up in these discussions? What do people from other countries say?

SWOT Analysis: From a career standpoint, periodically, evaluate your strengths and weaknesses as well as potential opportunities and threats to your career. In addition, strive to seek input from trusted peers and colleagues.

General Environment: Evaluate the element of the general environment facing your firm. Identify such factors as rapid technological change, which can provide promising career opportunities as well as possibilities for you to add value for your organization. In doing this, do not focus solely on internal factors of your organization.

Five-forces Analysis: Consider the five forces affecting the industry within which your organization competes. How does the picture look? What are the likely trends on each of the forces? How are they likely to change going forward? If the forces are unfavourable, the long-term profit potential of the industry may be unattractive. Are things likely to change? If not, there will likely be fewer resources and fewer career opportunities available.

EXPERIENTIAL EXERCISE

Select one of the following industries: personal computers, airlines, or automobiles. For this industry, evaluate the strength of each of Porter's five forces as well as complementors.

Industry Force	High? Medium? Low?	Why?
1. Threat of new entrants		
2. Power of buyers		
3. Power of suppliers		
4. Power of substitutes		
5. Rivalry among competitors		
6. Complementors		

APPLICATION QUESTIONS AND EXERCISES

1. Imagine yourself as the CEO of a large firm in an industry that interests you. Then (a) identify major trends in the general environment, (b) analyze their impact on the firm, and (c) identify major sources of information to monitor these trends. (Use the Internet and your library's resources.)

2. Analyze movements across the strategic groups in the Canadian retail industry. How do these movements within this industry change the nature of competition?

3. What are the major trends in the general environment that have impacted the Canadian financial services industry?

4. Have you participated or contributed in a particular crowdsourcing initiative? What has been your experience? Would you engage again? Why or why not?

5. Go to the Internet, and look up www.magna.ca. What are some of the forces driving industry competition that are affecting the profitability of this firm?

ETHICS AND CORPORATE SOCIAL RESPONSIBILITY QUESTIONS

1. What are some of the legal and ethical issues involved in collecting competitor intelligence in the following situations?

    a. A firm hires an MBA student to collect information directly from the competition; during his contacts with the competitors, the student claims that the information is for a course project.

    b. A firm advertises a non-existent position and interviews a rival's employees to obtain competitor information.

    c. A hotel sends an employee posing as a potential client to a competitor to find out how it handles new clients and who its major corporate customers are.

2. What are some of the legal and ethical concerns when engaging in a crowdsourcing activity? Consider, in turn, both the initiator and the contributor sides.

3. What are some of the ethical concerns that arise when a firm tries to exploit its power over a supplier? How can such efforts impede value creation?

CHAPTER THREE

Analyzing the Internal Environment of the Firm

LEARNING OBJECTIVES

After reading this chapter, you should have a good understanding of:

LO 1 How managers can use value-chain analysis to gain insights into a firm's internal environment.

LO 2 How individual activities within the firm add value and how interrelationships among activities within the firm, as well as between the firm and its suppliers and customers, create value.

LO 3 How managers can use the resource-based view of the firm to gain insights into a firm's internal environment.

LO 4 The four criteria that a firm's resources must possess to maintain a sustainable advantage and how value created can be appropriated by employees.

LO 5 How financial ratio analysis and other metrics of performance as well as meaningful comparisons across firms inform managers' understanding of the workings of their own organization.

LO 6 The value of recognizing how the interests of a variety of stakeholders can be interrelated.

CASE STUDY

The Canadian Broadcasting Corporation, popularly known as the CBC, has had a rich history and formed strong bonds with the Canadian population. Opening its doors in the early 1940s, the company has been the premier provider of news from a uniquely Canadian perspective since World War II.[1] The CBC brand has been consistently aligned with the Canadian identity and is in itself an inextricable aspect of modern Canadian history. In recent years, however, CBC has been plagued by scandals that have often been poorly mismanaged, reflecting serious miscalculations of the organization's strengths and weaknesses. If such mismanagement persists, it is unclear whether CBC will be able to maintain its popularity and strong brand identity in the future.

Lester Balajadia/Shutterstock.com

The most public scandal was that of Jian Ghomeshi, host of the successful radio show *Q*. In late 2014, Ghomeshi was fired amid allegations that he had sexually assaulted women, allegations of which he was later acquitted following a lengthy trial. Regardless of the outcome of the trial, the Ghomeshi affair tarnished CBC's brand by its association with a man who, in an independent report by employment lawyer Janice Rubin, was said to have created "an intimidating, humiliating, hostile or offensive work environment." Later in her report, Rubin noted that management had failed to take steps in accordance with CBC policies, concluding that CBC management had condoned Ghomeshi's behaviour. Ghomeshi was fired only after third-party journalists began looking into his personal life and CBC executives were shown what was described as "graphic evidence that he had physically injured a woman."

Following the Jian Ghomeshi scandal came a trifecta of conflicts of interest involving CBC personnel. In January 2015, senior business correspondent Amanda Lang came under the spotlight for conflicts of interest in her reporting on RBC. One month later, *The National* anchorman, Peter Mansbridge, generated similar concern over his journalistic integrity after he was paid to deliver a speech to petroleum producers. Then, Rex Murphy, a high-profile freelancer for the CBC, had past speeches on the oil sands come under attack, although his freelancer status made the ethical issue a bit less straightforward. Unlike Amanda Lang and Peter Mansbridge, both of whom had clear conflicts of interest in their reporting for the CBC, as a freelancer, Rex Murphy was not required to disclose his other sources of income. However, regardless of the specifics of each ethical dilemma, the damage to the CBC's integrity had been done. After a long history of high regard as an essential aspect of Canada and the Canadian news industry, the CBC was being associated with sexual assault allegations and conflicts of interest, damaging the integrity and credibility of their reporting.

Then, in June of 2015, Evan Solomon, the Ottawa-based host of TV's *Power and Politics* and *The House* on CBC radio, was fired for using his position as a journalist for the CBC to gain access to wealthy, influential people in order to advance his business as an art broker. Solomon solicited buyers from his television and radio programs, failed to disclose that he was being paid fees for introducing buyers and sellers, and took in commissions in excess of $300,000 for several pieces of art, as investigated by *The Toronto Star*. The CBC Code of Ethics specifically states that employees "must not use their positions to further their personal interests." Although Solomon issued a personal statement claiming that he had never intentionally used his position at the CBC to promote the art business, one of the initial clients in his side business met with him only after Solomon had requested that he appear on *Power and Politics*.

Tainted by sexual assault allegations, conflicts of interest, and purported use of CBC fame to further personal interests, the nation's public broadcaster, long known for the quality of its journalism, spent much of 2014 and 2015 in the headlines itself due to ethical breakdowns and scandals. It seems the CBC had placed too much emphasis on select on-air personalities as their primary strength and the source of their sustained competitive advantage, forgetting that a sustained competitive advantage is, by definition, difficult to imitate. The loyal CBC fan base, who had been tuning in to the CBC for its journalistic integrity since the 1940s, had been their true strength and the path-dependent source of inimitability all along; it was their sustained competitive advantage. A more insightful internal analysis and better understanding of their true strengths could have greatly improved the organization's reactions to and management of the scandals that plagued them. ■

CBC's strategic challenges underscore the uniqueness of individual situations and the need to complement the analysis of the external environment with a detailed assessment of what takes place inside each organization. Furthermore, the problems experienced by the public broadcaster clearly demonstrate the interrelatedness between ethical and economic concerns. As we learned in Chapter 2, a SWOT analysis consists of a careful listing of a firm's **S**trengths, **W**eaknesses, **O**pportunities, and **T**hreats.

Although the "OT" elements are likely to be rather common across different firms within an industry, the "SW" elements are unique and constitute the starting point for a discussion of a firm's competitive advantage. Yet, as we discussed in Chapter 2, SWOT by itself cannot show managers how to achieve a competitive advantage. Managers need to proceed to an analysis of the system of activities that creates its products and an analysis of the resources that are used in unique ways to successfully fulfil the customer's requirements. SWOT is a very helpful starting point, which can form the basis for evaluating a firm's situation, but it cannot answer the critical questions about competitive advantage. For that, we need to turn to a more in-depth analysis of the inner workings of the organization and develop insights about the processes that create value within the organization.

LO 1 VALUE-CHAIN ANALYSIS

Value-chain analysis views the organization as a sequential process of value-creating activities. It is based on the simple notion that a firm engages in a series of activities which combine the various necessary inputs to create the product offering that the firm brings to the marketplace. It disaggregates a firm into its various activities to help understand the ways all inputs are deployed and costs are incurred in creating a firm's products and services. Value-chain analysis provides the foundation for understanding the building blocks of competitive advantage. This approach was described in Michael Porter's book *Competitive Advantage*.[2] In competitive terms, value is the amount that buyers are willing to pay for what a firm provides them. Value can be measured by total revenue, a reflection of the price a firm's product commands and the quantity it can sell. A firm is profitable in economic and accounting terms to the extent that the value it receives exceeds the total costs involved in creating its product or service. Creating value for buyers that exceeds the costs of production represents the firm's profit margin and is a key concept used in analyzing a firm's competitive position.

Porter described two different categories of activities. First, five primary activities—inbound logistics, operations, outbound logistics, marketing and sales, and service—contribute to the physical creation of the product or service, its sale and transfer to the buyer, and its service after the sale. Second, support activities—procurement, technology development, human resource management, and firm infrastructure—add value either by themselves or through important relationships with both primary activities and other support activities. Exhibit 3-1 illustrates Porter's value chain.

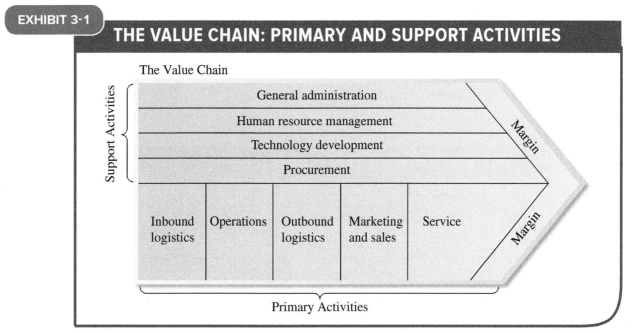

EXHIBIT 3-1

THE VALUE CHAIN: PRIMARY AND SUPPORT ACTIVITIES

To get the most out of value-chain analysis, managers need to view the concept in its broadest context irrespective of the boundaries of their own organization. That is, they must place their organization within a more encompassing value system that includes the firm's suppliers, customers, and alliance partners. For example, steel producers, auto parts makers, vehicle assemblers, and car dealers constitute the automobile industry value system, and the value chain of one player contributes to the creation of value at another player. In effect, the efficient business operations of an auto parts maker, such as Magna, contribute to the value chain of an assembler that is striving to produce an attractive, reasonably priced car.

Understanding how value is created within the organization is, therefore, not enough. Apple might be doing the creative design and engineering for its products but almost all the components and assembly of its phones is done halfway around the world. And while the ubiquitous Apple stores might be selling truckloads of iPhones, most of its sales actually come from telecommunications providers who put cell phone plans together for their customers. Over the life of a phone, a consumer spends a lot more money in paying his or her monthly bill for using the phone than he or she paid for the original cost of the device. Managers must become aware of how value is created by other organizations that are involved in the overall supply chain or distribution channel in which the firm participates.[3] Moreover, they need to appreciate that companies add value by means of relationships among activities within the organization as well as activities outside the organization, such as those associated with customers and suppliers.[4] In the following sections, we discuss each of the categories of activities and present examples that highlight those interrelationships, as well as the application of the value chain in both the manufacturing and the service sectors.

The value chain is often viewed as being primarily relevant to manufacturing operations. Indeed, basic concepts, such as inbound logistics, operations, and procurement, draw from the traditional ideas about creating value that have arisen in the physical production of goods. However, we can readily see that the process of transforming inputs into outputs (operations) takes place as much in accounting firms, law firms, airline companies, and retail stores as in factories. Moreover, our examples suggest that how the primary and support activities of a given firm are configured and deployed will often depend on industry conditions and the extent to which the company is service oriented or manufacturing oriented. Exhibit 3-2 provides a model of how the value chain might look in a service industry, such as retailing. Although the support activities would likely be the same, as the retailer still would be engaged in general administration, human resource management, technology development, and procurement, the primary activities would relate more to relationships with vendors, purchasing of merchandise (as distinct from procurement), managing and distributing inventory, operating stores, marketing and sales, and after-sales service. Retailers seek ways to add unique value through their various activities; for example, Walmart uses its clout as well as its financial resources not only to extract the best possible prices and terms from its vendors but also to develop close relationships with them. It invests heavily with its vendors to integrate information systems and facilitate seamless and speedy processing of orders as well as achieve coordination between individual stores and the vendor's distribution facilities to ensure that stores never run out of stock and that there is no excess and dated inventory on any of its shelves.

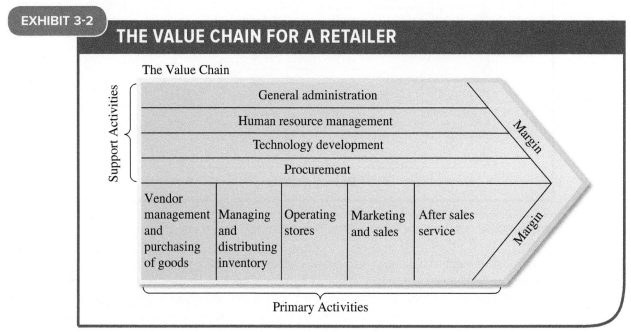

EXHIBIT 3-2

THE VALUE CHAIN FOR A RETAILER

The Value Chain

Support Activities

General administration

Human resource management

Technology development

Procurement

| Vendor management and purchasing of goods | Managing and distributing inventory | Operating stores | Marketing and sales | After sales service |

Margin

Primary Activities

Source: Adapted with the permission of The Free Press, a division of Simon & Schuster Adult Publishing Group, from *Competitive Advantage: Creating and Sustaining Superior Performance* by Michael E. Porter. Copyright © 1985, 1998 by Michael E. Porter. All rights reserved.

LO 2 Primary Activities

Five generic categories of primary activities are involved in competing in any industry, as shown in Exhibit 3-3. Each category is divisible into a number of distinct activities based on the particular industry and the firm's strategy.[5]

EXHIBIT 3-3   THE VALUE CHAIN: SOME FACTORS TO CONSIDER IN ASSESSING A FIRM'S PRIMARY ACTIVITIES

Inbound Logistics

- Location of warehousing and distribution facilities to minimize shipping distances and reduce shipping times; adoption of just-in-time or other appropriate shipping schedules to maximize capacity utilization while minimizing inventory costs
- Facilities' layouts and designs to increase efficiency of operations for incoming components and materials
- Automated materials handling with the use of robotics to maximize space utilization and inventory handling
- Quality control processes to ensure inbound materials meet specifications

Operations

- Efficient plant designs to minimize costs and speed workflow
- Efficient plant designs to minimize employee fatigue
- Processes to minimize waste and down time
- Efficient processes to minimize turn-down and turn-up of equipment for maintenance and scheduling

Outbound Logistics

- Efficient processes to speed deliveries, minimize errors, and eliminate damages to goods
- Shipping in lots to minimize transportation costs
- Shipping protocols to minimize customers' stock-outs and seamlessly connect with their inbound logistics

Marketing and Sales

- Strong market intelligence; effective monitoring of customer segment needs and trends
- Innovative approaches to advertising and promotion
- Effective customer relations, solution-driven sales approaches, and adoption of appropriate customer relationship management (CRM) protocols

Service

- Quick response time to customer needs
- Quality of service personnel and ongoing training
- Effective management of replacement parts and customer maintenance scheduling
- Effective handling of warranties and guarantees

Sources: Adapted from Porter, M.E. 1985. Competitive Advantage: Creating and Sustaining Superior Performance. New York: Free Press.

Inbound Logistics

Inbound logistics are primarily associated with receiving, storing, and distributing inputs to the product. They include material handling, warehousing, inventory control, vehicle scheduling, and returns to suppliers.

Just-in-time (JIT) inventory systems, for example, were designed to achieve efficient inbound logistics. Toyota epitomizes JIT inventory systems, in which parts deliveries arrive at the assembly plants only hours before they are needed. JIT systems play a vital role in making good on Toyota's commitment to fulfil a buyer's order for a new car in just five days.[6] This standard exists in sharp contrast to most competitors who require approximately 30 days' notice to build vehicles. How can Toyota achieve such a fast turnaround? Its 360 key suppliers are linked on the Web with the company in a virtual assembly line: Suppliers load parts onto trucks in the order in which they will be installed; parts are stacked on trucks in the same place each time to help workers unload them quickly; and deliveries are required to meet a rigid schedule, with as many as 12 trucks a day and no more than four hours between trucks.

Operations

Operations encompass all activities associated with transforming inputs into the final product and include machining, packaging, assembly, testing, printing, and facility operations.

Creating environmentally friendly manufacturing is one way a firm can use operations to achieve competitive advantage. Shaw Industries (now part of Berkshire Hathaway), a world-class competitor in the floor-covering industry, is well known for its strong concern for the environment.[7] It has been successful in reducing the expenses associated with the disposal of dangerous chemicals and other waste products from its manufacturing operations. Its environmental endeavours have multiple payoffs. Shaw has received numerous awards for its recycling efforts—awards that have enhanced its corporate reputation.

An example of how Shaw's commitment to the environment is paying off is evident in the development of a carpet fibre called Eco Solution Q. The industry's first nylon covering containing recycled content, Eco Solution

Q was the most successful product launch in the company's history. Shaw's residential staple polyester carpet, made from 100-percent petroleum-based materials, keeps one billion plastic containers out of landfills each year through recycling. Shaw is also pioneering other innovative recycling solutions, including recycled nylon for automotive underhood applications and ground-up carpet as an ingredient in road materials and fibre-reinforced concrete.

Outbound Logistics

The activities of outbound logistics are associated with collecting, storing, and distributing the product or service to buyers. They include finished goods, warehousing, material handling, delivery vehicle operation, order processing, and scheduling.

Campbell's Soup uses an electronic network to facilitate its continuous replenishment program with its most progressive retailers, including Loblaw and Walmart.[8] Each morning, retailers electronically inform Campbell's of their product needs and of the level of inventories in their distribution centres. Campbell's uses that information to forecast future demand and to determine which products require replenishment (based on the inventory limits previously established with each retailer). Trucks leave Campbell's shipping plant that afternoon and arrive at the retailers' distribution centres the same day. The program cuts the inventories of participating retailers from about a four-week supply to a two-week' supply. Campbell's Soup achieved this improvement because it knows the inventories of key retailers and can deploy supplies when they are most needed.

The Campbell's Soup example also illustrates the win–win benefits of exemplary value-chain activities. Both the supplier (Campbell's) and its buyers (retailers) come out ahead. Since the retailer makes more money on Campbell's products delivered through continuous replenishment, it has an incentive to carry a broader line and give the company greater shelf space. Campbell's found that after it introduced the program, sales of its products grew twice as fast through participating retailers as through all other retailers. Not surprisingly, supermarket chains love such programs.

Marketing and Sales

Marketing and sales include a firm's efforts to gather market intelligence and understand its customers, the activities associated with purchases of products and services by end users, and the inducements used to get them to make purchases.[9] These efforts include market research, consumer analysis, advertising, promotion, sales force, quoting, channel selection, channel relationships, and pricing.[10,11] It is not always enough to have a great product.[12] Managers must also convince their channel partners that it is in their best interests not only to carry the product but also to market it in a way that is consistent with their strategy.[13] Consider Monsanto's efforts at educating distributors to improve the value proposition of its line of Saflex® windows.[14] Its products, introduced in the early 1990s, had a superior attribute: The window design permitted laminators to form an exceptional type of glass by sandwiching a plastic sheet interlayer between two pieces of glass. Not only is this product stronger and a better shield against ultraviolet radiation compared with regular glass, but also, when the glass cracks, it adheres to the plastic sheet— an excellent safety feature for both cars and homes.

Despite these benefits, Monsanto had a hard time convincing laminators and window manufacturers to carry products made with Saflex. According to Melissa Toledo, brand manager at Monsanto, "Saflex was priced at a 30-percent premium above traditional glass, and the various stages in the value chain (distributors and retailers) didn't think there would be a demand for such an expensive glass product." Monsanto's solution? It subsequently reintroduced Saflex as KeepSafe® and worked to coordinate the product's value propositions. By analyzing the experiences of all of the players in the supply chain, it was able to create marketing programs that helped each build a business aimed at selling its products. Toledo stated, "We want to know how they go about selling those types of products, what challenges they face, and what they think they need to sell our products. This helps us a lot when we try to meet these needs." Thus, marketing is often a key element of competitive advantage. To that effect, Strategy Spotlight 3.1 discusses how Staples Business Depot redirected its marketing efforts.

3.1 STRATEGY SPOTLIGHT

Redirecting Marketing Efforts at Staples

On his first day as CEO of Staples Business Depot, one of North America's largest office supply chains, Ron Sargent put on the black pants, black shoes, and red shirt that associates wear and headed to the Staples store in Brighton, Massachusetts. This is Staples' first store (opened in May 1986), and by going there on his first day, he was trying to rally the Staples troops around a concept called "Back to Brighton." It was a symbolic message to the members of the organization that they were going to improve service and refocus on their core customer base: the small-business customer. After growing rapidly for most of its 16 years, in 2000, Staples encountered its first decline in performance. To make matters worse, its main rival, Office Depot, was experiencing a competitive rebound. Thus, Staples was forced to re-examine every aspect of its business.

The company had started catering to the casual customer, but this was not a profitable segment. So Ron removed 600 items that appealed to the casual customer and replaced them with 700 items that appealed to the small-business customer. The chain improved the quality of the merchandise it offered because businesses have more demanding needs compared with the casual customer. It stopped advertising in the Sunday newspapers, which are not usually read by businesspeople, and put more money into direct marketing. It also upgraded its website and doubled its direct sales force. Taking the money that was originally allocated to advertising, Ron invested it in the training of associates and added more store staff to provide better service.

Sources: M. Roman, "Ronald Sargent: Straightening Out Staples," *BusinessWeek,* September 17, 2001, pp. 9–11; and A. Overholt, "New Leaders, New Agenda," *Fast Company,* June 2002, p. 52.

Service consists of the range of activities associated with enhancing or maintaining the value of the product, such as installation, maintenance, support, repair, training, parts supply, and product adjustment.

Service

Internet-based retailers (e-tailers) provide many examples of how superb customer service is critical for adding value. Nearly all e-tailers figured that the Web's self-service model should save them millions in customer service-related expenses. But that was the last place they could afford to shave costs.[15] According to market researcher Datamonitor, 7.8 percent of abandoned online shopping carts—an impressive $6.1 billion in lost annual sales—could be salvaged through an effective customer service solution. Bill Bass, senior vice president of e-commerce at catalogue retailer Lands' End, Inc., claimed, "If there's a train wreck to happen, it's going to be around customer service." At Sephora.com, a customer service representative taking a phone call from a repeat customer has instant access to, for example, what shade of lipstick the customer likes best. This helps the representative cross-sell by suggesting a matching shade of lip gloss. CEO Jim Wiggett expects such personalization to build loyalty and boost sales per customer. Swisschalet.ca guides customers to build personal profiles of their food preferences to make ordering online easier, and Pizza Pizza, an Ontario-based pizza chain, allows online customers to repeat their recent orders with a single click and its phone customers with the press of a single button.

Support Activities

Support activities might not directly add value to the creation of the product, but they provide for and facilitate the primary activities and ensure that they take place efficiently and effectively. Support activities can be divided into four generic categories, as shown in Exhibit 3-4. As with primary activities, each category is divisible into a number of distinct value activities that are specific to a particular industry. For example, technology development's discrete activities may include component design, feature design, field testing, process engineering, and technology selection. Similarly, procurement may be divided into such activities as qualifying new suppliers, purchasing different groups of inputs, and monitoring supplier performance.

EXHIBIT 3-4   **THE VALUE CHAIN: SOME FACTORS TO CONSIDER IN ASSESSING A FIRM'S SUPPORT ACTIVITIES**

General Administration

- Effective strategic management systems to attain overall goals and objectives
- Efficient processes to coordinate and control activities across the organization
- Excellent relationships with diverse stakeholder groups
- Effective systems to both gather and distribute information across the various value-creating activities

Human Resource Management

- Effective recruiting, development, and retention mechanisms for employees
- Quality work environment to maximize overall employee performance and minimize absenteeism
- Reward and incentive programs to motivate all employees

Technology Development

- Effective research and development (R&D) activities for process and product initiatives
- Culture to enhance creativity and innovation
- Excellent professional qualifications of personnel

Procurement

- Procurement of raw material inputs to optimize quality and speed and to minimize the associated costs
- Development of collaborative "win–win" relationships with suppliers
- Analysis and selection of alternative sources of inputs; proper choices among lease and buy options

Sources: Adapted from Porter, M.E. 1985. Competitive Advantage: Creating and Sustaining Superior Performance. New York: Free Press.

General Administration

General administration consists of a number of activities, including general management, planning, finance, accounting, legal and government affairs, quality management, and information systems. Administration typically supports the entire value chain and not individual activities.

Although general administration is sometimes viewed only as overhead, it can be a powerful source of competitive advantage. In a telephone operating company, for example, negotiating and maintaining ongoing relationships with regulatory bodies can be among the most important activities for competitive advantage. In a similar vein, effective information systems can contribute significantly to cost position, and in some industries, top management plays a vital role in dealing with important buyers.[16]

In 2009, the chief executive officer of Bell Canada Enterprises (BCE) Inc., Michael Sabia, declined his bonus for the second time in three years. He did not accept the $1.47-million award, even though the firm did meet its targets. His refusal was a response to billing glitches, which plagued the wireless unit and led thousands of frustrated customers to complain about the service. Such decisions demonstrate exemplary management of general administration.

Legal services can contribute real value to a firm in many ways. One example is ensuring the protection of a firm's intellectual property through patents, trademarks, and copyrights. Although many companies are not aware of the earnings potential of their patent holdings, Texas Instruments (TI) is one notable exception.[17] In essence, in the mid-1980s when it was facing bankruptcy, out of desperation, TI began investigating the income-generation potential of its patent portfolio. Since then, TI has earned an impressive $4 billion in patent royalties; its licensing revenues are estimated to be $800 million per year.

Strategy Spotlight 3.2 discusses how Gary Kelly, Southwest Airlines' chief financial officer, adds value for his company.

3.2 STRATEGY SPOTLIGHT

How a Firm's General Administration Can Create Value

A firm's general administration can significantly impact a firm's performance. Southwest's chief financial officer (CFO), Gary Kelly, is a key contributor to the airline's solid financial performance.

When the rest of the airline industry was laying off workers by the thousands, Southwest did not furlough anyone. Its ability to shine in dire times is a result of its conservative financial culture that values a large cash balance and low debt. Southwest began conserving funds in 2000, when it saw a recession on the horizon. After installing a new computer system and renegotiating contracts with vendors, it managed to boost its cash on hand from $600 million to about $1 billion.

Through the years, Wall Street analysts have criticized Kelly's conservative approach and goaded him to use the extra cash to make acquisitions or buy back stock. Goldman Sachs' airline analyst actually called the balance sheet "too strong." Yet it is such fiscal preparedness that has kept the company's debt-to-capital ratio at around 40 percent (compared with the industry average of about 70 percent), which allows for more flexibility during tough times.

Kelly has frequently come up with creative measures to get through the economic cycles that are a common characteristic of the airline industry. For example, in 2001, during another down-turn of the market, he rescheduled the delivery of 19 planes from Boeing by developing an arrangement between Boeing and a collection of banks involved in the original financing of the planes. Under the arrangement, the banks took delivery from Boeing as scheduled and stored the planes in the Mojave Desert until Southwest needed them. The idea was to strike a balance between maintaining the good relationship with Boeing, its only supplier of planes, and holding off spending the cash on the planes it did not yet need. Darryl Jenkins, director of the Aviation Institute at George Washington University, attributes Southwest's success to two things: "Consistency, and the fact that they don't listen to other people."

Sources: W. Zellner and M. Arnadt, "Holding Steady," *BusinessWeek,* February 3, 2003; and I. Mount, "Southwest's Gary Kelly: A Tip of the Hat to the CFO at the One Airline Still Making Money," *Business 2.0,* February 12, 2002, pp. 5–7.

Human Resource Management

Human resource management consists of activities involved in the recruiting, hiring, training, development, and compensation of all types of personnel.[18] It supports both primary and support activities (e.g., hiring of engineers and scientists) and the entire value chain (e.g., negotiations with labour unions).

Starbucks' baristas are unquestionably the soul of the corporation and essential to its success. Lululemon's "ambassadors" and its in-store "educators" exemplify the company's passion for a healthy lifestyle and fitness that make the premium apparel's products so sought after by young women across North America. Like all great service companies, JetBlue Airways Corporation is concerned about hiring great employees.[19] But this company found it difficult to entice college graduates to commit to a career as a flight attendant. JetBlue developed a highly innovative recruitment program—a one-year contract that gives employees a chance to travel, meet people, and then whether they wish to become a member of the traditional flight crew, or move on to other career options. JetBlue also introduced the idea of hiring two flight attendants together to share one full-time job, with details of who covers each shift to be determined between the employees. With such employee-friendly initiatives, JetBlue has been very successful in attracting talent.

Employees often leave a firm because they have reached a plateau and want new opportunities and challenges.[20] AT&T strives to retain such employees with Resource Link, an in-house temporary service that enables employees with diverse management, technical, or professional skills to market their abilities to different departments within the firm for short-term assignments. This not only enables professionals to broaden their experience base but also provides a mechanism for other parts of the organization to benefit from new sources of ideas.

Hamilton, Ontario-based Dofasco's motto, "Our product is steel. Our strength is people," was well known within and outside its industry and reflected the company's deep-seated belief in the value of its human capital. This belief was manifested in many aspects of the company's operations—in the selection and training of its employees, in the exclusive promotions from within its ranks, and in its legendary annual staff social events. It is worth noting that since Dofasco was acquired by the global steel giant ArcelorMittal, most of those unique HR practices have been discontinued and that Dofasco's performance has also been affected.

Strategy Spotlight 3.3 describes how SAS Institute's innovative approach to human resources provides an insightful financial justification for the broad array of benefits it provides to employees.

3.3 STRATEGY SPOTLIGHT

SAS and Employee Turnover

Jeffrey Pfeffer, professor of organizational behaviour at Stanford University, asked a managing partner at a San Francisco law firm about its employee turnover rate. Turnover had increased from 25 percent to 30 percent over the past few years. The law firm's solution: Increase recruitment of new employees. Pfeffer's response: "What kind of doctor would you be if your patient was bleeding faster and faster and your only response was to increase the rate of transfusion?"

It is not difficult to calculate the cost of a new hire, but what does it cost a firm when employees leave? Consider the approach taken by SAS Institute, a software developer with 5,000 employees. David Russo, director of human resources, estimates that the average turnover in the industry is 20 percent per year. SAS's turnover rate is only 4 percent. SAS employees earn, on average, $60,000 a year. Multiplying the difference in the turnover rate by the number of employees, their average annual salary shows that SAS has a cost savings of nearly $50 million.

What can a firm do with an extra $50 million? SAS spends a large portion of this sum on its employees. The SAS gym, cafeteria (with a pianist), on-site medical and child care, flexible work schedules, employer retirement contributions of 15 percent of an employee's pay, and a host of other family-friendly programs help keep SAS's employee turnover level well below the industry average. Even after spending on all these perks, SAS still has money left over.

Russo's message? "This is not tree-huggery. This is money in the bank."

Sources: R. Levering and M. Moskowitz, "The 100 Best Companies to Work For," *Fortune,* January 20, 2003, pp. 127–52; and A. M. Webber, "Danger: Toxic Company," *Fast Company,* November 1998, pp. 152–61.

Jeffrey Immelt, chairman of General Electric (GE), addresses the importance of effective human resource management in the following:

> Human resources has to be more than a department. GE recognized early on, some 50 or 60 years ago, that in a multibusiness company, the common denominators are people and culture. From an employee's first day at GE, she discovers that she's in the people-development business as much as anything else. You'll find that most good companies have the same basic HR processes that we have, but they're discrete. HR at GE is not an agenda item, it is the agenda.[21]

Strategy Spotlight 3.4 discusses a rather unique approach to individual performance evaluations at a global corporation with operations in many countries with different cultures.

3.4 STRATEGY SPOTLIGHT

Removing Individual Metrics in Performance Evaluations

William Taylor, ITT China's former president, discovered a disturbing reality about the unusually high employee turnover in the Shanghai sales office. If the regional manager gave his team members an average score of 3 on the 1–5 performance scale, they would stop talking to him, and some would quit shortly thereafter. The manager lamented: "They're losing face within the organization. It would be great if we could do something about the scores."

Comments like that popped up in ITT's facilities around the world. For example, in southern Europe, the focus on individual performance did not sit well with the region's more "collective" ethos. And in Scandinavia, where there is more of a "sense of equality between bosses and workers," some workers asked their managers, "What gives you the right to rate me a 3?" That led ITT to make the radical decision to ditch performance ratings altogether.

Most employees cheered the changes. In one of the ITT plants in Shenyang, China, the new system has helped cut the attrition rate in half. The change is not as popular in the United States, where some metrics-loving engineers in the defence business remain attached to the old rankings. Still, most people have come around. According to the director of talent development, it has to do with the fact that everyone likes being treated as an adult in this discussion.

Sources: J. McGregor, "Case Study: To Adapt, ITT Lets Go of Unpopular Ratings," *BusinessWeek*, January 28, 2008, p. 46.

Technology Development

Every value-chain activity embodies technology.[22] The array of technologies employed in most firms is very broad, ranging from technologies used to prepare documents and transport goods to those embodied in processes and equipment or in the product itself. Technology development related to the product and its features supports the entire value chain, whereas other types of technology development are associated with particular primary or support activities. Shoppers Drug Mart's "HealthWATCH Med Ready"™ program serves to protect patients against overmedication or competing medications and to increase the filling, refilling, and transfers of prescriptions by its customers. Walmart invests heavily in technology to support its inbound logistics and its operations. All its suppliers are linked electronically in real time and receive information directly from the stores. Suppliers are expected to work with the company to ensure that goods are always in stock and on the shelves.[23] Walmart has been also investing heavily in radiofrequency identification (RFID) tags that aim to streamline the processing of inventory in its warehouses and throughout the delivery network. Already, crates and pallets from its larger suppliers, such as Procter & Gamble, Kimberly-Clark, and Levi Strauss, are tagged with microchips so that electronic readers at the entrances and exits of Walmart's massive storage facilities pick up the signals and track the goods electronically as they move in and out. The technology offers massive benefits in tracking and locating goods, improving both speed and accuracy in the handling of billions of dollars of inventory that passes through the channel.

Procurement

Procurement refers to the function of purchasing inputs to be used in the firm's value chain. Purchased inputs include raw materials, supplies, and other consumable items, as well as assets, such as machinery, laboratory equipment, office equipment, and buildings. Note that the issues here refer to the activities relating to purchasing inputs rather than the inputs themselves.

Microsoft has enhanced its procurement process (and the quality of its suppliers) by providing formal reviews to its suppliers. For example, one of Microsoft's divisions has extended the review process used for employees to its outside suppliers.[24] The evaluation system that Microsoft developed has helped clarify its expectations. An executive noted, "We had one supplier—this was before the new system—that would have scored a 1.2 out of 5. After we started giving this feedback, and the supplier understood our expectations, its performance improved dramatically. Within six months, it scored a 4. If you'd asked me before we began the feedback system, I would have said that was impossible."

Creating Shared Value by Redefining Productivity in the Value Chain

In Chapter 1, we talked about new and more ethical ways to think about strategy. One of the frameworks discussed was the Shared Value approach proposed by Michael Porter and Mark Kramer. They explain the important role a value-chain analysis plays in this regard, as a company's value chain can both affect and be affected by social and ethical issues, such as the use of water and other natural resources, health, safety and working conditions, as well as equity concerns. They note that opportunities to create shared value arise because most of the ethical and social problems companies regularly contend with can also have a negative economic impact that will be seen in the firm's value chain.

Porter and Kramer cite the example of Walmart, which in 2009 was able to address both ethical and economic issues by reducing its packaging and rerouting its trucks to cut 100 million miles from its delivery routes, saving $200 million while it shipped even more goods across the continent. Further innovations by Walmart in handling plastic materials used in its stores have saved the company millions by lowering disposal costs to landfills.

The Shared Value Creation perspective emphasizes the significant opportunities that can be found by thoughtful managers who look closely at productivity in the value chain as a means of advancing social and ethical concerns. They lament, however, that far too few companies have reaped the full productivity benefits in areas such as health, safety, environmental performance, and employee retention and capability. But there are signs of change as a growing consensus emerges around the necessity to start thinking about how firms can use their value chain to create both social and economic benefits for multiple stakeholders.

The "Prosumer" Concept: Integrating Customers into the Value Chain

When addressing the value-chain concept, it is important to focus on the interrelationship between the organization and its most important stakeholder—its customers.[25] A key to success for some leading-edge firms is to team up with their customers to satisfy their particular needs. Firms can do this in one of two ways.

First, they can employ the "prosumer" concept and directly team up with customers to design and build products to satisfy their particular needs. Working directly with customers in this process provides multiple potential benefits for the firm. As the firm develops individualized products and relationship marketing, it can benefit from greater customer satisfaction and loyalty. Additionally, the interactions with customers can generate insights that lead to cost-saving initiatives and more innovative ideas for the producing firm.

As stated in a 2008 IBM Global CEO Study:

> In the future, we will be talking more and more about the "prosumer"—a customer/producer who is even more extensively integrated into the value chain. As a consequence, production processes will be customized more precisely and individually.[26]

Customers using ATM machines to do their own banking are a precursor of this trend, but we have already seen signs elsewhere, such as commercial airlines working with the major airliner manufacturers in the design and finishing of new planes.

Including customers in the actual production process can create greater satisfaction among them. It also has the potential to result in significant cost savings and to generate innovative ideas for the firm, which can be transferred to the customer in the form of lower prices and higher-quality products and services.

In terms of how a firm views its customers, the move to create the prosumer stands in rather stark contrast to the conventional marketing approach, in which the customer merely consumes the products produced by the company. Another area where this approach differs from conventional thinking concerns the notion of tying the customer into the company through, for example, loyalty programs and individualized relationship marketing.

Second, firms can leverage the power of crowdsourcing. As introduced in Chapter 2, crowdsourcing occurs when firms tap into the knowledge and ideas of a large number of customers and other stakeholders, typically through online forums. The rise of social media has generated tremendous opportunities for firms to engage with customers. In contrast to prosumer interactions, which allow the firm to gain insights on the needs of a particular customer, crowdsourcing offers the opportunity to leverage the wisdom of a larger crowd. Many companies have encouraged customers to participate in value-creating activities, such as brainstorming advertising taglines or product ideas. These activities not only enable firms to innovate at low cost but also to engage their customers. Clearly, a marketer's dream! At the same time, crowdsourcing has some significant risks.

Understanding the Perils of Crowdsourcing

While crowdsourcing offers great promise, in practice such programs are difficult to run.[27] At times, customers can "hijack" them. Instead of offering constructive ideas, customers jump at the chance to raise concerns and even ridicule the company. Such hijacking is one of the biggest challenges companies face. Research has shown about half of such campaigns fail. Consider the following marketing-focused crowdsourcing examples:

- In 2006, General Motors tried a "fun" experiment, one of the first attempts to utilize user-generated advertising. The company asked the public to create commercials for the Chevy Tahoe—ads the company hoped would go viral. Unfortunately, some of the ads did go viral! These include: "Like this snowy wilderness. Better get your fill of it now. Then say hello to global warming. Chevy Tahoe," and "Seventy dollars to fill up the tank, which will last less than 400 miles. Chevy Tahoe."
- McDonald's set up a Twitter campaign to promote positive word of mouth. But this initiative became a platform for people looking to bash the chain. Tweets such as the following certainly didn't help the firm's cause: "I lost 50 lbs in six months after I quit working and eating at McDonald's," and "The McRib contains the same chemicals used to make yoga mats, mmmmm."

Research has identified three areas of particular concern in crowdsourcing:

- **Strong brand reputation.** Companies with strong brands need to protect them. After all, they have the most to lose. They must be aware that efforts like those of GM and McDonald's, above, provide consumers the opportunity to tarnish the brand. Strong brands are typically built through consistent, effective marketing, and companies need to weigh the potential for misbehaving customers to thwart their careful efforts.
- **High demand uncertainty.** Firms are generally more likely to ask for customer input when market conditions are changing. However, this often backfires when demand is highly uncertain, because customers in such markets often don't know what they want or what they will like. For example, Porsche received a lot of negative feedback when it announced plans to release an SUV, but it went ahead with the plan anyway, and the Porsche Cayenne was a great success.
- **Too many initiatives.** Firms typically benefit from working repeatedly with the same customers. Often, the quality, quantity, and variety of inputs decrease as the frequency of engagement increases. A study of the Dell IdeaStorm program (in which customers were encouraged to submit product or service ideas) discovered that the same people submitted ideas repeatedly—including submitting ones for things the company already provided. And customers whose ideas were implemented tended to return with additional ideas that were quite similar to their initial suggestions.

How Procter & Gamble Embraced the Prosumer Concept

In the early 2000s, P&G's people were not clearly oriented toward any common purpose. The corporate mission "To meaningfully improve the everyday lives of the customers" had not been explicitly or inspirationally rolled out to the employees. To more clearly focus everyone's efforts, P&G expanded the mission to include the idea that "the consumer is the boss." This philosophy became one in which people who buy and use P&G products are valued not just for their money but also as *a rich source of information and direction.* "The consumer is the boss" became far more than a slogan in P&G. It became a clear, simple, and inclusive cultural priority for both employees and the external stakeholders, such as suppliers.

P&G's efforts in the fragrance areas are one example. P&G transformed this small under-performing business area into a global leader and the world's largest fine fragrance company. They accomplished this by clearly and precisely defining the target consumer for each fragrance brand and by identifying subgroups of consumers for some brands. P&G still kept the partnerships with established fashion houses, such as Dolce & Gabbana, Gucci, and Lacoste. The efforts here are a model of co-creation, where the company was able to focus on innovations that were meaningful to consumers, including, for instance, fresh new scents, distinctive packaging, and proactive marketing, by working directly with the targeted stakeholder. In addition, P&G streamlined the supply chain to reduce complexity and lower its cost structure.

"The consumer is the boss" idea goes even further. It also means that P&G tries to build social connections through digital media and other forms of interactions. Baby diapers are one example. P&G used to use handmade diapers for its product tests. Today, however, the product is shown digitally and created in alternatives in an onscreen virtual world. Changes can be made immediately as new ideas emerge, and it can be redesigned onscreen. Thus, P&G is creating a social system with consumers (and potential consumers) that enables the firm to co-design and co-engineer new innovations with buyers. At P&G, the philosophy of "the consumer is the boss" set a new standard.

Applying the Value-Chain Concept to Service Organizations

The concepts of inbound logistics, operations, and outbound logistics suggest managing the raw materials that might be manufactured into finished products and delivered to customers. However, these three steps do not apply only to manufacturing. They correspond to any transformation process in which inputs are converted through a work process into outputs that add value. For example, accounting is a sort of transformation process that converts daily records of individual transactions into monthly financial reports. In this example, the transaction records are the inputs, accounting is the operation that adds value, and financial statements are the outputs.

What are the "operations," or transformation processes, of service organizations? At times, the difference between manufacturing and service is in providing a customized solution rather than mass production as is common in manufacturing. For example, a travel agent adds value by creating an itinerary that includes transportation, accommodations, and activities that are customized to the client's budget and travel dates. A law firm renders services that are specific to a client's needs and circumstances. In both cases, the work process (operation) involves the application of specialized knowledge based on the specifics of a situation (inputs) and the outcome that the client desires (outputs).

The application of the value chain to service organizations suggests that the value-adding process may be configured differently, depending on the type of business a firm is engaged in. As the preceding discussion on support activities suggests, activities, such as procurement and legal services, are critical for adding value. Indeed, the activities that may only provide support to one company may be critical to the primary value-adding activity of another firm.

In the retail industry, there are no manufacturing operations. A firm, such as Best Buy, adds value by developing expertise in the procurement of finished goods and by displaying them in their stores in a way that enhances sales. Thus, the value chain makes procurement activities (i.e., partnering with vendors and purchasing goods) a primary rather than a support activity. Operations should include the many tasks of running Best Buy's retail stores.

For an engineering services firm, R&D provides inputs, the transformation process is the engineering itself, and innovative designs and practical solutions are the outputs. Arthur D. Little, for example, is a large consulting firm with offices in 20 countries. In its technology and innovation management practice, A. D. Little strives to make the best use of the science, technology, and knowledge resources available to create value for a wide range of industries and client sectors. This involves activities associated with R&D, engineering, and creating solutions as well as downstream activities, such as marketing, sales, and service. How the primary and support activities of a given firm are configured and deployed will often depend on industry conditions and whether the company is service and/or manufacturing oriented.

LO 3 RESOURCE-BASED VIEW OF THE FIRM

To carry out the activities of its value chain, a firm needs resources. These comprise all the inputs necessary for the performance of each of the activities, irrespective of who owns or controls those resources. A firm may contract out for the use of certain resources and also own other resources outright that it can deploy at will. In either case, how resources are used by the organization is a critical decision, and success depends, to a large extent, on the appropriateness of such decisions made by the management of the organization. Managers also recognize that the ability of a firm's resources to confer competitive advantage(s) cannot be determined without taking into consideration the broader competitive context. To that end, the resource-based view (RBV) of the firm combines two perspectives: (1) the internal analysis of phenomena within a company and (2) an external analysis of the industry and its competitive environment. The RBV goes beyond the traditional SWOT analysis by integrating internal and external perspectives. It is a useful framework for gaining insights into why some competitors are more profitable than others. It is also helpful in developing strategies for individual businesses and diversified firms, since it reveals how core competencies embedded in a firm can help it exploit new product and market opportunities.

In the two sections that follow, we discuss the three key types of resources that firms possess: (1) tangible resources, (2) intangible resources, and (3) organizational capabilities. Then, we address the conditions under which these resources can enable a firm to attain a sustainable competitive advantage.

It is important to note that resources by themselves typically do not yield a competitive advantage. Even if a basketball team recruited an all-star centre, there would be little chance of victory if the other members of the team were continually outplayed by their opponents or if the coach's attitude were such that all the players, including the centre, became unwilling to put forth their best efforts. And imagine how many World Series titles Joe Torre would have won as manager of the New York Yankees if none of the players he signed could throw fastballs over 70 miles per hour. Although the all-star centre and the baseball manager are unquestionably valuable resources, they cannot enable the organization to attain advantages under these circumstances.

The RBV allows managers to build on the insights from their SWOT analysis. SWOT is useful for identifying internal strengths and capabilities but does not reveal ways to turn them into a competitive advantage; nor does it reveal how rapidly the environment could change, allowing imitators to come into the market and erode such advantage. A firm's strengths and capabilities, no matter how unique or impressive, may not enable it to achieve a competitive advantage in the marketplace. It can be compared to a highly creative but expensive product designer being employed by a firm that produces low-cost commodity products. If anything, the additional expense could erode the firm's cost advantage. If a firm builds its strategy on a capability that, by itself, cannot create or sustain competitive advantage, it is, in essence, wasting its resources. RBV explicitly directs managers to integrate internal and external perspectives and helps them develop strategies that build on core competencies and enable the firm to achieve sustainable competitive advantages.

Types of Firm Resources

Resources come in numerous forms. They are the inputs into a firm's production processes and range from widely available commodities to extremely scarce and hard-to-develop unique skills that might be responsible for the ultimate success of the firm's products. Resources include all assets, capabilities, organizational processes, information, knowledge, systems, and so forth controlled by a firm, which enable it to develop and implement value-creating strategies. Resources are fundamental to the firm's operations, and each firm possesses a unique bundle of resources. Moreover, resource accumulation is typically constrained and time consuming. A firm's strategic choices are limited by the resources that are available to it at a particular time and by its ability to accumulate additional resources.[28] Below, we define the three major types of resources.

Tangible Resources

Assets that are relatively easy to identify, measure, and value are called *tangible resources*. They include physical assets, such as real estate, cash, production facilities and equipment, raw materials, and components. Their value arises from their physical characteristics, such as their location, capacity, and features. They may represent essential inputs to a firm's operations, but only seldom can they provide the basis for competitive advantage, mainly because they are easy to identify, describe, and imitate. Among its tangible resources, a firm can list its cash and cash equivalent assets, accounts receivable, borrowing capacity, natural resources and raw materials (either in the ground or on hand), components, parts, inventory, plant, machinery and equipment, facilities, and physical proximity to customers and suppliers.

Intangible Resources

Assets that are harder to identify and quantify are called *intangible resources*. They are not concrete and can be elusive; yet they are potentially invaluable inputs into a firm's operations. They include brand name, company reputation, knowledge, technology, patents, copyrights and trademarks, trade secrets, expertise, and experience.

Intangible assets are combined with tangible assets to create the firm's product offerings. Interestingly, it is not the relative amounts of tangible and intangible inputs that determine the nature or the value of the output. For example, Holt Renfrew, the upscale retail store chain, and Club Monaco, the specialty fashion retailer, utilize real estate, store fixtures, cash machines, computer networks, and merchandise—all tangible assets. To produce the value that is desired by their clientele, these are combined with their brand names, experienced staff, marketing campaigns, accumulated reputation for quality, service, and support, management systems, and policies and procedures for ordering, pricing, merchandising, and selling. Although substantial tangible resources are required for the retail value to be produced, all the real value, at least what is most desirable to their customers, is created by the intangibles.

Intangible resources are much more difficult for competitors (and for a firm's own managers) to account for or imitate, since they are typically embedded in unique routines and practices that have evolved and accumulated over time. These include human resources (e.g., experience and capability of employees, as well as trust in and effectiveness of work teams), innovation resources (e.g., technical and scientific expertise and ideas), and reputation resources (e.g., brand name, reputation with suppliers for fairness and with customers for reliability and product quality). A firm's culture may also be a resource that provides competitive advantage.[29]

One might not think that motorcycles, clothes, toys, and restaurants have much in common. Yet Harley-Davidson has entered all these product and service markets by capitalizing on its strong brand image, a valuable intangible resource.[30] It has used that image to sell accessories, clothing, and toys, and it has licensed the Harley-Davidson Café in New York City for further exposure of its brand name and products.

Organizational Capabilities

Organizational capabilities are not specific tangible or intangible assets but the competencies and skills that a firm employs to transform those assets into outputs.[31] In short, they refer to what a firm does with the resources in its control. They concern an organization's capacity to make decisions, coordinate the use of tangible and intangible resources, and leverage these to bring about a desired end. Organizational capabilities are, in effect, the processes and routines that arise from numerous exchanges of information and knowledge and that guide the interactions of the firm's employees. Examples of organizational capabilities are lean manufacturing, excellent product development capabilities, superb innovation processes, and flexibility in manufacturing processes.

Gillette's capability to combine several technologies has been one of the keys to its unparalleled success in the wet-shaving industry. Technologies that are central to its product development efforts include its expertise with regard to the physiology of facial hair and skin, the metallurgy of blade strength and sharpness, the dynamics of a cartridge moving across skin, and the physics of a razor blade severing the hair—highly specialized areas in which

Gillette has unique capabilities. Combining these technologies has helped the company to develop innovative products, such as the MACH 3 and the Fusion shaving systems.

Unquestionably, 3M also has developed a competitive advantage using intangible resources that bring innovative products to its markets. Not only does it employ a large number of highly knowledgeable and curious scientists in its laboratories, but it frees 15 percent of their time for unrestricted experimentation and tinkering. It encourages the sharing of findings and best practices among its entire staff, and, finally, it sets minimum sales targets that contain at least 30 percent of sales from products less than five years old. As a result, it has one of the highest numbers of patents to its name and has brought to the market almost 50,000 innovations within its 100-year-plus history.[32]

LO 4 FIRM RESOURCES AND SUSTAINABLE COMPETITIVE ADVANTAGES

As we have mentioned earlier, resources alone are not the basis for competitive advantages, nor are advantages sustainable over time. In some cases, a resource or a capability may help a firm increase revenues or lower costs, but the firm derives only a temporary advantage because competitors quickly imitate or substitute its product. Many e-commerce businesses saw their profits seriously eroded because new (or existing) competitors easily duplicated their business model. Consider, for example, Priceline.com whose offerings enabled customers to place bids online for airline tickets and a wide variety of other products. Its resources (i.e., its software development knowledge) and its capabilities (i.e., its means to expand from one product line to others) were not sufficient foundations for a sustainable competitive advantage. It was simply too easy for competitors—a consortium of major airlines—to duplicate Priceline's products and services.

For a resource or a capability to provide a firm with the potential for a sustainable competitive advantage, it must meet four criteria.[33] These criteria are summarized in Exhibit 3-5. First, the resource must be valuable in the sense that it exploits opportunities, neutralizes threats in the firm's environment, or both. Second, the resource must be rare among the firm's current and potential competitors. Third, the resource must be difficult for competitors to imitate. Fourth, the resource must have no strategically equivalent substitutes. Let us examine each of these criteria.

EXHIBIT 3-5 FOUR CRITERIA FOR ASSESSING RESOURCES AND CAPABILITIES

Is the resource or capability . . .	
Valuable	• contributes value to the customer • exploits opportunities or neutralizes threats • possessed by few competing firms
Rare	• physical uniqueness (location, rights)
Inimitable	• path dependency (unique historical conditions) • causal ambiguity (difficult to disentangle causes or how it could be recreated) • social complexity (culture, trust, reputation)
Difficult to substitute	• no equivalent strategic resource or capability

Is the Resource Valuable?

Resources can be a source of competitive advantage only when they are valuable. They are valuable when they contribute to the fulfilment of customers' needs at a price the customers are willing to pay—that is, when they can be deployed to meet underserved needs better than the competitors can and when their cost of deployment is lower than the value placed by the customer on the fulfilment of the need. Under these conditions, resources are valuable because they enable a firm to formulate and implement strategies to exploit opportunities, minimize threats, and improve its efficiency and effectiveness.

The fact that firm resources must be valuable to be considered potential sources of competitive advantage reveals an important complementary relationship among environmental models (e.g., the SWOT analysis and the five-forces analysis) and the resource-based model. Environmental models isolate those firm resources that exploit opportunities, neutralize threats, or both. The resource-based model then suggests what additional characteristics these resources must possess if they are to support a sustained competitive advantage.

Is the Resource Rare?

If competitors or potential competitors also possess the same valuable resource, it is not a source of competitive advantage because all of these firms can potentially exploit that resource in the same way. Common strategies based on such a resource would give no single firm an advantage. For a resource to provide competitive advantage, it must be uncommon—that is, rare relative to other competitors.

This argument can apply to bundles of valuable firm resources that are used to formulate and develop strategies. Some strategies require a mix of resources—tangible assets, intangible assets, and organizational capabilities. If a particular bundle of firm resources is not rare, then a number of firms will be able to conceive of and implement the strategies in question. Thus, such strategies will not be a source of competitive advantage, even if the resources in question are valuable.

Can the Resource Be Imitated Easily?

Inimitability (difficulty in imitating) is a key to value creation because it constrains competition.[34] If a resource is inimitable, then any advantages generated are more likely to be sustainable. Having a resource that competitors can easily copy generates only temporary value. Inimitability has important implications. Frequently, managers fail to apply this test and base long-term strategies on resources that are imitable. Iowa Beef Processors (IBP) became the first meat-packing company in North America to modernize by building a set of assets (automated plants located in the cattle-producing states) and capabilities (low-cost "disassembly" of carcasses) that earned returns on assets of 1.3 percent in the 1970s. During the 1980s, however, ConAgra and Cargill imitated these resources, and IBP's profitability fell by nearly 70 percent, to 0.4 percent.

Monster.com entered the executive-recruiting market by providing, in essence, a substitute for traditional bricks-and-mortar headhunting firms. Although Monster.com's algorithms, software technology, and other resources were rare and valuable, they were subject to imitation by new rivals—other dot-com firms. Indeed, headhunter.com, jobsearch.com, and hotjobs.com are but a few of the many firms that have entered this market, and some 30,000 online job boards exist today. It would be difficult for any firm to attain a sustainable advantage in this industry.

Nonetheless, an advantage based on inimitability will not last forever either. Competitors will eventually discover a way to copy the most valuable resources. However, managers can forestall this and sustain profits for a while longer by developing strategies around resources that have at least one of the four characteristics described below.[35]

Physical Uniqueness

The first source of inimitability is physical uniqueness, which, by definition, is inherently difficult to copy. A beautiful resort location, mineral rights, or Merck & Co.'s pharmaceutical patents simply cannot be imitated. Locations, technologies, patents, monopoly licences, and exclusive permits are among the resources that convey uniqueness and could possibly lead to competitive advantage.

Interestingly, many managers believe that several of their resources fall into this category, but on close inspection, few do. Moreover, many of those advantages diminish with time as alternative locations are developed, patents and permits expire, and monopolists become regulated.

Path Dependency

A greater number of resources cannot be imitated because of what economists refer to as *path dependency*. This simply means that these resources are unique and, therefore, scarce because of all that has happened in the course of their development, accumulation, or both. Competitors cannot go out and buy them quickly and easily; the resources must be built up over time in ways that are difficult to accelerate.

The Gerber Products Co. brand name for baby food is an example of a resource that is potentially inimitable. Recreating Gerber's brand loyalty would be a time-consuming process that competitors cannot expedite, even with expensive marketing campaigns. Similarly, the loyalty and trust that Southwest Airlines employees feel for their firm and its co-founder Herb Kelleher are the result of a resource that has been built up over a long period. Also, a crash R&D program generally cannot replicate a successful technology when research findings accumulate. Clearly, these path-dependent conditions build protection for the original resource. The benefits from experience and learning through trial and error cannot be duplicated overnight.

Causal Ambiguity

Inimitability may also arise because it is impossible to disentangle the causes or possible explanations for either what the valuable resource is or how it can be recreated. What is the root of 3M's innovation process? One can study it and draw up a list of possible factors, but it is a complex, multilayered process that is difficult to understand and would be hard to imitate.

In many cases, causally ambiguous resources are organizational capabilities. They often involve a complex web of social interactions that may even depend on particular individuals. When Continental and United tried to mimic the successful low-cost strategy of Southwest Airlines, the planes, routes, and fast gate turnarounds were not the most difficult aspects to copy. These were all rather easy to observe and, at least in principle, easy to duplicate. However, they could not replicate Southwest's culture of fun, family, frugality, and focus, since no one can clearly specify exactly what that culture is or how it came to be.

Social Complexity

A firm's resources may be inimitable because they reflect a high level of social complexity. Such phenomena are typically beyond the ability of firms to systematically manage or influence. When competitive advantages are based on social complexity, it is difficult for other firms to imitate them.

A wide variety of firm resources may be considered socially complex. Examples include interpersonal relationships among the managers of a firm, its culture, or its reputation with its suppliers and customers. In many of these cases, it is easy to specify how these socially complex resources add value to a firm. Hence, there is little or no causal ambiguity surrounding the link between them and competitive advantage. But an understanding that certain firm attributes, such as quality relationships among managers, can improve a firm's efficiency does not necessarily lead to systematic efforts to imitate them. Such social engineering efforts are beyond the capabilities of most firms.

Although complex physical technology is not included among the sources of inimitability, the exploitation of physical technology in a firm typically involves the use of socially complex resources. That is, several firms may possess the same physical technology, but only one of them may have the social relationships, culture, group norms, and so on to fully exploit the technology in implementing its strategies. Many firms have attempted to replicate IKEA's success, but none has been able to come even close to the results achieved by its unique culture and values. If such complex social resources are not subject to imitation (and assuming they are valuable and rare and no substitutes exist), a firm may obtain a sustained competitive advantage from exploiting its physical technology more effectively than other firms can. (See Strategy Spotlight 3.5.)

3.5 STRATEGY SPOTLIGHT

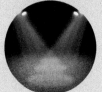

Amazon Prime: Very Difficult for Rivals to Copy

Amazon Prime is a membership program that, among other things, guarantees delivery of most products within two days for an annual fee of $99. According to *Bloomberg Businessweek*, it may be the most ingenious and effective customer loyalty program in all of e-commerce, if not retail in general. It converts casual shoppers, who gorge on the

(Continued)

gratification of having purchases reliably appear one or two days after they are ordered, into Amazon addicts. Analysts describe Prime as one of the main factors driving Amazon's stock price up. Also, it is one of the primary reasons why Amazon's sales grew 30 percent during the recession, while other retailers suffered.

Analysts estimate that Amazon Prime has more than four million members in the United States, a small slice of Amazon's 121 million active buyers worldwide. However, analysts claim that Prime members increase their purchases on the site by about 150 percent after they join and may be responsible for as much as 20 percent of Amazon's overall sales in the United States. Such shoppers are considered the "whales" of the $140-billion U.S. e-commerce market, one of the fastest-growing parts of U.S. retail. And, according to Hudson Square Research, Amazon, with a hefty 8 percent of the U.S. e-commerce market, is the single biggest online retailer in the United States.

Prime was introduced in 2004. It was the result of a years-long search for the right loyalty program. An Amazon software engineer named Charlie Ward first suggested the idea of a free shipping service via a suggestion box feature on Amazon's internal website. Bing Gordon, an Amazon board member and venture capitalist, came up with the name "Prime." Other executives, including CEO Jeffrey Bezos, devised the two-day shipping offer—which exploited Amazon's ability to accelerate the handling of individual items in its distribution centres.

Amazon Prime has proven to be extremely hard for rivals to copy. Why? It capitalizes on Amazon's wide selection, low prices, network of third-party merchants, and finely tuned distribution system. All that while also playing on that faintly irrational human need to maximize the benefits of a club that you have already paid to join.

Several years after the program's creation, rivals—both online and off—have realized the increasing threat posed by Prime and are rushing to respond. For example, in October 2010, a consortium of more than 20 retailers, including Barnes & Noble, Sports Authority, and Toys 'R' Us, banded together to offer their own copycat $79, two-day shipping program, Shop Runner, which applies to products across their websites. However, as noted by Fiona Dias, the executive who administers the program, "As Amazon added more merchandising categories to Prime, retailers started feeling the pain. They have finally come to understand that Amazon is an existential threat and that Prime is the fuel of the engine."

Sources: Stone, B. 2010. What's in the box? Instant gratification. Bloomberg Businessweek, November 29–December 5: 39–40; Kaplan, M. 2011. Amazon Prime: 5 million members, 20 percent growth. www.practicalcommerce.com, September 16: np; Fowler, G. A. 2010. Retailers team up against Amazon. www.wsj.com, October 6: np; Halkias, M. 2012. Amazon to collect sales tax in Texas. Dallas Morning News, April 28: 4A.

Are Substitutes Readily Available?

Of course, if competitors can substitute the contributions that a particular resource makes, even if that resource is valuable, rare, and inimitable, its ability to become the source of competitive advantage will diminish. Two valuable resources are strategically equivalent when each one can be exploited separately to implement the same strategies. Substitutability can take different forms. It may be impossible for a firm to imitate exactly another firm's resource, but it may be able to substitute a similar resource that enables it to develop and implement the same strategy. A firm seeking to imitate another firm's high-quality top management team would be unable to replicate the team exactly, short of hiring them all away from the competitor. However, it might be able to develop its own unique management team and develop its own strategically equivalent resource. Moreover, very different resources can become strategic substitutes. Online sellers, such as Amazon.ca, diminish the uniqueness of prime retail locations by substituting bricks-and-mortar locations with the convenience of the Internet. Several pharmaceutical firms have, similarly, seen the value of patent protection erode in the face of new drugs that are based on different chemical properties; although they might behave differently, they can be used in similar treatment regimens. Furthermore, radical changes might arise within the pharmaceutical industry in the near future from the substitution of chemotherapy with genetics-based therapies.[36]

Dynamic Capabilities

The key to attaining and sustaining a competitive advantage is being unique. Yet there are many facets to uniqueness that a firm hoping to be competitive over the long-term must contend with. For example, many analysts agree that one of the defining characteristics of the current competitive environment facing firms is a historically unprecedented rate of high-velocity change. In such a turbulent competitive environment, it is likely that the main threat to a firm's competitive advantage might not arise from efforts of rival firms within their industry to imitate the unique set of rare and valuable resources the firm has developed. Rather, the primary challenge facing the firm is likely to be the realization that many of their current resources are accelerating toward obsolescence rapidly and their value to the firm is diminishing. As such, the strategic focus of a firm finding itself in this situation shifts toward how the current stock of rare, valuable and difficult to imitate resources can be renewed in such a rapidly changing environment.

To speak directly to this challenge, the dynamic capabilities perspective emerged. Under this view, attention is turned away from a focus on the resources themselves and toward the ability of firms facing an environment of high-velocity change to constantly create new resources, or renew or alter their resource mix to support a sustainable competitive advantage.[37] A dynamic capability is defined as the firm's ability to integrate, build, and reconfigure internal and external competencies to address a rapidly changing competitive environment. The novelty in the dynamic capabilities perspective is found in the focal shift from assets broadly defined to abilities, specifically involving the capacity of a firm to integrate or coordinate valuable, rare, and difficult-to-imitate resources across the organization. These capabilities are typically developed internally by the firm over time (and not bought) and directly result in the attainment of a sustained competitive advantage.

Dynamic capabilities explain how firms sense the threats that may devalue their rare resources, and seize the opportunities to reconfigure or create new resources to maintain competitiveness. Good strategy in a highly volatile competitive setting involves making the appropriate choices with regard to the development, reconfiguration, integration, and even release of these resources. A focus on dynamic capabilities helps the contemporary manager steer the firm toward ongoing competitiveness.

Competitive Advantages and Competitive Parity

Recall that resources and capabilities must be valuable, rare, and difficult to imitate or substitute to enable a firm to attain competitive advantages that are sustainable over time.[38] When a firm's resources and capabilities do not meet any of the four criteria, it would be difficult to develop any type of competitive advantage. The resources and capabilities it possesses will not enable the firm to exploit environmental opportunities or to neutralize environmental threats. When a firm possesses resources and capabilities that are at least valuable, the firm can, at the least, achieve competitive parity with its competitors. However, if those resources and capabilities are not difficult for competitors to imitate, that parity will only allow a temporary competitive advantage, which will be eroded, sooner or later, by imitation or substitution. It is only when all four criteria are satisfied, that competitive advantages can be sustained over time.

By 2006, Dell Inc. had attained annual revenues of $56 billion and net profits of $3.6 billion. It had made its mark by competing in a quasi-commodity market for personal computers, but it differentiated itself by pioneering a direct sales approach, with user-configurable products to address the diverse needs of the individual, corporate, and institutional customer bases. Dell integrated many tangible resources, intangible resources, and organizational capabilities, and continued to maintain its competitive advantage by further strengthening its value-chain activities and the interrelationships that are critical to satisfy the largest market opportunities. It achieved this by (1) implementing e-commerce direct sales and support processes that took into account the sophisticated buying habits of the largest markets and (2) matching its operations to purchase options by adopting flexible assembly processes, leaving inventory management to the extensive supplier network. It sustained those advantages by investing in such intangible resources as proprietary assembly methods and packaging configurations, which help protect against the threat of imitation. However, recently Dell's competitive advantages have started to erode, and Dell is now challenged to sustain its financial performance and market successes of the past. Dell focused so much on costs that it failed to pay attention to its brand, and customers increasingly began to see the product as a commodity. Much of the growth in the personal computer industry came from laptops, and customers demanded sleeker and better-designed machines. In pursuit of lower costs, Dell outsourced its customer service function to foreign locations, and customer support declined, further eroding Dell's brand value. Dell's effort to duplicate its made-to-order strategy to other products, such as printers and storage devices, proved to be a failure. Customers saw little need for customization of these products. Finally, rivals, such as Hewlett-Packard (HP), improved their product designs and reduced their own costs achieving parity with Dell while enjoying better brand images and the support of extensive dealer networks.[39]

The Generation and Distribution of a Firm's Profits: Extending the Resource-Based View of the Firm

The resource-based view of the firm has been useful in determining when firms will create competitive advantages and enjoy high levels of profitability. However, it does not address how a firm's profits will be distributed to a firm's management and employees.[40] This becomes an important issue because a firm may be successful in creating competitive advantages that can be sustained for a certain period, while much of the profits can be retained (or "appropriated") by its employees and managers instead of flowing to the owners of the firm (i.e., the shareholders).

For a simple illustration, let us first consider Viewpoint DataLabs International, a company that made sophisticated three-dimensional models and textures for film production companies, video game makers, and car manufacturers. Not only was Viewpoint (later bought out by software giant Computer Associates) a highly successful firm, its employees were also able to appropriate a high proportion of the profits.

Walter Noot, Viewpoint's head of production, was having trouble keeping his highly skilled Generation X employees happy with their compensations. Each time one of them was lured away with more money, everyone else in Viewpoint would want a raise. "We were having to give out raises every six months—30 to 40 percent—then six months later they'd expect the same. It was a big struggle to keep people happy."[41] At Viewpoint Data-Labs, much of the profits were generated by the highly skilled professionals who worked together on a variety of projects. They were able to exercise their power by successfully demanding higher financial compensation. In part, management was powerless because the employees were united in their demands and because their work involves a certain amount of social complexity and causal ambiguity.

In general, profits will flow to the owners of the valuable, rare, and inimitable resources that are responsible for the creation of those profits. Four factors help explain the extent to which employees and managers will be able to obtain a proportionately high level of the profits that they generate.[42]

- *Employee bargaining power.* If employees are vital to forming a firm's unique capability, they will earn disproportionately high wages. For example, marketing professionals may have access to valuable information that helps them understand the intricacies of customer demands and expectations, or engineers may understand the unique technical aspects of products or services. Additionally, in some industries, such as consulting, advertising, and tax preparation, clients tend to be extremely loyal to individual professionals employed by the firm rather than to the firm itself. This client loyalty enables the professionals to "take the clients with them" when they leave, which enhances their bargaining power.

- *Employee replacement cost.* If employees' skills are idiosyncratic and rare (a source of resource-based advantage), they should have high bargaining power because the cost of replacing them is high for the firm. For example, Raymond Ozzie, the software designer who was critical to the development of Lotus Notes, was able to dictate the terms under which IBM acquired Lotus.

- *Employee exit costs.* This factor tends to reduce an employee's bargaining power. An individual may face high personal costs when leaving the organization. Thus, that individual's threat of leaving may not be credible. In addition, some of the expertise of an employee may be firm specific, so it would be of limited value to other firms. A related factor is that of causal ambiguity, which would make it difficult for the employee to explain his or her specific contribution to a given project. A rival firm might then be less likely to pay a high wage premium, since it would be unsure of the employee's unique contribution to the firm's success.

- *Manager bargaining power.* Managers' power is based on how well they create resource-based advantages. They are generally charged with creating value through the process of organizing, coordinating, and leveraging employees as well as other forms of capital, such as plant, equipment, and financial capital (issues we address in more detail in Chapter 4). Such activities provide managers with sources of information that may not be readily available to others. Thus, although managers may not know as much about the specific nature of customers and technologies, they are in a position to have a more thorough, integrated understanding of the total operation.

In Chapter 10, we discuss the conditions under which top-level managers (such as CEOs) of large corporations have been, at times, able to obtain levels of total compensation that would appear to be significantly disproportionate to their contributions to the firm's wealth generation and disproportionate to the level of compensation of top executives in peer organizations. Here, corporate governance becomes a critical control mechanism. Such diversion of profits from the owners of the business to top management is far less likely when the board does not consist of a high proportion of the firm's management and when board members are truly independent outsiders (i.e., do not have close ties to management). In general, given the external market for top talent, the level of compensation that executives receive is based on factors similar to those discussed above, which determine the level of their bargaining power.[43]

EVALUATING FIRM PERFORMANCE

If strategy is about an organization's success, assessing and measuring a firm's performance becomes a critical input to the analysis of the internal environment. Two approaches are typically used to evaluate a firm's performance. The first is financial ratio analysis, which, in general, identifies how a firm is performing according to its balance sheet and income statement. When performing a financial ratio analysis, managers must take into account the firm's performance from a historical perspective (not just at one point in time); the analysis should also take into account how the firm's performance compares with industry norms and the performance of key competitors.[44]

The second perspective may be considered a broader stakeholder perspective. Firms must satisfy a broad range of stakeholders, including employees, customers, and owners, to ensure long-term viability. Central to this discussion is a well-known approach, the balanced scorecard, which has been popularized by Robert Kaplan and David Norton.[45]

LO 5 Financial Ratio Analysis

The beginning point in analyzing the financial position of a firm is to compute and analyze five different types of financial ratios:

- Short-term solvency or liquidity
- Long-term solvency measures
- Asset management (or turnover)
- Profitability
- Market value

Financial analysis is the staple of the disciplines of accounting and finance. Extensive literature and a plethora of textbooks are available to guide students and managers through the logic, the technical analyses, and the thoughtful interpretation of these analyses. The Appendix at the end of the book provides detailed explanations of the five types of ratios and examples of how each is calculated.

A meaningful ratio analysis must go beyond the calculation and interpretation of financial ratios.[46] It must include an analysis of how ratios change over time and also how they are interrelated. For example, a firm that takes on too much long-term debt to finance operations will see an immediate impact on its indicators of long-term financial leverage. The additional debt will also have a negative impact on the firm's short-term liquidity ratio (i.e., current and quick ratios), since the firm must pay interest and principal on the additional debt each year until it is retired. Additionally, the interest expenses must be deducted from revenues, reducing the firm's profitability.

A firm's financial position should not be analyzed in isolation. Important reference points are needed. To make financial analysis more meaningful, historical comparisons, comparisons with industry norms, and comparisons with key competitors must be taken into account.

Historical Comparisons

When managers evaluate a firm's financial performance, it is very useful to examine changes in its financial position over time. This provides a means of evaluating trends. For example, Home Depot reported revenues of $77.3 billion and net income of $4.2 billion in 2007.[47] This is an impressive performance that many corporations would be extremely happy to be able to declare. Compare these results with the $77 billion in revenues and the $5.6 billion in net income that Home Depot achieved in 2005; there is not much to boast about anymore. Moreover, in 2005, Home Depot had only 2,042 stores, while it took 2,234 stores to achieve the 2007 results. From the perspective of its history, the company's performance looks much less remarkable. Exhibit 3-6 illustrates a 10-year period of return on sales (ROS) for a hypothetical company. As indicated by the dotted trend lines, the rate of growth (or decline) differs substantially over the various periods shown.

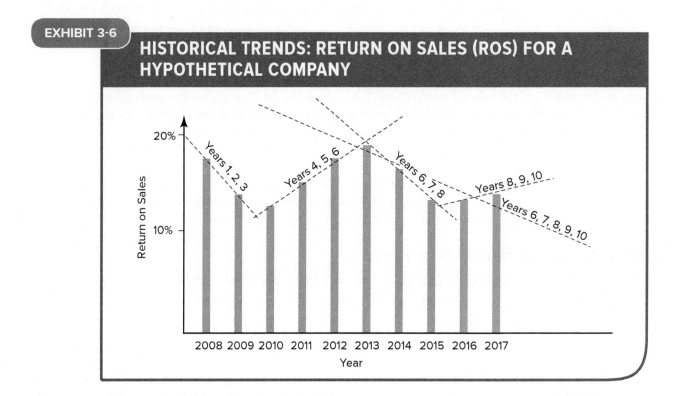

EXHIBIT 3-6

HISTORICAL TRENDS: RETURN ON SALES (ROS) FOR A HYPOTHETICAL COMPANY

Comparison with Industry Norms

When managers evaluate a firm's financial performance, they also compare it with industry norms. A firm's current ratio or profitability may appear impressive at first glance. However, it may pale in comparison with industry standards or norms.

By comparing a firm with all other firms in its industry, its relative performance can be calculated. Banks and other lending institutions often use such comparisons when evaluating a firm's creditworthiness. Exhibit 3-7 includes a variety of financial ratios for three industries: semiconductors, grocery stores, and skilled-nursing facilities. Why is there such variation among the financial ratios for these three industries? There are several reasons. With regard to the collection period, grocery stores operate mostly on a cash basis, so they have a very short collection period. Semiconductor manufacturers sell their output to other manufacturers (e.g., computer makers) on terms such as 2/15 net 45, which means they give a 2 percent discount on bills paid within 15 days and start charging interest after 45 days. Skilled-nursing facilities would also have a longer collection period compared with grocery stores because they typically rely on payments from insurance companies.

EXHIBIT 3-7   HOW FINANCIAL RATIOS DIFFER ACROSS INDUSTRIES

Financial Ratio	Semiconductors	Grocery Stores	Skilled-Nursing Facilities
Quick ratio (times)	1.9	0.6	1.2
Current ratio (times)	3.9	1.9	1.6
Total liabilities to net worth (%)	30.2	71.4	156.9
Collection period (days)	49.0	2.6	30.3
Assets to sales (%)	147.3	19.5	113.9
Return on sales (%)	24	1.1	2.4

Sources: Dun & Bradstreet. Industry Norms and Key Business Ratios, 2010–2011. One Year Edition, SIC #3600–3699 (Semiconductors); SIC #5400–5499 (Grocery Stores); SIC #8000–8099 (Skilled-Nursing Facilities). New York: Dun & Bradstreet Credit Services.

The industry norms for return on sales also highlight some differences among these industries. Grocery stores, with very slim margins, have a lower return on sales than either skilled-nursing facilities or semiconductor manufacturers. But how might we explain the differences between skilled-nursing facilities and semiconductor manufacturers? Health care facilities, in general, are limited in their pricing structures by government health regulations and by insurance reimbursement limits, but semiconductor producers have pricing structures determined by the market. If their products have superior performance, semiconductor manufacturers can charge premium prices.

Comparison with Key Competitors

Recall from Chapter 2 that firms with similar strategies are considered members of a strategic group in an industry. Furthermore, competition tends to be more intense among competitors within groups than across groups. Thus, we can gain valuable insights into a firm's financial and competitive position if we make comparisons between a firm and its most direct competitors. Consider Procter & Gamble's ill-fated efforts to enter the highly profitable pharmaceutical industry. Although P&G is a giant in consumer products, its efforts over two decades in the pharmaceutical market have produced nominal profits at best. In 1999, P&G spent $380 million on R&D of drugs—some 22 percent of its total corporate R&D budget. However, its drug division contributed only 2 percent to the company's $40 billion sales. The reason is that although $380 million is hardly a trivial amount of investment, its key competitors dwarfed P&G. *BusinessWeek's* take on P&G's chances, in an article entitled "Just Say No to Drugs," was this: "Don't bet on it. P&G may be a giant in detergent and toothpaste, but the consumer-products maker is simply outclassed by the competition."[48]

LO 6   Integrating Financial Analysis and Stakeholder Perspectives: Balanced Scorecards, Strategy Maps, and Executive Dashboards

It is always useful to see how a firm is performing over time in terms of several financial ratios. However, such a traditional approach to performance assessment can be a double-edged sword.[49] Many important actions that managers undertake—investments in R&D, employee training and development, advertising and promotion of key brands, and new product development—may greatly expand a firm's market potential and create significant long-term shareholder value. But such critical investments are not reflected positively in short-term financial reports. Why? Because financial reports typically measure expenses, not the value created. Thus, managers may be penalized for spending money in the short term to improve their firm's long-term competitive viability!

Now consider the other side of the coin. A manager may be destroying the firm's future value by operating in a way that makes customers dissatisfied, depletes the firm's stock of good products coming out of R&D, or damages the morale of valued employees. Such underinvestment, however, may lead to very good short-term financial outcomes. The manager may look good in the short run and even receive credit for improving the firm's performance. In essence, such a manager has mastered denominator management whereby decreasing investments makes the return on investment (ROI) ratio larger, even though the actual return remains constant or shrinks.

Various tools have been proposed to provide a meaningful integration of the many issues that come into evaluating a firm's performance. Among them, the most popular are balanced scorecards, strategy maps, and executive dashboards. Through a variety of formats and types of logic, these tools link strategic objectives, operational activities, and organizational outcomes. Probably the most widely adopted has been the balanced scorecard developed by Robert Kaplan and David Norton.[50] In its original form, it contains a set of measures that provide top managers with a fast but comprehensive view of the business. It includes financial measures that reflect the results of actions already taken, but it complements these indicators with operational measures of customer satisfaction, internal processes, and the organization's innovation and improvement activities—operational measures that drive future financial performance.

Balanced Scorecard

The balanced scorecard enables managers to consider their business from four key perspectives:

- *Customer perspective:* How do customers see us?
- *Internal business perspective:* What must we excel at?
- *Innovation and learning perspective:* Can we continue to improve and create value?
- *Financial perspective:* How do we look to shareholders?

Customer Perspective   The way in which a company is performing from its customers' perspective is a top priority for management. The balanced scorecard requires that managers translate their general mission statements on customer service into specific measures that reflect the factors that really matter to customers. For the balanced scorecard to work, managers must articulate goals for four key categories of customer concerns: time, quality, performance and service, and cost. For example, lead time may be measured as the time from the company's receipt of an order to the time it actually delivers the product or service to the customer. Also, quality measures may indicate the level of defective incoming products, as perceived by the customer, as well as the accuracy of the company's delivery forecasts.

Internal Business Perspective   Although customer-based measures are important, they must be translated into indicators of what the firm must do internally to meet customers' expectations. Excellent customer performance results from processes, decisions, and actions that occur throughout organizations in a coordinated fashion, and managers must focus on those critical internal operations that enable them to satisfy customer needs. The internal measures should reflect business processes that have the greatest impact on customer satisfaction. These include factors that affect cycle time, quality, employee skills, and productivity. Firms also must identify and measure the key resources and capabilities they need to ensure continued strategic success.

Innovation and Learning Perspective   Given the rapid rate of change in markets, technologies, and global competition, the criteria for success are constantly changing. To survive and prosper, managers must not only make frequent changes to existing products and services but also introduce entirely new products with expanded capabilities. A firm's ability to improve, innovate, and learn is tied directly to its value. Simply put, only by developing new products and services, creating greater value for customers, and increasing operating efficiencies can a company penetrate new markets, increase revenues and margins, and enhance shareholder value. A firm's ability to do well from the innovation and learning perspective is critically dependent on its intangible assets. Three categories of intangible assets are important: (1) human capital (skills, talents, and knowledge), (2) information capital (information systems and networks), and (3) organizational capital (culture and leadership).

Financial Perspective   Measures of financial performance indicate whether the company's strategy, implementation, and execution are, indeed, contributing to the improvement of the bottom line. Typical financial goals include profitability, growth, and shareholder value. Periodic financial statements remind managers that improved quality, response time, productivity, and innovative products benefit the firm only when they result in improved sales, increased market share, reduced operating expenses, or higher asset turnover.

Exhibit 3-8 provides an example of the balanced scorecard for a semiconductor manufacturer, ECI. Its managers saw the scorecard as a way to clarify, simplify, and then operationalize the vision at the top of the firm. The scorecard was designed to focus the attention of top executives on a short list of critical indicators of current as well as future performance. For example, to track the specific goal of providing a continuous stream of attractive solutions, ECI measured the percentage of sales from new products and the percentage of sales from proprietary products (customer perspective). After deciding that manufacturing excellence was critical to success, managers determined that cycle time, unit costs, and yield would be the most viable indicators (internal business perspective). Like many companies, ECI determined that the percentage of sales from new products is a key measure of innovation and improvement (the innovation and learning perspective). Finally, ECI decided on three key financial goals—survive, succeed, and prosper—with the corresponding measures of cash flow, quarterly sales growth or operating income by division, and increased market share and return on equity, respectively.

EXHIBIT 3-8   ECI'S BALANCED BUSINESS SCORECARD

Customer Perspective

Goals	Measures
• New products • Responsive supply • Customer partnership	• Percentage of sales from new products • On-time delivery (defined by customer) • Number of co-operative engineering efforts

Internal Business Perspective

Goals	Measures
• Manufacturing excellence	• Cycle time • Unit cost
• Design productivity • New product introduction	• Silicon efficiency • Engineering efficiency • Actual introduction schedule versus plan

Innovation and Learning Perspective

Goals	Measures
• Technology leadership • Manufacturing learning • Product focus • Time to market	• Time to develop next generation • Process time to maturity • Percentage of products that equal 80 percent of sales • New product introduction versus competition

Financial Perspective

Goals	Measures
• Survive • Succeed • Prosper	• Cash Flow • Quarterly sales growth and operating income by division • Market share growth • Return on investment; return on equity

Sources: Adapted with permission of *Harvard Business Review.* Exhibit from "The Balanced Scorecard: Measures that Drive Performance," by R. S. Kaplan and D. P. Norton, 69, no. 1 (1992). Copyright © 1992 by the Harvard Business School Publishing Corporation, all rights reserved.

Utilizing data analytics, a national retailer developed what it called its *total performance indicators,* or TPI—a set of indicators that showed how well the company was doing with customers, employees, and investors. Their model shown a strong causal relationship among employee attitudes, customer attitudes, and financial outcomes.[51] According to the analysis, a 5-percent improvement in employee attitudes led to a 1.3-percent improvement in customer satisfaction, which, in turn, would drive a 0.5-percent improvement in revenue. Thus, if a single store improved its employee attitude by 5 percent on a survey scale, they could predict, with confidence, that with revenue growth in the district as a whole at 3 percent, the revenue growth in that particular store would be 3.5 percent. Managers consider such numbers as rigorous as any others that they work with every year.

A key implication is that managers do not need to look at their jobs as primarily balancing stakeholder demands. They do not have to ask, "How many units in employee satisfaction do I have to give up to get some additional units of customer satisfaction or profits?" In contrast, the balanced scorecard provides a win–win approach, a means of simultaneously increasing satisfaction among various organizational stakeholders, including employees (at all levels), customers, and shareholders.

Although the balanced scorecard promises many advantages, it has been frequently viewed as a quick fix that can be easily installed and manipulated. In a study of medium-sized Canadian firms, more users expressed skepticism than claimed positive results from the adoption of various balanced scorecards. Moreover, many commented that their scorecards quickly became number-crunching exercises with only dubious effectiveness.[52]

Strategy Maps

Strategy maps attempt to more explicitly link strategic objectives with activities and anticipated outcomes. They also help employees see how their jobs are related to the overall objectives of the organization.[53] Scores of different strategy maps have been developed, each with its own idiosyncrasies and unique elements to capture the specificity or each organization. Some common elements across these maps are the visual representation of the main strategic objectives; arrows connecting objectives and placing them in causal relationships; banners or balloons representing different performance perspectives as those have been articulated in a balanced scorecard or otherwise; hierarchical interdependencies between the objectives across the various perspectives; performance metrics associated with each of the objectives; and activities that are associated with particular objectives and should yield the desirable outcomes. The simple visual representation of the strategic objectives, the visual cues illustrating the different perspectives, and the causal arrows employed aim to facilitate the discussion within the management team regarding such issues as the selection of objectives, the links between objectives across the organization's different units, and the actual performance achieved. Moreover, the visual simplicity aids management in communicating its choices throughout the organization and engaging employees to more readily identify with the objectives and recognize the links across the different levels of the organization.

Executive Dashboards

Executive dashboards are also visual representations of an organization's functions and performance. Among the countless formats that have been developed, some literally resemble traditional instruments in a car's dashboard. Executive dashboards draw data from multiple sources, databases, and information systems throughout the organization. They process the information in real time and display it in an easy-to-understand format so that management can appreciate the current conditions, make decisions, and more effectively run the business.[54] Dashboards show specific dimensions of an organization's performance as it happens and should not be confused with scorecards or maps, which effectively convey what "ought to be" as opposed to "what is." Dashboards can be customized to track each function within the organization and report on whatever activity or outcome a manager needs to monitor, and they can measure efficiencies or inefficiencies, monitor trends, identify correlations, and provide reports at different levels of detail.

SUMMARY

In the traditional approaches to assessing a firm's internal environment, the primary goal of managers would be to determine their firm's relative strengths and weaknesses. Such is the role of the SWOT analysis, wherein managers analyze their firm's strengths, weaknesses, and the opportunities and threats in the external environment. In this chapter, we discussed why this may be a good starting point but hardly the best approach to take in performing a sound analysis. There are many limitations to the SWOT analysis, including its static perspective, its potential to overemphasize a single dimension of a firm's strategy, and the likelihood that a firm's strengths do not necessarily help the firm create value or competitive advantages.

We identified two frameworks that serve to complement the SWOT analysis in assessing a firm's internal environment: value-chain analysis and the resource-based view of the firm. In conducting a value-chain analysis, the first step is to divide the firm into a series of value-creating activities. These include primary activities, such as inbound logistics, operations, and service, as well as support activities, such as procurement and human resource management. The next step is to analyze how each activity adds value and also how interrelationships among value activities in the firm and between the firm and its customers and suppliers add value. Thus, instead of merely determining a firm's strengths and weaknesses, per se, we analyze them in the overall context of the firm and its relationships with customers and suppliers—the value system.

The resource-based view of the firm considers the firm as a bundle of resources: tangible resources, intangible resources, and organizational capabilities. Competitive advantages that are sustainable over time generally arise from the creation of bundles of resources and capabilities. For advantages to be sustainable, four criteria must be satisfied: value, rarity, inimitability, and exploitability. Such an evaluation requires a sound knowledge of the competitive context in which the firm exists. The owners of a business may not capture all of the value created by the firm. The appropriation of value created by a firm between the owners and employees is determined by four factors: employee bargaining power, replacement cost, employee exit costs, and manager bargaining power.

An internal analysis of the firm would not be complete unless we evaluate its performance and make appropriate comparisons. Determining a firm's performance requires an analysis of its financial situation and a review of how well it is satisfying a broad range of stakeholders, including customers, employees, and shareholders. We discussed the concept of the balanced scorecard, in which four perspectives must be addressed: customer, internal business, innovation and learning, and financial. Central to the balanced scorecard is the idea that the interests of various stakeholders can be interrelated and improving a firm's performance does not need to involve making trade-offs among different stakeholders. We introduced strategy maps and executive dashboards, additional tools commonly used to evaluate a firm's performance. These tools allow managers to connect strategic objectives with activities and outcomes and facilitate links between objectives at different levels of the organization. Finally, we discussed why assessing the firm's performance is more useful if it is evaluated in terms of how it changes over time, compares with industry norms, and compares with the performances of key competitors.

Summary Review Questions

1. Briefly describe the primary and support activities in a firm's value chain.
2. How can managers create value by establishing important relationships among the value-chain activities both within their firm and between the firm and its customers and suppliers?
3. Briefly explain the four criteria for the sustainability of competitive advantages.
4. Under what conditions are employees able to appropriate some of the value that is created by their firm?
5. What are the advantages and disadvantages of conducting a financial-ratio analysis of a firm?
6. Summarize the concept of the balanced scorecard. What are its main advantages?

REFLECTING ON CAREER IMPLICATIONS

The Value Chain: Carefully analyze where you can add value in your firm's value chain. How might your firm's support activities help you accomplish your assigned tasks more effectively?

The Value Chain: Consider important relationships among activities within your firm as well as between your firm and its suppliers, customers, and alliance partners.

Resource-Based-View of the Firm: Are your skills and talents rare, valuable, and difficult to replicate or substitute? If so, you are in a better position to add value for your firm and earn rewards for your contributions.

How can your skills and talents be enhanced to help satisfy these criteria to a greater extent? Would more training help? What about changing positions within the firm? What about career options in other organizations?

Balanced Scorecard: In your decision making, strive to balance the four perspectives: customer, internal business, innovation and learning, and financial. Do you focus too much on short-term profits? Do your personal career goals provide opportunities to develop your skills in all four directions?

EXPERIENTIAL EXERCISE

Dell Computer is a leading firm in the personal computer industry, which as part of Dell Technologies posted annual revenues in excess of $61 billion during its 2016 fiscal year. Dell has created a very strong competitive position via its "direct model," whereby it manufactures its personal computers to detailed customer specifications. However, its advantage has been recently eroded by strong rivals, such as Lenovo and HP. Among many initiatives, Dell has recently introduced the Dell India Direct to enhance its competitive stance in the online Indian computer market.

Below we address several questions that focus on Dell's value-chain activities and interrelationships among them as well as whether they are able to create sustainable competitive advantage(s). In preparation for this exercise, in addition to reviewing our discussions earlier in the chapter, you may choose to do some online research into Dell's strategies and operations.

1. Where in its value chain is Dell creating value for its customers?

Value-Chain Activity	How Does Dell Create Value for the Customer?
Primary:	
Inbound logistics	
Operations	
Outbound logistics	
Marketing and sales	
Service	
Support:	
Procurement	
Technology development	
Human resource management	
General administration	

2. What are the important relationships among Dell's value-chain activities? What are the important inter-dependencies? For each activity, identify the relationships and interdependencies.

	Inbound logistics	Operations	Outbound logistics	Marketing and sales	Service	Procurement	Technology development	Human resource management	General administration
Inbound logistics									
Operations									
Outbound logistics									
Marketing and sales									
Service									
Procurement									
Technology development									
Human resource management									
General administration									

3. What resources, activities, and relationships enable Dell to achieve a sustainable competitive advantage?

	Is It Valuable?	Is It Rare?	Is It Inimitable?	Is It Exploitable?
Inbound logistics				
Operations				
Outbound logistics				
Marketing and sales				
Service				
Procurement				
Technology development				
Human resource management				
General administration				

APPLICATION QUESTIONS AND EXERCISES

1. Using published reports, select two CEOs who have recently made public statements regarding a major change in their firms' strategies. Discuss how the successful implementation of such strategies requires changes in the firms' primary and support activities.

2. Select a firm that competes in an industry in which you are interested. Draw on published financial reports, and complete a financial-ratio analysis. On the basis of changes over time and a comparison with industry norms, evaluate the firm's strengths and weaknesses in terms of its financial position.

3. How might exemplary human resource practices enhance and strengthen a firm's value-chain activities?

4. Learn about your university or college by visiting its website. What are some of its key value-creating activities that provide competitive advantages?

ETHICS AND CORPORATE SOCIAL RESPONSIBILITY QUESTIONS

1. What are some of the ethical issues that may arise when a firm tries to improve each of its primary activities?

2. What are some of the ethical dilemmas that may arise when a company imposes its own value system on its suppliers?

3. What are some of the ethical issues that might occur when a firm becomes overly zealous in advertising its products?

4. What are some of the ethical issues that may arise from a firm's procurement activities? Are you aware of any of these issues from your personal experience or from businesses you are familiar with?

CHAPTER FOUR

Assessing the Intellectual Assets of the Firm

LEARNING OBJECTIVES

After reading this chapter, you should have a good understanding of:

LO 1 The increasing value of intellectual assets for today's corporations and for the prosperity of a country.

LO 2 Why the management of knowledge and knowledge professionals is so critical in today's organizations.

LO 3 The importance of recognizing the interdependence of attracting, developing, and retaining human capital.

LO 4 The key role of social capital in leveraging human capital within and across an organization.

LO 5 The importance of social networks in knowledge management.

LO 6 The vital role of technology in leveraging knowledge and human capital.

LO 7 The challenge of protecting intellectual property and the importance of a firm's dynamic capabilities.

CASE STUDY

esearch in Motion (RIM) grew out of groundbreaking research into computer and telecommunications technology at the University of Waterloo. From humble beginnings and small amounts of seed capital to develop wireless modems and pagers in the mid 1980s, and through aggressive research and product development efforts, RIM introduced in 2000 the first BlackBerry and kick-started what today is a $120-billion global market in smartphones.[1] Yet RIM, which later changed its name to BlackBerry to better identify with its early achievements, was not able to sustain its success and eventually saw Apple, Samsung, and dozens of other players surpass it and render it irrelevant.

THE CANADIAN PRESS IMAGES/Lars Hagberg

BlackBerry has a tumultuous history in the Canadian business landscape. Previously a golden gem of Canadian research and development, the smartphone manufacturer experienced a meteoric rise between 2001 and 2007, followed by a significant financial decline resulting in precipitous erosion of both the company's market share and market value. In late 2013, CEO Thorsten Heins was replaced by John S. Chen, whose first move was to release a positive statement regarding the company's future: "We are committed to reclaiming our success."

Notwithstanding Chen's optimism, the statement did little to impress shareholders convinced of the company's imminent demise. In recent years, however, Chen's actions have demonstrated his dedication to reclaiming BlackBerry's sustained competitive advantage; that is, its intellectual property and patent portfolio.

BlackBerry's patent portfolio typically ranks in the top 75 annual patent recipients in the U.S., and Chen recognizes their value. "We have today about 44,000 patents. The good thing about this is that we also have one of the youngest patent portfolios in the entire industry, so monetization of our patents is an important aspect of our turnaround." Chen notes the fine balance between monetizing and protecting their patents. On the one hand, protecting their patents through lawsuits represents a short-term form of income; on the other hand, monetizing the patents through collaborative licensing agreements provides a long-term form of income.

As of 2017, Blackberry is well on its way to achieving that balance. In July 2016, the company filed an enforcement action alleging patent infringement against multinational technology company Avaya Inc; in August, an enforcement action was filed against BLU Products, alleging infringement of seven Blackberry patents. Most recently, the company filed an enforcement action against Nokia Oyj in the U.S., alleging willful and deliberate infringement of 11 standard essential patents. If successful, an action alleging willful and deliberate patent infringement could triple the amount awarded by the court.

In addition, BlackBerry's USB power patent portfolio was recently acquired by Fundamental Innovation Systems International, representing a move toward monetizing the patents through long-term licensing agreements. Maulin Shah, the managing attorney for Envision IP, a company researching the value of BlackBerry's patent portfolio, noted that "the company certainly seems to be placing a higher emphasis on monetizing its patents via licensing and litigation than it has in the past." While BlackBerry may still have a long path to tread toward recovery, it is clear that they are making the right steps in order to do so.

Beyond litigation and licensing, other recent strategic moves clearly show that BlackBerry recognizes that its future lies in its intellectual property and not in the manufacturing of smartphones. In September 2016, Black-Berry agreed to a licensing partnership with an Indonesian company, setting up a new joint venture called "BB Merah Putih," in which the partner company assumes responsibility for the manufacturing of their handsets. This move has since been lauded as showing BlackBerry's commitment to innovation and intellectual property. Having a third party complete their manufacturing allows BlackBerry to focus on what is most important for their long-term success: the continued research and development of their patent portfolio.

BlackBerry, after a few rocky years, is on the path to recovery. While their past success was dependent on their smartphone manufacturing and advanced security, Chen recognizes that their sustained competitive advantage, going forward, will be deeply rooted in intellectual property and their patent portfolio. By choosing to have a third party complete their manufacturing, BlackBerry has enabled itself to focus on monetizing their patent portfolio through a combination of litigation and licensing agreements, both of which have been profitable for the firm thus far.

Technology, knowledge, and human capital, as well as brand names and trademarks, all make critical contributions to a firm's competitive advantage and represent an increasingly important proportion of a company's wealth. As such, beyond analyzing its external and internal environments, all firms, not only BlackBerry must critically assess their intellectual assets and how they are vitally connected to their value creation activities. Peter Drucker convincingly argued that the "knowledge workers" and the knowledge they possess are the primary resource of the economy overall, emphasizing that these are far more valuable than material or financial resources for the long-term prosperity of a country and its firms.[2] Even in resource-based economies similar to Canada's, success depends on the ability of individual firms to create technological innovations that transform raw materials to value-added goods.

Silicon Valley in California has been the breeding ground for much talent in a range of technology-intensive industries. Individual firms within the Valley find new talent by tapping into the social contacts of existing owners and employees. New firms develop out of workers' previous experiences; experience involves contact with former employers and co-workers. Intricate networks of relationships facilitate the screening and selection of suitable candidates for new and existing firms alike. Individuals often have more loyalty to their peers, including those in competing firms, than they to their current employer. This makes the social network even more crucial. Individuals typically do not work for the same company for a lifetime. In fact, job changes are frequent and common. John Doerr of venture capital firm Kleiner Perkins Caufield & Byers (KPCB) is fond of saying that Silicon Valley is the only place where you can change jobs and keep your parking space![3]

The Waterloo region in southern Ontario is another such breeding ground. It is a traditional manufacturing centre, which, in the past, produced household names, such as Seagram's whisky, Bauer skates, Hush Puppies shoes, and Schneider's meats. The area has seen many of those product lines disappear, taking numerous manufacturing jobs with them. Yet in spite of the huge swings in the fortunes of BlackBerry, the region is thriving and adding jobs by the thousands, as the likes of Open Text Corporation, Vidyard, and Thalmic Labs are creating world-leading products and establishing new firms for the New Economy.[4] Tom Jenkins, chairman and chief strategy officer of Open Text, takes the view that the ongoing success of the region does not depend on erecting barriers to keep existing companies there and foreign competition out; instead, it relies on creating an environment that promotes education and rewards entrepreneurship to ensure that new firms continue to be spawned.

THE CENTRAL ROLE OF INTELLECTUAL CAPITAL IN TODAY'S ECONOMY

For much of business history, including most of the twentieth century, managers were primarily concerned with tangible resources, such as land, equipment, and money, as well as intangibles, such as brands, image, and customer loyalty. Efforts were directed toward the efficient allocation of labour and capital—the two traditional factors of production.

LO 1

Today, more than 50 percent of the gross domestic product (GDP) in the developed economies is knowledge based; that is, it is based on intellectual assets and intangible people skills.[5] Intellectual and information processes create most of the value for firms in large service industries (e.g., software, medical care, communications, and education), which provide 65 percent of Canada's GDP. In the manufacturing sector, intellectual activities, such as R&D, process design, product design, logistics, marketing, or technological innovation, produce the preponderance of value added.[6] Consider the perspective of Gary Hamel and C. K. Prahalad, two leading writers in strategic management:

> The machine age was a physical world. It consisted of things. Companies made and distributed things (physical products). Management allocated things (capital budgets), and management invested in things (plant and equipment). In the machine age, people were ancillary, and things were central. In the information age, things are ancillary, and knowledge is central. A company's value derives not from things, but from knowledge, know-how, intellectual assets, competencies—all embedded in people.[7]

In the knowledge economy, wealth is increasingly created through the effective management of intellectual assets and knowledge workers instead of by the efficient control of physical and financial assets. The growing importance of knowledge, coupled with the move by labour markets to reward knowledge work, tells us that someone who invests in a company is, in essence, paying for a set of talents, capabilities, skills, and ideas—intellectual capital—not physical and financial resources. The implications of this, of course, are that the values of a firm become more critical than ever. Motivating and inspiring people, getting them to be committed to a firm and its strategic objectives, is a more value-laden strategic task than turning on a machine.

The following examples should illustrate this point. People do not buy Microsoft's stock because of its software factories; it does not own any. Rather, the value of Microsoft rests on the company's ability to set standards for personal-computing software, exploit the value of its name, and forge alliances with other companies. Amazon and Apple are even starker examples of the same principles. Similarly, Merck did not become the "Most Admired" company for seven consecutive years in *Fortune's* annual survey because it can manufacture pills but, rather, because its scientists can invent new medicines. P. Roy Vagelos, who was CEO of Merck during its long run atop the "Most Admired" survey said, "A low-value product can be made by anyone anywhere. When you have knowledge no one else has access to—that's dynamite. We guard our research even more carefully than our financial assets."[8] Two Canadian knowledge powerhouses, Biovail and Cognos, during their formative years generated billions of dollars in market value from the creation and application of technology developed in the fields of biotechnology and medicine, and business intelligence. Their facilities, plants, and equipment represented a small fraction of the total value ascribed to them by the financial markets. Notably, Cognos had revenues of $ 979 million and less than one billion in physical assets when IBM paid $4.9 billion to acquire it in 2008. And firms that do not take values seriously are less likely to succeed in a people-centric economy.

To apply some numbers to our arguments, let us ask: What is a company worth? Start with the "big three" financial statements: income statement, balance sheet, and statement of cash flow. If these statements tell a story that investors find useful, then a company's market value should roughly (but not precisely, because the market looks forward and the books look backward) be the same as the value that accountants ascribe to it—the book value of the firm. However, this is not the case. A study compared the market value with the book value of 3,500 U.S. companies over a period of two decades. In 1978, the two were quite similar: Book value was 95 percent of market value. However, market values and book values have diverged significantly. Within 20 years, the S&P industrials were—on average— trading at 2.2 times the book value. Robert A. Howell, an expert on the changing role of finance and accounting, muses that "The big three financial statements . . . are about as useful as an 80-year-old Los Angeles road map."

The gap between a firm's market value and book value is far greater for knowledge-intensive corporations than for firms with strategies based primarily on tangible assets. Exhibit 4-1 shows the ratio of market-to-book value for some well-known companies. In firms where knowledge and the management of knowledge workers are relatively important contributors to developing products and services—and physical resources are less critical—the ratio of market-to-book value tends to be much higher.

EXHIBIT 4-1   RATIO OF MARKET VALUE TO BOOK VALUE FOR SELECTED COMPANIES

Company	Annual Sales ($ billions)	Market Value ($ billions)	Book Value ($ billions)	Ratio of Market to Book Value
Apple	215.63	798.32	193.68	4.13
Google	90.27	678.80	38.49	17.84
Microsoft	85.32	544.98	121.47	4.49
Oracle	37.04	187.29	65.18	2.87
Intel	59.38	169.38	57.36	2.96
International Paper	23.08	22.16	23.68	0.93
Southwest Airlines	20.04	35.25	15.33	2.30

Note: The data on market valuations are as of December 31, 2016. All other financial data are based on the most recently available balance sheets and income statements.

Sources: www.Ycharts.com, Data and Charts provided by Ycharts.

As shown in Exhibit 4-1, such firms as Apple, Google, Microsoft, and Oracle have very high market-to-book ratios because of their high investment in knowledge resources and technological expertise. In contrast, firms in more traditional industry sectors, such as International Paper, Nucor, and Southwest Airlines, have relatively low market-to-book ratios. This reflects their greater investments in physical resources and lower investment in knowledge resources.

How do companies create value in the knowledge-intensive economy? The answer rests on their ability to manage their intellectual assets and to attract and effectively leverage human capital through mechanisms that create products and services of value. Thus, for us to understand and appreciate the sources of a firm's competitive advantage, we must first take a close look at and analyze how that firm handles its intellectual capital. Remember from the previous chapter that the resource-based view of the firm recognizes that a firm's competitive advantage emerges from its valuable, rare, and inimitable socially complex resources. But before we further develop the role of intellectual assets and human capital in wealth creation, let us delineate some of the basic concepts as they are presented in Exhibit 4-2.

EXHIBIT 4-2   TYPES OF INTELLECTUAL CAPITAL (INTELLECTUAL ASSETS)

Human Capital	Social Capital	Intellectual Property
Individuals' • capabilities • knowledge, both tacit and explicit • skills • experiences	Relationships • formal and informal • personal and professional • organizational Networks	Copyrights Trademarks Patents

First, consider intellectual capital. **Intellectual capital** consists of intangible assets, such as human capital, social capital, intellectual property, brands and trademarks, which all contribute to a firm's ability to create value through new knowledge and its useful applications. Innovation rests at the heart of economic development, and the management of intellectual capital is arguably the only source of sustainable competitive advantage. Managing intellectual assets entails the whole life cycle of creation, codification, valuation, protection, and leveraging of such assets.[9] This broad definition includes such assets as reputation, employee loyalty and commitment, customer relationships, company values, brand names, and the experience and skills of employees. Thus, simplifying, we have:

Intellectual capital = Market value of the firm − Book value of the firm[10]

Second, **human capital** consists of the *"individual* capabilities, knowledge, skills, and experience of the company's employees and managers." This concerns knowledge that is relevant to the task at hand and the capacity to add to the reservoir of knowledge, skills, and experience through learning.[11]

Third, **social capital** involves "the network of relationships that individuals have throughout the organization." Relationships are critical in sharing and leveraging knowledge and in acquiring resources. Social capital extends beyond the organizational boundaries to include relationships between the firm and its suppliers, customers, alliance partners and a wide array of other committed stakeholders.[12]

Fourth is the concept of "knowledge," which comes in two different forms. On the one hand, there is **explicit knowledge,** which is codified, documented, easily reproduced, and widely distributed. Examples include engineering drawings, software code, sales collateral, and patents. On the other hand, there is **tacit knowledge.**[13] This is knowledge that is, in essence, in the minds of employees and is based on their experiences and backgrounds. Tacit knowledge is shared only with the consent and participation of the individual.

Fifth is the concept of **intellectual property.** Ideas, innovations, and creations contribute to sustainable competitive advantage only when a firm is able to protect its exclusive right to extract value from them for a long period and prevent others from copying or imitating them for their own benefits. As Conley and Szobocsan have pointed out, the careful and purposeful management of copyrights and trademarks is the single most important reason Disney has been able to maximize the economic life of its animation classics over many years. *Snow White,* after all, is 80 years old, and it still sells briskly when the Disney folks periodically offer another round of videos, compact discs, and toys for sale.[14]

New knowledge is constantly being created in organizations. It involves the continual interaction of explicit and tacit knowledge. Consider, for example, two software engineers working together on a computer code. The computer code itself is the explicit knowledge. By sharing ideas, which arise from each individual's experience—that is, their tacit knowledge—new knowledge is created as they make modifications to the existing code. Another important issue is the role of "socially complex processes," noted in the resource-based view of the firm as an inimitable source of competitive advantage, which include leadership, culture, and trust.[15] These processes play a central role in the creation of knowledge. They represent the "glue" that holds the organization together and helps create a working environment where individuals are more willing to share their ideas, work in teams, and, in the end, create products and services of value.

LO 2

Numerous books have been written on the subject of knowledge management and the central role that it plays in creating wealth in organizations and countries throughout the developed world.[16] Here, we focus on the central resource itself, human capital, and some guidelines on how it can be attracted, developed, and retained. Tom Stewart, former editor of the *Harvard Business Review,* noted that organizations must also carry out significant efforts to protect their human capital. A firm may "diversify the ownership of vital knowledge by emphasizing teamwork, guard against obsolescence by developing learning programs, and shackle key people with golden handcuffs."[17] In addition, people are less likely to leave an organization if there are effective structures to promote teamwork and information sharing, strong leaders to encourage innovation, and cultures that demand excellence and ethical behaviour. Such issues are also central to the topic of this chapter. We provide more detail in later chapters as we discuss organizational structure and design in Chapter 9; organizational controls (culture, rewards, and boundaries) in Chapter 10; and a variety of leadership and entrepreneurship topics in Chapters 11 and 12.

HUMAN CAPITAL: THE FOUNDATION OF INTELLECTUAL CAPITAL

To be successful, organizations must recruit talented people—employees at all levels with the proper sets of skills and capabilities coupled with the right values and attitudes. Such skills and attitudes must be continually developed, strengthened, and reinforced, and each employee must be motivated and focused on the organization's goals and objectives.

The rise to prominence of the knowledge worker as a vital source of competitive advantage is changing the balance of power in today's organization. Knowledge workers frequently place professional development and personal enrichment (financial and otherwise) above company loyalty. Attracting, recruiting, and hiring "the best and the brightest," are critical first steps in the process of building intellectual capital. At a symposium for chief executive officers (CEOs), Bill Gates said, "The thing that is holding Microsoft back . . . is simply how [hard] we find it to go out and recruit the kind of people we want to grow our research team."[18]

Hiring is only the first of three vital processes in which all successful organizations must engage to build and leverage their human capital. Firms must also *develop* employees at all levels and specialties so that they fulfil their potential and, in doing so, maximize their joint contributions. Finally, firms must provide the working environment and intrinsic and extrinsic rewards to *retain* their best and brightest; without employee retention, the first two processes are rendered meaningless.

These three activities are highly interrelated. They constitute a three-legged stool (Exhibit 4-3).[19] If one leg is weak or broken, the stool collapses. Poor hiring impedes the effectiveness of development and retention processes. In a similar vein, ineffective retention efforts place additional burdens on hiring and development. Recall from the previous chapter Jeffrey Pfeffer's likening of stepping up recruitment efforts aimed at compensating for poor retention to a doctor who tries to treat a bleeding patient by increasing the speed of transfusion.[20] Although there are no simple, easy-to-apply answers, we can learn from what leading-edge firms are doing to attract, develop, and retain human capital in today's highly competitive and rapidly changing marketplace. In assessing a firm's intellectual capital then, one must delve into an analysis of the management of its human capital.

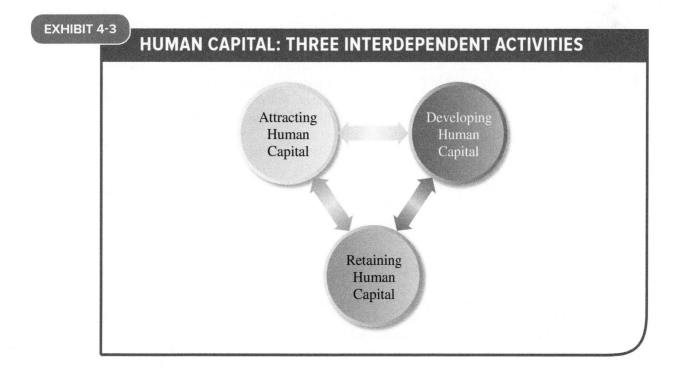

EXHIBIT 4-3

HUMAN CAPITAL: THREE INTERDEPENDENT ACTIVITIES

Attracting Human Capital

Developing Human Capital

Retaining Human Capital

Attracting Human Capital

> "All we can do is bet on the people we pick. So my whole job is picking the right people."
>
> —**Jack Welch,** former chairman, General Electric Company[21]

The first step in the process of building superior human capital is input control: attracting and selecting the right person. Many human resource professionals still approach employee selection from a "lock and key" mentality—that is, fit a key (a job candidate) into a lock (the job). Such an approach involves a thorough analysis of both the person and the job. Only then can the right decision be made as to how well the two will fit together. How can you fail, the theory goes, if you get a precise match of knowledge, ability, and skill profiles? Frequently, however, the precise matching approach places its primary emphasis on task-specific skills (e.g., motor skills, specific information gathering and processing capabilities, and communication skills) and puts less emphasis on broader aspects, such as general knowledge and experience, social skills, values, beliefs, and attitudes of employees.

Many have questioned the "precise matching" approach. They argue that firms can identify top performers by focusing on key employee mindsets, attitudes, social skills, and general orientations that lead to success in nearly all jobs. It is believed that if firms get these elements right, the task-specific skills can be learned in relatively short order. (This does not imply, however, that task-specific skills are unimportant; rather, it suggests that the requisite skill sets must be viewed as a necessary but not sufficient condition.) This leads us to a phrase that is popular with many organizations today and serves as the heading of the next section.

"Hire for Attitude, Train for Skill"

Organizations are increasingly placing their emphasis on the general knowledge and experience, social skills, values, beliefs, and attitudes of employees. Consider the hiring practices of Southwest Airlines (SWA), which involve a strong focus on employee values and attitudes. Given its strong team orientation, SWA uses an "indirect" approach. For example, the interviewing team asks a group of employees to prepare a five-minute presentation about themselves. During the presentations, the interviewers observe which candidates are enthusiastically supporting their peers and which candidates are focused on polishing their own presentations while the others are presenting.[22] The former, of course, are favoured.

Social skills are also important. Being pleasant and collegial are requirements of Rosenbluth International, a travel management company based in Philadelphia, with annual revenues over $4 billion. Here, job applicants are asked to play a trial game of softball with the company team. Potential executives are frequently flown to the firm's North Dakota ranch to help repair fences or drive cattle. Do athletic ability or ranching skills matter? Not at all. According to Keami Lewis, former Rosenbluth diversity manager, "You can teach a person almost anything. But you can't teach him or her how to be nice."[23] Or, as Tom Stewart has suggested, "You can make a leopard a better leopard, but you can't change its spots."[24]

Many have argued that the most common—and fatal—hiring mistake is to select individuals with the right skills but the wrong mindset on the assumption that "we can change them." According to Alan Davidson, an industrial psychologist, "The single best predictor of future behaviour is past behaviour. Your personality (largely reflecting values, beliefs, attitudes, and social skills) is going to be essentially the same throughout your life."[25]

Sound Recruiting Approaches and Networking

Companies that take hiring seriously must also take recruiting seriously. The number of jobs that successful knowledge-intensive companies must fill is astonishing. Ironically, many companies still have no shortage of applicants. Southwest Airlines typically gets 150,000 résumés a year, and hires about 5,000 new employees. Netscape reviews 60 résumés for every hire.[26] The challenge becomes having the right job candidates, not the greatest number of them.

Few firms are as thorough as Microsoft when it comes to recruiting. Each year, the firm scans the entire pool of 25,000 U.S. and 2,000 Canadian computer science graduates and identifies the 8,000 in whom they are interested. After further screening, 2,600 are invited for on-campus interviews at their universities. Out of these, only 800 are invited to the company's Redmond, Washington, headquarters. Of this group, 500 receive offers, and usually 400 accept. These massive efforts, however, meet less than 20 percent of the company's hiring needs. For the rest of its human capital needs, Microsoft maintains a team of 300 recruiting experts whose full-time job is to locate the best and the brightest in the industry.[27] Other firms, such as GE Medical Systems and BlackBerry have found that current employees are the best source for new ones. When someone refers former colleagues or friends for a job, his or her own reputation is also on the line. Employees tend to be careful in recommending people for employment unless they are reasonably confident that these people will work out well. This provides a good "screen" for the firm in deciding whom to hire. After all, hiring the right people makes things a lot easier: fewer rules and regulations, less need for monitoring and hierarchy, and greater internalization of organizational norms and objectives.

Developing Human Capital

It is not enough to hire top-level talent and expect that the skills and capabilities of those employees remain current throughout the duration of their employment. Rather, training and development must take place at all levels of the organization. For example, Solectron assembles printed circuit boards and other components for its Silicon Valley clients. Its employees receive an average of 95 hours of company-provided training each year. Chairman Winston Chen observed, "Technology changes so fast that we estimate 20 percent of an engineer's knowledge becomes obsolete each year. Training is an obligation we owe to our employees. If you want high growth and high quality, then training is a big part of the equation."[28] Since being purchased by Flextronics International, Selectron continues with its emphasis on employee training and development and vouches for their effectiveness. Although the financial returns on training may be hard to calculate, most experts believe it is not only real but also essential. One company that has calculated the benefits derived from training is Motorola. This high-technology (high-tech) firm has calculated that every dollar spent on training returns $30 in productivity gains over the following three years. In addition to training, the effective development of human capital throughout the organization entails widespread involvement, monitoring of progress, and continuous evaluation and feedback.

Encouraging Widespread Involvement

The development of human capital requires the active involvement of leaders at all levels throughout the organization. Such development will not be successful if it is viewed only as the responsibility of the human resource department. Each year at General Electric (GE), 200 facilitators, 30 officers, 30 human resource executives, and many young managers actively participate in GE's orientation program at the firm's impressive Crotonville training centre outside New York City. Topics include global competition, winning on the global playing field, and personal examination of each new employee's core values vis-à-vis GE's values. As a senior manager once commented, "There is nothing like teaching Sunday school to force you to confront your own values."

Monitoring Progress and Tracking Development

Whether a firm uses on-site formal training, off-site training (e.g., universities), or on-the-job training, tracking individual progress—and sharing this knowledge with both the employee and key managers—becomes essential. At Citibank, a talent inventory program keeps track of roughly 10,000 employees worldwide—how they are doing, what skills they need to work on, and where else in the company they might thrive. Larry Phillips, head of human resources, considers the program critical to the company's global growth.[29]

GlaxoSmithKline, the global pharmaceutical giant, places increasingly greater emphasis on broader experiences over longer periods. Dan Phelan, senior vice-president and director of human resources, explains, "We ideally follow a two-plus-two-plus-two formula in developing people for top management positions." The formula reflects the belief that GlaxoSmithKline's best people should gain experience in two business units, two functional units (such as finance and marketing), in two countries.

Evaluating Human Capital

In today's competitive environment, collaboration and interdependence have become vital to organizational success. Individuals must share their knowledge and work together constructively to achieve collective, not just individual, goals. To address the "softer" dimensions of communications and social skills, the values, beliefs, and attitudes that go beyond technical skills, organizations have begun to use 360-degree evaluation and feedback systems.[30] In these systems, superiors, direct reports, colleagues, and even internal and external customers rate a person's skills. Managers also rate themselves so that they can have a personal benchmark. The 360-degree feedback system complements teamwork, employee involvement, and organizational flattening. Moreover, as organizations continue to push responsibility downward, traditional top-down appraisal systems become insufficient. A manager who previously managed the performance of three supervisors might now be responsible for 10 and is less likely to have the in-depth knowledge needed to appraise and develop each sufficiently and fairly.

To assist its managers in the task of appraisal, GE's 360 leadership assessment evaluates all managers on 10 distinct characteristics—namely, vision, customer/quality focus, integrity, accountability/commitment, communication/influence, shared ownership/being boundaryless, team building/empowerment, knowledge/expertise/intellect, initiative/speed, and global mindset. Each of these characteristics has four performance criteria, and those around a manager are asked to rate that person on those criteria. With respect to vision, for example, the four criteria are (1) the ability to develop and communicate a clear, simple, customer-focused vision/direction for the organization; (2) the ability to be forward thinking, stretch horizons, challenge imaginations; (3) the ability to inspire and energize others to commit to vision, capture minds, and lead by example; and (4) as appropriate, the ability to update vision to reflect constant and accelerating change affecting the business.

Finally, evaluation systems must ensure that a manager's success does not come at the cost of compromising the organization's core values. It is understood that such conduct leads only to short-term wins for both the manager and the organization. The organization typically suffers long-term losses in terms of morale, turnover, productivity, and so on. Accordingly, Merck's former chairman, Ray Gilmartin, told his employees, "If someone is achieving results but not demonstrating the core values of the company, at the expense of our people, that manager does not have much of a career here."

Retaining Human Capital

It has been said that talented employees are like "frogs in a wheelbarrow."[31] That is, they can jump out any time. Today's leaders can either provide the work environment and incentives to keep productive employees and management from wanting to bail out, or they can rely on legal means, such as employment contracts and non-compete clauses.[32] Automotive industry supplier Magna International has a keen focus on cultivating the creative potential of its workforce and retaining its talent. Its strategy—to foster the entrepreneurial spirit—is relatively simple. Each division within the $26-billion multinational firm operates as a separate "Automotive Systems Corporation," with its own profit centre. According to Magna's corporate constitution, 10 percent of pre-tax profits are allocated to employees, and up to 6 percent may be distributed to senior managers. In addition, no less than 20 percent of after-tax profits must be distributed to shareholders. This "Fair Enterprise System" is designed to keep good employees prospering within the Magna family and the corporation prospering because of them.[33]

An individual's identification with the organization's mission and values, challenging work and a stimulating environment, and financial and non-financial rewards and incentives all play a critical role in retaining a firm's human capital.

Identifying with an Organization's Mission and Values

People who identify with and are committed to the core mission and values of the organization are less likely to stray or bolt to the competition. Researchers have long known that people are motivated by a host of non-economic factors, and values are chief amongst them. Consider BC Biomedical Laboratories of Surrey, British Columbia. It was named Canada's "Best Employer" for the three years running. BC Biomedical's CEO, Doug Buchanan, attributed the recognition squarely to the fact that management and employees shared the same goals and attitudes; all were driven by their desire to be able to help others in times of need. A flat organization allowed every employee to be in direct contact with patients and to have a clear image of where the business was going. During the same period, BC Biomedical recorded a mere 1 percent turnover among its 412 employees.[34]

Employees form strong bonds with organizations that create simple and straightforward missions—strategic intents—that channel efforts and generate intense loyalties.[35] Examples include Canon's passion to "beat Xerox" and Honda's early commitment to build fuel-efficient and environmentally friendly cars, even when those characteristics were not popular. Likewise, leaders can arouse passions and loyalty by reinforcing their firm's quest to "topple Goliath" or by constantly communicating a history of overcoming adversity and life-threatening challenges.[36] For example, CEO Richard Branson of the Virgin Group constantly uses David-and-Goliath imagery, pitting his company against such powerful adversaries as British Airways and Coca-Cola.

Challenging Work and a Stimulating Environment

Arthur Schawlow, winner of the 1981 Nobel Prize in physics, was once asked what he believed made the difference between highly creative and less creative scientists. He replied, "The labour of love aspect is very important. The most successful scientists often are not the most talented. But they are the ones impelled by curiosity. They've got to know what the answer is."[37]

Such insights highlight the importance of intrinsic motivation: the motivation to work on something because it is interesting, exciting, satisfying, or personally challenging. To keep competitors from poaching talent, organizations keep employees excited about the challenges and opportunities available. Scott Cook, chairman of Intuit, understands this reality: "I wake up every morning knowing that if my people don't sense a compelling vision and a big upside, they'll simply leave."[38]

Financial and Non-financial Rewards and Incentives

As we will discuss more extensively in Chapter 9, financial rewards are a vital organizational control mechanism. Money—whether in the form of salary, bonuses, or stock options—can mean many different things to people. For some, it might mean security; to others, recognition; and to still others, a sense of freedom and independence.

Nevertheless, most surveys show that money is not the most important reason why people take or leave jobs. In fact, in some surveys, money doesn't even make the top 10.[39] Consistent with these findings, Tandem Computers (now part of Hewlett-Packard) never used to tell people being recruited what their salaries would be. People who asked were told that their salaries were competitive. If they persisted along this line of questioning, they would not be offered a position. Why? Tandem recognized a rather simple reality: People who come for money will leave for money.

Without proper retention mechanisms, organizations can commit time and resources to inadvertently helping the competition develop their human capital.[40] And, given the importance of networking and teams, losses tend to multiply and intensify. The exodus of talent can erode a firm's competitive advantages in the marketplace.

The departure of David Kassie from the top job at CIBC World Markets, and his overtures to other high-flying investment bankers and equity traders, created tremors. Their loyalty appeared to be directed more toward their former boss and his promise of big bonuses and partnerships in an upstart investment firm than it was to their corporate employer.[41]

At various firms, rewards and incentives may include an impressive array of amenities aimed at retaining employees, such as on-site stores, dry-cleaning services, banks, automatic teller machines (ATMs), first-class cafeterias, and athletic facilities. Non-financial rewards also involve accommodating working families with children. Coping with the conflicting demands of family and work is a challenge at some point for virtually all employees. Whirlpool Canada offers additional "work–life balance" days to each employee. CIBC estimated that it saved more than 6,800 employee days and enjoyed savings of $1.4 million by providing emergency babysitting services to the staff in its Toronto locations through a two-year pilot project, which it then rolled out in select locations across Canada and the U.S. In a recent study, 13 percent of women with preschoolers indicated that they would work more hours if additional or better child care were provided.[42]

Similar initiatives are developed not only to address and capitalize on the increasing diversity of the workforce but also to deal with the cultural differences of an increasingly heterogeneous population and customer base. Gender, race, ethnicity, and nationality are but the most recognized dimensions of diversity. Organizations that compete globally recognize the benefits of effectively managing a diverse workforce in the atmosphere of enhanced creativity, diversity of ideas and solutions, greater flexibility, and better attraction of people and resources that directly impact the nurturing of competitive advantages.[43] Strategy Spotlight 4.1 describes the advantages MTV draws from its diverse workforce.

4.1 STRATEGY SPOTLIGHT

MTV: Benefiting from a Diverse Workforce

Managers know that heterogeneous workforces are rich seedbeds for ideas. Companies, though, seldom tap employees for insights and experiences specific to their cultures. Further, barriers of language, geography, and association often prevent diverse employees from collaborating on innovation efforts.

To address these issues, MTV Networks created the firm's first executive vice-president and chief diversity officer position with the responsibility to lead MTV's global initiatives and foster the highest levels of diversity throughout every aspect of the business. MTV's CEO at the time stated:

> We are completely committed to diversity and inclusion because it's the most creative and vibrant thing we can do for our future. The audience for our content is increasingly global, diverse in thought, demographic, and lifestyle. Over the years, no other initiative has so enriched MTV Networks or made us more relevant and successful.

MTV has benefited from these initiatives in many ways. One cross-cultural group discovered marketing opportunities in the similarities between North American country music and Latin American music, which use many of the same instruments, feature singers with similar vocal styles, and appeal to much the same audience. Other groups have influenced the multicultural content of Nickelodeon's children's programming. Tom Freston, MTV's former CEO says:

> Those teams are diverse by design to generate innovation. The probability that you will get a good, original, innovative idea with that type of chemistry is simply much higher.

Sources: Johansson, F., 2005, Masters of the Multicultural, *Harvard Business Review*, 83 (10) 18-19; Anonymous, 2006, MTV Networks Names Billy Dexter s Chief Diversity Officer, *PRNewswire*, October 28, np.

Enhancing Human Capital: Redefining Jobs and Managing Diversity

Before moving on to our discussion of social capital, it is important to point out that companies are increasingly realizing that the payoff from enhancing their human capital can be substantial. Firms have found that redefining jobs and leveraging the benefits of a diverse workforce can go a long way in improving their performance.

Enhancing Human Capital: Redefining Jobs

Recent research by McKinsey Global Institute suggests that by 2020, the worldwide shortage of highly skilled, college-educated workers could reach 38 to 40 million, or about 13 percent of demand.[44] In response, some firms are taking steps to expand their talent pool, for example, by investing in apprenticeships and other training pro-grams. Some are going further: They are redefining the jobs of their experts and transferring some of their tasks to lower-skilled people inside or outside their companies, as well as outsourcing work that requires less-scarce skills and is not as strategically important. Redefining high-value knowledge jobs can not only help organizations address skill shortages but can also lower costs and enhance job satisfaction.

Consider the following examples:

- Orrick, Herrington & Sutcliffe, a San Francisco-based law firm with nine U.S. offices, shifted routine dis-covery work previously performed by partners and partner-tracked associates to a new service centre in West Virginia staffed by lower-paid attorneys.

- In the United Kingdom, a growing number of public schools are relieving head teachers (or principals) of administrative tasks such as budgeting, facilities maintenance, human resources, and community relations so that they can devote more time to developing teachers.

- The Narayana Hrudayalaya Heart Hospital in Bangalore has junior surgeons, nurses, and technicians handle routine tasks such as preparing the patient for surgery and closing the chest after surgery. Senior cardiac surgeons arrive at the operating room only when the patient's chest is open and the heart is ready to be oper-ated on. Such an approach helps the hospital lower the cost to a fraction of the cost of U.S. providers while maintaining U.S.-level mortality and infection rates.

Breaking high-end knowledge work into highly specialized pieces involves several processes. These include identifying the gap between the talent your firm has and what it requires; creating narrower, more-focused job descriptions in areas where talent is scarce; selecting from various options to fill the skills gap; and rewiring processes for talent and knowledge management.

Enhancing Human Capital: Managing Diversity

A combination of demographic trends and accelerating globalization of business has made the management of cultural differences a critical issue.[45] Reflecting demographic changes in the overall population, workplaces will become increasingly heterogeneous along dimensions such as gender, race, ethnicity, and nationality. For example, demographic trends in the United States indicate a growth in Hispanic Americans from 6.9 million in 1960 to over 35 million in 2000, with an expected increase to over 59 million by 2020 and 102 million by 2050. Similarly, the Asian-American population should grow to 20 million in 2020 from 12 million in 2000 and only 1.5 million in 1970. And the African-American population is expected to increase from 12.8 percent of the U.S. population in 2000 to 14.2 percent by 2025.[46]

Such demographic changes have implications not only for the labour pool but also for customer bases, which are also becoming more diverse.[47] This creates important organizational challenges and opportunities.

The effective management of diversity can enhance the social responsibility goals of an organization.[48] How-ever, there are many other benefits as well. Six other areas where sound management of diverse workforces can improve an organization's effectiveness and competitive advantages are (1) cost, (2) resource acquisition, (3) mar-keting, (4) creativity, (5) problem solving, and (6) organizational flexibility.

- **Cost argument.** As organizations become more diverse, firms effective in managing diversity will have a cost advantage over those that are not.

- **Resource acquisition argument.** Firms with excellent reputations as prospective employers for women and ethnic minorities will have an advantage in the competition for top talent. As labour pools shrink and change in composition, such advantages will become even more important.

- **Marketing argument.** For multinational firms, the insight and cultural sensitivity that members with roots in other countries bring to marketing efforts will be very useful. A similar rationale applies to subpopulations within domestic operations.

- **Creativity argument.** Less emphasis on conformity to norms of the past and a diversity of perspectives will improve the level of creativity.

- **Problem-solving argument.** Heterogeneity in decision-making and problem-solving groups typically produces better decisions because of a wider range of perspectives as well as more thorough analysis. Jim Schiro, former CEO of PricewaterhouseCoopers, explains, "When you make a genuine commitment to diversity, you bring a greater diversity of ideas, approaches, and experiences and abilities that can be applied to client problems. After all, six people with different perspectives have a better shot at solving complex problems than sixty people who all think alike."[49]

- **Organizational flexibility argument.** With effective programs to enhance workplace diversity, systems become less determinant, less standardized, and therefore more fluid. Such fluidity should lead to greater flexibility to react to environmental changes. Reactions should be faster and less costly.

Most managers accept that employers benefit from a diverse workforce. However, this notion can often be very difficult to prove or quantify, particularly when it comes to determining how diversity affects a firm's ability to innovate.[50]

New research provides compelling evidence that diversity enhances innovation and drives market growth. This finding should intensify efforts to ensure that organizations both embody and embrace the power of differences.

LO 4 THE VITAL ROLE OF SOCIAL CAPITAL

Successful firms are well aware that the attraction, development, and retention of talent are *necessary but not sufficient conditions* for creating competitive advantage. In the knowledge economy, it is not the stock of human capital but the extent to which it is combined and leveraged that is important. In a sense, developing and retaining human capital becomes less important as key players (talented professionals, in particular) take the role of "free agents" and bring with them the requisite skill. Instead, the development of social capital (i.e., the friendships and working relationships among talented individuals) becomes increasingly important as it helps tie knowledge workers to a given firm.[51] Knowledge workers often exhibit greater loyalties to their colleagues and their profession than to their employing organization, which may be "an amorphous, distant, and sometimes threatening entity."[52] Thus, a firm must find ways to create "ties" among its knowledge workers.

To illustrate, let us look at a hypothetical example. Two pharmaceutical firms are fortunate enough to hire Nobel Prize-winning scientists to work in their laboratories.[53] In one case, the scientist is offered a very attractive salary, outstanding facilities, and equipment and is told to "Go to it!" In the second case, the scientist is offered approximately the same salary, facilities, and equipment, but will be working in a laboratory with 10 highly skilled and enthusiastic scientists. Part of the job is to collaborate with these peers and jointly develop promising drug compounds. There is little doubt as to which scenario will lead to a higher probability of retaining the scientist. The interaction, sharing, and collaboration are likely to create a situation in which the scientist will develop firm-specific ties and be less likely to "bolt" for a higher salary offer. Such ties are critical because knowledge-based resources tend to be more tacit in nature, as we mentioned earlier in this chapter. Therefore, they are much more difficult to protect against loss (i.e., the individual quitting the organization) than other types of capital, such as equipment, machinery, and land.

Recall the resource-based view of the firm that we discussed in Chapter 3. Competitive advantages tend to be harder for competitors to copy if they are based on "unique bundles" of resources.[54] If employees are working effectively in teams, sharing their knowledge, and learning from each other, not only will they be more likely to add value to the firm, but they also will be less likely to leave the organization because of the loyalties and social ties that they develop over time. Strategy Spotlight 4.2 discusses how Nucor, a highly successful steel manufacturer, develops social capital among its employees and managers. This promotes the sharing of ideas within and across its manufacturing plants. Nucor does not use any unique or proprietary technology in its mills, yet it has consistently outperformed competitors and is one of the most efficient steel producers in the world.

4.2 STRATEGY SPOTLIGHT

How Nucor Shares Knowledge within and between Its Manufacturing Plants

A key aspect of steel-producer Nucor's strategy is to develop strong social relationships and a team-based culture throughout the firm. It is effectively supported by a combination of work-group, plant-level, and corporate-wide financial incentives and rewards, wherein knowledge and best practices are eagerly shared by everyone in the organization. How does Nucor do it?

Within-Plant Knowledge Transfers. Nucor strives to develop a social community within each plant that promotes trust and open communication. People know each other very well throughout each plant, and they are encouraged to interact. To accomplish this, the firm's policy is to keep the number of employees at each plant between 250 and 300. Such a relatively small number, combined with employees' long tenure, fosters a high degree of interpersonal familiarity. Additionally, each plant's general manager regularly holds dinner meetings for groups of 25 to 30, inviting every employee once a year. The format is open and includes a few ground rules: All comments are to remain business-related and are not to be directed to specific individuals. In turn, managers guarantee that they will carefully consider and respond to all suggestions and criticisms.

Between-Plant Knowledge Transfers. Nucor uses several mechanisms to transfer knowledge among its plants. First, detailed performance data on each mill are regularly distributed to all of the plant managers. Second, all general managers of the plants meet as a group three times a year to review each facility's performance and develop formal plans on how to transfer best practices. Third, plant managers, supervisors, and machine operators regularly visit each other's mills. These visits enable operations personnel to go beyond performance data so that they can understand first-hand the factors that make particular practices superior or inferior. After all, they are the true possessors of process knowledge. Fourth, given the inherent difficulties in transferring complex knowledge, Nucor selectively assigns people from one plant to another on the basis of their expertise.

Sources: Reprinted from "Knowledge Management's Social Dimension: Lessons from Nucor Steel," by A. K. Gupta and V. Govindarajan, Organizational Dynamics, Fall 2000, pp. 71–80, by permission of publisher. Copyright © 2000 by *Massachusetts Institute of Technology.* All rights reserved.

How Social Capital Helps Attract and Retain Talent

The importance of social ties among talented professionals is creating an important challenge (and opportunity) for organizations today. Writers describe the increasing prevalence of a "Pied Piper effect," in which teams or networks of people are leaving one company for another.[55] The trend is to recruit job candidates at the pinnacle of social networks in organizations, particularly if they are seen as having the potential to bring with them a raft of valuable colleagues. This is a process that is referred to as "hiring via personal networks." The corollary of this human capital mobility is the departure of talent from an organization to form startup ventures. For instance, Northern Telecom laboratories are credited with having supplied the inspiration and the key personnel for scores of technology and telecommunications firms in the Ottawa region during the 1980s and 1990s.[56] Microsoft is perhaps the best-known example of this phenomenon.[57] Professionals have frequently left Microsoft—en masse—to form venture capital and technology startups built around teams of software developers. One example is Ignition Corporation of Bellevue, Washington, which was formed by Brad Silverberg, a former Microsoft senior vice-president. Eight former Microsoft executives, among others, founded the company.[58] Social networks can provide important mechanisms for obtaining both resources and information from individuals and organizations outside the boundary of a firm.[59]

LO 5 Social Network Analysis

Managers face many challenges driven by such factors as rapid changes in globalization and technology. Leading a successful company is more than a one-person job. As Tom Malone put it in *The Future of Work,* "As managers, we need to shift our thinking from command and control to coordinate and cultivate—the best way to gain power is sometimes to give it away." The move away from top-down bureaucratic control to more open, decentralized network models makes it more difficult for managers to understand how work is actually getting done, who is interacting with whom both within and outside the organization, and the consequences of these interactions for the long-term health of the organization.[60] In short, coordination, cultivation, and collaboration are increasingly becoming the mode of work at every level.[61]

But how can this be achieved? **Social network analysis** depicts the pattern of interactions among individuals and helps to diagnose effective and ineffective patterns.[62] It helps identify groups or clusters of individuals that comprise the network, individuals who link the clusters, and other network members. It helps diagnose communication patterns and, consequently, communication effectiveness.[63] Such analysis of communication patterns is helpful because the configuration of group members' social ties within and outside the group affects the extent to which members connect to individuals who:

- convey needed resources,
- have the opportunity to exchange information and support,
- have the motivation to treat each other in positive ways, and,
- have the time to develop trusting relationships that might improve the groups' effectiveness.

However, such relationships do not "just happen."[64] Developing social capital requires interdependence among group members. Social capital erodes when people in the network become independent. And increased interactions between members aid in the development and maintenance of mutual obligations in a social network. Online social networks, such as Facebook, may facilitate increased interactions among members via Internet-based communications.

There are two primary types of mechanisms through which social capital will flow: *closure relationships* and *bridging relationships.* In the former relationships, one member is central to the communication flows in a group. In contrast, in the latter relationship, one person "bridges" or brings together groups that would have been otherwise unconnected. Both closure and bridging relationships have important implications for the effective flow of information in organizations and for the management of knowledge.

Closure Relationships

With closure, many members have relationships (or ties) with other members. Through closure, group members develop strong relationships with each other, high levels of trust, and greater solidarity. High levels of trust help ensure that informal norms in the group are easily enforced and there is less "free riding." Social pressure will prevent people from withholding effort or shirking their responsibilities. In addition, people in the network are more willing to extend favours and "go the extra mile" on a colleague's behalf because they are confident that their efforts will be reciprocated by another member in their group. Another benefit of a network with closure is the high level of emotional support. This becomes particularly valuable when setbacks occur that may destroy morale or an unexpected tragedy happens that might cause the group to lose its focus. Social support helps the group to rebound from misfortune and get back on track.

But high levels of closure often come with a price. Groups that become too closed can become insular. They cut themselves off from the rest of the organization and fail to share what they are learning from people outside their group. Research shows that while managers need to encourage closure up to a point, if there is too much closure, they need to encourage people to open up their groups and infuse new ideas through bridging relationships.[65]

Bridging Relationships

The closure perspective rests on an assumption that there is a high level of similarity among group members. However, members can be quite heterogeneous with regard to their positions in either the formal or informal structures of the group or the organization. Such heterogeneity exists because of, for example, vertical boundaries (different levels in the hierarchy) and horizontal boundaries (different functional areas).

In contrast to closure, bridging stresses the importance of ties connecting people. Employees who bridge disconnected people tend to receive timely, diverse information because of their access to a wide range of heterogeneous information flows. Such bridging relationships span a number of different types of boundaries.

The University of Chicago's Ron Burt originally coined the term **structural holes** to refer to the social gap between two groups. Structural holes are common in organizations. When they occur in business, managers typically refer to them as "silos" or "stovepipes." Sales and engineering are a classic example of two groups whose members traditionally interact with their peers rather than across groups.

A study that Burt conducted at Raytheon, a $25-billion U.S. electronics company and military contractor, provides further insight into the benefits of bridging.[66] Burt studied several hundred managers in Raytheon's supply chain group and asked them to write down ideas to improve the company's supply chain management. Then he asked two Raytheon executives to rate the ideas. The conclusion: *The best suggestions consistently came from managers who discussed ideas outside their regular work group.*

Burt found that Raytheon managers were good at thinking of ideas but bad at developing them. Too often, Burt said, the managers discussed their ideas with colleagues already in their informal discussion network. Instead, he said, they should have had discussions outside their typical contacts, particularly with an informal boss, or someone with enough power to be an ally but not an actual supervisor.

Before we address how to overcome barriers to collaboration and the implications of social network theory on a company's success, one might ask: Which is the more valuable mechanism to develop and nurture social capital—closure or bridging relationships? Of course, they are both useful in most cases, although we should explore which one should be more prevalent in different situations. As with many aspects of strategic management, the answer becomes: "It all depends." So let us look at a few contingent issues.[67]

First, consider firms in competitive environments characterized by rapidly changing technologies and markets. Such firms should bridge relationships across networks because they need a wide variety of timely sources of information. Also, innovation is facilitated if there are multiple, interdisciplinary perspectives. In contrast, firms competing in a stable environment would typically face less unpredictability. Thus, the cohesive ties associated with network closure would help to ensure the timely and effective implementation of strategies.

A second contingent factor would be the type of business strategies that a firm may choose to follow (a topic that we address in Chapter 5). Managers with social networks characterized by closure would be in a preferred position if their firm is following an overall low-cost strategy.[68] Here, there is a need for control and coordination to implement strategies that are constrained by pressures to reduce costs. Alternatively, the uncertainties generally associated with differentiation strategies (i.e., creating products that are perceived by customers as unique and highly valued) would require a broad range of information sources and inputs. Social networks characterized by bridging relationships across groups would access the diverse informational sources needed to deal with more complex, multifaceted strategies.

Nonetheless, some companies have been damaged by a certain amount of social capital that breeds "groupthink" and other detrimental effects. We discuss those and other downsides to social capital below, in the section titled "The Potential Downsides of Social Capital." In general, however, the effects of high social capital are strongly positive. Engagement, collaboration, loyalty, persistence, and dedication are important benefits.[69] Some firms, such as United Parcel Service, Hewlett-Packard, Four Seasons Hotels and Resorts, and Tim Horton's, have made significant investments in social capital that enable them to attract and retain talent and help them do their best work. Such companies rarely face any imminent danger from an overdose of a good thing.

Overcoming Barriers to Collaboration

Social capital within a group or organization develops through repeated interactions among its members and the resulting collaboration.[70] However, collaboration does not "just happen." There are various reasons why people sometimes don't collaborate. Effective collaboration requires overcoming four barriers:

- The not-invented-here barrier (people aren't willing to provide help)
- The hoarding barrier (people aren't willing to share)

- The search barrier (people are unable to find what they are looking for)

- The transfer barrier (people are unable to work with the people they don't know well)

All four barriers need to be low before effective collaboration can take place. Each one is sufficient on its own to prevent people from collaborating well. The key is to identify which barriers are present in an organization and then to devise appropriate ways to overcome them.

Different barriers require different solutions. Motivational barriers require leaders to pull levers that make people more willing to collaborate. Ability barriers mean that leaders need to pull levers that enable motivated people to collaborate throughout the organization.

To be effective, leaders can choose a mix of three levers. First, when motivation is the problem, they can use the unification lever, wherein they craft compelling common goals, articulate a strong value of cross-company teamwork, and encourage collaboration in order to send strong signals to lift people's sights beyond their narrow interests toward a common goal.

Second, with the people lever, the emphasis isn't on getting people to collaborate more. Rather, it's on getting the right people to collaborate on the right projects. This means cultivating what may be called T-shaped management: people who simultaneously focus on the performance of their unit (the vertical part of the T) and across boundaries (the horizontal part of the T). People become able to collaborate when needed but are disciplined enough to say no when it's not required.

Third, by using the network lever, leaders can build nimble interpersonal networks across the company so that employees are better able to collaborate. Interpersonal networks are more effective than formal hierarchies. However, there is a dark side to networks: When people spend more time networking than getting work done, collaboration can adversely affect results.

The Potential Downsides of Social Capital

Let's close our discussion of social capital by addressing some of its limitations. First, as mentioned earlier, some firms have been adversely affected by very high levels of social capital because it may breed **"groupthink"**—a tendency not to question shared beliefs.[71] Such thinking may occur in networks with high levels of closure where there is little input from people outside the network. In effect, too many warm and fuzzy feelings among group members prevent people from rigorously challenging each other. Two firms that were well known for their collegiality, strong sense of employee membership, and humane treatment—Digital Equipment (now part of Hewlett-Packard) and Polaroid—suffered greatly from market misjudgments and strategic errors. The aforementioned aspects of their culture contributed to their problems.

Second, if there are deep-rooted mindsets, there will be a tendency to develop dysfunctional human resource practices. That is, the organization (or group) will continue to hire, reward, and promote like-minded people who tend to further intensify organizational inertia and erode innovation. Such homogeneity increases over time and decreases the effectiveness of decision-making processes.

Third, the socialization processes (orientation, training, etc.) can be expensive in terms of both financial resources and managerial commitment. Such investments can represent a significant opportunity cost that should be evaluated in terms of the intended benefits. If such expenses become excessive, profitability would be adversely affected.

Finally, individuals may use the contacts they develop to pursue their own interests and agendas, which may be inconsistent with the organization's goals and objectives. Thus, they may distort or selectively use information to favour their preferred courses of action or withhold information in their own self-interest to enhance their power to the detriment of the common good.

LO 6 USING TECHNOLOGY TO LEVERAGE HUMAN CAPITAL AND KNOWLEDGE

Sharing knowledge and information throughout the organization can be a means of conserving resources, developing products and services, and creating new opportunities. Technology can be used to leverage human capital and knowledge within organizations as well as with customers and suppliers beyond their boundaries. Examples range from simple applications, including the use of email and networks for product development, to more sophisticated uses that enhance the competitive position of knowledge-intensive firms in industries such as consulting, health care, and personal computers, and that help firms retain employees' knowledge, even when they leave.

Consider email—an effective means of communicating a wide variety of information across various parts of an organization and with suppliers and customers. It is quick, easy, and almost costless. Of course, it can become a problem when employees use it excessively or for personal reasons. Nevertheless, email can be an effective means for top executives to communicate information efficiently, share ideas, and relate decisions. Employees use email extensively to relate information, coordinate tasks, contribute to a discussion, and participate in decisions.

Technology also enables professionals to work in virtual teams and enhance the speed and effectiveness with which products are developed. For example, Microsoft has concentrated much of its development around virtual teams that are networked together throughout the company.[72] This helps accelerate design and testing of new software modules that use the Windows-based framework as their central architecture. Microsoft is able to foster specialized technical expertise while rapidly sharing knowledge throughout the organization. This helps the firm learn how its new technologies can be applied rapidly to new business ventures, such as cable television, broadcasting, travel services, and financial services.

Codifying Knowledge for Competitive Advantage

We have identified two different kinds of knowledge. On the one hand, *tacit knowledge* is embedded in personal experience and shared only with the consent and participation of the individual. *Explicit (or codified) knowledge,* on the other hand, is knowledge that can be documented, widely distributed, and easily replicated. One of the challenges of knowledge-intensive organizations is to capture and codify the knowledge and experience that, in effect, resides in the heads of its employees. Otherwise, they will have to constantly "reinvent the wheel," which is both expensive and inefficient. Also, the "new wheel" may not necessarily be superior to the "old wheel."[73]

Once a knowledge asset (e.g., a software code or processes/routines for a consulting firm) is developed and paid for, it can be reused many times at very low cost, assuming that it does not have to be substantially modified each time. Let us take the case of the consulting company Accenture.[74] Since the knowledge of its consultants has been codified and stored in electronic repositories, it can be employed in many jobs by a huge number of consultants. Additionally, since the work has a high level of standardization (i.e., there are strong similarities across the numerous client engagements), there generally tends to be a rather high ratio of some 30 consultants to each partner. As one might expect, there must be extensive training of the newly hired consultants for such an approach to work. The recruits are trained at Accenture's Center for Professional Education, a 150-acre campus in St. Charles, Illinois. Using the centre's knowledge-management repository, the consultants work through many scenarios designed to improve business processes. In effect, the information technologies enable the consultants to be "implementers, not inventors."

Access Health, a call-in medical centre, also uses technology to capture and share knowledge. When someone calls the centre, a registered nurse uses the company's "clinical decision architecture" to assess the caller's symptoms, rule out possible conditions, and recommend a home remedy, doctor's visit, or trip to the emergency room. The company's knowledge repository contains algorithms of the symptoms of more than 500 illnesses. According to CEO Joseph Tallman, "We are not inventing a new way to cure disease. We are taking available knowledge and inventing processes to put it to better use." At Access Health, the codified knowledge is in the form of software algorithms. The algorithms were very expensive to develop, but the investment has been repaid many times over. The first 300 algorithms that Access Health developed have each been used an average of 8,000 times a year since the process was developed. Further, the company's paying customers—insurance companies and provider groups—save money because many callers would have made expensive trips to the emergency room or the doctor's office had they not been diagnosed over the phone.

The use of information technology to codify knowledge can also help a firm to integrate its internal value-chain activities with its customers and suppliers. Dell Computer Corporation uses a sophisticated knowledge management system to assemble and sell over 11 million personal computers (PCs) per year. It offers some 40,000 possible configurations compared with about 100 used by its competitors.[75] Dell employs an army of talented engineers and invests heavily upfront to determine the necessary configurations and then to develop and codify the process of assembly for each configuration. Although each configuration is used, on average, only about 275 times each year, the investment pays off in the cost containment that is passed on to consumers. Dell's knowledge-management system integrates its processes with the assembly activities of its suppliers, giving customers the flexibility to order PCs to their desired specifications and itself an edge in the intensely competitive PC market.

Retaining Knowledge When Employees Leave

All organizations suffer the adverse consequences of voluntary turnover. However, many leading firms are devising ways to minimize the loss of knowledge when employees leave.

Information technology can often help employers cope with turnover by saving some tacit knowledge that the firm would otherwise lose.[76] Customer relationship software, for example, automates sales and provides salespeople with access to client histories, including prior orders and complaints. This enables salespeople to quickly become familiar with client accounts (about which they might otherwise know nothing). Similarly, groupware applications, such as IBM Notes, can standardize interactions and keep records of decisions and crucial contextual information, providing something like an electronic record of employee knowledge. Other programs, such as Waterloo-based Open Text's Livelink, enable all employees to track and share documents on their firm's intranet. New simulation software for team-based project management, such as Thinking Tools' Project Challenge, enables new teams to learn how to work together much more rapidly than on-the-job experience alone would permit.

Strategy Spotlight 4.3 discusses what 3M does to help retain key knowledge that might otherwise be lost when employees leave the firm.

4.3 STRATEGY SPOTLIGHT

How 3M Retains Knowledge

As the issue of retiring employees becomes more critical at 3M, retaining employee knowledge has become a high priority. 3M applies what it calls high-tech, low-tech, and no-tech methods to a gamut of knowledge retention measures.

The company's searchable knowledge base, called Maven, makes information gleaned from 2,000 technical-service engineers across the globe accessible to all 3M employees. Maven is a high-tech extension of the database system already in place at 3M's call centres. Historically, if call centre representatives could not find an answer to a technical question, they would call a technical service engineer. The rep would typically call their favourite tech engineer, who would send an electronic file or a lengthy email with the response. With the new process, that information goes into a corporate knowledge base, and it is searchable by anyone within the entire company.

Another tool in the 3M knowledge retention arsenal is storytelling, considerably less formal than Maven. How does it work? A 3M department will identify business scenarios that, though they do not crop up often, happen often enough to merit consideration and, when they do come up, can throw a wrench into day-to-day plant operations. Examples include a switchover to a new machine or a repair to production equipment that takes it offline. After a situation is identified, the knowledge-management department creates a group of experts, including production, maintenance, and engineering employees who have previously encountered similar situations. They bring them together in a conference room and have facilitators ask pertinent questions. Software is used to map out the diagnosis of what happened and what the experts did as a result. After the responses are polished and streamlined, they become available online so that other operators, in their spare time or when something happens, can do a quick search and find the answers.

Sources: Excerpted from Thilmany, J., 2008, Passing on know-how: knowledge retention strategies can keep employees' workplace-acquired wisdom from walking out the door when they retire, *HR Magazine,* June, with permission of the Society for Human Resource Management (SHRM).

As a summary of the preceding discussion, Exhibit 4-4 poses a series of questions managers should consider in determining (1) how effective their organization is in attracting, developing, and retaining human capital and (2) how effective they are in leveraging human capital through social capital and technology.

EXHIBIT 4-4   ISSUES TO CONSIDER IN CREATING VALUE THROUGH HUMAN CAPITAL, SOCIAL CAPITAL, AND TECHNOLOGY

Human Capital

Recruiting "Top-Notch" Human Capital

- Does the organization assess attitude and "general makeup" instead of focusing primarily on skills and background in selecting employees at all levels?
- How important are creativity and problem-solving ability? Are these properly considered in hiring decisions?
- Do people throughout the organization engage in effective networking activities to obtain a broad pool of worthy potential employees? Is the organization creative in such endeavours?

Enhancing Human Capital through Employee Development

- Does the development and training process inculcate an "organization-wide" perspective?
- Is there widespread involvement, including that of top executives, in the preparation and delivery of training and development programs?
- Is the development of human capital effectively tracked and monitored?
- Are there effective programs for succession at all levels of the organization, especially the top-most levels?
- Does the firm effectively evaluate its human capital? Is a 360-degree evaluation used? Why? Why not?
- Are mechanisms in place to assure that a manager's success does not come at the cost of compromising the organization's core values?

Retaining the Best Employees

- Are there appropriate financial rewards to motivate employees at all levels?
- Do people throughout the organization strongly identify with the organization's mission?
- Are employees provided a stimulating and challenging work environment that fosters professional growth?
- Are valued amenities provided (e.g., flex time, child-care facilities, telecommuting) that are appropriate given the organization's mission, strategy, and how work is accomplished?
- Is the organization continually devising strategies and mechanisms to retain top performers?

Social Capital

- Are there positive personal and professional relationships among employees?
- Is the organization benefiting (or being penalized) by hiring (or by voluntary turnover) en masse?
- Does an environment of caring and encouragement, rather than of competition, enhance team performance?
- Do the social networks within the organization have the appropriate levels of closure and bridging relationships?
- Does the organization minimize the adverse effects of excessive social capital, such as excessive costs and "groupthink"?

Technology

- Has the organization used technologies, such as email and networks, to develop products and services?
- Does the organization effectively use technology to transfer best practices across the organization?
- Does the organization use technology to leverage human capital and knowledge both within the boundaries of the organization and among its suppliers and customers?
- Has the organization effectively used technology to codify knowledge for competitive advantage?
- Does the organization try to retain some of the knowledge of employees when they decide to leave the firm?

Sources: Adapted from Dess, G. G., & Picken, J. C. 1999. Beyond Productivity: 63–64. New York: AMACON.

LO 7 PROTECTING THE INTELLECTUAL ASSETS OF THE ORGANIZATION: INTELLECTUAL PROPERTY AND DYNAMIC CAPABILITIES

In today's dynamic and turbulent world, unpredictability and fast change dominate the business environment. Economic prosperity rests on the useful application of knowledge, and access to the underlying information—in terms of technology, human capital, or research and design networks—is fairly even among firms. Developing dynamic capabilities is the only avenue providing firms with the opportunity to reconfigure their knowledge and activities so that they can achieve sustainable competitive advantage. What would give a sustainable competitive advantage to firms and then prevent others from copying their valuable ideas?[77] Protecting a firm's intellectual capital requires a concerted effort. After all, employees can become disgruntled, and patents do expire. The management of intellectual property involves contracts with confidentiality and non-compete clauses, copyrights, patents, and the development of trademarks. Moreover, developing dynamic capabilities is the only avenue providing firms with the ability to reconfigure their knowledge and activities to achieve a sustainable competitive advantage.

The management of intellectual property and intellectual property rights has its conceptual roots in individual rights, especially the right to own property. Such rights can be found in many societies, going back centuries. Simply put, if those rights are not reliably protected by the state, no individual will build private long-term assets and make investments, activities that constitute the foundation of a growing economy. Property rights have been enshrined in constitutions and rules of law in many countries. In the information era, though, adjustments need to be made to accommodate the new realities of knowledge. Knowledge and information are fundamentally different assets from the physical ones that property rights have been designed to protect.

Intellectual property typically has no diminishing returns; much of production is characterized by constant, if not zero, marginal costs. Indeed, it may take a substantial investment to develop a software program, an idea, or a digital music tune. Once developed, though, their reproduction and distribution cost may be almost zero, especially if the Internet is used. Effective protection of intellectual property is necessary before any investor will finance such an undertaking. Appropriation of their returns is harder to police, since possession and deployment are not as readily observable. Unlike physical assets, intellectual property can be stolen simply by broadcasting it; recall Napster and all the debates about counterfeit software, music CDs, and DVDs coming to the West from developing countries, such as China. Part of the problem is that using an idea does not prevent others from simultaneously using it for their own benefit, something that is impossible with physical assets. Also, new ideas are frequently and easily built on old ideas and, thus, are not easily traceable. Strategy Spotlight 4.4 describes the trajectory of IMAX, the globally successful Canadian firm that started out as an experiment and, through many ups and downs, has succeeded in capitalizing on its unique intellectual capital to build an enviable position in the entertainment world.

4.4 STRATEGY SPOTLIGHT

IMAX's Capability to Evolve

IMAX's giant screens using unique projection equipment were developed in the late 1960s as a revolutionary film system to entertain and educate crowds at the EXPO pavilions in Montreal (1967) and Osaka, Japan (1971). Their first permanent installation at Ontario Place's Cinesphere in Toronto in 1971 heralded the introduction of an extraordinary movie experience that since then has brought three-dimensional (3D) images, Hollywood blockbusters, and special-purpose films to audiences around the world.

In its early days, IMAX installed systems in museums, exhibition halls, and special-purpose locations; for the most part, it had to produce its own shows to fully take advantage of the exceptional features of its systems, as the oversized equipment required specialized handling and was not compatible with most of the traditional movie studio work. Nonetheless, the uniqueness of the technology and the spectacular results had brought the small Canadian firm to the centre of the entertainment industry, albeit as a specialized niche player.

Through the 1990s, the extraordinary shows, management's technical accomplishments, and a commitment to deliver on a strategy of growth and profitability impressed the financial markets. By 2000, though, a glut of multiplex screens and a softening economy put many of IMAX's customers into financial trouble and investors questioned IMAX's inability to deliver on the promises of market penetration and financial performance. The company had to take drastic measures. New faces were brought in to join the senior management team, and some of the old guard were let go. IMAX embarked on a new strategy of commercial installations, actively sought closer collaboration with Hollywood studios, and pursued a business model involving partnerships with exhibitors. In a very competitive marketplace, the old business model requiring theatre owners to fork over $1.6 million upfront to build and equip a venue did not cut it anymore. IMAX began to shoulder the construction and equipment costs and to operate the screens as joint ventures. A flurry of activity ensued. By March 2011, IMAX had been crowned the undisputed leader in delivering unique movie experiences, enjoyed a healthy backlog of over 300 new installation orders for IMAX 3D systems, and had a series of digital re-mastering film deals that would convert regular movies to extraordinary 3D shows.

Sources: Lieberman, D., 2008, "IMAX Makes a Dramatic Comeback," *USA Today,* May 9: 12; Anonymous, 2007, "IMAX CEO Richard Gelfond on What's Next for the Big Screen,"*Knowledge@Wharton,* July 25; "IMAX, China in Movie Screen Deal,"*Bloomberg* and *The Globe and Mail,* March 25, 2011; the company's financial statements and 10K filings, as well as its website.

Economists and jurists alike admit that many of the issues around intellectual property have not been resolved yet and that our current thinking still mainly rests on relatively archaic principles. Politicians have attempted to legislate new patent regulations for very important new pharmaceutical compounds, new research fields, such as stem cell research and biotechnology, or the protection of Canadian culture through the awarding of restrictive licences for such services as satellite radio. The relative effects of intellectual property rights and economic growth need to be analyzed. However, a firm that is faced with this challenge today cannot wait for the legislators to resolve the political and economic issues. It has to embark on the next technological development, drug, software solution, electronic game, online service, or any of myriad other products and services that contribute to our economic prosperity and the creation of wealth for those entrepreneurs who have the idea first and risk bringing it to the market.

Dynamic capabilities entail the capacity to build and protect a competitive advantage, which rests on knowledge, assets, competencies, and complementary assets and technologies, as well as the ability to sense and seize new opportunities, generate new knowledge, and reconfigure existing assets and capabilities. According to organizational theorist David Teece, dynamic capabilities are related to the entrepreneurial side of the firm and are built within a firm through its environmental and technological "sensing" apparatus, its choices of organizational form, and its collective ability to strategize. Dynamic capabilities are about the ability of an organization to challenge the conventional wisdom within its industry and market, learn and innovate, adapt to the changing world, and continuously adopt new ways to serve the evolving needs of the market.

SUMMARY

Firms throughout the industrial world are recognizing that the knowledge worker is the key to success in the marketplace. However, we also recognize that human capital, although vital, is still only a necessary but not sufficient condition for creating value. We began the first section of the chapter by addressing the importance of human capital and how it can be attracted, developed, and retained. We then discussed the role of social capital and technology in leveraging human capital for competitive success. We pointed out that intellectual capital—the difference between a firm's market value and its book value—has increased significantly over the past few decades. This is particularly true of firms in knowledge-intensive industries, such as software development, where there are relatively few tangible assets.

The second section of the chapter addressed the attraction, development, and retention of human capital in more detail. We viewed these three activities as a "three-legged stool"—that is, it is difficult for firms to be successful if they ignore or are unsuccessful in any one of these activities. Among the issues we discussed in *attracting* human capital were "hiring for attitude, training for skill" and the value of using social networks to attract human capital. In particular, it is important to attract employees who can collaborate with others, given the importance of collective efforts, teams, and task forces. With regard to *developing* human capital, we discussed the need to encourage widespread involvement throughout the organization, monitor progress and track the development of human capital, and evaluate human capital. Among the practices that are widely acknowledged in evaluating human capital is the 360-degree evaluation system. Employees are evaluated by their superiors, peers, direct reports, and even internal and external customers. Finally, some mechanisms for *retaining* human capital are employees' identification with the organization's mission and values, providing challenging work and a stimulating environment, financial and non-financial rewards and incentives, and providing flexibility and amenities. A key issue here is that a firm should not overemphasize financial rewards. After all, if individuals join an organization for money, they are also likely to leave for money. With money as the primary motivator, there is little chance that employees will develop firm-specific ties to keep them with the organization.

The third section of the chapter discussed the importance of social capital in leveraging human capital. Social capital refers to the network of relationships that individuals have throughout the organization as well as with customers and suppliers. Such ties can be critical in obtaining both information and resources. With regard to recruiting, for example, we saw how some firms are able to hire, en masse, groups of individuals who are part of social networks. Social relationships can also be very important in the effective functioning of groups. Nonetheless, we also identified some of the potential downsides of social capital, including the potential for "groupthink" wherein individuals are reluctant to express divergent (or opposing) views on an issue because of social pressures to conform.

The fourth section addressed the role of technology in leveraging human capital. We discussed relatively simple means of using technology, such as email and networks, through which individuals can collaborate. We also addressed more sophisticated uses of such technology as management systems. Here, knowledge can be codified and reused at very low cost, as we saw in the examples of firms in the consulting, health care, and high-tech industries. Also, given that there will still be some turnover—voluntary or involuntary—even in the most desirable places to work, technology can be a valuable means of preserving knowledge when individuals terminate their employment with a firm.

The final section addressed the importance of the protection of intellectual property through the use of patents, copyrights, and trademarks, and it considered the development of dynamic capabilities for supporting a sustainable competitive advantage.

Summary Review Questions

1. Explain the role of knowledge in today's competitive environment.
2. Why is it important for managers to recognize the interdependence of factors in the attraction, development, and retention of talented professionals?
3. What are some of the potential downsides for firms that engage in a "war for talent"?
4. Discuss the need for managers to use social capital in leveraging their human capital both within their firm and across firms.
5. Discuss the key role of technology in leveraging knowledge and human capital.

REFLECTING ON CAREER IMPLICATIONS

Human Capital: Does your organization effectively attract, develop, and retain talent? What are some of the practices that most effectively and least effectively accomplish these tasks?

Human Capital: Does your organization value diversity? What kinds of diversity seem to be encouraged? If not, what missed opportunities do you identify?

Social Capital: Does your organization have effective programs to build and develop social capital such that professionals develop strong ties to the organization? Alternatively, is social capital so strong that you see the occurrence of such effects as "groupthink"? From your own perspective, how might you better leverage social capital toward pursuing other career opportunities?

Technology: Does your organization provide and effectively use technology to help you leverage your talents and expand your knowledge base? Do you recognize opportunities for improvement either through low-tech or high-tech applications?

EXPERIENTIAL EXERCISE

Johnson & Johnson, a leading health care firm with $72 billion in revenues, is often rated as one of *Fortune*'s "Most Admired Firms." It is considered an excellent place to work and has generated high return to shareholders. Clearly, the firm values its human capital. Using the Internet, library resources, or both, identify some of the actions and strategies that attract, develop, and retain human capital in Johnson & Johnson. What are their implications?

Activity	Actions/Strategies	Implications
Attracting human capital		
Developing human capital		
Retaining human capital		

APPLICATION QUESTIONS AND EXERCISES

1. Look up successful firms in a high-tech industry as well as two successful firms in more traditional industries such as automobile manufacturing and retailing. Compare their market values and book values. What are some implications of these differences?

2. Select a firm for which you believe its social capital—both within the firm and among its suppliers and customers—is vital to its competitive advantage. Support your arguments.

3. Choose a company you are familiar with. What are some of the ways in which it uses technology to leverage its human capital?

4. Using the Internet, look up a company you are familiar with. What are some of the policies and procedures that it uses to enhance the firm's human and social capital?

ETHICS AND CORPORATE SOCIAL RESPONSIBILITY QUESTIONS

1. Recall an example of a firm that recently faced an ethical crisis. How do you think the crisis and the management's handling of it affected the firm's human capital and social capital?

2. On the basis of your experiences or what you have learned in your previous classes, are you familiar with any companies that used unethical practices to attract talented professionals? What do you feel were the short-term and long-term consequences of such practices?

3. Who does or should own the knowledge created within a firm? Research outcomes, new processes, or even client feedback and insights are frequently possessed by individuals, but the firm pays their salaries and provides the resources to make things happen. Should individual employees have ownership rights to such valuable assets?

4. Legislation within the European Union gives artists who have sold their creations subsequent rights to future price appreciation of their work. Is full ownership transferred with the sale of an artistic piece? Is selling a painting different from selling a music CD? Is selling a CD different from assigning patent rights to an invention? Is streaming videos different from purchasing a DVD?

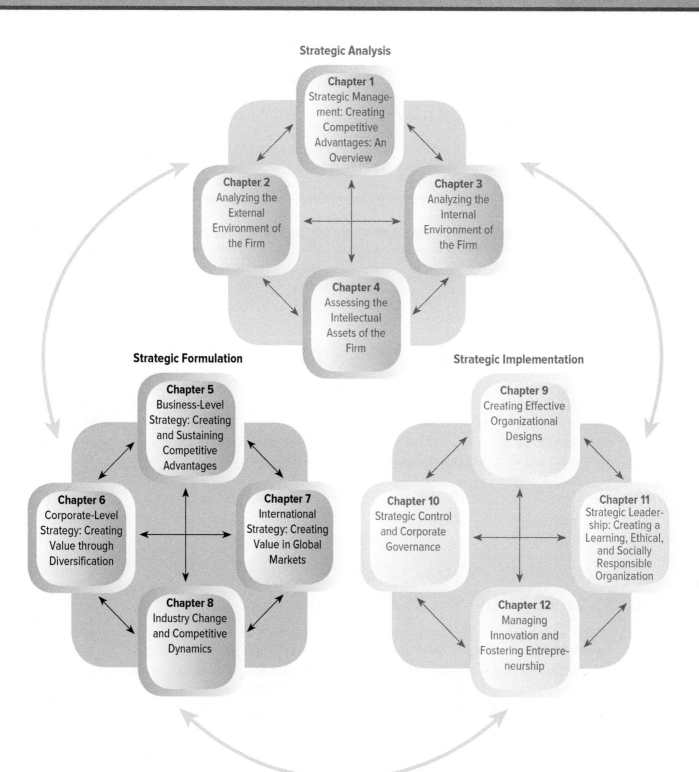

Strategic Analysis

Chapter 1
Strategic Management: Creating Competitive Advantages: An Overview

Chapter 2
Analyzing the External Environment of the Firm

Chapter 3
Analyzing the Internal Environment of the Firm

Chapter 4
Assessing the Intellectual Assets of the Firm

Strategic Formulation

Chapter 5
Business-Level Strategy: Creating and Sustaining Competitive Advantages

Chapter 6
Corporate-Level Strategy: Creating Value through Diversification

Chapter 7
International Strategy: Creating Value in Global Markets

Chapter 8
Industry Change and Competitive Dynamics

Strategic Implementation

Chapter 9
Creating Effective Organizational Designs

Chapter 10
Strategic Control and Corporate Governance

Chapter 11
Strategic Leadership: Creating a Learning, Ethical, and Socially Responsible Organization

Chapter 12
Managing Innovation and Fostering Entrepreneurship

Board: © Everythingpossible/Dreamstimecom; Tablet: VICTOR DE SCHWANBERG

CHAPTER FIVE

BUSINESS-LEVEL STRATEGY:
Creating and Sustaining Competitive Advantages

LEARNING OBJECTIVES

After reading this chapter, you should have a good understanding of:

LO 1 The central role of competitive advantage in the study of strategic management.

LO 2 The three generic strategy choices: market focus, cost leadership, and differentiation.

LO 3 How the successful attainment of generic strategies can improve a firm's relative power vis-à-vis the five forces that determine an industry's average profitability.

LO 4 The pitfalls managers must avoid in striving to attain generic strategies.

LO 5 How firms can effectively combine elements of generic strategies.

LO 6 How strategies can be evaluated before they are implemented.

CASE STUDY

S trategy, in essence, is supposed to answer some seemingly simple questions: How can we outrun our competitors? How can we achieve our objectives? A firm's competitive strategy is about creating value for its customers and having these customers reward the firm for the superior value they receive. Consider how one of the largest retailers in North America fared along those lines.

Paul McKinnon/Shutterstock.com

In the massive American discount retail landscape, Target and its customers viewed the popular "one-stop-shop" as existing at a level above its major competitor, Walmart. Target had seen great success with American customers and was a popular retailer for Canadians shopping south of the border.[1] Initially, its proposed expansion to Canada was greeted with excitement; Canadians assumed Target would bring the same range of products and prices to their local shopping centres as they had enjoyed when shopping in the U.S. Instead, Target's aggressive expansion, which involved the opening of 124 stores within 10 months of their initial entry into Canada, ended in momentous failure. Target racked up nearly $2 billion in losses before choosing to abandon their expansion efforts in early 2015 and retreat from Canada altogether.

There are many reasons why Target failed. Notably, most of these can be understood in terms of Target's failure to successfully implement one of the two basic types of generic strategies. That is, Target was neither able to provide low-cost offerings, nor to successfully differentiate.

Target was rightly lambasted in the media for poor product selection and availability. This went beyond not maintaining parity with the products available in the company's U.S. locations. On many occasions, news sources showed pictures of empty shelves, and one source noted that there were weeks when the products advertised in weekly flyers were entirely unavailable in the stores. A number of factors contributed to this, including the decision to implement a new software system for the Canadian expansion. Target's software system in the U.S was unable to deal with Canadian dollars and French characters, so Target purchased and introduced a new system from an outside vendor. Typically, an operating business implementing a new system successfully will require a slow launch over several years. Target did not have such luxury; the rushed execution meant that Target's employees were unprepared and made errors in data entry that caused serious delays of critical shipments.

Equal responsibility for the poor supply chain management should be attributed to inaccurately forecasting demand. The first stores in Ontario garnered much attention from customers used to visiting Target in the U.S., and Target was unprepared for the number of shoppers. Additionally, demand forecasts were based on information from U.S. stores, and were not altered to adjust for Canadian buying habits.

Canadian shoppers were familiar with Target's prices in the U.S. and recognized that similar products in the Canadian stores were more expensive, for reasons that were not always due to Target's internal issues nor its arrangements with its suppliers on each side of the border. These price differences sparked a number of complaints, forcing Target to rush to lower its prices. In addition, major competitors, such as Walmart and Loblaws, had moved to lower their prices and increase their product offerings in groceries and clothing just before the entry of Target in the market, in anticipation of the new competitor's expansion. This added to the level of competition in the industry.

Without a strong product selection and with limited availability in stores, Target Canada failed to differentiate its offering from Walmart, and customers, unable to actually purchase the products on their shopping list, soon turned away. Target's inability to position itself as competitive on price, and the intense competition in the Canadian retail industry, ensured that it was unable to deliver superior value to its customers. ■

LO 1

Since all firms endeavour to achieve above-average returns but only some can do so at any given time, the question of how management should go about achieving this goal is a core issue in strategic management. Strategy formulation, the second main aspect of strategic management, is about the thought processes and the decisions managers make to address (1) what businesses they should be in, and (2) how to compete in these businesses. The former is primarily addressed in a firm's corporate strategy, whereas the latter is the focus of business strategy.

Business-level strategy is about the particular ways a firm competes in its chosen business. A firm presumably chooses to compete in certain ways to create superior value compared with its competitors. The superiority is manifested in the marketplace's response to its products and services. Do buyers rush to buy what the firm has to offer, such as Apple's iPhone or Toyota's Prius? A firm also strives to sustain such superiority over a long period. Sustainability usually results from the ongoing relevance and robustness of the competitive advantage against the assaults of competitors, including their attempts to bypass or imitate it, and the firm's ability to continuously outpace them. For not-for-profit organizations, the key issues are, again, sustainability, accomplishing objectives, attracting the support of external constituencies, and generating the resources to pursue the organization's mission.

The business strategy choices available to organizations depend largely on what one views as important considerations and how one views the process by which managers choose their strategies. Different schools of strategic management emphasize different perspectives of strategy and highlight formal or informal processes, all with different fundamental principles.[2] The design school and the planning school articulate formal processes of external and internal analyses followed by systematic conclusions and recommendations, which incorporate various elements of managerial values and responsibilities. Other schools regard managers as protagonists or as members of teams, who continuously experiment, learn, perceive, react, or negotiate with others in their efforts to further their businesses.

The two most dominant schools are arguably the positioning school and the resource-based school. The former views business strategy and the corresponding role of managers as identifying and striving to occupy the most attractive competitive positions in the marketplace. It is an outside–in perspective that emphasizes the importance of external analysis and alignment of the firm's activities to pursue a desirable position against external forces. The latter school starts with the resources within the firm and the uniqueness of those resources, and it views the choices for exploitation of those resources as the firm's strategy. It is, by contrast, an inside–out perspective. Both perspectives provide invaluable insights for managers and reveal different, but largely complementary, facets of business strategies. They also suggest alternative bases of competitive advantage. Those who have studied how managers arrive at their strategic choices frequently report that, in reality, managers strive to reconcile a combination of perspectives.

For pedagogical purposes, we choose to use the outside–in perspective, but with a twist. We start with identifying attractive competitive positions but also emphasize how internal resource bundles and activities are used to achieve sustainable competitive advantages. The dominant writings of the outside–in perspective derive from the work of Michael Porter of the Harvard Business School, who observed that avenues of competitive advantage may take several forms but, at their core, they are all about two choices: target market and type of competitive advantage.[3] The first is essentially about focusing on a narrow strategic target versus going after the whole industry, whereas the second is about pursuing a low-cost strategy versus uniqueness and differentiation. Those choices create four generic strategies, as shown in Exhibit 5-1. It should be noted that Porter and many writers following his work prefer to consider only three generic strategies—namely, overall low cost, differentiation, and focus. In their writings, a generic focus strategy is simply subdivided into cost focus and differentiation focus. We follow this convention but emphasize the distinct choices that need to be made. Moreover, we consider how firms can successfully combine multiple strategies.

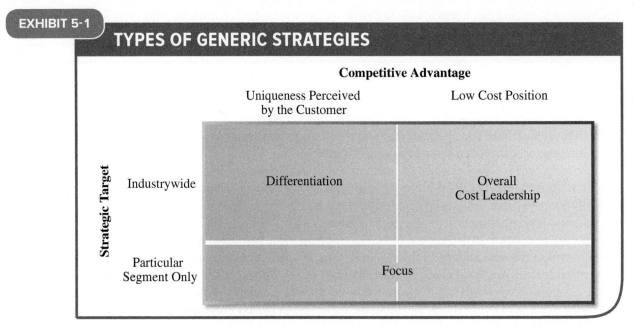

EXHIBIT 5-1

TYPES OF GENERIC STRATEGIES

TYPES OF COMPETITIVE ADVANTAGE AND SUSTAINABILITY

Michael Porter identified three generic strategies that a firm can use to align best with the five forces and achieve competitive advantage: cost leadership, differentiation, and focus. Each of Porter's generic strategies has the potential to allow a firm to outperform its rivals within the industry. The first, overall cost leadership, is based on creating a low-cost position relative to a firm's peers. With this strategy, a firm must manage the relationships in the entire value chain and be devoted to lowering costs throughout the chain. The second, differentiation, requires a firm to create products and services that are unique and valued as such in the eyes of its customers. Here, the primary emphasis is on the "non-price" attributes, including supporting a firm's ethical posture, for which customers will gladly pay a premium.

When a firm decides to pursue one type of competitive advantage (e.g., low cost), it must attain parity on the basis of other competitive advantages (e.g., differentiation) relative to competitors. To generate above-average performance, a firm following an overall cost leadership position needs to be able to stay "on par" with competitors with respect to differentiated products.[4] Parity on the basis of differentiation permits a cost leader to translate cost advantages into higher profits than those achieved by competitors and earn above-average returns.[5] For example, a supermarket chain, such as No Frills or FreshCo, although pursuing an overall cost leadership position, still needs to pay attention to updating and enlarging its current stores, offering extended operating hours, improving shoppers' convenience, and experimenting with new ideas, such as organics and green products.

Finally, a firm following a focus strategy must direct its attention (or "focus") toward narrow product lines, buyer segments, or targeted geographic markets. A firm emphasizing a focus strategy must still attain advantages either through differentiation or through cost leadership; however, these advantages are targeted at a narrow market focus as opposed to industrywide.

LO 2 Overall Cost Leadership

The first generic strategy is overall cost leadership. Cost leadership requires a tight set of interrelated efforts that include the following:

- Aggressive construction of efficient-scale facilities
- Vigorous pursuit of cost reductions from experience
- Tight cost and overhead control
- Avoidance of marginal customer accounts
- Cost minimization in all activities in the firm's value chain, such as research and development (R&D), service, sales force, and advertising

Exhibit 5-2 draws on the value-chain concept to provide examples of how a firm can attain an overall cost leadership strategy in its primary and support activities. Contrast this list with Target's activities in the opening

EXHIBIT 5-2

VALUE-CHAIN ACTIVITIES: EXAMPLES OF OVERALL COST LEADERSHIP

Firm infrastructure	Few management layers to reduce overhead costs.	Standardized accounting practices to minimize personnel required.
Human resource management	Effective policies to minimize costs associated with employee turnover.	Effective orientation and training programs to maximize employee productivity.
Technology development	Effective use of automated technology to reduce scrappage rates.	Expertise in process engineering to reduce manufacturing costs.
Procurement	Effective policy guidelines to ensure low-cost raw materials (with acceptable quality levels).	Shared purchasing operations with other business units.

Inbound logistics	Operations	Outbound logistics	Marketing and sales	Service
Effective layout of receiving dock operations.	Effective use of quality control inspectors to minimize rework on the final product.	Effective utilization of delivery fleets.	Purchase of media in large blocks.

Effective territory management to maximize sales force productivity. | Thorough service repair guidelines to minimize repeat maintenance calls.

Use of single type of repair vehicle to minimize costs. |

Margin

Source: Adapted from: Porter, M.E. 1985. *Competitive Advantage: Creating and Sustaining Superior Performance.* New York: Free Press.

case of this chapter. The value chain can be used as an analytical tool to identify specific activities and the costs and assets associated with them. As Porter explains, analyzing the behaviour of specific cost drivers and assessing the relative costs of competitors for each activity can demonstrate areas where a firm can develop sustainable cost advantages.

Two important concepts related to the overall cost leadership strategy are (1) economies of scale and (2) the experience curve. *Economies of scale* refer to the decline in per-unit costs that usually come with larger production runs, larger facilities, and allocating fixed costs (such as marketing and research and development) across more units produced. The *experience curve* refers to how a business "learns" to lower costs as it gains experience with production processes. In most industries, with experience, unit costs of production decline as output increases. The experience curve concept is discussed in Strategy Spotlight 5.1 and illustrated in Exhibit 5-3.

5.1 STRATEGY SPOTLIGHT

The Experience Curve

The experience curve, as articulated by the Boston Consulting Group, is a way of looking at efficiencies developed through a firm's cumulative experience. In its basic form, the experience curve relates production costs to production output. As cumulative output doubles, costs decline by 10 to 30 percent. For example, if it costs $10 per unit to produce the first 100 units, the per-unit cost could decline to between $9 and $7 in the production of the next 100 units.

What factors account for this increased efficiency? It takes time to learn new tasks, people get better at the same task as they repeat it, and firms continuously introduce product modifications and changes in the manufacturing processes.

Each time the accumulated output doubles, a firm can expect per-unit costs to decline. Of course, as output accumulates, it takes longer for the total output to double again, making further gains from experience harder to register. The early stages of a product's life cycle are typically characterized by rapid gains in technological advances in production efficiency. Most experience curve gains come early in the product life cycle.

The inherent technology of the product offers opportunities for enhancement through gained experience. High-tech products give the best opportunity for gains in production efficiencies. As technology is developed, "value engineering" of innovative production processes is implemented, driving down the per-unit costs of production.

A product's sensitivity to price strongly affects a firm's ability to exploit the experience curve. Cutting the price of a product with high demand elasticity—where demand increases substantially with modest price decreases—creates significant new consumer purchases of the new product. By cutting prices, a firm can increase demand for its product. The increased demand, in turn, increases product manufacture, thus increasing the firm's experience in the manufacturing process. So, by decreasing price and increasing demand, a firm gains manufacturing experience in that particular product, which drives down per-unit production costs.

The Japanese automobile manufacturers Toyota and Nissan used the lessons of the experience curve early on in their entry into the North American market. They aggressively priced their cars, with an eye on the cost structures that they would enjoy after having traversed lower on the curve. Their long-term orientation paid off handsomely, as buyers responded to the lower prices and happily bought huge volumes of vehicles, which allowed the manufacturers to ride the experience curve to lower costs even faster.

Sources: P. Ghemawat, "Building Strategy on the Experience Curve," *Harvard Business Review,* March–April 1985, pp. 143–49; M. E. Porter, *On Competition* (Boston: Harvard Business Review Press, 1996); S. M. Oster, *Modern Competitive Analysis,* 2nd ed. (New York: Oxford University Press, 1994).

EXHIBIT 5-3

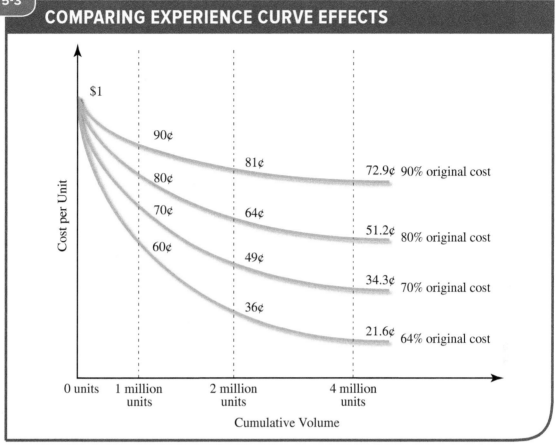

COMPARING EXPERIENCE CURVE EFFECTS

In an article in the *Harvard Business Review,* Pankaj Ghemawat recommended answering these questions when considering an experience curve strategy:

- Does my industry exhibit a significant experience curve?
- Have I defined the industry broadly enough to take into account interrelated experiences?
- What is the precise source of cost reduction? Can my company keep cost reductions proprietary?
- Is demand sufficiently stable to justify the use of the experience curve?
- Is cumulated output doubling fast enough for the experience curve to provide significant strategic leverage?
- Do the returns from an experience curve strategy warrant the risks of technological obsolescence?
- Is the demand price sensitive?
- Are there well-financed competitors who are already following an experience curve strategy or are likely to adopt one if my company does?

Whether to base strategy on the experience curve depends on what specifically causes the decline in costs. For example, if costs drop from economies of scale or efficient production facilities, the experience curve is not helpful. The experience curve can help managers analyze costs when efficient learning, rather than efficient machinery, is the source of cost savings.

A business that strives for a low-cost advantage must attain an absolute cost advantage relative to its rivals. This is typically accomplished by offering a no-frills product or service to a broad target market using standardization to derive the greatest benefits from economies of scale and experience. However, such a strategy may fail if a firm is unable to attain parity on important dimensions of differentiation, such as quick responses to customer requests for design changes. IKEA, the global furniture retailer based in Sweden, achieves competitive advantage in different ways and at different points in its value chain. Strategy Spotlight 5.2 describes how IKEA achieves

5.2 STRATEGY SPOTLIGHT

IKEA's Successful Overall Cost Leadership Strategy

IKEA began in 1943 as a one-person mail-order company in a small farming village in the southern part of Sweden. The founder, Ingvar Kamprad, only 17 years old at the time, initially arranged for the local county milk van to transport goods to the nearby train station. This cost-effective way of thinking has been the guiding force behind IKEA's success ever since. Today, through its unique, low-cost strategy, the IKEA Group has 120,000 employees and revenues of $37 billion. Interbrand, a marketing research firm, rated IKEA 26th on its list of the top 100 best global brands in 2016, along with the likes of Pepsi, Harley-Davidson, and Apple.

Everything at IKEA is done with an eye to cutting costs, reducing waste, and simplifying activities to achieve a successful cost leadership strategy. Even its decision to enter the North American marketplace was driven by the same cost leadership considerations. IKEA chose to come first into Canada, which required a lower investment, lower marketing costs, less risk, and less expensive modifications to its product lines, before embarking on the more expensive and risky entry into the larger U.S. market. IKEA honed its skills for five years in Canada before opening its first store in the United States. IKEA learned how to operate efficiently on a different continent, where cities are further apart, people own larger homes, and the labour force is much more diverse and heterogeneous.

How does IKEA achieve parity on differentiation? Most traditional furniture stores are found in downtown locations, have elaborate showrooms with expensive display samples, employ several salespeople likely on commission, and source products from third-party manufacturers who may require up to eight weeks to deliver an order. IKEA takes a totally different approach. It serves customers who are happy to trade off some of that complexity and service for lower prices. Rather than have a salesperson follow customers around the store, IKEA uses a self-service model based on clear in-store displays. IKEA does not rely on third-party manufacturers. Instead, it designs its own low-cost, modular, ready-to-assemble furniture, and it contracts out manufacturing capacity to mass produce in high volumes and supply over 340 stores in 28 countries. Within each store, IKEA displays every product in room-like settings. Thus, customers do not need a decorator to help them imagine what the pieces would look like put together. Next to the finished showrooms is a warehouse containing products in boxes on pallets. Customers do their own pickup and delivery. They can even rent an IKEA van or a roof rack for their car in order to take their purchases home right away. Delivery can also be arranged at a reasonable price.

What is central to IKEA's strategy? Good quality at a low price. It sells furniture that is well designed, well made, and inexpensive but not "cheap," at prices that are generally 30 to 50 percent below those of the competition. IKEA's emphasis on lowering costs across the whole value chain means that while rivals' prices may rise over time, IKEA is able to reduce its retail prices on a continuous basis, capitalizing on experience curve effects. At IKEA, the process of driving down costs starts the moment a new item is conceived and continues relentlessly throughout its production run.

Sources: K. Kling and I. Goteman, "IKEA CEO Anders Dahlvig on International Growth and IKEA's Unique Corporate Culture and Brand Identity," *Academy of Management Executive* 17(1), 2003, pp. 31–37; L. Margonelli, "How IKEA Designs Its Sexy Price Tags," *Business 2.0,* October 2002:pp. 45–50; and M. E. Porter, "What Is Strategy?," *Harvard Business Review* 74(4), 1996, p. 65.

a successful cost leadership strategy while at the same time countering perceptions of poor quality or "cheap" merchandise—thus achieving relative parity on differentiation.

LO 3   Overall Cost Leadership: Improving Competitive Position vis-à-vis the Five Forces

An overall low-cost position enables a firm to achieve above-average returns despite strong competition. It protects a firm against rivalry from competitors because lower costs allow a firm to earn returns, even if its competitors are eroding profits through intense rivalry. A low-cost position also protects firms against powerful buyers. Buyers can exert power to drive down prices only to the level of the next most efficient producer. Also, a low-cost position provides more flexibility to cope with demands from powerful suppliers for input cost increases. The factors that lead to a low-cost position also provide substantial entry barriers from economies of scale and cost advantages. Finally, a low-cost position puts the firm in a favourable position with respect to substitute products introduced by new and existing competitors.

A few examples will illustrate these points. IKEA's close attention to costs helps protect the firm from both buyer power and the intense rivalry of competitors. It designs its own furniture and orders in large quantities. Thus, it is able to drive down unit costs and enjoy relatively strong power over its suppliers. Rona, a building and home-improvement retailer based in Quebec, and now owned by Lowe's Canada, has aligned itself with ITM, one of the world's largest distributors of hardware, giving Rona's 600 stores across Canada enormous purchasing power and the ability to compete head-on with Home Depot from Atlanta. Strategy Spotlight 5.3 discusses ING Direct, a financial services company that provides no-frills services but very generous rates on savings accounts and other retail banking products.

5.3 STRATEGY SPOTLIGHT

ING Direct: A Highly Successful Low-Cost Strategy

ING Direct, considered the fast-food chain of the financial services industry, is a perfect, if not extreme, example of a low-cost strategy. This company has been enormously successful in an industry that is losing huge amounts of money. From its humble beginnings in Canada in 1997 as an outpost of the large Dutch financial conglomerate ING Group, it grew to become a multinational financial powerhouse serving over 30 million clients in nine countries, with assets exceeding $300 billion. (As a side note, in 2012, ING Direct sold its Canadian assets to Scotiabank, which operates it today as a direct banking subsidiary, under the name Tangerine.)

ING Direct offers a limited line-up of financial services, including savings accounts, guaranteed investment certificates (GICs), mutual funds, and mortgages. It attracts people who need very little hand holding and are looking for higher interest rates on their savings. The company's Orange Savings Account recently was paying 2.6 percent on the entire balance, compared with the 0.56 percent average rate for a moneymarket account at a bank. It is able to offer such enticing rates because 75 percent of its transactions occur online, and it avoids such amenities as chequing accounts or a branch network service. A unique aspect of ING Direct's approach to driving down costs is that it typically "fires" about 0.2 percent of its clients each year. It saves about $1 million annually by getting rid of customers who are too time consuming, thereby ruthlessly driving down its costs per account to about one-third of the industry average. CEO Arkadi Kuhlmann provides an interesting perspective on how ING Direct gets rid of its overly demanding customers:

> The difference between us and the rest of the financial industry is like the difference between takeout food and a sitdown restaurant. The business isn't based on relationships; it's based on a commodity product that is high-volume and low-margin. We need to keep expenses down, which doesn't work well when customers want a lot of empathetic contact.

(Continued)

If the average customer phone call costs us $5.25 and the average account revenue is $12 per month, all it takes is 100,000 misbehaving customers for costs to go through the roof. So, when a customer calls too many times or wants too many exceptions, our sales associated can basically say, "Look this doesn't fit you. You need to go back to your community bank and get the kind of contact you are comfortable with." Of course, we have to use judgment. In some cases, people have legitimate questions. But often, it's customers with large balances who are used to special treatment. They like premiums, platinum cards, and special rates. But you don't get that kind of stuff at the take-out window.

Sources: A. Stone, "Bare Bones, Plump Profits," *BusinessWeek,* March 14, 2005, p. 88; E. Esfahani, "How to Get Tough with Bad Customers," *Business 2.0,* October, 2004, p. 52; and www.ingdirect.ca.; www.tangerine.ca, www.ingdirect.au; www.ingdirect.it; www.ingdirect.com

LO 4 Potential Pitfalls of Overall Cost Leadership Strategies

Although the benefits from following a strategy of overall cost leadership are well documented, one should also be aware of certain pitfalls that must be avoided:

- *Too much focus on one or a few value-chain activities.* Firms need to pay attention to all activities in the value chain and to manage their overall costs. Too often, managers make big cuts in operating expenses but do not question year-to-year spending on capital projects. Or managers may decide to cut selling and marketing expenses but leave manufacturing expenses untouched. Managers should explore all valuechain activities—including relationships among them—as possibilities for cost reductions.

- *Vulnerability to raw material costs.* Firms that compete on overall low-cost strategies are exceedingly vulnerable to price increases in the factors of production. Since they are competing on the basis of low costs, they are less able to pass on price increases because the customers they target are more price sensitive and constantly look for lower prices. Jetsgo, a "low-frills" airline based in Montreal, had to file for bankruptcy as a result of rising fuel costs. Although such costs had burdened all airlines, they had a devastating effect on a company that had staked its strategy on being a low-cost provider.

- *A strategy that is imitated too easily.* A firm's strategy may consist of value-creating activities that are easy to imitate.[6] Such was the case with online brokers, the low cost equivalent of financial brokerage firms.[7] Although the economics of the business could profitably support between 5 and 10 firms, the ease with which one could set up shop resulted in over 100 firms adopting very similar operating models and offering similar products. Not surprisingly, most of them did not last very long and were forced to exit the business after incurring substantial losses.

- *A lack of parity on differentiation.* Firms endeavouring to attain cost leadership advantages, nonetheless, need to obtain a level of parity on differentiation. Consider, for example, organizations providing online degree programs to adults working full time. Although such firms may offer low prices, they may not be successful unless they can offer instruction that is perceived as comparable with traditional providers. For them, parity can be achieved on differentiation dimensions, such as reputation and quality, and through signalling mechanisms, such as national and regional accreditation agencies.

- *Erosion of cost advantages when the pricing information available to customers increases.* The Internet dramatically increases the amount of information available to consumers about price and cost structures, challenging competitors to lower prices to remain competitive. For example, one study found that for each 10-percent increase in consumer use of the Internet, there is a corresponding reduction in life insurance prices to consumers of 3 to 5 percent.[8]

LO 2 Differentiation

The strategy of differentiation consists of creating differences in the firm's product or service offering by creating something that is perceived industry-wide as unique and valued by customers. Differentiation can take many forms:

- Prestige or brand image (BMW, Roots clothing, Holt Renfrew retail)
- Quality (Lexus, President's Choice, Pusateri's food)
- Technology (Martin guitars, Marantz stereo components, North Face camping gear)
- Innovation (Medtronic medical equipment, Cervélo bicycles, 3M, Cirque du Soleil)
- Features (Cannondale bicycles, Honda Goldwing motorcycles, Mountain Equipment Co-op)
- Customer service (Nordstrom retail, Four Seasons Hotels and Resorts)
- Dealer network (Caterpillar, Canadian Tire)
- Ethical posture (Ethical Fruit Company Ltd., Whole Foods)

Exhibit 5-4 draws on the concept of the value chain to provide examples of how firms may differentiate themselves in primary and support activities. The value chain provides an analytical tool, which highlights the fact that differentiation, as a strategy, is more than simply being different or having different products and different marketing strategies. It also demonstrates that differentiation can derive from anywhere in the value chain.

EXHIBIT 5-4

VALUE-CHAIN ACTIVITIES: EXAMPLES OF DIFFERENTIATION

Source: Adapted from Porter, M.E. 1985. Competitive Advantage: Creating and Sustaining Superior Performance. New York: Free Press.

Firms may differentiate themselves along several different dimensions at once. For example, BMW is known for its high prestige, superior engineering, and high-quality automobiles. Harley-Davidson differentiates itself on image and dealer services.[9]

Firms achieve and sustain differentiation advantages and attain above-average performances when their price premiums exceed the extra costs incurred in being unique.[10] Both BMW and Harley-Davidson charge higher prices to offset higher manufacturing costs and added marketing expenses. A differentiator will always seek out ways of distinguishing itself from similar competitors to justify price premiums greater than the costs incurred for differentiating. Clearly, a differentiator cannot ignore costs. After all, its premium prices would be eroded by a markedly inferior cost position. Therefore, it must attain a level of cost parity relative to its competitors. Differentiators can do this by reducing costs in all areas that do not affect differentiation. Porsche, for example, invests heavily in engine design—an area in which its customers demand excellence—but it is less concerned about and spends fewer resources in the design of the instrument panel.[11]

Many companies successfully follow a differentiation strategy.[12] For example, some firms offer products with an excellent image and strong brand identification. Holt Renfrew, a purveyor of fashionable clothing, caters to the affluent and all those who are willing to pay top dollars for the latest designer outfits. Ferrari's lower-priced model, the California T, posts a price tag starting at over U.S. $200,000, although fully equipped models can command twice as much. There is an 18-month to 2-year waiting list for the roadster, and it is broadly speculated that the waiting list adds to the unique appeal and desirability of the brand.[13] Premium apparel retailer Lululemon bases its differentiation on both the uniqueness of its designs and the materials used in its clothing, although the premium service and the personalized attention given to all who enter the store does not hurt either. Strategy Spotlight 5.4 describes how Lexus, the premium automobile nameplate, successfully achieves differentiation.

5.4 STRATEGY SPOTLIGHT

Lexus: Quality and Service

Lexus, a division of Toyota, was introduced as a luxury car line to both Japanese and American markets in the late 1980s, much later than traditional top name brands, such as Mercedes, Jaguar, and Audi. By the mid-1990s, Lexus cars had soared to the top of J. D. Power & Associates' customer satisfaction ratings.

One of Lexus's competitors hired Custom Research Inc. (CRI), a marketing research firm, to find out why Lexus owners were so satisfied. CRI conducted a series of focus groups in which Lexus drivers eagerly offered anecdotes about the special care they received from their dealers. It became clear that although Lexus was manufacturing cars with few mechanical defects, it was the extra attention shown by the sales and service staff that had resulted in such satisfied customers. Such pampering is reflected in the feedback from one customer who, after initially claiming she had never had a problem with her Lexus, clarified that as follows: "Well, I suppose you could call the four times they had to replace the windshield a 'problem.' But, frankly, they took care of it so well and always gave me a loaner car, so I never really considered it a problem until you mentioned it now." An insight gained in CRI's research is that perceptions of product quality (design, engineering, and manufacturing) can be strongly influenced by downstream activities in the value chain (marketing and sales, service).

Lexus recognizes that strong relationships among value activities reinforce and strengthen the customer's total perception of value. Lexus maintains exceptionally close ties with its dealers and generously provides them with resources, such as advertising materials, training, parts, supplies, and automobile inventories. Yet one could easily imagine the futility of Lexus's superb marketing, sales, and service efforts if the company could not maintain high production quality or if procurement were unable to acquire high-quality components. *Consumers Reports,* a magazine published by the consumer advocacy group Consumers Union, consistently rates Lexus cars among the best designed and built in the market. Superb marketing and service alone would be inadequate to support Lexus's strategy.

Sources: Reprinted from "Strategic Innovation" by C. Markides, *MIT Sloan Management Review,* 38 (3), pp. 9–23, by permission of publisher. Copyright © 1997 from MIT Sloan Management Review/Massachusetts Institute of Technology. All rights reserved. Distributed by Tribune Content Agency, LLC; G. G. Dess and J. C. Picken, *Mission Critical* (Burr Ridge, IL: Irwin Professional Publishing, 1997), p. 84.

Strategy Spotlight 5.5 provides the example of a Canadian company that has succeeded against an American powerhouse competitor. Like Lexus, its success can be partially explained by its excellence in downstream activities, such as customer service, as well as by its reputation for product excellence.

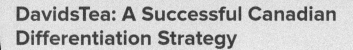

5.5 STRATEGY SPOTLIGHT

DavidsTea: A Successful Canadian Differentiation Strategy

In October of 2013, Montreal-based DavidsTea found itself at the crux of an issue whose solution was integral for its future growth. Starbucks had acquired DavidsTea's main competitor, Teavana, and was in the process of opening its first café tea bar, a hybrid between a specialty tea store, such as Teavana or DavidsTea, and the café setting for which Starbucks is so expansively known. While the number of Canadian DavidsTea locations had doubled in the previous two years and their American counterparts had grown by an even more impressive 700 percent, two questions still remained: How exactly could DavidsTea differentiate itself in order to compete with the hot beverage giant? And what did they need to do to ensure their ability to continue growing in the future?

Founded in 2007 by David Segal, a 28-year-old tea-loving entrepreneur, DavidsTea had opened its first store in the trendy Queen Street West area of Toronto and by the time of Starbucks's acquisition of Teavana had grown to more than 100 locations across North America. CEO Jevin Eagle attributed the brand's explosive growth to a business model developed around expensive rent in high-traffic malls, almost zero paid advertising, and extensive training of its "tea guides" (sales-level employees) in order to provide a better overall customer experience. Customers were able to engage with the company actively through DavidsTea's Twitter account, which had a descriptor reading "Talk tea with us. It's kind of our thing."

New tea guides received a nine-hour tea education session, on-the-job training, and had access to extensive learning materials for each of the 150-plus tea blends in the store—outlining the ingredients, location of origin, and health benefits of each tea—as well as all the merchandise that generated the bulk of DavidsTea's revenues. PR director Bradley Grill described the investment in employee training as critical in enhancing the "show and tell" experience for customers.

Only time will tell whether the strategies that helped establish DavidsTea will be enough for it to continue to differentiate itself and effectively compete against Starbucks's might, its 500-plus Canadian outlets, and the leverage from a global network of over 23,000 stores.

Sources: The case material draws on Benoit, D., 2012, Tea Time for Starbucks: Coffee Giant to Spend $620 Million on Teavana, Deal Journal RSS, November 4; Haynes, M, 2013, Brands of the Year: David's Tea Brews up Growth, Strategy Online, October 3; as well as the company's financial statements and website.

LO 3   Differentiation: Improving Competitive Position vis-à-vis the Five Forces

Differentiation provides protection against rivalry, since brand loyalty lowers customer sensitivity to price and raises customer switching costs.[14] A positive firm reputation offers further protection, and customers rely on such reputation as a signal for what the firm stands for and ignore alternative messages by competitors. By increasing a firm's margins, differentiation also avoids the need for a low-cost position. Lexus has enjoyed enhanced power over buyers because its top J. D. Power & Associates ranking makes buyers more willing to pay a premium price. Differentiation reduces buyers' power because buyers lack comparable alternatives. Higher entry barriers result from differentiation because of customer loyalty and the firm's ability to provide uniqueness in its products or services. Differentiation provides higher margins, which enable a firm to deal with supplier power. Supplier power is also decreased because there is a certain amount of prestige associated with being the supplier to a producer of highly differentiated products and services. The prestige associated with upper-crust brand names, such as Holt Renfrew and Ferrari, along with suppliers' desire to be associated with these prestigious brands, reduces their ability to drive up prices. Finally, a firm that uses differentiation will enjoy high customer loyalty and experience less threat from substitutes compared with its competitors. The loyalty and "peace of mind" associated with such firms as Coach and Holt Renfrew make these firms less vulnerable to rivalry from other firms or to pressures from substitute products and services.

Shared Value in the Value Chain

As discussed in Chapters 1 and 3, Porter & Kramer's shared-value perspective offers a framework for managers to use their understanding of the firm's value chain to find methods of differentiation that not only improve the firm's position in relation to the five forces but also create value for society.

For example, McDonald's revisited how it creates value in outbound logistics and decided to change its approach to packaging and disposal in a way that reduces its environmental footprint and allows it to stand out from its rivals, encourages its suppliers to take a greener approach with it, and lets its customers feel better about consuming its food. The company also looked at the marketing and advertising components of its value chain and realized that there was an opportunity to be more ethical and transparent in its message via a special questions and answers forum on their website.[15] In fact, its disclosure that there are 19 ingredients in its french fries went viral and garnered much criticism, but it is nevertheless a testament to the company's commitment to rethink advertising and use its promise of transparency as a source of differentiation, even if the specific message going out is not necessarily the one McDonald's would like emphasized.

LO 4   Potential Pitfalls of Differentiation Strategies

Along with the benefits of differentiation, there are also pitfalls:

- *Uniqueness that is not valuable.* A differentiation strategy must provide unique bundles of products and services that customers value highly. It is not enough just to be "different." An example is Gibson's Dobro bass guitar. Gibson came up with a unique idea: design and build an acoustic bass guitar with sufficient sound volume so that amplification was not necessary. The problem with other acoustic bass guitars was that they did not project enough volume because of the low-frequency bass notes. By adding a resonator plate on the body of the traditional acoustic bass, Gibson increased the sound volume. Gibson believed this product would serve a particular niche market—bluegrass and folk artists who played in small group "jams" with other acoustic musicians. Unfortunately, Gibson soon discovered that its targeted market was content with its existing options: an upright bass amplified by a microphone and an acoustic electric guitar. Thus, Gibson developed a unique product, but it was not perceived as valuable by its potential customers.[16]

- *Too much differentiation.* Firms may strive for quality or service that is higher than what their customers desire, leaving themselves vulnerable to competitors who provide an acceptable level of quality at a lower price. Consider, for example, the high-end Mercedes Benz S-Class series, which ranges in price from $105,000 to $275,000. In 2004, *Consumer Reports* described these cars as sumptuous, quiet, luxurious, and a delight to drive, but the magazine also considered them among the least reliable sedans available. According to David Champion, who ran the testing program at *Consumer Reports,* the problems were electronics related. "The engineers have gone a little wild," he said. "They have put in every bell and whistle that they think of, and sometimes they don't have the attention to detail to make those systems work." Some of the features included a computer-driven suspension that reduces body roll as the vehicle whips around a corner;

cruise control that automatically slows the car if it gets too close to another car; seats that are adjustable 14 ways and that are ventilated by a system that uses eight fans to whisk away perspiration; and memory settings for a number of adjustments depending on who drives the car.

- *Too high a price premium.* Customers may desire the product, but they may also be put off by the price premium. For example, Duracell (a division of Berkshire Hathaway) at one point charged too high a price for its batteries.[17] The firm tried to sell consumers on its superior-quality products, but the market was not convinced. The price differential was simply too high. A four-pack of Energizer AA batteries sold for $2.99 compared with a Duracell four-pack at $4.59. Not only did Duracell lose market share, but its profits declined by over 30 percent.

- *Differentiation that is easily imitated.* Firms may strive for, and even attain, a differentiation strategy that is successful for a time; however, competitors may erode these advantages through imitation. Consider the frequent flyer programs of airlines or the loyalty credit cards that are aligned with automobile manufacturers (e.g., TD Canada Trust, GM, Visa), which allow holders to accumulate points toward the purchase of vehicles. The ease of imitation by competitors significantly undermines the value of such differentiation strategies. Strategy Spotlight 5.6 describes a very successful differentiator who quickly went out of business when its products were easily copied by Chinese manufacturers who flooded the market and eroded any remaining advantage.

5.6 STRATEGY SPOTLIGHT

Crocs Shoes' Walk from Stardom to Also-Rans

Those clunky and gaudy shoes that were the must-have footwear of 2006 and sold over 10 million pairs in 2007 were first introduced in 2002 by Foam Creations Inc., the Quebec City company that invented a light but durable resin and designed the shoes. Boaters and surgeons alike found the loose-fitting clogs irresistible. The colourful and comfortable, yet admittedly ugly, shoes came in a myriad of colours and sizes to fit every taste and age, from toddlers to seniors. Priced between $35 and $50, they were worn in the garden, at home, in the office, in the store, at the hospital, in the school, and on the street to walk, run, hike, or climb. The clogs were distinctly bulky, with perforations around the toes for ventilation and comfort. Crocs's CEO was on top of the world when the firm's initial public offering (IPO) became the highest ever for a shoe manufacturer, and the company embarked on a shopping spree to acquire design firms and shoe, sandal, accessories, and apparel manufacturers that would allow it to transition from a one-hit wonder to a diversified powerhouse with operations across the globe. At one point, the financial markets ascribed Crocs a price–earnings (P/E) ratio of 50 with growth expectations hitting the stratosphere and valued the company at $6 billion. After all, those odd shoes could possibly one day be worn by six billion people.

Yet, by 2008, imitations from China had started appearing everywhere. Despite the company's efforts to protect it, the design could easily be altered slightly to circumvent the patents. Worse still, competitors' lawyers successfully argued that clogs had existed well before the company's trademarks were registered. The proprietary resin could be substituted with something just a bit different, but more importantly, the Chinese and Vietnamese knockoffs were selling for a fraction of the price of a pair of Crocs, sometimes for as low as $8 a pair. Soon, the firm found its stock down to $1 and its warehouses full of Crocs!

Admirably, although Crocs did get hit hard and almost went under, it has reinvented itself as a multi-platform, multi-type shoe company and it now has a thriving global business in the broader shoe market.

Sources: C. Sethi, "Kudos for Shoes Yet to Crocs' Stock," *The Globe and Mail,* June 15, 2006, p. B20; T. Perkins, "Keeping One Step Ahead of a Shoe Craze," *The Globe and Mail,* April 14, p. B3; D. Lacey, "Crocs Lose Footing," *National Post,* April 16, 2008, p. FP3; www.crocs.com.

- *Dilution of brand identification through productline extensions.* Firms may erode their quality-brand image by adding products or services with lower prices and quality. Although this can increase short-term revenues, it may be detrimental in the long-run. Profits do not necessarily follow revenues. The case of Gucci illustrates this point.[18] In the 1980s, Gucci was determined to capitalize on its prestigious brand name by launching an aggressive strategy of revenue growth. It added a set of lower-priced canvas goods to its product line. It also pushed goods heavily into department stores and duty-free channels, and it allowed its name to appear on a host of licensed items, such as watches, eyeglasses, and perfumes. In the short term, this strategy worked. Sales soared. However, the strategy carried a high price. Gucci's indiscriminate approach to expanding its products and channels tarnished its sterling brand. Sales of its high-end goods (with higher profit margins) fell, causing profits to decline.

- *Perceptions of differentiation that vary between buyers and sellers.* The issue here is that "beauty is in the eye of the beholder." Companies must realize that although they may perceive their products and services as differentiated, their customers may view them as commodities. Indeed, in today's marketplace, many products and services have been reduced to commodities.[19] Thus, a firm could overprice its offerings and lose margins altogether if it has to lower prices to reflect market realities.

Many products and services that used to be differentiated are now sold at online auctions, such as FreeMarkets (an online business-to-business auction house), where several competing sellers fight for big pieces of business purely on price. Personal computers, servers, data storage capacity, hotel rooms, bandwidth, generic drugs, and ocean shipping have been traded at online auctions featuring readily available information about competing products and services. This does not mean that it is impossible for a firm to achieve differentiation strategies in these industries, but certainly differentiation is becoming more difficult.

LO 2 Focus

Focus is based on the choice of a narrow competitive scope within an industry. A firm following this strategy selects a segment or group of segments and tailors its strategy to serve them. The focuser achieves competitive advantages by dedicating itself to these segments exclusively. The essence of focus is the exploitation of a particular market niche that is unique within the industry. As one might expect, narrow focus itself (like merely "being different" as a differentiator) is simply not sufficient for above-average performance. The focus strategy, as indicated in Exhibit 5-1, has two variants: (1) cost focus and (2) differentiation focus.

Cost Focus

With a cost focus strategy, a firm strives to create a cost advantage in its target segment and serve customers within that segment with a price lower than the prices of rivals, who may either target the whole industry or be unable to match the lower-cost position. It exploits differences in cost behaviour in a particular segment and takes advantage of potentially lower costs that arise from purposefully limiting the firm's customer base to a well-defined segment.

Staples, Canada's reigning retailer of office supplies, is deliberately limiting its selection in an explicit effort to shed customers.[20] In response to an onslaught from retailers, such as Walmart, Costco, Canadian Tire, and Loblaw Companies, fighting to take a piece of the profitable stationery and office supplies business, Staples has aggressively targeted the small-business and home-office clients by increasing the number of private label items it carries, offering jumbo-size packs, and passing on the savings of its bulk buying power to customers by cutting prices. At the same time, its collection of single-pack highlighters and teen-targeted backpacks and binders has all but disappeared from its stores' shelves. Staples has succeeded in retaining its dominant position in the highly competitive marketplace and continues to open new stores across the country.

In another example, NetApp has developed a more cost-effective way to store and distribute computer files.[21] Its larger rival, EMC Corporation, makes mainframe-style products, priced over $1 million, which store files and Internet traffic. NetApp makes devices that cost under $200,000 for particular storage jobs, such as caching (temporary storage) of Internet content. Focusing on such narrow segments has certainly paid off for NetApp; it has ranked in the Fortune 500 since 2012.

Differentiation Focus

A firm pursuing a differentiation focus strategy will seek to differentiate itself within a narrow segment. The dimensions of differentiation are similar to those presented earlier; however, in this case, the firm aims to provide better service, prestige, image, or quality to a well-defined and rather narrow segment.

The Keg Steakhouse & Bar has developed a simple operating formula that serves it with a stable business, and its customers with perfect steaks, every time.[22] The Keg has purposefully limited its menu and has stayed away from food fashions and fads, such as nachos and pizzas; it targets young families and the après-work crowd. Suppliers of meats and vegetables are monitored extremely closely and are expected to meet very specific standards. Cooks follow head office's detailed preparation instructions; service, food quality, and portion size are precisely maintained. Customers have rewarded The Keg with frequent visits and praise. The Keg was the only chain not to be affected by the "perfect storm" that so greatly impacted the food-services sector in Canada during the outbreak of SARS (severe acute respiratory syndrome) in 2002, the incidence of a case of "mad cow" disease (bovine spongiform encephalopathy, BSE) in Alberta in the spring of 2003, and the occurrence of a blackout in northeastern parts of North America in August 2003. The industry's sales plunged by more than 13 percent, but The Keg's sales slid only by 2.4 percent and completely rebounded soon after. Similarly, the financial downturn that began in 2008 did not even make a dent in The Keg's operations.

Hermès, the upscale French design house, has for years catered to an exclusive clientele with its line of leather goods and silk scarves and ties. It has retained an exclusive image, religiously guarded the quality and design of its products, and succeeded in maintaining the allure of rarity and glamour while safeguarding its presence in 40 countries and more than 300 store locations around the world.

LO 3   Focus: Improving Competitive Position vis-à-vis the Five Forces

Focus requires a firm to have a low-cost position with its strategic target, a high differentiation, or both. As we discussed with regard to cost and differentiation strategies, these positions provide defences against each competitive force. Focus is also used to select niches that are least vulnerable to substitutes or wherein competitors are weakest. For example, The Keg experiences less rivalry and lower bargaining power among buyers by providing products and services to a targeted market segment that is less price sensitive. New rivals would have difficulty attracting customers away from these firms only on the basis of lower prices. Similarly, the image and quality that these brands evoke heighten the entry barriers for rivals trying to gain market share. Additionally, such firms enjoy some protection against substitute products and services because of their relatively high reputation, brand image, and customer loyalty. Consider Network Appliances' strategy of cost focus. The successful rival to EMC in the computer storage industry was better able to absorb price increases from suppliers as a result of its lower-cost structure. Thus, the effects of supplier power were lessened.

LO 4   Potential Pitfalls of Focus Strategies

Along with the benefits, managers must be aware of the pitfalls of a focus strategy:

- ***Erosion of cost advantages within the narrow segment.*** The advantages of a cost focus strategy may be fleeting if the cost advantages are eroded over time. For example, Dell's pioneering direct-selling model in the personal computer industry has been eroded by its rivals, such as Hewlett-Packard, as they have gained experience with Dell's distribution method. Similarly, other firms have seen their profit margins drop as competitors enter their product segment.

- ***Possible competition from new entrants and from imitation.*** Some firms adopting a focus strategy may enjoy temporary advantages because they select a small niche with few rivals. However, their advantages may be short-lived as rivals invade their market niche. A notable example is the multitude of dot-com firms that specialize in very narrow segments, such as pet supplies, ethnic foods, and vintage automobile accessories. Entry barriers tend to be low, there is little buyer loyalty, and competition becomes intense. And since the marketing strategies and technologies employed by most rivals are largely non-proprietary, imitation is easy. Over time, revenues fall, profit margins are squeezed, and only the strongest players survive the shakeout.

- *Too much focus on satisfying buyer needs.* Some firms attempting to attain competitive advantages through a focus strategy may have a product or service that is too narrow. Examples include many retail firms. Hardware chains, such as True Value, are losing market share to their rivals, such as Rona and Home Depot, who offer a full line of home and garden equipment and accessories. Similarly, many specialty ethnic and gourmet food stores may see their sales and profits shrink as large national grocers, such as Loblaws, expand their already broad product lines to include similar items. And given the enormous purchasing power of the national chains, it would be difficult for such specialty retailers to attain parity on costs.

LO 5 Combination Strategies: Integrating Overall Low Cost and Differentiation

There has been ample evidence—in the popular press and in research studies—about the strategic benefits of combining generic strategies. One study analyzed 1,789 strategic business units and found that businesses combining multiple forms of competitive advantage (differentiation and overall cost leadership) outperformed businesses that used only a single form. The lowest performers were those that did not identify with even a single type of advantage. They were classified as "stuck in the middle"—that is, unable or unwilling to make choices about how to compete, having tried to do everything and accomplishing nothing particularly well. The results of this study are presented in Exhibit 5-5. Results from other studies on a wide variety of industries, such as paints and allied products, Korean electronics, apparel, and screw machine products, are consistent with these findings.[23]

EXHIBIT 5-5   COMPETITIVE ADVANTAGE AND BUSINESS PERFORMANCE

	Competitive Advantage					
	Differentiation and Cost	Differentiation	Cost	Differentiation and Focus	Cost and Focus	Stuck in the Middle
Performance						
Return on investment (%)	35.5	32.9	30.2	17.0	23.7	17.8
Sales growth (%)	15.1	13.5	13.5	16.4	17.5	12.2
Gain in market share (%)	5.3	5.3	5.5	6.1	6.3	4.4
Sample size	123	160	100	141	86	105

Perhaps the primary benefit to be enjoyed by firms that successfully integrate low-cost and differentiation strategies is that the integrated strategy is generally harder for competitors to duplicate or imitate. An integrated strategy enables a firm to provide two types of value to customers: differentiated attributes (e.g., high quality, brand identification, reputation) and lower prices (because of the firm's lower costs in value-creating activities). The goal becomes one of providing unique value to customers in an efficient manner.[24] Some firms are able to attain both types of advantages simultaneously. For example, superior quality can lead to lower costs because of less need for rework in manufacturing, fewer warranty claims, a reduced need for customer service personnel to resolve customer complaints, and so forth. Thus, the benefits of combining advantages can be additive, instead of involving trade-offs. Consider three approaches to combining overall low-cost and differentiation competitive strategies.

Automated and Flexible Manufacturing Systems

Given the advances in manufacturing technologies, such as CAD/CAM (computer-aided design and computer-aided manufacturing) and information technologies, many firms have been able to manufacture unique products in relatively small quantities at lower costs—a concept known as "mass customization."[25]

Let us consider the case of Andersen Windows, a $1 billion manufacturer of windows for the building industry.[26] For many years, Andersen was a mass producer of a variety of standard windows that were manufactured in small batches. However, to meet changing customer needs, Andersen kept adding to its product line, resulting in catalogues of ever-increasing size and a bewildering array of choices for both homeowners and contractors. Over a six-year period, the number of products tripled, price quotes began to take several hours to put together, and the error rate increased—not only damaging the company's reputation but also adding to its manufacturing expenses.

To bring about a major change, Andersen developed an interactive computer version of its paper catalogues for distributors and retailers. Salespersons can now customize each window to meet the customer's needs, check the design for structural soundness, and provide a price quote quickly. The system is virtually error free, customers get exactly what they want, and the time to develop the design and furnish a quotation has been cut by 75 percent. Each showroom computer is connected to the factory, and customers are assigned a code number that permits them to track their order. The manufacturing system has been developed to use some common finished parts (e.g., mullions, the vertical or horizontal strips separating window panes and sashes), but it also allows considerable variation in the final products. Despite the huge investment in time and money, Andersen found that the new system lowered costs, enhanced quality and variety, and improved its response time to customers.

Other examples of flexible production systems that enable firms to offer mass customization to their customers include Lands' End, which offers customers the ability to order customized shirts and pants by specifying style parameters, measurements, and fabrics through the firm's website.[27] Moreover, by saving these settings, customers can easily order duplicate items later. Similarly, Cannondale permits consumers to specify the parameters that define a road bike frame, including custom colours and inscriptions. Customers can then arrange for the delivery of the customized bike through a dealer.

Using Data Analytics

Corporations are increasingly collecting and analyzing data on their customers, including data on customer characteristics, purchasing patterns, employee productivity, and physical asset utilization. This information, commonly referred to as "Big Data," has the potential to allow firms to better customize their product and service offerings to customers while more efficiently and fully using the resources of the company. For example, Pepsi used data analytics to develop an algorithm that lowers the rate of inventory out-of-stocks and has shared the algorithm with partners and retailers. Similarly, Kaiser Permanente collects petabytes of data on the health treatment of its 8 million health care members. This has allowed Kaiser to develop insights on the cost, efficacy, and safety of the treatments provided by doctors and procedures in hospitals—leading to more effective and cost-conscious treatment patterns.[28]

Exploiting the Profit Pool Concept for Competitive Advantage

A profit pool can be defined as the total profits in an industry at all points along the industry's value chain.[29] Although the concept is relatively straightforward, the structure of the profit pool can be complex. The potential pool of profits will be deeper in some segments of the value chain than in others, and the depths will vary within an individual segment. Segment profitability may vary widely by customer group, product category, geographic market, or distribution channel. Additionally, the pattern of profit concentration in an industry is very often different from the pattern of revenue generation.

Consider the automobile industry profit pool in Exhibit 5-6. Here, we see little relationship between the generation of revenues and the capturing of profits. Manufacturing generates most of the revenue, but this value activity is far smaller in terms of profit than other value activities, such as financing and extended warranty operations. Thus, even though a car manufacturer may be under tremendous pressure to produce cars efficiently, much of the profit (at least proportionately) can be captured in the aforementioned downstream operations. It is no wonder that all car manufacturers and dealers today are happy to arrange lease financing for their customers. It would be unwise for a carmaker to focus solely on manufacturing and leave downstream operations to others through outsourcing.

EXHIBIT 5-6

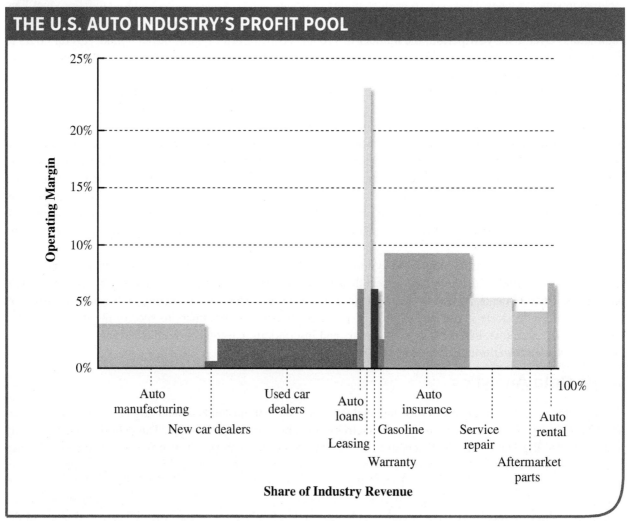

THE U.S. AUTO INDUSTRY'S PROFIT POOL

Source: Adapted and reprinted by permission of Harvard Business Review. Exhibit from "Profit Pools: A Fresh Look at Strategy," by O. Gadiesh and J. L. Gilbert, May–June 1998. Copyright © 1998 by the Harvard Business School Publishing Corporation; all rights reserved.

Coordinating the "Extended" Value Chain by Way of Information Technology

Many firms have achieved success by integrating activities throughout the "extended value chain" and using information technology to link their own value chain with the value chains of their customers and suppliers. As noted in Chapter 3, this approach enables a firm to add value through its own value-creating activities and to pass this value to its customers and suppliers.

Such a strategy often necessitates redefining the industry's value chain. A number of years ago, Walmart took a close look at its industry's value chain and decided to reframe the competitive challenge.[30] Although its competitors were primarily focused on retailing—merchandising and promotion—Walmart determined that it could unleash more value in the logistics and communications parts of its business than in the retailing part. Here, linkages in the extended value chain became central. That became Walmart's chosen battleground. By redefining the rules of competition such that they played to its strengths, Walmart has attained competitive advantages and dominates its industry.

Integrated Overall Low-Cost and Differentiation Strategies: Improving Competitive Position vis-à-vis the Five Forces

Firms that successfully integrate both differentiation and cost advantages create an enviable position relative to industry forces. For example, Walmart's integration of information systems, logistics, and transportation helps it drive down costs and provide outstanding product selection. This dominant competitive position, along with its excellent reputation, serves to erect high entry barriers to potential competitors that have neither the financial nor the physical resources to compete head to head. Walmart's size, with its $485 billion sales in 2016, provides the chain with enormous bargaining power over suppliers. Its low pricing and wide selection of merchandise reduce the power of buyers (its customers) because there are relatively few competitors that can provide a comparable cost–value proposition. This reduces the possibility of intense head-to-head rivalry and protracted price wars. Finally, Walmart's overall value proposition makes potential substitute products (e.g., Internet competitors) a less viable threat.

Strategy Spotlight 5.7 describes how a small Canadian firm revolutionized the global beverage market through a combination of low-cost and differentiation strategies. As a cautionary tale, though, we should not forget that when Cott forgot what its strategy really was, it got itself into trouble and compromised its narrow but powerful position.

5.7 STRATEGY SPOTLIGHT

Low Cost and Differentiation Redefining the Cola Wars

The soft drinks and beverage business is not just global but also cutthroat, where each single market share point translates into billions of dollars of sales. Two giants dominate the space, with the annual revenues of each exceeding $30 billion, and they are followed by myriad smaller players who vie for a slice of the lucrative pie. Something happened, however, in 1989, which not only revolutionized the beverage industry but forever changed the global retail food industry. That year, Sam and Gerry Pencer, sons of the Canadian owner of beverage company Cott Corporation, secured a contract to supply the line of President's Choice soft drinks, the premium private label of Loblaw Companies Ltd. Loblaw itself had recently turned the corner as an ailing food retailer by launching its President's Choice line of products to improve customers' perceptions of the supermarket chain's quality, build customer loyalty, and increase margins.

Soon the President's Choice soft drinks surpassed the combined sales of Coke and Pepsi products within Loblaws stores. Cott's success drew new customers from Canada and the United States. By 1993, the client roster consisted of all major Canadian chains in addition to Loblaws, including A&P (now Metro), Shoppers Drug Mart, and Sobeys, as well as the large American retailers Walmart, Safeway, Price Club, and 7-Eleven. On the supply side, Cott had secured a long-term agreement with RC Cola, which provided Cott with the only reliable alternative source of cola syrup. Cott also capitalized on the presence of substantial excess bottling capacity in the United States and enlisted many independent bottlers to help it meet demand. The recipe was simple: Produce a quality product at or exceeding the leading national brands, eliminate marketing and distribution costs by adopting the retailer's brand and utilizing the retailer's own distribution and warehousing capacity, and price the product at a substantially lower point to provide the retailer with a better margin than the powerful national brands.

In 1993, Cott brought on board its new president, Heather Reisman, a strategic change consultant with strong connections in the Canadian corporate world. Reisman's mission: Convert the small beverage firm to a global powerhouse that would develop "total product service bundles" for

(Continued)

major retailers, and champion the private label movement in changing food retailing around the world. As part of the plan, Cott acquired a controlling interest in The Watt Group, a world-known corporate design house that was responsible for the creation of many successful corporate images and product designs for such firms as Nestlé and Kraft. Cott and Watt also founded Retail Brands Inc., a consulting firm that would guide retailers through the development and active marketing of their private labels. Cott acquired interests in the manufacturers of snack foods, pet foods, and beer in an effort to replicate the success of the soft drinks and broaden its product offerings.

Whether it was because of pressure to deliver impressive growth and the expectation of higher and higher free cash flows that led to aggressive accounting practices or simply that senior managers ended up stretched too thin as they embarked on a global endeavour to preach the retail revolution and offer a range of marketing and merchandising consulting services, Cott found itself embroiled in a number of controversies. Analysts started questioning its financial results, and operational problems appeared in many of its facilities.

Sales in 1998 declined by 8.5 percent from the previous year, and the firm experienced a net loss of almost $30 million. New management, led by Frank Weise, was brought in to clean house. The first order of business was to focus the company on the premium soft drink business in three markets (Canada, the United States, and the United Kingdom), close down small facilities in faraway markets, such as Norway and New Zealand, divest non-core businesses, and prune the company's extensive product line. Production efficiencies were introduced throughout the corporation, with an emphasis on streamlining operations, directing production toward the most efficient plants, and simplifying operations by eliminating costly auxiliary services. Over the next two years, the company divested its operations in many markets in Europe, Latin America, and the Pacific and sold its prized corporate design outfit, The Watt Group, along with its marketing and merchandising advisor firm, Retail Brands Inc. The firm soon returned to its roots as an efficient supplier of premium private-label soft drinks for major retailers.

Annual sales in 2003 reached $1.6 billion, and the stock price climbed back to the mid-$40 range. This turn of events occurred in response to the concerted efforts of the new management and strong endorsement by major shareholders, who invested additional capital to fund the firm's growth plans. The summer of 2004 saw very healthy demand and an expanding range of customers, requiring a greater assortment of products. Each of the firm's plants was making a broad range of products for its local market.

However, by the end of the summer, Cott had again started to experience operational problems. The firm's capacity was stretched, and it was unable to handle the increasing demand. It had to resort to the costly move of outsourcing its products to other bottlers. By January 2005, the stock had fallen to below $28, reflecting the market's disappointment with management. The new CEO, John Sheppard, found himself busy assuring analysts and shareholders that the company had not lost its focus and that it would start to rationalize production, streamline operations, put more emphasis on its core products, stop the production of less-popular items, and even introduce external audits of the efficiency of its plants.

Sheppard seemed to have stemmed the tide, and soon he was looking, again, to introduce new product lines, add customers, and enhance services. In pursuit of the energy drink rage that had swept the market, Cott launched Red Rain and Red Rave to compete with the highly successful Red Bull drink. Ready-to-drink teas, sports drinks, and flavoured waters followed. Brent Willis, an experienced executive from the beer industry, took over as the CEO to lead the company in its new direction. Only a few months later, though, he had to acknowledge that the company's operations were suffering from "growing pains"—supply-chain problems and higher costs for some of its raw materials. The stock took another beating; in 2008, it was trading as low as $2, and a new CEO, David Gibbons, a veteran of the consumer packaged goods business, was brought in to turn the company around one more time.

Ten years later, Cott has managed to regroup and turn things around one more time by consolidating operations in North America and the U.K. and narrowing the product range. The

Potential Pitfalls of Integrated Overall Cost-Leadership and Differentiation Strategies

Along with the benefits, managers must be aware of the pitfalls that can potentially arise in pursuing combination strategies:

- *Failing to attain both strategies and ending up "stuck in the middle."* A key issue in strategic management is the creation of competitive advantages that enable a firm to enjoy above-average returns. Some firms may become "stuck in the middle" if they try to attain both cost and differentiation advantages but achieve neither. Eaton's, Canada's original department store, was known for its famous pledge of "Goods satisfactory or money refunded." It was the first company to sell from a catalogue and build large open-concept stores, and it subsequently became the purveyor of choice for generations of Canadians. In the early 1980s, Eaton's lost direction in a highly competitive retail market as it tried to achieve differentiation and cost control at the same time but failed on both. It struggled to fend off discounters, such as Walmart, on one front, department stores, such as The Bay, on another, and the more popular specialty clothing stores, such as Club Monaco, Gap, and Roots, on a third. Eventually, Eaton's filed for bankruptcy and folded after 100 years because it could not identify with and succeed by using any one strategy, while other retailers around it adapted and prospered.

- *Underestimating the challenges and expenses associated with coordinating value-creating activities in the extended value chain.* Successfully integrating activities across a firm's value chain with the value chain of suppliers and customers involves significant investment in financial and human resources. Managers must not underestimate the expenses linked to technology investment, managerial time and commitment, and the involvement and investment required by the firm's customers and suppliers. The firm must be confident that it can generate a sufficient scale of operations and revenues to justify all associated expenses.

- *Miscalculating sources of revenue and profit pools in the firm's industry.* Firms may fail to accurately assess sources of revenue and profits in their value chain. This can occur for several reasons. For example, a manager's bias may arise from his or her functional area background, work experiences, and educational background. A manager with a background in engineering might be more inclined to perceive that proportionately greater revenue and margins are being created in manufacturing, product, and process design compared with a person whose background is in a "downstream" value-chain activity, such as marketing and sales. Allocating fixed costs, transfer pricing mechanisms, or even politics may yield an inaccurate picture of where costs and revenues are generated within a firm. A related problem is directing an overwhelming amount of managerial time, attention, and resources to activities that create the greatest margins and paying little attention to other important, although less profitable, activities. For example, an automobile manufacturer may focus too much on downstream activities, such as warranty fulfilment and financing operations, to the detriment of differentiation and the cost of manufacturing of the automobiles themselves.

Limitations of Porter's Generic Strategies Model

Although the generic strategies model presented here has tremendous advantages deriving mainly from simplicity, determinism, formality, and tight analytical prescriptions, it also falls short on a number of fronts. Some writers have criticized the model for focusing too narrowly on economic analysis and not enough on the social, political, and cognitive aspects.[31] Moreover, the strategic choices are largely restricted to a very short list of options, discouraging the creation of truly unique strategies.

The model itself lacks dynamism, although industry evolution and realignment of strategic choices are not excluded from its conceptualization. It emphasizes stability—identifying and staying in an attractive position, rather than analyzing how one gets there. Managers must think outside the model if they are to identify the tools and choices that will ultimately move their firm to a new competitive position or allow them to respond to the complexity and unpredictability of the business environment that is typical today.

In an attempt to address at least some of these criticisms, in Chapter 8, we look at the industry life-cycle concept and discuss its implications for strategic decisions. We will also explore turnaround strategies—that is, strategies that are necessary to reverse performance erosion and regain a competitive position.

LO 6 EVALUATING BUSINESS STRATEGY

How do managers know that the strategy they have selected is the right one or, at least, that it is not the wrong one? How can an outside observer, an industry analyst, a potential supplier, or a potential major client assess the quality of a company's strategy before initiating substantial business dealings with that company? Using the various analytical tools, as described in the previous three chapters, is the first step in selecting a good strategy, but a thorough assessment should go beyond that. Moreover, evaluating a strategy is not the same as evaluating a firm's performance. The latter is an ex-post assessment of a business's success; it is an outcome following all actions and events that have unfolded over a period, and it is a composite measure to determine not only whether the chosen strategy was good but also whether it was executed well and whether the industry, as a whole, did well and the firm was somewhat lucky! Indeed, outcomes are complex and, for the most part, difficult to ascribe to individual causes. Nonetheless, outcomes are about results and the ultimate performance of a business.

Evaluating strategy, however, is, or ought to be, an ex-ante prerequisite before the strategy is put to action, resources are allocated, and commitments are made. Managers should have in place a process that is integral to strategy formulation and allows them to assess whether their choices are good, just good enough, or simply poor. In their day-to-day professional lives, managers make many decisions—such as the design of a new plant, choice of a particular location, options among information systems, or introducing automation processes—where, indeed, they can judge whether something is optimal or at least compare the options by using technical features and quantitative methods to determine which one will give them the highest payoff. In strategy management, we can only talk about assessing a strategy to determine whether it is better than alternative strategies or whether, at least, it does not have any critical flaws—not whether it is the best. Given the unique nature of strategy, it is impossible to demonstrate before implementation that a particular strategy is the most advantageous or even to guarantee that it will work. Ex-ante, our examination is mostly qualitative, but we can systematically test for the consistency and consonance of a strategy, whether it provides a competitive advantage, and whether it is, indeed, feasible.[32]

- *Consistency* refers to whether the strategy is in alignment with the organization's goals and objectives, whether it introduces contradictions among different goals, and whether it will be pulling the organization (or different parts of it) into competing dimensions. Consistency arises from a strategy whose components are well aligned with a company's vision and its values. All participants can readily identify and appreciate the direction, the commitments, the choices made, the expectations, and the desirable outcomes. Consistency also occurs when all the elements of the strategy mutually underpin and do not undermine each other.

- *Consonance* refers to the fit between the strategy and the external environment. Does the strategy take into account what is going on in the environment, what trends are emerging, and what the various stakeholders would support? This is both about responding to and incorporating the external environment. Does it capitalize on opportunities? Does it promise to create value that will be worth more than the cost of its creation? Does it address threats that are arising from the environment? Does it allow the firm to convert the value created into wealth (i.e., can the firm appropriate some of the value it creates)?

- *Advantage* refers to the competitive stance of the strategy and whether it is creating and exploiting competitive advantages that are both enduring and difficult to duplicate. Does the strategy give the firm an advantageous position relative to competitors? Can the strategy be pursued more economically compared with competitors' strategies? What are the elements of superiority against competitors that are embedded in the strategy? This is essentially about doing something "better" not "well." The issue here is whether the firm can perform activities and serve markets better than competitors can. Managers should also ask whether the strategy capitalizes on or erects entry barriers that would create obstacles for competitors. Can competitors imitate the strategy? Does it allow the firm to continue to innovate and stay ahead of competitors on particular dimensions?

- *Feasibility* refers to the capacity of the firm to achieve what it is embarking on. Is the strategy realistic? Does the organization possess, or can it gain access to, the necessary resources to carry out the strategy? Does the strategy explicitly address resource constraints? Does the organization possess the human capacity and managerial talent to implement what the strategy calls for? Does it explicitly exploit key resources and capitalize on unique competencies, skills, and capabilities within the organization? Does it create unsolvable problems? Does it spread the organization too thin? Does it explicitly address the organizational requirements to execute and support the different elements of the strategy?

Can Competitive Strategies Be Sustained? Integrating and Applying Strategic Management Concepts

Thus far, this chapter has addressed how firms can attain competitive advantages in the marketplace. We discussed the three generic strategies—overall cost leadership, differentiation, and focus—as well as combination strategies. Next, we discussed the importance of linking value-chain activities (both those within the firm and those linkages between the firm's suppliers and customers) to attain such advantages. We also showed how successful competitive strategies enable firms to strengthen their position vis-à-vis the five forces of industry competition as well as how to avoid the pitfalls associated with the strategies.

Competitive advantages are, however, often short-lived. The firms that constitute the Fortune 500 list has experienced significant turnover in its membership over the years—reflecting the temporary nature of competitive advantages. And recall Dell's fall from grace (Chapter 3). Here was a firm whose advantages in the marketplace seemed unassailable in the early 2000s. In fact, it was *Fortune's* "Most Admired Firm" in 2005. However, cracks began to appear in 2007, and its competitive position has since been severely eroded by rivals, such as Hewlett-Packard. In short, Dell focused so much on operational efficiency and perfecting its "direct model" that it failed to deliver innovations that an increasingly sophisticated market demanded. Also, Dell continues to face further pricing pressures as a result of the commoditization of the personal computer industry.

Clearly, "nothing is forever" when it comes to competitive advantages. Rapid changes in technology, globalization, and actions by rivals from within—as well as outside—the industry can quickly erode a firm's advantages. It is becoming increasingly important to recognize that the duration of competitive advantages is declining, especially in technology-intensive industries.[33] Even in industries which are normally viewed as "low tech," the increasing use of technology has suddenly made competitive advantages less sustainable.[34] Amazon's success in book retailing at the cost of Barnes & Noble, the former industry leader, as well as Blockbuster's struggle against Netflix in the video rental industry serve to illustrate how difficult it has become for industry leaders to sustain competitive advantages that they once thought would last forever.

What are the factors that determine whether a strategy is sustainable over a long period? To answer this question, we can draw on some of the strategic management concepts developed in the textbook already. To illustrate our points, we look at a company, Atlas Door, which created an innovative strategy in its industry and enjoyed superior performance for several years. Our discussion of Atlas Door draws on a *Harvard Business Review* article by George Stalk, Jr.[35] It was published in 1988, which provides us the benefit of hindsight to make our points about the sustainability of competitive advantage. After all, the strategic management concepts we have been addressing in the text are quite timeless in their relevance to practice. A brief summary follows:

Atlas Door: A Case Example   Atlas Door, a U.S.-based company, has enjoyed remarkable success. It has grown at an average annual rate of 15 percent in an industry with an overall annual growth rate of less than 5 percent. Recently, its pre-tax earnings were 20 percent of sales—about five times the industry average. Atlas is debt free and by its 10th year, the company achieved the number one competitive position in its industry.

Atlas produces industrial doors—a product with almost infinite variety, involving limitless choices of width and height and material. Given the importance of product variety, inventory is almost useless in meeting customer orders. Instead, most doors can be manufactured only after the order has been placed.

How Did Atlas Door Create Its Competitive Advantages in the Marketplace?   *First,* Atlas built just-in-time factories. Although simple in concept, they require extra tooling and machinery to reduce changeover times. Further, the manufacturing process must be organized by product and scheduled to start and complete with all of the parts available at the same time.

Second, Atlas reduced the time to receive and process an order. Traditionally, when customers, distributors, or salespeople called a door manufacturer with a request for price and delivery, they would have to wait more than one week for a response. In contrast, Atlas first streamlined and then automated its entire order-entry, engineering, pricing, and scheduling process. Atlas can price and schedule 95 percent of its incoming orders while the callers are still on the phone. It can quickly engineer new special orders because it has preserved on computer the design and production data of all previous special orders—which drastically reduces the amount of re-engineering necessary.

Third, Atlas tightly controlled logistics so that it always shipped only fully complete orders to construction sites. Orders require many components, and gathering all of them at the factory and making sure that they are with the correct order can be a time-consuming task. Of course, it is even more time consuming to get the correct parts to the job site after the order has been shipped! Atlas developed a system to track the parts in production and the purchased parts for each order. This helped to ensure the arrival of all necessary parts at the shipping dock in time—a just-in-time logistics operation.

The Result   When Atlas began operations, distributors had little interest in its product. The established distributors already carried the door line of a much larger competitor and saw little to no reason to switch suppliers except, perhaps, for a major price concession. But as a startup, Atlas was too small to compete on price alone. Instead, it positioned itself as the door supplier of last resort—the company people came to if the established supplier could not deliver or missed a key date.

Of course, with an average industry order fulfilment time of almost four months, some calls inevitably came to Atlas. And when it did get the call, Atlas commanded a higher price because of its faster delivery. Atlas not only got a higher price, but its effective integration of value-creating activities saved time and lowered costs. Thus, it enjoyed the best of both worlds.

In 10 short years, the company replaced the leading door suppliers in 80 percent of the distributors in the United States. With its strategic advantage, the company could be selective—becoming the supplier for only the strongest distributors.

Are Atlas Door's Competitive Advantages Sustainable?   We will now take both the "pro" and "con" position as to whether or not Atlas Door's competitive advantages will be sustainable for a very long time. It is important, of course, to appreciate that Atlas Door's strategy is unique in the industry, and the central issue becomes whether or not rivals will be able to easily imitate their strategy or create a viable substitute strategy.

"Pro" Position: The Strategy Is Highly Sustainable   Drawing on Chapter 2, it is quite evident that Atlas Door has attained a very favourable position vis-à-vis the five forces of industry competition. For example, it is able to exert power over its customers (distributors) because of its ability to deliver a quality product in a short period of time. Also, its dominance in the industry creates high entry barriers for new entrants. It is also quite evident that Atlas Door has been able to successfully integrate many value-chain activities within the firm—a fact that is integral to its just-in-time strategy. As noted in Chapter 3, such integration of activities provides a strong basis for sustainability because rivals would have difficulty in imitating this strategy due to causal ambiguity and path dependency (i.e., it is difficult to build up in a short period of time the resources that Atlas Door has accumulated and developed as well as disentangle the causes of what the valuable resources are or how they can be re-created). Further, as noted in Chapter 4, Atlas Door benefits from the social capital that they have developed with a wide range of key stakeholders (Chapter 1). These would include customers, employees, and managers (a reasonable assumption, given how smoothly the internal operations flow and their long-term relationships with distributors). It would be very difficult for a rival to replace Atlas Door as the supplier of last resort—given the reputation that it has earned over time for "coming through in the clutch" on time-sensitive orders. Finally, we can conclude that Atlas Door has created competitive advantages in both overall low cost and differentiation (Chapter 5). Its strong linkages among value-chain activities—a requirement for its just-in-time operations—not only lower costs but enable the company to respond quickly to customer orders. As noted earlier, many of the value-chain activities associated with a differentiation strategy reflect the element of speed or quick response.

"Con" Position: The Strategy Can Be Easily Imitated or Substituted   An argument could be made that much of Atlas Door's strategy relies on technologies that are rather well known and nonproprietary. Over time, a well-financed rival could imitate its strategy (via trial and error), achieve a tight integration among its value-creating activities, and implement a just-in-time manufacturing process. Because human capital is highly mobile (Chapter 4), a rival could hire away Atlas Door's talent, and these individuals could aid the rival in transferring Atlas Door's best practices. A new rival could also enter the industry with a large resource base, which might enable it to price its doors well under Atlas Door to build market share (but this would likely involve pricing below cost and would be a risky and nonsustainable strategy). Finally, a rival could potentially "leapfrog" the technologies and processes that Atlas Door has employed and achieve competitive superiority. With the benefit of hindsight, it could use the Internet to further speed up the linkages among its value-creating activities and the order entry processes with its customers and suppliers. (But even this could prove to be a temporary advantage, since rivals could relatively easily do the same thing.)

What Is the Verdict?   Both positions have merit. Over time, it would be rather easy to see how a new rival could achieve parity with Atlas Door—or even create a superior competitive position with new technologies or innovative processes. However, two factors make it extremely difficult for a rival to challenge Atlas Door in the short term: (1) the success that Atlas Door has enjoyed with its just-in-time scheduling and production systems—which involve the successful integration of many value-creating activities—helps the firm not only lower costs but also respond quickly to customer needs, and (2) the strong, positive reputational effects that it has earned with multiple stakeholders—especially its customers.

Finally, it is important to also understand that it is Atlas Door's ability to appropriate most of the profits generated by its competitive advantages that make it a highly successful company. As we discussed in Chapter 3, profits generated by resources can be appropriated by a number of stakeholders, such as suppliers, customers, employees, or rivals. The structure of the industrial door industry makes such value appropriation difficult: The suppliers provide generic parts, no one buyer is big enough to dictate prices, the tacit nature of the knowledge makes imitation difficult, and individual employees may be easily replaceable. Still, even with the advantages that Atlas Door enjoys, it needs to avoid becoming complacent or it may suffer the same fate as the dominant firm it replaced.

SUMMARY

How firms succeed and why some outperform others are two issues that go to the heart of strategic management. In this chapter, we identified three generic strategies and discussed how firms are able to not only attain advantages over competitors but also sustain such advantages over time. Why do some advantages become long lasting, whereas others are quickly imitated by competitors?

The generic strategies—overall cost leadership, differentiation, and focus—form the core of this chapter. We began with a brief description of each generic strategy and provided examples of firms that have successfully implemented these strategies. Successful generic strategies invariably enhance a firm's position vis-à-vis the five forces of its industry—a point that we stressed and illustrated with examples. However, there are pitfalls to each of the generic strategies. Thus, the sustainability of a firm's advantage is always challenged because of imitation or substitution by new or existing rivals. Such competition erodes a firm's advantage over time.

We also discussed the viability of combining (or integrating) the generic strategies of overall cost leadership and differentiation. When successful, such integration can enable a firm to enjoy superior performance and improve its competitive position. However, this is challenging, and managers must be aware of the potential downsides and risks associated with this kind of initiative.

Finally, we discussed the necessity and unique nature of evaluating strategic choices before these choices are put in place and acted on. We identified four tests and argued that a strategy should be internally consistent, be consonant with the environment, build and protect competitive advantages, and be feasible to deliver, given the organization's skills, capabilities, and resources.

Summary Review Questions

1. Explain why the concept of competitive advantage is central to the study of strategic management.
2. Briefly describe the three generic strategies: overall cost leadership, differentiation, and focus.
3. Explain the relationship between the three generic strategies and the five forces that determine the average profitability within an industry.
4. What are some of the ways in which a firm can attain a successful turnaround strategy?
5. Describe some of the pitfalls associated with each of the three generic strategies.
6. Can firms combine the generic strategies of overall cost leadership and differentiation? Why, or why not?

REFLECTING ON CAREER IMPLICATIONS

Types of Competitive Advantage: Always be aware of your organization's business level strategy. What do you do to help your firm either increase differentiation or lower costs? What are some ways that your role in the firm can help realize these outcomes?

Combining Sources of Competitive Advantage: Are you engaged in activities that simultaneously help your organization increase differentiation and reduce costs?

EXPERIENTIAL EXERCISE

1. Go online, and search newspaper articles and other publications on Lululemon, the sensational apparel retailer. Check also the company's own website. What are some examples of primary and support activities that enable Lululemon, a $1.8-billion integrated apparel firm, to achieve success? How do these activities contribute to Lululemon's business strategy? What would you characterize as Lululemon's business strategy? Why? What pitfalls could you envision that you would advise Lululemon's management to pay attention to for its future?
2. Consider some of Lululemon's main competitors, such as Under Armour or Nike retail. On the table below, create an additional column for each competitor and list their corresponding primary and support activities. What are the differences? How do they reflect and result in different competitive strategies?

Value-Chain Activity	How Does Lululemon Create Value for the Customer?
Primary:	
Inbound logistics	
Operations	
Outbound logistics	
Marketing and sales	
Service	
Support:	
Procurement	
Technology development	
Human resource management	
General administration	

3. Look for up-to-date information on Cott. Use the Internet and the company's own website. Has the company been able to sustain its business strategy? What elements have they had to change recently? How have they adjusted their business strategy?

APPLICATION QUESTIONS AND EXERCISES

1. Go to the Internet, and look up www.CanadianTire.ca. How has this firm been able to combine overall cost leadership and differentiation strategies?

2. Choose a firm in your local business community that you are familiar with. Is the firm successful in following its generic strategies? Why, or why not? What do you think are some of the challenges it faces in implementing these strategies in an effective manner?

3. Think of a firm that has attained a differentiation focus or cost focus strategy. Are its advantages sustainable? Why, or why not? (*Hint:* Consider its position vis-à-vis Porter's five forces.)

4. Think of a firm that has successfully achieved a combination strategy of overall cost leadership and differentiation. What can be learned from this example? Are these advantages sustainable? Why, or why not? (*Hint:* Consider its competitive position vis-à-vis Porter's five forces.)

ETHICS AND CORPORATE SOCIAL RESPONSIBILITY QUESTIONS

1. Can you think of a company that suffered ethical consequences as a result of an overemphasis on cost leadership or differentiation strategy? What do you think were the financial and non-financial implications?

2. Detractors of Walmart and other low-cost competitors argue that the processes that set them apart also create major social, environmental, and personal problems for thousands of communities, local businesses, and individuals. "The high cost of low price" and "the high price of low cost" are two positions taken by a range of skeptics in reaction to the proliferation of Walmarts and easyJets. On the Internet, search the two statements and their associated positions. What issues do they raise? Do you have an opinion?

CHAPTER SIX

CORPORATE-LEVEL STRATEGY: Creating Value through Diversification

LEARNING OBJECTIVES

After reading this chapter, you should have a good understanding of:

LO 1 Why firms engage in diversification efforts and how managers can create value through diversification initiatives.

LO 2 How corporations can use related diversification to achieve synergistic benefits through economies of scope and market power.

LO 3 How corporations can use unrelated diversification to achieve synergistic benefits through corporate restructuring, parenting, and portfolio analysis.

LO 4 The various means of engaging in diversification: mergers and acquisitions, strategic alliances and joint ventures, and internal development.

LO 5 The value of real options analysis (ROA) in making resource allocation decisions under conditions of high uncertainty.

LO 6 The reasons for the failure of many diversification efforts.

LO 7 How corporate-level strategies can be evaluated before they are implemented.

Stantec Inc. is a global design firm founded in Edmonton in 1954 as D. R. Stanley Associates.[1] Since its inception, the firm has experienced impressive growth and today, its 22,000 employees provide engineering, architecture, interior design, landscape architecture, surveying, environmental sciences, project management, and project economics services from Stantec's more than 400 locations worldwide. How did a small Albertan firm grow into a global force?

Stantec's growth did not come without challenges. Even though the first twenty-five years of its existence were good to the firm, the early 1980s saw the firm struggling to respond to the National Energy Program, a short-lived but intensive intervention by the federal government to support self-sufficiency targets for energy and fossil fuels. The effects of the policy were felt particularly hard in Alberta, and Stantec had to take measures to respond, which included reducing staff. At the same time, Stantec focused on business and geographic diversification–a strategy that has provided stability in other times of economic recession.

Fast forward ten years and the road to Stantec's eventual global success included some seminal milestones and a new president and CEO. Specifically, in 1998, Tony Franceschini, a former vice-president and current board member at Stantec, became president and CEO of a much smaller version of the firm, with only 2,000 employees in 40 locations. "Our vision is to grow the company into a 10,000 employee, billion-dollar firm by 2008," Franceschini pledged early in his tenure as CEO, setting a ten-year vision of growth and prosperity. While the company only narrowly missed their staffing goal–achieving a size of 8,000 employees–they did surpass their goals for revenue, hitting $1.4 billion by 2008 and continuing to increase that in the following years.

What elements of Franceschini's leadership supported this strong pivot to success? Many will argue that the answer lies in a clear, aggressive strategy of consistent, value-creating acquisitions.

Stantec's acquisition history since the early 2000s is impressive, boasting more than 100 successful acquisitions during the time period. In 2016, Stantec acquired MWH, a global professional services firm with a strong expertise in water resources infrastructure. With the acquisition of MWH, Stantec became a global leader in water and infrastructure markets while simultaneously allowing the firm to expand its geographic footprint and create additional service diversification opportunities through MWH's global presence.

Datacraft Co Ltd/Getty Images

Stantec's acquisition history since the early 2000s is impressive, boasting more than 90 successful acquisitions during this time period. Most recently, Stantec acquired MWH, a global professional services firm with a strong expertise in water resources infrastructure. There are clear synergies and strengths to the acquisition; notably, through pursuing related diversification, the acquisition will allow Stantec to expand their expertise into water and infrastructure markets, add water-related construction capabilities to their repertoire, and simultaneously allow the firm to enlarge its geographic footprint and create additional growth opportunities through MWH's global presence. Interestingly, the firm prioritizes these strengths and potential synergies over the financial benefits of the acquisition, which are equally strong.

Other recent acquisitions include Bury Inc. in March 2016, VOA Associates Inc. in May 2016, Edwards & Zuck in September 2016, Tkalcic Bengert Architecture in December 2016, and Inventrix Engineering Inc. in April 2017 among many, many others. With so many firms acquired, it would be reasonable to expect that some of the acquisitions would fail, yet the success of the firm would suggest that most deals go well.

Considering the rate by which most acquisitions fail (some studies peg the failure rate in excess of 75 percent), this growth and success rate are astounding. The secret to Stantec's successful acquisitions lies in their metrics for determining an acquisition target. Stantec's first concern when considering a potential acquisition target is cultural fit. If they do not believe that a potential target could be fully integrated into their team, then they do not continue with the acquisition process. By placing such importance on culture and fit with the team, Stantec has developed a strong competence in successful acquisitions.

After acquiring a firm, Stantec's focus is on leadership engagement. Stantec believes that the best method of fully integrating acquisition targets is through engaging the leaders at the acquisition target to help them see the value in merging the companies so that their enthusiasm will trickle down to the staff. With the MWH acquisition, this was Stantec's central approach. They tied up multiple members of the MWH leadership team with employment agreements to ensure that they would be keeping the talent at the firm and improving the ease of the acquisition. This two-step process of focusing on cultural fit and leadership engagement ensures that Stantec's aggressive acquisition strategy will continue to be successful long into the future. ∎

What criteria should managers consider as they contemplate opportunities for growth? Why do some diversification efforts pay off and others produce extremely disappointing results? Chapter 5 focused on business-level strategy—that is, how to achieve sustainable advantages in a given business or product market. This chapter addresses corporate-level strategy—that is, the choice of businesses a corporation should compete in and how those businesses should be managed to jointly create more value than if they were free-standing units. Getting answers to this general question requires us to look at the various types of diversification that can potentially be considered (related and unrelated diversification), the rationale for contemplating each type of diversification, and the means to achieve diversification.

Michael Porter has said that corporate strategy is what makes the corporate whole add up to more than the sum of its business unit parts. It is not just about finding new spaces to compete in but integrating these new value-creating activities in a way that truly transforms the corporation. Although we discuss business-level and corporate-level strategies in separate chapters in this text, they are quite intimately related and interdependent. Managers need to be mindful of these connections and always move between levels as they formulate strategy.

LO 1 MAKING DIVERSIFICATION WORK: AN OVERVIEW

Diversification initiatives—whether through mergers and acquisitions, strategic alliances and joint ventures, or internal development—must be justified by the creation of value for shareholders and other important stakeholders. Firms may diversify for a host of reasons, including the desire to bring new stakeholders into the firm's competitive landscape or exploit opportunities for value creation that emerge through the successful management of existing stakeholder relationships.

Interestingly, however, evidence that a diversification initiative was actually successful in creating new value is not always readily found. For example, looking at a classic economic measure of value creation, acquiring firms typically pay high premiums to capture a target. In contrast, individuals, as private investors, can diversify their own portfolios of stocks. Moreover, with the advent of the intensely competitive online brokerage industry, investors can acquire hundreds of shares for a transaction fee of as little as $10, a far cry from the 30 to 40 percent (or higher) premiums that corporations typically must pay to acquire companies.[2]

Given the seemingly high inherent downside risks and uncertainties, it might be reasonable to ask why companies should even bother with diversification initiatives. The answer, in a word, is *synergy* (derived from the Greek word *synergos,* which means "working together").[3] Synergy can be achieved in many different ways, and it is not always immediately obvious when it has been achieved. In fact, as we discussed earlier in this book, competitive advantage emerges from inimitable resources born of complexity and causal ambiguity. The most advantageous synergies are often those that emerge organically. But there are still a few elements that managers hoping to find these synergies need to think about.

First, a firm may diversify into *related* businesses. Here, the primary potential benefits to be derived come from sharing intangible resources (e.g., sales forces, brand names, technologies, or even a unique culture) and tangible resources (e.g., production facilities, distribution channels) across multiple businesses that can use the same resources and spread their costs over a larger revenue base. Maple Leaf Foods has built a successful corporation in processed meats, prepared foods, and baked goods—all businesses benefiting from a common sales and distribution network. Additionally, firms can enhance their market power by increasing dominance in a market, becoming a more critical supplier to their customers, or by increasing their hold on the business through vertical integration. It should be noted that firms can simultaneously enjoy multiple benefits from their related diversification moves, including shared costs and increased market power.

Second, a corporation may diversify into *unrelated* businesses. In these instances, the primary potential benefits derive largely from value created by the corporate office. Examples include leveraging some of the support activities in the value chain, such as information systems or human resource practices. Onex Corporation, a $22-billion conglomerate based in Toronto, has followed a successful strategy of unrelated diversification.[4] There are few similarities in the products it makes or the industries in which it competes. Its businesses include Sky Chefs, an airline catering business with operations across the world; plants in Kansas and Oklahoma that make wings, fuselages, and struts for Boeing jets; Emergency Medical Services, a U.S. ambulance and emergency room service company; Celestica, an electronics manufacturer with facilities around the world; Husky, one of the world's largest injection moulding equipment manufacturers; J. L. French Automotive, an auto parts supplier for the major automobile manufacturers; and a fragrance manufacturer based in New Jersey. Moreover, through the personal investments of CEO Gerry Schwartz it controls Indigo Books and Music, the parent company of booksellers Indigo, Chapters, and Coles, along with a small stake in Vincour, a winery with holdings in North America and Australia. The corporate office adds value through such activities as planning, performance evaluation, and budgeting systems.

It is important to note that the benefits derived from related and unrelated relationships are not mutually exclusive. Many firms that diversify into related areas benefit from the information technology expertise in the corporate office, and firms diversifying into unrelated areas often benefit from the "best practices" of sister businesses, even though their products, markets, and technologies may differ dramatically.

LO 2 RELATED DIVERSIFICATION: ECONOMIES OF SCOPE AND REVENUE ENHANCEMENT

Related diversification enables a firm to benefit from relationships across different businesses within the diversified corporation by leveraging core competencies and sharing activities (e.g., production facilities and distribution facilities). This enables a corporation to benefit from *economies of scope.* Economies of scope are cost savings from leveraging core competencies, sharing resources, or sharing related activities among businesses within the corporation. A firm can also enjoy greater revenues if two businesses, combined, attain higher levels of sales than either company could attain independently.

For example, a sporting goods store may build or acquire other stores in different locations, cities, or even countries. This enables it to leverage, or reuse, many of its key resources, such as reputation, expert staff and management skills, or efficient purchasing operations, which constitute the basis of its competitive advantage(s), over a larger number of stores.[5]

Leveraging Core Competencies

The concept of core competencies can be illustrated by the imagery of the diversified corporation as a tree.[6] The trunk and major limbs represent core products; the smaller branches are business units; and the leaves, flowers, and fruit are end products. The core competencies are represented by the root system, which provides nourishment, sustenance, and stability to the whole tree. Managers often misread the strength of competitors by looking only at their end products, just as one can fail to appreciate the strength of a tree by looking only at its leaves or counting how many flowers have bloomed. Core competencies may also be viewed as the "glue" that binds existing businesses together or as the engine that drives new business growth.

Core competencies reflect the collective learning in organizations—how to coordinate diverse production skills, integrate multiple streams of technologies, and market and merchandise diverse products and services. The theoretical knowledge necessary to put a radio on a chip does not in itself assure a company of the skill needed to produce a miniature radio approximately the size of a business card. To accomplish this, Casio, a giant electronic-products producer, must synthesize know-how in miniaturization, microprocessor design, material science, and ultra-thin precision castings. These are the same skills that it applies in its miniature card calculators, pocket TVs, and digital watches.

For a core competence to create value and provide a viable basis for synergy among the businesses in a corporation, it must meet three criteria:[7]

1. ***The core competence must enhance competitive advantage(s) by creating superior customer value.*** It must enable the business to develop strengths relative to the competition. Every value-chain activity has the potential to provide a viable basis for building on a core competence. At Gillette, for example, scientists developed the Mach 3 and Sensor Excel after the introduction of the tremendously successful Sensor System and through a thorough understanding of several phenomena that underlie shaving. These include the physiology of facial hair and skin, the metallurgy of blade strength and sharpness, the dynamics of a cartridge moving across skin, and the physics of a razor blade severing hair. These innovations are possible only with an understanding of such phenomena and the ability to combine technologies into innovative products. Customers have consistently been willing to pay more for such technologically differentiated products.

2. ***Different businesses in the corporation must be similar in at least one important way related to the core competence.*** It is not essential that the products or services themselves be similar. Rather, at least one element in the value chain must require similar skills in creating competitive advantage if the corporation is to capitalize on its core competence. At first glance, one might think that motorcycles, clothes, and restaurants don't have anything in common. But at Harley-Davidson, they do.[8] Harley-Davidson has capitalized on its exceptionally strong brand image as well as its merchandising and licensing skills to sell accessories, clothing, and toys; it has also licensed the Harley-Davidson Café in New York City. Loblaw Companies Ltd. operates a range of food stores under the banners of Provigo, No Frills, Fortinos, Loblaws, and Zehrs. Even though each caters to a different customer segment, they all rely on an intimate knowledge of the Canadian consumer and the merchandising skills of the parent company. Moreover, Loblaw has developed the very successful private label line of President's Choice, which reflects much of the corporation's knowledge about consumer tastes. Finally, Loblaw uses the enhanced negotiating power that arises from its larger scale to extract preferential terms from its suppliers.

3. ***The core competence must be difficult for competitors to imitate or find substitutes for.*** As we discussed in Chapter 5, competitive advantages will not be sustainable if the competition can easily imitate or substitute them. Similarly, if the skills associated with a firm's core competencies are easily imitated or replicated, they are not a sound basis for sustainable advantages. Consider Sharp Corporation, a $34 billion consumer electronics giant.[9] It has a set of specialized core competencies in optoelectronics technologies that are difficult to replicate and that contribute to its competitive advantages in its core businesses.

Its most successful technology has been liquid crystal displays (LCDs), which are critical components in nearly all of Sharp's products. Its expertise in this technology enabled Sharp to succeed in video cassette recorders (VCRs), with its innovative LCD viewfinder, and led to the creation of its Wizard, a personal electronic organizer that was innovative for its time.

Consider Amazon's retailing operations. To dominate the online book industry, Amazon developed strong competencies in Internet retailing, website infrastructure, warehousing, and order fulfilment. It used these competencies along with its brand name to expand into a range of online retail businesses. Competitors in these other market areas have had great difficulty imitating Amazon's competencies, and many have simply stopped trying. Instead, they have partnered with Amazon and contracted with Amazon to provide these services for them.[10]

Strategy Spotlight 6.1 provides the insights of Steve Jobs, the late, legendary CEO of Apple, on the importance of a firm's core competencies and how they form the basis for venturing into new business lines.

6.1 STRATEGY SPOTLIGHT

Steve Jobs Discusses Apple's Core Competence

"One of our biggest insights, years ago, was that we didn't want to get into any business where we didn't own or control the primary technology, because you'll get your head handed to you. We realized that for almost all future consumer electronics, the primary technology was going to be software. And we were pretty good at software. We could do the operating system software. We could write applications like iTunes on the Mac or even PC. We could write the software in the device, like you might put in an iPod or an iPhone. And we could write the back-end software that runs on a cloud, like iTunes. So we could write all these different kinds of software and make it work seamlessly. And you ask yourself: What other companies can do that? It's a pretty short list."

Sources: A. Fisher, "America's Most Admired Companies," *Fortune*, March 17, 2008, p. 74.

Sharing Activities

As we saw above, leveraging core competencies involves transferring accumulated skills and expertise across business units in a corporation. When carried out effectively, this leads to advantages that can become quite sustainable over time. Corporations can also achieve synergy by sharing activities across their business units. These include value-creating activities, such as common manufacturing facilities, distribution channels, and sales forces. Sharing activities can potentially provide two primary payoffs: cost savings and revenue enhancements.

Deriving Cost Savings through Sharing Activities

Typically, this is the most common type of synergy and the easiest to estimate. Peter Shaw, former head of mergers and acquisitions at ICI, the British chemical and pharmaceutical company (taken over by AkzoNobel in 2008), referred to cost savings as "hard synergies" and contended that the level of certainty of their achievement is quite high. Cost savings come from many sources, including elimination of jobs, facilities, and related expenses that are no longer required when functions are consolidated, or from economies of scale in purchasing. Cost savings are generally highest when one company acquires another from the same industry in the same country. Rogers Wireless was able to obtain immediate savings from its acquisition of Microcell through consolidation of back office operations and technical support as well as through higher capacity utilization of its infrastructure. At the same time, the clients of Fido, Microcell's main retail brand name, instantly gained broader market coverage and better reception for their phones. Of course, while efficiencies are found through consolidation, eliminating jobs has also an impact on the culture of the corporation, which is equally important in assuring success from an acquisition. Non-economic measures of value creation must always be considered alongside dollar benefits.

Sharing activities inevitably entails costs, such as greater coordination, that the benefits must outweigh. Even more important is the need to compromise the design or performance of an activity so that it can be shared. For example, a salesperson handling the products of two business units must operate in a way that is usually not what either unit would prescribe were it independent. If the compromise erodes the unit's effectiveness, then sharing may reduce rather than enhance competitive advantage.

Enhancing Revenue and Differentiation through Sharing Activities

Often, two businesses may achieve a higher level of sales growth together than either one could on its own. Shortly after Gillette acquired Duracell it confirmed its expectation that selling Duracell batteries through Gillette's existing channels for personal care products would increase sales, particularly internationally. Gillette sold Duracell products in 25 new markets in the first year after the acquisition and substantially increased sales in established international markets. In a similar vein, a target company's distribution channel can be used to improve the sales of an acquiring company's product. This was the case when Gillette acquired Parker Pen. Gillette estimated that it could gain an additional $25 million in sales of its own Waterman pens by taking advantage of Parker's distribution channels.

Firms can also enhance the effectiveness of their differentiation strategies by means of sharing activities among business units. A shared order-processing system, for example, may permit new features and services that a buyer will value. Also, sharing can reduce the cost of differentiation. For instance, a shared service network may make more advanced, remote service technology economically feasible. To illustrate the potential for enhanced differentiation through sharing, consider the $7 billion VF Corporation—producer of such well-known brands as Lee, Wrangler, Vanity Fair, and Jantzen. VF's acquisition of Nutmeg Industries and H. H. Cutler provided it with several large customers that it did not have before, increasing its plant utilization and productivity. But more importantly, Nutmeg designs and makes licensed apparel for sports teams and organizations, and Cutler manufactures licensed brand-name children's apparel, including Walt Disney kids' wear. Such brand labelling enhances the differentiation of VF's apparel products. According to former VF president Mackey McDonald, "What we're doing is looking at value-added knitwear, taking our basic fleece from Basset-Walker (one of its divisions), embellishing it through Cutler and Nutmeg, and selling it as a value-added product." Additionally, Cutler's advanced high-speed printing technologies will enable VF to be more proactive in anticipating trends in the fashion-driven fleece market. Claims McDonald, "Rather than printing first and then trying to guess what the customer wants, we can see what's happening in the marketplace and then print it up."[11]

On a cautionary note, managers must keep in mind that sharing activities among businesses in a corporation can have a negative effect on a given business's differentiation. For example, following the merger of Chrysler and Daimler-Benz, many consumers could have lowered their perceptions of Mercedes's quality and prestige if they felt that common production components and processes were being used across the two divisions. Mercedes eventually divested Chrysler, in no small measure because it was not able to create incremental value through the sharing of any activities. Strategy Spotlight 6.2 discusses how Canadian Tire, the storied retailer, leverages its core competencies and shared activities to create multiple revenue streams through new acquisitions.

6.2 STRATEGY SPOTLIGHT

Canadian Tire: Growing to Stay on Top

Canadian Tire has expanded from its origins as a well-known retailer of automotive supplies to a broadly diversified mix of businesses under three very distinct subsidiaries: FGL Sports Ltd, Mark's, and Canadian Tire Financial Services. FGL Sports Ltd. owns brands such as Sport Chek, a chain of reputable sporting goods stores; Mark's sells fashionable clothing, uniforms, and work attire in some 380 stores across the country; and Canadian Tire Financial Services offers branded credit cards as well as lines of credit and personal loans. The activities of the three subsidiaries complement the flagship retail operations.

Ninety percent of Canadians are said to live within 15 minutes of one of Canadian Tire's 490 stores. Each store is independently owned by an associate dealer in an arrangement that requires commitment from dealers and gives them the autonomy to run their own stores the best they can and the right to veto decisions made by the centre that would not work in their local community.

While Canadian Tire enjoys enviable brand recognition and is considered a Canadian retail icon, it has also been under enormous pressure to remain competitive in the new retail environment. The company is struggling to figure out what it needs to do to remain an industry leader. In response to Amazon and other online retailers, Canadian Tire has been slow to roll out a new e-commerce website and to support the development of a stand-out digital retail strategy. Up against stiff competition in Home Depot and Walmart, the company still prides itself on its 30-million square feet of retail space and the fact that its printed flyers are the most read in Canada. These are laudable points of differentiation in the old competitive landscape, yet the two competitive giants continue to erode Canadian Tire's market share.

Without a doubt, Canadian Tire's diversification efforts have successfully strengthened the firm through a host of related business lines while reinforcing its core strategic strengths. But in the new retail landscape, will this be enough to assure that they continue to stay ahead of the competition?

Sources: Anonymous, Canada's Changing Retail Market, Industry Canada, 2 Aug 2013; Anonymous, Canadian Tire Corporation, Ltd, Reference for Business, 2014; Anonymous, Canadian Brands Top 40, Canadian Business, 2014; Nguyen, Linda, Canadian Tire to Launch E-Commerce Site, CTV News, 7 Nov. 2013; Offman, Craig, How to fix Canadian Tire, The Globe and Mail, 23 June 2011; the company's financial statements and website.

Market Power

Working together with similar businesses or affiliation to a strong parent can strengthen an organization's bargaining position in relation to suppliers and customers as well as enhance its position vis-à-vis competitors. Compare, for example, the position of an independent food manufacturer with the same business within Nestlé. Being part of Nestlé Corporation provides a business with significant clout—greater bargaining power with suppliers and customers—since it is part of a firm that makes large purchases from suppliers and provides a wide variety of products to its customers. Access to the parent's deep pockets increases the business's strength relative to rivals. Further, the Nestlé unit enjoys greater protection from substitutes and new entrants. Not only would rivals perceive the unit as a more formidable opponent, but the unit's association with Nestlé would also provide greater visibility and an improved image.

Consolidating an industry can also increase a firm's market power. This has been a trend in the multimedia industry.[12] Several blockbuster deals have been completed, most notably the merger of Time Warner Inc. with America Online Inc. In Canada, Globe media brought together the assets of a national newspaper (*The Globe and Mail*) and a television network (CTV) under the joint ownership of the world's largest information company (The Thomson Corporation, based in Toronto), and the country's largest telephone company (BCE, based in Montreal). Its competitor, CanWest, of Winnipeg, owns its own newspapers (including *National Post,* Montreal's *The Gazette,* and *The Vancouver Sun*), a television network (Global), and Canadian radio stations along with radio and television stations in Australia and New Zealand. All of these strategic moves have a common goal: to control and leverage as many news and entertainment channels as possible. The enhanced scale and scope of each company were seen as critical to competing more effectively and growing more rapidly in two consolidating industries—newspaper and television broadcasting. The combined company would increase its power by providing a "one-stop shop" for advertisers desiring to reach consumers through multiple media in enormous markets, such as New York, Los Angeles, Toronto, London, and Sydney. It would also increase its power relative to its suppliers. A company's enhanced size could be expected to lead to increased efficiencies when purchasing newsprint and other commodities.[13]

When acquiring related businesses, a firm's potential for pooled negotiating power vis-à-vis its customers and suppliers can be very enticing. However, managers must carefully evaluate how the combined businesses may affect relationships with actual and potential customers, suppliers, and competitors. For example, when PepsiCo diversified into the fast-food industry with its acquisitions of KFC, Taco Bell, and Pizza Hut (since spun off as Tricon Inc. and now part of Yum! Brands), it clearly benefited from its position over these units that served as a captive market for its soft drink products. However, some of its customers, such as McDonald's, have since refused to consider PepsiCo as a supplier of their own soft drink needs because of competition with Pepsi's divisions in the fast food industry. Simply put, McDonald's did not want to patronize the enemy! Thus, although acquiring related businesses can enhance a corporation's bargaining power, it must be aware of the potential for retaliation by others.

It is also important to recognize that managers have limits on their ability to use market power for diversification because government regulations can sometimes restrict the ability of a business to gain very large shares of a particular market.

When General Electric (GE) announced a $41-billion bid for Honeywell, the European Union stepped in. GE's market clout would have expanded significantly as a result of the deal, with GE supplying over one-half the parts needed to build several aircraft engines. The commission's concern, causing it to reject the acquisition, was that GE could use its increased market power to dominate the aircraft engine parts market and edge out competitors.[14] When Air Canada acquired Canadian Airlines, the federal government imposed numerous restrictions on routes, fares, and potential layoffs. These restrictions were intended to ensure that the overwhelming power, which was to be accumulated under one firm, would not be abused, and that the airline would continue to serve the Canadian public with competitive fares while retaining most of its employees. Although managers need to be aware of the strategic advantages of market power, they must, at the same time, be aware of regulations and legislation. Generally, it is most advantageous for a firm to deal with these issues before a regulatory or government body steps in. This is another example where non-economic measures of value and an understanding of social norms become critical. Strategy Spotlight 6.3 discusses how 3M's actions to increase its market power led to a successful lawsuit by a much smaller Canadian competitor.

6.3 STRATEGY SPOTLIGHT

How 3M's Efforts to Increase Market Power Backfired

In the spring and summer of 2006, 3M found itself in court facing three class-action lawsuits launched by consumers and retailers of transparent and invisible adhesive tape, generally known as "Scotch tape," 3M's brand. The suits alleged that 3M had unlawfully bullied its way into a monopoly position in the adhesive tape market and that, as a result, consumers had been deprived of their rightful amount of choice and had often paid up to 40 percent more for the tape. LePage's Inc., of North York, Ontario, the only significant competitor in the home and office adhesive tape market, was behind the suits. LePage's argued that 3M's practice of "bundled rebates" violated the legislation that limited monopoly power. 3M's program offered significant rebates, sometimes in the millions of dollars, to retailers as a reward for selling targeted amounts of six product lines. LePage's claimed that such selling targets were so large that retailers could only meet them by excluding competing products from store shelves. For example, LePage's argued that Kmart, which had constituted 10 percent of LePage's sales, dropped the account when 3M started offering the discount chain $1 million in rebates in return for selling more than $15 million worth of 3M products in a year.

The courts concluded that rebate bundling, even if above cost, may exclude equally efficient competitors from offering products: "They may foreclose portions of the market to a potential competitor who does not manufacture an equally diverse group of products and who therefore cannot make a comparable offer." The bundled rebates were judged to be an exploitation of 3M's monopoly power.

Sources: D. Bush & B. D. Gelb, "When Marketing Practices Raise Antitrust Concerns," *MIT Sloan Management Review,* 46(4), 2005, pp. 73–81; C. Campbell, "Tale of the Tape," *Canadian Business,* April 24, 2006, pp. 39–40; and B. Bergstrom, "$68M Jury Award Upheld against 3M in Antitrust Case," *The Associated Press,* March 26, 2003.

Vertical Integration

Vertical integration represents an expansion or extension of the firm by integrating preceding or successive productive processes.[15] That is, the firm incorporates more processes toward the original source of raw materials (backward integration) or toward the ultimate consumer (forward integration). For example, an automobile manufacturer might supply its own parts or make its own engines to secure sources of supply. Or it might control its own system of dealerships to ensure retail outlets for its products. Similarly, an oil refinery might secure land leases and develop its own drilling capacity to ensure a constant supply of crude oil. Or it could expand into retail operations by owning or licensing gasoline stations to guarantee customers for its petroleum products.

Vertical integration can be a viable strategy for many firms. Strategy Spotlight 6.4 discusses Canfor Corporation, a significant player in the international forest products sector. It has attained a dominant position in the industry via a strategy of vertical integration. Canfor has successfully implemented strategies of both forward and backward integration. Similarly, Dominion Diamond Corporation (formerly Aber Diamond Corporation), part owner of the Diavik diamond mine in the Northwest Territories, acquired Harry Winston Inc., an upscale chain of American-based jewellery stores, and saw immediate benefits in enhanced revenues and profits.[16]

6.4 STRATEGY SPOTLIGHT

Vertical Integration at Canfor

Canfor Corporation, based in Vancouver, British Columbia, is the world's largest SPF (spruce-pine-fir) lumber producer and a global leader in the forest products industry. Early in its corporate development, Canfor made the strategic choice to diversify into most aspects of the industry and expand both across stages of the value chain and across markets. Its senior management was convinced that such moves would allow it to better control its destiny and shield the company from the cyclical nature of various parts of the business. It has followed a very successful strategy of vertical integration pursuing both backward and forward integration through internal development as well as through acquisitions. Canfor recognized that prudent forest management is as critical to the economics of the business as building strong relationships with the communities where the corporation operates.

Today, it owns or controls vast amounts of timberland that provide the raw materials for its downstream businesses and a valuable supply of fibre. At the same time, it has pursued sustainable forest management certifications in all its woodlands operations and has built partnerships with local Indigenous communities. Further upstream, Canfor operates nurseries and seed orchards to feed those timberlands with new stock. At the other end of its business, it has a marketing and distribution arm that sells high-performance packaging, craft, and other specialty papers to markets around the world. In between, Canfor has built and acquired sawmills, panel and plywood production facilities, pulp and paper mills, and remanufacturing operations. Canfor sees its vertical and horizontal integration strategy as an effective response to the realities of the global forestry industry as it faces increasingly larger customers who also operate globally, are getting more dominant, and are exerting more pressure on their suppliers.

Sources: W. Stueck, "Confident Canfor Has an Eye for Acquisitions," *The Globe and Mail,* May 4, 2007, p. B5; Canfor Corporation Annual Reports; and www.canfor.com.

Benefits and Risks of Vertical Integration

Although vertical integration is a means for an organization to reduce its dependence on suppliers or its channels of distribution to end users, it represents a major decision that an organization must carefully consider. The benefits associated with vertical integration—backward or forward—must be carefully weighed against the risks.

The *benefits* of vertical integration include (1) a secure source of raw materials or distribution channels that cannot be "held hostage" to external markets where costs can fluctuate over time, (2) protection and control over assets and services required to produce and deliver valuable products and services, (3) access to new business opportunities and new forms of technologies, and (4) improved coordination of activities across the value chain.

The *risks* of vertical integration include (1) the costs associated with increased overhead and capital expenditures to provide facilities, raw material inputs, and distribution channels inside the organization; (2) a loss of flexibility resulting from the inability to respond quickly to changes in the external environment, as the huge investments in vertical integration activities are generally not easily deployed elsewhere; (3) problems associated with unbalanced capacities or unfilled demand along the value chain; and (4) additional administrative costs associated with managing a more complex set of activities.

In making decisions about vertical integration, four questions should be considered:[17]

1. ***Is the value provided by present suppliers and distributors satisfactory?*** If the performance of organizations in the vertical chain—both suppliers and distributors—is satisfactory, it may not, in general, be appropriate for the firm to perform these activities. Firms in the athletic footwear industry, such as Nike and Reebok, have traditionally outsourced the manufacture of their shoes to such countries as China and Indonesia, where labour costs are low. Since the strengths of these companies are typically in design and marketing, it would be advisable for them to continue to outsource production operations and focus on where they can add the most value.

2. ***Are there activities in the industry value chain presently being outsourced or performed independently by others that are a viable source of future profits?*** Even if a firm is outsourcing value-chain activities to companies that are doing a credible job, it may be missing out on substantial profit opportunities. As an illustration, consider the automobile industry's profit pool. As noted in Chapter 5, there has been much more potential profit in many downstream activities (e.g., leasing, warranty, insurance, and service) than in the manufacture of automobiles. Not surprisingly, carmakers, such as Ford and General Motors, have undertaken forward integration strategies to become bigger players in these high-profit activities.

3. ***Is there relative stability in the demand for the organization's products?*** High demand or sales volatility would not be conducive to a vertical integration strategy. Substantial fixed costs in plant and equipment, as well as operating costs that typically accompany vertical integration, can strain resources in times of high demand and result in unused capacity in times of low demand. The cycles of "boom and bust" in the automobile industry are a key reason why the manufacturers have increased the level of outsourcing in recent years.

4. ***Is there a source of core competence in the activity that is considered for outsourcing or vertical integration?*** Unlike most other retailers, Walmart has fully integrated all the upstream logistics of the handling, warehousing, transportation, and distribution of the goods it sells in all its stores. It is no wonder that those activities are what sets Walmart apart from the competition and are the greatest contributors to its success. Similarly, Intel both designs and manufactures all its microchips. Numerous writers have cautioned firms to be mindful of outsourcing their core competencies and thus, in effect, helping to establish their own formidable competitors.[18]

Analyzing Vertical Integration: The Transaction Cost Perspective

Another approach that has proven very useful in understanding vertical integration is the *transaction cost perspective.*[19] According to this perspective, every market transaction involves some *transaction costs.* First, a decision to purchase an input from an outside source leads to *search* costs (i.e., the cost to find where it is available, the level of quality, etc.). Second, there are costs associated with *negotiating.* Third, a *contract* needs to be written, spelling out future possible contingencies. Fourth, parties in a contract have to *monitor* each other. Finally, if a party does not comply with the terms of the contract, there are *enforcement* costs. Many of these transaction costs can be avoided by internalizing the activity—in other words, by producing the input in-house.

A related problem with purchasing a specialized input from outside is the issue of *transaction-specific investments.* For example, when an automobile company needs an input specifically designed for a particular car model, its supplier may be unwilling to make the investments in plant and machinery necessary to produce that component for two reasons. First, the investment may take many years to recover, but there is no guarantee the automobile company will continue to buy from them after the contract expires, typically in one or two years. Second, once the investment is made, the supplier has no bargaining power; that is, the automobile company knows that the supplier has no option but to supply at ever-lower prices because the investments were so specific that they cannot be used to produce alternative products. Given the reluctance of the supplier to undertake the investments, vertical integration may be the only option.

Finally, vertical integration also gives rise to *administrative costs*. Coordinating different stages of the value chain now internalized within the firm causes administrative costs to go up. Decisions about vertical integration are, therefore, based on a comparison of transaction costs and administrative costs. If transaction costs are lower than administrative costs, it is best to resort to market transactions and avoid vertical integration. For example, McDonald's may be the world's biggest buyer of beef, but it does not raise cattle. The market for beef has low transaction costs and requires no transaction-specific investments. Conversely, if transaction costs are higher than administrative costs, vertical integration becomes an attractive strategy. Most automobile manufacturers produce their own engines because the market for engines involves high transaction costs and transaction-specific investments.

Vertical Integration: Further Considerations

As many companies would attest, successfully executing strategies of vertical integration can be very difficult. For example, Unocal, a major petroleum refiner that once owned retail gas stations, was slow to capture the potential grocery and merchandise side business that might have resulted from customer traffic to its service stations. Unocal lacked the competencies to develop a separate retail organization and culture. The company eventually sold the assets and brand to Tosco (now part of ConocoPhillips). Eli Lilly, the pharmaceutical firm, tried to achieve forward integration by acquiring a pharmaceutical mail-order business in 1994, but it was unsuccessful in increasing market share because it failed to integrate its operations. Two years later, Lilly wrote off the venture.

Managers must carefully consider the impact that vertical integration may have on existing and future customers, suppliers, and competitors. After Lockheed Martin, a dominant defence contractor, acquired Loral Corporation, an electronics supplier, for $9.1 billion, it had an unpleasant surprise. Loral, as a captive supplier of Lockheed, is now perceived and treated as a competitor by many of its previous customers. McDonnell Douglas (MD), for example, announced that it would switch its business from Loral to other suppliers of electronic systems, such as Litton Industries or Raytheon. Thus, before Lockheed Martin can realize any net synergies from this acquisition, it must make up for the substantial lost business resulting from MD's (now part of Boeing) decision to switch suppliers.

(LO 3) UNRELATED DIVERSIFICATION: FINANCIAL SYNERGIES AND PARENTING

With unrelated diversification, potential benefits can be gained from the creation of synergies from the interaction of the corporate office with the individual business units. There are two main sources of such synergies. First, the corporate office can contribute to "parenting" and restructuring of (often acquired) businesses. Second, the corporate office can add value by viewing the entire corporation as a family or "portfolio" of businesses and allocating resources to optimize corporate goals of profitability, cash flow, and growth. Additionally, the corporate office enhances value by establishing appropriate human resource practices and financial controls for each of its business units.

Corporate Parenting and Restructuring

So far, we have discussed how corporations can add value through related diversification by exploring sources of synergy *across* business units. In this section, we discuss how value can be created *within* business units as a result of the expertise and support provided by the corporate office.

Parenting

The positive contributions of the corporate office have been referred to as the *parenting advantage.*[20] Many firms have successfully diversified their holdings without strong evidence of the more traditional sources of synergy (i.e., across business units). Diversified public corporations, such as Power Corporation, and Onex, and leveraged buyout firms, such as Kohlberg, Kravis, Roberts & Company, and Clayton, Dublilier & Rice, are a few examples.[21] These parent companies create value through management expertise. How? They improve plans and budgets and provide especially competent central functions, such as legal, financial, human resource management, procurement, and the like. They also help their subsidiaries make wise choices in their own acquisitions, divestitures, and new internal development decisions. Such contributions often help business units substantially increase their revenues and profits.

Consider Onex Corporation's record. It acquired Sky Chefs from American Airlines in 1984 for $99 million. Onex took over the airline catering business that, at the time, had only one captive customer; it established high quality standards, tightened operations, introduced management incentives, and started attracting outside customers. By the time Onex sold Sky Chefs to Lufthansa for $1.8 billion in 2001, it boasted over 200 airlines among other commercial customers. In 1996, Onex acquired Celestica, one of IBM's manufacturing divisions, for $262 million. It introduced closely monitored and controlled management processes throughout the operations and pushed to expand the customer base. The concerted efforts yielded spectacular results for the company; even after the technology meltdown of 2000 and the financial crisis of 2008, Celestica's value was estimated at $2 billion. In 2005, Onex purchased three of Boeing's component manufacturing facilities, at the equivalent of $3.33 per share, or approximately $375 million; in early 2011, it sold part of its holdings for $24.49 per share, valuing its holdings at $2.5 billion, and demonstrating again its shrewd investment skills and disciplined management intervention to yield long-term results.[22]

Restructuring

Restructuring is another means by which the corporate office can add substantial value to a business.[23] Here, the corporate office tries to find either poorly performing firms with unrealized potential or firms in industries on the threshold of significant, positive changes. The parent intervenes, often selling off parts of the business, changing the management, reducing payroll and unnecessary sources of expenses, revising strategies, and infusing the company with new technologies, processes, reward systems, and so forth. When the restructuring is complete, the firm can be either sold to monetize the added value or kept so that the corporate family can enjoy the financial and competitive benefits of enhanced performance.[24]

For the restructuring strategy to work, the corporate management must have the insight to detect undervalued companies (otherwise the cost of acquisition would be too high) or businesses competing in industries with a high potential for transformation.[25] Additionally, of course, management must have the requisite skills and resources to turn the businesses around, even if they may be in new and unfamiliar industries.

Restructuring can involve changes in assets, capital structure, or management.

- *Asset restructuring* involves the sale of unproductive assets or even whole lines of businesses that are peripheral. In some cases, it may involve acquisitions that strengthen the core business.

- *Capital restructuring* involves changing the debt–equity mix, or the mix between different classes of debt and equity. Although the substitution of equity with debt is more common in buyout situations, occasionally the parent may provide additional equity capital.

- *Management restructuring* typically involves changes in the composition of the top management team, organizational structure, and reporting relationships. Tight financial control, rewards based strictly on meeting short-term to medium-term performance goals, and reduction in the number of middle-level managers are common steps in management restructuring. In some cases, parental intervention may even result in changes in strategy as well as in infusion of new technologies and processes.

KKR, a venerable New York private equity firm, acquired Shoppers Drug Mart in 2000 for $2.7 billion and worked with management to design and execute a plan that would improve its operations, sales, and marketing, and also provide for expansion. KKR did an IPO just 15 months later for almost double the value; Shoppers' market value exceeded $10 billion as it opened its thousandth store. Similarly, KKR's leveraged buyout of Yellow Pages from BCE in 2002 involved restructuring to generate top-line growth, achieve cost optimization, and improve capital allocation. A short two years later, Yellow Pages had tripled in value.[26]

Portfolio Management

During the 1970s and early 1980s, several leading consulting firms developed the concept of portfolio matrices to achieve a better understanding of the competitive position of an overall portfolio (or family) of businesses, to suggest strategic alternatives for each of the businesses, and to identify priorities for the allocation of resources. Several studies have reported widespread use of portfolio analysis techniques among firms.[27]

The key purpose of portfolio models was to assist a firm in achieving a balanced portfolio of businesses.[28] This consisted of businesses whose profitability, growth, and cash flow characteristics would complement each other and add up to a satisfactory overall corporate performance. Imbalance could be caused either by excessive cash generation with too few growth opportunities or by insufficient cash generation to fund the growth requirements in the portfolio.

The Boston Consulting Group's (BCG) growth–share matrix is among the best known of the portfolio planning approaches.[29] In the BCG approach, each of the firm's strategic business units (SBUs) is plotted on a two-dimensional grid, in which the axes are relative market share and industry growth rate. The grid is broken into four quadrants. Exhibit 6-1 depicts the BCG matrix. The following are a few clarifications:

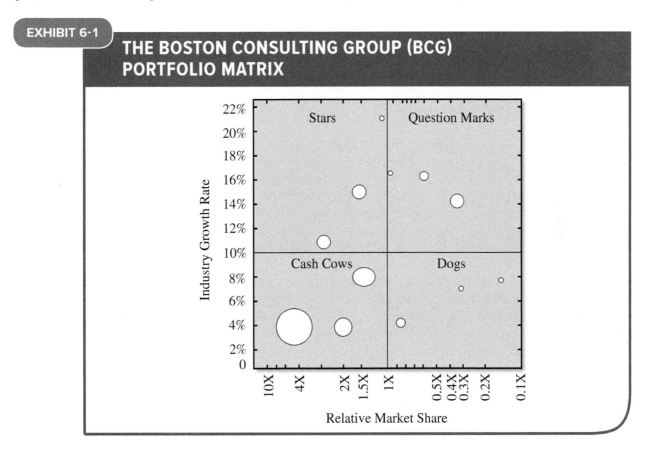

EXHIBIT 6-1

THE BOSTON CONSULTING GROUP (BCG) PORTFOLIO MATRIX

- Each circle represents one of the corporation's business units. The size of the circle represents the relative size of the business unit in terms of revenues.

- Relative market share, measured by the ratio of the business unit's size to that of its largest competitor, is plotted along the horizontal axis.

- Market share is central to the BCG matrix. This is because high relative market share leads to unit cost reduction (due to experience and learning curve effects) and, consequently, superior competitive position.

Each of the four quadrants of the grid has different implications for the SBUs that fall into that section or category:

- *Stars* are SBUs competing in high-growth industries with relatively high market shares. These firms have long-term growth potential and should continue to receive substantial investment funding.

- *Question marks* are SBUs competing in high-growth industries but having relatively weak market shares. Resources should be invested in them to enhance their competitive positions and help them increase their relative market share to become "stars"; otherwise, they are destined to become "dogs" and should be divested when the industry matures.

- *Cash cows* are SBUs with high market shares in low-growth industries. These units have limited long-run potential but represent a source of current cash flows to fund investments in "stars" and "question marks."

- *Dogs* are SBUs with weak market shares in low-growth industries. Because they have weak positions and limited potential, most analysts recommend that they be divested.

Another portfolio matrix that gained prominence is commonly known as the GE matrix. It is based on the same principles as those of the BCG matrix, with a few modifications. In the GE matrix, the vertical axis goes beyond the industry growth rate and looks at the overall attractiveness of the industry, emerging opportunities, intensity of competition, resource requirements, and uncertainty. The various business units are assessed as high, medium, or low on their industry attractiveness. The horizontal axis expands on the business unit's market position and competitive strength and includes such aspects as relative market share, relative costs, capabilities, relative product attributes, relative image, and reputation. SBUs are assessed as strong, average, or weak compared with those of competitors. The result is a matrix with nine cells. Similar to the BCG matrix, diversified corporations are expected to plot their businesses on the matrix and follow particular strategies corresponding to each of the cells.

Benefits of Portfolio Management

In using portfolio strategy approaches, a corporation tries to create synergies and shareholder value in a number of ways.[30] Since the businesses are unrelated, synergies that develop are those that result from the actions of the corporate office with the individual units instead of among business units. First, portfolio analysis provides a snapshot of the businesses in a corporation's portfolio; therefore, the corporation is in a better position to allocate resources among the business units according to prescribed criteria (e.g., the use of cash flows from the "cash cows" to fund promising "stars"). Second, the expertise and analytical resources in the corporate office provide guidance in determining what firms may be attractive (or unattractive) acquisitions. Third, the corporate office is able to provide financial resources to the business units on favourable terms that reflect the corporation's overall ability to raise funds. Fourth, the corporate office can provide high-quality review and coaching for the individual businesses. Fifth, portfolio analysis provides a basis for developing strategic goals and reward/evaluation systems for business managers. For example, managers of "cash cows" would have lower targets for revenue growth than managers of "stars," but the former would have higher threshold levels of profit targets on proposed projects than the managers of "star" businesses. Compensation systems would also reflect such realities: Managers of "cash cows" would, understandably, be rewarded more on the basis of cash that their businesses generated than would managers of "star" businesses. Similarly, managers of "star" businesses would be held to higher standards for revenue growth than managers of "cash cow" businesses.

To understand how companies can benefit from portfolio approaches, consider Ciba-Geigy (now called Novartis). In 1994, Ciba-Geigy, a $4-billion firm operating in a range of industries, adopted a portfolio planning approach to manage its business units, which competed across chemicals, dyes, pharmaceuticals, crop protection, and animal health.[31] It placed each business unit in a category corresponding to the BCG matrix. The business unit's goals, compensation programs, personnel selection, and resource allocation were strongly associated with the category within which the business was placed. For example, business units classified as "cash cows" had much higher hurdles for obtaining financial resources (from the corporate office) for expansion than "question marks," since the latter were businesses for which Ciba-Geigy had high hopes for accelerated future growth and profitability. Additionally, the compensation of a business unit manager in a "cash cow" would be strongly associated with its success in generating cash to fund other businesses, whereas a manager of a "question mark" business would be rewarded on his or her ability to increase revenue growth and market share. The portfolio planning approach appears to have worked. In 2001, Ciba-Geigy's revenues and net income stood at $18.5 billion and $4.0 billion, respectively, and by 2016, Novartis had reached $48 billion in revenue and over $6 billion in net income.

Limitations of Portfolio Management

Despite the potential benefits of portfolio models, there are also some notable downsides. First, they compare SBUs on only two dimensions, making the implicit but erroneous assumption that (1) those are the only factors that really matter, and (2) that every unit can be accurately compared on that basis. Second, the approach views each SBU as a stand-alone entity, ignoring common core business practices and value-creating activities that may hold promise for synergies across business units. Third, portfolio models do not explicitly incorporate an SBU's core competencies in the analysis, and they ignore the importance of nurturing and protecting those for the long-term viability and success of a business. Fourth, unless care is exercised, the process can become largely mechanical, substituting an oversimplified graphic model for the important contributions of the CEO's (and other corporate managers') experience and judgment. Fifth, a strict reliance on the rules regarding resource allocation across SBUs can be detrimental to a firm's long-term viability. For example, according to one study, over half of all the businesses that should have been cash users (based on the BCG matrix) were instead cash providers.[32] Finally, though it is colourful and easy to comprehend, the imagery of a portfolio matrix can lead to some troublesome and overly simplistic prescriptions. As one author noted:

> The dairying analogy is appropriate (for some cash cows), so long as we resist the urge to oversimplify it. On the farm, even the best-producing cows eventually begin to dry up. The farmer's solution to this is euphemistically called "freshening" the cow: The farmer arranges a date for the cow with a bull, she has a calf, the milk begins flowing again. Cloistering the cow—isolating her from everything but the feed trough and the milking machines—assures that she will go dry.[33]

Caveat: Is Risk Reduction a Viable Goal of Diversification?

One of the purposes of diversification is ostensibly to reduce the risk that is inherent in a firm's variability in revenues and profits over time. In essence, the argument is that if a firm enters new products or markets that are affected differently by seasonal or economic cycles, its performance over time will be more stable. Bombardier's introduction of the Sea-Doo was driven by the success and seasonality of the Ski-Doo. A firm manufacturing a luxury line of household furniture may introduce a lower-priced line, since affluent and lower-income customers are affected differently by economic cycles.

At first glance, such reasoning may make sense, but there are some problems with it. First, a firm's shareholders can diversify their portfolios at a much lower cost than a corporation. Individuals can purchase shares with almost no premium (e.g., only a small commission is paid to a discount broker), and they do not have to worry about integrating the acquisition into their portfolio. Second, economic cycles and their impact on a given industry (or firm) are difficult to predict with any degree of accuracy.

Nevertheless, some firms have benefited from diversification by lowering the variability (or risk) in their performance over time. Consider Emerson Electric, an American multinational corporation that in 2014 celebrated its 58th consecutive year of earnings growth! It produces a wide variety of products, including measurement devices for heavy industry, temperature controls for heating and ventilation systems, and power tools sold at Home Depot. A few years ago, many analysts questioned Emerson's purchase of companies that sell power systems to the volatile telecommunications industry. Why?

This industry was expected to experience, at best, minimal growth. However, CEO David Farr maintained that such assets could be acquired inexpensively because of the aggregate decline in demand in this industry. Additionally, he argued that the other business units, involving the sales of valves and regulators to the booming oil and natural gas companies, were able to pick up the slack. Therefore, net profits in the electrical equipment sector (Emerson's core business) sharply decreased, but Emerson's overall corporate profits increased by 1.7 percent.

In summary, risk reduction in and of itself is rarely a viable way to create shareholder value. It must be undertaken with a view of a firm's overall diversification strategy.

LO 4   THE MEANS TO ACHIEVE DIVERSIFICATION

So far, we have addressed the types of diversification (e.g., related and unrelated) that a firm may undertake to achieve synergies and create value for its shareholders and other important stakeholders. Next, we address the means by which a firm can go about pursuing such diversification.

Firms have three different means at their disposal. First, through *mergers and acquisitions,* corporations can directly acquire the assets and competencies of other firms. Second, corporations may agree to pool the resources of other companies with their own resource base. This approach is commonly known as a *strategic alliance* or *joint venture.* Third, corporations may diversify into new products, markets, and technologies through internal development. This approach—sometimes called *corporate entrepreneurship, green field,* or *organic growth*—involves the leveraging and combining of a firm's own resources and competencies to create synergies and enhance shareholder value.

All three approaches are valuable strategic alternatives, and managers consider all three as means to pursue their strategies. Although mergers and acquisitions tend to command the lion's share of publicity, firms typically engage in any one of the three, as appropriate, to address different situations and achieve different results. Each one has its advantages and disadvantages, mainly relating to speed and timing, risk, investment and cost requirements, ease of execution, control, and flexibility.

Mergers and Acquisitions (M&A)

Growth through M&A has played a critical role in the success of many corporations in a wide variety of economic sectors, including resources and energy, manufacturing, services, as well as the high-technology and knowledge-intensive industries. Canada experienced a dramatic increase in such activity emanating from aggressive global firms that found Canadian assets attractive and relatively undervalued. Canadian corporate icons, such as Alcan, Inco, Falconbridge, and Dofasco, changed ownership and became subsidiaries and divisions of American, European, or Asian corporations. The shareholders of those firms reaped great financial gains, but the firm headquarters and the strategic decisions have effectively moved overseas, taking with them senior management positions and, some would argue, Canada's ability to control its economic destiny.[34] Of course, Canadian firms have themselves always been active acquirers, both domestically and internationally. Bombardier's global success is, in part, the outcome of a series of acquisitions: Canadair, de Havilland, Learjet (U.S.), Short (Ireland) and Skyjet (U.S.) aerospace firms; and Lohnerwerke (Austria), Alco (U.S.), BN (Belgium), ANF (France), CNCF (Mexico), Waggonfabrik Tablot (Germany), and Adtranz (Germany) in rail transportation. Yet not many acquisitions end up creating the promised value. Some of the most celebrated disasters include the 2001 AOL–Time Warner $350 billion merger, which destroyed almost $150 billion in value, and the Vodafone–Mannesmann $340 billion deal, where the combined entity, eight years later, was valued less than $100 billion.

Motives and Benefits

Although the motivations for merging with or acquiring another firm may vary, managers ascribe similar reasons for their proposed deals. Market and technology changes can occur very quickly and unpredictably; therefore, *speed*—speed to market, speed to positioning, and speed to becoming a viable company—is critical in some industries. For example, Alex Mandl, AT&T's president in the early 1990s, was responsible for the acquisition of McCaw Cellular. Although many industry experts felt the price was too steep, he believed that cellular technology was a critical asset for the telecommunications business and that it would have been extremely difficult to build that business from the ground up. Mandl claimed, "The plain fact is that acquiring is much faster than building."[35] Similarly, in 2010, Apple acquired Siri Inc. so that it could quickly integrate Siri's natural-language voice recognition software into its own operating system, the Apple iOS.

M&A can also be a means of *obtaining valuable resources* that can help an organization expand its product offerings and services. For example, Cisco Systems, a dominant player in networking equipment, acquired more than 70 companies from 1993 to early 2000 and another 300 since then.[36] These companies provided Cisco with access to the latest in networking equipment. But Cisco also learned the importance of integrating the acquired companies efficiently and effectively.[37] It used its excellent sales force to market the acquired technology to its corporate customers and telephone companies, and it put in place strong incentives for the staff of acquired companies to stay on.

Corporations often use acquisitions to gain critical human capital. These acquisitions have been referred to as acq-hires. In an acq-hire, the acquiring firm believes it needs the specific technical knowledge or the social network contacts of individuals in the target firm. This is especially important in settings where the technology or consumer preferences are highly dynamic. For example, in 2014, Apple purchased Beats Electronics for $3 billion. While Apple valued the product portfolio of Beats, its primary aim was to pull the founders of Beats, Jimmy Iovine and Dr. Dre (aka Andrew Young), into the Apple family. Apple's iTunes business had hit a wall in growth, experiencing a 1 percent decline in 2013, and Apple wanted to acquire new management talent to turn the business around. In addition to their experience at Beats, Iovine and Dr. Dre could each bring over 20 years of experience in the music industry; Iovine had founded InterScope Records and Dr. Dre was a hip-hop pioneer and music producer. With this acquisition, Apple brought in a wealth of knowledge about the music business, the ability to identify music trends and up-and-coming talent, and industry contacts needed to rejuvenate its music business.[38]

M&A activity can also lead to consolidation within an industry and give firms instant *scale to respond to external pressures.* In the pharmaceutical industry, the patents for many top-selling drugs have started to expire; one of the observed consequences is heightened M&A activity.[39] Although health care providers and patients are happy about the lower-cost generic options that arrive following the expiry of drug patents, pharmaceutical firms are being pressed to make up for lost revenues and are required to undertake major and risky investments to develop new drugs.

Combining top firms, such as Pfizer Inc. and Warner-Lambert Co., as well as Glaxo Wellcome and SmithKline Beecham, has many potential long-term benefits. It not only promises significant post-merger cost savings, but the increased size of the combined companies also brings greater research and development (R&D) possibilities.

Molson Inc. of Montreal, Quebec, and Adolph Coors Co. of Golden, Colorado, merged their operations in an attempt to create a firm that could stand up to the continuing consolidation in the global beer industry. They could achieve synergies by rationalizing production across the two countries, improving the effectiveness of marketing efforts, and cross-selling brands in Europe and Latin America, where the two firms have local operations.[40] Molson was responding to its arch-rival Labatt's acquisition by Interbrew (now InBev) of Belgium and to the subsequent purchase of Sleeman's by Sapporo of Japan. Three years later, MolsonCoors had achieved annual savings of $175 million and had successfully integrated and rationalized operations globally.

Corporations can use M&A *to leverage core competencies, share activities,* and *build market power*—the three bases of synergy. Consider Procter & Gamble's $57 billion acquisition of Gillette.[41] First, it helps P&G to leverage its core competencies in marketing and product positioning in the area of personal care brands. Second, there are opportunities to share value-creating activities; Gillette benefits from P&G's strong distribution network in developing countries where the potential for growth for the industry's products is much higher than in the traditional markets of North America and Europe.

Corporations can also *enter new markets* and new market segments by way of acquisitions. In 1998, Loblaw Companies Limited—having a strong presence in Ontario and western Canada but with no footprint in the Quebec grocery market—acquired Provigo, that province's second largest chain, to gain entry into the highly competitive market. The move enabled the firm to quickly enter the new market and acquire local skills and competencies.

Potential Limitations

Nonetheless, there are also many potential downsides associated with M&A. Among these are the *expensive and excessive premiums* that are frequently paid to acquire a business. Premiums of 20, 30, or even 80 percent are not uncommon, and the acquiring firm must create enough value to recoup the investment. Although synergies and economies of scale, which should result in increased sales and market gains, may, indeed, materialize, the performance hurdle has already been set quite high. Other difficulties relate to integrating the activities and resources of the acquired firm into the corporation's own operations as well as identifying "synergies" that are quickly imitated by the competition.

Moreover, *managers' egos and credibility* can sometimes get in the way of sound business decisions. Size is not always important for the success of a business, but senior managers may be preoccupied with the personal prestige of leading the largest firm in their industry, even if that means paying excessive amounts of money to accumulate enough entities to become the biggest player. At other times, if the acquisition does not perform as planned, managers who pushed for the deal find their reputations at stake. To protect their credibility, and against better business judgment, these managers might funnel more resources and escalate their commitment toward an inevitably doomed venture.

Finally, there are many *cultural issues* that may bring calamity to a well-intended M&A endeavour. Consider, for example, the insights of Joanne Lawrence who played an important role, as vice-president and director of communications and investor relations at SmithKlineBeecham, in the merger of SmithKline and the Beecham Group, a diversified consumer-oriented group headquartered in the United Kingdom:

> The key to a strategic merger is to create a new culture. This was a mammoth challenge during the SmithKlineBeecham merger. We were working at so many different cultural levels, it was dizzying. We had two national cultures to blend—American and British—that compounded the challenge of selling the merger in two different markets with two different shareholder bases. There were also two different business cultures: One was very strong, scientific, and academic; the other was much more commercially oriented. And then we had to consider within both companies the individual businesses, each of which has its own little culture.[42]

Divestitures: The Flip Side of Acquisitions

When firms acquire other businesses, it typically generates quite a bit of "press" in business publications. It makes for exciting news; large acquiring firms automatically improve their standing in the various size-based rankings, such as Fortune 500. However, managers must also carefully consider the strategic implications of exiting business.[43] Divestments, the exit of a business from a firm's portfolio, are quite common. One study found that large U.S. companies divested more acquisitions than they kept.[44] Some of the best known divestitures in business history include Daimler-Benz's acquisition (at that time, it was called a "merger") of Chrysler for $36 billion in 1998, which was sold to a private equity firm in 2007 for just over $7 billion; Novell's purchase of WordPerfect for $1.4 billion, which it later sold to Corel for $124 million; and Quaker Oats' purchase of Snapple for $1.7 billion, unloaded three years later for $300 million.

Divesting a business can accomplish different objectives, such as reversing an acquisition that did not work out as planned. Divestitures can also enable managers to focus their efforts on the firm's core businesses, provide the firm with more resources to spend on more attractive alternatives, and raise cash to help fund existing businesses. Frequently, firms also divest businesses to monetize successful restructuring and turnarounds. Firms can divest their businesses in a number of ways. Sell-offs, spin-offs, equity carve-outs, asset sales, and split-ups are some such modes of divestment.

Divesting can enhance a firm's competitive position only to the extent that it reduces its tangible (such as maintenance, investment) or intangible (such as opportunity costs, managerial attention) costs without sacrificing a current competitive advantage. To be effective, divesting requires a thorough understanding of a business unit's current ability and future potential to contribute to a firm's value creation.

Strategy Spotlight 6.5 discusses why Campbell Soup divested Godiva, even though the chocolatier had a very strong market position and financial performance.

6.5 STRATEGY SPOTLIGHT

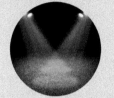

Campbell Soup Divests Godiva to Focus on Its Core Business

In August 2007, Campbell Soup decided to sell Godiva, its super-premium chocolate business, which had been a very profitable brand for them for the previous 35 years. Campbell did not base the decision on financial considerations. Rather, it made the move because Godiva was not consistent with Campbell's values, competencies, and aspirations of nutrition and simplicity. Doug Conant, then Campbell's CEO, stated, "Although the premium chocolate category is experiencing strong growth and Godiva is well positioned for the future, the premium chocolate business does not fit Campbell's focus on simple meals."

The firm reached an agreement with Yildiz Holding, a conglomerate which also owns the largest consumer goods manufacturer in the Turkish food sector, for $850 million. Godiva's annual sales of $500 million in that year suggest that Campbell got full value for the brand, relying on its identity, rather than on financial projections, and making the decision to sell the unit quickly and painlessly.

Sources: J. Camilus, 2008, "Strategy as a Wicked Problem," *Harvard Business Review*, 86(5), pp. 98–108; "Campbell Completes Sale of Godiva," *Yahoo Finance*, August 31, 2008.

Strategic Alliances and Joint Ventures

Strategic alliances are cooperative relationships between two or more firms. Alliances can be either formal or informal, that is, involving written contracts. Joint ventures are special types of alliances in that the firms contribute assets to form a new legal entity. Strategic alliances and joint ventures are assuming an increasingly prominent role in the strategy of leading firms, both large and small.[45] Such cooperative relationships have many potential advantages. Among these are entering new markets; reducing purchasing, manufacturing, and other costs in the value chain; and developing and diffusing new technologies.

Entering New Markets

Often, a company that has a successful product or service wants to introduce it into a new market. However, it may not have the requisite marketing expertise because it does not understand customer needs, know how to promote the product, or have access to the proper distribution channels.

Couche-Tard of Quebec, which also operates Mac's convenience stores in Ontario, has partnered with Convenience Retail Asia, an established chain of convenience stores in Hong Kong and mainland China, to embark on an aggressive growth strategy in China.[46] Its Circle K banner has been employed to expand aggressively into the United States and Mexican markets, using partnerships with large integrated oil companies that provide it with ready access to prime locations and market knowledge of local customers. Couche-Tard has over 13,000 stores worldwide and generated $34 billion in revenue in 2016.

In other situations, a company may be prevented from entering a new market because of regulatory, reputational, or legal barriers. High-flyer Nortel used joint ventures during its 1990s meteoric growth to enter many markets in Asia and Latin America. Partners provided capital, and, more importantly, local knowledge, along with legitimacy and access to governments, for the telecommunications infrastructure projects that were the bread and butter of Nortel's telecommunications systems.

Reducing Costs in the Value Chain

Strategic alliances often enable firms to pool capital, value-creating activities, or facilities to reduce costs. For example, in the late 1980s, Molson Companies and Carling O'Keefe Breweries formed a joint venture to merge their brewing operations. While Molson had a modern and efficient brewery in Montreal, Carling's was outdated. However, Carling had the better facilities in Toronto. In addition, Molson's Toronto brewery was located on the waterfront and had substantial real estate value. Overall, the synergies gained by the efficient use of their combined facilities added $150 million of pre-tax earnings during the initial year of the venture. Economies of scale were realized, and the facilities were better utilized.

Developing and Diffusing New Technologies

Strategic alliances may also be used to build on the technological expertise of two or more companies to develop products that are technologically beyond the capability of the companies acting independently. Consider the following examples: STMicroelectronics (ST), a high-tech company based in Geneva, Switzerland, has thrived—largely because of the success of its strategic alliances.[47] The firm develops and manufactures computer chips for a variety of applications: mobile phones, set-top boxes, smart cards, and flash memories. In 1995, it teamed up with Hewlett-Packard (HP) to develop powerful new processors for various digital applications. A few years later, it also formed a strategic alliance with Nokia to develop a chip that would give Nokia's phones a longer battery life. ST produced a chip that tripled the standby time to 60 hours—a breakthrough that gave Nokia cellphones a huge advantage in the marketplace. The firm's CEO, Pasquale Pistorio, was among the first in the industry to form R&D alliances with other companies. Soon, ST's top 12 customers, including HP, Nokia, and Nortel, accounted for 45 percent of revenues. Pistorio stated, "Alliances are in our DNA." Such relationships helped ST keep better-than-average growth rates, even in difficult times. This is possible because close partners are less likely to defect to other suppliers. ST's financial results were consistently impressive.

But strategic alliances are not just for smaller firms. Magna International, the global automobile parts manufacturer based in Aurora, Ontario, has entered into numerous alliances over the years to continue innovating and retaining its leadership role in its very competitive field. For example, an alliance with IBM explored new systems designs, software development, and engineering that would lead to advanced driver information systems. Magna knows cars, and IBM knows software; together they could address technological challenges that would allow cars to respond to road signs or take evasive action to avoid a crash, even when the driver is distracted. Such technological developments will eventually lead to the self-driving cars that are bound to take over from a human activity that has defined human transport for over one hundred years.[48]

Potential Limitations

Despite their promise, many alliances and joint ventures fail to meet expectations for a variety of reasons. First, without the proper partner, an alliance can be unproductive, even if formed for the best of reasons. Each partner should bring the desired complementary strengths to the partnership. Ideally, the strengths contributed by the partners are unique so that synergies created can be more easily sustained and defended over the longer term. The goal must be to develop synergies between the contributions of the partners, which would ultimately result in a win–win situation for both. Second, partners must usually share control over the direction of their strategic alliance and defer to others over important decisions. In many cases, the partner is geographically quite distant, or the joint venture's operations might reside within the partner's own facilities. The consequences of a limited ability to control critical decisions may be compounded by the divergent goals of the partners and their different perspectives on the alliance. Goal alignment and monitoring of progress frequently impose significant tension on an alliance. Moreover, the partners must be compatible and be willing to trust each other. Often, however, little attention is given to nurturing the close working relationships and interpersonal connections that bring together the partnering organizations. The human factors are not carefully considered or, at worst, dismissed as unimportant.

Tim Hortons and Wendy's worked very hard to ensure compatibility of the partners. Although the companies' cultures were, indeed, quite similar, the executives of both firms spent literally thousands of hours in each other's operations.[49] Proceeding cautiously at first, they created working teams and cross-functional task forces consisting of members from both sides. They initially opened a few joint locations in Prince Edward Island and along Ontario's highways to provide Tim Hortons doughnuts, muffins, and its famous coffee as well as Wendy's sandwich fare and fries to motorists, thereby utilizing the facilities round the clock. Their success encouraged them to move forward and expand to city locations. After some further collaboration, the two firms merged to create a new corporation that consistently delivered excellent financial and market performances. Analysts attributed the firm's success to the ongoing effort by all managers to build on the unique cultures of the initial partners. Interestingly, with the changing of the guard at the very top of the combined firm, the two sides grew apart. Some claimed that the success of Tim Hortons started to bother the top brass in the United States. Eventually, Wendy's spun off Tim Hortons into an independent entity in 2006, and it was subsequently purchased by Burger King in 2014 for $11.4 billion.

Lululemon Athletica's seaweed-clothing scandal emanated from its German supplier's claims about the health benefits of the fabrics used in its top line of t-shirts. Special seaweed-blend cotton shirts were supposed to not only contain health-promoting substances that enhance blood flow and stimulate skin regeneration but also secrete vitamins, minerals, and amino acids that had stress-reducing and detoxifying properties.[50] Independent laboratories announced test results that challenged those claims. To complicate things further, the t-shirts were not even made by the German firm, which supplied the fibre to Asian manufacturers. Lululemon's health claims were based on the assurances of its partner, but it was its own stock that took a hit on the news.

Internal Development

Firms can also diversify by means of corporate entrepreneurship and new venture development. In today's economy, internal development is such an important means by which companies expand their businesses that we have devoted a whole chapter to it (see Chapter 12). Sony and the Minnesota Mining & Manufacturing Co. (3M) are among the companies best known for their dedication to innovation, R&D, and cutting-edge technologies. For example, 3M has developed its entire corporate culture to support its ongoing policy of generating at least 25 percent of total sales from products created within the most recent four-year period. During the 1990s, 3M exceeded this goal by achieving about 30 percent of sales per year from new, internally developed products.

Compared with M&A, internal development is able to capture the value created by a firm's own innovative activities without having to "share the wealth" with alliance partners or face the difficulties associated with combining activities across the value chains of several companies or merging corporate cultures. Another advantage is that the firm can often develop new products or services at a relatively lower cost and, thereby, rely on its own resources rather than turning to external funding. Moreover, internal development is fully customized to fit the company's existing culture, systems, and core competencies.

There are also potential disadvantages. Internal development may be time consuming; thus, firms may forfeit the benefits of speed that growth through M&A or strategic alliances can provide. This may be especially important among high-tech or knowledge-based organizations and in fast-paced environments where being an early mover is critical. Firms that choose to grow and diversify through internal development must, therefore, develop capabilities that allow them to move quickly from initial opportunity recognition to market introduction.

LO 5   REAL OPTIONS ANALYSIS: A USEFUL TOOL

In discussing the means of diversification, we briefly explore some recent developments in *real options analysis* (ROA), which has its roots in the field of finance and has slowly entered the tool kit of consultants and executives who aim to support strategic decision making in firms. What does ROA consist of, and how can it be appropriately applied to the investments required to initiate strategic decisions? To understand *real* options, it is first necessary to have a basic understanding of what *options* are.

An option gives its owner the right but not the obligation to engage in a specific transaction. The most common example is the stock option. A stock option grants the holder the right to buy (call option) or sell (put option) shares of the stock at a fixed price (strike price) at some time in the future.[51] In essence, a call option gives its holder the right to buy a stock at a predetermined price at a given point in time, no matter what the price of the stock will be at that time. If the stock does trade at a price above the strike price, the holder will only have to pay the strike price and can immediately pocket the difference by selling the stock in the open market. For the privilege, the holder has invested a very small amount in acquiring the option. Conversely, if the stock trades at a price below the strike price at the given point in time, the option is worthless, and the holder will allow it to expire, having lost the modest investment. An important aspect of stock options is that the investment to be made immediately is relatively small, whereas the investment to be made in the future can be substantial. For example, an option to buy a rapidly rising stock at a strike price of $50 might cost as little as $0.50.[52] An important point to note is that owners of such a stock option have limited their losses to $0.50 per share, whereas the upside potential is unlimited. This aspect of options is attractive because they offer the prospect of high gains with relatively small upfront investments that represent limited losses. At the same time, it should be understood that options can become totally worthless. The holder who invested $0.50 to acquire an option will lose all the investment if the stock's value falls even $0.01 below the strike price, whereas the holder of the stock will still be able to trade the stock for the going price.

The phrase "real options" applies to situations in which options theory and valuation techniques are applied to real assets, or physical things, as opposed to financial assets. Some of the most common applications of real options concern property and insurance. A real estate option grants the holder the right to buy or sell a piece of property at an established price sometime in the future. The actual market price of the property may rise above the established (or strike) price—or the market value may sink below the strike price. If the price of the property goes up, the owner of the option is likely to buy it. If the market value of the property drops below the strike price, the option holder is unlikely to execute the purchase. In the latter circumstance, the option holder has limited the loss to the cost of the option but during the life of the option retains the right to participate in whatever the upside potential might be. Casualty insurance is another variation of real options. With casualty insurance, the owner of the property has limited the loss to the cost of the insurance, whereas the upside potential is the actual loss, ranging, of course, up to the limit of the insurance.[53]

Applications of Real Options Analysis to Strategic Decisions

The concept of options can also be applied to strategic decisions in which management has flexibility; that is, the situation will permit management to decide whether to invest additional funds to grow or accelerate the activity, delay in order to learn more, shrink the scale of the activity, or even abandon it. The initial alliance between Tim Hortons and Wendy's can be evaluated as an option that provided both firms with the opportunity to learn more about each other and assess their initial investment before proceeding with a full merger. Decisions to invest in business activities, such as R&D, motion pictures, exploration and production of oil wells, and the opening and closing of copper mines, often have similar flexibility.[54] Some important issues to note include the following:

- Real options analysis is appropriate to use when investments can be staged; that is, a smaller investment up front can be followed by subsequent investments. In short, real options can be applied to an investment decision that gives the company the right, but not the obligation, to make follow-up investments.

- The strategic decision makers have "tollgates" or key points at which they can decide whether to continue, delay, or abandon the project. In short, the executives have flexibility. There are opportunities to make other go or no go decisions associated with each phase.

- It is expected that there will be increased knowledge about outcomes at the time of the next investment and that additional knowledge will help inform the decision makers about whether to make additional investments—that is, whether the option is in the money or out of the money.

Many strategic decisions tend to bear a series of options. This phenomenon is called "embedded options," a series of investments in which, at each stage of the investment, there is a go/no go decision. For example, pharmaceutical companies have successfully used real options analysis in evaluating decisions about investments in R&D projects and in forming alliances with start-up biotechnology firms.[55] Pharmaceuticals have at least four stages of investments: basic research yielding compounds and the three federally mandated phases of clinical trials. Generally, each phase is more expensive to undertake than the previous phase. However, as each phase unfolds, management knows more about the underlying drugs and the many sources of uncertainty, including technical difficulties related to the drugs themselves, as well as external market conditions, such as the results of competitors' research. Management can make the decision to invest more with the intent of speeding up the process, delay the start of the next phase, reduce investment, or even abandon the R&D.[56] Merck famously applied real options analysis to its relationship with Biogen, one of the earlier biotechnology firms developing technology which Merck did not really understand and could not assess. Eli Lilly used it to proceed cautiously and eventually to acquire Hybritech when it established that, indeed, the drugs under development had real potential in the marketplace.[57]

LO 6 HOW MANAGERIAL MOTIVES CAN ERODE VALUE CREATION

Thus far in the chapter, we have implicitly assumed that CEOs and top executives are "rational beings" who act in the best interests of shareholders to maximize long-term shareholder value. The real world and agency theory have shown, however, that this is not the case. Frequently, managers may act in their own self-interest. Below, we address some managerial motives that can serve to erode, rather than enhance, value creation. These include "growth for growth's sake," excessive egotism, and the introduction of a wide variety of anti-takeover tactics to protect the entrenchment of current management.

Growth for Growth's Sake

There are huge incentives for executives to increase the size of their firms, and many of these incentives are hardly consistent with increasing shareholder wealth. Top managers, including the CEO, of larger firms typically enjoy more prestige, higher rankings for their companies on various corporate lists, such as Fortune 500 (which are based on revenues, not cash flows or profits), greater incomes, more job security, and so on. There is also the excitement and associated recognition of making a major acquisition. As noted by Harvard's Michael Porter, "There's a tremendous allure to mergers and acquisitions. It's the big play, the dramatic gesture. With one stroke of the pen, you can add billions to size, get a front-page story, and create excitement in markets."[58]

At times, executives' overemphasis on growth can result in a plethora of ethical lapses, which can have disastrous outcomes for their companies. A good example of bad practice is Joseph Bernardino's leadership at Andersen Worldwide. Bernardino had a chance, early on, to take a hard line on ethics and quality in the wake of earlier scandals at such clients as Waste Management and Sunbeam. Instead, according to former executives, he put too much emphasis on revenue growth. The accounting firm's reputation quickly eroded when it audited and signed off on the highly flawed financial statements of such infamous firms as Enron, Global Crossing, Qwest Communications, and WorldCom. Bernardino ultimately resigned in disgrace in March 2002, and his firm was dissolved later that year.[59]

Egotism

A healthy ego helps make a leader confident, clear-headed, and able to cope with change. CEOs, by their very nature, are often fiercely competitive people whether in the office or on the tennis court or golf course. However, when pride is at stake, individuals will sometimes go to great lengths to win—or at least to not back down.

Few executives (or lower-level managers) are immune to the potential dangers of too much ego. GE's former CEO, Jack Welch, considered by many to be one of the world's most admired executives, admitted to his regrettable decision to acquire the soon-to-be-troubled Wall Street firm Kidder Peabody.[60] According to Welch, "My hubris got in the way in the Kidder Peabody deal. I got wise advice from Walter Wriston and other directors who said, 'Jack, don't do this.' But I was bully enough and on a run to do it. And I got whacked right in the head." In addition to poor financial results, Kidder Peabody was wracked by a widely publicized trading scandal that tarnished the reputations of both it and GE. GE eventually divested Kidder and registered a multi-billion dollar loss.

The business press has included many stories of how egotism and greed creep into organizations. Some incidents are rather astonishing, for example, Tyco's former CEO Dennis Kozlowski's well-chronicled purchase of a $6,000 shower curtain and a vodka-spewing, life-size replica of Michelangelo's David.[61] Other well-known examples of egos and power grabs include executives at Enron; the Regis family, who defrauded Adelphia of roughly $1 billion; Bernie Ebbers, the former CEO of WorldCom, originally from Alberta, who granted himself a $408 million personal loan from the company while orchestrating an accounting fraud to inflate company profits; and Ross Johnson, CEO of Nabisco, originally from Winnipeg and the protagonist in the book *Barbarians at the Gate.* Frank Dunn of Nortel, Conrad Black of Hollinger International, and Miles Nadal of MDC are other executives who have allegedly tested the limits of the law and the pockets of their shareholders.

Few would disagree that Frank Stronach is the soul and the genius behind the tremendous global success of Magna International, a company he founded in Aurora, Ontario, back in 1957 and led to become one of the world's largest and most profitable automobile parts manufacturers. Yet Frank will be forever haunted by the consequences of Magna's ventures into gaming and horse racing; the creation of Magna Entertainment Corp—with millions of dollars thrown into a black hole that just does not seem to know how to make a profit—does, however, cater to Frank's personal love of horses and thoroughbred racing.[62]

Anti-takeover Tactics

Unfriendly or hostile takeovers can occur when a company's stock becomes undervalued. A competing organization can buy the outstanding stock of a takeover candidate in sufficient quantity to become a large shareholder. It then makes a tender offer to gain full control of the target company. If the shareholders of the target company accept the offer, the hostile firm buys the target company and either fires the target firm's management team or strips them of their power.

A number of anti-takeover tactics can be used to preserve the corporate status quo. Among the most common are poison pills, frequently put in place but seldom exercised; greenmail, a well-known tactic in the United States that is prohibited in Canada; controlling shareholders; staggered boards; lock-up agreements; white knights; and golden parachutes. Although such tactics have been defended by management and boards of directors as protecting the rights of shareholders, those scrutinizing these takeover activities have questioned the motives behind these tactics and have argued that, by and large, they only help senior management and board members to entrench themselves and protect their jobs.[63] We briefly comment on each tactic below.

Poison pills, or *shareholder rights plans,* allow existing shareholders, under certain conditions, to have the option to buy additional shares at a discount to the current market price. This action is typically triggered when a new shareholder accumulates more than a set percentage of ownership, usually 20 percent. Managers fear that the new shareholder might be masterminding a takeover of the company. In the name of protecting existing shareholders, newly issued stock is offered at a steep discount to all shareholders except the alleged aggressor. As the existing shareholders buy the discounted shares, the stock is diluted significantly, since there are now more shares, each with a lower value. If there has been a takeover bid at a set price per share, the overall price offered for the company immediately goes up by a substantial amount, since more shares are now outstanding. This assures shareholders of receiving a high price for the company. Of course, the takeover bidder is aware of the poison pill provision and is likely to stop just short of accumulating shares beyond the trigger level. Senior management and the board will usually negotiate better terms before removing the poison pill. Often, however, the board will also negotiate to keep senior management and itself in place as part of the deal to remove the pill.

Greenmail is an effort by the target firm to prevent an impending takeover. When a hostile firm buys a large block of outstanding target company stock and the target firm's management feels that a tender offer is imminent, they offer to buy the stock back from the hostile company at a higher price than the unfriendly company paid for it. The positive effect is that this often prevents a hostile takeover. On the downside, the same price is not offered to pre-existing shareholders. Greenmail is illegal in Canada because it deprives shareholders of the right to choose whether or not to tender their shares to the bid. There is also something morally suspect when the senior managers and the directors of a public company use the existing shareholders' money to buy out a potential acquirer in order to protect their own jobs.

Controlling shareholders could be members of a founder's family or others in a privileged ownership position. Either through majority ownership or through ownership of special classes of shares involving multiple voting rights, they can effectively block any unwanted takeover attempt. The family of Ted Rogers at Rogers Communications Inc. and Laurent Beaudoin at Bombardier Inc. own relatively small percentages of those public companies but, through dual-share structures, can effectively dictate the strategic decisions made by their boards. At Bombardier, in particular, institutional shareholders are calling for corporate reforms in light of the federal and provincial governments' involvement in funding development of the next generation of passenger jets.[64]

Staggered boards limit the number of board members that are elected each year, usually to one-third of all seats. This effectively delays any unwanted suitor from controlling the board for at least two years, even after gaining control of voting shares.

Lock-up agreements and break-up fees are commitments that senior managers and boards make to friendly firms to consummate transactions with them, even if a superior offer were to come forth. Allegedly, such fees serve to cover the friendly suitor's expenses for its troubles in getting involved; in essence, they make the superior offer that much more expensive for the unwanted offering party, which will have to pay penalties on completion of the deal. Creo of Vancouver, British Columbia, signed a break-up fee of $32 million to signal its support for Kodak's offer of $980 million. Similarly, Canadian Airlines signed an operating agreement with American Airlines for over $100 million in its attempt to block Air Canada's hostile bid.

White knights represent firms that are invited by the target firm's management to step in during a hostile bid and offer a higher price for the firm in exchange for the cooperation of management. Springfield served as a white knight for Schneider's when the family-controlled firm wanted to block the attempt by Maple Leaf Foods to acquire the largest hog producer and manufacturer of processed meat products in Canada.

Golden parachutes are prearranged employment contracts between companies and their managers specifying that in the event of a hostile takeover, the firm's managers will be paid a significant severance package. Although top managers may lose their jobs, the golden parachute provisions offer them substantial extraordinary compensation.

Clearly, anti-takeover tactics often raise serious ethical issues and highlight the divergence of interests between individual shareholders and the managers who undertake diversification moves—supposedly on behalf of the shareholders.

LO 7 EVALUATING CORPORATE STRATEGY

As we noted in the previous chapter on business-level strategies, evaluating a firm's strategy needs to be undertaken before any action is taken. And as we have tried to make clear throughout this chapter, business and corporate level strategies need to be integrated. As such, the goal of evaluating a corporate-level strategy is not to demonstrate that a particular strategy is guaranteed to work, which is an impossible task, but to test for its consistency with the goals of the firm, including its business-level strategy, how it too contributes to the pursuit of a competitive advantage, and whether it is feasible.

- *Consistency* refers to whether the diversification strategy is in alignment with the organization's goals and objectives. Does this manner of diversification introduce contradictions among different goals; for example, is it consistent with the firm's choice of generic business-level strategy? Can all participants readily identify and appreciate the direction, the commitments, the choices made, the expectations, and the desirable outcomes?

- *Consonance* refers to the fit between the corporate-level strategy and the external environment. Does the proposed diversification strategy take into account what is going on in the environment, what trends are emerging, and what the various stakeholders would support? For example, does vertical integration capitalize on a unique opportunity to create value that will be worth more than the cost of taking on the activity in-house? Does the acquisition address threats that are arising from the environment?

- *Advantage* refers to the competitive stance of the corporate strategy and whether it is creating inimitable advantages. Will the merger give the firm an advantageous position relative to competitors? Can the strategy be pursued more economically compared with competitors' strategies? Once again, the question is whether the strategic move would allow the firm to do something better relative to its competitors, not do it well in an objective sense.

- *Feasibility* refers to the capacity of the firm to achieve what it is embarking on. Is the diversification strategy realistic? Or is the diversification motivated by a managerial bias, such as growth for growth's sake? Does the organization possess, or can it gain access to, the necessary resources to carry out the strategy? Does the strategy explicitly address resource constraints? Does the organization possess the human capacity and managerial talent to implement what the strategy calls for? Too many alliances and mergers fail because of a clash of corporate cultures and a lack of personal fit.

Michael Porter offers a complimentary tool for evaluating a diversification strategy.[65] It consists of three critical tests:

1. *The attractiveness test* Successful efforts at diversification must be directed toward attractive industries or, at the very least, industries that managers have identified as having a strong potential to become attractive in the near future. Some indicators of attractiveness include industries with high entry barriers, low customer and supplier bargaining power, and few substitute products.

2. *The cost-of-entry test* Diversifying successfully means that the cost the firm must bear to enter the new venture does not outweigh all future profits. If the cost of entry is so high that it negatively affects the potential return on investment, profitability is eroded before the firm even begins to integrate the activity into its broader strategy and should therefore be avoided.

3. *The better-off test* A successful diversification initiative means that the acquisition will provide a competitive advantage to either the acquirer or the acquired. There must be evidence of some form of potential synergy as advantage emerges for the new unit via its link to the company, or vice versa.

SUMMARY

A key challenge for today's managers is to create "synergy" when engaging in diversification activities. As we discussed in this chapter, corporate managers do not, in general, have a very good track record in creating value through such endeavours, particularly mergers and acquisitions. Among the factors that serve to erode shareholder values are paying an excessive premium for the target firm, failing to integrate the activities of the newly acquired businesses into the corporate family, and undertaking diversification initiatives that are too easily imitated by the competition.

We addressed two major types of corporate-level strategy: related and unrelated diversification. With *related diversification* the corporation strives to enter areas in which key resources and capabilities of the corporation can be shared or leveraged. Synergies come from relationships between business units. Cost savings and enhanced revenues can be derived from three major sources. First, economies of scope can be achieved from the leveraging of core competencies and the sharing of activities. Second, market power can be attained from greater negotiating power, and third, benefits can be derived from vertical integration.

When firms undergo *unrelated diversification,* they enter product markets that are dissimilar to their present businesses. Thus, there is generally little opportunity to either leverage core competencies or share activities across business units. Here, synergies are created from relationships between the corporate office and the individual business units. With unrelated diversification, the primary ways to create value are through corporate restructuring and parenting as well as the use of portfolio analysis techniques.

Corporations have three primary means of expanding their activities and diversifying their product markets. These are mergers and acquisitions, strategic alliances and joint ventures, and internal development. There are key trade-offs associated with each of these. For example, mergers and acquisitions are typically the quickest means to enter new markets and provide the corporation with a high level of control over the acquired business. However, with the high premiums that often need to be paid to the shareholders of the target firm and the challenges associated with integrating acquisitions, they can also be quite expensive. Strategic alliances between two or more firms, may be a means of reducing risk, since they involve the sharing and combining of resources. But such joint initiatives also provide a firm with less control (than it would have with an acquisition), since governance is shared between two independent entities. In addition, there is a limit to the potential upside for each partner because returns must be shared as well. Finally, through internal development, a firm is able to capture all of the value from its initiatives (as opposed to sharing it with a merger or alliance partner). However, diversification by means of internal development can be very time consuming—a disadvantage that becomes even more critical in fast-paced competitive environments.

Traditional tools, such as net present value (NPV) analysis, are not always very helpful in making resource allocation decisions under uncertainty. Real options analysis (ROA) is increasingly used to make better-quality decisions in such situations.

Finally, some managerial behaviours may erode shareholder returns. Among these are "growth for growth's sake," egotism, and anti-takeover tactics. As we discussed in this chapter, some of these issues—particularly anti-takeover tactics—raise ethical questions because the managers of the firm may not be acting in the best interests of the shareholders.

Summary Review Questions

1. Discuss how managers can create value for their firm through diversification efforts.
2. What are some of the reasons that many diversification efforts fail to achieve desired outcomes?
3. How can companies benefit from related diversification? Unrelated diversification? What are some of the key concepts that can explain such success?
4. What are some of the important ways in which a firm can restructure its business?
5. Discuss some of the various means that firms can use to diversify. What are the pros and cons associated with each of these?
6. Discuss some of the actions of managers that erode shareholder value.

REFLECTING ON CAREER IMPLICATIONS

Corporate-Level Strategy: Be aware of your firm's corporate-level strategy. Can you come up with an initiative that will create value both within and across business units?

Core competencies: What do you see as your core competencies? How can you leverage them within your business unit as well as across other business units?

Sharing infrastructures: What infrastructure activities and resources, such as information systems or legal frameworks, are available in the corporate office that would help you create value for your business unit or another business unit?

Diversification: From your career perspective, what actions can you take to diversify your employment risk (e.g., course work at a local university; obtaining professional certification, such as a chartered financial accountant (CFA); or networking through a professional affiliation)? During periods of retrenchment, such actions will provide you with a greater number of career options.

EXPERIENTIAL EXERCISE

Rogers Communications is a firm that follows a strategy of related diversification. Evaluate their success (or lack thereof) with regard to how well they have (1) built on core competencies, (2) shared infrastructures, and (3) increased market power.

Rationale for Related Diversification	Successful/Unsuccessful?	Why?
1. Build on core competencies		
2. Share infrastructures		
3. Increase market power		

APPLICATION QUESTIONS AND EXERCISES

1. What were some of the largest mergers and acquisitions over the last two years? What was the rationale for these actions? Do you think they will be successful? Explain.

2. Discuss some examples from business practice in which an executive's actions appear to be in the interest of himself or herself rather than that of the corporation.

3. Discuss some of the challenges that managers must overcome in making strategic alliances successful. What are some strategic alliances you are familiar with? Were they successful or not? Explain.

4. Use the Internet to select a company that has recently undertaken diversification into new product markets. What do you feel were some of the reasons for this diversification (e.g., leveraging core competencies, sharing infrastructures)?

ETHICS AND CORPORATE SOCIAL RESPONSIBILITY QUESTIONS

1. In recent years, there has been a rash of corporate downsizing and layoffs. Do the ethical considerations merit attention? Are there strategic implications tied to the ethical concerns? Why, or why not?

2. What are some of the ethical issues that arise when managers act in a manner that is counter to their firm's best interests? What are the long-term implications for both the firms and the managers themselves?

3. Consider Lululemon's predicament reported earlier in the chapter. What were some of the issues related to the company's support of its supplier's claims? How can a partner in a strategic alliance be committed to the partnership and also retain its independence?

CHAPTER SEVEN

INTERNATIONAL STRATEGY:
Creating Value in Global Markets

LEARNING OBJECTIVES

After reading this chapter, you should have a good understanding of:

LO 1 The importance of international expansion as a viable diversification strategy.

LO 2 The sources of national advantage—that is, why an industry in a given country is more (or less) successful than the same industry in another country.

LO 3 The motivations, benefits, and the risks associated with international expansion.

LO 4 The two opposing forces—cost reduction and adaptation to local markets—that firms face when entering international markets.

LO 5 The advantages and disadvantages associated with each of the four basic strategies for achieving competitive advantage in global markets: international, global, multidomestic, and transnational.

LO 6 The six basic types of entry strategies and the relative benefits and risks associated with each of them.

LO 7 The emergence of offshoring and outsourcing as vehicles for firms to disperse their value chains across countries.

CASE STUDY

anopy Growth Corporation, formerly Tweed Marijuana Inc., is a medical marijuana company based in Smith Falls, Ontario.[1] The first federally regulated cannabis producer in North America, it trades on the Toronto Stock Exchange as WEED. As of the time of this writing, marijuana is legal in Canada exclusively for medicinal purposes, and Canopy Growth is licensed by Health Canada under the *Access to Cannabis for Medical Purposes Regulations*. The company has been described as one of the world's premier (and Canada's first) exporter of marijuana, and has recently expanded abroad to Germany.

photolona/Shutterstock.com

Germany's regulatory environment is today quite similar to Canada's. Germany legalized access to medical marijuana in 2005, but has yet to consider legalizing the drug for recreational use. Canada's current Liberal government, on the other hand, is expected to do so by 2018. Nonetheless, and unlike Canada, Germany has no domestic producers, and the industry relies entirely on imports. By entering the German market now, Canopy Growth is positioning itself to take advantage of an open market, build international brand recognition, and enjoy a head start into selling marijuana for domestic use, should the regulatory environment change.

This expansion was facilitated through an all-stock acquisition of the German-based MedCann, which gave Canopy Growth a German distribution network. MedCann is a pharmaceutical distributor which, as of late 2016, had already successfully placed Canopy's cannabis strains into German pharmacies. By acquiring a local distributor, Canopy benefits from their domestic expertise, allowing them to navigate the complicated regulatory environment surrounding the sale of medical marijuana.

Specifically, German legislation requires a strong track record of producing consistent strains of marijuana that yield reliable profiles harvest over harvest. "Germans need access to high-quality cannabis and [Canopy's] products are proving to be up to the very strict standards set by the federal government," said Dr. P. Debs, founder of MedCann, following the announcement of the acquisition. "Working together as one team will allow Canopy Growth through Tweed, Tweed Farms, and future production sites, to supply the unmet demand that has been building over the past decade." As Canopy is able to meet these quality requirements, it ensures that the acquisition is mutually beneficial: MedCann is given access to high quality products, and Canopy is able to take advantage of their local expertise in navigating regulatory policies.

Canopy's international interests are not limited to Germany. Earlier in 2016, Canopy announced its intention to set up a new Brazilian partnership. For their Brazilian expansion, Canopy is not acquiring a local distributor, as they did with MedCann; instead they have developed a joint venture with Entourage Phytolab to form a new,

Brazilian subsidiary of Bedrocan Brasil with local partners. In Brazil, Canopy intends to begin a clinical study for the development of a plant targeting epilepsy and pain management, intended to be registered with the Brazilian health authorities in early 2018.

With these ventures, Canopy reaps the benefits of utilizing different types of expansion strategies in different locations. With the German regulatory environment being considerably more complicated than that of Brazil, acquiring a distributor with expertise in the local environment was essential. Acquiring an existing company also ensured their speed of entry, which was necessary to take advantage of an open market with no local manufacturers. In Brazil, however, absent the same concerns as it had with German regulations, Canopy chose instead to develop a partnership and a joint venture agreement, reducing the level of risk involved with their expansion, and positioning themselves well to maintain their status as a high-quality international cannabis producer.

LO 1   THE GLOBAL ECONOMY: A BRIEF OVERVIEW

Canopy's apparent ease navigating the oceans of global business and its success in expanding internationally provide an informative example of smart expansion and a business's successful efforts to venture overseas. Nonetheless, many firms have taken the plunge, only to discover that competing internationally can be much more challenging than even the fiercest battles at home. Foreign markets can provide many opportunities for firms to increase their revenue base and their profitability. Bombardier, CAE, SNC Lavalin, and Aldo are some of the Canadian firms that have prospered internationally. How do these firms create value and achieve competitive advantages in the global marketplace? What factors can explain the success of a particular industry in a particular country? How can firms become successful when they diversify and expand the scope of their business to include international operations? International strategy choices present unique sets of challenges to executives who consider foreign markets for further expansion of their current business operations and for diversification opportunities.

Managers face many opportunities and risks when they venture abroad. Opportunities abound. Trade among nations has increased dramatically. It was estimated that in 2015, the trade *across* nations exceeded the trade *within* nations. In a variety of industries, such as semiconductors, automobiles, commercial aircraft, telecommunications, computers, and consumer electronics, it is virtually impossible for a firm to survive unless it scans the world for competitors, customers, human resources, suppliers, and technology.[2]

GE's wind energy business benefits by tapping into talent around the world. The firm has built research centres in China, Germany, India, and the United States. "We did it," says CEO Jeffrey Immelt, "to access the best brains everywhere in the world." All four centres played a key role in GE's development of huge 92-tonne turbines:[3]

- Chinese researchers in Shanghai designed the microprocessors that control the pitch of the blade.

- Mechanical engineers in India (Bangalore) devised mathematical models to maximize the efficiency of materials in the turbine.

- Power-systems experts in the United States (Niskayuna, New York, which has researchers from 55 countries) do the design work.

- Technicians in Munich, Germany, have created a "smart" turbine that can calculate wind speeds and signal sensors in other turbines to produce maximum electricity.

The rise of globalization and market capitalism around the world has contributed to the economic boom in the new economy, where knowledge is the key source of competitive advantage and value creation. In 2005 it was estimated that globalization had brought phone service to about 300 million households in developing nations and a transfer of nearly $2 trillion from rich countries to poor countries through equity, bond investments, and commercial loans.[4]

At the same time, there have been extremes in the effects of global capitalism on national economies and poverty levels around the world. The economies of East Asia have attained rapid growth, but there has been comparatively little progress in the rest of the world. For example, income in Latin America grew by only 6 percent in the past two decades—just as the continent was opening up to global capitalism. Inflation-adjusted average incomes in sub-Saharan Africa and the old Eastern European bloc have actually declined. The World Bank estimates that the number of people living on $1.90 or less per day has *increased* to 1.3 billion over the past decade, even if as a percentage of the total population there has been a slight drop.

Such disparities in wealth among nations raise an important question: Why do certain countries and their citizens enjoy the fruits of global capitalism, whereas others are mired in poverty? Why do some governments make the best use of inflows of foreign investment and know-how and others do not? There are many explanations. For one thing, governments need to have track records of business-friendly policies to attract multinationals. Furthermore, governments need to encourage local entrepreneurs, invest in modern technology, and nurture local suppliers and managers. Also, it means carefully managing the broader economic factors in an economy, such as interest rates, inflation, unemployment, and so on, as well as having a good legal system that protects property rights, strong educational systems, and a society where prosperity is widely shared.

The above policies are the type that East Asia—in locations such as Hong Kong, Taiwan, South Korea, and Singapore—has employed to evolve from the sweatshop economies of the 1960s and 1970s to the industrial powers of the 21st century. Conversely, many countries have moved in the other direction. Consider, for example, Guatemala, a country in Central America. Here, less than 50 percent of males complete fifth grade, an astonishing 40 percent of the population subsists on less than $1 per day, and the country ranks 31st out of 33 Latin American countries in the human development index. By comparison, the corresponding numbers for South Korea are 98 percent and less than 2 percent, respectively. Moreover, in Guatemala, 70 percent of the land rests in the hands of only 2 percent of the population in a country that is still predominantly agricultural.[5] Taxes and decades of ill-designed economic policies have kept the country's masses in poverty. Yet, as Strategy Spotlight 7.1 reports, marketing to the "bottom of the pyramid" allows multinational firms to target their goods and services to the nearly five billion poor people in the world who inhabit developing countries. Collectively, they represent a very large market with $14 trillion in purchasing power.

7.1 STRATEGY SPOTLIGHT

Marketing to the "Bottom of the Pyramid"

Many executives wrongly believe that profitable opportunities to sell consumer goods exist only in countries where income levels are high. Even when they expand internationally, they often tend to limit their company's marketing to only the affluent segments within the developing countries. Such narrow conceptualizations of the market lead them to ignore the vast opportunities that exist at the "bottom of the pyramid," according to C. K. Prahalad, one of the best global thinkers of strategic management. The bottom of the pyramid refers to the nearly five billion people inhabiting developing countries. Surprisingly, this group represents $14 trillion in purchasing power, and they are looking for products and services that can improve the quality of their lives. Multinationals are missing out on growth opportunities if they ignore this vast segment of the world market.

How can the poor buy if they do not have the money? The key is to bring the cost structures of the companies and their product offerings within the reach of low-income customers. Unilever, the Anglo-Dutch maker of such brands as Dove, Lipton, and Vaseline, started marketing single-serve sachets of shampoo to the poor in India several years ago. Selling for about a penny each, single sales account for 60 percent of the total value of shampoo sold in India today. A 500 millilitre (mL) bottle of shampoo may cost more than a farm worker's daily income and thus may be out of her reach. But the need for shampoo is almost universal. The challenge is to sell it in such a way that the poor can have their need for shampoo satisfied and the company can still make a profit.

Grameen Bank in Bangladesh is very different from the money-centre banks of London or New York. Pioneers of the concept of micro-credit, Grameen Bank extends small loans, sometimes as small as $20, to the thousands of struggling microbusiness entrepreneurs who have no credit histories or collateral to offer. The value of micro-credit loans soared from $4 million to $1.3 billion between 1996 and 2006. Not only are micro-credit loan recovery rates comparable with those of the big banks, but such lenders are also changing the lives of thousands of people who, because of small loans, are able to start and finance their own small businesses.

Casas Bahia, the Brazilian retailer, has built a $2.5 billion-per-year chain selling to the poor who live in the *favelas,* the illegal shanty towns on the outskirts of cities. Aravind Eye Care, an Indian hospital that specializes in cataract surgeries, has become the largest eye-care facility in the world, performing more than 200,000 procedures per year. The surgeries cost only about $25 compared with some $3,000 in North America. And, best of all, Aravind has a return on equity of more than 75 percent.

As the above examples demonstrate, to sell to the bottom of the pyramid, managers must rethink their costs, quality, scale of operations, and even their use of capital. What prevents managers from selling to this vast market? Often, they are the victims of their own false assumptions. First, they think that the poor have no purchasing power. But $14 trillion can buy a lot. Second, they assume that poor people have no use for new technologies. We only have to see the demand for cell phones from entrepreneurs who run microbusinesses in villages in India to dispel this myth. Third, managers assume that the poor have no use for their companies' products and services. They seem to ignore that shampoo, detergents, and financial services offered by banks are needs that all people have, not just the affluent. Fourth, they assume that working in these markets may not be exciting. Yet, recent experiences show that this may be a more invigorating environment than the mature markets of developed countries with its dogfights over fractions of market share.

Sources: J. McGregor, "The World's Most Influential Companies," *BusinessWeek,* December 22, 2008, pp. 43–53; C. Miller, "Easy Money," *Forbes,* November 27, 2006, pp. 134–138; C. K. Prahalad, "Why Selling to the Poor Makes for Good Business," *Fortune,* 150(9), 2004, pp. 32–33; A. Overholt, "A New Path to Profit," *Fast Company,* January, 2005, pp. 23–26; and C. K. Prahalad, *The Fortune at the Bottom of the Pyramid: Eradicating Poverty through Profits* (Philadelphia: Wharton School Publishing, 2005).

In the next section, we discuss in more detail why some nations' particular industries are more competitive than others. This discussion establishes an important context for the remainder of the chapter; after we discuss why some *nations and their industries* outperform others, we can better address the various strategies that *firms* can take to create competitive advantage when they expand internationally.

LO 2 FACTORS AFFECTING A NATION'S COMPETITIVENESS

Michael Porter of Harvard University conducted a four-year study in which he and a team of 30 researchers looked at the patterns of competitive success in 10 leading trading nations.[6] He concluded that there are four broad attributes of nations that individually, and as a system, constitute what is termed "the diamond of national advantage." In effect, the following attributes, together, determine the playing field that each nation establishes and operates for its industries:

- *Factor endowments.* The nation's position in factors of production, such as skilled labour or infrastructure, necessary to compete in a given industry.
- *Demand conditions.* The nature of home-market demand for the industry's product or service.

- *Related and supporting industries.* The presence or absence in the nation of supplier industries and other related industries that are internationally competitive.

- *Firm strategy, structure, and rivalry.* The conditions in the nation governing how companies are created, organized, and managed as well as the nature of domestic rivalry.

Factor Endowments

Classical economics suggests that factors of production, such as land, labour, and capital, are the building blocks that create usable consumer goods and services.[7,8] However, companies in advanced nations seeking competitive advantage over firms in other nations *create* many of the factors of production. For example, a country or industry dependent on scientific innovation must have a skilled human resource pool to draw on. This resource pool is not inherited; it is created through investment in industry-specific knowledge and talent. The supporting infrastructure of a country— that is, its transportation and communication systems as well as its banking system—are also critical. Factors of production must be developed that are industry specific and firm specific. In addition, the pool of resources a firm or a country has at its disposal is less important than the speed and efficiency with which these resources are deployed. Thus, firm-specific knowledge and skills created within a country—that are rare, valuable, difficult to imitate, and rapidly and efficiently deployed—are the factors of production that ultimately lead to a nation's competitive advantage. For example, the island nation of Japan has little land mass, making the warehouse space needed to store inventory prohibitively expensive. But by pioneering just-in-time inventory management, Japanese companies managed to create a resource from which they gained advantage over companies in other nations that spent large sums to warehouse their inventories.

Demand Conditions

Demand conditions are the demands that consumers place on an industry for goods and services. Consumers who demand highly specific, sophisticated products and services force firms to create innovative, advanced products and services to meet the demand. This consumer pressure presents challenges to a country's industries. But in response to these challenges, improvements to existing goods and services often result, creating conditions necessary for competitive advantage over firms in other countries.

Countries with demanding consumers drive firms in that country to meet high standards, upgrade existing products and services, and create innovative products and services. The conditions of consumer demand then influence how firms view a market, with more demanding consumers stimulating advances in products and services. This, in turn, helps a nation's industries better anticipate future global demand conditions and proactively respond to product and service requirements before competing nations are even aware of the need for such products and services.

Denmark, for instance, is known for its environmental awareness. Demand from consumers for environmentally safe products has spurred Danish manufacturers to become leaders in water pollution control equipment— products it successfully exports to other nations. Canada's vast landmass has always created unique challenges in bringing people and goods together, and a global industry for telecommunications has sprung from these challenges. Similarly, the wealth of metals and mineral resources in Canada has not only created a world-renowned mining industry but has also provided the conditions for the rise of mining engineering, exploration and drilling, and other specialized industries that today successfully compete around the world.

Related and Supporting Industries

Related and supporting industries enable firms to manage inputs more effectively. For example, countries with a strong supplier base benefit by adding efficiency to downstream activities. A competitive supplier base helps a firm obtain inputs using cost-effective, timely methods, thus reducing manufacturing costs. Also, close working relationships with suppliers provide the potential to develop competitive advantages through joint research and development and the ongoing exchange of knowledge.

Related industries offer similar opportunities through joint efforts among firms. In addition, related industries create the probability that new entrants will appear on the market, increasing competition and forcing existing firms to become more competitive through efforts, such as cost control, product innovation, and novel approaches to distribution. When combined, these give the home country's industries a source of competitive advantage.

Supporting industries in Italian footwear show how such relationships can lead to national competitive advantage. In Italy, shoe manufacturers are located near their suppliers. The manufacturers have ongoing interactions with leather suppliers and learn about new textures, colours, and manufacturing techniques while a shoe is still in the prototype stage. The manufacturers are able to project future demand and gear their factories for new products long before companies in other nations become aware of the new styles.

Firm Strategy, Structure, and Rivalry

Rivalry is particularly intense in nations with conditions of strong consumer demand, strong supplier bases, and high new-entrant potential from related industries. This competitive rivalry, in turn, increases the efficiency with which firms develop, market, and distribute products and services within the home country. Domestic rivalry thus provides a strong impetus for firms to innovate and find new sources of competitive advantage.

The intense rivalry forces firms to look outside their national boundaries for new markets, setting up the conditions necessary for global competitiveness. Among all the points on Porter's "diamond" of national advantage, domestic rivalry is, perhaps, the strongest indicator of global competitive success. Firms that have experienced intense domestic competition are more likely to have designed strategies and structures that allow them to successfully compete in world markets. In the United States, for example, intense rivalry spurred some companies, such as Dell Computer, to find innovative ways to produce and distribute its products. This was largely a result of competition from IBM and Hewlett-Packard.

It should be noted that Porter's diamond does not imply that one managerial style is best across industries; different strategies and different organizational structures have been instrumental in creating world-class competitors. Small- and medium-sized family-owned firms dominate the Italian footwear industry, and large multinationals have given Switzerland its leadership position in the pharmaceutical industry. Strategy Spotlight 7.2 discusses India's software industry. It provides an integrative example of how the insights from Porter's diamond can help to explain the relative degree of success of an industry in a given country.

7.2 STRATEGY SPOTLIGHT

India and the Diamond of National Advantage

Consider the following facts:

- SAP, the German software company, has developed new applications for notebook PCs at its Bangalore facility that employs 500 engineers.

- General Electric invested close to $100 million and hired 2,000 scientists to create one of the world's largest research and development laboratory in Bangalore, India.

- Over the last ten years, Microsoft has invested over a billion dollars in new research partnerships in India.

- One quarter of Fortune 1000 companies outsource their software requirements to firms in India.

- Indian software exports soared from less than $6 billion in 2000 to close to $100 billion in 2016 and the sector has been growing 12 percent per year during the same period. India is the second largest exporter of IT services in the world.

- More than 10,000 firms in India are involved in software services as their primary activity.

- Software and information technology (IT) firms in India are estimated to have directly employed over 4 million people by 2016 and provided auxiliary and indirect employment to over 10 million.

(Continued)

INDIA'S VIRTUAL DIAMOND IN SOFTWARE

Domestic rivalry

No regulatory barriers to entry or start-up; 800 firms, mostly small, in fierce rivalry; growing number of MNC software-development centres in India.

Factor endowments

Domestic demand conditions

U.S. demand conditions

Large pool of skilled labour; low salaries; English-language capability.

Large, growing market; sophisticated customers; cutting-edge applications.

Related and supporting industries

Large network of public and private educational institutions; weak but rapidly improving communications infrastructure; duty-free access to imported computers and software, following economic liberalization.

Note: Dashed lines represent weaker interactions.

Source: From D. Kampur and R. Ramamurti, "India's Emerging Competition Advantage in Services," *Academy of Management Executive: The Thinking Manager's Source.* Copyright © 2001 by Academy of Management. Reproduced with permission of Academy of Management via Copyright Clearance Center.

First, *factor endowments* are conducive to the rise of India's software industry. Through investment in human resource development with a focus on industry-specific knowledge, India's universities and software firms have literally created this essential factor of production. For example, India produces the second largest annual output of scientists and engineers in the world, behind only the United States. In a knowledge-intensive industry, such as software, development of human resources is fundamental to both domestic and global success.

Second, *demand conditions* require that software firms stay on the cutting edge of technological innovation. India has already moved toward globalization of its software industry; consumer demand conditions in developed nations, such as Germany, Denmark, parts of Southeast Asia, and the United States, created the consumer demand necessary to propel India's software makers toward sophisticated software solutions.[*]

Third, India has the *supplier base as well as the related industries* needed to drive competitive rivalry and enhance competitiveness. IT hardware prices declined rapidly in the 1990s. Furthermore, rapid technological change in IT hardware meant that latecomers, such as India, were not locked into older-generation technologies. Thus, both the IT hardware and software industries could "leapfrog" older technologies. In addition, relationships among knowledge workers in these IT hardware and software industries offer the social structure for ongoing knowledge exchange, promoting further enhancement of existing products. Further infrastructure improvements are occurring rapidly.

Fourth, with over 800 firms in the software services industry in India, *intense rivalry forces firms to develop competitive strategies and structures.* Although such firms as TCS, Infosys, and Wipro have become huge, with annual revenues in the tens of billions of dollars, they were quite small only a few years ago. And dozens of small- and mid-sized companies are aspiring to catch up, exploring and venturing in the latest spaces of e-commerce, artificial intelligence, and knowledge outsourcing. This intense rivalry is one of the primary factors driving Indian software firms to develop overseas distribution channels, as predicted by Porter's diamond of national advantage.

It is worth mentioning, though, that the cost advantage of Indian firms has been eroding. For example, TCS, Infosys, and Wipro engineers' salaries have soared. Part of the reason is that global firms, such as IBM and Accenture, are aggressively building their Indian operations and hiring tens of thousands of sought-after young Indian engineers. Even with the increased salaries, this still costs these firms a fraction of what a similar employee would cost in North America or Europe to produce similar work. Also, other Asian companies are trying to steal Indian firms' clients by offering to do relatively simple tasks at lower prices.

Sources: P. Ghemawat and T. Hout, "Tomorrow's Global Giants," *Harvard Business Review,* 86(1), 2008, pp. 80–88; S. K. Mathur, "Indian IT Industry: A Performance Analysis and a Model for Possible Adoption," ideas.repec.org, January 1, 2007, n.p.; M. Kripalani, "Calling Bangalore: Multinationals Are Making it a Hub for High-Tech Research," *BusinessWeek,* November 25, 2002, pp. 52–54; D. Kapur and R. Ramamurti, "India's Emerging Competitive Advantage in Services," *Academy of Management Executive,* 15(2), 2001, pp. 20–33;. Rajalakshmi, "It is time for Ctl+alt+dlt" The Hindu, Feb 26, 2017,; World Bank, *World Development Report* (New York: Oxford University Press, Reuters, 2001); "Oracle In India Push, Taps Software Talent," *Washington Post Online,* July 3.

* Although India's success cannot be explained in terms of its home market demand (according to Porter's model), the nature of the industry enables software to be transferred among different locations simultaneously by way of communications links. Thus, competitiveness of markets outside India can be enhanced without a physical presence in those markets.

Concluding Comments on Factors Affecting a Nation's Competitiveness

Porter based his conclusions on case histories of firms in more than 100 industries. Despite the differences in strategies employed by successful global competitors, a common theme did emerge: Firms that succeeded in global markets had first succeeded in intense competition in their home markets.

Competitive advantage for global firms typically grows out of relentless, continuing improvement, innovation, and change. Within this framework, governments act either as facilitators or as inhibitors through their policies on education, innovation, standards, regulations, taxation, and the removal of obstacles to firms' competitiveness. At the same time, chance can always play a determinant role in the development of globally competitive industries.

Canada's unique circumstances call for some modifications to the diamond analogy. Canada's international trade is responsible for some 70 percent of its gross domestic product (GDP), one of the highest levels among developed nations. Goods worth more than $1 billion cross the border between Canada and the United States each day. It is impossible to consider Canada's automotive sector without acknowledging the role of the U.S. market in every factor. The same applies to the lumber, pulp and paper, agriculture, energy, minerals, and metals industries. For example, most of the automobile manufacturers, such as General Motors (GM), Ford, Chrysler, Honda, and Toyota, have operations in both countries, but their strategic and tactical decisions are made on a North American basis; the integration of the industry is such that many of their parts suppliers, such as Magna, are responsible for moving components and sub-assemblies back and forth multiple times during the various stages of the value chain. It is quite possible for a simple stamped material from Canada to be shipped south of the border for refinement and be brought up again to become part of a subassembly. The sub-assembly could be shipped south to be installed on a component that crosses the border again for an assembly plant in Canada, where it could then become part of a car that is likely sold to a dealer in the south! Our notion of a national diamond and of the associated factors has to incorporate demand and factor conditions in both countries, rivalry among global players, related and support industries, as well as the role of two independent governments in assessing the viability and future prospects of the members of the industry.

Having highlighted the important role that nations play in international strategy, we turn next to the level of the individual firm. In the following section, we discuss a company's motivations for and the risks associated with international expansion.

LO 3 INTERNATIONAL EXPANSION: A COMPANY'S MOTIVATIONS AND RISKS

Motivations for International Expansion

Many reasons push companies to pursue international expansion. The most obvious one is to *increase the size of potential markets* for a firm's products and services.[9] The world's population exceeds 7.4 billion, with Canada representing less than 0.5 percent. Exhibit 7-2 lists the population of Canada compared with other major markets abroad and contrasts their per-capita purchasing power.

EXHIBIT 7-2 POPULATIONS AND PER-CAPITA GROSS DOMESTIC PRODUCT OF SELECTED NATIONS

Country	Population*	Per-Capita GDP in US$**
China	1,382,323,332	8,069
India	1,326,801,576	1,593
United States	324,118,787	56,115
Indonesia	260,581,100	3,346
Brazil	209,567,920	8,667
Japan	126,323,715	46,720
Germany	80,682,351	41,178
Congo	79,722,624	456
Canada	36,286,378	43,315
Norway	5,079,808	74,482
Luxembourg	576,243	99,717
The World	7,432,663,275	10,112

Sources: www.geohive.com/earth and World Development Indicators, World Bank national accounts data, and OECD National Accounts data files.

* Estimates as of March 2014.

** Per-capita GDP estimates are from 2012.

Many multinational firms have intensified their efforts to market their products and services to such countries as India and China, where the ranks of the middle class have increased over the past decade. Procter & Gamble has successfully achieved a 50-percent share in China's shampoo market, and PepsiCo has made impressive inroads in the Indian soft-drink market.[10]

Yet it is not only multinationals that are seeking to increase the sizes of their potential markets. Small firms might also be tempted or forced to look overseas for new customers. Lingo Media of Toronto, in spite of its small base as a Canadian publisher, has successfully penetrated the Chinese market, selling over 75 million units of English language educational material; it serves 65 percent of the Chinese ESL (English as Second Language) primary textbook market. Many successful Canadian firms have frequently looked to the neighbouring U.S. market for growth. Molson has been selling beer to U.S. consumers for almost a century; most of the Canadian forestry and energy firms have typically served U.S. customers; and many Canadian retailers, such as Loblaw, Jean Coutu, Couche-Tard, Canadian Tire, Aldo, La Senza, and Future Shop, when starting to think about foreign ventures, have looked first to the United States for opportunities, albeit with varying degrees of success.

Expanding a firm's global presence automatically increases its scale of operations, providing it with a larger revenue and asset base. As we noted in Chapter 5 in discussing overall cost leadership strategies, an increase in revenues and asset base potentially enables a firm to *attain economies of scale.* This provides multiple benefits. One advantage is the spreading of fixed costs, such as research and development, over a larger volume of production. Examples include the sale of Bombardier aircraft and Microsoft's operating systems in many foreign countries. IMAX knows very well that every new theatre that it opens somewhere in the world lowers the per-theatre cost of production of its unique movies. The Mississauga firm has built over 1,100 special theatres in 69 countries around the world, and each new theatre adds to the firm's capacity to produce more films for all the theatres in the chain.

Another advantage would be *reducing the costs of research and development as well as operating costs.* Recall, for example, the establishment of software development operations by Microsoft and other firms in talent-rich India (see Strategy Spotlight 7.2). A final advantage would be the attainment of greater purchasing power by pooling purchases. As Cott increases the number of facilities it has all over the world, it is able to place larger orders for equipment and supplies, thus increasing its bargaining power with suppliers.

Taking advantage of *arbitrage opportunities* is another advantage of international expansion. Arbitrage involves buying something from a place where it is cheap and selling it in another place where it commands a higher price. The possibilities for arbitrage are not necessarily confined to simple trading opportunities. It can be applied to virtually any factor of production and every stage of the value chain. For example, a firm may locate its call centre in India, its manufacturing plants in China, and its research and development (R&D) in Europe, where the specific types of talented personnel may be available at the lowest possible price. In today's integrated global financial markets, a firm can borrow anywhere in the world where capital is cheap and use it to fund a project in a country where capital is expensive. Such arbitrage opportunities are even more attractive to global corporations because their larger size enables them to buy in huge volumes, thus increasing their bargaining power over their suppliers. However, international expansion brings its own challenges, as Walmart has found in its aggressive pursuit of the Mexican market, a case described in Strategy Spotlight 7.3.

7.3 STRATEGY SPOTLIGHT

How Walmart Used Bribes to Solidify Its Position in Mexico

With revenues over $400 billion and net income of $14 billion, Walmart is considered among the most successful companies in the world. In recent years, Walmart has embarked on an ambitious international expansion agenda, opening stores in such countries as China, Japan, and England. Walmart today has 6,369 stores outside its home market in the United States.

Walmart's above-average industry profitability has been attributed to various factors, such as superior logistics, strict control over overhead costs, and effective use of information systems. But a *New York Times* investigation found that Walmart de Mexico frequently and aggressively used bribes to get its way. It began with $16 million in self-described "donations" to local

(Continued)

governments to speed up bureaucratic processes, then it expanded to over $24 million in alleged bribes that were used to pay off government officials to allow Walmart to engage in illegal activity. It is alleged that Walmart used bribes to have zoning maps redrawn, subvert public votes, circumvent regulatory safeguards, and outflank its rivals. After a public outcry and prolonged media pressure, Walmart launched an investigation. In March 2014, it announced that the two-year inquiry into the Mexican bribery scandal had cost the company $439 million, making it one of the most expensive probes in U.S. history. Meanwhile, the U.S. government is investigating Walmart's possible violation of the *Foreign Corrupt Practices Act,* Mexican authorities are exploring the company's violation of their laws, and Walmart shareholders are launching their own lawsuits in light of the skyrocketing costs that are emerging from this scandal.

Sources: D. Voreacos and R. Dudley, 2014, "Wal-Mart Says Bribe Probe Cost $439 Million in Two Years," *Business Week,* March 26; D. Barstow and A. Xanic von Bertrab, 2012, "The Bribery Aisle: How Wal-Mart Got Its Way in Mexico," *The New York* Times, December 17; P. Ghemawat, *Redefining Global Strategy* (Boston: Harvard Business School Press, 2007); R. E. Scott, "The Wal-Mart Effect," epi.org, June 26, 2007, n.p.

International expansion can also *extend the life cycle of a product* that is in its maturity stage in a firm's home country but has greater demand potential elsewhere. Products generally go through a four-stage life cycle: introduction, growth, maturity, and decline. During much of the 1990s, many Western telecommunications equipment manufacturers frequently sold their earlier-generation telephone switches to developing countries at lower costs and used the revenues to fund further research and development. Volkswagen continued to produce its original Beetle in Brazil long after it had stopped selling it in Europe and North America.

Finally, international expansion can enable a firm to *optimize the physical location for every activity in its value chain.* All firms have to make critical decisions as to where each activity will take place.[11] Very much in the form of arbitrage, a firm optimizing the location for every activity in the value chain can reap one or more of three strategic advantages: performance enhancement, cost reduction, and risk reduction.

Performance Enhancement

Microsoft's decision to establish a corporate research laboratory in Cambridge, England, is an example of a location decision that was guided mainly by the goal of building and sustaining world-class excellence in selected value-creating activities.[12] This strategic decision provided Microsoft with access to outstanding technical and professional talent. Location decisions can affect the quality with which any activity is performed in terms of the availability of needed talent, speed of learning, and the calibre of external and internal coordination.

Cost Reduction

Two location decisions founded largely on cost-reduction considerations are Nike's decision to source the manufacture of athletic shoes from Asian countries, such as China, Vietnam, and Indonesia, and the decision of many multinational companies to set up production operations just south of the United States–Mexico border to access lower-cost labour. These operations are called *maquiladoras.* Such location decisions affect the cost structure and are based on the availability of local manpower and other resources, transportation and logistics, and government incentives and the local tax structure.

Strategy Spotlight 7.4 discusses how Deere & Co, the $28-billion construction and farm equipment manufacturer, developed a new tractor at its research facility in Pune, India, for the local market and how that tractor created a viable alternative to a competitor's offering back in North America.

Performance enhancement and cost-reduction benefits parallel the business-level strategies (discussed in Chapter 5) of differentiation and overall cost leadership. They can, at times, be attained simultaneously. Consider

7.4 STRATEGY SPOTLIGHT

How Deere & Co. Learned from Its Indian Operations

Companies are increasingly discovering that their international operations are coming up with ideas that resonate far beyond local markets. Case in point: Deere & Co. is pursuing a new market in the United States—recreational farmers. And they have innovations developed at their research facility in Pune, India, to thank for it.

Deere, based in Moline, Illinois, opened the Pune centre in 2001 as a way to enter the Indian market. The move was quite unexpected. After all, Deere is known for its heavy-duty farm equipment and big construction gear, and many of India's farmers still use oxen-pulled plows. However, Deere saw potential, and its engineers in Pune responded with four no-frills models. Although they did not include a global positioning system (GPS) or air conditioning, they were sturdy enough to handle the rigours of commercial farming.

The tractors cost between $8,400 and $11,600 in India and were so basic that Deere never considered selling them in the United States until Indian tractor maker Mahindra & Mahindra started selling its no-frill tractors in the United States, targeting a market that Deere had largely ignored—hobbyists and bargain hunters. Such buyers did not need many advanced features. And it turned out that they coveted the same qualities that Indian farmers did: affordability and manoeuvrability.

Deere, taking a cue from its rival, brought a slightly modified version (with softer seats and higher horsepower) of the Indian line of tractors to the American market. Called the 5003 model, it sold for $14,400 in the United States, and by 2008, half the Deere tractors produced in India were making their way overseas. "These tractors are like Swiss Army knives. They get used for anything: mowing, transporting bales of hay, pushing dirt, and removing manure," explained Mike Alvin, a product manager at Deere.

Raj Kalathur, then the managing director of Deere's Indian division, said the 5003 tractors were born out of "frugal engineering." Such innovation is not just global—it is good business.

Sources: J. Mero, "John Deere's Farm Team," *Fortune*, April 14, 2008, pp. 119–124; and "No-Frills Indian Tractors Find Favor with US Farmers," www.thaindian.com, April 29, 2008, n.p.

our example, in the previous section, of the Indian software industry. When Oracle set up a development operation in that country, the company benefited from lower labour costs and operational expenses as well as from performance enhancements realized through the hiring of superbly talented professionals.

Managing across borders also gives rise to challenging ethical dilemmas. One issue that has received a good deal of attention is child labour. Strategy Spotlight 7.5 discusses the approaches of two multinationals in addressing this issue.

7.5 STRATEGY SPOTLIGHT

Child Labour: How Two Companies Have Addressed This Issue

The issue of child labour has been raised frequently since the early 1990s, when the proliferation of goods from China and Southeast Asia started hitting the North American retail shelves, although experts would explain that children had been exploited for centuries in sweatshops and factories producing goods for local consumption and export. How have

(Continued)

companies responded to these concerns? Consider Nike, one of the first companies to be publicly criticized for the practice. The company initially tried to distance itself from the issue by pointing the finger at its independent subcontractors. Nike has revised its code of conduct a number of times since 1992, making changes that include increasing the minimum age from 14 to 18 for footwear factory workers and from 14 to 16 for equipment and apparel workers. Both these standards are higher than the codes of other companies and of the convention of the International Labour Organization (ILO). The company also has started an internal compliance program, supplemented with external monitoring. These actions, however, do not seem to have silenced the critics. Nike's website reflects the way in which the company tries to openly address this criticism, providing ample information about the monitoring of facilities and the dilemmas the company faces after introducing its latest code.

In contrast, Chiquita Banana almost completely follows the SA 8000 standard, including all references to international conventions, but with appropriate modifications to account for workplace issues specific to agriculture. The SA 8000 standard was developed by the Council on Economic Priorities Accreditation Agency and is widely recognized and accepted; it is based on ILO and United Nations conventions. The company's strict child labour provisions do not apply to family farms or to small-scale holdings in the seasonal, non-banana businesses that do not regularly employ hired workers. This is also meant to allow for employment of a farmer's own children in seasonal activities. Chiquita tries to address the problem associated with children working in supplier factories by giving support to enable them to remain in school until they are old enough to work.

Sources: Reprinted from A. Kolk and R. V. Tulder, "Ethics in International Business: Multinational Approaches to Child Labor," Journal of World Business, 39, 2004, pp. 49–60, Copyright 2004, with permission from Elsevier

Risk Reduction

Given the erratic swings in the exchange ratios between the U.S. dollar and the Japanese yen (in relation to each other as well as to other major currencies), an important basis for cost competition between Ford and Toyota has been their relative ingenuity at managing currency risks. One of the ways for such competitors to manage currency risks has been to spread the high-cost elements of their manufacturing operations across a few select and carefully chosen locations around the world. Such location decisions can affect the overall risk profile of the firm with respect to political, economic, and currency risks.[13]

Learning Opportunities

By expanding into new markets, corporations expose themselves to differing market demands, R&D capabilities, functional skills, organizational processes, and managerial practices. This provides opportunities for managers to transfer the knowledge that results from these exposures back to their home office and to other divisions in the firm. Thus, expansion into new markets provides a range of learning opportunities. For example, when L'Oréal, a French personal care product manufacturer, acquired two U.S. firms that developed and sold hair care products to African-American customers, L'Oréal gained knowledge on what is referred to in the industry as "ethnic hair care." It then took this knowledge and built a new ethnic hair care division in Europe and later began making inroads in African markets. More generally, research suggests that overseas expansion leads to valuable learning at home. One study found that, rather than distracting the firm from its efforts in its home market, overseas acquisitions led to substantial performance improvements, averaging of a 12 percent increase, in home markets.[14]

Exploring Reverse Innovation

Finally, exploring possibilities for reverse innovation has become a major motivation for international expansion. Many leading companies are discovering that developing products specifically for emerging markets can pay off in a big way. In the past, multinational companies typically developed products for their rich home markets and then tied to sell them in developing countries with minor adaptations. However, as growth slows in rich nations and demand grows rapidly in developing countries, such as India and China, this approach becomes increasingly inadequate. Instead, companies like GE have committed significant resources to developing products that meet the needs of developing nations, products that deliver adequate functionality at a fraction of the cost. Interestingly, these products have subsequently found considerable success in value segments in wealthy countries as well. Hence, this process is referred to as reverse innovation, a new motivation for international expansion.

As $3,000 cars, $300 computers, and $30 mobile phones bring what were previously considered luxuries within the reach of the middle class of emerging markets, it is important to understand the motivations and implications of reverse innovation. *First,* it is impossible to sell first-world versions of products with minor adaptations in countries where the average annual income per person is between $1,000 and $4,000, as is the case in most developing countries. To sell in these markets, entirely new products must be designed and developed by local technical talent and manufactured with local components. *Second,* although these countries are relatively poor, they are growing rapidly. *Third,* if the innovation does not come from first-world multinationals, there are any number of local firms that are ready to grab the market with low-cost products. *Fourth,* as the consumers and governments of many first-world countries are rediscovering the virtues of frugality and are trying to cut down expenses, these products and services originally developed for the first world may gain significant market shares in developing countries as well.

Potential Risks of International Expansion

When a company expands its international operations, it does so to increase its profits or revenues. As with any other investment, however, potential risks accompany the anticipated returns.[15] To help companies assess the risk of entering foreign markets, rating systems have been developed to evaluate political, economic, and financial and credit risks. *Euromoney* magazine publishes a semiannual "Country Risk Rating" that evaluates political, economic, and other risks faced by potential entrants. Exhibit 7-3 depicts a sample of country risk ratings, published by the World Bank, from the 178 countries that *Euromoney* evaluates. In the exhibit, note that the lower the score, the higher the country's expected level of risk. Firms contemplating international expansion typically consider four types of risk—namely, political, economic, currency, and management risk.

EXHIBIT 7-3   A SAMPLE OF INTERNATIONAL COUNTRY RISK RANKINGS

Rank	Country	Total Risk Assessment	Economic Performance	Political Risk	Total of Debt Indicators	Total of Credit and Access to Finance Indicators
1	Norway	93.44	90.40	92.97	20.00	30.00
2	Luxembourg	91.03	81.00	93.67	20.00	30.00
3	Switzerland	89.59	82.50	87.23	20.00	30.00
9	Canada	86.17	73.50	88.97	20.00	29.75
15	United States	81.60	60.67	85.25	20.00	30.00
25	Japan	74.66	53.80	76.79	18.54	28.42
40	China	63.55	66.88	48.47	16.44	23.69
56	India	56.96	57.00	49.66	12.78	19.78
57	Russia	56.83	61.56	44.30	13.66	20.16
89	Pakistan	40.34	24.64	34.40	11.99	13.59
183	Afghanistan	12.66	8.40	2.93	0.00	1.23
185	Iraq	7.40	1.84	2.20	0.00	0.83

Sources: Based on figures from www.worldbank.org and A. Mortimer, "Country Risk, March 2015: Middle East Drops, Sub-Saharan Africa Rises," *Euromoney.*

Political and Economic Risks

Generally, the business climate in Canada is very favourable. Other countries around the globe, though, present elevated levels of political risk. Forces such as social unrest, military turmoil, demonstrations, and even violent conflict and terrorism can pose serious threats.[16] Consider, for example, the ongoing tensions and violence in the Middle East associated with social unrest, terrorist acts and civil wars in a host of countries including Egypt, Libya, Syria and Iraq.[17] Because such conditions increase the likelihood of destruction of property as well as non-payment for goods and services, countries that are viewed as bearing high political and economic risks are less attractive for most types of business. Nevertheless, firms that choose to operate in those environments, such as Canadian firms in Afghanistan and U.S. firms in Iraq, would expect substantially higher returns from their operations there to compensate for the additional risk.

Political risk can also arise from boycotts directed toward the home government of a corporation and its policies. Many U.S. firms have suffered overseas as a result of the U.S. government's stance in the Middle East, and Canadian firms around the world have been the targets of animal rights groups that do not approve of seal hunting in Newfoundland and the Canadian Arctic.

Another source of political risk in many countries is the absence of the **rule of law.** The absence of rules or the lack of uniform enforcement of existing rules leads to what might often seem to be arbitrary and inconsistent decisions by government officials. This can make it difficult for foreign firms to conduct business.

For example, consider Renault's experience in Russia. Renault paid $1 billion to acquire a 25 percent ownership stake in the Russian automaker AvtoVAZ in 2008. Just one year later, Russian prime minister Vladimir Putin threatened to dilute Renault's ownership stake unless it contributed more money to prop up AvtoVAZ, which was then experiencing a significant slide in sales. Renault realized its ownership claim may not have held up in the corrupt Russian court system. Therefore, it was forced to negotiate and eventually agreed to transfer over $300 million in technology and expertise to the Russian firm to ensure its ownership stake would stay at 25 percent.[18]

Interestingly, while corporations have historically been concerned about rule-of-law issues in developing markets, such issues have also become a significant concern in developed markets, most critically in the United States. In the 2012 World Economic Forum *Global Competitive Report* examining the quality of governmental institutions and the rule of law, the United States fared poorly.

Starkly, the United States was ranked among the top 20 countries on only 1 of the 22 measures of institutional quality included in the survey. In line with these findings, the International Finance Corporation (IFC) found that governmental hurdles faced by businesses have become a greater challenge in the U.S. in recent years. The IFC compiles data annually on the burdens of doing business that are put in place by governments and found that the U.S. is one of only a few countries surveyed in which doing business has become more burdensome, not less. In nearly 90 percent of countries, governmental burdens have eased since 2006, but the U.S. has bucked that trend, becoming a more difficult location in which to operate. As institutions deteriorate, the U.S. loses its lustre as a place to base operations. This sentiment was reflected in a survey of business executives who are alumni of the Harvard Business School. When asked whether they had recently favoured basing new operations in the U.S. or in a foreign location, an overwhelming majority, 84 percent, responded that they had chosen the foreign location. Thus, advanced economies, such as the U.S., risk losing out to other countries if they fail to reinforce and strengthen their legal and political institutions.[19]

The laws, as well as the enforcement of laws, associated with the protection of intellectual property rights can be another significant potential risk in entering new countries. Microsoft, for example, has lost billions of dollars in potential revenue through piracy of its software products in many countries, including China. Other areas of the globe, such as the former Soviet Union and some eastern European nations, have piracy problems as well. Firms rich in intellectual property have encountered financial losses as imitations of their products have grown through a lack of law enforcement of intellectual property rights.[20]

Currency Risks

Currency fluctuations can pose substantial risks. A company with operations in several countries must constantly monitor the exchange rate between its own currency and that of the host country. Even a small change in the exchange rate can result in a significant difference in the cost of production or net profit when doing business overseas. When the dollar appreciates against other currencies, Canadian goods can be more expensive to consumers in foreign countries. Many Canadian firms started reporting reduced profits after 2004 from their U.S. operations, simply because of the appreciation of the loonie. Gold and oil companies, in contrast, benefited enormously from the decline of the U.S. dollar and the simultaneous global price increases of their commodities, even if those prices were marked in U.S. dollars.

It is important to note that even when government intervention is well intended, the macroeconomic effects of such action can be very negative for multinational corporations. Such was the case in 1997 when Thailand suddenly chose to devalue its currency, the baht, after months of trying to support it at an artificially high level. This, in effect, made the baht worthless compared with other currencies. In 1998, Russia not only devalued its ruble but also elected not to honour its foreign debt obligations. Of course, 10 years later, flush with cash from oil and gas exports, Russia paid back its debt with depressed dollars.

Management Risks

Management risks reflect the challenges that managers face when they must respond to the inevitable differences that they encounter in foreign markets. These concern a variety of factors: culture, customs, language, income levels, customer preferences, distribution systems, and so on.[21]

Differences in cultures across countries pose unique challenges for managers. Cultural symbols can evoke deep emotions.[22] For example, in a series of advertisements aimed at Italian vacationers, Coca-Cola executives turned the Eiffel Tower, the Empire State Building, and the Tower of Pisa into the familiar Coke bottle. However, when the white marble columns of the Parthenon that crowns the Acropolis in Athens were turned into Coke bottles, the Greeks became outraged. Greeks refer to the Acropolis as the "holy rock," and a government official insisted that the Parthenon is an "international symbol of excellence" and that "whoever insults the Parthenon insults international culture." Coca-Cola apologized for the advertisement. Exhibit 7-4 highlights how cultures vary across countries and some of the implications for the conduct of business across national boundaries.

 **EXHIBIT 7-4** ## HOW CULTURE VARIES ACROSS NATIONS: IMPLICATIONS FOR BUSINESS

France

- Most English-speaking French have learned British-style English, which can lead to communication breakdowns with speakers of American-style English. For example, in the United States, a presentation that "bombs" has failed, but in England it has succeeded.
- Words in French and English may have similar roots but different meanings or connotations. For example, a French person might "demand" something because in French *demander* means "to ask."

Hong Kong

- Negotiations occur over cups of tea. Always accept an offer of tea whether you want it or not. When you are served, wait for the host to drink first.
- Chinese negotiators commonly use teacups as visual aids. One cup may be used to represent your company and another cup to represent the Hong Kong company. The positions of the cups will be changed to indicate how far apart the companies are on the terms of an agreement.
- Also, avoid any gifts of knives, scissors, or cutting tools; these suggest the severing of a friendship to the Chinese. If you are giving flowers, give an even number of them; an odd number would be considered very unlucky.

Ecuador

- Dinner at an Ecuadorian home lasts many hours. Expect drinks and appetizers around 8:00 p.m., with dinner not served until 11:00 p.m. or midnight. You will dismay your hosts if you leave as early as 1:00 a.m. A party at an Ecuadorian home will begin late and end around 4:00 a.m. or 5:00 a.m. Late guests may sometimes be served breakfast before they leave.

Sources: T. Morrison, W. Conaway, and G. Borden, *Kiss, Bow, or Shake Hands* (Avon, MA: Adams Media Corporation, 1994); and www.executiveplanet.com/business-culture/112565157281.html.

Let us now look at how firms can attain competitive advantages when they move beyond the boundaries of their home nation.

ACHIEVING COMPETITIVE ADVANTAGE IN GLOBAL MARKETS

Firms are pulled by two opposing forces when they expand into global markets: cost reduction and adaptation to local markets. In responding to the relative pressure from these forces, firms choose among four basic types of international strategies: international, global, multidomestic, and transnational.

LO 4   Two Opposing Forces: Reducing Costs and Adapting to Local Markets

Pressures to lower costs derive from the standardization or even commoditization of many products; meaningful differences among producers' diverse offerings may be difficult to discern, and price then becomes the main competitive weapon. Pressure further intensifies when competition arises from producers located in low-cost countries. Standardization promotes substantial economies of scale; supplying global markets with standard products allows for global manufacturing decisions and the adoption of global marketing efforts. Both promise significant savings. In response, economist Theodore Levitt advocated strategies that favour global products and brands. He suggested that firms should standardize all of their products and services for all of their worldwide markets. Such an approach would help a firm lower its overall costs by spreading its investments over as large a market as possible. Levitt's thesis rests on extensive observations about our world.[23] Television, newspapers, global publications, inexpensive travel, and the Internet have brought people closer together than ever before. Most luxury brands from France (Louis Vuitton, Hermès, Chanel, Dior), Italy (Gucci, Armani, Dolce & Gabbana), Germany (Hugo Boss), and the United States (Ralph Lauren, Calvin Klein) are well recognized and have set up stores in the high-fashion streets of each of dozens of metropolises around the world. Aldo, the successful Montreal-based fashion shoe company, operates 850 stores in over 40 countries on five continents, selling identical designs of shoes and accessories. Club Monaco, another Canadian fashion icon, owns six stores in its founding city, Toronto, and has already opened five stores in Beijing. Coca-Cola, McDonald's, Levi's, Sony, Apple, and Microsoft are among many brands used daily by hundreds of millions of consumers around the world. Industrial customers of commodities, such as steel, aluminum, oil, and gold, have identical needs and shop globally for supplies. Levitt also argues that people around the world are willing to sacrifice idiosyncratic preferences in product features, functions, and design for lower prices at high quality.

Although pressures for cost reductions might, indeed, direct firms toward standardized global products, one cannot ignore the opposite reality that is also prevalent in the world's markets today.[24] Countless local firms thrive by offering products that cater to the specific needs of local consumers. Many global firms customize their products and services to target local market segments. In Japan, Coca-Cola markets Georgia (a tonic drink) as well as Classic Coke, and Hi-C. McDonald's serves wine in France and lamb-based hamburgers in India. Couche-Tard uses the banner Circle K in the United States, where the range of products in its convenience stores differs markedly from its Quebec and Ontario stores. Many consumers might be willing to sacrifice product attributes for lower prices, but many more are likely to want more features, higher product quality, and enhanced services.

Transportation costs and other diseconomies of scale put a damper on the ability of firms to build very large facilities in the most cost-efficient locations to supply distant markets. Moreover, flexible factory automation technologies enable economies of scale to be attained at lower levels of output and do not require production of a single standardized product. Sales, service, and distribution are inherently localized activities and increasingly represent a substantial part of a product's total value to consumers.

Although Harley-Davidson motorcycles, Bombardier planes, and some of Coca-Cola's soft-drink products are rightly designed the same for all markets throughout the world, managers usually strive to tailor their products to the culture of the country in which they are attempting to do business. Few would argue that "one size fits all" applies generally.

Managers face two opposing pressures when they compete in markets beyond their national boundaries, and these pressures place conflicting demands on their firms as they strive to be competitive.[25] On the one hand, competitive pressures require that firms do what they can to lower unit costs so that consumers will not perceive their product and service offerings as too expensive. This may lead them to consider locating manufacturing facilities in areas where labour costs are low and to develop products that are highly standardized across multiple countries.

On the other hand, in addition to responding to pressures to lower costs, managers must strive to be responsive to local pressures and to tailor their products to the demand of the local market in which they do business. This requires differentiating their offerings and strategies from country to country to reflect consumer tastes and preferences as well as making changes to reflect differences in distribution channels, human resource practices, and governmental regulations. However, since the strategies and tactics to differentiate products and services to local markets can involve additional expenses, a firm's costs will tend to rise.

The two opposing pressures result in four different basic strategies that companies can use to compete in the global marketplace: international, global, multidomestic, and transnational. The strategy that a firm selects depends on the degree of pressure that it is facing with respect to cost reductions and the need to adapt to local markets. Exhibit 7-5 shows the conditions under which each of these strategies would be most appropriate.

EXHIBIT 7-5

OPPOSING PRESSURES AND FOUR STRATEGIES

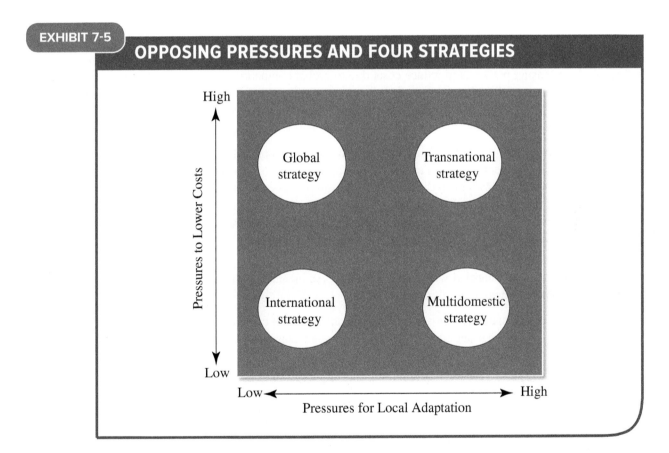

LO 5 Opposing Pressures and Four Strategies

As one would expect, there are advantages and disadvantages associated with each of these strategies. In the following sections, we consider each of the strategies in their basic, or pure, form. In practice, though, firms frequently employ a mix of the elements of all four strategies.

International Strategy

There are a small number of industries in which pressures for both local adaptation and reducing costs are rather low. An extreme example of such an industry is the "orphan" drug industry, which produces medicines for diseases that are severe but affect only a small number of people (e.g., Gaucher's disease and Fabry's disease). Such companies as Alexion and Vertex are active in this segment of the drug industry. There is virtually no need to adapt their products to the local markets. And the pressures to reduce costs are low; even though only a few thousand patients are affected, the revenues and margins are significant because patients receiving treatments for these diseases are charged up to $100,000 per year.

An international strategy is based on diffusion and adaptation of the parent company's knowledge and expertise to foreign markets. Country units are allowed to make some minor adaptations to products and ideas coming from the head office, but they enjoy little independence and autonomy. The primary goal of the strategy is worldwide exploitation of the parent firm's knowledge and capabilities. All sources of core competencies are centralized.

For most of its history, Ericsson, a Swedish telecommunications firm, has followed this strategy. Because its home market (Sweden) was too small to support the R&D effort necessary in the industry, Ericsson built its strategy on its ability to transfer and adapt its innovative products and process technologies to international markets. This strategy of sequential diffusion of innovation that it developed at home helped it to compete successfully against NEC, which followed a global strategy, and ITT, which followed a multidomestic strategy.[26]

The majority of large multinational firms pursued the international strategy in the decades following World War II. These companies centralized R&D and product development but established manufacturing facilities as well as marketing organizations abroad. Such companies as McDonald's and Kellogg are examples of firms still following this strategy. Although these companies do make some local adaptations, these are of a rather limited nature. With increasing pressures to reduce costs due to global competition, especially from low-cost countries, opportunities to successfully employ international strategy are becoming more limited. This strategy is most suitable in situations where a firm has distinctive competencies that local companies in foreign markets lack.

Certain challenges and risks are associated with an international strategy:

- Different activities in the value chain typically have different optimal locations. That is, R&D may be optimally located in a country that has an abundant supply of scientists and engineers, whereas assembly may be better conducted in a low-cost location. Nike, for example, designs its shoes in the United States, but all the manufacturing is done in such countries as China and Thailand. The international strategy, with its tendency to concentrate most of its activities in one location, fails to take advantage of the benefits of an optimally distributed value chain.

- The international strategy is susceptible to higher levels of political risk and currency risk. The company is often too closely identified with a single country. An increase in the value of the currency may suddenly make the product unattractive abroad.

- The lack of local responsiveness may result in the alienation of customers. Worse still, the firm's inability to be receptive to new ideas and innovation from its foreign subsidiaries may lead to missed opportunities.

Global Strategy

A firm whose emphasis is on lowering costs tends to follow a global strategy. Competitive strategy is centralized and controlled to a large extent by the corporate office. Since the primary emphasis is on controlling costs, the corporate office strives to achieve a strong level of coordination and integration across the various businesses.[27] Firms following a global strategy strive to offer standardized products and services as well as to locate manufacturing, R&D, and marketing activities in only a few locations.[28]

Bombardier follows a global strategy for its airplanes as well as its public transit systems. Although each individual airline customer may require some customization in terms of fitting the interior of the planes with certain colours and configurations, the planes are, for the most part, standardized and produced in a single location for worldwide distribution. Bombardier also provides its customers with technical support, spare parts, and maintenance, which adhere to global standards.

A global strategy emphasizes economies of scale due to the standardization of products and services and the centralization of operations in a few locations. One advantage of this may be that innovations, which come about through efforts of either a business unit or the corporate office, can be transferred more easily to other locations. Although costs may be lower, the firm following a global strategy may, in general, have to forgo opportunities for revenue growth, since it does not invest extensive resources in adapting product offerings from one market to another.

A global strategy is most appropriate when there are strong pressures for reducing costs and comparatively weak pressures for adaptation to local markets. Identifying potential economies of scale becomes an important consideration.[29] Advantages to increased volume may come not only from larger production plants or runs but also from more efficient logistics and distribution networks. Worldwide volume is also especially important in supporting high levels of investment in R&D. As we would expect, many industries requiring high levels of R&D, such as pharmaceuticals, semiconductors, and jet aircraft, follow global strategies.

Another advantage of a global strategy is that it can enable a firm to create a standard level of quality throughout the world. Here is what Tom Siebel, former chairman of Siebel Systems, the $2-billion developer of e-business application software (acquired by Oracle in 2006), had to say about global standardization:

> Our customers—global companies like IBM, Zurich Financial Services, and Citicorp— expect the same high level of service and quality, and the same licensing policies, no matter where we do business with them around the world. Our human resources and legal departments help us create policies that respect local cultures and requirements worldwide, while at the same time maintaining the highest standards. We have one brand, one image, one set of corporate colors, and one set of messages, across every place on the planet. An organization needs central quality control to avoid surprises.[30]

Strategy Spotlight 7.6 describes how Gildan, a Canadian firm, benefits from manufacturing and marketing activewear around the world.

7.6 STRATEGY SPOTLIGHT

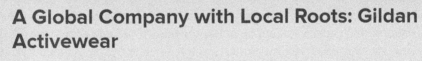

A Global Company with Local Roots: Gildan Activewear

Check the label! Chances are, your school t-shirt and fleece are made by Gildan. Across North America and Europe, over 50 percent of all decorated activewear sold by and on behalf of thousands of colleges, schools and universities, sports franchises, entertainment venues, and summer camps, as well as corporate imprinted promotional golf shirts, are made by the Montreal-based company founded by Greg and Glenn Chamandy over 30 years ago.

From its humble beginnings, Gildan has become a billion-dollar, global firm that sources, manufactures, markets, sells, and distributes across the world. The company is the leading supplier of basic, quality branded activewear for the wholesale imprinted sportswear market. Essentially, it sells blank t-shirts, sports shirts, and fleece in large quantities to wholesalers, who have them

(Continued)

emblazoned with designs and logos by screen printers. Consumers purchase Gildan's products at schools, sports events, corporate functions, and travel and tourism destinations. Gildan has also ventured into supplying athletic socks, underwear, and activewear to mass-market retailers in North America and overseas. Including Walmart as one of its major customers has taken Gildan to Latin America, Central America, Europe, and Asia, in addition to its traditional markets in North America.

Although its headquarters are still in Montreal, few of Gildan's 42,000 employees can be found there, as very little of the spinning, cutting, sewing, assembly, or manufacturing takes place in Canada. All the strategic decisions are made near Mount Royal, but most of the raw materials come from the United States and Asia, and the spinning takes place in southern United States and in Central America. The bulk of the manufacturing work is spread across some 10 facilities in the Caribbean and Central America. Sales and distribution offices are strategically located in North America, Europe, and Asia. Consider the following figures: 75 percent of Gildan's fixed assets are located in the Caribbean Basin and in Central America, 5 percent can be found in Canada, and approximately 15 percent are in the United States. The United States accounts for 85 percent of sales, in part because the headquarters of Walmart and of other global customers are in the United States, and thus their sales are booked in that country to be distributed and sold around the world. Canada accounts for just over 4 percent of total sales. Gildan's gross margins are continually affected by the differential exchange rates across its multiple facilities in different countries, as well as by the different levels of efficiency achieved in the various locations. Gildan is a proud Canadian company whose little label adorns millions of college students' favourite activewear, across the world. In the process, Gildan has rewarded its shareholders with continuous earnings growth.

As a postscript to Gildan's global strategy, it is also worth mentioning that the company has come under criticism for closing Canadian, U.S., and Mexican facilities to move operations to Haiti, Honduras, Nicaragua, and the Dominican Republic—all countries that have been frequently connected with sweatshop and unethical labour practices. In response to such criticism, Gildan has committed to adhering to the Fair Labour Association's (FLA) labour compliance program and, in 2013, was the first activewear manufacturer to be accredited by the FLA.

Sources: B. Marotte, "Gildan CEO Reducing Stake; Stock Split Set," *The Globe and Mail*, May 4, 2007, p. B4; "Gildan Activewear Beats Expectations, Boosts Guidance," *The Globe and Mail*, August 4, 2006, p. B5; Maquila Solidarity Network at www.en.maquilasolidarity.org; company annual reports, financial statements and proxy circular; www.gildan.com.

There are, of course, some risks associated with a global strategy.[31]

- A firm can enjoy economies of scale only by concentrating scale-sensitive resources and activities in one or few locations. Such concentration, however, becomes a "double-edged sword." For example, if a firm has only one manufacturing facility, it must export its output (e.g., components, subsystems, or finished products) to other markets, some of which may be a great distance from the operation. Thus, decisions about locating facilities must weigh the potential benefits from concentrating operations in a single location against the higher transportation and tariff costs that result from such concentration.

- The geographic concentration of any activity may also tend to isolate that activity from the targeted markets. Such isolation could be risky, since it may hamper the facility's ability to quickly respond to changes in market conditions and needs.

- Concentrating an activity in a single location also makes the rest of the firm dependent on that location. Dependency on a sole source implies that unless the location has world-class competencies, the firm's competitive position can be eroded if problems arise. A European executive of Ford Motor Co., reflecting on the firm's concentration of activities during a global integration program in the mid-1990s, lamented, "Now if you misjudge the market, you are wrong in 15 countries rather than only one."

Multidomestic Strategy

A firm whose emphasis is on differentiating its product and service offerings to adapt to local markets follows a multidomestic strategy. Decisions evolving from a multidomestic strategy tend to be decentralized to permit the firm to tailor its products and respond rapidly to changes in demand. This enables a firm to expand its market and to charge different prices in different markets. For firms following this strategy, differences in language, culture, income levels, customer preferences, and distribution systems are only a few of the many factors that must be considered. Even in the case of relatively standardized products, at least some level of local adaptation is often necessary. Consider Honda motorcycles. Although one could argue that a good product knows no national boundaries, there are subtle differences in ways that a product is used and in what customers expect of it in different countries. Although Honda uses a common basic technology, it must develop different types of motorcycles for different regions of the world. For example, North Americans primarily use motorcycles for leisure and sports; thus, aggressive looks and high horsepower are key. In Southeast Asia, motorcycles are a basic means of transportation; thus, they require low cost and ease of maintenance. And in Australia and New Zealand, shepherds use motorcycles to herd sheep; therefore, they demand low-speed torque, rather than high speed.[32]

In addition to the products themselves, the way they are packaged must sometimes be adapted to local market conditions. Some consumers in developing countries are likely to have packaging preferences very different from those of consumers in the West. For example, single-serve packets, or sachets, are very popular in India.[33] They permit consumers to purchase only what they need, experiment with new products, and conserve cash at the same time. Products as varied as detergents, shampoos, pickles, and cough syrup are sold in sachets in India. It is estimated that they make up between 20 and 60 percent of the total volume sold in their categories. In China, sachets are also spreading as a marketing device for such items as shampoos. This brings to the fore the importance of considering all activities in a firm's value chain when determining where local adaptations may be advisable.

Maple Leaf Foods, for example, customizes its prepared meat recipes to meet local tastes in each of the countries in which it sells processed foods. Similarly, La Senza adapts its customer service processes to match the different perceptions about lingerie in each of the 23 countries in which it operates.

Cultural differences may also require a firm to adapt its personnel practices when it expands internationally.[34] Dofasco had to seriously review its famous "Our strength is people" motto and its unique policy of extending empowerment to all employees as it embarked on its venture in Mexico. Mexican workers typically expect more hierarchical structures and are more comfortable under managers who will supervise and make the decisions on all aspects of the daily work life. Dofasco's highly successful strategy and organizational design in Canada is far removed from those principles and has embraced empowerment and delegation of responsibility to the lowest possible levels of the organization. Dofasco had to revisit some of its policies and also spend additional resources in the training of its local employees to establish a successful operation in Mexico.

Strategy Spotlight 7.7 describes how multinationals have adapted to the problem of bribery in various countries while adhering to strict federal laws on corrupt practices at home.

7.7 STRATEGY SPOTLIGHT

Dealing with Bribery Abroad

Most multinational firms experience difficult dilemmas when it comes to the question of adapting rules and guidelines, both formal and informal, while operating in foreign countries. The *Foreign Corrupt Practices Act*, in fact, makes it illegal for U.S. companies to bribe officials to gain business or facilitate approvals and permissions. Canada's equivalent, the *Corruption of Foreign Public Officials Act*, similarly prohibits individuals and organizations from engaging in any one of a series of activities, such as bribes, loans, facilitation payments, rewards, or advantages for the purposes of using the official's position to influence a decision or act

(Continued)

by the foreign state. In other countries, though, the only provision is that such payments constituting bribes cannot be deducted for tax purposes, To complicate matters further, the *Sarbanes-Oxley Act* in the United States effectively makes the U.S. rules applicable to all foreign firms whose shares trade in American stock exchanges.

Unfortunately, in many parts of the world, bribery is a way of life, with large payoffs to government officials and politicians being necessary to win government contracts. At a lower level, goods will not clear customs unless notionally illegal, but routine and well-accepted, payments are made to officials. What is a foreign company to do in such situations?

Intel follows a strict rule-based definition of bribery as "a thing of value given to someone with the intent of obtaining favorable treatment from the recipient." The company strictly prohibits payments to expedite a shipment through customs if the payment did not "follow applicable rules and regulations, and if the agent gives money or payment in kind to a government official for personal benefit." Texas Instruments, in contrast, follows a middle approach. It requires its employees to "exercise good judgment" in questionable circumstances "by avoiding activities that could create even the appearance that our decisions could be compromised." And Analog Devices has set up a policy manager as a consultant to overseas operations. The policy manager does not make decisions for country managers. Instead, the policy manager helps country managers think through the issues and provides information on how the corporate office has handled similar situations in the past.

Sources: T. M. Begley and D. P. Boyd, "The Need for a Corporate Global Mind-Set," *MIT Sloan Management Review,* Winter 2003, pp. 25–32. http://laws-lois.justice.gc.ca/eng/acts/c-45.2

As one might expect, there are some risks associated with a multidomestic strategy. These are listed below:

- Typically, local adaptation of products and services will increase a company's cost structure. In many industries, competition is so intense that most firms can ill afford any competitive disadvantages on the dimension of cost. A key challenge of managers is to determine the trade-off between local adaptation and its cost structure. For example, cost considerations led Procter & Gamble to standardize its diaper design across all European markets. This was done despite research data indicating that Italian mothers, unlike those in other countries, preferred diapers that covered the baby's navel. Later, however, P&G recognized that this feature was critical to these mothers, so the company decided to incorporate this feature for the Italian market despite its adverse cost implications.

- At times, local adaptations, even when well intentioned, may backfire. When the U.S. restaurant chain TGI Fridays entered the South Korean market, it purposely incorporated many local dishes, such as kimchi (hot, spicy cabbage), into its menu. Company analysis of the weak market acceptance indicated that Korean customers anticipated a visit to TGI Fridays as a visit to the United States. Thus, finding Korean dishes was inconsistent with their expectations.

- Consistent with other aspects of global marketing, the optimal degree of local adaptation evolves over time. In many industry segments, a variety of factors, such as the influence of global media, greater international travel, and declining income disparities across countries, may lead to increasing global standardization. However, in other industry segments, especially where the product or service can be delivered over the Internet (such as music), the need for even greater customization and local adaptation may increase over time. Firms must recalibrate the need for local adaptation on an ongoing basis; excessive adaptation extracts a price as surely as underadaptation.

Transnational Strategy

Let us briefly review global and multidomestic strategies before we discuss how a transnational strategy can be a vehicle for overcoming the limitations of each of these strategies and, in effect, "getting the best of both worlds."[35]

With a *global strategy,* resources and capabilities are concentrated at the centre of the organization. Authority is highly centralized. Thus, a global company achieves efficiency primarily by exploiting potential economies of scale in all of its value-chain activities. Since innovation is highly centralized in the corporate office, there is often a lack of understanding of the changing market needs and production requirements outside the local market, and there are few incentives to adapt.

The *multidomestic strategy* can be considered the exact opposite of the global strategy. Resources are dispersed throughout many countries in which a firm does business, and a subsidiary of the multinational company can more effectively respond to local needs. However, such fragmentation inevitably carries efficiency penalties. Learning also suffers because knowledge is not consolidated in a centralized location and does not flow among the various parts of the company.

A multinational firm following a *transnational strategy* strives to optimize the trade-offs associated with efficiency, local adaptation, and learning.[36] It seeks efficiency not for its own sake but as a means to achieve global competitiveness. It recognizes the importance of local responsiveness but as a tool for flexibility in international operations.[37] Innovations are regarded as an outcome of a larger process of organizational learning that includes the contributions of everyone in the firm.[38] Additionally, a core tenet of the transnational model is that a firm's assets and capabilities are dispersed according to the most beneficial location for a specific activity. Thus, managers avoid the tendency to either concentrate activities in a central location (as with a global strategy) or disperse them across many locations to enhance adaptation (as with a multidomestic strategy). Peter Brabeck-Letmathe, the former CEO of food giant Nestlé, provides such a perspective:

> We believe strongly that there isn't a so-called global consumer, at least not when it comes to food and beverages. People have local tastes based on their unique cultures and traditions—a good candy bar in Brazil is not the same as a good candy bar in China. Therefore, decision making needs to be pushed down as low as possible in the organization, out close to the markets.
>
> Otherwise, how can you make good brand decisions? That said, decentralization has its limits. If you are too decentralized, you can become too complicated—you get too much complexity in your production system. The closer we come to the consumer, in branding, pricing, communication, and product adaptation, the more we decentralize. The more we are dealing with production, logistics, and supply-chain management, the more centralized decision making becomes. After all, we want to leverage Nestlé's size, not be hampered by it.[39]

Nestlé illustrates a common approach to determining whether or not to centralize or decentralize a value-chain activity. Typically, primary activities that are "downstream" (e.g., marketing, sales, and service) or closer to the customer tend to require more decentralization to adapt to local market conditions. However, primary activities that are "upstream" (e.g., logistics and operations), or further away from the customer, tend to be centralized. This is because there is less need for adapting these activities to local markets and the firm can benefit from economies of scale. Additionally, many support activities, such as information systems and procurement, tend to be centralized to increase the potential for economies of scale.

A central philosophy of the transnational organization is enhanced adaptation to all competitive situations as well as flexibility by capitalizing on communication and knowledge flows throughout the organization.[40] A principal characteristic is the integration of unique contributions of all units into worldwide operations. Thus, a joint innovation by headquarters and by one of the overseas units can potentially lead to the development of relatively standardized and yet flexible products and services that are suitable for multiple markets.

Asea Brown Boveri (ABB) is a firm that successfully follows a transnational strategy. ABB, with its home bases in Sweden and Switzerland, illustrates the trend toward cross-national mergers that lead firms to consider multiple headquarters. ABB is managed as a flexible network of units, and one of management's main functions is the facilitation of information and knowledge flows between units. ABB's subsidiaries have complete responsibility for product categories on a worldwide basis. Such a transnational strategy enables ABB to benefit from access to new markets and the opportunity to use and develop resources wherever they may be located.

As with the other strategies, there are some unique risks and challenges associated with a transnational strategy:

- The choice of a seemingly optimal location cannot guarantee that the quality and cost of factor inputs (i.e., labour, materials) will be optimal. Managers must ensure that the relative advantage of a location is actually realized, not squandered because of weaknesses in productivity and the quality of internal operations. Ford Motor Co., for example, has benefited from having some of its manufacturing operations in Mexico. Although some have argued that the benefits of lower wage rates will be partly offset by lower productivity, this does not always have to be the case. Since unemployment in Mexico is higher than in the United States, Ford can be more selective in its hiring practices for its Mexican operations. And, given the lower turnover among its Mexican employees, Ford can justify a high level of investment in training and development. Thus, the net result could be not only lower wage rates but also higher productivity than in the United States.

- Although knowledge transfer can be a key source of competitive advantages, it does not take place automatically. For knowledge to be effectively transferred from one subsidiary to another, it is important for the source of the knowledge, the target units, and the corporate headquarters to recognize the potential value of such unique know-how. Given that there can be significant geographic, linguistic, and cultural distances separating subsidiaries, the realization of knowledge transfer can become very difficult to achieve. Firms must create mechanisms to systematically and routinely uncover the opportunities for knowledge transfer.

Exhibit 7-6 summarizes the relative advantages and disadvantages of international, global, multidomestic, and transnational strategies.

EXHIBIT 7-6   STRENGTHS AND LIMITATIONS OF VARIOUS STRATEGIES

Strategy	Strengths	Limitations
International	• Leveraging and diffusion of parent's knowledge and core competencies. • Lower costs because of less need to tailor products and services. • Greater level of worldwide coordination.	• Limited ability to adapt to local markets. • Inability to take advantage of new ideas and innovations occurring in local markets.
Global	• Strong integration across various businesses. • Standardization leading to higher economies of scale, which lowers costs. • Potential to create uniform standards of quality throughout the world.	• Limited ability to adapt to local markets. • Concentration of activities leading to increased dependence on a single facility. • Potential for higher tariffs and transportation costs from single locations.
Multidomestic	• Ability to adapt products and services to local market conditions. • Ability to detect potential opportunities for attractive niches in a given market, enhancing revenue.	• Less ability to realize cost savings through scale economies. • Greater difficulty in transferring knowledge across countries. • Potential for "overadaptation" as conditions change.
Transnational	• Ability to attain economies of scale. • Ability to adapt to local markets. • Ability to locate activities in optimal locations. • Ability to increase knowledge flows and learning.	• Unique challenges in determining optimal locations of activities to ensure cost and quality. • Unique managerial challenges in fostering knowledge transfer.

Having discussed the types of strategies that firms pursue in international markets and their relative advantages and disadvantages, let us now turn to the types of entry modes that companies may use to enter international markets.

GLOBAL OR REGIONAL? A SECOND LOOK AT GLOBALIZATION

Thus far, we have suggested four possible strategies from which a firm must choose once it has decided to compete in the global marketplace. In recent years, many writers have asserted that the process of globalization has caused national borders to become increasingly irrelevant.[41] Yet scholars have also challenged this perspective, arguing that it is unwise for companies to rush into full-scale globalization.[42]

Before answering questions about the extent of firms' globalization, let us try to clarify what "globalization" means. Traditionally, a firm's globalization is measured in terms of its foreign sales as a percentage of total sales. However, this measure can be misleading. For example, consider a U.S. firm that has expanded its activities into Canada. Clearly, this initiative is qualitatively different from achieving the same sales volume in a distant country, such as China. Similarly, if a Malaysian firm expands into Singapore or a German firm starts selling its products in Austria, this would represent an expansion into a geographically adjacent country. Such nearby countries would often share many common characteristics in terms of language, culture, infrastructure, and customer preferences. In other words, this is more a case of regionalization than globalization.

Extensive analysis of the distribution data of sales across different countries and regions led Alan Rugman and Alain Verbeke to conclude that there is a stronger case to be made in favour of regionalization than globalization. According to their study, a company would have to have at least 20 percent of its sales in each of the three major economic regions—North America, Europe, and Asia—to be considered a global firm. However, they found that only nine of the world's 500 largest firms at the time met this standard! Even when they relaxed the criterion to 20 percent of sales each in at least two of the three regions, the number only increased to 25. *Thus, most companies are regional or, at best, bi-regional—not global—even today.* Exhibit 7-7 provides a listing of the large firms that met each of these two criteria.

EXHIBIT 7-7   GLOBAL OR REGIONAL? SALES DISTRIBUTION OF THE *FORTUNE* GLOBAL 500 FIRMS[*]

Firms with at least 20 percent sales in Asia, Europe, and North America each but with less than 50 percent sales in any one region		
IBM	Nokia	Coca-Cola
Sony	Intel	Flextronics
Philips	Canon	LVMH
Firms with at least 20 percent sales in at least two of the three regions (Asia, Europe, North America) but with less than 50 percent sales in any one region		
BP Amoco	Alstom	Michelin
Toyota	Aventis	L'Oreal
Nissan	Diageo	Electrolux
Unilever	Sun Microsystems	BAE
Motorola	Bridgestone	Lafarge
GlaxoSmithKline	Roche	

(Continued)

Firms with at least 20 percent sales in at least two of the three regions (Asia, Europe, North America) but with less than 50 percent sales in any one region		
EADS	3M	
Bayer	Skanska	
Ericsson	McDonald's	
Firms with at least 50 percent of their sales in one of the three regions—other than their home region		
News Corporation	Santander	Sodexho Alliance
ING Group	Delhaize "Le Lion"	Manpower
Royal Ahold	Astra Zeneca	Wolseley
Honda		

Sources: Peng, M.W. 2010. *Global Strategy,* 2nd ed. Mason, OH: Thomson Southwestern; and Rugman, A.M., & Verbeke, A. 2004. A Perspective on Regional and Global Strategies of Multinational Enterprises. *Journal of International Business Studies,* 35: 3–18.

* This chart is for illustrative and discussion purposes. In a dynamic global competitive environment, the global/regional mix is likely to change year to year.

In a world of instant communication, rapid transportation, and governments that are increasingly willing to open up their markets to trade and investment, why are so few firms "global"? The most obvious answer is that distance still matters. After all, it is easier to do business in a neighbouring country than in a geographically distant country, all else being equal. Distance, in the final analysis, may be viewed as a concept with many dimensions, not just a measure of geographic distance. For example, both Canada and Mexico are the same distance from the United States. However, U.S. companies find it easier to expand operations into Canada than into Mexico. Why? Canada and the United States share many commonalities in terms of language, culture, economic development, legal and political systems, and infrastructure development. Thus, if we view distance as having many dimensions, the United States and Canada are very close, whereas there is greater distance between the United States and Mexico. Similarly, when we look at what we might call the "true" distance between the United States and China, the effects of geographic distance are multiplied by distance in terms of culture, language, religion, and legal and political systems between the two countries. Conversely, although the United States and Australia are geographically distant, the "true" distance is somewhat less when one considers distance along the other dimensions.

Another reason for regional expansion is the rise of the trading blocs. The European Union originally started in the 1950s as a regional trading bloc. Over the years, though, it has achieved a much larger degree of economic and political integration in terms of common currency and common standards that many thought infeasible, if not impossible, only 20 years ago. The resulting economic benefits have led other regions to consider similar moves. For example, the North American Free Trade Agreement (NAFTA) has the eventual abolition of all barriers to the free movement of goods and services among Canada, the United States, and Mexico as its goal. Other regional trading-blocs include MERCOSUR (consisting of Argentina, Brazil, Paraguay, Uruguay, and Venezuela) and the Association of Southeast Asian Nations (ASEAN) (consisting of about ten Southeast Asian countries).

Regional economic integration has progressed at a faster pace than global economic integration and the trade and investment patterns of the largest companies reflect this reality. After all, regions represent the outcomes of centuries of political and cultural history that result not only in commonalities but also mutual affinity. For example, stretching from Algeria and Morocco in the west to Oman and Yemen in the east, more than 30 countries share the Arabic language and the Islamic religion, making these countries a natural regional bloc. Similarly, the countries of South and Central America share the Spanish language (except Brazil), Catholic religion, and a shared history of Spanish colonialism. No wonder firms find it easier and less risky to expand within their region than to other regions.

LO 6 ENTRY MODES OF INTERNATIONAL EXPANSION

A firm has many options available to it when it decides to expand into international markets. Because of the challenges associated with such entry, many firms first start on a small scale and then increase their level of investment and risk as they gain greater experience with the overseas market in question.[43]

Exhibit 7-8 illustrates a wide variety of modes of foreign entry, including exporting, licensing, franchising, strategic alliances, joint ventures, and wholly owned subsidiaries.[44] As the exhibit indicates, the various types of entry form a continuum that ranges from exporting (low investment and risk, low control) to a wholly owned subsidiary (high investment and risk, high control).[45]

EXHIBIT 7-8

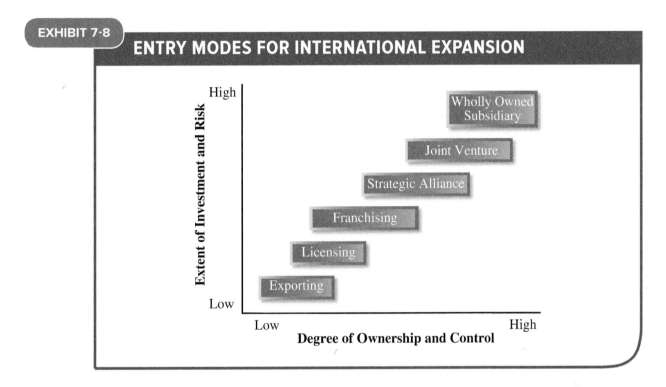

ENTRY MODES FOR INTERNATIONAL EXPANSION

Admittedly, there can, at times, be frustrations and setbacks as a firm evolves its international entry strategy from exporting to more expensive types, including wholly owned subsidiaries. According to the CEO of a large U.S. specialty chemical company,

> In the end, we always do a better job with our own subsidiaries; sales improve, and we have greater control over the business. But we still need local distributors for entry, and we are still searching for strategies to get us through the transitions without battles over control and performance.[46]

Exporting

Exporting consists of producing goods in one country to sell in another. This entry strategy enables a firm to invest the least amount of resources in terms of its product, its organization, and its overall corporate strategy. Not surprisingly, many host countries dislike this entry strategy because it provides less local employment than other modes of entry.[47]

Multinationals often stumble onto a stepwise strategy for penetrating markets, beginning with the exporting of products. This often results in a series of unplanned actions to increase sales revenues. As the pattern recurs with entries into subsequent markets, this approach, named a "beachhead strategy," becomes official policy in many organizations.

Such an approach definitely has its advantages. After all, firms start from scratch in sales and distribution when they enter new markets. Because many foreign markets are nationally regulated and dominated by networks of local intermediaries, firms need to partner with local distributors to benefit from their valuable expertise and knowledge of their own markets. Multinationals generally recognize that they cannot master local business practices, meet regulatory requirements, hire and manage local personnel, or gain access to potential customers without some form of local partnership.

In addition to the need to partner with local firms, multinationals also want to minimize their own risk. They do this by hiring local distributors and investing very little in the undertaking. In essence, the firm gives control of strategic marketing decisions to the local partners—much more control than they would be willing to give up in their home market.

As one might expect, exporting is a relatively inexpensive way to enter foreign markets. However, it can still have significant downsides. In a study of 250 instances in which multinational firms used local distributors to implement their exporting entry strategy, the results were dismal. In the vast majority of the cases, the distributors were bought (to increase control) by the multinational firm or fired. By contrast, successful distributors shared two common characteristics:

- They carried product lines that complemented, rather than competed with, the multinational's products.
- They behaved as if they were business partners with the multinationals. They shared market information with the corporations, they initiated projects with distributors in neighbouring countries, and they suggested initiatives in their own or nearby markets. Additionally, these distributors took on risk themselves by investing in such areas as training, information systems, and advertising and promotion to increase the business of their multinational partners.

The key point is the importance of developing collaborative, win–win relationships.

To ensure more control over operations without incurring significant risks, many firms have used licensing and franchising as a mode of entry. Let us now discuss these and their relative advantages and disadvantages.

Licensing

Licensing as an entry mode enables a company to receive a royalty or fee in exchange for the right to use its trademark, patent, trade secret, or other valuable item of intellectual property.[48] In international markets, the advantage is that the firm granting the licence incurs little risk, since it does not have to invest any significant resources into the country itself. In turn, the licensee (the firm receiving the licence) gains access to the trademark, patent, and so on and is able to potentially create competitive advantages. In many cases, the country also benefits from the product being manufactured locally. For example, Yoplait yogourt is licensed by General Mills from Sodima, a French co-operative, for sale in the United States, and it is produced and sold by Ultima Foods in Canada. Licensing technology is very common in telecommunications, software, and pharmaceuticals.

There are, of course, some important disadvantages to this type of entry. For example, the licensor gives up control of its product and forgoes potential revenues and profits. Furthermore, the licensee may eventually become so familiar with the patent and trade secrets that it may become a competitor; in effect, the licensee may make some modifications to the product and manufacture and sell it independently of the licensor without having to pay a royalty fee. This situation is aggravated in countries that have relatively weak laws to protect intellectual property. Additionally, if the licensee selected by the multinational firm turns out to be a poor choice, the brand name and reputation of the product may be tarnished.[49]

Franchising

Although licensing and franchising are both forms of contractual arrangements, franchise contracts generally include a broader range of factors in an operation and involve a longer period. Franchising has the advantage of limiting the risk exposure that a firm has in overseas markets while expanding the revenue base of the parent company. The other side of the coin is that the multinational firm receives only a portion of the revenues, in the form of franchise fees, instead of the entire revenue— as would be the case if the firm set up the operation itself (e.g., a restaurant) through direct investment.

As a vehicle for international expansion, franchising remains an overwhelmingly American form of business, although some notable examples from Canada include Tim Hortons, La Senza, and The Keg. La Senza, as a case in point, operates some 280 corporate stores in Canada but has resorted to franchising for its international expansion. It has established relationships with master franchisees in each of 23 countries, who have built and operate some 300 stores according to La Senza's directions. Today, the company sells its collection of lingerie products through those stores—from the United Kingdom to Indonesia. This strategic choice has allowed La Senza to expand internationally and enter all those countries much faster and with significantly less capital requirements compared with attempting to do it all on its own. Its global success did attract the attention and eventual acquisition by the much larger multi-brand retailer, Limited Brands.

The International Franchise Association (IFA) lists in excess of 1,300 franchisers and ten times as many franchisees; more than 400 U.S. franchisers have international exposure.[50] This is greater than the combined totals of the next four largest franchiser home countries—France, the United Kingdom, Mexico, and Austria.

Strategic Alliances and Joint Ventures

Strategic alliances can take many forms, including joint research and development, joint exploration initiatives, joint production, or co-distribution of two partners' products. Frequently, a multinational will engage in a strategic alliance with a local firm to produce a product for the local market, using the multinational's technology and brand name but the local firm's management and market knowledge. Unlike licensing, though, the multinational retains substantially more control over the strategic and operational decisions. Joint ventures are a unique form of strategic alliance in that they entail the creation of a third legal entity, owned by the partners, with a clear mandate and a separate organizational structure.

As we discussed in Chapter 6, strategic alliances have been effective in helping firms to increase revenues and reduce costs and also to enhance learning and diffuse technologies. They enable firms to share risks as well as potential returns. Also, by gaining exposure to new sources of knowledge and technologies, such partnerships can help firms develop core competencies that can lead to competitive advantages in the marketplace.[51] Finally, entering into partnerships with host country firms can provide very useful information on local market tastes, competitive conditions, legal matters, and cultural nuances.[52] Strategy Spotlight 7.8 discusses how Microsoft has used a variety of partnerships to strengthen its position in East Asia.

7.8 STRATEGY SPOTLIGHT

Microsoft's Partnerships in East Asia

Microsoft has been forming strategic alliances and joint ventures with companies in East Asia to complement its own strategic presence and make inroads in the many diverse markets of the region. Rather than competing with existing firms, Microsoft has often entered countries by co-operating with these firms. For example, it initially entered the Japanese and Taiwanese markets by joining efforts with mobile phone operator NTT DoCoMo, which had already established itself as a successful provider of cellular phone service through its Mobimagic service. By teaming with Microsoft, NTT could stand to profit by integrating Microsoft's software applications into the existing service of mobile phone subscribers.

Another partner, GigaMedia, offering online sports, music, entertainment, gaming, and online karaoke, is using the Microsoft platforms to move its services seamlessly between computers, televisions, and mobile phones. In exchange for its contribution, Microsoft gleans 2 percent of GigaMedia's

(Continued)

broadband subscriber fees and significant revenue from GigaMedia's e-commerce sales. In a similar move, the Koos Group, owner of KG Telecom, the second largest cell phone operator in Taiwan, joined ranks with Microsoft to integrate Internet capabilities on the televisions and cell phones of its subscribers.

Microsoft also partnered with Tata Consulting Services, India's largest information technology outsourcing company, and three Chinese state-owned companies to form a software development centre in Beijing, China. The venture aims to leverage the complementary strengths of the parties in technology, software development, and talent training while giving a foothold in the world's second largest market to two of the world's largest software companies.

Microsoft has used a forward-thinking vision to achieve win–win relationships through several joint ventures and strategic alliances across the globe. By doing so, it is successfully exporting its influence from an entrenched position in the United States to a global presence. This is good not only for Microsoft and its shareholders, but for the shareholders of other firms around the world who also stand to prosper from the co-operative agreements Microsoft has forged with their firms. In addition, the added competition from a powerhouse such as Microsoft forces other international firms to compete for efficiencies, thus increasing the potential for overall economic prosperity.

Sources: N. Chowdhury, "Gates & Co. Attack Asia," *Fortune.com,* April 17, 2000; G. Mariano, "Palm to Groove with Liquid Audio Music," *New York Times Online,* April 11, 2001; J. Leahy, "Asian Partnership Takes Off," www.ft.com, Dec. 5, 2006, p. 3; Anonymous, "TCS and Microsoft Intend to Establish Joint Venture with Chinese Firms," *Microsoft Press Release,* June 30, 2005.

Despite the potential benefits, managers must be aware of the risks associated with strategic alliances and joint ventures and how these risks can be minimized.[53] First, there must be well-articulated goals to guide the strategic alliance, and the partners must agree on a set of related, clearly defined criteria to measure progress. A well-defined strategy must be strongly supported by the organizations that are party to the partnership. Otherwise, the firms may work at cross-purposes and not achieve any of their goals. Second, there must be a clear understanding of the capabilities and resources that will be central to the partnership. Without such understanding, there will be fewer opportunities for learning and developing the competencies that could lead to competitive advantages. Third, trust is a vital element. Phasing in the relationship between alliance partners permits them to get to know each other better and develop trust. According to Philip Benton Jr., former president of Ford Motor Co. (which has been involved in multiple international partnerships over the years), "The first time two companies work together, the chances of succeeding are very slight. But once you find ways to work together, all sorts of opportunities arise." Without trust, one party may take advantage of the other by, for example, withholding its fair share of resources and gaining access to privileged information through unethical (or illegal) means. Fourth, cultural issues, which could potentially lead to conflict and dysfunctional behaviours, need to be addressed. An organization's culture is the set of values, beliefs, and attitudes that influence the behaviour and goals of its employees. Thus, recognizing cultural differences as well as striving to develop elements of a "common culture" for the partnership is vital. Without a unifying culture, it will become difficult to combine and leverage the kinds of resources that are increasingly important in knowledge-intensive organizations (as discussed in Chapter 4).[54]

Finally, the success of a firm's alliance should not be left to chance.[55] To improve their odds of success, many companies have carefully documented alliance-management knowledge by creating guidelines and manuals to help them manage specific aspects of the entire alliance life cycle (e.g., partner selection and alliance negotiation and contracting). For example, Lotus Corp. (part of IBM) created what it calls its "35 rules of thumb" to manage each phase of an alliance, from formation to termination. Hewlett-Packard developed 60 different tools and templates, which it placed in a 300-page manual, for guiding decision making in specific alliance situations. The manual included such items as a template for making the business case for an alliance, a partner evaluation form, a negotiations template outlining the roles and responsibilities of different departments, a list of the ways to measure alliance performance, and an alliance termination checklist.

Wholly Owned Subsidiaries

A wholly owned subsidiary is a business in which a multinational company owns 100 percent of the stock. There are two means by which a firm can establish a wholly owned subsidiary. It can either acquire an existing company in the home country or it can develop a totally new operation. The latter is often referred to as a "greenfield venture." Establishing a wholly owned subsidiary is the most expensive and risky of the various entry modes. However, as expected, it can also yield the highest returns. In addition, it provides the multinational company with the greatest degree of control over all activities, including manufacturing, marketing, distribution, and technology development.[56]

As we saw in the opening case of Chapter 6, Stantec Inc., an Edmonton-based engineering and architectural firm, is growing by acquiring design firms in second-tier markets in the United States and preparing for a major push into primary centres, such as New York City and Chicago.[57] Stantec's CEO, Tony Franceschini, is betting on a global consolidation that will see a handful of giant firms offering a range of services to clients around the world and he is determined to be among the top 10 global design firms within a decade. Establishing new offices in different markets would simply take too long.

Wholly owned subsidiaries as well as direct investment in greenfield ventures are most appropriate when a firm already has the necessary knowledge and capabilities to leverage across multiple locations in many countries. Examples range from restaurants to semiconductor manufacturers. To lower costs, for example, Intel Corporation builds semiconductor plants throughout the world—all of which use virtually the same blueprint. In establishing wholly owned subsidiaries, knowledge can be further leveraged by the hiring of managers and professionals from the firm's home country, often seeking out talent from competitors.

As noted, wholly owned subsidiaries are typically the most expensive and risky of the various modes for entering international markets. With franchising, strategic alliances, or joint ventures, the risk is shared with the firm's partners. In the case of wholly owned subsidiaries, the entire risk is assumed by the parent company. The risks associated with doing business in a new country (i.e., political, cultural, and legal) can be lessened by hiring local talent.

One should not consider entry strategies as a clear-cut progression from exporting through to the creation of wholly owned subsidiaries. Many firms, such as La Senza or The Keg, follow rather unique entry paths. For example, The Keg belongs in the casual dining restaurant segment, where one finds mostly franchise operations, especially those that move internationally; yet the company has chosen to only open its own stores in the United States. Although this decision has certainly slowed its expansion, it has ensured that the company can maintain the atmosphere, unique service, and knowledgeable staff that have allowed it to develop a loyal following in its Canadian operations. Moreover, international expansion is not the exclusive purview of large firms that have first succeeded in their local markets. Many medium- and small-sized Canadian firms, such as Lingo Media and Hydrogenics, with little local presence at home, have directed all their efforts to overseas markets.

LO 7   Global Dispersion of Value Chains: Outsourcing and Offshoring

Beyond the traditional entry modes of international expansion, firms have recently explored the dispersion of their value chains across different countries; that is, the various activities that constitute the value chain of a firm are now spread across several countries and continents. Such dispersion of value occurs mainly through increasing offshoring and outsourcing.

Detroit's automobile manufacturers have done so for over 40 years with subsidiaries in Canada, under the protection of the Auto Pact, signed between the two countries in 1965. Parts and components produced in one country would be transported to be assembled in facilities in the other country without any tariff or other restrictions. Yet, although rather unique at the time, the Auto Pact was primarily driven by tariffs and customs considerations. Today, we are increasingly witnessing outsourcing and offshoring taking place to capitalize on comparative and competitive advantages outside the home country's own boundaries.

Outsourcing

This occurs when a firm decides to utilize other firms to perform value-creating activities that were previously performed in-house.[58] It may be a new activity that the firm is perfectly capable of undertaking but chooses to have someone else perform for cost or quality reasons. Outsourcing can be to either a domestic or foreign firm.

Offshoring

This takes place when a firm decides to shift an activity that it was performing in a domestic location to a foreign location.[59] For example, both Microsoft and Intel have substantial R&D facilities in India, employing a large number of Indian scientists and engineers. Often, offshoring and outsourcing go together; that is, a firm may outsource an activity to a foreign supplier, thereby causing the work to be offshored as well.[60] Spending on offshore information technology was estimated to have nearly tripled between 2004 and 2010 to reach $60 billion, according to pertinent research by Gartner. And while the trend has continued since, there is also a wave of repatriation of activities occurring as automation mutes the labour-cost advantage of developing countries from South East Asia and Central America.[61]

The explosion in the volume and variants of outsourcing and offshoring we have witnessed during the last thirty years has been caused by a variety of factors. Until the 1960s, for most companies, the entire value chain was in one location. Further, to keep transportation costs under control, the production took place close to where the customers were. In the case of service industries, it was generally believed that offshoring was not possible because the producer and consumer had to be present at the same place at the same time. After all, a haircut could not be performed if the barber and the client were in two different locations!

For manufacturing industries, the rapid decline in transportation and coordination costs has enabled firms to disperse their value chains over different locations. For example, Nike's R&D takes place in the United States; raw materials are procured from a multitude of countries; actual manufacturing takes place in China, Indonesia, or Vietnam; advertising is produced in the United States; and sales and service take place in practically all the countries. Each value-creating activity is performed in the location where the cost is the lowest or the quality is the best. Without finding optimal locations for each activity, Nike could not have attained its position as the world's largest shoe company.

The experience of the manufacturing sector was also repeated in the service sector by the mid-1990s. A trend that began with the outsourcing of low-level programming and data entry work to such countries as India and Ireland suddenly grew many times over, encompassing a variety of white-collar and professional activities ranging from call centres to R&D. The cost of a long distance call from the North America to India has decreased from about $3 to $0.03 in the last 20 years, thereby making it possible to have call centres located in the subcontinent, where a combination of low labour costs and English proficiency presents an ideal mix of factor conditions.

Consider, for example, that in recent years, more and more U.S. tax returns are prepared in Bangalore, India. Also in India, U.S.-licensed radiologists interpret chest X-rays and computed tomography (CT) scans from U.S. hospitals for half the cost. The advantages from offshoring go beyond mere cost savings today. In many specialized occupations in science and engineering, there is a shortage of qualified professionals in developed countries, whereas such countries as India and China have what seems like an inexhaustible supply.[62]

For much of the twentieth century, domestic companies catered to the needs of local populations. Local production seemed to suffice for the local needs, few companies ventured abroad, and fewer competed across many countries. However, with the increasing globalization of customer needs and the institutionalization of free trade and investment (especially after the creation of the World Trade Organization (WTO)), competition has become truly global. To survive, whether they are local or multinational, firms must keep their costs low, find the best suppliers and the most skilled workers, and locate each stage of the value chain in places where factor conditions are most conducive.[63] Thus, outsourcing and offshoring are no longer mere options to consider but imperatives for competitive survival. Yet, in a sign of the dynamism of the global economy, many companies have also developed flexible manufacturing and micro-manufacturing capabilities that allow them to repatriate some of the production capacity and bring back to their home countries some of the activities they had shipped overseas.

SUMMARY

We live in a highly interconnected global community, where many of the best opportunities for growth and profitability lie beyond the boundaries of a company's home country. Along with the opportunities, of course, there are many risks associated with diversification into global markets.

The first section of the chapter addressed the factors that determine a nation's competitiveness in a particular industry. The framework was developed by Michael Porter of Harvard University and was based on a four-year study that explored the competitive success of 10 leading trading nations. The four factors, collectively termed the "diamond of national advantage," are factor conditions; demand conditions; related and supporting industries; and firm strategy, structure, and rivalry.

The discussion of Porter's "diamond" helped, in essence, set the broader context for exploring competitive advantage at the firm level. In the second section, we discussed the primary motivations and the potential risks associated with international expansion. The primary motivations include increasing the size of the potential market for the firm's products and services, achieving economies of scale, extending the life cycle of the firm's products, and optimizing the location for every activity in the value chain. However, the key risks include political and economic risks, currency risks, and management risks. Management risks are the challenges associated with responding to the inevitable differences that exist across countries, such as customs, culture, language, customer preferences, and distribution systems.

Next, we addressed how firms can go about attaining competitive advantage in global markets. We began by discussing the two opposing forces—cost reduction and adaptation to local markets—which managers must contend with when entering global markets. The relative importance of these two factors plays a major part in determining which of the four basic types of strategies to select: international, global, multidomestic, or transnational. The chapter covered the benefits and risks associated with each type of strategy.

Finally, we discussed the six types of entry strategies that managers may undertake when entering international markets. The key trade-off in each of these strategies is the level of investment or risk versus the level of control. The strategies include (in order of their progressively greater investment, risk, and control) exporting, licensing, franchising, strategic alliances and joint ventures, and wholly owned subsidiaries. The relative benefits and risks associated with each of these strategies were addressed. We also explored the reasons and opportunities associated with offshoring and outsourcing, as firms disperse their value chains across the world.

Summary Review Questions

1. What are some of the advantages and disadvantages associated with a firm's expansion into international markets?

2. What are the four factors described in Porter's "diamond of national advantage"? How do the four factors explain why some industries in a given country are more successful than others?

3. Explain the two opposing forces—cost reduction and adaptation to local markets—that firms must deal with when they go global.

4. There are four basic strategies for achieving competitive advantage in global markets—international, global, multidomestic, and transnational. What are the advantages and disadvantages associated with each?

5. Describe the basic entry strategies that firms have available when they enter international markets. What are the relative advantages and disadvantages of each?

REFLECTING ON CAREER IMPLICATIONS

- *International Strategy:* Are you aware of your organization's international strategy? What percentage of the total firm activity is international? What skills are needed to enhance your company's international efforts? How can you get more involved in your organization's international strategy? For your career, what conditions in your home country might cause you to seek careers abroad?

- *International Career Opportunities:* Work assignments in other countries can often provide a career boost. Be proactive in pursuing promising career opportunities in other countries. Anticipate how such opportunities will advance your short-term and long-term career aspirations.

- *Cultural diversity:* Develop cultural sensitivity. Be sensitive and seek to appreciate individuals from different cultures in your home-based organization as well as in your overseas experience.

- *Outsourcing and Offshoring:* How much of what is done in your organization today could more effectively be done either by another firm or overseas? What activities in your organization can or should be outsourced or offshored? Can you competitively provide outsourcing for other firms? Do you continually take inventory of your talents, skills, and competencies and compare them with others to decide who could best perform each activity?

EXPERIENTIAL EXERCISE

1. Canada is considered a world leader in the mining industry. Using Porter's "diamond" framework for national competitiveness, explain the success of this industry.

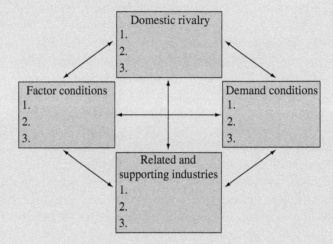

2. What elements of your analysis of the mining industry do not fit neatly inside the diamond? What adjustments to the framework would you suggest?

APPLICATION QUESTIONS AND EXERCISES

1. Global changes occur rapidly and daily, and their impact on a firm's global strategy becomes even more prolific. Pick a current article (less than one month old) from the business press, and apply it to the concepts discussed in this chapter.

2. The Internet has lowered the entry barriers for smaller firms that wish to diversify into international markets. Why is this so? Provide an example.

3. In spite of the successful examples we discussed in this chapter, many firms fail when they enter into strategic alliances with companies based in other countries. What are some reasons for this failure? Provide an example.

4. Canadian engineering and exploration firms have been very successful in the international marketplace. How can Porter's diamond explain their success?

ETHICS AND CORPORATE SOCIAL RESPONSIBILITY QUESTIONS

1. Over the past few decades, many North American and European firms have relocated their operations to countries that pay lower wages, such as Mexico, India, and China. What are some of the ethical issues that such actions may raise?

2. As shareholders, pensioners, and mutual fund holders, Canadians, Americans, and Europeans want the firms whose stock they own to maximize profits and pay dividends. As employees and members of the local community, they also want to keep the factories and offices in their own countries. What contradictions and challenges do these positions raise for the executives and managers of global firms?

3. Business practices and customs vary throughout the world. What are some of the ethical issues concerning payments that must be made in a foreign country to obtain business opportunities?

CHAPTER EIGHT

INDUSTRY CHANGE AND COMPETITIVE DYNAMICS

LEARNING OBJECTIVES

After reading this chapter, you should have a good understanding of:

LO 1 The importance of considering the industry life cycle and determining the relative forces shaping the competitive landscape.

LO 2 How industries evolve and how different drivers influence the paths to industry change.

LO 3 How disruptive innovation can completely revolutionize an industry and permanently upset the competitive order.

LO 4 How different strategic responses may be more effective over the phases of the industry life cycle.

LO 5 How turnaround strategies can reinvigorate a firm.

LO 6 How competitive actions, such as the entry of new competitors into a marketplace, may launch a cycle of actions and reactions among close competitors.

LO 7 The components of competitive dynamics analysis—new competitive action, threat analysis, motivation and capability to respond, types of competitive actions, and likelihood of competitive reaction.

The story of the taxi industry's plight against Uber is well known.[1] Media reports showcase global protests against Uber. Highlights include London's "go-slow" movement bringing traffic to a standstill and protests in the large cities of Brazil, Italy, Belgium, France, India, and Australia. Famously, Toronto taxi drivers blocked traffic in the downtown core for 12 hours in December, 2015—and that wasn't the end of the protests. When Uber was granted a licence as a Private Transportation Company (PTC)—the first such licence in Canada—taxi drivers went back to the streets to disrupt and protest anew, with some calling for the resignation of Tracey Cook, the city's executive director of licensing and standards.

Mr.Whiskey/Shutterstock.com

The main complaint of Toronto taxi drivers is that Uber isn't subjected to the same regulatory environment as taxicabs. Instead of levelling the playing field and forcing traditional taxi firms to innovate, as Uber claims, they are only skirting the rules that taxis are required to obey.

However, three clear points of differentiation arise for Uber. Firstly, e-hailing a cab is convenient. In the age of screen-happy millennials who prefer texting to calling, the ability to hail a cab through an app is undeniably attractive. Secondly, costs are lower. In the post-2008 economy, discretionary spending on small luxuries such as cabs has significantly decreased; Uber prices average 36 percent lower than Toronto cab fares, with the cheapest Uber option, UberX, being close to half the price of a regular Toronto taxicab. And finally, in the wake of the taxi protests another point of differentiation arose: customer service. Uber drivers, hoping to keep their five-star ratings, keep their cars clean and inviting and are polite and friendly with their customers. Op-eds singing the praises of Uber often tell horror stories about Toronto taxis, such as that of one individual who jumped into a Toronto taxicab only to find himself covered in a white, viscous liquid—likely some sort of fat or oil. Upon contacting Beck Taxi to have the dry-cleaning costs covered, the individual was told that the cabs are licensed out to individual drivers and Beck had no responsibility in the matter.

While it might not be able to improve customer service among Toronto taxi drivers, at least one Canadian app is trying to address another of the industry's shortcomings. CellWand Communications, a technology company located in downtown Toronto, has created an app called The Ride, an e-hailing service that connects users with nearby taxicabs, much like the e-hailing convenience of Uber. Unlike Uber, however, the app provides multiple transportation options and a comparison of taxi-versus-transit transportation times, allowing users to compare expected arrival times and the pricing of various options.

Unlike Uber, though, The Ride has been unable to lower the exorbitant taxicab prices in Toronto. Even worse, The Ride charges an additional fee for the convenience of e-hailing. After the first month of use, e-hailing charges a $2 "convenience fee" with every ride, or, in smaller towns where the app hasn't been picked up yet, $1 to connect the customer to a local dispatch centre. While the app is a step in the right direction for the taxicab industry, it doesn't fully address the advantages Uber has over traditional taxicab companies.

Nevertheless, it does have a few advantages over Uber. The Ride platform, unlike Uber, does not employ surge pricing, a common method Uber uses to get drivers onto the roads during peak times by raising fare prices. In addition, all drivers with The Ride are fully insured, and the app has been sponsored by Mothers Against Drunk Driving (MADD) Canada. Keeping prices consistent, ensuring the safety provided by a fully insured driver, and the MADD sponsorship are likely to help The Ride when looking to compete with Uber for the older generation.

The battle between the Toronto taxicabs and Uber is one that shows a traditional industry in decline. Taxicabs have long been lambasted for their licensing process, poor customer service, and high prices. With the advent of Uber, the taxicab industry is being forced to innovate in order to continue to compete—and The Ride is one of the first innovations that may help the industry work toward becoming competitive with Uber. ■

In this chapter, we consider the topic of change by looking at the industry life cycle and other tools to facilitate the analysis of competitive dynamics in support of better strategy formulation. Shifting social trends, the introduction of new technologies, and sudden changes in the business environment present strategic challenges for a firm. Like products, entire industries can experience a life cycle that starts with an introductory phase and flows through growth into maturity and eventual decline. Take Indigo, for example. There is no question that the modern book publishing industry, an industry that was once very profitable for Indigo, is now in decline. But there is also no question that the decline was fuelled by the somewhat unpredictable effects of new technologies. We say they are *somewhat* unpredictable because there has long been evidence of disruptive technologies destroying other classic media industries. It was only a matter of time before such disruptions would move from newspapers to CDs to books. But firms like Indigo need not necessarily throw in the towel. They need to consider, as we will, competitive dynamics—the actions and responses of firms to competitors' moves. Each of these elements allows us to appreciate the dynamism of strategic management, the challenges facing firms in an ever-changing world, and the options available to managers to steer their firms toward creating sustainable competitive advantages.

LO 1 INDUSTRY LIFE CYCLE STAGES: STRATEGIC IMPLICATIONS

The life cycle of an industry refers to four stages that all industries experience: introduction, growth, maturity, and decline. In considering the industry life cycle, it is useful to think in terms of broad product lines, such as personal computers (PCs), photocopiers, or long-distance telephone service. Yet the industry life cycle concept can be explored from several levels, from the life cycle of an entire industry to the life cycle of a single variation or model of a specific product or service.

Why is it important to consider industry life cycles?[2] The emphasis on various generic strategies, functional areas, value-creating activities, and overall objectives varies over the course of an industry's life cycle. Managers must become even more aware of their firm's strengths and weaknesses in many areas to attain competitive advantages. For example, firms depend on their research and development (R&D) activities in the introductory stage of the life cycle. R&D is the source of new products and features that everyone hopes will appeal to customers. Firms develop products and services to stimulate consumer demand. Later, during the maturity phase, the functions of the product have been defined, more competitors have entered the market, and competition becomes intense. Managers then place greater emphasis on production efficiencies and process (as opposed to the product) engineering to lower manufacturing costs. This helps protect the firm's market position and extends the product life cycle because the firm's lower costs can be "passed on" to consumers in the form of lower prices, and price-sensitive customers will find the product more appealing.

Exhibit 8-1 illustrates the four stages of the industry life cycle and how such factors as generic strategies, market growth rate, intensity of competition, and overall objectives change over time. Managers must strive to emphasize the key functional areas during each of the four stages and attain a level of parity in all functional areas and value-creating activities. For example, even though controlling production costs may be a primary concern during the maturity stage, managers should not totally ignore other functions, such as marketing and R&D. If they do, they can become so focused on lowering costs that they miss market trends or fail to incorporate important product or process designs. In such cases, the firm may attain low-cost products that have limited market appeal.

EXHIBIT 8-1 STAGES OF THE INDUSTRY LIFE CYCLE

	Stage Factor			
	Introduction	**Growth**	**Maturity**	**Decline**
Generic strategies	Differentiation	Differentiation	Differentiation Overall cost leadership	Overall cost leadership Focus
Market growth rate	Low	Very large	Low to moderate	Negative
Number of segments	Very few	Some	Many	Few
Intensity of competition	Low	Increasing	Very intense	Changing
Emphasis on product design	Very high	High	Low to moderate	Low
Emphasis on process design	Low	Low to moderate	High	Low
Major functional area (s) of concern	Research and development	Sales and marketing	Production	General management and finance
Overall objective	Increase market awareness	Create consumer demand	Defend market share and extend product life cycles	Consolidate, maintain, harvest, or exit

LO 2

What might be the factors that push industries forward to the next phase? How do the various characteristics of the industry change? Is this change gradual or rapid? What determines the pace and direction of change? These and other questions underlie the concept of industry life cycle and, admittedly in some respects, undermine it and render it less than a theory. We cannot predict when an industry will transition from one phase to the next and can only describe that moment after the fact. Moreover, as we will see below, industries can rejuvenate and revert to an earlier stage of growth. It is important to note that although the life cycle idea is clearly analogous to a living organism (i.e., birth, growth, maturity, and death), the comparison does have limitations.[3] Products and services go through many cycles of innovation and renewal. For the most part, only fad products have a single life cycle. The maturity stages of an industry can be "transformed" or followed by a stage of rapid growth if consumer tastes change, technological innovations take place, or new developments occur in the general environment. The cereal industry is a good example. When medical research indicated that oat consumption reduced a person's cholesterol, sales of Quaker Oats increased dramatically.[4]

In general, the industry life cycle implies an evolutionary change and a gradual progression from one stage to the next. Although this may frequently be the case and such evolution may unfold over many years, equally common is the phenomenon of revolutionary change when rapid and discontinuous change takes place, leading to a quick and unpredictable industry transformation. Industries are transformed by innovation or major shifts in the external environment, such as regulation, globalization, and dramatic changes in the economy. Frequently, though, the change comes from within, as competitors jockey for position and develop different competitive advantages; customers' preferences shift; and suppliers use technology, regulation, or consolidation to gain bargaining power. We consider these forces each in turn.

By far the most potent forces for industry change are technology and innovation. In Chapter 2, we discussed the role played by the Internet and digital technologies in drastically altering many industries' five forces. Other types of technological innovations also dramatically change industries. For example, biotechnology has had tremendous impact on the pharmaceutical industry and the ways new medicines are invented. We distinguish between sustaining innovations—that serve to improve existing products and cement the incumbents' positions in an industry—from disruptive technological changes—that arise from new breakthrough technologies introduced by new firms that upset the competitive advantages of incumbent firms, rendering their competencies irrelevant.[5] The personal computer was one such disruptive technological innovation, which completely revolutionized the mainframe computer industry. Smartphones changed the mobile phone industry forever. Nokia and Motorola were the powerhouses of the mobile phone industry until smartphones from Blackberry and Apple made their products look tired and inferior. Now Blackberry's products look tired next to Apple's iPhones and Samsung's very successful Galaxy lineup.

Disruptive technologies can be both product based and process based. Although the product-focused ones are more obvious and are directed toward developing different products for consumers, process innovations, though less obvious, can be just as powerful, revolutionizing the ways products are made and industry value-chains are defined. Henry Ford's assembly line, Toyota's just-in-time inventory management, and Honda's total quality management are but three process revolutions that forever changed the automobile industry and replaced dominant incumbent firms with newcomers. Similarly, Walmart's emphasis on logistics was initially discounted by the incumbents as peripheral to retailing, and Walmart was relegated to serving smaller and rural communities away from the dominance of traditional retailers on the main street and in the shopping malls. Notably, in each case, the newcomers were initially dismissed by the mainstream of the industry as inferior, and the new products were offered at a lower price. They targeted customers who were not considered attractive enough to be courted by the existing players, but these customers provided the underpinning of growth markets and helped the newcomers to eventually dominate their industries.

Regulation and deregulation can also drastically alter an industry and compel it to take a different configuration. The deregulation of the airline industry completely upset the bases of competition and led to the dramatic realignment of the dominant companies and their competitive advantages. It heralded the birth of low-cost carriers with radically different business models, such as WestJet, Porter Airlines, Southwest Airlines, Ryanair, and EasyJet, and witnessed the crash landing of many icons of the industry, such as PanAm, Canadian Airlines, and Swissair. Changes in patent laws facilitated the emergence of generic drug manufacturers and revolutionized the pharmaceutical industry, introducing new dimensions of competition, lower prices, and extensive litigation. Consumers have benefited tremendously in both cases by the regulatory changes and have enjoyed better access, lower costs, and more variety of products and services.

An industry whose core activities or core assets face obsolescence will follow one of four change trajectories, as they are depicted in Exhibit 8-2.

Radical change occurs when core activities and core assets both face the threat of obsolescence. For example, the overnight delivery industry is beginning to experience this problem. The availability of cheap and instantaneous document delivery through fax machines and the Internet has made the core assets (delivery trucks, airplanes, and a central hub) and core activities (document tracking) of such firms as Federal Express (FedEx) suddenly less relevant. A similar situation was faced by typewriter manufacturers decades ago when relatively inexpensive PCs became widely available.

Intermediating change occurs when core assets are not threatened but core activities are. Automobile dealerships are an example of an industry facing intermediating change, as customers can get all the information they need online. Second, as the quality and longevity of cars improve, individual purchases have become less frequent. Moreover, car manufacturers are increasingly sharing the task of customer relations with the dealers, and, in some cases, have even completely taken over this function. Finally, inventory management and financing are now subject to significant economies of scale that only large, integrated companies can take advantage of.

When core assets are threatened but core activities are not, industries tend to follow the creative change trajectory. Some industries undergoing creative change include the film production industry, the pharmaceutical industry, oil and gas exploration, and pre-packaged software. In each of these industries, there is rapid asset turnover but relatively stable relationships with suppliers and customers. For example, in the pharmaceutical industry, patents

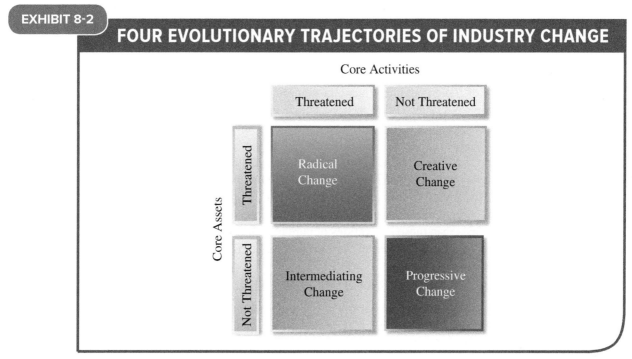

EXHIBIT 8-2

FOUR EVOLUTIONARY TRAJECTORIES OF INDUSTRY CHANGE

Core Activities

	Threatened	Not Threatened
Threatened (Core Assets)	Radical Change	Creative Change
Not Threatened (Core Assets)	Intermediating Change	Progressive Change

for some drugs expire while new drugs are being approved, but the core activities of commercialization and marketing continue to be relevant.

Finally, progressive change occurs in industries where neither core assets nor core activities face imminent threat of obsolescence. Change does occur, but it is within the existing framework of the industry. At any given moment, incremental changes may be occurring, but over time, these events accumulate to result in substantial change. The commercial airline industry and the discount retailing industry are both experiencing progressive change. Their suppliers and the customers have not changed, and the core assets and activities have changed only incrementally, but over the last decade, both these industries have experienced significant changes.

LO 3   Disruptive Innovation and the Innovator's Dilemma

Harvard Professor Clayton Christensen differentiates between "sustaining" and "disruptive" innovations.[6] Although the pace of a firm's innovations may be faster than the evolving needs of its customers, companies can, nonetheless, pursue these "sustaining innovations" at the higher tiers of their markets. They can charge high prices for these innovative products to their most demanding and sophisticated customers at the top of the market and, thus, use these innovations to sustain their profitability.

However, while focusing on these sustaining innovations at the top of the market, these companies often open the door to new competitors who introduce "disruptive innovations." Disruptive innovations allow a whole new population of consumers at the bottom of a market access to a product or service that was historically only accessible to consumers at the top. Disruptive innovations are frequently simpler, cheaper and more accessible and can decimate an industry leader who keeps on making very profitable, perfectly good products better and better.

Because these lower tiers of the market offer lower gross margins, they are unattractive to other firms moving upward in the market, creating space at the bottom of the market for new disruptive competitors to emerge. The innovator's dilemma involves figuring out how much energy to put into supporting an innovation that has now risen to the top, knowing that someone at the bottom is waiting to unseat you with a disruptive innovation. Too many companies focus on sustaining innovations geared toward the top of their industry and do not see the disruptive innovations coming until it is too late.

In 2013, Christensen and colleagues revisited the theory of disruptive innovation.[7] They realized that the predictions hold true when a product or service's utility is the dominant consideration. However, if the innovation is challenging a product or service's identity function, something else happens. Identity refers to values, ethics, and relationships. Every product or service has both a utility function and an identity function. When customers focus on the utility function, getting the job done, they were happy to abandon one technology for another.

Think of the example of Indigo, and how many customers are happily abandoning the printed book for the ebook (see Strategy Spotlight 8.1, later in this section). Those customers are most interested in the utility of the product, which, in this case, is getting access to the material they want to read. But other customers stay loyal to printed books; they privilege the identity function. Although it might be more economical to have 100 books on their Kobo, they may pride themselves on having in their homes a dedicated room where they can lovingly house hundreds of hard copy books printed on the finest paper—something once called a library!

Christensen and colleagues argue that there is a continuum for all products and services for each person and group, which they call the utility–identity curve. They note that innovations that challenge identity will have a much different set of dynamics than those innovations of pure utility. Focusing only on utility and not on identity, or the values of a firm's stakeholders, could result in missed opportunities, or worse.

LO 4 Industry Life Cycle: Strategies in the Introduction Stage

In the introduction stage, products are unfamiliar to consumers.[8] Market segments are not well defined, and product features are not clearly specified. The early development of an industry typically involves low sales growth, rapid technological change, operating losses, and the need for strong sources of cash to finance operations. Since there are few players and not much growth, competition tends to be limited.

Success in the introduction stage requires an emphasis on research and development and marketing activities to enhance awareness of the product or service. The challenge involves (1) developing the product and finding a way to get users to try it and (2) generating enough exposure so that the product emerges as the standard by which all other competitors' products are evaluated.

There is an advantage to being the "first mover" in a market.[9] Consider Coca-Cola's success in becoming the first soft drink company to build a recognizable global brand. Moving before others enabled Caterpillar to get a lock on overseas sales channels and service capabilities. Being a first mover in the mid-1990s allowed RIM (now BlackBerry Ltd.), based in Waterloo, Ontario, to establish its BlackBerry as the global standard for personal digital assistants (PDAs).

However, there can also be a benefit to being a "late mover." U.S. retailer Target carefully thought out the decision to delay its Internet strategy. In comparison with its competitors Walmart and Kmart, Target was definitely the industry laggard. It patiently waited to learn from the mistakes of the first movers and made sure it understood how to attract online customers before it launched its own website. The wait paid off and, before long, Target had equal online market presence to its larger competitors.[10]

Examples of products currently in the introduction stage of the industry life cycle include electric vehicles, where models, platforms, and formats are still getting settled; self-driving cars, where regulatory frameworks and legal issues are as fluid as the competing technologies jostling for dominance; and applications of Artificial Intelligence (AI) and the Internet of Things (IoT).

Industry Life Cycle: Strategies in the Growth Stage

The second stage of the industry life cycle, growth, is characterized by strong increases in sales. The potential for strong sales (and profits) attracts other competitors who also want to benefit. During the growth stage, the primary key to success is to build consumer preferences for specific brands. This requires strong brand recognition, differentiated products, and the financial resources to support a variety of value chain activities, such as marketing and sales, customer service, and R&D. In the introduction stage, marketing and sales initiatives were mainly directed at spurring aggregate demand, that is, demand for all such products, whereas efforts in the growth stage are directed toward stimulating selective demand—that is, demand for a firm's product offerings instead of those of its rivals.

Revenues in the growth stage increase at an accelerating rate because (1) new consumers are trying the product and (2) a growing proportion of satisfied consumers are making repeat purchases.[11] In general, as a product moves through its life cycle, the proportion of repeat buyers to new purchasers increases. Yet new products and services often fail if there are relatively few repeat purchases. This is especially true of many consumer products that are characterized by relatively low prices and infrequent purchases. For example, Alberto-Culver introduced Mr. Culver's Sparklers, which were solid air fresheners that looked like stained glass. Although the product quickly went from the introduction stage to the growth stage, sales subsequently plummeted. Why? Unfortunately, there were few repeat purchasers because buyers treated the air fresheners as inexpensive window decorations, left them on the windows, and felt little need to purchase new ones. Examples of products currently in the growth stage of the industry life cycle include Internet servers, smartphones, and computer tablets.

Industry Life Cycle: Strategies in the Maturity Stage

In the third stage, maturity, aggregate industry demand begins to slow. Since markets are becoming saturated, there are few opportunities to attract new adopters. It is no longer possible to "grow around" the competition, so direct competition becomes predominant.[12] With few attractive prospects, marginal competitors begin to exit the market. At the same time, rivalry among existing competitors intensifies because there is often fierce price competition as expenses associated with attracting new buyers rise. Advantages based on efficient manufacturing operations and process engineering become more important for keeping costs low as customers become more price sensitive. It also becomes more difficult for firms to differentiate their offerings once users have a greater understanding of products and services.

An article in *Fortune* magazine that addressed the intensity of rivalry in mature markets was aptly titled "A Game of Inches." It stated, "Battling for market share in a slowing industry can be a mighty dirty business. Just ask laundry soap archrivals Unilever and Procter & Gamble."[13] These two firms have been locked in a battle for market share since 1965. Why is the competition so intense? There is not much territory to gain. In 2000, total sales for the industry were flat at $6 billion a year. A Lehman Brothers analyst noted, "People aren't getting any dirtier." Thus, the only way to win is to take market share from the competition. To increase its share, Procter & Gamble (P&G) spends $100 million a year promoting its Tide brand on television, billboards, subways, buses, magazines, and the Internet. But Unilever is not standing still. Armed with a new $80-million budget, it launched a soap tablet product named Wisk Dual Action Tablets. It delivered samples of this product to 24 million U.S. homes with the Sunday newspapers, followed by a series of TV ads. P&G launched a counteroffensive: Tide Rapid Action Tablets ads showed side-by-side comparisons of the two products dropped into beakers of water. In the promotion, P&G claimed that its product was superior because it dissolved faster than Unilever's product.

Many product classes and whole industries, such as beer, automobiles, televisions, furniture, home renovations, and airlines, are in the maturity stage. Firms, however, do not need to be "held hostage" to the life cycle curve. By positioning or repositioning their products in unexpected ways, firms can change how customers mentally categorize them. Thus, firms are able to rescue products floundering in the maturity phase of their life cycles and return them to the growth phase. Firms can "strip" away traditional features and attributes of a product and introduce new ones, as did some Credit Unions by simplifying the endless variations of chequing and savings accounts.[14] Firms can also reposition their products to be associated with a radically different category, as in the case of Swatch, the Swiss watch, which was introduced as a new concept, that of a casual, fun, and relatively disposable accessory, in contrast to the traditional notion of a watch as a jewellery timepiece.

Industry Life Cycle: Strategies in the Decline Stage

Although all decisions in the phases of an industry life cycle are important, they become particularly critical in the decline stage. Difficult choices must be made, and firms must face up to the fundamental strategic choice between either exiting or staying and attempting to consolidate their position in the industry.[15]

The decline stage occurs when industry sales and profits begin to fall. Typically, changes in the business environment are at the root of an industry or product group entering this stage.[16] Changes in consumer tastes or a technological innovation can push a product into decline. Typewriters went into the decline stage because of the word processing capabilities of PCs. Compact discs (CDs) forced cassette tapes into decline in the pre-recorded music industry, and digital video discs (DVDs) replaced CDs and were then replaced themselves by digital file streaming and downloads. About 35 years ago, of course, cassette tapes had caused the demise of long-playing records (LPs).

Products in the decline stage, often consume a large share of management time and financial resources relative to their potential worth. As sales and profits decline, competitors may start drastically cutting their prices to raise cash and remain solvent in the short term. The situation is further aggravated by the wholesale liquidation of assets, including inventory, of some of the competitors that have failed. This further intensifies the price competition.

In the decline stage, a firm's strategic options become dependent on the actions of its rivals. On the one hand, if many competitors decide to leave the market, sales and profit opportunities increase. On the other hand, prospects are limited if all competitors remain.[17] If some competitors merge, their increased market power may erode the opportunities for the remaining players. Managers must carefully monitor the actions and intentions of competitors before deciding on a course of action.

Four basic strategies are available in the decline phase: maintaining, harvesting, exiting, or consolidating.[18]

- *Maintaining* refers to keeping a product going without significantly reducing marketing support, technological development, or other investments, in the hope that competitors will eventually exit the market. Some offices still use typewriters for filling out forms and carrying out functions that cannot be completed on a PC. In some rural areas, rotary (or dial) telephones continue to exist because of the older technology used in central switching offices. Thus, if a firm remains in the business and others exit, there may still be the potential for revenues and profits.

- *Harvesting* involves taking as much profit as possible from the business and making absolutely minimal investments. It requires that sales volume be maximized and costs be reduced quickly. To cut associated budgets and wring out as much profit as possible, managers must review all of the firm's value-creating activities. All value-chain activities should be considered for cost cutting, including primary activities, such as operations and sales and marketing, as well as support activities, such as procurement, information systems, and technology development.

- *Exiting* the market involves dropping the product from a firm's portfolio. Since a residual core of consumers may continue to use the product, eliminating it should be considered carefully. If the firm's exit involves product markets that affect important relationships with other product markets in the corporation's overall portfolio, an exit could have repercussions for the whole corporation. For example, it may involve the loss of valuable brand names or human capital with a broad variety of expertise in many value-creating activities, such as marketing, technology, and operations.

- *Consolidation* involves one firm acquiring a number of its competitors in a declining industry. The surviving firm enhances its market power and acquires valuable assets. It retains the best facilities and effectively rationalizes its operations. It takes production capacity out of the system in an orderly fashion and prevents a bloody price war that could severely hurt its profits. Certain firms in the North American steel industry undertook an ambitious strategy of consolidation during the late 1990s and created fewer but better-positioned players with much more competitive cost structures. Another example of consolidation took place in the U.S. defence industry at about the same time. As the cliché goes, "peace broke out" at the end of the Cold War, and overall U.S. defence spending levels plummeted.[19] Many companies saw more than 50 percent of their market disappear. Only one-quarter of the 120,000 companies that once supplied the Department of Defense were around by 2001; the others shut down their defence business or dissolved altogether. But one key player, Lockheed Martin, became a dominant rival by pursuing an aggressive strategy of consolidation. During the 1990s, it purchased 17 independent entities, including General Dynamics' tactical aircraft and space systems divisions, GE Aerospace, Goodyear Aerospace, and Honeywell Electro-Optics. These combinations enabled Lockheed Martin to emerge as the top provider to three governmental customers: the Department of Defense, the Department of Energy, and the National Aeronautics and Space Administration (NASA). Even before the defence and security build-up that followed the September 11, 2001, terrorist attacks, the firm was ranked among the largest 25 industrial concerns in the United States and was posting healthy profits.

Examples of products currently in the decline stage of the industry life cycle include automotive spark plugs (replaced by electronic fuel ignition), video cassette recorders (replaced by DVD players), DVD players (replaced by streaming and downloading of movies and music) 35-mm photographic equipment (replaced by digital cameras), digital cameras (replaced by the ubiquitous cellphones) and PC zip drives (replaced by DVD drives and Universal Serial Bus (USB) ports, which as of late have all been eclipsed by "the cloud").[20]

As a case in point, Strategy Spotlight 8.1 describes how a venerated Canadian icon has attempted to respond to the declining stages of an industry, it once dominated.

8.1 STRATEGY SPOTLIGHT

Indigo and the Declining Book Sales

In 2014, Indigo was struggling to stay afloat in an industry that was changing. In-store book sales had been decreasing rapidly. Indigo's great e-commerce hope was not yet materializing, as online sales experienced only a marginal offsetting increase of 0.7 percent. The historical pseudo-monopoly that Indigo had previously enjoyed was now lost to increased competition from the online giant, Amazon. The time had come for Indigo to reevaluate the industry in which it operates in order to determine how to do more than simply stay afloat.

In 2001, Indigo had acquired Chapters, and its controlling shareholders ended up with 70.5 percent of the company. As a result of the acquisition, Indigo Books & Music became the largest book retailer in Canada, progressively pushing many small retailers out of business and becoming something akin to a monopoly in literary retail in Canada. In the same year, the online website chapters.indigo.ca was created. However, the entry of Amazon and e-readers helped to neutralize the monopolistic power of Indigo, creating other attractive alternatives within the Canadian book market.

Many bookstores were shutting their doors as a result of decreased sales attributed to a consumer base that was switching to the lower cost, more convenient alternatives of e-books. This phenomenon was not without precedent. It has significant parallels with the 1990s crisis within the newspaper industry and a similar upheaval during the early 2000s within the music industry. It seems that into the 2010s, bricks-and-mortar book retailers, along with the entire publishing industry, are facing existential crises and are under the serious threat of becoming totally obsolete.

Indigo is attempting to boost its profitability by offering more high-margin products, such as toys and lifestyle items. The adaptation process continues as the company introduces more "stuff" to its lifestyle section. Indigo's main growth categories are paper, toys, and gift products, such as home and fashion accessories. By September 28, 2013, Indigo had launched its first 12 Indigo Tech shops, and more followed. These stores, located within the larger bookstores, sell Kobo and Apple products as well as other electronic accessories. While Indigo is delving into more diverse product categories, it claims that the core of the business remains the love of books, and strives to relate non-book merchandise back to the joy of reading and the lifestyle of a book reader.

Sources: Anonymous, Chapters & Indigo Unveil Merger Details, CBC News, 13 Jan. 2001; Kopun, Francine, Indigo Struggles as Transformation Continues, Toronto Star Newspapers Ltd, 5 Nov 2013; Shaw, Hollie, Indigo to Open 40 Apple In-store Shops as Retailer Works through 'difficult transformation', National Post, 25 Jun 2013; Anonymous, A New Chapter for Indigo, The Canadian Press, 25 Jun 2013; Anonymous, Disappearing Ink, The Economist, 10 Sept 2011; the company's financial statements and website.

LO 5 Turnaround Strategies

One problem with the life cycle analogy is that we tend to think that decline is inevitably followed by death. In the case of businesses, however, decline can be reversed by strategies that lead to turnaround and rejuvenation. Such a need for turnaround may occur at any stage in the life cycle; however, it is more likely to occur during the maturity or decline stage.

Most successful turnarounds start with a careful analysis of the external and internal environments.[21] The external analysis leads to identification of market segments or customer groups that may still find the product attractive.[22]

Internal analysis points to opportunities for reduced costs and higher efficiency. Typically, a firm needs to undertake a mix of both internally and externally oriented actions to effect a turnaround.[23]

A study of 260 mature businesses in need of a turnaround identified three strategies used by successful companies:[24]

- *Asset and cost surgery.* Very often, mature firms tend to have accumulated assets that do not produce any returns. These include real estate, buildings, or fine art pieces; even equipment, such as airplanes, needs to be considered. Outright sales or sale-and-leaseback free up considerable cash and improve returns. Investment in new plants and equipment can be deferred. Firms in turnaround situations try to aggressively cut administrative expenses and inventories and speed up the collection of receivables. Costs can also be reduced by outsourcing the production of various inputs, for which market prices may be cheaper elsewhere compared with in-house production costs.

- *Selective product and market pruning.* Most of the mature or declining firms have many product lines that are marginally profitable or losing money. One strategy is to discontinue unsuccessful product lines, cut off unprofitable and usually difficult clients, and focus all of the resources on a few core profitable areas. For example, in the early 1980s, faced with possible bankruptcy, Chrysler Corporation sold off all of its non-automotive businesses as well as all of its production facilities abroad. Focus on the North American market and identification of a profitable niche—namely, minivans—were key to Chrysler's eventual turnaround.

- *Piecemeal productivity improvements.* There are hundreds of ways in which a firm can eliminate costs and improve productivity. Although individually these are small gains, they accumulate over a period to yield substantial gains. Improving business processes by re-engineering them, benchmarking specific activities against industry leaders, encouraging employee input to identify excess costs, reducing R&D and marketing expenses, increasing capacity utilization, and improving employee productivity lead to significant overall gain.

Software maker Intuit provides an example of a quick but well-implemented turnaround strategy. After stagnating and stumbling during the dot-com bust, Intuit, which is known for its QuickBooks and TurboTax software, hired Stephen M. Bennett, a 22-year GE veteran. He immediately discontinued Intuit's online finance, insurance, and bill-paying operations, which were losing money. Instead, he focused on software for small businesses that employ less than 250 people. He also instituted a performance-based reward system that greatly improved employee productivity. Within a couple of years, Intuit was once again making substantial profits, and its stock went up by 42 percent.[25]

Even when an industry is in overall decline, pockets of profitability remain. These are segments with customers who are relatively price insensitive. For example, the replacement demand for vacuum tubes affords its manufacturers an opportunity to earn above-normal returns, although the product itself is technologically obsolete. Surprisingly, within declining industries, there may still be segments that are either stable or growing. Cigars and chewing tobacco are examples of profitable segments within the tobacco industry. Although fountain pens ceased to be the writing instrument of choice a long time ago, the fountain pen industry has successfully reconceptualized the product as a high margin luxury item that signals accomplishment, success, and appreciation of the finer things in life. Every business has the potential for rejuvenation. But it takes creativity, persistence, and, most of all, a clear strategy to translate that potential into reality.

LO 6 COMPETITIVE DYNAMICS

New entry into markets, whether by startups or by incumbent firms, nearly always threatens existing competitors. This is partly true because except in very new markets, nearly every market need is already being met, either directly or indirectly, by existing firms. As a result, the competitive actions of a new entrant are very likely to provoke a competitive response from companies that feel threatened. This, in turn, is likely to evoke a reaction to the response. As a result, a competitive dynamic—action and response—begins among the firms competing for the same customers in a given marketplace.

Competitive dynamics—intense rivalry among similar competitors—has the potential to alter a company's strategy. New entrants may be forced to change their strategies or develop new ones to survive competitive challenges by incumbent rivals. New entry is among the most common reasons a cycle of competitive actions and reactions gets started. It might also occur because of threatening actions among existing competitors, such as aggressive cost cutting. Thus, studying competitive dynamics helps explain why strategies evolve and reveals how, why, and when to respond to the actions of close competitors. Exhibit 8-3 identifies the factors that competitors need to consider when determining how to respond to a competitive act.

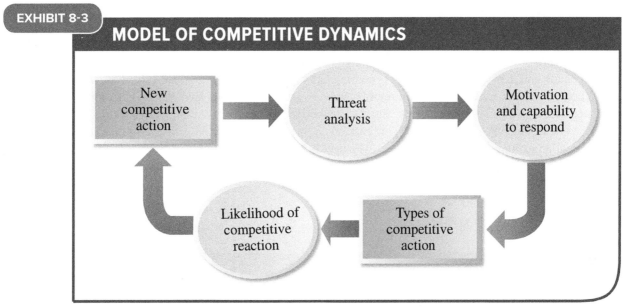

EXHIBIT 8-3

MODEL OF COMPETITIVE DYNAMICS

New competitive action → Threat analysis → Motivation and capability to respond → Types of competitive action → Likelihood of competitive reaction → (back to New competitive action)

Source: Adapted from M. J. Chen, "Competitor Analysis and Interfirm Rivalry: Toward a Theoretical Integration," *Academy of Management Review,* 21(1), 1996, pp. 100–134; D. J. Ketchen, C. C. Snow, and V. L. Hoover, "Research on Competitive Dynamics: Recent Accomplishments and Future Challenges," *Journal of Management,* 30(6), 2004, pp. 779–804; and K. G. Smith, W. J. Ferrier, and C. M. Grimm, "King of the Hill: Dethroning the Industry Leader," *Academy of Management Executive,* 15(2), 2001, pp. 59–70.

Pankaj Ghemawat identifies four threats to the sustainability of a firm's value creating activities:[26]

- *Imitation.* The threat that competitors may be able to replicate the value-creating elements over time.
- *Substitution.* The concern that new products or services launched by competitors may decrease the value customers see in the current product or service offerings of the firm.
- *Slack.* The worry that complacency on the part of the firm will dissipate value over time.
- *Hold-up.* The fear that other players in the firm's network can capture the value created by the firm through exercising their superior bargaining power.

New Competitive Action

Entry into a market by a new competitor is a good starting point to begin describing the cycle of actions and responses characteristic of a competitive dynamic process.[27] However, new entry is only one type of competitive action. Price cutting, imitating successful products, or expanding production capacity are other examples of competitive actions that might provoke competitors to react.

Why do companies launch new competitive actions? There are several reasons:

- To improve market position
- To capitalize on growing demand
- To expand production capacity
- To provide an innovative new solution
- To obtain first-mover advantages

Underlying all of these reasons is the desire to strengthen financial outcomes, capture some of the extraordinary profits that industry leaders enjoy, and grow the business. Some companies are also motivated to launch competitive challenges because they want to build their reputation for innovativeness or efficiency. For example, Southwest Airlines, once an upstart airline with only a few routes, has become phenomenally successful and an industry leader. For years, it went virtually unchallenged. But Southwest's costs have crept up, and now start-up airlines, such as JetBlue, are challenging the industry leader with their own low-cost strategies.[28] This is indicative of the competitive dynamic cycle. As former Intel Chairman Andy Grove stated, "Business success contains the seeds of its own destruction. The more successful you are, the more people want a chunk of your business and then another chunk and then another until there is nothing left."[29]

When a company enters a market for the first time, it can be considered an attack on existing competitors. As indicated earlier in the chapter, any of the entry strategies can be used to take competitive action. But competitive attacks come from many sources besides new entrants. Some of the most intense competition is among incumbent rivals intent on gaining strategic advantages. "Winners in business play rough and don't apologize for it," according to Boston Consulting Group authors George Stalk, Jr., and Rob Lachenauer in their book *Hardball: Are You Playing to Play or Playing to Win?*[30] Exhibit 8-4 outlines their five strategies.

EXHIBIT 8-4   FIVE "HARDBALL" STRATEGIES

Strategy	Description	Examples
Devastate rivals' profit sanctuaries	Not all business segments generate the same level of profits for a company. Through focused attacks on a rival's most profitable segments, a company can generate maximum leverage with relatively smaller-scale attacks. Recognize, however, that companies closely guard the information needed to determine just what their profit sanctuaries are.	In 2005, Walmart began offering low-priced extended warranties on home electronics after learning that its rivals, such as Best Buy, derived most of their profits from extended warranties.
Plagiarize with pride	Just because a close competitor comes up with an idea first does not mean it cannot be successfully imitated. Second movers, in fact, can see how customers respond, make improvements, and launch a better version without all the market development costs. Successful imitation is harder than it may appear and requires the imitating firm to keep its ego in check.	Blockbuster copied the online DVD rental strategy of its rival Netflix. Not only did Blockbuster continue to struggle even after this imitation, but Netflix sued Blockbuster for patent violations as well. It should be noted that Blockbuster's strategy was not enough to revive its fortunes. The company ended up in bankruptcy nonetheless.
Deceive the competition	A good gambit sends the competition off in the wrong direction. This may cause the rivals to miss strategic shifts, spend money pursuing dead ends, or slow their responses. Any of these outcomes support the deceiving firms' competitive advantage. Companies must be sure not to cross ethical lines during these actions.	Boeing spent several years touting its plans for a new high-speed airliner. After it became clear the customer valued efficiency over speed, Boeing quietly shifted its focus. When Boeing announced its new 7e7 (now 787) Dreamliner, its competitor, Airbus Industries, was surprised and caught without an adequate response, which helped the 787 set new sales records.
Unleash massive and overwhelming force	Although many hardball strategies are subtle and indirect, this one is not. This is a full-frontal attack, where a firm commits significant resources to a major campaign to weaken rivals' positions in certain markets. Firms must be sure they have the mass and stamina required to win before they declare war against a rival.	Southwest Airlines took on US Airways in Baltimore and drove US Airways' market share from over 50 percent to 10 percent. Southwest began flying to Philadelphia and Pittsburgh as well—additional key markets for US Airways.

(Continued)

Strategy	Description	Examples
Raise competitors' costs	If a company has superior insight into the complex cost and profit structure of the industry, it can compete in a way that steers its rivals into relatively higher cost or lower profit arenas. This strategy uses deception to make the rivals think they are winning, when, in fact, they are not. Again, companies using this strategy must be confident that they understand the industry better than their rivals do.	Ecolab, a company that sells cleaning supplies to businesses, encouraged a leading competitor, Diversity, to adopt a strategy to go after the low-volume, high-margin customers. What Ecolab knew that Diversity did not is that the high servicing costs involved with this segment make the segment unprofitable—a situation Ecolab ensured by bidding high enough to lose the contracts to Diversity but low enough to ensure the business lost money for Diversity.

Sources: Berner, R. 2005. Watch Out, Best Buy and Circuit City. BusinessWeek, November 10; Stalk, G. Jr. 2006. Curveball Strategies to Fool the Competition. Harvard Business Review, 84(9): 114–121; and Stalk, Jr., G. & Lachenauer, R. 2004. Hardball: Are You Playing to Play or Playing to Win? Cambridge, MA: Harvard Business School Press. Reprinted by permission of Harvard Business School Press from G. Stalk, Jr. and R. Lachenauer. Copyright 2004 by the Harvard Business School Publishing Corporation; all rights reserved; Lam, Y. 2013. FDI companies dominate Vietnam's detergent market. www.saigon-gpdaily.com.vn, January 22: np; Vascellaro, J. 2012. Apple wins big in patent case. www.wsj.com, August 25: np; and Pech, R. & Stamboulidis, G. 2010. How strategies of deception facilitate business growth. Journal of Business Strategy, 31(6): 37–45.

The likelihood that a competitor will launch an attack depends on many factors. In the remaining sections, we discuss such factors as competitor analysis, market conditions, types of strategic actions, and the resource endowments and capabilities that companies need to take competitive action.

Threat Analysis

Prior to actually observing a competitive action, companies may need to become aware of potential competitive threats. That is, companies need to have a keen sense of who their closest competitors are and the kinds of competitive actions they might be planning.[31] This may require some environmental scanning and monitoring of the sort described in Chapter 2. Awareness of the threats posed by industry rivals allows a firm to understand what type of competitive response, if any, may be necessary.

For example, Netflix founder and chief executive officer (CEO) Reed Hastings has faced numerous competitive threats since launching Netflix as an online movie rental company in 1997. According to Hastings, however, not all potential threats need to be taken seriously:

> We have to recognize that now there are tens and maybe hundreds of start-ups who think that they are going to eat Netflix's lunch. The challenge for a management team is to figure out which are real threats and which aren't. . . . It's conventional to say, "only the paranoid survive," but that's not true. The paranoid die because the paranoid take all threats as serious and get very distracted.
>
> There are markets that aren't going to get very big, and then there are markets that are going to get big, but they're not directly in our path. In the first camp, we have small companies likeMovielink—a well-run company but not an attractive model for consumers, sort of a $4-download to watch a movie. We correctly guessed when it launched four years ago that this was not a threat and didn't react to it.

(Continued)

> The other case I brought up is markets that are going to be very large markets, but we're just not the natural leader. Advertising supported online video, whether that's at CBS.com or YouTube—great market, kind of next door to us. But we don't do advertising-supported video, we do subscription, so it would be a huge competence expansion for us. And it's not a threat to movies."[32]

Being aware of competitors and cognizant of whatever threats they might pose is the first step in assessing the level of competitive threat. Once a new competitive action becomes apparent, companies must determine how threatening it is to their business. Competitive dynamics are likely to be most intense among companies that are competing for the same customers or who have highly similar sets of resources.[33] Two factors are used to assess whether or not companies are close competitors:

- *Market commonality.* Whether or not competitors are vying for the same customers and how many markets they share in common. For example, aircraft manufacturers Boeing and Airbus have a high degree of market commonality because they make very similar products and have many buyers in common.

- *Resource similarity.* The degree to which rivals draw on the same types of resources to compete. For example, the home pages of Google and Bing may look very different, but behind the scenes, they both rely on the talent pool of high-calibre software engineers to create the cutting-edge innovations that help them compete.

When any two firms have both a high degree of market commonality and highly similar resource bases, a stronger competitive threat is present. Such a threat, however, may not lead to competitive action. On the one hand, a market rival may be hesitant to attack a company with which it shares a high degree of market commonality because this could lead to an intense battle. On the other hand, once attacked, rivals with high market commonality will be much more motivated to launch a competitive response. This is especially true in cases where the shared market is an important part of a company's overall business.

How strong a response an attacked rival can mount will be determined by its strategic resource endowments. In general, the same set of conditions holds true with regard to resource similarity. Companies that have highly similar resource bases will be hesitant to launch an initial attack but pose a serious threat if required to mount a competitive response.[34] Greater strategic resources increase a firm's capability to respond. Strategy Spotlight 8.1 addresses how the dynamics of market commonality and resource similarity have shaped the battle between chipmakers Intel and Advanced Micro Devices (AMD) and intensified their competitive rivalry.

8.2 STRATEGY SPOTLIGHT

AMD and Intel: Related Rivals

Few business battles are as intensely reported as the one between chipmakers Intel and Advanced Micro Devices (AMD). For years, Intel aggressively advertised its brand by pushing its "Intel Inside" logo to average consumers. In an effort to develop a stronger presence among consumers, AMD launched a successful initiative labelled internally, "War in the Store" to promote the sales of AMD-based computers in retailers, such as Best Buy. The effort prompted retaliation by Intel, which lowered the cost of chips enough to decrease PC prices by $200. Meanwhile, AMD won a round when Dell announced it would start using AMD chips in its servers.

Why is the battle between the two companies so intense? The reason is that they are so much alike. Both companies were founded in the late 1960s in Silicon Valley and were partners during their early histories. But in 1986, Intel cancelled a key licensing agreement with AMD to manufacture microprocessors and refused to turn over technical details. AMD sued, and after years of litigation, the Supreme Court of California forced Intel to pay AMD over $1 billion in compensation for contract violations. The two companies have been battling each other ever since.

Consider how comparable the two companies are in terms of markets and resources.

Market Commonality

A key issue facing the two chipmakers is that to continue growing, they have to enter each other's market space. This is a major reason why the competition has become so heated. For example, Intel dominated that high-end server business in 2003. Now AMD holds 26 percent of the U.S. server chip business and supplies a 48-percent share of the multicore processors (which feature two or more chips on one slice of silicon). To maintain its status as the number-one supplier, Intel launched a new family of processors called Core 2 Duo, which combines the performance of the Pentium 4 with the energy saving features of its notebook computer processors. "We intend to energetically compete for every single microprocessor opportunity," said Sean M. Maloney, Intel's executive vice-president.

Resource Similarity

Intel is the world's number-one supplier of semiconductors and has five manufacturing plants across the globe. Because of new manufacturing techniques at three of its plants, it can squeeze more transistors onto a chip and its processors cost less to make than AMD's. In contrast, AMD has just two manufacturing plants, but it has moved aggressively to match Intel's muscle. In 2005, it paid $5.4 billion to acquire graphics chipmaker ATI Technologies and outsourced more manufacturing to Chartered Semiconductors. One result has been that AMD, now the number-two maker of processors and graphic cards, doubled semiconductor sales within three years.

The battle between the two companies has been costly. When Intel retaliated against AMD's rapid gains, the result was slower sales for AMD and first quarter 2006 revenues of $1.23 billion, not the $1.55 billion that analysts expected. Meanwhile, Intel was hurt when Dell decided to begin installing AMD chips in its servers after years of using Intel exclusively. "The competitive dynamics have been more intense than we expected," commented Kevin B. Rollins, Dell's former CEO.

Sources: C. Edwards, "AMD: Chipping Away at Intel's Lead," *BusinessWeek,* June 12, 2006, pp. 72–73; C. Edwards, "Intel Sharpens its Offensive Game," *BusinessWeek,* July 31, 2006, p. 60; A. Gonsalves, "AMD Pays the Price in Awakening Intel Goliath," *InformationWeek,* www.informationweek.com, April 9, 2007; S. Gaudin, "AMD Cracks Top 10 Chip Ranking, Intel Sales Slump," *InformationWeek,* www.informationweek.com, December 5, 2006; and www.wikipedia.org.

Motivation and Capability to Respond

Once attacked, competitors are faced with deciding how to respond. Before deciding, however, they need to evaluate not only how they will respond but also their reasons for responding and their capability to respond. Companies need to be clear about what problems a competitive response is expected to address and what types of problems it might create.[35] There are several factors to consider.

First, how serious is the impact of the competitive attack to which the competitors are responding? For example, a large company with a strong reputation that is challenged by a small or unknown company may elect to simply keep an eye on the new competitor rather than react quickly or too much. Part of the story of online retailer Amazon's early success is attributed to Barnes & Noble's overreaction to Amazon's claim that it was "the earth's biggest bookstore." Because Barnes & Noble was already using the phrase "the world's largest bookstore," it sued

Amazon, but lost. The confrontation made it to the front pages of *The Wall Street Journal,* and Amazon was on its way to becoming a household name.[36]

Companies planning to respond to a competitive challenge must also understand their motive for responding. What is the intent of the competitive response? Is it merely to blunt the attack of the competitor, or is it an opportunity to enhance its own competitive position? Sometimes, the most a company can hope for is to minimize the damage caused by a competitive action.

A company that seeks to improve its competitive advantage may be motivated to launch an attack rather than merely respond to one. For example, Walmart is known for its aggressive efforts to live up to its "everyday low prices" corporate motto. Strategy Spotlight 8.3 describes the retailer's assault on rivals Circuit City and Best Buy. A company must also assess its capability to respond. What strategic resources can be deployed to fend off a competitive attack? Does the company have an array of internal strengths it can draw on, or is it operating from a position of weakness?

8.3 STRATEGY SPOTLIGHT

Walmart's Cutthroat Pricing Schemes

Walmart has a reputation as a relentless competitor in its pursuit of an overall cost-leader strategy. Most of that reputation has come from its efforts to drive down costs in its dealings with suppliers. Walmart sometimes goes on the offensive with rivals by also driving down prices.

The retail giant took on Circuit City and Best Buy, with whom it competes head-on in the consumer electronics market. First, Walmart made big improvements in the electronics departments of 1,300 of its 3,100 U.S. stores by spiffing up displays and adding high-end products, such as Apple iPods, Toshiba laptops, and Sony liquid-crystal-display (LCD) televisions. Then, it delivered the two rivals a proverbial one-two punch—offering low-cost extended warranties and slashing prices on flat-panel TVs.

- *Extended warranties.* These are the multiyear protection plans that salespeople offer at the close of a sale on such items as TVs and computers. For both Circuit City and Best Buy, they are one of the most profitable segments of their businesses, accounting for at least a third of their operating profits. In late 2005, Walmart launched its own extended warranty program at prices nearly 50 percent lower than those of Best Buy and Circuit City.

- *Flat-panel TVs.* This includes both LCD and big-screen plasma models, which, until the 2006 holiday season, had never sold below $1,000. Walmart broke that barrier by offering a 42-inch flat-panel TV for $998. The cuts were not limited to lesser-known brands, such as Viore TV. Walmart also lowered the 42-inch Panasonic high-definition TV by $500 to $1,294. The response was immediate. Circuit City lowered the price on the same Panasonic TV to $1,299, and Best Buy began offering a 42-inch Westinghouse LCD TV for $999.

Circuit City was among the hardest hit by this cutthroat competition. After several attempts to cut costs and bolster revenues, it filed for bankruptcy in 2008 and was liquidated in 2009. Best Buy, the largest electronic retailer, did a better job of absorbing the shock. Still, its stock fell by 9 percent during the first quarter of 2007. Other retailers were also hit hard by the audacious pricing that has been labelled the "Walmart effect," including CompUSA, which slashed 126 of its 229 stores, and Tweeter's, which closed 49 of its 153 stores and laid off 650 workers.

Sources: M. Boyle and A. McConnon, "Circuit City Files for Bankruptcy," www.businessweek.com, November 10, 2008, n.p.; R. Berner, "Watch Out, Best Buy and Circuit City," *BusinessWeek Online,* www.businessweek.com, November 10, 2005; and P. Gogoi, "How Wal-Mart's TV Prices Crushed Rivals," *BusinessWeek Online,* www.businessweek.com, April 27, 2007.

Consider the role of the age and size of a firm in calculating its ability to respond. Most entrepreneurial new ventures start out small. The smaller size makes them more nimble compared with large firms, so they can respond quickly to competitive attacks. Because they are not well known, startups also have the advantage of the element of surprise in how and when they attack. Innovative uses of technology, for example, allow small firms to deploy resources in unique ways.

Because they are young, however, startups may not have the financial resources needed to follow through with a competitive response. In contrast, older and larger firms may have more resources and a repertoire of competitive techniques they can use in a counterattack. Large firms, however, tend to be slower to respond. Older firms tend to be predictable in their responses because they often lose touch with the competitive environment and rely on strategies and actions that have worked in the past.

Strategy Spotlight 8.4 describes how Microsoft struggled in the early 2000s to convert new ideas into successful businesses and lists a range of failed attempts to gain dominance in the rapidly changing mobile world.

8.4 STRATEGY SPOTLIGHT

Microsoft's Struggles with Corporate Entrepreneurship

Microsoft was used to dominating the market for PC operating system and office suite application software, yet its stock languished for the better part of ten years, until around 2014. Investors had little confidence that Microsoft would produce blockbuster products that could replace the revenues of its core PC software products as the information technology market moves into the post-PC phase.

It is not that Microsoft has failed to generate innovative ideas. The firm typically spends over $10 billion a year on R&D. More than 10 years ago, engineers at Microsoft developed a tablet PC and an eBook system, two rather hot technology products. They also pioneered Web-TV. But they failed to turn these design efforts into marketable products. In other markets they have seen limited success with products they have designed to meet emerging challengers. The Zune music player was supposed to challenge the iPod but was a flop in the market. The Xbox 360 has arguably been Microsoft's most successful product launch designed to take on a pioneering rival, but even there, the firm is competitive but not dominating the market. Only its latest inroads into the "cloud" under the new CEO, Satya Nadella, has produced meaningful results.

With all of its resources, why has Microsoft struggled to translate its innovations into market successes? Let us look at three reasons that have been talked about in the business press.

First, the dominance of the Windows and Office software has made it difficult to launch new products. Developers of new products have, at times, had to justify how their new product fit into the core Microsoft product line. Dick Brass, a former VP at Microsoft, states, "The company routinely manages to frustrate the efforts of its visionary leaders." For example, when Brass and his team developed an innovative technology to display text on a screen, called ClearType, engineers in the Windows group hampered the product by falsely arguing it had bugs and would not display some colours properly. Others in the firm stated they would support the technology only if they could control it. In the end, it took 10 years to get ClearType integrated into Windows.

Second, Microsoft has a difficult time attracting the top software designers. The firm is not seen as a hip place to work. It is seen by developers as too bureaucratic, and their flat stock price makes it hard to entice top designers with promises of wealth from rising stock options—a common compensation element for technology talent.

Third, great innovations are increasingly the output of collaborative, open-source design, but Microsoft is reluctant to fully embrace the open-source development model. It developed a system

(Continued)

where startup firms can sign on to a program to gain access to free Microsoft software and provide development ideas to Microsoft. Even though 35,000 firms have signed up, the system is still more bureaucratic than those of its competitors. As one entrepreneur commented about working with Microsoft, "We got introduced to Microsoft through our investors. They don't do this for just anybody." As a result, Microsoft has lost those "anybodies" as development partners and future customers.

In 2010, Microsoft launched the Windows Phone and again found their product struggling to gain market share. In 2011, Microsoft announced a partnership with Nokia, where Windows Phone would be Nokia's primary smartphone operating system. In September 2013, Microsoft announced that they would acquire Nokia's mobile phone division outright, as it was no longer researchers at Microsoft, but rather developers at Nokia, who were driving the R&D of the Windows Phone platform to better match their products.

In 2014, Nokia began producing Android phones that had replaced Google software with Microsoft software. This is certainly an aggressive move—will it turn the tide for Microsoft? Some analysts believe this may be the case, as an MS-Android will have unique advantages over rival products. One of the unique dynamics of this industry is that Android is open source—so Microsoft can easily step in and modify work done by its competitors. It is much easier to tweak a popular Android phone than redesign a Windows Phone.

Sources: Vaughan-Nichols, S.J., 2014, Worstall, T., 2013, "Five Reasons Microsoft Could Become a Top Android Smartphone Company," *ZDnet,* March 10; "The Real Reason Microsoft Bought Nokia," *Forbes,* September 8; Vance, A., 2010, "At Top of Business but Just Not Cool, *International Herald Tribune,* July 6: 2; Clarke, G., 2010, "Inside Microsoft's Innovation Crisis," *Theregister.co.uk,* February 5: n.p.; Brass, D., 2010, "Microsoft's Creative Destruction," *NYTimes.com,* February 4: n.p.; and the company website.

Other resources may also play a role in whether a company is equipped to retaliate. For example, one avenue of counterattack may be launching product enhancements or new product and service innovations. For that approach to be successful, a company needs to have both the intellectual capital to put forward viable innovations and the teamwork skills to prepare a new product or service and get it to market. Such resources as cross-functional teams and the social capital that makes production through teamwork effective and efficient represent the type of human capital resources that enhance a company's capability to respond.

Types of Competitive Actions

Once an organization determines whether it is willing and able to launch a competitive action, it must determine what type of action is appropriate. The actions taken will be determined by both its resource capabilities and its motive for responding. There are also marketplace considerations. What types of actions are likely to be most effective given a company's internal strengths and weaknesses as well as market conditions?

Two broadly defined types of competitive action include strategic actions and tactical actions. Strategic actions represent major commitments of distinctive and specific resources. Examples include launching a breakthrough innovation, building a new production facility, or merging with another company. Such actions require significant planning and resources and, once initiated, are difficult to reverse.

Tactical actions include refinements or extensions of strategies. Examples of tactical actions include cutting prices, improving gaps in service, or strengthening marketing and distribution efforts. Such actions typically draw on general resources and can be implemented quickly.

Some competitive actions take the form of frontal assaults, that is, actions aimed directly at taking business from another company or capitalizing on industry weaknesses. This can be especially effective when firms use a low-cost strategy. The airline industry provides a good example of this head-on approach. When Southwest Airlines began its no-frills, no-meals strategy in the late-1960s, it represented a direct assault on the major carriers of the day. In Europe, Ryanair has directly challenged the traditional carriers with an overall cost leadership strategy.

Founded in 1985, Ryanair is one-seventh the size of British Airways (BA) in terms of revenues, but in 2006, due to cost-cutting measures that significantly improved operating margins, it had a higher market capitalization of $7.6 billion compared with BA's $7.3 billion.[37]

Guerilla offensives and selective attacks provide an alternative for firms with fewer resources.[38] These draw attention to products or services by creating a buzz or generating enough shock value to get some free publicity. The open-source software movement, which has been gaining momentum as major corporations are becoming aware of its potential, still lacks the market power and the omnipresence that software giant Microsoft enjoys.[39] Loyal users of open-source software, such as Linux, stay connected and share software through online blogs. They also pull the occasional publicity stunt. In 2006, users of Firefox, the open-source browser developed by the Mozilla Corporation, created a crop circle in Oregon based on the Firefox logo. The effort made the local news and garnered thousands of mentions on open-source blogs and on Internet news organizations.

Some companies limit their competitive responses to defensive actions. Such actions rarely improve a company's competitive advantage, but a credible defensive action can lower the risk of being attacked and deter new entry. This may be especially effective during such periods as an industry shake-up when pricing levels or future demand for a product line become highly uncertain. At such times, such tactics as lowering prices on products that are easily duplicated, buying up the available supply of goods or raw materials, or negotiating exclusive agreements with buyers and suppliers can insulate a company from a more serious attack.

Several of the factors discussed earlier in the chapter, such as types of entry strategies and the use of cost leadership versus differentiation strategies, can guide the decision about what types of competitive actions to take. Before launching a given strategy, however, assessing the likely response of competitors is a vital step.[40]

Likelihood of Competitive Reaction

The logic of competitive dynamics suggests that once competitive actions are initiated, it is likely they will be met with competitive responses.[41] Thus, before mounting an attack, a firm should evaluate how competitors are likely to respond. Evaluating potential competitive reactions helps companies plan for future counterattacks. It may also lead to a decision to hold off—that is, not to take any competitive action at all because of the possibility that a misguided or poorly planned response will generate a devastating competitive reaction.

How a competitor is likely to respond will depend on three factors: market dependence, competitor's resources, and the reputation of the firm that initiates the action (actor's reputation). The implications of each of these are described briefly in the following sections.

Market Dependence

A company with a high concentration of its business in a particular industry has more at stake because it depends on that industry's market for its sales. Single-industry businesses are more likely to mount a competitive response. Young and small firms with a high degree of market dependence may be limited in how they respond due to resource constraints. JetBlue, itself an aggressive competitor, is unable to match some of the perks its bigger rivals can offer, such as first-class seats or international travel benefits.

Competitor's Resources

Previously, we examined the internal resource endowments that a company must evaluate when assessing its capability to respond. Here, it is the competitor's resources that need to be considered. For example, a small firm may be unable to mount a serious attack due to lack of resources. As a result, it is more likely to react to tactical actions, such as incentive pricing or enhanced service offerings, because they are less costly to attack than large-scale strategic actions. In contrast, a firm with financial "deep pockets" may be able to mount and sustain a costly counterattack. As a way to combat these differences in market power, young firms can strengthen their resource positions by forming strategic alliances. Yahoo!, for example, pressed hard by its young but powerful rival Google, allied itself with a group of seven newspaper chains that publish a total of 176 U.S. dailies in a content sharing arrangement. Both Yahoo! and the newspaper chains were trying to stay ahead of Google as it moved aggressively beyond ads on its search pages.

Actor's Reputation

Whether a company should respond to a competitive challenge will also depend on who launched the attack against it. In previous examples, we have noted that some companies, such as Walmart and Intel, are capable of bold offences. These competitive actors also have the ability and motivation to mount overwhelming counterattacks. Competitors are more likely to respond to competitive moves by market leaders than to those by relatively smaller firms with little market power. Another consideration is how successful prior attacks have been. For example, price cutting by the big automakers usually has the desired result—increased sales to price-sensitive buyers—at least in the short run. Given that history, when GM offers discounts or incentives, its rivals Ford and Chrysler cannot afford to ignore the challenge, and they quickly follow suit.

Choosing Not to React: Forbearance and Co-opetition

The above discussion suggests that there may be many circumstances in which the best reaction is no reaction at all. This is known as *forbearance*—refraining from reacting at all as well as holding back from initiating an attack. For example, none of the Japanese automakers attempted to match the employee discount pricing war that cost the big U.S. automakers heavily in terms of lower profits and lost jobs. Yet, during the same period, Honda, Toyota, and Nissan enjoyed substantial sales increases over the previous year.

Related to forbearance is the concept of *co-opetition*. This is a term that was coined by Raymond Noorda, founder and former CEO of the network software company Novell, to suggest that companies often benefit most from a combination of competition and co-operation.[42] Close competitors that differentiate themselves in the eyes of consumers may work together behind the scenes to achieve industry-wide efficiencies.[43] For example, the three top Canadian breweries, Labatt, Molson Coors, and Sleeman co-operate in owning and running the Beer Store, the only private retailer allowed to sell beer in Ontario. As long as the benefits of co-operating are enjoyed by all participants in a co-opetition system, the practice can help companies avoid intense and damaging competition.[44]

Despite the potential benefits of co-opetition, companies need to guard against co-operating to such a great extent that their actions are perceived as collusion, a practice that has legal ramifications in the United States. Satellite radio competitors XM and Sirius, after years of intense rivalry, faced several challenges recently related to their efforts to merge their operations.

Once a company has evaluated a competitor's likelihood of responding to a competitive challenge, it can decide what type of action is most appropriate. Competitive actions can take many forms: the entry of a startup into a market for the first time, an attack by a lower-ranked incumbent on an industry leader, or the launch of a breakthrough innovation that disrupts the industry structure. Such actions forever change the competitive dynamics of a marketplace. Thus, the cycle of actions and reactions that occur in business every day is a vital aspect of entrepreneurial strategy that leads to continual new value creation and the ongoing advancement of economic well-being.

SUMMARY

The concept of the industry life cycle is a critical contingency that managers must take into account in striving to create and sustain competitive advantages. We identified the four stages of the industry life cycle—introduction, growth, maturity, and decline—and suggested how these stages can affect the decisions that managers must make at the business level. These decisions include overall strategies as well as the relative emphasis on functional areas and value-creating activities. We also discussed the innovator's dilemma, and the unique threat posed by disruptive innovations. We pointed out the need to consider both the utility and identity elements inherent in a product or service to aid in assessing the appropriate strategic response to a possibly threatening competitor innovation.

When a firm's performance erodes severely, turnaround strategies are needed to reverse the situation and enhance the firm's competitive position. We discussed three approaches—asset and cost surgery, selective product and market pruning, and piecemeal productivity improvements.

The entry of a new company into a competitive arena can be considered a competitive attack on incumbents in that arena. Such actions often provoke a competitive response, which may, in turn, trigger a reaction to the response. As a result, a competitive dynamic—action and response—begins among close competitors. In deciding whether to attack or counterattack, companies must analyze the seriousness of the competitive threat, their ability to mount a competitive response, and the type of action—strategic or tactical—that the situation requires. At times, competitors find it is better not to respond at all or to find avenues to co-operate with, rather than challenge, close competitors.

Summary Review Questions

1. Explain why the concept of industry life cycle is an important factor in determining a firm's business-level strategy.

2. What are the main forces that cause radical industry changes?

3. What does the term *competitive dynamics* mean?

4. Explain the difference between strategic actions and tactical actions, and provide examples of each.

REFLECTING ON CAREER IMPLICATIONS

- *Industry Life Cycle:* If your firm is in the mature stage of the industry life cycle, can you think of ways to enhance your firm's level of differentiation to make customers less price sensitive to your organization's goods and services?

- *Industry Life Cycle:* If you sense that your career inside a firm is maturing or in the decline phase, what actions can you take to restore growth and momentum?

- *Competitive Dynamics:* Is your organization "on the offence" with its close competitors or "playing defence"? What types of strategic and/or tactical actions have been taken by your close rivals recently to gain competitive advantages?

ETHICS AND CORPORATE SOCIAL RESPONSIBILITY QUESTIONS

1. In the introduction phase of the industry life cycle, what are some of the unethical practices that managers could engage in to enhance their firm's market position? What could be some of the long-term implications of such actions?

2. In the decline phase of the industry life cycle, what are some of the unethical practices that managers could engage in to prolong their firm's survival and consolidate their positions?

3. Intense competition, such as price wars, are an acceptable practice in certain markets and sometimes even desirable. In other markets, co-operation between companies is also welcomed. What are the ethical considerations for firms that find themselves in such situations?

4. Imitation strategies are based on the idea of copying another firm's idea and using it for one's own purposes. Is this unethical or simply a smart business practice? Discuss the ethical implications of this practice (if any).

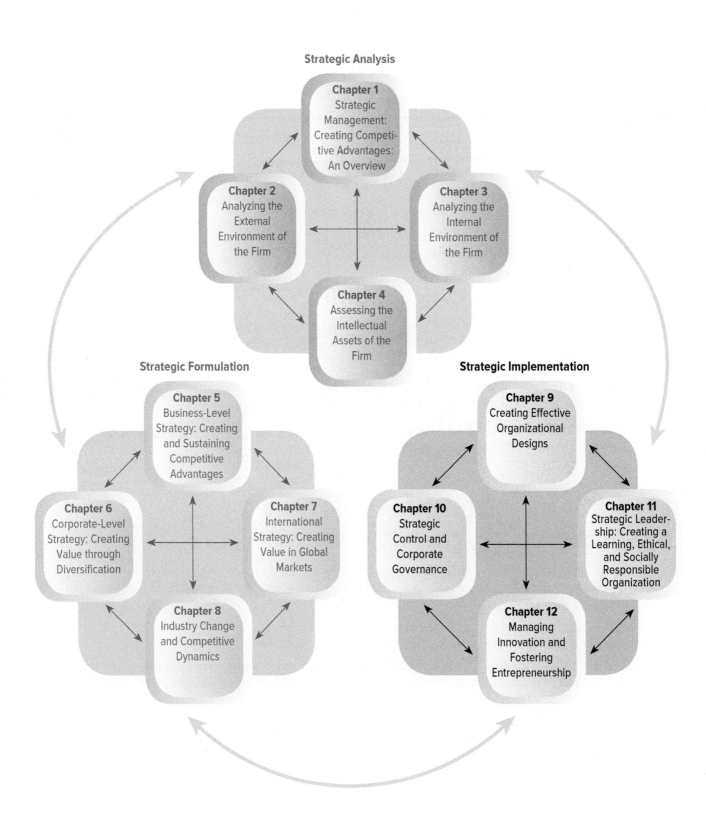

Strategic Analysis

Chapter 1
Strategic Management: Creating Competitive Advantages: An Overview

Chapter 2
Analyzing the External Environment of the Firm

Chapter 3
Analyzing the Internal Environment of the Firm

Chapter 4
Assessing the Intellectual Assets of the Firm

Strategic Formulation

Chapter 5
Business-Level Strategy: Creating and Sustaining Competitive Advantages

Chapter 6
Corporate-Level Strategy: Creating Value through Diversification

Chapter 7
International Strategy: Creating Value in Global Markets

Chapter 8
Industry Change and Competitive Dynamics

Strategic Implementation

Chapter 9
Creating Effective Organizational Designs

Chapter 10
Strategic Control and Corporate Governance

Chapter 11
Strategic Leadership: Creating a Learning, Ethical, and Socially Responsible Organization

Chapter 12
Managing Innovation and Fostering Entrepreneurship

Board: © Everythingpossible/Dreamstimecom; Tablet: VICTOR DE SCHWANBERG

CHAPTER NINE

CREATING EFFECTIVE ORGANIZATIONAL DESIGNS

LEARNING OBJECTIVES

After reading this chapter, you should have a good understanding of:

LO 1 The growth patterns of major corporations and the relationship between a firm's strategy and its structure.

LO 2 The traditional types of organizational structure: simple, functional, divisional, and matrix.

LO 3 The implications of a firm's international operations for organizational structure.

LO 4 Why there is no "one best way" to design strategic reward and evaluation systems, and the important contingent roles of business-level and corporate-level strategies.

LO 5 The different types of boundaryless organizations—barrier-free, modular, and virtual—and their relative advantages and disadvantages.

LO 6 The need for creating ambidextrous organizational designs that enable firms to explore new opportunities and effectively integrate existing operations.

Bell Media, the mass media subsidiary of Bell Canada Enterprises, is responsible for a variety of iconic Canadian media productions.[1] These include the broadcasting and production of both CTV and CTV Two, radio broadcasting through Bell Media Radio, digital streaming through CraveTV, and Internet services through sympatico.ca. Although once considered a media giant, Bell Media has recently undergone significant restructuring, with a number of layoffs starting in late 2015, and continuing until early 2017.

Jeff Whyte/Shutterstock.com

The initial rounds of layoffs included directors and vice-presidents, along with 380 production, editorial, sales, and administrative jobs in Toronto and Montreal. Further staff reductions announced in November of that year included high-profile on-air talent from television media groups in Ottawa, Toronto, and Vancouver. The layoffs were in essence the company's response to the new industry environment, the rise of Netflix, and changing Canadian Radio-television and Telecommunications Commission (CRTC) requirements. While the layoffs did initially yield positive financial results, they were not enough to allow Bell Media to stay competitive.

In early 2017, Bell Media announced a second round of layoffs. Scott Henderson, a Bell Media spokesperson, confirmed via email with multiple major news outlets the intention of the company to restructure operations in order to remain competitive. "We are undergoing a restructuring at Bell Media that includes local radio and TV stations," he explained. "The restructuring is the result of the challenges Bell Media and other Canadian media companies are facing due to increasing international competition, the evolution of broadcast technologies, and advertising and regulatory pressure."

Two major changes in the Canadian media industry have impacted this situation. The first of these is the rise of "cord-cutters," or traditional cable subscribers who have chosen to cancel their subscriptions in order to pursue streaming services such as Netflix. The second change involves new CRTC requirements regarding advertising during the Super Bowl.

As of 2016, more than half of all Canadians had used Netflix to watch media content, posing a considerable threat to the broadcasting industry. Indeed, the phenomenon of cord-cutting is rising, with a Solutions Research Group report estimating that in 2016, 46 percent of Canadians were considering cancelling their cable TV services, a rise from 38 percent in 2015, and 28 percent in 2012. As the trend indicates, streaming services pose an undeniable threat to traditional cable services.

In addition, changes to advertising regulations for the Super Bowl, one of the most profitable sports events in broadcasting, decreased Bell Media revenue and ratings for the popular winter weekend. As of 2015, the CRTC banned "simultaneous substitution" during the Super Bowl. Under simultaneous substitution, the Canadian broadcast of the game, along with Canadian ads, would be run over top of the signal on the U.S. channels for Canadian cable subscribers. With the banning of this practice, Bell Media, which owns the TV rights to the game in Canada, saw their ratings drop by 39 percent for the 2017 broadcast. Additionally, many Canadian businesses chose to purchase ad time on U.S. networks, redirecting advertising money away from Bell Media. Although Bell Media intends to fight the new CRTC policy, that fight is likely to a be a long-term battle, and in the interim they have little choice but to continue with their restructuring.

Although the 2017 layoffs at Bell Media included some high-profile names, such as 40-year CHUM veteran Ingrid Schumacher, CHOM host Heather Backman, TSN Radio Vancouver hosts Scott Rintoul and Peter Shaad, and CTV Vancouver anchor Coleen Christie, restructuring the business to further reduce costs in the face of a very competitive media environment will hopefully prove beneficial for Bell Media's long-term success. What is essential, however, is that profitable or popular departments are not lost in their entirety, as this could stimulate further cord-cutting.

Bell Media's continual restructuring efforts recognize that changing corporate structures and reassigning priorities may be necessary tactics for particular industry environments, and they demonstrate one form of responsiveness to difficult industry changes.

To implement strategies successfully, firms must have appropriate organizational designs. These include the processes and integrating mechanisms necessary to ensure that boundaries among internal activities and external parties, such as suppliers, customers, and alliance partners, are flexible and permeable. A firm's performance will suffer if its managers do not carefully consider both of these organizational design attributes.

In the first section, we begin by discussing the growth patterns of large corporations to address the important relationships between the strategy that a firm follows and its corresponding structure. For example, as firms diversify into related product–market areas, they change their structure from functional to divisional. We then address the different types of traditional structures—simple, functional, divisional, and matrix—and their relative advantages and disadvantages. We close with a discussion of the implications of a firm's international operations for the structure of its organization.

The second section takes the perspective that there is no "one best way" to design an organization's strategic reward and evaluation system. Here, we address two important contingencies: business-level strategy and corporate-level strategy. For example, when strategies require a great deal of collaboration, as well as resource and information sharing, there must be incentives and cultures that encourage and reward such initiatives.

The third section discusses the concept of the "boundaryless" organization. We do *not* argue that organizations should have no internal and external boundaries. Instead, we suggest that in rapidly changing and unpredictable environments, organizations must strive to make their internal and external boundaries both flexible and permeable. We suggest three different types of boundaryless organizations: barrier-free, modular, and virtual.

The fourth section focuses on the need for managers to recognize that they typically face two opposing challenges: (1) being proactive in taking advantage of new opportunities and (2) ensuring the effective coordination and integration of existing operations. This suggests the need for ambidextrous organizations, that is, firms that can be efficient both in managing existing assets and competencies and in taking advantage of opportunities in rapidly changing and unpredictable environments—conditions that are becoming more pronounced in today's global markets.

TRADITIONAL FORMS OF ORGANIZATIONAL STRUCTURE

Organizational structure refers to the formalized patterns of interactions that link a firm's tasks, technologies, and people.[2] Structures help ensure that resources are used effectively in accomplishing an organization's mission. Structure provides a means of balancing two conflicting forces: (1) a need for the division of tasks into meaningful groupings and (2) the need to integrate such groupings to ensure efficiency and effectiveness. As we saw in the Bell Media case that opens this chapter, the way companies are structured can sometimes lead to more problems instead of achieving the efficiencies that are being sought. Structure identifies the executive, managerial, and administrative organization of a firm and indicates responsibilities and hierarchical relationships. It also influences the flow of information as well as the context and nature of human interactions.[3]

Most organizations begin very small and either die eventually or remain small. Those that survive and prosper embark on strategies designed to increase the overall scope of operations and enable them to enter new product–market domains. Such growth places additional pressure on executives to control and coordinate the firm's increasing size and diversity. The most appropriate type of structure depends on the nature and magnitude of growth.

LO 1 Patterns of Growth of Large Corporations: Strategy–Structure Relationships

A firm's strategy and structure change as it increases in size, diversifies into new product markets, and expands its geographic scope.[4] Exhibit 9-1 illustrates the common growth patterns of firms.

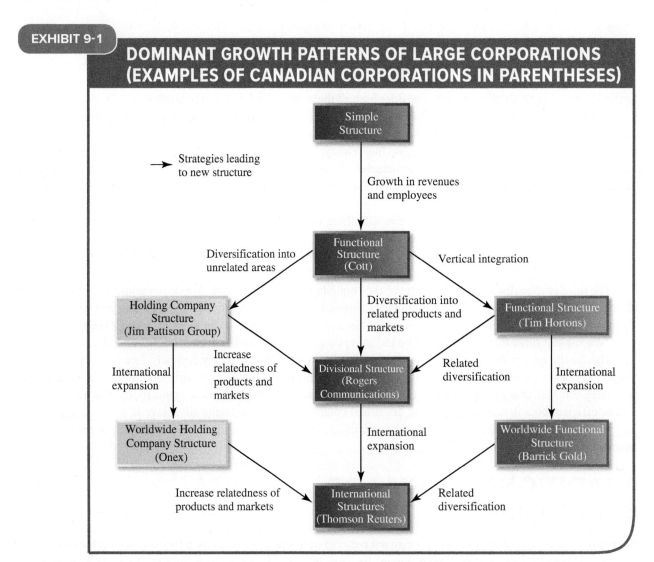

EXHIBIT 9-1

DOMINANT GROWTH PATTERNS OF LARGE CORPORATIONS (EXAMPLES OF CANADIAN CORPORATIONS IN PARENTHESES)

Simple Structure

→ Strategies leading to new structure

Growth in revenues and employees

Functional Structure (Cott)

Diversification into unrelated areas

Vertical integration

Holding Company Structure (Jim Pattison Group)

Diversification into related products and markets

Functional Structure (Tim Hortons)

International expansion

Increase relatedness of products and markets

Divisional Structure (Rogers Communications)

Related diversification

International expansion

Worldwide Holding Company Structure (Onex)

International expansion

Worldwide Functional Structure (Barrick Gold)

Increase relatedness of products and markets

International Structures (Thomson Reuters)

Related diversification

Source: Adapted from J. R. Galbraith and R. K. Kazanjian. Strategy Implementation: Structure, Systems and Process, 2nd ed. Copyright © 1986.

A new firm with a *simple structure* typically increases its sales revenue and volume of outputs over time. It may also engage in some vertical integration to secure sources of supply (backward integration) as well as channels of distribution (forward integration). The simple-structure firm then implements a *functional structure* to concentrate efforts on both increasing efficiency and enhancing its operations and products. This structure enables the firm to group its operations into functions, departments, or geographic areas. As its initial markets mature, a firm looks beyond its present products and markets for possible expansion.

A strategy of related diversification involves reorganizing around product lines or geographic markets. This leads to a *divisional structure.* As the business expands in terms of sales revenues, and domestic growth opportunities become somewhat limited, a firm may seek opportunities in international markets. A firm has a wide variety of structures to choose from. These include *international division, geographic area, worldwide product division, worldwide functional division,* and *worldwide matrix.* Deciding on the most appropriate structure when a firm has international operations depends on three primary factors: (1) the extent of international expansion, (2) the type of strategy (global, multidomestic, or transnational), and (3) the degree of product diversity.[5]

Some firms may find it advantageous to diversify into several product lines rather than focusing their efforts on strengthening distributor and supplier relationships through vertical integration. They would organize themselves according to product lines by implementing a divisional structure. Also, some firms may choose to move into unrelated product areas, typically by acquiring existing businesses. Frequently, their rationale is that acquiring assets and competencies is more economical or expedient than developing them internally. Such an unrelated, or conglomerate, strategy requires relatively little integration across businesses and sharing of resources. Thus, a *holding company structure* becomes appropriate.

Today's firms frequently bypass some of the stages and aggressively outsource substantial elements of their value-creating activities, capitalizing on globalization and information technologies. As well, young firms expand internationally much earlier than their predecessors did because of lower communication and transportation costs.[6]

LO 2 Simple Structure

The simple organizational structure is the oldest, and most common, organizational form. Most organizations are very small and have a single or very narrow product line in which the owner-manager (or top executive) makes most of the decisions. The owner-manager controls all activities, and the staff serves as an extension of the top executive.

Advantages

The simple structure is highly informal, and the coordination of tasks is accomplished by direct supervision. Decision making is highly centralized; there is little specialization of tasks; few rules and regulations exist; and an informal evaluation and reward system is in place. Although the owner-manager is intimately involved in almost all phases of the business, a manager is often employed to oversee day-to-day operations.

Disadvantages

A simple structure may foster creativity and individualism, since there are generally few rules and regulations. However, such "informality" may lead to some problems. Employees may not clearly understand their responsibilities, which can lead to conflict and confusion. Furthermore, employees may take advantage of the lack of regulations and act in their own self-interest, possibly in unethical manners, which can erode motivation and lead to the misuse of organizational resources. Small organizations have flat structures that limit opportunities for upward mobility. Without the potential for future advancement, recruiting and retaining talent may become very difficult.

Functional Structure

When an organization is small (15 employees or fewer), it is not necessary to have a variety of formal arrangements and groupings of activities. However, as firms grow, excessive demands may be placed on the owner-manager to obtain and process all of the information necessary to run the business. Chances are the owner will not be skilled in all functions and will need to hire specialists in the various functional areas. Such growth in the overall scope and complexity of the business necessitates a functional organizational structure wherein the major functions of the firm are grouped internally. The coordination and integration of the functional areas becomes one of the most important responsibilities of the chief executive of the firm (Exhibit 9-2).

EXHIBIT 9-2

FUNCTIONAL ORGANIZATIONAL STRUCTURE

Functional structures are generally found in organizations in which there is a single or closely related product or service, high production volume, and some vertical integration. As expansion activities increase the scope and complexity of the operations, a functional structure provides for a high level of centralization that helps ensure integration and control over the related product–market activities or multiple primary activities (from inbound logistics to operations to marketing, sales, and service) in the value chain (discussed in Chapters 3 and 4). Strategy Spotlight 9.1 provides an example of an effective functional organizational structure—Parkdale Mills.

9.1 STRATEGY SPOTLIGHT

Parkdale Mills: A Successful Functional Organizational Structure

For more than 80 years, Parkdale Mills, a $1-billion yarn manufacturer, has been the industry leader in the production of cotton and cotton-blend yarns. Its expertise comes through concentrating on a single product line, perfecting processes, and welcoming innovation. "I think we've probably spent more than any two competitors combined on new equipment and robotics," explains CEO Andy Warlick. "We do this because we have to compete in a global market where a lot of the competition has a lower wage structure and gets subsidies that we don't receive, so we really have to focus on consistency and cost control." Yarn making is generally considered a commodity business, and Parkdale is the industry's low-cost producer.

Tasks are highly standardized, and authority is centralized with founder and chairman Duke Kimbrell and Warlick. The firm operates a bare-bones staff with a small group of top executives. Kimbrell and Warlick are considered shrewd about the cotton market, technology, customer loyalty, and incentive pay.

Sources: C. Stewart, "The Perfect Yarn," *The Manufacturer.com*, July 31, 2003, www.parkdalemills.com; P. Berman, "The Fast Track Isn't Always the Best Track," *Forbes*, November 2, 1987, pp. 60–64; and Personal Communication with Duke Kimbrell, March 11, 2005.

Advantages

By bringing together specialists into functional departments, a firm is able to enhance its coordination and control within each of the functional areas. Decision making in the firm will be centralized at the top of the organization.

This enhances the organizational-level perspective across the various functions. In addition, the functional structure provides for a more efficient use of managerial and technical talents, since functional area expertise is pooled in a single department (e.g., marketing) instead of being spread across a variety of product–market areas. Finally, career paths and professional development in specialized areas are facilitated.

Disadvantages

The differences in values and orientations among functional areas may impede communication and coordination. Edgar Schein, a former professor at the Massachusetts Institute of Technology (MIT) has argued that shared assumptions, often based on similar backgrounds and experiences of members, form around functional units in an organization. This leads to "silos," in which departments view themselves as isolated, self-contained units with little need for interaction and coordination with other departments. More worrisome is that functional groups may not only have different goals but also attribute differing meanings to specific words and concepts. According to Schein:

> The word "marketing" will mean product development to the engineer, studying customers through market research to the product manager, merchandising to the salesperson, and constant change in design to the manufacturing manager. When they try to work together, they will often attribute disagreements to personalities and fail to notice the deeper, shared assumptions that color how each function thinks.[7]

Such narrow functional orientations also may lead to short-term thinking that is based largely on what is best for the functional area, not for the entire organization. In a manufacturing firm, sales may want to offer a wide range of customized products to appeal to the firm's customers; research and development (R&D) may overdesign products and components to achieve technical elegance; and manufacturing may favour no-frills products that can be produced at low cost by means of long production runs. Functional structures may overburden the top executives in the firm because conflicts have a tendency to be "pushed up" to the top of the organization, since there are no managers who are responsible for the specific product lines.

Divisional Structure

The divisional organizational structure (sometimes called the *multidivisional structure* or the *M-form)* is organized around products, projects, or markets. Each of the divisions, in turn, includes its own functional specialists, who are typically organized into departments.[8] A divisional structure encompasses a set of relatively autonomous units governed by a central corporate office. The operating divisions are relatively independent and consist of products and services that are different from those of the other divisions.

An extreme approach to this type of organizational design is what is described in Strategy Spotlight 9.2, where we explore the restructuring efforts of Sears, the Canadian subsidiary of the U.S. retailer. Not surprisingly, operational decision making in a large business places excessive demands on the firm's top management. To attend to broader, longer-term organizational issues, top-level managers must delegate decision making to lower-level managers. Divisional executives play a key role: They help determine the product–market and financial objectives for the division as well as their division's contribution to overall corporate performance.[9] In the Sears example, the CEO believed that he would best be able to make important decisions if each divisional manager was competing for his attention. He established a rewards system based largely on measures of financial performance, such as net income and revenue, to motivate the managers. Exhibit 9-3 illustrates a divisional structure.

EXHIBIT 9-3

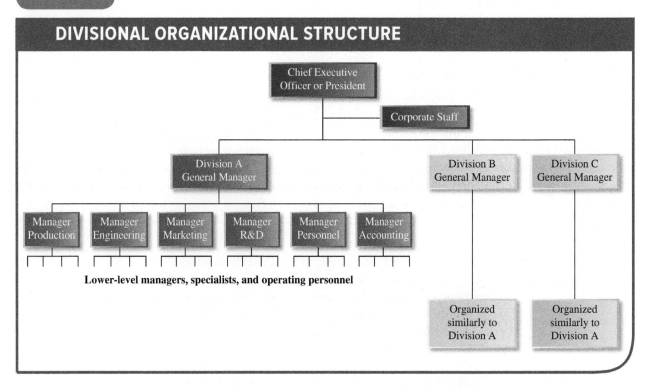

DIVISIONAL ORGANIZATIONAL STRUCTURE

General Motors was among the earliest firms to adopt the divisional organizational structure.[10] In the 1920s, the company formed five major product divisions (Cadillac, Buick, Oldsmobile, Pontiac, and Chevrolet) as well as several industrial divisions. Since then, many firms have discovered that as they diversified into new product–market activities, functional structures—with their emphasis on single functional departments—were unable to manage the increased complexity of the entire business.

9.2 STRATEGY SPOTLIGHT

Sears Canada: A Divisional Structure for Better Times

Although once an icon of Canadian retail, Sears Canada has been experiencing significant financial trouble over the past dozen years, translating into a $2.2-billion decline in revenues since 2002. Originally established in 1953, Sears not only offers sales through its bricks-and-mortar retail locations but also through the Sears catalogue, issued to more than three million households, as well as through its online shopping outlet. Sears Canada, in fact, has Canada's most extensive general merchandise catalogue, a comprehensive website, and a wide variety of home-related products. It offers a coast-to-coast product repair services network, travel offices, hair care centres, optical services, health food shops, portrait studios, income tax services, carpet, upholstery and air duct cleaning, flowers, and home-installed products and services. However, with numerous retail giants on the stage, the Canadian retail industry is highly competitive, and Sears Canada's revenue has been declining significantly.

In July 2011, Calvin McDonald was brought in as the chief executive officer (CEO) with a mandate to change the product mix and revive the existing brands in response to the continuous decline in revenues. To really understand the context of Sears Canada's struggles, however, one needs to look at what was happening south of the border. In 2008, Eddie Lampert, CEO of the parent company, Sears, introduced an organizational design model that allowed him to run Sears like a hedge fund portfolio, forcing the different parts of the company to act as autonomous businesses competing for resources. This meant that the American arm of Sears (Sears Domestic as it was referred to), Sears Canada, and Kmart became separate entities from an operational standpoint, and a multidivisional structure was introduced within each of these entities to facilitate further internal competition. Lampert believed that if the company's various leaders were told to act selfishly, they would run their divisions in a more efficient manner. However, his instinct was off, and the divisions, instead, turned against each other as they battled over fewer resources. One former executive says the model created a "warring tribes" culture that destroyed any hope for co-operation and collaboration.

In this environment, Sears Canada launched a three-year turn-around plan in 2012, which included a new focus on key categories of products, a change in pricing strategy, sprucing up the stores, cutting jobs, outsourcing its information technology (IT) and accounting, and selling off store leases back to the owners. The strategic independence given to Calvin McDonald by the controversial design structure, coupled with a mandate to compete for resources, resulted in approximately 2,000 non-core and head office positions being cut over a two-year period. Sears Canada also decided to exit any and all locations where the landlords offered deals that made better overall financial sense to the company than running the stores. McDonald has said that there are non-strategic assets that Sears Canada owns today and that if the opportunity is right to create value through those assets, Sears Canada will explore and engage the opportunities. Yet, despite these efforts, the decline in revenues continues. Furthermore, by vacating numerous popular urban locations, Sears is facilitating U.S. chains Nordstrom, Saks Fifth Avenue, and Bloomingdale's to make inroads into Canada, further intensifying competition.

McDonald resigned from his position in early September 2013 and was replaced by Douglas Campbell, the previous Chief Operating Officer at Sears Canada. Campbell announced a plan to continue on with the three-year strategy put in place by McDonald. However, he was also intent on evaluating the operating efficiency of the company by looking at the existing networks, store base, logistics facilities, and costs. After meeting with employees at multiple levels and departments, he introduced salary decreases at the head office level, and streamlined category management and purchasing decisions. Campbell was replaced as CEO by Ronald Boire in 2014, who in turn ceded the top job to Carrie Kirkman, who took over with the new title of President and Chief Merchant. Less than a year later Kirkman, too, left the company.

In 2016, Sears Canada unveiled a new logo and a series of new store concepts in what it called "Sears 2.0." Since then, and in spite of all the efforts to save it, Sears continued to struggle through consistent downsizing and realignments and finally sought and was granted court approval to close down its remaining stores and layoff its entire remaining staff. Of course, this battle does not only belong to Sears; the entire retail industry continues to be disrupted and reinvented as new players, such as Amazon and Alibaba, more effectively respond to the habits of digital-savvy consumers.

Sources: The case material draws on Kimes, M, 2013, At Sears, Eddie Lampert's Warring Divisions Model Adds to the Troubles, *BusinessWeek,* July 11; Shaw, H, 2014, Sears Canada revenue falls for 8th year in row as winter storms cost 220 store hours, *Financial Post,* February 26; Shaw, H, 2014, Sears Canada CEO works to rebalance top-heavy executive structure, *Financial Post,* April 24; Anonymous, Forget retail - Sears Canada's future lies in selling off real estate, *Financial Post,* 2013; Anonymous, Sears Canada announces new pricing strategy, *Financial Post,* 2013; Anonymous, Sears Canada cuts 245 jobs, outsourcing IT positions to India and the Philippines, *Financial Post,* 2013; Anonymous, Sears Canada Q2 revenue falls 9.6 per cent; deal to vacate stores offsets loss, *Macleans,* 2013; Anonymous, Sears Canada revenue falls yet again, *Reuters,* 21 August 2013; the company's financial statements and website.

Advantages

By creating separate divisions to manage individual product markets, there is a separation of strategic control and operating control. Divisional managers can focus their efforts on improving operations in the product markets for which they are responsible, and corporate officers can devote their time to overall strategic issues for the entire corporation. The focus on a division's products and markets—by the divisional executives—provides the corporation with an enhanced ability to respond quickly to important changes. Since there are functional departments within each division of the corporation, the problems associated with sharing resources across functional departments are minimized. Because there are multiple levels of general managers (executives responsible for integrating and coordinating all functional areas), the development of general management talent is enhanced. Strategy Spotlight 9.3 discusses the rationale behind Brinker Corporation's change in structure from functional to divisional.

9.3 STRATEGY SPOTLIGHT

Brinker International Changes to a Divisional Organizational Structure

Although Brinker International had a traditional functional structure, changes in its competitive outlook forced management to take a closer look at the organizational design of the firm, which controlled a variety of restaurant chains and bakeries, including Wildfire, Big Bowl, Maggiano's and Chili's.

With all these interests under one corporate roof, management of the disparate entities became difficult. The fragmented $330-billion restaurant and bakery industry caters to highly focused market niches. The original functional design of the Brinker chain had some disadvantages as the company grew. With areas separated by function, it became hard to focus efforts on a single restaurant chain. The diverse markets served by the bakeries and restaurants began to lose their focus. Brinker also had diverse growth options domestically and internationally that could not be addressed effectively through the old structure.

As a result, Brinker International changed to a divisional organizational structure. This allowed the company to consolidate individuals who worked with a single restaurant or bakery chain into a separate division. Brinker referred to these as concept teams, with each concept team responsible for the operation of a single line of business. This focused effort strengthened the company's ability to concentrate on the market niche served by each of its restaurants and bakeries. Investments in technology to streamline operations and enhance customer experience could better be targeted at the individual business, further strengthening the main brands, Chili's and Maggiano's.

Sources: The discussion draws on the company's latest annual reports and quarterly filings and various press releases that can be found in the company's website www.brinker.com and under the ticker EAT at the New York Stock Exchange, as well as an interview of Ronald A. McDougall, CEO, Brinker International. reported in a *Wall Street Transcript,* January 20, 1999, pp. 1–4 and S. Strom, "Chipotle Posts Another Quarter of Billion Dollar Sales," *The New York Times,* April 21, 2015.

Disadvantages

The divisional structure can be very expensive. Costs can increase because of the duplication of personnel, operations, and investment, since each division must staff multiple functional departments—which is why Sears Canada ultimately decided to outsource some of these functions. There can also be dysfunctional competition among divisions, because each division tends to become concerned solely about its own operations, what was described as a "tribal" mentality in the Sears case. Divisional managers are often evaluated on common measures, such as return on assets and sales growth. If goals are conflicting, there can be a sense of a "zero-sum" game that would discourage sharing ideas and resources among the divisions for the common good of the corporation. Ghoshal and Bartlett, two leading strategy scholars, note:

As their label clearly warns, divisions divide. The divisional model fragmented companies' resources; it created vertical communication channels that insulated business units and prevented them from sharing their strengths with one another. Consequently, the whole of the corporation was often less than the sum of its parts.[11]

With many divisions providing different products and services, there is the chance that differences in image and quality may occur across divisions. One division may offer no-frills products of lower quality that may erode the brand reputation of another division that has top-quality, highly differentiated offerings. Since each division is evaluated in terms of financial measures, such as return on investment and revenue growth, there is often an urge to focus on short-term performance. If corporate management uses quarterly profits as the key performance indicator, divisional management may tend to put significant emphasis on "making the numbers" and minimizing activities, such as advertising, maintenance, and capital investments, which would detract from short-term performance measures. As a result, two variants of the divisional form have been frequently adopted to counter some of the disadvantages: the strategic business unit (SBU) and holding company structures. These are discussed briefly below.

Strategic Business Unit (SBU) Structure

Highly diversified corporations, such as George Weston Ltd., a $30-billion food producer and retailer, may consist of dozens of different divisions.[12] If Weston were to use a purely divisional structure, it would be nearly impossible for the corporate office to plan and coordinate activities because the span of control would be too large. To attain synergies, Weston has put its diverse businesses into three primary SBUs: bakeries, retail, and food processing.

With an SBU structure, divisions with similar products, markets, and/or technologies are grouped into homogeneous units to achieve some synergies. These include those discussed in Chapter 6 for related diversification, such as leveraging core competencies, sharing infrastructures, and market power. Generally, the higher the number of related businesses within a corporation, the fewer will be the SBUs required. Each of the SBUs in the corporation operates as a profit centre.

Advantages The SBU structure makes the task of planning and control by the corporate office more manageable. Also, with greater decentralization of authority, individual businesses can react more quickly to important changes in the environment than if all divisions had to report directly to the corporate office.

Disadvantages Since the divisions are grouped into SBUs, it may become difficult to achieve synergies across SBUs. If divisions in different SBUs have potential sources of synergy, it may become difficult for them to be realized. The additional level of management increases the number of personnel and overhead expenses, while the additional hierarchical level removes the corporate office further from the individual divisions. The corporate office may become unaware of key developments that could have a major impact on the corporation.

Holding Company Structure

The holding company structure (sometimes referred to as a *conglomerate)* is also a variation of the divisional structure. Whereas the SBU structure is often used when similarities exist between the individual businesses (or divisions), the holding company structure is appropriate when the businesses in a corporation's portfolio do not have much in common. Thus, the potential for synergies is limited.

Holding company structures are most appropriate for firms with a strategy of unrelated diversification. Some companies, such as Onex Corporation, Power Corporation, and the Jim Pattison Group, have used holding company structures to implement their unrelated diversification strategies. Since there are few similarities across the businesses, the corporate offices in these companies provide a great deal of autonomy to operating divisions and rely on financial controls and incentive programs to obtain high levels of performance from the individual businesses. Corporate staff at these firms tends to be small because of limited involvement in the overall operation of their various businesses.[13]

Advantages The holding company structure has the cost savings associated with fewer personnel and the lower overhead resulting from a small corporate office and fewer hierarchical levels. The autonomy of the holding company structure increases the motivational level of divisional executives and enables them to respond quickly to market opportunities and threats.

Disadvantages There is an inherent lack of control of corporate-level executives have over divisional executives and little strategic dependence of divisional executives on their corporate counterparts, other than financial oversight. Major problems could arise if key divisional executives leave the firm because the corporate office has very little "bench strength"—additional managerial talent ready to quickly fill key positions. If problems arise in a division, it may become very difficult to turn around individual businesses because of limited staff support in the corporate office.

Matrix Structure

One approach that tries to overcome the inadequacies inherent in the other structures is the matrix organizational structure. It is a combination of the functional and divisional structures. Most commonly, functional departments are combined with product groups on a project basis. Exhibit 9-4 illustrates a matrix structure.

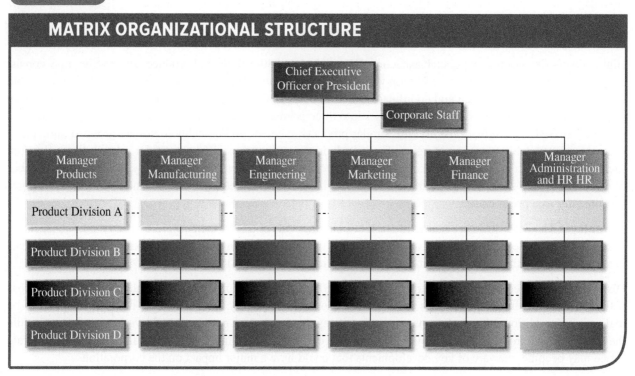

Some large multinational corporations rely on a matrix structure to combine product groups and geographic units. Product managers have global responsibility for the development, manufacturing, and distribution of their own lines, whereas managers of geographic regions have responsibility for the profitability of the businesses in their regions. In the mid-1990s, Caterpillar, Inc. implemented this type of structure.

Dell Computer relies on the matrix concept, with its dual reporting responsibility, to enhance accountability and also to develop general managers. According to former CEO Kevin Rollins:

> We're organized in a matrix of sales regions and product groups. Then we break each of those groups down to a pretty fine level of sub-products and sales sub-segments. Dell has more P&L managers, and smaller business units, than most companies its size. This not only increases accountability to the customer, it helps train general managers by moving them from smaller to larger businesses as their skills develop.

Our matrix organization has a third level—our business councils. For example, we have a small-business sales group in each country, along with product development people who become very familiar with what small-business customers buy. In addition, we have our worldwide small-business council made up of all our small-business GMs and product managers. Everyone in these councils sees everyone else's P&L, so it provides another set of checks and balances.[14]

Advantages

The matrix structure facilitates the use of specialized personnel, equipment, and facilities. Instead of duplicating functions, as would be the case in a divisional structure based on products, the resources are shared. Individuals with high expertise can divide their time among multiple projects. Such resource sharing and collaboration enable a firm to use resources more efficiently and to respond more quickly and effectively to changes in the competitive environment. The flexibility inherent in a matrix structure provides professionals with a broader range of responsibility. Such experience enables them to develop their skills and competencies.

Disadvantages

The dual-reporting structures can result in uncertainty and lead to intense power struggles and conflict over the allocation of personnel and other resources. Working relationships become more complicated. This may result in excessive reliance on group processes and teamwork, along with a diffusion of responsibility, which, in turn, may erode timely decision making.

LO 3 International Operations: Implications for Organizational Structure

Today's managers must maintain an international outlook with regard to their firm's businesses and competitive strategies. In the global marketplace, managers must ensure consistency between their strategies (at the business, corporate, and international levels) and the structure of their organization. As firms expand into foreign markets, they generally follow a pattern of change in structure that parallels the changes in their strategies. Three major contingencies that influence the chosen structure are (1) the type of strategy that is driving a firm's foreign operations, (2) product diversity, and (3) the extent to which a firm is dependent on foreign sales.[15]

As international operations become an important part of a firm's overall operations, managers must make changes that are consistent with their firm's structure. The primary types of structures used to manage a firm's international operations are:[16]

- International division
- Geographic-area division
- Worldwide functional division
- Worldwide product division
- Worldwide matrix

Multidomestic strategies are driven by political and cultural imperatives requiring managers within each country to respond to local conditions. The structures consistent with such a strategic orientation are the *international division* and *geographic-area division* structures. Here, local managers are provided with a high level of autonomy to manage their operations within the constraints and demands of their geographic market. As a firm's foreign sales increase as a percentage of its total sales, it will likely change from an international division to a geographic-area division structure. And, as a firm's product and/or market diversity becomes large, it is likely to benefit from a *worldwide matrix* structure.

Global strategies are driven by economic pressures that require operations in different geographic areas to be managed for overall efficiency. The structures consistent with the efficiency perspective are the *worldwide functional division* and *worldwide product division* structures. Here, divisional managers view the marketplace as homogeneous and devote relatively little attention to local market, political, and economic factors. The choice between these two types of structures is guided largely by the extent of product diversity. Firms with relatively low levels of product diversity may opt for a worldwide product division structure. However, if significant product–market diversity results from highly unrelated international acquisitions, a worldwide holding company structure should be implemented. Such firms have very little commonality among products, markets, or technologies, and have little need for integration.

Global Startups

International expansion occurs rather late for most corporations, typically after possibilities of domestic growth are exhausted. Increasingly, though, we are seeing two interrelated phenomena. First, many firms now expand internationally relatively early in their history. Second, some firms are "born global"—that is, from the very beginning, many startups are global in their activities. For example, Logitech Inc., a leading producer of personal computer accessories, was global from day one. Founded in 1982 by a Swiss and two Italians, the company was headquartered both in California and in Switzerland. R&D and manufacturing were also conducted in both locations and, subsequently, in Taiwan and Ireland.[17]

The success of such companies as Logitech challenges the conventional wisdom that a company must first build up assets, internal processes, and experience before venturing into faraway lands. It also raises a number of questions: What exactly is a global startup? Under what conditions should a company start out as a global startup? What does it take to succeed as a global startup?

A *global startup* has been defined as a business organization that from inception seeks to derive significant competitive advantage from the use of resources and the sale of outputs in multiple countries. Right from the beginning, it uses inputs from around the world and sells its products and services to customers around the world. Geographic boundaries of nation-states are irrelevant for a global startup.

There is no reason for every startup to go global. Being global necessarily involves higher communication, coordination, and transportation costs. Therefore, it is important to identify the circumstances under which going global from the beginning is advantageous.[18] First, if the required human resources are globally dispersed, going global may be the best way to access those resources. For example, Italians are masters in fine leather, and Europeans are leaders in ergonomics. Second, in many cases, foreign financing may be easier to obtain and more suitable. Traditionally, U.S. venture capitalists have shown greater willingness to bear risk, but they have shorter time horizons in their expectations for return. If a U.S. startup is looking for patient capital, it may be better off looking overseas. Third, the target customers in many specialized industries are located in other parts of the world. Fourth, in many industries a gradual move from domestic markets to foreign markets is no longer possible because if a product is successful, foreign competitors may immediately imitate it. Therefore, pre-emptive entry into foreign markets may be the only option. Finally, because of high up-front development costs, a global market is often necessary to recover the costs. This is particularly true for startups from smaller nations that do not have access to large domestic markets. Strategy Spotlight 9.4 discusses two global startups.

Successful management of a global startup presents many challenges. Communication and coordination across time zones and cultures are always problematic. Since most global startups have far fewer resources than

9.4 STRATEGY SPOTLIGHT

Global Startup BRCK Works to Bring Reliable Internet Connectivity to the World

BRCK is a notable technology pioneer, bringing a novel and potentially very valuable product to the market, and it does so as a truly global startup. BRCK's first product is a surge-resistant, battery-powered router to provide Internet service, which the firm is simply calling the BRCK. In many parts of the world, power systems are unreliable and offer only intermittent service. Moreover, they are prone to generate power surges that can sometimes fry electronic products, including Internet routers. For example, in 2013, a single power-surge event in Nairobi, Kenya, blew out more than 3,000 routers. BRCK has developed a product to address these issues. Its router has a built-in battery that charges up whenever the power grid is operating. The router then runs off the battery for up to eight hours when the power grid goes down. It can also handle power surges of up to 400 volts. Even better, the BRCK is flexible as to how it connects to the Internet. It can connect directly to an ethernet line, link up with a Wi-Fi network in its area, and connect via a wireless phone connection.

BRCK is aiming to sell its product to small and medium-size businesses, schools, and medical facilities. Its routers allow up to 20 users to simultaneously connect to the Internet. The technologies it uses are not cutting edge, but the end product itself is innovative and meets a market need.

What really sets BRCK apart is that it is a global startup that turns the table on typical global structures. Most tech-oriented global firms design their products in a technology centre in the developed world and manufacture the products in a developing country. BRCK has flipped this model. BRCK designs its products in a developing country and manufactures in a developed country. Its corporate headquarters are in Nairobi, Kenya, at a technology centre that houses a small group of entrepreneurs. The firm employs a dozen engineers to design its products in its corporate headquarters. While its offices look a bit like those in Silicon Valley, the building is equipped with backup power for the inevitable times when the Kenyan power grid goes down. The firm sources most of the components for its routers from Asia and manufactures its products in Austin, Texas. Even its sales are going global right from the start. As of 2014, the firm had sold 700 BRCKs to customers in 45 countries.

Sources: Cary, J. 2014. Made in Kenya, assembled in America: This Internet-anywhere company innovates from silicon savannah. fastcoexist.com, September 4: np; and Vogt, H. 2014. Made in Africa: A gadget startup. wsj.com, July 10

well-established corporations, one key for success is to internalize few activities and outsource the rest. Managers of such firms must have considerable prior international experience so that they can successfully handle the inevitable communication problems and cultural conflicts. Another key for success is to keep the communication and coordination costs low. The only way to achieve this is by creating less costly administrative mechanisms. The boundaryless organizational designs that we discuss in the next section are particularly suitable for global startups because of their flexibility and low cost.

LO 4 How an Organization's Structure Can Influence Strategy Formulation

Discussions of the relationship between strategy and structure usually strongly imply that structure follows strategy. The strategy that a firm chooses (e.g., related diversification) dictates such structural elements as the division of tasks, the need for integration of activities, and authority relationships within the organization. However, an existing structure can influence strategy formulation. Once a firm's structure is in place, it is very difficult and expensive to change.[19] Executives may not be able to modify their duties and responsibilities greatly or may not welcome the disruption associated with a transfer to a new location. There are costs associated with hiring, training, and replacing executive, managerial, and operating personnel. Strategy cannot be formulated without considering structural elements.

An organization's structure can also have an important influence on how it competes in the marketplace. Furthermore, it can strongly influence a firm's strategy, day-to-day operations, and performance.[20] For example, we discussed Brinker International's move to a divisional structure to organize its restaurant groups into different units to focus on market niches. This new structure should enable the firm to adapt to change more rapidly and innovate more effectively with the various restaurant brands. Brinker's management did not feel that they were as effective with their previous functional organizational structure.

LINKING STRATEGIC REWARD AND EVALUATION SYSTEMS TO BUSINESS-LEVEL AND CORPORATE-LEVEL STRATEGIES

The effective use of reward and evaluation systems can play a critical role in motivating managers to conform to organizational strategies, achieve performance targets, and reduce the gap between organizational and individual goals. In contrast, reward systems, if improperly designed, can lead to behaviours that either are detrimental to organizational performance or can lower morale and cause employee dissatisfaction.

As we will see in this section, there is no "one best way" to design reward and evaluation systems. Instead, the most suitable method will be contingent on many factors. Two of the most important factors are a firm's business-level strategy (see Chapter 5) and its corporate-level strategy (see Chapter 6).

Business-Level Strategy: Reward and Evaluation Systems

In Chapter 5, we discussed two approaches that firms may take to secure competitive advantages: overall cost leadership and differentiation.[21] As we might expect, implementing these strategies requires fundamentally different organizational arrangements, approaches to control, and reward and incentive systems.

Overall Cost Leadership

This strategy requires that product lines remain rather stable and that innovations deal mostly with production processes. Given the emphasis on efficiency, costly changes even in production processes tend to be rare. Since products are fairly standardized and change infrequently, procedures can be developed to divide work into its basic components—those that are routine, standardized, and ideal for semiskilled and unskilled employees. As such, firms competing on the basis of cost must implement tight cost controls, frequent and comprehensive reports to monitor the costs associated with outputs, and highly structured tasks and responsibilities. Incentives tend to be based on explicit financial targets, since innovation and creativity are expensive and might tend to erode competitive advantages.

Nucor, a highly successful steel producer with $16 billion in revenues, competes primarily on the basis of cost and has a reward and incentive system that is largely based on financial outputs and financial measures.[22] Nucor uses four incentive compensation systems that correspond to the levels of management.

1. *Production incentive program.* Groups of 20 to 40 people are paid a weekly bonus based on either anticipated product time or tonnage produced. Each shift and production line is in a separate bonus group.
2. *Department managers.* Bonuses are based on divisional performance, primarily measured by return on assets.
3. *Employees not directly involved in production.* These include engineers, accountants, administration, receptionists, and others. Bonuses are based on two factors: divisional and corporate return on assets.
4. *Senior incentive programs.* Salaries are lower than in comparable companies, but a significant portion of total compensation is based on return on stockholder equity. A portion of pre-tax earnings is placed in a pool and divided among officers as bonuses that are part cash and part stock.

The culture at Nucor reflects its reward and incentive system. Since incentive compensation can account for more than half of their paycheques, employees become nearly obsessed with productivity and apply a lot of pressure on each other. Ken Iverson, a former CEO, recalled an instance in which one employee arrived at work wearing sunglasses instead of safety glasses, preventing the team from doing any work. Other workers who were infuriated by this chased him around the plant with a piece of angle iron!

Differentiation

This strategy involves the development of innovative products and services that require experts who can identify the crucial elements of intricate, creative designs and marketing decisions. Highly trained professionals, such as scientists and engineers, are essential for devising, assessing, implementing, and continually changing complex product designs. This also requires extensive collaboration and co-operation among specialists and functional managers from different areas within a firm. They must evaluate and implement a new design, constantly bearing in mind marketing, financial, production, and engineering considerations.

Given the need for co-operation and coordination in many functional areas, it becomes difficult to evaluate individuals using set quantitative criteria. It is also difficult to measure specific outcomes of such efforts and attribute outcomes to particular individuals. More behavioural measures (how effectively employees collaborate and share information) and intangible incentives and rewards become necessary to support a strong culture and to motivate employees. Consider 3M, a highly innovative company whose core value is innovation.

> Rewards are tied closely to risk-taking and innovation-oriented behavior. Managers are not penalized for product failures. Instead, those same people are encouraged to work on another project that borrows from their shared experience and insight. A culture of creativity and "thinking out of the box" is reinforced by their well-known "15 percent rule," which permits employees to set aside 15 percent of their work time to pursue personal research interests. And a familiar 3M homily, "Thou shall not kill new ideas for products," is known as the 11th commandment. It is the source of countless stories, including one that tells how L. D. DeSimone (3M's former CEO) tried five times (and failed) to kill the project that yielded the 3M blockbuster product, Thinsulate.[23]

Corporate-Level Strategy: Reward and Evaluation Systems

In Chapter 6, we discussed two broad types of diversification strategies: related and unrelated. The type of diversification strategy that a firm follows has important implications for the type of reward and evaluation systems that it should use.

For example, Sharp Corporation, a $36-billion Japanese consumer electronics giant, follows a strategy of *related* diversification.[24] Its most successful technology has been liquid crystal displays (LCDs) that are critical components in nearly all of the firm's products, as well as many products and components it sells to other manufacturers. With their expertise in this area, they have successfully moved into high-end displays for cellular telephones, handheld computers, and tablets.[25]

Given the need to leverage such technologies across multiple product lines, Sharp needs a reward and evaluation system that fosters co-operation and sharing. It must focus more on individuals' behaviour rather than on short-term financial outcomes. Promotion is a powerful incentive, generally based on seniority and subtle skills exhibited over time, such as teamwork and communication. It helps to ensure that the company's reward system will not reward short-term self-interested orientations.

Like many Japanese companies, Sharp's culture reinforces the view that the firm is a family whose members should co-operate for the greater good. With the policy of lifetime employment, turnover is low. This encourages employees to pursue what is best for the entire company. Such an outlook lessens the inevitable conflict over sharing important resources, such as R&D knowledge.

In contrast to Sharp, Hanson PLC (a British conglomerate, now known as Hanson Ltd.) followed a strategy of unrelated diversification for most of its history. At one time, it owned as many as 150 operating companies in such diverse areas as tobacco, footwear, building products, brewing, and food. There were limited product similarities across businesses and therefore little need for sharing of resources and knowledge across divisional boundaries. James Hanson and Gordon White, founders of the company, actually did not permit any sharing of resources between operating companies, even if it was feasible!

Their reward and evaluation system placed such heavy emphasis on individual accountability that they viewed resource sharing, with its potential for mutual blaming, as unacceptable. The operating managers had more than 60 percent of their compensation tied to the annual financial performance of their subsidiaries. All decision making was decentralized so that subsidiary managers could be held responsible for the return on capital they achieved. However, there was one area in which managers had to obtain approval from the corporate office. No subsidiary manager was allowed to incur a capital expenditure greater than $3,000 without permission from the corporate office. Hanson managed to be successful with a very small corporate office because of its decentralized structure, tight financial controls, and an incentive system that motivated managers to meet financial goals. In fact, Gordon White was proud to claim that he had never visited any of the operating companies that were part of the Hanson empire.[26]

The key issue becomes the need for *in*dependence versus *inter*dependence. With cost leadership strategies and unrelated diversification, there tends to be less need for interdependence. The reward and evaluation systems focus more on the use of financial indicators because unit costs, profits, and revenues can be easily attributed to a given business unit or division.

In contrast, firms that follow related diversification strategies have intense needs for tight interdependencies among the functional areas and business units. Sharing of resources, including raw materials, R&D knowledge, marketing information, and so on, is critical to organizational success. It is more important to achieve synergies with value-creating activities and business units than with cost leadership or unrelated strategies. Reward and evaluation systems tend to incorporate more behavioural indicators.

Exhibit 9-5 suggests guidelines on how an organization should match its strategies to its evaluation and reward systems. However, all organizations must have combinations of *both* financial and behavioural rewards. Both overall cost leadership and unrelated diversification strategies require a need for collaboration and the sharing of best practices across value-creating activities *and* business units. For example, General Electric has developed many integrating mechanisms to enhance sharing "best practices" across what would appear to be rather unrelated businesses, such as jet engines, appliances, and network television. For both differentiation and related diversification strategies, financial indicators, such as revenue growth and profitability, should not be overlooked at either the business-unit or corporate levels.

| EXHIBIT 9-5 | SUMMARY OF RELATIONSHIPS BETWEEN REWARD AND EVALUATION SYSTEM AND BUSINESS-LEVEL AND CORPORATE-LEVEL STRATEGIES |

Level of Strategy	Types of Strategy	Need for Interdependence	Primary Type of Reward and Evaluation System
Business-level	Overall cost leadership	Low	Financial
Business-level	Differentiation	High	Behavioural
Corporate-level	Related diversification	High	Behavioural
Corporate-level	Unrelated diversification	Low	Financial

LO 5 BOUNDARYLESS ORGANIZATIONAL DESIGNS

The term *boundaryless* may bring to mind a chaotic organizational reality in which "anything goes." This is not the case. As Jack Welch, former CEO of General Electric Company (GE), has suggested, *boundaryless* does not imply that all internal and external boundaries vanish completely, but that they become more open and permeable.[27] Strategy Spotlight 9.5 discusses four types of boundaries.

9.5 STRATEGY SPOTLIGHT

Boundary Types

There are primarily four types of boundaries that place limits on organizations. In today's dynamic business environment, different types of boundaries are needed to foster varying levels of permeability and high degrees of interaction with outside influences.

1. *Vertical boundaries between levels in the organization's hierarchy.* SmithKline Beecham (now GlaxoSmithKline) asks employees at different hierarchical levels to brainstorm ideas for managing clinical trial data. The ideas are incorporated into action plans that significantly cut the new product approval time of its pharmaceuticals. This would not have been possible if the barriers between levels of individuals in the organization had been too high.

2. *Horizontal boundaries between functional areas.* Fidelity Investments makes the functional barriers more porous and flexible among divisions, such as marketing, operations, and customer service, to offer customers a more integrated experience when conducting business with the company. Customers can take all their questions to one person, thus reducing the chance that customers will "get the runaround" from employees who feel that customer service is not their responsibility. At Fidelity, customer service is everyone's business, regardless of functional area.

3. *External boundaries between the firm and its customers, suppliers, and regulators.* GE Lighting, by working closely with retailers, functions throughout the value chain as a single operation. This allows GE to track point-of-sale purchases, giving it better control over inventory management.

4. *Geographic boundaries between locations, cultures, and markets.* The global nature of today's business environment spurred PricewaterhouseCoopers to use a global groupware system. This allows the company to instantly connect to its offices worldwide.

Source: R. Ashkenas, "The Organization's New Clothes." In F. Hesselbein, M. Goldsmith, and R. Beckhard (Eds.), *The Organization of the Future* (San Francisco: Jossey Bass, 1997), pp. 104–106.

We are not suggesting that boundaryless organizational designs should replace traditional forms of organizational structure; instead, they should complement them. Sharp Corp. has implemented a functional structure to attain economies of scale with its applied research and manufacturing skills. However, to bring about this key objective, Sharp has relied on several integrating mechanisms and processes:

> To prevent functional groups from becoming vertical chimneys that obstruct product development, Sharp's product managers have responsibility—but not authority—for coordinating the entire set of value-chain

(Continued)

activities. And the company convenes enormous numbers of cross-unit and corporate committees to ensure that shared activities, including the corporate R&D unit and sales forces, are optimally configured and allocated among the different product lines. Sharp invests in such time-intensive coordination to minimize the inevitable conflicts that arise when units share important activities.[28]

We discuss three approaches to making boundaries more permeable, which help facilitate the widespread sharing of knowledge and information across both the internal and external boundaries of the organization. The *barrier-free* type of organization involves making all organizational boundaries—internal and external—more permeable. The *modular* and *virtual* types of organizations focus on the need to create seamless relationships with external organizations, such as customers or suppliers. The modular type emphasizes the outsourcing of noncore activities, whereas the virtual (or network) organization focuses on alliances among independent entities formed to exploit specific market opportunities.

The Barrier-Free Organization

The "boundary" mindset is deeply ingrained into bureaucracies. It is evidenced by such clichés as "That's not my job," and "I'm here from corporate to help" or by the endless battles over transfer pricing. In the traditional company, boundaries are clearly delineated in the design of organizational structure. Their basic advantage is that the roles of managers and employees are simple, clear, well-defined, and long-lived. One major shortcoming of boundaries was pointed out to the authors of this text during an interview with a high-tech executive: "Structure tends to be divisive; it leads to territorial fights."

Today, structures are being replaced by fluid, ambiguous, and deliberately ill-defined tasks and roles. But just because work roles are no longer clearly defined, it does not mean that differences in skills, authority, and talent disappear. A *barrier-free organization* enables a firm to bridge real differences in culture, function, and goals to find common ground that facilitates information sharing and other forms of co-operative behaviour. Eliminating the multiple boundaries that stifle productivity and innovation can enhance the potential of the entire organization. Strategy Spotlight 9.6 describes how McDonald's is using the concept of boundaryless organization to revitalize its brand and attract customers.

9.6 STRATEGY SPOTLIGHT

New Structure at McDonald's

Growing from a single restaurant opened by two brothers in California in 1940 to over 36,000 restaurants worldwide in 2016, McDonald's has experienced nearly continuous growth and success. With over $25 billion in sales in the U.S., McDonald's generates nearly three times the revenue of its closest competitor, Subway.

But that doesn't mean that McDonald's is immune to struggles. In 2014, it faced a real challenge to remain relevant as an attractive option for customers and saw its U.S. sales drop by 4.1 percent compared to sales in 2013. This negative turn in the firm's performance most likely resulted in the surprise retirement of McDonald's CEO, Don Thompson, in February 2015.

So how did things unfold as such? To modern, nutrition-conscious consumers, McDonald's menu appeared stale and unhealthy. Customers started flocking to competing restaurants, such as Panera, Boston Chicken, and Chipotle, which were seen as offering healthier food, and having fresher ingredients and more interesting menu items. As retired McDonald's U.S.A. president Mike Andres admitted, "What has worked for McDonald's for the past decade is not sufficient to propel the business forward in the future."

McDonald's insiders mused that one cause of its struggles in the U.S. lay in the structure of the firm. McDonald's has long aimed for consistency across its units. To maintain this consistency, it has used a central testing kitchen to develop new products that could then be rolled out across the firm.

It has also relied on a regional structure, with Eastern, Central, and Western divisions. When a new initiative or product was rolled out, the firm would introduce it in each region, moving from north to south. Thus, customers in Minnesota and Louisiana would have the same menu, but new products would be introduced first in Minnesota and later in Louisiana. This structure has hampered the restaurant chain, leaving it unable to respond to regional taste differences and slow to adapt to changing customer tastes and preferences. As a result, according to Andres, within McDonald's "there are too many layers, redundancies in planning and communication, competing priorities, barriers to efficient decision making, and too much talking to ourselves instead of to and about our customers." In other words, the firm has been burdened by organizational boundaries that slow communication and hinder the ability to talk to and respond to customers and other stakeholders.

To shake things up, in October 2014, McDonald's announced it would eliminate layers of management and create a new organizational structure. The aim of the changes was to allow the firm to be more responsive to local tastes and to variations in customer demands. At the top level, the chain moved to four regional divisions: Northeast, South, Central, and West. In management's assessment, this new structure more effectively clusters together customers with similar tastes and preferences. At a lower level, McDonald's gave its leaders in 22 regional groups greater autonomy in making local menu and marketing decisions. In Andres's words, "We need to be more sophisticated in how we use local intelligence to address specific consumer needs . . . and to put decision making closer to our customers." As part of this effort, McDonald's looked to the regions to learn about emerging customer preferences, and it created a learning lab on the west coast to better understand what consumers in that region want.

As the case of McDonald's illustrates, for all firms, the open question is whether or not structural changes within the organization can help a brand to refresh its image and pull in more customers. Only time can tell.

Sources: Lorenzetti, L. 2014. McDonald's struggling to stay relevant with millennials. *fortune.com,* August 25: np; Anonymous. 2014. McDonald's profit, sales decline amid ongoing struggles around the world. *foxbusiness.com,* October 21: np; Jargon, J. 2014. McDonald's plans to change U.S. structure. *wsj.com,* October 30: np; and Jargon, J. & Prior, A. 2014. McDonald's expects further challenges. *wsj.com,* July 22: np.

Creating Permeable Internal Boundaries

For barrier-free organizations to work effectively, the level of trust and shared interests among all parts of the organization must be raised. The organization needs to develop among its employees the skill level needed to work in a more democratic organization. Barrier-free organizations also require a shift in the organization's philosophy from executive to organizational development and from investments in high-potential individuals to investments in leveraging the talents of all individuals. Teams frequently develop more creative solutions to problems because they can share each individual's knowledge.

Teams can be an important aspect of barrier-free structures.[29] Jeffrey Pfeffer, author of several insightful books, including *The Human Equation,* suggests that teams have three primary advantages.[30] First, teams substitute peer-based control for hierarchical control of work activities. Employees control themselves, reducing the time and energy management needs to devote to controlling. Second, teams frequently develop more creative solutions to problems because they encourage the sharing of the tacit knowledge held by individuals.[31] Brainstorming, or group problem solving, involves the pooling of ideas and expertise to enhance the chances that at least one group member will think of a way to solve the problems at hand. Third, by substituting peer control for hierarchical control, teams permit the removal of layers of hierarchy and absorption of administrative tasks previously performed by specialists. This avoids the costs of having people whose sole job is to watch the people who watch other people do the work.

Some have argued for the need to move more radically to discard formal hierarchical structures and work toward a more democratic team organizational structure.[32] One version of such systems is called a *holacracy.* In a holacracy, there is no formal organizational structure in the traditional sense. Instead, employees self-identify into roles, undertaking the types of tasks that they are highly skilled at and interested in. Most employees will have multiple roles. Employees then group together into self-organized teams—or, in the terminology of holacracy, circles—in which they work together to complete tasks, such as circles for service delivery or product development. Since individual employees have multiple roles, they typically belong to multiple circles. This overlapping membership facilitates communication and coordination between circles. The circles within a firm change over time to meet the evolving situation of the firm. Each circle elects a lead, called a "lead link." This lead link guides meetings and sets the general agenda for the circle, although the members of the circle decide democratically on how the circle will complete tasks. The lead link also serves as a member of a higher-level circle. Overseeing it all is the general company circle, a collection of lead links who serve as the leadership team for the firm.

Most firms that have moved to implement a holacracy in their organization are small technology firms. These firms see little need for hierarchical authority, and they are attracted to the promises of improved agility and creativity, and higher employee morale, that are associated with this flexible, autonomous type of structure. In 2014, online retailer Zappos decided to transition its entire 1,500 employees to a holacracy structure. The new structure initially consisted of 250 circles, though it may grow to 400 circles as the new system gets fully implemented. Tony Hsieh, formerly Zappos's CEO and now lead link of the Experiential SWAT Team, explains that he wants Zappos "to function more like a city and less like a top-down bureaucratic organization." In making this change, Zappos will serve as a real-world experiment in determining whether or not larger firms can operate as holacracies.

Effective barrier-free organizations must go beyond achieving close integration and coordination within divisions in a corporation. Research on multidivisional organizations has stressed the importance of interdivisional coordination and resource sharing.[33] This requires interdivisional task forces and committees, reward and incentive systems that emphasize interdivisional co-operation, and common training programs.

Frank Carruba (former head of Hewlett-Packard's labs) found that the difference between mediocre teams and good teams could generally be attributed to varying levels of motivation and talent.[34] But what explained the difference between good teams and truly superior teams? The key difference—and this explained a 40-percent overall difference in performance—was the way members treated each other: the degree to which they believed in one another and created an atmosphere of encouragement rather than competition. Vision, talent, and motivation could carry a team only so far. What clearly stood out in the "super" teams were higher levels of authenticity and caring, which allowed the full synergy of their individual talents, motivation, and vision.

Developing Effective Relationships with External Constituencies

In barrier-free organizations, managers must also create flexible, porous organizational boundaries and establish communication flows and mutually beneficial relationships with internal (e.g., employees) and external (e.g., customers) constituencies.[35] Michael Dell, founder and CEO of Dell Technologies, is a strong believer in fostering close relationships with his customers:

> We're not going to be just your PC vendor anymore. We're going to be your IT department for PCs. Boeing, for example, has 100,000 Dell PCs, and we have 30 people that live at Boeing, and if you look at the things we're doing for them or for other customers, we don't look like a supplier, we look more like Boeing's PC department. We become intimately involved in planning their PC needs and the configuration of their network.
>
> It's not that we make these decisions by ourselves. They're certainly using their own people to get the best answer for the company. But the people working on PCs together, from both Dell and Boeing, understand the needs in a very intimate way. They're right there living it and breathing it, as opposed to the typical vendor who says, "Here are your computers. See you later."[36]

Barrier-free organizations create successful relationships between both internal and external constituencies, but there is one additional constituency—competitors—with whom some organizations have benefited as they developed co-operative relationships. In one example, after years of seeing its empty trucks return from warehouses back to production facilities following deliveries, General Mills teamed up with 16 of its competitors. They formed an e-commerce business to help the firms find carriers with empty cargo trailers to piggyback freight loads to distributors near the production facilities.[37] This increased revenue for all network members and reduced fuel costs.

Risks, Challenges, and Potential Downsides

Many firms find that creating and managing a barrier-free organization can be frustrating.[38] Puritan-Bennett Corporation, a manufacturer of respiratory equipment, found that its product development time more than doubled after it adopted team management. Roger J. Dolida, director of R&D, attributed this failure to a lack of top management commitment, high turnover among team members, and infrequent meetings. Often, managers trained in rigid hierarchies find it difficult to make the transition to the more democratic, participatory style that teamwork requires.

Christopher Barnes, a consultant with PricewaterhouseCoopers, previously worked as an industrial engineer for Challenger Electrical Distribution (a subsidiary of Westinghouse, now part of CBS) at a plant which produced circuit-breaker boxes. His assignment was to lead a team of workers from the plant's troubled final-assembly operation with the mission: "Make things better." That vague notion set the team up for failure. After a year of futility, the team was disbanded. In retrospect, Barnes identified several reasons for the debacle: (1) limited personal credibility—he was viewed as an "outsider"; (2) a lack of commitment to the team—everyone involved was forced to be on the team; (3) poor communications—nobody was told why the team was important; (4) limited autonomy—line managers refused to give up control over team members; and (5) misaligned incentives—the culture rewarded individual performance over team performance. Barnes's experience has implications for all types of teams, whether they are composed of managerial, professional, clerical, or production personnel.[39] The pros and cons of barrier-free structures are summarized in Exhibit 9-6.

EXHIBIT 9-6   PROS AND CONS OF A BARRIER-FREE STRUCTURE

Pros	Cons
• Leverages the talents of all employees. • Enhances co-operation, coordination, and information sharing among functions, divisions, small business units, and external constituencies. • Enables a quicker response to market changes through a single-goal focus. • Can lead to coordinated win–win initiatives with key suppliers, customers, and alliance partners.	• Difficulties in overcoming political and authority boundaries inside and outside the organization. • Requires strong leadership and common vision; otherwise, can lead to coordination problems. • Includes time-consuming and difficult-to-manage democratic processes. • Requires high levels of trust, which can impede performance. • Difficulties in assigning individual responsibility and allocating individual incentives and rewards.

The Modular Organization

Charles Handy, author of *The Age of Unreason,* noted:

> While it may be convenient to have everyone around all the time, having all of your workforce's time at your command is an extravagant way of marshaling the necessary resources. It is cheaper to keep them outside the organization . . . and to buy their services when you need them.[40]

The modular organization outsources nonvital functions, tapping into the knowledge and expertise of "best in class" suppliers, but retains strategic control. Outsiders may be used to manufacture parts, handle logistics, or perform accounting activities.[41] The value chain can be used to identify the key primary and support activities performed by a firm to create value: Which activities do we keep "in-house," and which activities do we outsource to suppliers?[42] The organization becomes a central hub surrounded by networks of outside suppliers and specialists and parts can be added or taken away. Both manufacturing and service units may be modular.[43]

Firms in the apparel industry have adopted the modular type quite successfully. Nike and Adidas, for example, concentrate on their strengths: designing and marketing high-tech, fashionable sportswear. Between them, they have few production facilities. They contract virtually all their footwear production to suppliers in China, Vietnam, and other countries with low-cost labour. Most of their sportswear is also manufactured in these countries. Avoiding large investments in fixed assets helps them derive large profits on minor sales increases. Nike and Adidas can keep pace with changing tastes in the marketplace because their suppliers have become experts at rapidly retooling to produce new products.[44]

In a modular company, outsourcing noncore functions offers three advantages:

1. A firm can decrease overall costs, stimulate new product development by hiring suppliers with superior talent to that of in-house personnel, avoid idle capacity, reduce inventories, and steer clear of being locked into a particular technology.
2. A company can focus scarce resources on areas where it holds a competitive advantage. These benefits can translate into more funding for R&D, hiring the best engineers, and providing continuous training for sales and service staff.
3. An organization can tap into the knowledge and expertise of its specialized supply chain partners, adding critical skills and accelerating organizational learning.[45]

The modular structure enables a company to leverage relatively small amounts of capital and a small management team to achieve seemingly unattainable strategic objectives.[46] Certain preconditions are necessary before the modular approach can be successful, however. First, the company must work closely with suppliers to ensure that the interests of each party are being fulfilled. Companies need to find loyal, reliable vendors who can be trusted with trade secrets. They also need assurances that suppliers will dedicate their financial, physical, and human resources to satisfy strategic objectives, such as lowering costs or being first to market.

Second, the modular company must be sure that it selects the proper competencies to keep in-house. For Nike and Adidas, the core competencies are design and marketing, not shoe manufacturing; for Honda, the core competency is engine technology. These firms are unlikely to outsource any activities that involve their core competencies. Exhibit 9-7

EXHIBIT 9-7

EXAMPLES OF MODULAR ORGANIZATIONS

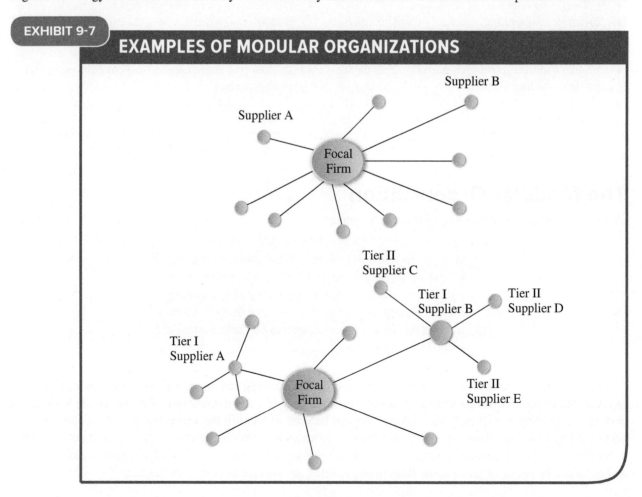

presents examples of modular structures from the computer and automobile manufacturing industries. In each case, the focal organization is connected with others in the value-creation process and relies on them for delivering some of the primary and support activities.

Strategic Risks of Outsourcing

The main strategic concerns with outsourcing are (1) loss of critical skills or developing the wrong skills, (2) loss of cross-functional skills, and (3) loss of control over a supplier.[47]

Too much outsourcing can result in a firm "giving away" too much skill and control. Outsourcing relieves companies of the requirement to maintain skill levels needed to manufacture essential components of their products.[48] For instance, at one time, semiconductor chips seemed like a simple technology to outsource, but they have since become a critical component of a wide variety of products. Companies that have outsourced the manufacture of these chips run the risk of losing the ability to manufacture them as the technology escalates. They thus become more dependent on their suppliers.

Cross-functional skills refer to the skills acquired through the interaction of individuals in various departments within a company.[49] Such interaction assists a department in solving problems as employees interface with others across functional units. However, if a firm outsources key functional responsibilities, such as manufacturing, communication across departments can become more difficult. A firm and its employees must now integrate their activities with a new, outside supplier.

Finally, outsourced products may give suppliers too much power over the manufacturer. Suppliers that are key to a manufacturer's success can, in essence, hold the manufacturer "hostage." Nike manages this potential problem by sending full-time "product expatriates" to work at the plants of its suppliers. Also, Nike often brings top members of supplier management and technical teams to its headquarters. This way, Nike keeps close tabs on the pulse of new developments, builds rapport and trust with suppliers, and develops long-term relationships with suppliers to prevent hostage situations.

Strategy Spotlight 9.7 discusses how Sony outsources for talent to develop products for its highly successful video game business. Exhibit 9-8 summarizes the pros and cons of modular structures.[50]

9.7 STRATEGY SPOTLIGHT

Outsourcing for Talent: How Sony Develops Video Games

The convergence of Hollywood and Silicon Valley has led to the explosive growth of the worldwide video game industry. By some estimates, it has more than doubled the movie industry's box office receipts. While broadcast TV audiences are dwindling and movie-going is stagnating, gaming is emerging as the newest and perhaps strongest pillar in the media world. So, it is no surprise that film studios, media giants, game makers, and Japanese electronics companies are all battling to win the "Game Wars." According to former Sony Entertainment Chairman, Michael Lynton, "This is a huge shift we're seeing, and nobody wants to be left behind."

Sony sells hardware with its PlayStation 4 (PS4) consoles, and has developed a handheld PlayStation Portable (PSP) and the PS VR headset to enhance the system. It develops a slew of games to be played on the consoles, such as the popular *Gran Turismo* racing and *EverQuest* online. The corporation also owns Sony Pictures and MGM movie studios, whose *Spider-Man* and *James Bond* franchises have been mega hit games for Activision and EA. The real payoff for Sony comes in game software sales. Although Sony and other console makers sell their hardware for a loss, they typically make $5 to $10 in royalties for every game sold on their platforms and more on those they produce in-house. PS3 had more than 300 software titles by 2012 and PS4 is on track to surpass this volume.

(Continued)

Starting in 2002 with the previous-generation game console, the PS2, Sony has used outside developers to produce most of its games. It has even reached out to gamers themselves. "We didn't want outside developers to be peripheral to our business model," says Andrew House, an early PlayStation team member and president and Global CEO of Sony Interactive Entertainment. "We knew that the widest variety of content possible was the best way to build the largest consumer base possible." Sony has searched high and low for talent. In 1997, it launched a developer kit aimed at hobbyists. "We sent it to budding college developers who wanted to try their hands," House says. Ideas from those amateurs made their way into commercial games in Japan. Meanwhile, externally developed titles, like *Final Fantasy and Madden NFL Football,* helped put Sony's PS2 at the top of the heap in 2001. Sony also launched a Linux developer kit for just $199 in 2002. "It's our way of feeding the market for the future. Some of the first great games were developed by people at home in their garages," says House. "If we're not getting people involved and looking for opportunities very early on, we really are missing out."

Sources: www.sony.com, 2009; Euromonitor International, 2009, Consumer Electronics Report, Global Market Information Database; A. House, "Sony," *Fast Company,* April, 2004, p. 65; and R. Grover, C. Edwards, I. Rowley, and I. Moon, "Game Wars," *BusinessWeek,* February 28, 2005, pp. 35–40.

EXHIBIT 9-8   **PROS AND CONS OF A MODULAR STRUCTURE**

Pros	Cons
• Directs a firm's managerial and technical talent to the most critical activities.	• Inhibits common vision through reliance on outsiders.
• Maintains full strategic control over most critical activities (core competencies).	• Diminishes future competitive advantages if critical technologies or other competencies are outsourced.
• Achieves "best in class" performance at each link in the value chain.	• Increases the difficulty of bringing back into the firm activities that add value due to market shifts.
• Leverages core competencies by outsourcing with smaller capital commitment.	• May lead to an erosion of cross-functional skills.
• Encourages information sharing and accelerates organizational learning.	• Decreases operational control and, potentially, control over a supplier.
• Increases flexibility and reduces resource commitments.	

The Virtual Organization

In contrast to the "self-reliant" thinking that guided traditional organizational designs, the strategic challenge today has become doing more with less and looking outside the firm for opportunities and solutions to problems. The virtual organization provides a new means of leveraging resources and exploiting opportunities.[51]

The *virtual organization* is a continually evolving network of independent companies—suppliers, customers, even competitors—linked together to share skills, costs, and access to one another's markets.[52] The members of a virtual organization, by pooling and sharing the knowledge and expertise of each of the component organizations, simultaneously "know" more and can "do" more than any one member of the group could know or do alone. By working closely together, each gains in the long run from individual and organizational learning.[53] The term *virtual,* meaning "being in effect but not actually so," is commonly used in the computer industry. A computer's ability to appear to have more storage capacity than it really possesses is called *virtual memory.* Similarly, by assembling resources from a variety of entities, a virtual organization may seem to have more capabilities than it really possesses.[54]

The virtual organization is a grouping of units from different organizations that have joined in an alliance to exploit complementary skills in pursuing common strategic objectives. A case in point is Lockheed Martin's use of specialized coalitions between and among three entities—the company, academia, and government—to enhance competitiveness. According to former CEO Norman Augustine:

> The underlying beauty of this approach is that it forces us to reach outward. No matter what your size, you have to look broadly for new ideas, new approaches, new products. Lockheed Martin used this approach in a surprising manner when it set out during the height of the Cold War to make stealth aircraft and missiles. The technical idea came from research done at the Institute of Radio Engineering in Moscow in the 1960s that was published, and publicized, quite openly in the academic media.
>
> Despite the great contrasts among government, academia and private business, we have found ways to work together that have produced very positive results, not the least of which is our ability to compete on a global scale.[55]

Virtual organizations need not be permanent and participating firms may be involved in multiple alliances. Virtual organizations may involve different firms performing complementary value activities, or different firms involved jointly in the same value activities, such as production, R&D, and distribution. The percentage of activities that are jointly performed with partners may vary significantly from alliance to alliance.[56]

How does the virtual type of structure differ from the modular type? Unlike the modular type, in which the focal firm maintains full strategic control, the virtual organization is characterized by participating firms that give up part of their control and accept interdependent destinies. Participating firms pursue a collective strategy that enables them to cope with uncertainty through co-operative efforts. The benefit is that, just as virtual memory increases storage capacity, the virtual organizations enhance the capacity or competitive advantage of participating firms. Strategy Spotlight 9.8 discusses the benefits of a virtual organization serving the scientific community. Exhibit 9-9 presents an example of a virtual organization from the oil exploration field.

9.8 STRATEGY SPOTLIGHT

Using Internet-Based Collaboration to Foster Innovation

Innocentive, launched in 2001, is the first online, incentive-based scientific network created specifically for the global research and development community. Innocentive's online platform has enabled world-class scientists and R&D-based companies to collaborate to attain innovative solutions to complex challenges.

Innocentive offers "seeker companies" the opportunity to increase their R&D potential by posting challenges without violating their confidentiality and intellectual property interests. Seeker companies might be looking for a chemical to be used in art restoration, for example, or the efficient synthesis of butane tetracarboxylic acid. David Bradin, a patent attorney from Seattle, was paid $4,000 for his tetracarboxylic acid formula. And Procter & Gamble claims that Innocentive has increased the share of its new products originating outside the company from 20 to 35 percent.

Often, individuals outside of the seeker company find the best solutions to the company's problem. By using Innocentive to post their problems, companies do not have to admit publicly that they

(Continued)

need help, yet they get access to a much broader range of ideas than can be generated inside the firm. Within firms, even those firms hiring the best and brightest scientists and engineers, ideas are tossed around by the same few people over and over. This situation can create a narrowing of the possible solutions to a problem (i.e., "groupthink" can occur), rather than searching over the broadest range of ideas. Anne Goldberg, technical knowledge manager at Solvay Pharmaceuticals, said, "The benefits [of Innocentive] are mainly in the simultaneous access to a lot of different scientific backgrounds that could bring new perspectives on sometimes old problems."

Sources: B. Libert and J. Spector, *We Are Smarter Than Me* (Philadelphia: Wharton School Publishing, 2008); K. Lakhani and L. Jeppesen, "Getting Unusual Suspects to Solve R&D Puzzles," *Harvard Business Review*, 85(5), 2007, pp. 30–32; T. Caldwell, "R&D Finds Answers in the Crowd," *Information World Review*, 236, 2007, p. 8.

EXHIBIT 9-9

EXAMPLE OF A VIRTUAL ORGANIZATION

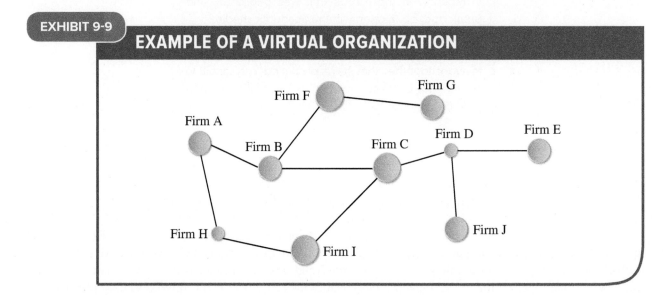

Each company that links up with others to create a virtual organization contributes only what it considers its core competencies. It will mix and match what it does best with the best of other firms by identifying its critical capabilities and the necessary links to other capabilities.[57]

Challenges and Risks

Such alliances often fail to meet expectations. The alliance between IBM and Microsoft soured in early 1991 when Microsoft began shipping Windows in direct competition to OS/2, which they had jointly developed. The runaway success of Windows frustrated IBM's ability to set an industry standard. In retaliation, IBM formed an alliance with Microsoft's archrival, Novell, in developing network software to compete with Microsoft's LAN Manager.

The virtual organization demands that managers build relationships with other companies, negotiate win–win deals for all parties find the right partners with compatible goals and values, and provide the right balance of freedom and control. Information systems must be designed and integrated to facilitate communication with current and potential partners.

Managers must be clear about the strategic objectives when forming alliances. Some objectives are time-bound, and those alliances need to be dissolved once the objective is fulfilled. Some alliances may have relatively long-term objectives and will need to be clearly monitored and nurtured to produce mutual commitment and avoid bitter fights for control. The highly dynamic personal computer industry is characterized by multiple temporary alliances among hardware, operating systems, and software producers.[58] But alliances in the more stable automobile industry, such as those involving Nissan and Volkswagen, have long-term objectives and tend to be relatively stable.

The virtual organization is a logical culmination of joint-venture strategies of the past. Shared risks, costs, and rewards are the facts of life in a virtual organization.[59] When virtual organizations are formed, they involve tremendous challenges for strategic planning. As with the modular corporation, it is essential to identify core competencies. However, for virtual structures to be successful, a strategic plan is also needed to determine the effectiveness of combining core competencies.

The strategic plan must address the diminished operational control and the overwhelming need for trust and common vision among the partners. This new structure may be appropriate for firms whose strategies require merging technologies (e.g., computing and communication) or for firms exploiting shrinking product life cycles that require simultaneous entry into multiple geographic markets. It may be effective for firms that want to be quick to the market with a new product or service. The profusion of alliances among airlines was primarily motivated by the need to provide seamless travel demanded by the full-fare paying business traveller. Exhibit 9-10 summarizes the advantages and disadvantages of a virtual structure.

EXHIBIT 9-10 PROS AND CONS OF A VIRTUAL STRUCTURE

Pros	Cons
• Enables the sharing of costs and skills. • Enhances access to global markets. • Increases market responsiveness. • Creates a "best of everything" organization, since each partner brings core competencies to the alliance. • Encourages both individual and organizational knowledge sharing and accelerates organizational learning.	• Difficulties in determining where one company ends and another begins, due to close interdependencies among players. • Leads to potential loss of operational control among partners. • Results in loss of strategic control over emerging technology. • Requires new and difficult-to-acquire managerial skills.

Sources: R. E. Miles and C. C. Snow, "Organizations: New Concepts for New Forms," *California Management Review,* Spring, 1986, pp. 62–73; Miles and Snow, "Causes of Failure in Network Organizations," *California Management Review,* Summer, 1999, pp. 53–72; and H. Bahrami, "The Emerging Flexible Organization: Perspectives from Silicon Valley," *California Management Review, Summer,* 1991, pp. 33–52.

Boundaryless Organizations: Making Them Work

Designing an organization that simultaneously supports the requirements of an organization's strategy, is consistent with the demands of the environment, and can be effectively implemented by the people around the manager is a tall order for any manager.[60] The most effective solution is usually a combination of organizational types. That is, a firm may outsource many parts of its value chain to reduce costs and increase quality, engage simultaneously in multiple alliances to take advantage of technological developments or penetrate new markets, and break down barriers within the organization to enhance flexibility.

When an organization faces external pressures, resource scarcity, and declining performance, it tends to become more internally focused, rather than directing its efforts toward managing and enhancing relationships with existing and potential external stakeholders. This may be the most opportune time for managers to carefully analyze their value-chain activities and evaluate the potential for adopting elements of modular, virtual, and barrier-free organizational types.

Achieving the coordination and integration necessary to maximize the potential of an organization's human capital involves much more than just creating a new structure. Techniques and processes to ensure the coordination and integration of an organization's key value-chain activities are critical. Teams are key building blocks of the new organizational forms, and teamwork requires new and flexible approaches to coordination and integration.

Managers trained in rigid hierarchies may find it difficult to make the transition to the more democratic, participative style that teamwork requires. As Douglas K. Smith, co-author of *The Wisdom of Teams,* pointed out, "A completely diverse group must agree on a goal, put the notion of individual accountability aside, and figure out how to work with each other. Most of all, they must learn that if the team fails, it's everyone's fault."[61] Within the framework of an appropriate organizational design, managers must select a mix and balance of tools and techniques to facilitate the effective coordination and integration of key activities. Some of the factors that must be considered include:

- Common culture and shared values
- Horizontal organizational structures
- Horizontal systems and processes
- Communications and information technologies
- Human resource practices

Common Culture and Shared Values

Shared goals, mutual objectives, and a high degree of trust are essential to the success of boundaryless organizations. In the fluid and flexible environments of the new organizational architectures, common cultures, shared values, and carefully aligned incentives are often less expensive to implement and a more effective means of strategic control than rules, boundaries, and formal procedures.

Horizontal Organizational Structures

These structures, which group similar or related business units under common management control, facilitate sharing resources and infrastructures to exploit synergies among operating units and help create a sense of common purpose. Consistency in training and the development of similar structures across business units facilitates job rotation and cross-training and enhances understanding of common problems and opportunities. Cross-functional teams and interdivisional committees and task groups represent important opportunities to improve understanding and foster co-operation among operating units.

Horizontal Systems and Processes

Organizational systems, policies, and procedures are the traditional mechanisms for achieving integration among functional units. Existing policies and procedures often do little more than institutionalize the barriers that exist from years of managing within the framework of the traditional model. Beginning with an understanding of basic business processes in the context of "a collection of activities that takes one or more kinds of input and creates an output that is of value to the customer," Michael Hammer and James Champy's 1993 best-selling *Reengineering the Corporation* outlined a methodology for redesigning internal systems and procedures that has been embraced by many organizations.[62] Successful re-engineering lowers costs, reduces inventories and cycle times, improves quality, speeds response times, and enhances organizational flexibility. Others advocate similar benefits through total quality management, and the like.

Communications and Information Technologies

The effective use of IT can play an important role in bridging gaps and breaking down barriers between organizations. Email and videoconferencing can improve lateral communications across long distances and multiple time zones and circumvent many of the barriers of the traditional model. IT can be a powerful ally in the redesign and streamlining of internal business processes and in improving coordination and integration between suppliers and customers. Internet technologies have eliminated paperwork in many buyer–supplier relationships, enabling co-operating organizations to reduce inventories, shorten delivery cycles, and reduce operating costs. IT must be viewed more as a prime component of an organization's overall strategy rather than simply in terms of administrative support.

Human Resource Practices

Change always involves and affects the human dimension of organizations. The attraction, development, and retention of human capital are vital to value creation. As boundaryless structures are implemented, processes are re-engineered, and organizations become increasingly dependent on sophisticated ITs, the skills of workers and managers alike must be upgraded to realize the full benefits.

LO 6 CREATING AMBIDEXTROUS ORGANIZATIONAL DESIGNS

"Ambidexterity" involves the ability to manage two contradictory challenges faced by today's managers.[63] First, managers must explore new opportunities and adjust to volatile markets to avoid complacency. They must ensure that they maintain *adaptability* and remain proactive in expanding and/or modifying their product–market scope to anticipate and satisfy market conditions. Such competencies are especially challenging when change is rapid and unpredictable.

Second, managers must also effectively exploit the value of their existing assets and competencies. They need to have *alignment,* which is a clear sense of how value is being created in the short term and how activities are integrated and properly coordinated. Firms that achieve both adaptability and alignment are considered *ambidextrous organizations*—aligned and efficient in how they manage today's business but flexible enough to changes in the environment so that they will prosper tomorrow.

Handling such opposing demands is difficult because there will always be some degree of conflict. Firms often suffer when they place too strong a priority on either adaptability or alignment. If it places too much focus on adaptability, the firm will suffer low profitability in the short term. If managers direct their efforts primarily at alignment, they will likely miss out on promising business opportunities.

An ambidextrous organization has a clear and compelling vision, consistently communicated by the company's senior management team. Breakthrough efforts are organized within structurally independent units, each having its own processes, structures, and cultures. However, they are integrated into the existing senior management structure, enabling cross-fertilization while avoiding cross-contamination. The tight coordination and integration at the managerial levels allows the newer units to share important resources from the traditional units, such as cash, talent, and expertise. Such sharing is encouraged and facilitated by effective reward systems that emphasize overall company goals. The organizational separation ensures that the new units' distinctive processes, structures, and cultures are not overwhelmed by the forces of "business as usual." The established units are shielded from the distractions of launching new businesses, and they continue to focus all of their attention and energy on refining their operations, enhancing their products, and serving their customers.

Ambidextrous Organizations: Key Design Attributes

Charles O'Reilly and Michael Tushman[64] provide some insights into how some firms are able to create successful ambidextrous organizational designs. They investigated companies that attempted to simultaneously pursue modest, incremental innovations as well as more dramatic, breakthrough innovations. The team investigated 35 attempts to launch breakthrough innovations undertaken by 15 business units in nine different industries. They studied the organizational designs and the processes, systems, and cultures associated with the breakthrough projects as well as their impact on the operations and performance of the traditional businesses.

Companies structured their breakthrough projects in one of four primary ways:

- Seven were carried out within existing *functional organizational structures.* The projects were completely integrated into the regular organizational and management structure.

- Nine were organized as *cross-functional teams.* The groups operated within the established organization but outside of the existing management structure.

- Four were organized as *unsupported teams.* Here, they became independent units set up outside the established organization and management hierarchy.

- Fifteen were conducted within *ambidextrous organizations.* Here, the breakthrough efforts were organized within structurally independent units, each having its own processes, structures, and cultures. However, they were integrated into the existing senior management structure.

The performance results of the 35 initiatives were tracked along two dimensions:

- Their success in creating desired innovations was measured by either the actual commercial results of the new product or the application of practical market or technical learning.
- The performance of the existing business was evaluated.

The study found that the organizational structure and management practices employed had a direct and significant impact on the performance of both the breakthrough initiative and the traditional business. The ambidextrous organizational designs were more effective than the other three designs on both dimensions: launching breakthrough products or services (i.e., adaptation) and improving the performance of the existing business (i.e., alignment).

Why Was the Ambidextrous Organization the Most Effective Structure?

The study found that there were many factors. A clear and compelling vision, consistently communicated by the company's senior management team, was critical in building the ambidextrous designs. The structure enabled cross-fertilization while avoiding cross-contamination. The tight coordination and integration at the managerial levels enabled the newer units to share important resources from the traditional units such as cash, talent, and expertise. Such sharing was encouraged and facilitated by effective reward systems that emphasized overall company goals. The organizational separation ensured that the new units' distinctive processes, structures, and cultures were not overwhelmed by the forces of "business as usual." The established units were shielded from the distractions of launching new businesses, and they continued to focus all of their attention and energy on refining their operations, enhancing their products, and serving their customers.

SUMMARY

Successful organizations must ensure that they have the proper type of organizational structure. Furthermore, they must ensure that their firms incorporate the necessary integration and processes so that the internal and external boundaries of the firms are flexible and permeable. Such a need is increasingly important as the environments of firms become more complex, rapidly changing, and unpredictable.

In the first section of the chapter, we discussed the growth patterns of large corporations. Although most organizations remain small or die eventually, some firms continue to grow in terms of revenues, vertical integration, and diversity of products and services. In addition, their geographic scope may increase to include international operations. We traced the dominant pattern of growth, which evolves from a simple structure to a functional structure as a firm grows in terms of size and increases its level of vertical integration. After a firm expands into related products and services, its structure changes from a functional form to a divisional form of organization. Finally, when the firm enters international markets, its structure again changes to accommodate the change in strategy.

We also addressed the different types of organizational structure—simple, functional, divisional (including two variations—strategic business unit and holding company), and matrix—as well as their relative advantages and disadvantages. We closed the section with a discussion of the implications for structure when a firm enters international markets. The three primary factors to take into account when determining the appropriate structure are type of international strategy, product diversity, and the extent to which a firm is dependent on foreign sales.

In the second section, we took a contingency approach to the design of reward and evaluation systems. That is, we argued that there is no one best way to design such systems; rather, the optimal approach is dependent on a variety of factors. The two that we discussed are business-level and corporate-level strategies. With an overall cost leadership strategy and unrelated diversification, it is appropriate to rely primarily on cultures and reward systems that emphasize the production outcomes of the organization because it is rather easy to quantify such indicators. In contrast, differentiation strategies and related diversification require cultures and incentive systems that encourage and reward creativity initiatives as well as the co-operation among professionals in many different functional areas. Here, it becomes more difficult to measure accurately each individual's contribution, and more subjective indicators become essential.

The third section of the chapter introduced the concept of the boundaryless organization. We did not suggest that the concept of the boundaryless organization replaces the traditional forms of organizational structure. Rather, it should complement them. This is necessary to cope with the increasing complexity and change in the competitive environment. We addressed three types of boundaryless organizations. The *barrier-free type* focuses on the need for the internal and external boundaries of a firm to be more flexible and permeable. Some go further to abolish all formal structures in a holacracy. The *modular type* emphasizes the strategic outsourcing of noncore activities. The *virtual type* centers on the strategic benefits of alliances and the forming of network organizations. We discussed both the advantages and disadvantages of each type of boundaryless organization and also suggested some techniques and processes that are necessary to successfully implement them. These are common culture and values, horizontal organizational structures, horizontal systems and processes, communications and information technologies, and human resource practices.

Finally, we addressed the need for managers to develop ambidextrous organizations. In today's rapidly changing global environment, managers must be responsive and proactive to take advantage of new opportunities. At the same time, they must effectively integrate and coordinate existing operations. Such requirements call for organizational designs that establish project teams that are structurally independent units, each having its own processes, structures, and cultures. But at the same time, each unit needs to be effectively integrated into the existing management hierarchy.

Summary Review Questions

1. Why is it important for managers to carefully consider the type of organizational structure they use to implement their strategies?

2. Briefly trace the dominant growth pattern of major corporations from simple structure to functional structure to divisional structure. Discuss the relationship between a firm's strategy and its structure.

3. What are the relative advantages and disadvantages of the types of organizational structure—simple, functional, divisional, matrix—discussed in the chapter?

4. When a firm expands its operations into foreign markets, what are the three most important factors to take into account in deciding what type of structure is most appropriate? What are the types of international structures discussed in the text, and what are the relationships between strategy and structure?

5. Briefly describe the three different types of boundaryless organizations: barrier-free, modular, and virtual.

6. What are some of the key attributes of effective groups? Ineffective groups?

7. What are the advantages and disadvantages of the three types of boundaryless organizations: barrier-free, modular, and virtual?

8. When are ambidextrous organizational designs necessary? What are some of their key attributes?

REFLECTING ON CAREER IMPLICATIONS

- *Strategy–Structure:* Is there an effective "fit" between your organization's strategy and its structure? If not, there may be inconsistencies in how you are evaluated, which often leads to role ambiguity and confusion. A poor fit could also affect communication among departments as well as across the organization's hierarchy.

- *Matrix Structure:* If your organization employs elements of a matrix structure (e.g., dual reporting relationships), are there effective structural supporting elements (e.g., culture and rewards)? If not, there could be a high level of dysfunctional conflict among managers.

- *The "Fit" between Rewards and Incentives and "Levels of Strategy" (Business-Level and Corporate-Level):* What metrics are used to evaluate the performance of your work unit? Are there strictly financial measures of success, or are you also rewarded for achieving competitive advantages (through effective innovation, organizational learning, or other activities that increase knowledge but may be costly in the short run)?

- *Boundaryless Organizational Designs:* Does your firm have structural mechanisms (e.g., culture, human resource practices) that facilitate sharing of information across boundaries? If so, you should be better able to enhance your human capital by leveraging your talents and competencies.

EXPERIENTIAL EXERCISE

Many firms have recently moved toward a modular structure. For example, they have increasingly outsourced many of their information technology (IT) activities. Identify three such organizations. Using secondary sources, evaluate (1) the firm's rationale for IT outsourcing and (2) the implications for performance.

Firm	Rationale	Implication(s) for Performance
1.		
2.		
3.		

APPLICATION QUESTIONS AND EXERCISES

1. Select an organization that competes in an industry in which you are particularly interested. Go to the Internet, and determine what type of organizational structure this organization has. In your view, is it consistent with the strategy that it has chosen to implement? Why? Why not?

2. Choose an article from *Canadian Business, BusinessWeek, Report on Business Magazine, Fortune, Forbes, Fast Company,* or any other well-known publication that deals with a corporation that has undergone a significant change in its strategic direction. What are the implications for the structure of this organization?

3. Go to the Internet, and look up some of the public statements or speeches of an executive in a major corporation about a significant initiative, such as entering a joint venture or launching a new product line. What do you feel are the implications for making the internal and external barriers of the firm more flexible and permeable? Does the executive discuss processes, procedures, integrating mechanisms, or cultural issues that should serve this purpose? Or are other issues discussed that enable a firm to become more boundaryless?

4. Look up a recent article in the publications listed in question 2 above that addresses a firm's involvement in outsourcing (modular organization) or in strategic alliance or network organizations (virtual organization). Was the firm successful or unsuccessful in this endeavour? Why? Why not?

ETHICS AND CORPORATE SOCIAL RESPONSIBILITY QUESTIONS

1. If a firm has a divisional structure and places extreme pressures on its divisional executives to meet short-term profitability goals (e.g., quarterly income), could this raise some ethical considerations? Why? Why not?

2. A firm participating in a strategic alliance will normally refrain from exercising direct control and expressing opinions about the management and treatment of its partner's employees (in terms of culture, compensation, rewards, and incentives). What ethical issues could this stance raise? What could be the potential long-term and short-term downsides for the firm?

3. A matrix structure is said to be potentially stressful to some employees who cannot handle the ambiguity of roles and divided responsibilities. What is the ethical obligation of the corporation toward those employees?

CHAPTER TEN

STRATEGIC CONTROL AND CORPORATE GOVERNANCE

LEARNING OBJECTIVES

After reading this chapter, you should have a good understanding of:

LO 1 The value of effective strategic control systems in strategy formulation and implementation.

LO 2 The key differences between financial and strategic control systems and the role they play in the success of an organization.

LO 3 The benefits of having the proper balance among the three levers of behavioural control: culture, rewards and incentives, and boundaries.

LO 4 The three key participants in corporate governance: shareholders, management (led by the chief executive officer), and the board of directors.

LO 5 The role of corporate governance mechanisms in ensuring that the interests of managers are aligned with those of an organization's shareholders and other stakeholders.

CASE STUDY

The Toronto Dominion Bank, commonly knows as TD, was formed in 1955 through the merger of the Bank of Toronto and the Dominion Bank, both of which were founded in the mid-1800s.[1] The rich history of both banks and their respective sizes propelled TD to a position at the forefront of the Canadian banking industry. TD is currently the second largest bank in Canada by market capitalization, and a top-10 bank in North America. TD's recent history includes many accolades, such as being named among Canada's Top 100 Employers by *Maclean's* magazine in 2008 and as one of Canada's Top 10 Employers by the *Financial Post* in 2011. Yet, recently TD has come under fire for—among other questionable tactics—imposing unreasonable sales targets on its front-line staff, generating a number of legal and ethical concerns.

DayOwl/Shutterstock.com

In a CBC report published in early 2017, three TD employees spoke out about what they claimed was "incredible pressure" to generate revenues from customers by signing them up for products and services that they may not need. Although there has always been a sales component to the job of front-line tellers, the employees reported that new, unrealistic sales goals were being enforced as a means of counterbalancing low interest rates and generating more capital in hand to protect against a downturn in the market.

No longer considered customer service representatives, tellers are now "front-line advisors" instructed to "advise" customers on services and products that the bank has on offer, even when the customer may not need them, in order to meet aggressive sales goals. When a customer meets with a teller, a gold star lights up on the teller's computer screen, indicating that "Advice Opportunities Exist." The teller then clicks on the star, and products and services the customer hasn't yet purchased pop up, such as overdraft protection, credit cards, or lines of credit. Each time a teller gets a customer to sign up for one of those options, it counts toward their sales goals.

Tellers are also encouraged to upsell on the accounts requested. When CBC investigators conducted a hidden-camera test at five Vancouver TD branches, tellers offered to "activate" overdraft protection, failing to mention the fees involved, and offered an account with monthly service fees of $29.95 when the basic chequing account with monthly fees of $3.95 had been requested. Investigators had similar experiences at other TD branches, showing the widespread nature of upselling in the company.

Tellers who spoke to the CBC felt that they had to leave their ethics aside when they came to work, and often chose not to do what was right for the customer. "I'm in survival mode now," said an anonymous teller who had worked at TD for more than 15 years, "because it's a choice between keeping my job and feeding my family . . . or doing what's right for the customer."

Sure enough, sales revenue goals for TD tellers have more than tripled in the past three years. A manager who spoke to the CBC reporters also highlighted the pressure being placed upon management by top executives. "The higher-ups are also putting more pressure on us to get tellers to achieve these goals," the manager explained. "And if they don't . . . our job is to make sure that they understand that they're no longer right for this job." Managers of the branches who had expressed concerns to upper management about the sales goals were promptly asked to consider whether they were still a good fit for their position.

After the report was published, TD Bank enlisted the help of an outside company to review its sales goal process, although CEO Bharat Masrani denied the presence of a widespread problem. The Financial Consumer Agency of Canada also launched its own investigation into banking industry practices since the publication of the CBC report. Aggressive sales goals imposed by management may point to a misalignment of interests between the top brass and the front-line employees. Higher sales certainly benefit top management, at least in the short-term, and in this case they did contribute to a strong financial performance for TD in 2016. However, tactics to achieve those sales may involve exploiting the trust many customers have in their front-line banking representatives—tactics including high-pressure upselling, setting customers up for higher fees, and selling them products they don't need. ▪

Organizations must employ effective strategic controls if they are to successfully develop and implement their strategies. This means having systems that allow the organization to effectively respond to environmental changes as well as balance and align the organization's culture, rewards, and boundaries. Overriding this is the goal of the firm's owners (shareholders) and their elected representatives (board of directors) to ensure that the firm's executives (management team) strive to fulfil their fiduciary duty and maximize the long-term value of the firm. A list of controls that are, or are supposed to be, in place for the functioning of each individual corporation and to ensure the presence of trust in the entire institution of public corporations includes the following:

- Effective corporate governance aligning managerial and stakeholder interests
- Effective informational controls ensuring that the organization is informed and that its strategies and goals remain aligned with the changing environment—that the organization does the right things
- Effective behavioural controls ensuring that all the members of the organization behave consistently and in coordination, to achieve desirable outcomes—that the organization does things right[2]

Complementing these controls are financial and operating controls, that is, quantitative measures that ensure that the firm's performance on multiple dimensions meets previously established targets. Among them are a range of financial and accounting measures, market-based measures, operating performance measures, and benchmarks against competitors.

LO 1

In this chapter, we first discuss financial and operating controls as feedback-based control systems that measure outcomes after a sufficient time has elapsed and that serve only to guide corrective action subsequent to the implementation of strategy and achievement of results. We then elaborate on informational and behavioural controls—the main strategic control systems at managers' disposal. We highlight their forward-looking nature as contrasted with feedback controls. We expand on their potential to inform and steer action concurrently with strategy formulation and execution. Finally, in the last part of this chapter, we focus on strategic control from a broader perspective—what is referred to as *corporate governance* and the mechanisms that guide managers to behave in the interests of the firm's key stakeholders, including its shareholders.

FEEDBACK CONTROL SYSTEMS

Traditional control mechanisms rely on measuring outcomes. Managers set targets and devise specific metrics to measure the achievement of those targets. The targets are established to match specific objectives and organizational goals. An appropriate time frame is also established that allows pursuit of those objectives and the delivery of results. Performance is measured against the targets. Targets can take the form of accounting metrics, such as return on investment (ROI), return on assets (ROA), return on equity (ROE), budgets, or adherence to financial audit standards, such as the Generally Accepted Accounting Principles (GAAP). Other targets correspond to market-based outcomes and take the form of sales quotas, market share figures, customer satisfaction scores, product introduction rates, brand coverage, and the like. Operating targets, such as production schedules, tolerance levels, waste rates, utilization, and productivity are also used.

Feedback control systems are placed at the end of a sequential process that starts with strategy formulation and proceeds to goal setting, strategy implementation and action, performance measurement, evaluation and feedback; and, if needed in response to that evaluation, the organization proceeds with steering and corrective action. There is usually no action taken to revise strategies, goals, and objectives until the end of the period in question, often tied to a firm's annual planning cycle.

Control is based on a feedback loop from performance measurement to strategy formulation. This process typically involves lengthy time lags, often tied to a firm's annual planning cycle.[3] Exhibit 10-1 illustrates the typical feedback loop of traditional control systems. They are most appropriate when the environment is stable and relatively simple, goals and objectives can be measured with a high level of certainty, and there is little need for complex measures of performance. Sales quotas, operating budgets, production schedules, and similar quantitative control mechanisms are typical.

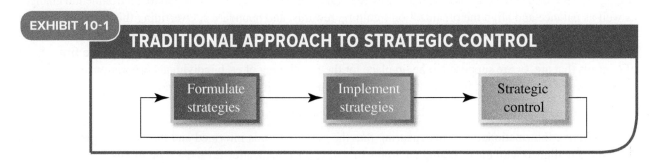

EXHIBIT 10-1

TRADITIONAL APPROACH TO STRATEGIC CONTROL

Formulate strategies → Implement strategies → Strategic control

LO 2

Such financial and operating control systems serve a number of essential functions within organizations and represent valuable management tools. Above all, they facilitate the articulation of clear, unambiguous, explicit, and concrete goals for the organization as a whole and for individual units within it. Each department knows exactly what is expected of it and the time frame within which its task is expected to be accomplished. These systems provide direct links between individual goals and organizational goals. A feedback-based control system communicates exactly what individual managers are accountable for. Specific results can be compared across units and provide the basis for corrective action. Finally, managers can look back to the actions that have led to the results and draw conclusions about cause and effect; they can use this understanding to inform their subsequent decisions, adjust plans, and take corrective action.

The power of financial and operating controls and feedback control systems, in general, rests on some simple premises that are linked to their very nature. First, there is a fundamental assumption that goals and objectives can be measured with a high level of certainty. Second, the environment is thought to be stable enough and simple enough that a well-managed company can move forward in accordance with detailed and precise plans, which can be set out well in advance of their execution. Third, it is believed that there is a clear and unambiguous connection between original plans and eventual outcomes. The appropriateness of the business strategy or standards of performance is seldom questioned.[4]

Many writers, however, have questioned the plausibility of those premises. Most notably, McGill University's Henry Mintzberg has written about leaders "crafting" a strategy.[5] Drawing on the parallel between the strategist and the potter at her wheel, Mintzberg pointed out that the potter begins work with some general idea of the artifact she wishes to create, but the details of design—even possibilities for a different design—emerge as the work progresses. For businesses facing complex and turbulent business environments, the craftsperson's method seems more appropriate than that provided by the traditional, more rational planner. It helps us deal with the uncertainty about how a design will work out in practice and allows for a creative element.

Mintzberg's observations cast doubt on the value of rigid planning and goal-setting processes. Fixed strategic goals become meaningless for firms competing in highly unpredictable competitive environments, where strategies need to change frequently and opportunistically. An inflexible commitment to predetermined goals and milestones can prevent the very adaptability that is often required of a good strategy. Grand designs with precise and carefully integrated plans seldom work. Rather, most strategic change proceeds incrementally, one step at a time.[6] A leader can best serve the organization by introducing some sense of direction and logic in incremental steps and not hampering its progress with elaborate financial controls that would constrain the managers' ability to anticipate the future. Even organizations that have been extremely successful in the past can become complacent. Often, they may fail to anticipate important changes in their environment and adapt their goals and strategies to the new conditions.

INFORMATIONAL CONTROL: RESPONDING EFFECTIVELY TO ENVIRONMENTAL CHANGE

Adapting to and anticipating both internal and external environmental change is an integral part of strategic control. The relationships between strategy formulation, implementation, and control are highly interactive, as suggested by Exhibit 10-2. *Informational control* is primarily concerned with whether or not the organization is "doing the right things." It deals with the internal environment as well as with the external strategic context. It addresses the assumptions and premises that provide the foundation for an organization's strategy.[7] The key question addressed by informational control is: Do the organization's goals and strategies still "fit" within the context of the current strategic environment?

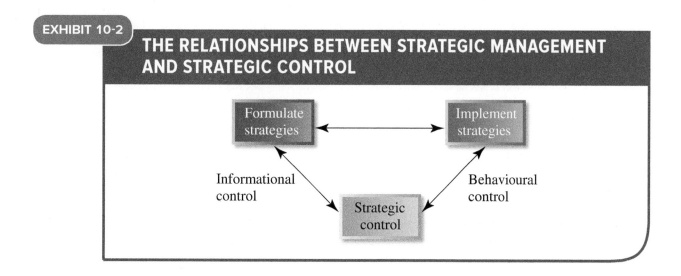

EXHIBIT 10-2   **THE RELATIONSHIPS BETWEEN STRATEGIC MANAGEMENT AND STRATEGIC CONTROL**

Informational control is part of an ongoing process of organizational learning that continuously updates and challenges the assumptions that underlie the organization's strategy. In such "double-loop" learning, the organization's assumptions, premises, goals, and strategies are continuously monitored, tested, and reviewed.[8] The benefits of continuous monitoring are evident—time lags are dramatically shortened, changes in the competitive environment are detected earlier, and the organization's ability to respond with speed and flexibility is enhanced.

Contemporary control systems must have four characteristics to be effective:[9]

1. The focus is on constantly changing information that has potential strategic importance.
2. The information is important enough to demand frequent and regular attention from all levels of the organization.
3. The data and information generated are best interpreted and discussed in face-to-face meetings.
4. The control system is a key catalyst for an ongoing debate about underlying data, assumptions, and action plans.

Strategic control systems track the strategic uncertainties that may keep senior managers awake at night. Depending on the type of business, such uncertainties may relate to changes in technology, customer tastes, government regulation, and industry competition. Since control systems must be designed to gather information that might challenge the strategic visions of the future, they are, by definition, hot buttons for senior managers.

An executive's decision to use the control system interactively—in other words, to invest the time and attention to review and evaluate new information—sends a clear signal to the organization about what is important. The dialogue and debate that emerge from such an interactive process can often lead to new strategies and innovations. Strategy Spotlight 10.1 discusses how executives at Google use an interactive control process.

10.1 STRATEGY SPOTLIGHT

Google's Interactive Control System

Google has attempted to introduce many hierarchical control systems typically found in large firms. Each time, the firm has reverted within weeks to its interactive control system. All of Google's roughly 5,000 product developers work in teams of three engineers. Larger projects simply assemble several teams of three workers. Within teams, there is a rotating "über-tech leader," depending on the project. Engineers tend to work in more than one team and do not need permission to switch teams. According to Shona Brown, former vice-president for business operations, "If at all possible, we want people to commit to things rather than be assigned to things." At Google, "employees don't need a lot of signoffs to try something new, but they won't get much in the way of resources until they've accumulated some positive user feedback."

Google's executives regularly review projects with project leaders and analyze data about projects. Google uses some of its own Web page ranking technology in the review of software and other business projects. Using their own employees as mini–test markets, managers often solicit employee opinions and analyze usage patterns of new product features and technologies. This interactive control of corporate information allows Google to make faster decisions about its business, including to

- compare the performances of customer usage and feedback among all components of the Google business in real time;
- quickly discover shortfalls before major problems arise;
- become aware of unexpected successes that have often led to innovations; and
- discontinue failing products and services in a timely manner to save the company money.

These manager meetings return significant rewards for Google. Innovations that have been implemented as a result of high information control include the following:

- Gmail, the email system that uses Google's core search features to help users organize and find email messages easily;

- Google News, a computer-generated news site that aggregates headlines from more than 4,500 English-language news sources worldwide, groups similar stories together, and displays them according to each reader's personalized interests; and

- Google AdSense, a service that matches ads to a website's content and audience and operates on a revenue-sharing business model.

As mentioned, Google managers are able to quickly analyze user feedback and revenue data to discontinue projects that are not working out as hoped. This information control allows managers to reallocate resources to more promising projects in a timely manner.

For instance, Google Lively, a virtual world simulation, was launched in 2008 and shut down after five months after management determined that the service was not competitive. Similarly, Google Print Ads, Google's automated method of selling ads through auctions to the newspaper industry, was terminated in early 2009 when managers analyzed the data and determined that the revenue stream was negligible compared with the costs of the program.

Sources: G. Hamel, "Break Free," *Fortune,* October 1, 156(7), 2007, pp. 119–126; B. Iyer and T. Davenport, "Reverse Engineering Google's Innovation Machine," *Harvard Business Review,* April 2008, pp. 59–68; A. Pham, "Google to End Virtual World, Lively, Launched by the Internet Giant Less Than Five Months Ago," *Los Angeles Times,* November 21, 2008, p. C3; and M. Helft, "Google Ends Sale of Ads in Papers after 2 Years," *New York Times,* January 21, 2009, p. B3.

LO 3 BEHAVIOURAL CONTROL: BALANCING CULTURE, REWARDS, AND BOUNDARIES

Behavioural control is focused on implementation—doing things right. Whereas financial and operating controls assess the results of implementing a strategy at the end of the period allocated for its execution, behavioural controls recognize the potential costs, lost opportunities, and risks associated with withholding intervention until the predetermined strategy and its execution do produce outcomes.

A number of reasons compel organizations to develop alternatives to the feedback systems described earlier. First, the competitive environment is increasingly complex and unpredictable, demanding both flexibility and quick response to its challenges. Organizations are frequently called upon, midstream, to make iterative adjustments in direction, alter management priorities in the face of new information and developments, and modify resource allocations during a plan's execution. Moreover, employees do not connect with an organization to the same degree that they did in the past, as professional careers now take very different forms, lateral moves are much more common, and employees move in and out of an organization more frequently.[10] The implicit long-term contract between an employee and the organization has been eroded. Young managers are conditioned to see themselves as free agents and view a career as a series of opportunities and challenges across multiple organizations. At the same time, work does not occur in neat and well-defined ways. Tasks are cross-functional and carried out by teams of workers and, although less repetitive, do not necessarily begin and end in the same time dimensions as the plan. Feedback control systems are rendered less useful in such circumstances because the individuals who set the plan and initiate its execution may not be around to witness the results and receive the feedback at the end.

Behavioural controls then become extremely useful, since they leverage the organization's culture, rewards, and incentives and define the boundaries of individuals and units. In doing so, they guide behaviour while strategy is unfolding, and they direct individuals' efforts toward desirable outcomes, which may, in fact, be continuously redefined. In effect, behavioural control systems use the three levers *culture, rewards,* and *boundaries* in a balanced and consistent manner to achieve results.

Building a Strong and Effective Culture

Organizational culture is a system of shared values (what is important) and beliefs (how things work) that shape a company's people, organizational structures, and control systems to produce behavioural norms (the way we do things around here).[11] Over the years, numerous bestsellers, such as *Theory Z, Corporate Cultures, In Search of Excellence,* and *Good to Great,* have emphasized the powerful influence of culture on what goes on within organizations and how they perform.[12] Collins and Porras argued in *Built to Last* that the key factor in sustained exceptional performance is a cult-like culture.[13] Some type of culture exists inside every organization. You cannot touch it or write it down, but it is there; its influence is pervasive; it can work for you or against you.[14] Effective leaders understand its importance and strive to shape and use it as one of their important levers of strategic control.[15]

Michael Watkins[16] has observed that while there is universal agreement that organizational cultures exist and play crucial roles in shaping behaviour in organizations, there is little consensus on what organizational culture actually is. He sought online feedback from senior executives on how they defined organizational culture and came up with the following:

- Culture is consistent, observable patterns of behaviour in organizations.

- Culture is powerfully shaped by incentives.

- Culture is a process of "sense making" in organizations.

- Culture is a carrier of meaning.

- Culture is a social control system.

- Culture is a form of protection that has evolved from situational pressures.

- Organizational culture is shaped by and overlaps with other cultures—especially the broader culture of the societies in which it operates.

- The cultures of organizations are never monolithic.

- Cultures are dynamic.

The Role of Culture

Culture wears many different hats, each woven from the fabric of those values that sustain the organization's primary source of competitive advantage. Some examples are as follows:

- Four Seasons Hotels and Southwest Airlines focus on customer service.

- Lexus and Hewlett-Packard emphasize product quality.

- Cirque du Soleil and 3M place a high value on innovation.

- Nucor Steel and Walmart are concerned, above all, with operational efficiency.

Culture sets implicit boundaries—unwritten standards of acceptable behaviour—in dress, ethical matters, and the way an organization conducts its business.[17] By creating a framework of shared values, culture encourages individual identification with the organization and its objectives. Culture acts as a means of reducing the costs of monitoring.[18]

Sustaining an Effective Culture

Powerful organizational cultures do not happen overnight, and they do not remain in place without a strong commitment—both in terms of words and deeds—by leaders throughout the organization.[19] A viable and productive organizational culture can be strengthened and sustained. However, it cannot be "built" or "assembled"; instead, it must be cultivated, encouraged, and "fertilized."[20]

Storytelling is one way effective cultures are maintained. Many are familiar with the story of how Art Fry's failure to develop a strong adhesive led to 3M's enormously successful Post-it Notes. Perhaps less familiar is the story of Francis G. Okie.[21] In 1922, Okie came up with the idea of selling sandpaper to men as a replacement for razor blades. The idea obviously did not pan out, but Okie was allowed to remain at 3M. Interestingly, the technology developed by Okie led 3M to develop its first blockbuster product: waterproof sandpaper, which became a staple in the automobile industry. Such stories foster the importance of risk taking, experimentation, freedom to fail, and innovation—all vital elements of 3M's culture.

Rallies or "pep talks" by top executives also serve to reinforce a firm's culture. The late Sam Walton was known for his pep rallies at local Walmart stores. Four times a year, the founders of Home Depot—former CEO Bernard Marcus and Arthur Blank—used to don orange aprons and stage Breakfast with Bernie and Arthur, a 6:30 a.m. pep rally, which was broadcast live over the firm's closed-circuit TV network to most of its 45,000 employees.[22]

Southwest Airlines' "Culture Committee" is a unique vehicle designed to perpetuate the company's highly successful culture. The following excerpt from an internal company publication describes its objectives:

> The goal of the Committee is simple—to ensure that our unique Corporate Culture stays alive . . . Culture Committee members represent all regions and departments across our system and they are selected based upon their exemplary display of the "Positively Outrageous Service" that won us the first-ever Triple Crown; their continual exhibition of the "Southwest Spirit" to our Customers and to their fellow workers; and their high energy level, boundless enthusiasm, unique creativity, and constant demonstration of teamwork and love for their fellow workers.[23]

Motivating with Rewards and Incentives

Reward and incentive systems represent a powerful means of influencing an organization's culture, focusing efforts on high-priority tasks, and motivating individual and collective task performance.[24] Just as culture deals with influencing beliefs, behaviours, and attitudes of people within an organization, the reward system—by specifying who gets rewarded and why—is an effective motivator and control mechanism.[25] Strategy Spotlight 10.2 shows how a firm distributes rewards on the basis of individuals' contributions.

10.2 STRATEGY SPOTLIGHT

Rewards That Count

When John Thompson, the new CEO of $11-billion software security firm Symantec, arrived at his new job, he learned that any executive who was promoted to vice-president automatically received a BMW. Senior management's bonuses were paid quarterly and were heavily skewed toward cash, not stock. Thompson says: "So if the stock didn't do

(Continued)

well, they didn't care. We now have a stock option plan that is broad-based but not universal. One of the things we recognized early on was that if we were going to grow at the rate that we were growing, we have to be more selective in who we gave options to so as not to dilute the value of our stock. And, the first thing we did was identify a range of employees who were valuable to the company but didn't need equity to come to work, and we focused their compensation around cash bonuses. Then we increased the equity we gave to the engineers and other people that were critical to our long-term success." By paying the two groups of people in different ways, the new compensation scheme recognizes their distinctive importance.

Source: G. L. Neilson, B. A. Pasternack and K. E. Van Nuys, "The Passive-Aggressive Organization," *Harvard Business Review,* 83(10), 2005, pp. 82–95.

Generally, people in organizations act rationally, each motivated by their own best interests.[26] However, the collective sum of individual behaviours of an organization's employees does not always result in what is best for the organization; individual rationality is no guarantee of organizational rationality. For example, sales and marketing personnel promise unrealistically quick delivery times to bring in business, much to the dismay of operations and logistics; overengineering by research and development (R&D) creates headaches for manufacturing; and so on. Conflicts also arise across divisions when divisional profits become a key compensation criterion. As ill will and anger escalate, personal relationships and performance may suffer.

To be effective, incentive and reward systems need to reinforce basic core values, enhance cohesion and commitment to goals and objectives, and meet with the organization's overall mission and purpose.[27] For example, at General Mills, to ensure a manager's interest in the overall performance of his or her unit, half of a manager's annual bonus is linked to business-unit results and half to individual performance.[28] If a manager simply matches a rival manufacturer's performance, his or her salary is roughly 5 percent lower. However, if a manager's product ranks in the industry's top 10 percent in earnings growth and return on capital, the manager's total pay can rise to nearly 30 percent beyond the industry norm.

Effective reward and incentive systems share a number of common characteristics:

- Objectives are clear, well understood, and broadly accepted.

- Rewards are clearly linked to performance and desired behaviours.

- Performance measures are clear and highly visible.

- Feedback is prompt, clear, and unambiguous.

- The compensation "system" is perceived as fair and equitable.

- The structure is flexible; it can adapt to changing circumstances.

The perception that a plan is "fair and equitable" is critically important. The firm must have the flexibility to respond to changing requirements as its direction and objectives change. In recent years, many companies have begun to place more emphasis on growth. Emerson Electric has shifted its emphasis from cost cutting to growth. To ensure that changes take hold, the management compensation formula has been changed from a largely bottom-line focus to one that emphasizes growth, new products, acquisitions, and international expansion. Discussions about profits are handled separately, and a culture of risk taking is encouraged.[29]

However, incentive and reward systems don't have to be all about money. Employees respond not only to monetary compensation but also to softer forms of incentives and rewards. In fact, a number of studies have found that for employees who are satisfied with their base salary, nonfinancial motivators are more effective than cash incentives in building long-term employee motivation.[30] Three key reward systems appear to provide the greatest incentives. First, employees respond to managerial praise. This can include formal recognition policies and events. For example, at Mars Central Europe, the company holds an event twice a year at which they celebrate innovative ideas generated by employees. Recognition at the Mars "Make a Difference" event is designed to motivate the winners and also other employees who want to receive the same recognition. Employees also respond well to informal recognition rewards, such as personal praise, written praise, and public praise. This is especially effective when it includes small perks, such as a gift certificate for dinner, some scheduling flexibility, or even an extra day off. Positive words and actions are especially powerful since almost two-thirds of employees in one study said management was much more likely to criticize them for poor performance than praise them for good work. Second, employees feel rewarded when they receive attention from leaders and, as a result, feel valued and involved. One survey found that the number-one factor employees valued was "managerial support and involvement"—having their managers ask for their opinions, involve them in decisions, and give them authority to complete tasks. Third, managers can reward employees by giving them opportunities to lead projects or task forces. In sum, incentives and rewards can go well beyond simple pay to include formal recognition and praise that enhance the self-esteem that comes from feeling valued.

Employees who are passionate about their jobs are more engaged in their jobs.[31] And employees who are more engaged in their jobs perform them better, according to new research. Employees who had job passion identified with their jobs intrinsically and believed their work was meaningful. Therefore, they were able to feel passionate about their jobs while balancing that passion with other aspects of their lives that were also important to them. This resulted in an intensity of focus on and deep immersion in their tasks while they were working. When they were deeply engrossed in work, the employees were not distracted by other activities or roles in their lives. In turn, this job absorption resulted in superior performance on the job.

While many managers attempt to tap into their employees' passions to motivate them to perform their jobs better, external incentives are not the best way to engender internal identification with work. Even positive feedback can become an external incentive if employees work toward receiving that recognition rather than working simply because they identify with and enjoy their jobs. A better way to nurture employees' identification with their work is to provide them with a sense of ownership over their work and, more importantly, to help them see how meaningful their jobs are. For example, to help their employees see the impact of their work on others, Cancer Treatment Centers of America in the Tulsa, Oklahoma, area recruits spouses of employees to form and run a nonprofit organization to raise money for cancer patients' nonmedical expenses.

Kevin Cleary, CEO of Clif Bar and Co., says success is contingent upon an "engaged, inspired and outrageously committed team." He breaks this down into these steps:

1. Engage your employees with the company's mission and vision. If you don't have a mission and vision statement, get employees' contributions to create one you believe in.
2. Once people understand the mission and vision, trust your employees to work. Do not micromanage or assume they need a held hand.
3. Have a business model in which people come first, second, and third.

Cleary says exceptional talent is valuable only when employees believe in the organization's mission.

Setting Boundaries and Constraints

In an ideal world, a strong culture and effective rewards should be sufficient to ensure that all individuals and subunits work toward the common goals and objectives of the whole organization.[32] However, this is not usually the case. Counterproductive behaviour can arise because of motivated self-interest, lack of a clear understanding of goals and objectives, or outright malfeasance. Boundaries and constraints can serve many useful purposes for organizations, including:

- focusing individual efforts on strategic priorities;
- providing short-term objectives and action plans to channel efforts;

- improving efficiency and effectiveness; and

- minimizing improper and unethical conduct.

Focusing Efforts on Strategic Priorities

Boundaries and constraints play a valuable role in focusing a company's strategic priorities. A well-known example of a strategic boundary is former CEO of General Electric, Jack Welch's, demand that any business in the corporate portfolio be ranked first or second in its industry. Similarly, Eli Lilly has reduced its research efforts to five broad areas of disease, down from eight or nine over a decade ago.[33] This concentration of effort and resources provides the firm with greater strategic focus and the potential for stronger competitive advantages in the remaining areas.

Norman Augustine, Lockheed Martin's former chairman, provided four criteria for selecting candidates for diversification into "closely related" businesses.[34] They must (1) be high tech, (2) be systems oriented, (3) deal with large customers (either corporations or government) as opposed to consumers, and (4) be in growth businesses. "We have found," Augustine explained, "that if we can meet most of those standards, then we can move into adjacent markets and grow."

Boundaries also have a place in the nonprofit sector. For example, a British relief organization uses a system to monitor strategic boundaries by maintaining a list of companies whose contributions it will neither solicit nor accept. Such boundaries are essential for maintaining legitimacy with existing and potential benefactors.

Providing Short-Term Objectives and Action Plans

In Chapter 1, we discussed the importance of a firm having a vision, a mission, and strategic objectives that are internally consistent and that provide strategic direction. Together, these elements set clear choices for all employees within the organization with respect to what is desirable, what the priorities are, and what the employees should strive for; they also define what is not a priority and what would not be in line with the organization's goals. Short-term objectives and action plans provide similar benefits. They represent boundaries that help to allocate resources in an optimal manner and to channel the efforts of employees at all levels throughout the organization.[35] To be effective, short-term objectives must have several attributes. They should

- be specific and measurable;

- include a specific time horizon for their attainment; and

- be achievable, yet challenging enough to motivate managers, who must strive to accomplish them.

Research has found that performance is enhanced when individuals are encouraged to attain specific, difficult, yet achievable, goals (as opposed to vague "do your best" goals).[36]

Short-term objectives must provide proper direction and also enough flexibility for the firm to keep pace with and anticipate changes in the external environment such as new government regulations, a competitor introducing a substitute product, or changes in consumer taste. Unexpected events within a firm may require a firm to make important adjustments in both strategic and short-term objectives. The emergence of new industries can have a drastic effect on the demand for products and services in more traditional industries.

Action plans are critical to the implementation of chosen strategies. Unless action plans are specific, there may be little assurance that managers have thought through all of the resource requirements for implementing their strategies. In addition, unless plans are specific, managers may not understand what needs to be implemented or have a clear time frame for completion. This is essential for the scheduling of key activities that must be implemented. Finally, individual managers must be held accountable for the implementation. This helps provide the necessary motivation and "sense of ownership" to implement action plans on a timely basis. Strategy Spotlight 10.3 illustrates how action plans fit into the mission statement and objectives of a small manufacturer of aircraft interior components.

10.3 STRATEGY SPOTLIGHT

Developing Meaningful Action Plans: ABC Aircraft Products, Inc.

ABC Aircraft Products, Inc., (not their real name) fulfils a small but highly profitable niche in the aviation industry with two key product lines. The first consists of patented, light-weight, self-contained window-shade assemblies. The second encompasses a range of interior cabin shells, which are state-of-the-art assemblies that include window panels, side panels, headliners, and suspension system structures. ABC's products have been installed on a variety of aircraft, such as the Gulfstream series, the Cessna Citation, and Boeing's 727, 737, 757, and 707.

Much of the firm's success can be attributed to carefully articulated action plans consistent with the firm's mission and objectives. During the past five years, ABC has increased its sales at an annual rate of 15 to 18 percent. It has also succeeded in adding many prestigious companies to its customer base. How do they do it? Besides having a great product range, ABC sports a clear mission statement, a series of well articulated objectives, as well as the action plans to achieve a 20-percent annual increase in sales.

Mission Statement

- Be recognized as an innovative and reliable supplier of quality interior products for the high-end, personalized transportation segments of the aviation, marine, and automotive industries.

- Design, develop, and manufacture interior fixtures and components that provide exceptional value to the customer through the development of innovative designs in a manner that permits decorative design flexibility while retaining the superior functionality, reliability, and maintainability of well-engineered, factory-produced products.

- Grow, be profitable, and provide a fair return, commensurate with the degree of risk, for owners and stockholders.

Objectives

1. Achieve sustained and profitable growth over the next three years:

    - 20-percent annual growth in revenues

    - 12-percent pretax profit margins

    - 18-percent return on shareholder's equity

2. Expand the company's revenues through the development and introduction of two or more new products capable of generating revenues in excess of $8 million a year within five years.

3. Continue to aggressively expand market opportunities and applications for the window-shade assemblies, with the objective of sustaining or exceeding a 20-percent annual growth rate for at least the next three years.

ABC's action plans are supported by detailed month-by-month budgets and strong financial incentives for its executives. Budgets are prepared by each department and include all revenue and cost items. Managers are motivated by their participation in a profit-sharing program, and the firm's two founders each receive a bonus equal to 3 percent of total sales. Exhibit 10-3 provides details of an action plan to fulfil one of the firm's objectives.

(Continued)

EXHIBIT 10-3   ACTION PLAN FOR OBJECTIVE 3

Description	Primary Responsibility	Target Date
1. Develop and implement current year marketing plan, including specific plans for addressing Falcon 20 retrofit programs and expanded sales of cabin shells.	R. H. Smith (V.P. Marketing)	December 15, 2018
2. Negotiate new supplier agreement with Gulfstream Aerospace.	M. Strong (President)	March 1, 2019
3. Continue and complete the development of the UltraSlim window and have a fully tested and documented design ready for production at a manufacturing cost of less than $900 per unit.	D. R. Perfect (V.P. Operations)	June 15, 2019
4. Develop a window design suitable for B-777 and similar wide-body aircraft and have a fully tested and documented design ready for production at a manufacturing cost comparable to the current Boeing window.	D. R. Perfect (V.P. Operations)	September 15, 2019

Sources: Internal company documents. For purposes of confidentiality, some of the information presented in this spotlight has been disguised. We would like to thank company management and external consultants for providing us with the information used in this application.

Improving Operational Efficiency and Effectiveness

Rule-based-controls are most appropriate in organizations with the following characteristics:

- Environments are stable and predictable.
- Employees are largely unskilled and interchangeable.
- Consistency in product and service is critical.
- The risk of malfeasance is extremely high (e.g., in banking or casino operations).[37]

McDonald's Corp. has extensive rules and regulations that regulate the operation of its franchises.[38] Its policy manual states, "Cooks must turn, never flip, hamburgers. If they haven't been purchased, Big Macs must be discarded in 10 minutes after being cooked and french fries in 7 minutes. Cashiers must make eye contact with and smile at every customer."

Guidelines can also be effective in setting spending limits and the range of discretion for employees and managers, such as the $2,500 limit that hotelier Ritz-Carlton uses to empower employees to placate dissatisfied customers. Regulations can also be initiated to improve an employee's use of their time at work.[39] Computer Associates restricts the use of email during the hours of 10 a.m. to noon and 2 p.m. to 4 p.m. each day.[40]

Minimizing Improper and Unethical Conduct

Guidelines can be useful in specifying proper relationships with a company's customers and suppliers.[41] Many companies have explicit rules regarding commercial practices, including the prohibition of any form of payment, bribe, or kickback. Cadbury Schweppes has followed a simple but effective step in controlling the use of bribes by specifying that all payments, no matter how unusual, are recorded on the company's books. Its former chairman, Sir Adrian Cadbury, contended that such a practice causes managers to pause and consider whether a payment is simply a bribe or a necessary and standard cost of doing business.[42]

Behavioural Control in Organizations: Situational Factors

Controls, especially behavioural controls, are put in place to ensure that the behaviour of individuals at all levels of an organization is directed toward achieving organizational goals and objectives. As we saw, there are three fundamental types of controls: (1) culture, (2) rewards and incentives, and (3) rules defining boundaries and constraints. An organization may pursue one or a combination of them on the basis of a variety of internal and external factors.

Not all organizations place the same emphasis on each type of control.[43] In high-tech firms engaged in basic research, members may work under high levels of autonomy. An individual's performance is generally quite difficult to measure accurately because of the long lead times involved in R&D activities. Thus, internalized norms and values become very important.

When the measurement of an individual's output or performance is quite straightforward, control depends primarily on granting or withholding rewards. Frequently, a sales manager's compensation is in the form of commission and bonus tied directly to his or her sales volume, which is relatively easy to determine. Here, behaviour is influenced more strongly by the attractiveness of the compensation than by the norms and values implicit in the organization's culture. The measurability of output precludes the need for an elaborate system of rules to control behaviour.

Control in bureaucratic organizations is dependent on members following a highly formalized set of rules and regulations. Most activities are routine and the desired behaviour can be specified in a detailed manner because there is generally little need for innovative or creative activity. Managing an assembly plant requires strict adherence to many rules as well as exacting sequences of assembly operations. In the public sector, provincial ministries of transportation must follow clearly prescribed procedures when issuing or renewing driver's licences.

Exhibit 10-4 lists alternative approaches to behavioural control and some of the situational factors associated with them.

EXHIBIT 10-4   ORGANIZATIONAL CONTROL: ALTERNATIVE APPROACHES

Approach	Some Situational Factors
Rules: Written and explicit guidelines that provide external constraints on behaviour.	• Associated with standardized output. • Tasks are generally repetitive and routine. • Little need for innovation or creative activity.
Rewards: The use of performance-based incentive systems to motivate.	• Measurement of output and performance is rather straightforward. • Most appropriate in organizations pursuing unrelated diversification strategies. • Rewards may be used to reinforce other means of control.
Culture: A system of unwritten rules that forms an internalized influence over behaviour.	• Often found in professional organizations. • Associated with high autonomy. • Norms are the basis for behaviour.

Evolving from Boundaries to Rewards and Culture

In most environments, organizations should strive to provide a system of rewards and incentives, coupled with a culture strong enough that boundaries become internalized. This reduces the need for external controls, such as rules and regulations.

First, the right people—individuals who already identify with the organization's dominant values and have attributes consistent with them—should be hired. Microsoft's David Pritchard is well aware of the consequences of failing to hire properly.

> If I hire a bunch of bozos, it will hurt us, because it takes time to get rid of them. They start infiltrating the organization and then they themselves start hiring people of lower quality. At Microsoft, we are always looking for people who are better than we are.[44]

Second, training plays a key role. For example, in elite military units, such as the Green Berets and Navy SEALs, the training regimen so thoroughly internalizes the culture that individuals, in effect, lose their identity. The group becomes the overriding concern and focal point of their energies. In some firms, such as FedEx, training not only builds skills but also plays a significant role in building a strong culture on the foundation of each organization's dominant values.

Third, managerial role models are vital. Andy Grove, former CEO and co-founder of Intel, did not need (or want) a large number of bureaucratic rules to determine who was responsible for what, who was supposed to talk to whom, and who got to fly first class (no one did). He encouraged openness by not having many of the trappings of success—he worked in a cubicle like all the other professionals in the company. Can you imagine any new manager asking whether or not they could fly first class? Grove's personal example eliminated such a need.

Fourth, reward systems must be clearly aligned with the organizational goals and objectives. Where do you think rules and regulations are more important in controlling behaviour—Home Depot, with its generous bonus and stock option plans, or Walmart, which does not provide the same level of rewards and incentives?

Linking Strategic Control to Business-Level and Corporate-Level Strategies

There is no "one best way" to design strategic control systems for an organization. Effective controls are contingent on many factors and are related to the choices made by the organization regarding its business-level and corporate-level strategies. For example, firms competing on the basis of overall cost leadership must implement tight cost controls, frequent and comprehensive reports to monitor the costs associated with outputs, and highly structured tasks and responsibilities. Not surprisingly, incentives tend to be based on explicit financial targets, since innovation and creativity are expensive and might tend to erode competitive advantages. However, firms pursuing a differentiation strategy would typically want to encourage the development of innovative products and services, requiring the employment of experts who can identify the crucial elements of intricate, creative designs and formulate innovative marketing decisions.

Given the need for co-operation and coordination among professionals in many functional areas, it becomes important to be able to measure and assess such activity. Yet it is difficult to measure such efforts on an individual basis or to attribute outcomes to specific individuals. Thus, more behavioural measures (such as how effectively employees collaborate and share information) become necessary, as well as intangible incentives and rewards that aim to support a strong culture of collaboration.

In appreciating the relationship between strategy and evaluation and control systems, a key issue that becomes apparent is the need to foster independence versus interdependence. In the cases of cost leadership strategies or unrelated diversification, there tends to be less need for interdependence. Thus, the reward and control systems focus more on the use of financial indicators because unit costs, profits, and revenues can be rather easily attributed to a given business unit or division.

In contrast, firms that follow differentiation or related diversification strategies have intense needs for tight interdependencies among the functional areas and business units within the corporation. In these firms, the sharing of resources, including raw materials, R&D knowledge, marketing information, and so on, is critical to organizational success. In other words, achieving synergies across value-creating activities and business units is more important than with cost leadership or unrelated strategies. To facilitate sharing and collaboration, reward and control systems tend to incorporate more behavioural indicators.

Finally, we must include an important caveat. In actual practice, organizations have combinations of financial and behavioural control systems. In fact, in both overall cost leadership and unrelated diversification strategies, there is a need for collaboration and the sharing of best practices across value-creating activities and business units. GE, for example, has developed many integrating mechanisms to enhance the sharing of "best practices" across what would appear to be rather unrelated businesses, such as jet engines, appliances, and network television. And, for both differentiation and related diversification strategies, financial indicators, such as revenue growth and profitability, should not be overlooked at either the business-unit or corporate level.

THE ROLE OF CORPORATE GOVERNANCE

Thus far, we have addressed how managers can exercise strategic control over the firm's overall operations through the use of informational and behavioural controls. But who should exercise control over management? The issue of strategic control in a broader perspective, typically referred to as corporate governance, addresses the need for both shareholders (the owners of the corporation) and their elected representatives, the board of directors, to actively ensure that management fulfils its overriding purpose of increasing long-term shareholder value.[45]

LO 4

Robert Monks and Nell Minow, two leading scholars in corporate governance, define it as "the relationship among various participants in determining the direction and performance of corporations. The primary participants are (1) the shareholders, (2) management (led by the CEO), and (3) the board of directors." Our discussion will centre on how corporations can succeed (or fail) in aligning managerial motives with the interests of the shareholders and their elected representatives, the board of directors.[46] In Chapter 1, we discussed the important role of boards of directors and provided some examples of effective and ineffective boards.[47]

Good corporate governance plays an important role in the investment decisions of major institutions, and a premium is often reflected in the price of securities of companies that practise it. The corporate governance premium is larger for firms in countries with sound corporate governance practices compared with countries with weaker corporate governance standards.[48] There is a strong correlation between strong corporate governance and superior financial performance.

At the same time, few topics in the business press generate as much interest and disdain as does corporate governance. Some notable examples of flawed corporate governance from the last decade include the following:[49]

- In 2014, three senior executives at Walmart resigned from the firm in the wake of accusations of bribery of government officials in Mexico. As soon as evidence started mounting about the impropriety, Walmart recognized the governance lapses in its regional organization and changed both the local leadership and its compliance structure.

- In 2012 Japanese camera and medical equipment maker Olympus Corporation and three of its former executives pleaded guilty to charges that they falsified accounting records over a five-year period to inflate the financial performance of the firm. The total value of the accounting irregularities came to $1.7 billion.

- In October 2010, Angelo Mozilo, the co-founder of Countrywide Financial, agreed to pay $67.5 million to the Securities and Exchange Commission (SEC) to settle fraud charges. He was charged with deceiving the home loan company's investors while reaping a personal windfall. He was accused of hiding risks about Countrywide's loan portfolio as the real estate market soured. Former Countrywide president David Sambol and former chief financial officer Eric Sieracki were also charged with fraud, as they failed to disclose the true state of Countrywide's deteriorating mortgage portfolio. The SEC accused Mozilo of insider trading, alleging that he sold millions of dollars worth of Countrywide stock after he knew the company was doomed.

- Satyam Computer Services, a leading Indian outsourcing company that serves more than a third of Fortune 500 companies, significantly inflated its earnings and assets for years. The chairman, Ramalinga Raju, resigned after admitting he had cooked the books. Mr. Raju said he had overstated cash on hand by $1 billion and inflated profits and revenues in the September 2008 quarter. Satyam shares sank by 78 percent, and the benchmark Sensex index lost 7.3 percent on the day of his admission (January 7, 2009).

- Former Brocade CEO Gregory Reyes was sentenced to 21 months in prison and fined $15 million for his involvement in backdating stock option grants. Mr. Reyes was the first executive to go on trial and be convicted over the improper dating of stock option awards, a practice which dozens of companies subsequently acknowledged they had engaged in to store up their executives' compensation packages when their stock performance did not improve as had been anticipated.

- Hewlett-Packard admitted that outside investigators, led by chairman Patricia Dunn, used a potentially illegal tactic to investigate board-level leaks in which they impersonated directors, journalists, and two employees to obtain personal phone records of HP board members and reporters who covered HP. Dunn subsequently resigned (September 12, 2006).

- Walter Forbes, former chairman of Cendant Corp. (now known as Avis Budget Group, Inc.), was sentenced to 12 years in prison and ordered to pay $3.3 billion in one of America's biggest accounting scandals. Forbes oversaw a decade-long accounting scheme that overstated income. He was convicted on one count of conspiracy and two counts of false reporting (January 17, 2006).

Because of the many lapses in corporate governance, we can see the benefits associated with effective practices.[50] Corporate managers may behave in their own self-interest, often to the detriment of shareholders. Next, we address the implications of the separation of ownership and management in the modern corporation, and some mechanisms that can be used to ensure consistency (or alignment) between the interests of shareholders and those of the managers to minimize potential conflicts.

The Modern Corporation: The Separation of Owners (Shareholders) and Management

Some of the proposed definitions for a *corporation* include the following:

- "The business corporation is an instrument through which capital is assembled for the activities of producing and distributing goods and services and making investments. Accordingly, a basic premise of corporation law is that a business corporation should have as its objective the conduct of such activities with a view to enhancing the corporation's profit and the gains of the corporation's owners, that is, the shareholders." (Melvin Aron Eisenberg, *The Structure of Corporation Law*)

- "A body of persons granted a charter legally recognizing them as a separate entity having its own rights, privileges, and liabilities distinct from those of its members." (*American Heritage Dictionary*)

Each of these definitions has some validity and each one reflects a key feature of the corporate form of business organization—its ability to draw resources from a variety of groups and establish and maintain its own persona that is separate from all of them.[51] As Henry Ford once said, "A great business is really too big to be human."

Simply put, a *corporation* is a mechanism created to allow different parties to contribute capital, expertise, and labour for the maximum benefit of each party.[52] The shareholders (investors) are able to participate in the profits of the enterprise without taking direct responsibility for the operations. The management can run the company without the responsibility of personally providing the funds. The shareholders have limited liability as well as rather limited involvement in the company's affairs. However, they reserve the right to elect directors who have the fiduciary obligation to protect their interests.

Over 70 years ago, Columbia University professors Adolf Berle and Gardiner C. Means addressed the divergence of the interests of the owners of the corporation from the professional managers who are hired to run it. They warned that widely dispersed ownership "released management from the overriding requirement that it serve stockholders." The separation of ownership from management has given rise to a set of ideas called "agency theory." Central to agency theory is the relationship between two primary players—the *principals,* who are the owners of the firm (shareholders), and the *agents,* who are the people paid by principals to perform a job on their behalf (management). The shareholders elect and are represented by a board of directors that has a fiduciary responsibility to ensure that management acts in the best interests of shareholders to ensure long-term financial returns for the firm.

Agency theory is concerned with resolving two problems that can occur in agency relationships.[53] The first is the agency problem that arises (1) when the goals of the principals and agents conflict and (2) when it is difficult or expensive for the principal to verify what the agent is actually doing. The board of directors, for example, may be unable to confirm that the managers are actually acting in the shareholders' interests because managers are "insiders" with regard to the businesses they operate and thus are better informed than the principals. Thus, managers may act "opportunistically" in pursuing their own interests—to the detriment of the corporation.[54] Managers may spend corporate funds on expensive perquisites (e.g., company jets and expensive art), devote time and resources to pet projects (initiatives in which they have a personal interest but that have limited market potential), engage in power struggles (where they may fight over resources for their own betterment and to the detriment of the firm), and negate (or sabotage) attractive merger offers because they may result in increased employment risk.[55]

The second issue is the problem of risk sharing. This arises when the principal and the agent have different attitudes and preferences toward risk. The executives in a firm may favour additional diversification initiatives because, by their very nature, they increase the size of the firm and thus the level of executive compensation.[56] At the same time, such diversification initiatives may erode shareholder value because they fail to achieve some of the synergies that we discussed in Chapter 6 (e.g., building on core competencies, sharing activities, or enhancing market power). Agents (executives) may have a stronger preference toward diversification than shareholders because it reduces their personal level of risk from potential loss of employment. Interestingly, executives who have large holdings of shares in their firms were more likely to have diversification strategies that were more consistent with shareholder interests—increasing long-term returns.[57] At times, top-level managers engage in actions that reflect their self-interest rather than the interests of shareholders.

LO 5   Governance Mechanisms: Aligning the Interests of Owners and Managers

As noted above, a key characteristic of the modern corporation is the separation of ownership from control. To minimize the potential for managers to act in their own self-interest, or opportunistically, the owners can implement some governance mechanisms.[58] First, there are two primary means of monitoring the behaviour of managers. These include (1) a committed and involved *board of directors* that acts in the best interests of the shareholders to create long-term value and (2) *shareholder activism* wherein the owners view themselves as share*owners* instead of share*holders* and become actively engaged in the governance of the corporation. Finally, there are managerial incentives, sometimes called "contract-based outcomes," which consist of *reward and compensation agreements.* Here, the goal is to carefully craft managerial incentive packages to align the interests of management with those of the shareholders.[59]

A Committed and Involved Board of Directors

The *board of directors* acts as a fulcrum between the owners and controllers of a corporation. They are the intermediaries who provide a balance between a small group of key managers in the firm based at the corporate headquarters and a sometimes vast group of shareholders. In the United States, the law imposes on the board a strict and absolute fiduciary duty to ensure that a company is run consistent with the long-term interests of the owners—the shareholders. The reality, as we have seen, is somewhat more ambiguous.[60]

The Business Roundtable, a group representing large public corporations, describes the duties of the board as follows:

1. Select, regularly evaluate, and, if necessary, replace the CEO. Determine management compensation. Review succession planning.

2. Review and, where appropriate, approve the financial objectives, major strategies, and plans of the corporation.

3. Provide advice and counsel to top management.

4. Select and recommend to shareholders for election an appropriate slate of candidates for the board of directors; evaluate board processes and performance.

5. Review the adequacy of the systems to comply with all applicable laws and regulations.[61]

Given these principles, what makes for a good board of directors?[62] According to the Business Roundtable, the most important quality is a board of directors who are active, critical participants in determining a company's strategies.[63] That does not mean board members should micromanage or circumvent the CEO. Rather, they should provide strong oversight going beyond simply approving the CEO's plans. A board's primary responsibilities are to ensure that strategic plans undergo rigorous scrutiny, to evaluate managers against high performance standards, and to take control of the succession process.

Although boards in the past were often dismissed as a CEO's rubber stamp, increasingly they are playing a more active role by forcing out CEOs who cannot deliver on performance.[64] According to the consulting firm Booz Allen Hamilton, the rate of CEO departures for performance reasons more than tripled, from 1.3 percent to 4.2 percent, between 1995 and 2002.[65] In 2006, turnover among CEOs had increased 30 percent over the previous year.[66] Well-known CEOs, such as Gerald M. Levin of AOL Time Warner and Jack M. Greenberg of McDonald's, paid the price for poor financial performance by being forced to leave. Others, such as Bernard Ebbers of World-Com, Inc. and Dennis Kozlowski of Tyco International, lost their jobs because of scandals. More recently, Uber's founder and CEO was ousted by the board, as were Roger Ailes of Fox News, Richard Anderson of Delta Airlines, and Mike Pearson of Valeant.

Another key component of top-ranked boards is director independence.[67] Governance experts believe that a majority of directors should be free of all ties to the CEO or to the company.[68] That means minimizing the number of "insiders" (past or present members of the management team) that serve on the board, and that directors and their firms should be barred from doing consulting, legal, or other work for the company.[69] Interlocking directorships—in which CEOs and other top managers serve on each other's boards—are not desirable. But perhaps the best guarantee that directors act in the best interests of shareholders is the simplest: Most good companies now insist that directors own significant amounts of shares in the company they oversee.[70]

Such guidelines are not always followed. At times, the practices of boards of directors are the antithesis of such guidelines. Take, for example, the Walt Disney Co. Over a five-year period, former CEO Michael Eisner pocketed an astonishing $531 million. He likely had very little resistance from his board of directors:

> Many investors view the Disney board as an anachronism. Among Disney's 16 directors is Eisner's personal attorney—who for several years was chairman of the company's compensation committee! There was also the architect who designed Eisner's Aspen home and his parents' apartment. Joining them are the principal of an elementary school once attended by his children and the president of a university to which Eisner donated $1 million. The board also includes actor Sidney Poitier, seven current and former Disney executives, and an attorney who does business with Disney. Moreover, most of the outside directors own little or no Disney stock. "It is an egregiously bad board—a train wreck waiting to happen," warns Michael L. Useem, a management professor at the University of Pennsylvania's Wharton School.[71]

This example also shows that "outside directors" are only beneficial to strong corporate governance if they are vigilant in carrying out their responsibilities.[72] As humorously suggested by Warren Buffett, founder and chairman of Berkshire Hathaway: "The ratcheting up of compensation has been obscene. . . . There is a tendency to put cocker spaniels on compensation committees, not Doberman pinschers."[73]

Many firms do have exemplary board practices. Below we list some of the excellent practices at Intel Corp., the world's largest semiconductor chip manufacturer, with $59 billion in revenues:[74]

- *Mix of inside and outside directors.* The board believes that there should be a majority of independent directors on the board. However, the board is willing to have members of management, in addition to the CEO, as directors.

- *Board presentations and access to employees.* The board encourages management to schedule attendance and presentations by managers who (1) can provide additional insight into the items being discussed because of personal involvement in these areas, or (2) have future potential that management believes should be given exposure to the board.

- *Formal evaluation of officers.* The Compensation Committee conducts, and reviews with the outside directors, an annual evaluation to help determine the salary and executive bonus of all officers, including the CEO.

Exhibit 10-5 shows how boards of directors can improve their practices. Strategy Spotlight 10.4 addresses some of the excellent practices at Manulife Financial Corporation, Canada's largest insurance company. In general, Canadian public firms have been urged to split the roles of CEO and chairperson of the board. By 2009, 79 percent of S&P (Standard & Poor) and TSX (Toronto Stock Exchange) index corporations had already followed suit, a much higher percentage than their U.S. counterparts, even though many of Canada's public companies are still dominated by families and have dual-class share structures.

EXHIBIT 10-5   BEST PRACTICE IDEAS: THE NEW RULES FOR DIRECTORS

Issue	Suggestion
Pay	**Know the Math**
Companies will disclose full details of CEO payouts. Activist investors are already drawing up hit lists of companies where CEO paycheques are out of line with performance.	Before approving any financial package, directors must make sure they can explain the numbers. They need to adopt the mindset of an activist investor and ask: What is the harshest criticism someone could make about this package?
Strategy	**Make It a Priority**
Boards have been so focused on compliance that duties like strategy and leadership oversight too often get ignored. Just over half the directors give their own boards high marks for their work in setting strategy.	To avoid spending too much time on compliance issues, move strategy up to the beginning of the meeting. Annual one-, two- or three-day offsite meetings on strategy alone are becoming standard for good boards.
Financials	**Put in the Time**
Although 95 percent of directors had said they were doing a good job of monitoring financials, the number of earnings restatements hit a new high in 2006, after breaking records in 2004 and 2005.	Even non-financial board members need to monitor the numbers and keep a close eye on cash flows. Audit committee members should prepare to spend 300 hours a year on committee responsibilities.
Crisis Management	**Dig in**
Some 120 companies are under scrutiny for options backdating, and the 100 largest companies have replaced 56 CEOs in the past five years—nearly double the terminations in the prior five years.	The increased scrutiny on boards means that a perfunctory review will not suffice if a scandal strikes. Directors can no longer afford to defer to management in a crisis. They must roll up their sleeves and move into watchdog mode.

Source: N. Byrnes and J. Sassen, "Board of Hard Knocks," *BusinessWeek,* January 22, 2007, pp. 36–39.

Shareholder Activism

As a practical matter, there are so many owners of the largest public corporations that it makes little sense to refer to them as "owners" in the sense of individuals becoming informed and involved in corporate affairs.[75] Nonetheless, every individual shareholder has several rights, including (1) the right to sell the shares, (2) the right to vote the proxy (which includes the election of board members), (3) the right to bring suit for damages if the corporation's directors or managers fail to meet their obligations, (4) the right to certain information from the company, and (5) certain residual rights following the company's liquidation (or its filing for reorganization under bankruptcy laws), once creditors and other claimants are paid off.[76]

Collectively, shareholders have the power to direct the course of corporations.[77] This may involve acts such as being party to shareholder action suits and demanding that key issues be brought up for proxy votes at annual board meetings.[78] The power of shareholders has intensified in recent years because of the increasing influence of large institutional investors, such as mutual funds (e.g., Appraisal Institute of Canada (AIC), Canadian Investments (CI), Fidelity Investments, Investors Group, and MacKenzie) and retirement systems (e.g., the OTPP and the Ontario Municipal Employees Retirement System (OMERS)).[79] Institutional investors hold over 50 percent of all listed corporate shares in Canada.

10.4 STRATEGY SPOTLIGHT

Manulife Financial Corporation: An Exemplary Governance Structure

One of the best examples of governance guidelines is that of Manulife Financial. The country's largest insurance company's practices address some of the most important issues in governance, such as director independence, meetings of outside directors, evaluation and compensation of directors and executives, auditing, and succession planning. The guidelines are posted on the company's website for everyone to see and represent another example of the board's commitment to communicate with shareholders in a timely, accurate, and straightforward fashion. Below are a few highlights:

Board Composition

- The board's independence is fundamental to its stewardship role and its effectiveness.

- All but one member (the current CEO) of the board are unrelated and independent.

- All committees of the board are composed solely of unrelated and independent directors.

- The positions of chair and CEO are separate. The chair must be an unrelated and independent director.

Compensation

- The board, with the assistance of independent external advisors, undertakes a biennial review of directors' compensations.

- Directors are required to hold an equity position having a minimum value of $300,000 in the company.

- A Compensation Committee, established by the board and consisting of unrelated and independent directors, oversees the company's global human resource strategy, approves appointments of senior management, and provides proper development, review, and compensation of all senior management. It also approves the annual performance assessment and compensation of senior executives.

Board Meetings

- Each meeting of the board and of its committees is followed by an "in camera" meeting that excludes all members of management.

- Individual shareholders can directly contact both non-management directors and the chair.

- The board and its committees may retain any outside advisors at the company's expense. Individual directors may also retain outside advisors at the company's expense to provide independent advice on any matter before the board or a board committee.

Business Conduct

- A Code of Business Conduct and Ethics, established by the board, provides a set of guidelines for all employees, executives (including the CEO), and all members of the board of directors; they periodically sign an acknowledgement confirming their commitment to the Code.

- The CEO and the chief financial officer (CFO) sign and certify the annual and quarterly financial statements.

- An Ethics Committee, established by the board and consisting exclusively of unrelated and independent directors, oversees such items as conflicts of interest, related party transactions, and confidential information. The Committee also reviews the company's compliance with legal requirements.

Sources: J. McFarland, and E. Church, "Do Better Boards Make Better Companies?," *The Globe and Mail*, October 24, 2006, p. B1; www.manulife.com; MFC Proxy Circular 2005.

Many institutional investors are aggressive in protecting and enhancing their investments. They are shifting from traders to owners, assuming the role of permanent shareholders and rigorously analyzing issues of corporate governance. In the process, they are reinventing systems of corporate monitoring and accountability.[80]

Consider the proactive behaviour of the OTPP, which manages approximately $85 billion in assets and is the largest pension fund in Canada and one of the largest in the world. Every year, the OTPP reviews the performance of all companies in its stock portfolio and identifies those that are among the lowest long-term relative performers and whose governance structures do not ensure full accountability to company owners. The OTPP meets with the directors and management to discuss performance and suggest specific governance reforms. It also follows a set of guidelines on all corporate governance issues and has frequently voted down items on shareholder annual meeting agendas or withheld its support for individual board members as well as entire boards of directors that do not conduct their affairs according to those guidelines. On its website, the OTPP lists and explains its voting decisions—on the principles of transparency and accountability—to the plan's beneficiaries, whom it sees as the ultimate owners of those public corporations.

Managerial Rewards and Incentives

Incentive systems must be designed to help a company achieve its goals.[81] From the perspective of governance, one of the most critical roles of the board of directors is to create incentives that align the interests of the CEO and top executives with the interests of owners of the corporation—long-term shareholder returns.[82] Shareholders rely on CEOs to adopt policies and strategies that maximize the value of their shares.[83] A combination of three basic policies may create the right monetary incentives for CEOs to maximize the value of their companies:[84]

1. Boards can require that the CEOs become substantial owners of company shares.
2. Salaries, bonuses, and stock options can be structured so as to provide rewards for superior performance and penalties for poor performance.
3. Threat of dismissal for poor performance can be a realistic outcome.

In recent years, the granting of stock options has enabled top executives of publicly held corporations to earn enormous levels of compensation. A 2015 report pegged the top Canadian CEOs' salaries at 159 times that of the average worker.[85] Over the past decade, the wages of rank-and-file workers increased only 30 percent, whereas the pay of CEOs climbed 300 percent. The numbers are even more staggering in the United States, where the average CEO earns 433 times the pay of the average worker.[86] The lion's share of such increases came from exercising options. Stock options can be a valuable governance mechanism to align the CEO's interests with those of the shareholders, and the extraordinarily high level of compensation can often be grounded in sound governance principles.

However, the "pay for performance" principle does not always hold. Consider, for example, that CoolBrands International's shares lost more than three-quarters of their value between 2004 and 2005—largely because of the loss of the contract to produce and sell Smart Ones, a frozen dessert, for the Weight Watchers brand name. At the same time, company president David Stein received a salary of $645,183 and exercised stock options worth $10.6 million, and the now-deceased Richard Smith received a salary of $1,711,710 and $8.3 million in stock options. Over the next two years, CoolBrands sold off many of its remaining assets to cover debts and other obligations. From its position as the third-largest ice cream maker in North America, it was left with a small processing facility in Arkansas employing less than 40 people. In 2008, CoolBrands was asked to de-list its stock from the TSX for dropping below one dollar in value for an extended period; just a few short years earlier, the shares were at an all-time high of over $25.

Many boards have awarded huge option grants despite poor executive performance, and others have made performance goals easier to reach. In 2002, nearly 200 companies in the United States swapped or re-priced their options—all to enrich wealthy executives who were already among the country's richest people.[87] In addition to the granting of stock options, boards of directors are often failing to fulfil their fiduciary responsibilities to shareholders when they lower the performance targets that executives need to meet to receive millions of dollars. TIAA-CREF (Teachers Insurance and Annuity Association – College Retirement Equities Fund) has provided several principles of corporate governance with regard to executive compensation.[88] As Exhibit 10-6 shows, these principles include the importance of aligning the rewards of all employees—rank-and-file as well as executives—to the long-term performance of the corporation; general guidelines on the role of cash compensation, shares, and "fringe benefits"; and the mission of a corporation's compensation committee.[89]

FIGURE 10-6

TIAA-CREF'S PRINCIPLES ON THE ROLE OF STOCK IN EXECUTIVE COMPENSATION

Stock-based compensation plans are a critical element of most compensation programs and can provide opportunities for managers whose efforts contribute to the creation of shareholder wealth. In evaluating the suitability of these plans, consideration of reasonableness, scale, linkage to performance, and fairness to shareholders and all employees also apply. TIAA-CREF, the largest pension system in the world, has set forth guidelines for proper stock-based compensation. The plans should display the following characteristics:

- Allow for creation of executive wealth that is reasonable in view of the creation of shareholder wealth. Management should not prosper through stock, while shareholders suffer.

- Have measurable and predictable outcomes that are directly linked to the company's performance.

- Be market oriented, within levels of comparability for similar positions in companies of similar size and business focus.

- Be straightforward and clearly described so that investors and employees can understand them.

- Be fully disclosed to the investing public and be approved by shareholders.

Source: Teachers Insurance and Annuity Association College Retirement Equities Fund. www.tiaa-cref.org/pubs.

CEO Duality: Is It Good or Bad?

CEO duality is one of the most controversial issues in corporate governance. It refers to the dual leadership structure where the CEO acts simultaneously as the chair of the board of directors.[90] Scholars, consultants, and executives who are interested in determining the best way to manage a corporation are divided on the issue of the roles and responsibilities of a CEO. Two schools of thought represent the alternative positions.

Unity of Command

Advocates of the unity of command perspective believe that when one person holds both roles, he or she is able to act more efficiently and effectively. CEO duality provides firms with a clear focus on both objectives and operations and eliminates confusion and conflict between the CEO and the chairperson. Thus, it enables smoother, more effective strategic decision making. Holding dual roles as CEO/chairperson creates unity across a company's managers and board of directors and ultimately allows the CEO to serve the shareholders even better. Having leadership focused in a single individual also enhances a firm's responsiveness and ability to secure critical resources. This perspective maintains that separating the two jobs—that of a CEO and that of the chairperson of the board of directors—may produce all types of undesirable consequences. CEOs may find it harder to make quick decisions. Ego-driven chief executives and chairpersons may squabble over who is ultimately in charge. The shortage of first-class business talent may mean that bosses find themselves second-guessed by people who know little about the business.

Agency Theory

Supporters of agency theory argue that the positions of CEO and chairperson should be separate. The case for separation is based on the simple principle of the separation of power. How can boards discharge their basic duty—monitoring the boss—if the boss is chairing its meetings and setting its agenda? How can a board act as a safeguard against corruption or incompetence when the possible source of that corruption and incompetence is sitting at the head of the table? CEO duality can create a conflict of interest that could negatively affect the interests of the shareholders.

Duality also complicates the issue of CEO succession. In some cases, a CEO/chairperson may choose to retire as CEO but keep his or her role as the chairperson. Although this splits up the roles, which appeases an agency perspective, it nonetheless puts the new CEO in a difficult position. The chairperson is bound to question some of the new changes put in place, and the board as a whole might take sides with the chairperson they trust and with whom they have a history. This conflict of interest would make it difficult for the new CEO to institute any changes, as the power and influence would still remain with the former CEO.[91]

Duality also serves to reinforce popular doubts about the legitimacy of the system as a whole and evokes images of bosses writing their own performance reviews and setting their own salaries. One of the first things that some of America's troubled banks, including Citigroup, Washington Mutual, Wachovia, and Wells Fargo, did when the financial crisis hit in 2007–2008 was to separate the two jobs. Firms like Siebel Systems, Disney, Oracle, and Microsoft have also decided to divide the roles between CEO and the chairperson and eliminate duality.

The increasing pressures for effective corporate governance have led to a sharp decline in duality. Firms now routinely separate the jobs of chairperson and chief executive. For example, in 2009, fewer than 12 percent of incoming CEOs were also made chairperson—compared with 48 percent in 2002.

These same pressures have led to other changes in corporate governance practices. For example, the New York Stock Exchange and NASDAQ have demanded that companies should have a majority of independent directors. Also, CEOs are held accountable for their performance and tossed out if they fail to perform, with the average length of tenure dropping from 8.1 years in 2000 to 6.3 years in 2009. Finally, more than 90 percent of S&P 500 companies with CEOs who also serve as chairperson of the board have appointed "lead" or "presiding" directors to act as a counterweight to a combined chairperson and chief executive.

The Role of the Board in Supporting an Ethical and Socially Responsible Orientation

Research has shown that managers are likely to turn to their firm's board of directors for strategic guidance during a period of crisis. But more important is the question of how corporate governance practices can prevent an organization from reaching the point of crisis in the first place? The authors of this text, David Weitzner and Theo Peridis, argue that corporate boards of directors need to place stronger emphasis on the ethical oversight of managerial decisions.[92] For a firm to be successful, a robust consideration of the potential for ethical harms and benefits to emerge from the value-creating activities of the firm must be fully integrated into corporate strategy. It cannot be viewed as an extraneous activity unconnected to the rigours of strategic planning and management. And it is the board of directors that are in the best position to set the strategic tone for the company due to their ultimate control of the incentive systems and resource-allocation processes that are most likely to shape the behaviour of the organization's actors.

Weitzner and Peridis discuss how different short- and long-term orientations, asymmetric assessments of both the benefits and harms that may potentially arise from different value-creating activities, and the divergence of personal, corporate, and social consequences have resulted in varying and limited degrees of managerial willingness to submit to meaningful board-led ethical oversight. What this means in practice is that boards of directors need to be more keenly aware of the potential social harms behind the value-creating activities of the firm—harms that for a variety of reasons managers tend to overlook. In this sense, it is incumbent on board members to become more active in exercising strategic control early in the value-creation process.

Managers tend to exhibit asymmetric perceptions of gains versus losses—they tend to focus on the potential returns of their activities and underestimate the risks. They are especially unlikely to take into account in their strategic calculations the full array of social and ethical risks behind the innovating activities of the firm. As such, when there is a high potential for significant social harm, corporate governance needs to be aggressively incorporated into the strategy-making process. This is illustrated in Exhibit 10-7. Boards must be vigilant in understanding the firm's value proposition and assessing the social risks and the orientation of management in the name of good corporate governance and to ensure the economic health of our society.

EXHIBIT 10-7

ASSESSMENT OF A FIRM'S VALUE PROPOSITION TO DETERMINE LEVEL OF BOARD INTERVENTION

Value Proposition	High-Potential Social Benefit	Low-Potential Social Benefit
High-Potential Social Harm	Strong need for strategic control or board most likely to encounter resistance	Need for strategic control to support compliance-based approach to ethics
Low-Potential Social Harm	Optimal alignment of interests or least need of board intervention	Financial control should be adequate governance

Source: With kind permission from Springer Science+Business Media: Weitzner, D. & Peridis, T. 2011. Corporate Governance as Part of the Strategic Process: Rethinking the Role of the Board. Journal of Business Ethics, 102: 33–42.

External Governance Control Mechanisms

Thus far, we have discussed internal governance mechanisms. Internal controls, however, are not always enough to ensure good governance. The separation of ownership and control that we discussed earlier requires multiple control mechanisms, some internal and some external, to ensure that managerial actions lead to shareholder value maximization. Further, society-at-large wants some assurance that this goal is met without harming other stakeholder groups. Now, we discuss several *external governance control mechanisms* that have developed in most modern economies. These include the market for corporate control, auditors, governmental regulatory bodies, banks and analysts, media, and public activists.

The Market for Corporate Control

Let us assume for a moment that internal control mechanisms in a company are failing. This means that the board is ineffective in monitoring managers and is not exercising the oversight required of them and that shareholders are passive and are not taking any actions to monitor or discipline managers. Under these circumstances managers may behave opportunistically.[93] Opportunistic behaviour can take many forms. First, managers can *shirk* their responsibilities. Shirking means that managers fail to exert themselves fully, as is required of them. Second, they can engage in *on-the-job consumption*. Examples of on-the-job consumption include private jets, club memberships, expensive artwork in the offices, and so on. Each of these represents consumption by managers that does not in any way increase shareholder value. Instead, they actually diminish shareholder value. Third, managers may engage in *excessive product–market diversification.*[94] As we discussed in Chapter 6, such diversification serves to reduce only the employment risk of the managers rather than the financial risk of the shareholders, who can more cheaply diversify their risk by owning a portfolio of investments. Is there any external mechanism to stop managers from shirking, consumption on the job, and excessive diversification?

The *market for corporate control* is one external mechanism that provides at least some partial solution to the problems described. If internal control mechanisms fail and the management is behaving opportunistically, the likely response of most shareholders will be to sell their shares rather than engage in activism.[95] As more shareholders vote with their feet, the value of the shares begins to decline. As the decline continues, at some point, the market value of the firm becomes less than the book value. A corporate raider can take over the company for a price less than the book value of the assets of the company. The first thing that the raider may do on assuming control over the company will be to fire the underperforming management. The risk of being acquired by a hostile raider is often referred to as the *takeover constraint.* The takeover constraint deters management from engaging in opportunistic behaviour.[96]

In theory at least, the takeover constraint is supposed to limit managerial opportunism, but in recent years, its effectiveness has become diluted as a result of a number of defence tactics adopted by incumbent management. In Chapter 6, we discussed such tactics, foremost among them "poison pills" and "golden parachutes."

Auditors

Even when there are stringent disclosure requirements, there is no guarantee that the information disclosed will be accurate. Managers may deliberately disclose false information or withhold negative financial information as well as use accounting methods that distort results based on highly subjective interpretations. Therefore, all accounting statements are required to be audited and certified to be accurate by external auditors. These auditing firms are independent organizations staffed by certified professionals who verify the firm's books of accounts. Audits can unearth financial irregularities, and they ensure that financial reporting by the firm conforms to standard accounting practices.

Developments leading to the bankruptcy of firms such as Enron and WorldCom and a spate of earnings restatements raise questions about the failure of the auditing firms to act as effective external control mechanisms. Why did an auditing firm, such as Arthur Andersen, with decades of good reputation in the auditing profession at stake, fail to raise red flags about accounting irregularities? First, auditors are appointed by the firm being audited. The desire to continue that business relationship sometimes makes them overlook financial irregularities. Second, most auditing firms also do consulting work and often have lucrative consulting contracts with the firms that they audit. Understandably, some of them tend not to ask too many difficult questions because they fear jeopardizing the consulting business, which is often more profitable than the auditing work.

Consider a restatement of earnings by Xerox as an example of the lack of independence of auditing firms. In January 2003, the U.S. Securities and Exchange Commission (SEC) filed a lawsuit against KPMG, the world's third-largest accounting firm, for allowing Xerox to inflate its revenues by $3 billion between 1997 and 2000. Of the $82 million that Xerox paid KPMG during those four years, only $26 million was for auditing. The rest was for consulting services. When one of the auditors objected to Xerox's practice of booking revenues for equipment leases earlier than it should have, Xerox asked KPMG to replace him. It did.[97] In response, the OTPP used its proxy voting rights to refuse the appointment of KPMG as the external auditor to public companies in which it held shares.

Banks and Analysts

Commercial and investment banks have lent money to corporations and therefore have to ensure that the borrowing firm's finances are in order and that the loan covenants are being followed. Stock analysts conduct ongoing in-depth studies of the firms that they follow and make recommendations to their clients to buy, hold, or sell. Their rewards and reputation depend on the quality of these recommendations. Their access to information, knowledge of the industry and the firm, and the insights they gain from interactions with the management of the company enable them to alert the investing community of both positive and negative developments relating to a company.

It is generally observed that analyst recommendations are often more optimistic than warranted by facts. "Sell" recommendations tend to be exceptions rather than the norm. Many analysts failed to grasp the gravity of the problems surrounding failed companies, such as Enron and Global Crossing, until the very end. Part of the explanation may lie in the fact that most analysts work for firms that also have investment banking relationships with the companies they follow. Negative recommendations by analysts can displease the management, who may decide to take their investment banking business to a rival firm. Otherwise independent and competent analysts may be pressured to overlook negative information or tone down their criticism. A related settlement between the SEC and the New York State Attorney General with 10 banks that were systematically biasing their analysts' opinions forced them to pay $1.4 billion in penalties and to fund independent research for investors.[98]

Regulatory Bodies

The extent of government regulation is often a function of the type of industry. Banks, utilities, and pharmaceuticals are subject to more regulatory oversight because of their importance to society. Public corporations are subject to more regulatory requirements than private corporations.[99]

All public corporations are required by bodies, such as the SEC, to disclose a substantial amount of financial information. These include quarterly and annual filings of financial performance, stock trading by insiders, and details of executive compensation packages. There are two primary reasons behind such requirements. First, markets can operate efficiently only when the investing public has faith in the market system. In the absence of disclosure requirements, the average investor suffers from a lack of reliable information and therefore may completely stay away from the capital market. This will negatively impact an economy's ability to grow. Second, disclosure of information, such as insider trading, protects the small investor to some extent from the negative consequences of information asymmetry. The insiders and large investors typically have more information than the small investor and can therefore use that information to buy or sell before the information becomes public knowledge.

The failure of a variety of external control mechanisms led the U.S. Congress to pass the *Sarbanes-Oxley Act* in 2002. This act calls for many stringent measures that would ensure better governance of U.S. corporations. Some of these measures include the following:[100]

- Auditors are barred from certain types of non-audit work. They are not allowed to destroy records for five years. Lead partners auditing a client should be changed at least every five years.

- CEOs and chief financial officers (CFOs) must fully reveal off-balance-sheet finances and vouch for the accuracy of the information revealed.

- Executives must promptly reveal the sale of shares in firms they manage and are not allowed to sell when other employees cannot.

- Corporate lawyers must report to senior managers any violations of securities law lower down.

Although the *Sarbanes-Oxley Act* has been a welcome move to clean up corporate boards and reinstate confidence in public markets, it has also had some unintended consequences. For example, in Canada, compliance with the relevant provisions of the act is estimated to cost hundreds of millions of dollars for the affected firms and has spun a small industry of lawyers and accountants to guide corporations through the regulatory maze. In other countries, such as the United Kingdom, Germany, and Japan, some provisions conflict with their current corporate laws and customs, and this is causing a furor in Europe and Asia.[101] Nevertheless, regulators in each of those countries are looking for ways to strengthen corporate governance. Canadian regulators have introduced

Rule 198 to address some of the same issues as those identified by the *Sarbanes-Oxley Act.* The Canadian Securities Administrators, an umbrella group for all provincial securities commissions, requires CEOs not only to certify their financial statements but also to guarantee the internal processes, such as computer and accounting systems, used to create them. In Japan, legislation is promoting the importance of independent directors, and in Russia, extensive education on corporate governance is being promoted via a grant from the Canadian International Development Agency.

Media and Public Activists

The press is not usually recognized as an external control mechanism in the literature on corporate governance, but there is no denying that in all developed capitalist economies, the financial press and media play an important indirect role in monitoring the management of public corporations. In Canada, business magazines such as *Canadian Business;* the financial sections of national newspapers, such as the *Report on Business* and *Financial Post;* and television networks, such as RoBTV, are constantly reporting on companies. Public perceptions about a company's financial prospects and the quality of its management are greatly influenced by the media. Bethany McLean of *Fortune* magazine is often credited as the first to raise questions about Enron's long-term financial viability.[102]

Similarly, consumer groups and activist individuals often take a crusading role in exposing corporate malfeasance. Well-known examples include Pollution Probe in Canada and Ralph Nader and Erin Brockovich in the U.S., who played important roles in bringing to light the safety issues related to GM's Corvair and environmental pollution issues concerning Pacific Gas and Electric Company, respectively. Ralph Nader, in fact, has created over 30 watchdog groups, including the following:[103]

- *Aviation Consumer Action Project.* Works to propose new rules to prevent flight delays, impose penalties for deceiving passengers about problems, and push for higher compensation for lost luggage.

- *Center for Auto Safety.* Helps consumers find plaintiff lawyers and agitate for vehicle recalls, increased highway safety standards, and lemon laws.

- *Center for Study of Responsive Law.* This is Nader's headquarters and his original vehicle founded in 1968. It supports and conducts widely ranging research and sponsors projects to further the needs of the citizen-consumer focusing on environmental and health and safety issues.

- *Pension Rights Center.* This centre helped employees of IBM, GE, and other companies to organize themselves against cash-balance pension plans.

Corporate Governance: An International Perspective

The topic of corporate governance has long been dominated by agency theory and based on the explicit assumption of the separation of ownership and control.[104] The central conflicts are principal–agent conflicts between shareholders and management. However, such an underlying assumption seldom applies outside of the United States and the United Kingdom. This is particularly true in continental Europe, Canada, and Australia, as well as in emerging economies. In these countries, there is often concentrated ownership, along with extensive family ownership and control, business group structures; these are frequently coupled with weak legal protection for minority shareholders. Serious conflicts tend to exist between two classes of principals: controlling shareholders and minority shareholders. Such conflicts can be called *principal–principal conflicts,* as opposed to *principal–agent* conflicts. Exhibit 10-8 describes some of the differences.

Strong family control is one of the leading indicators of concentrated ownership. In East Asia (excluding China), approximately 57 percent of corporations have board chairmen and CEOs from the controlling families. In continental Europe, this number is 68 percent. A very common practice is the appointment of family members as the board chairperson, as CEOs, and as other top executives. This happens because the families are controlling (not necessarily majority) shareholders. In 2003, 30-year-old James Murdoch was appointed CEO of British Sky Broadcasting (BSkyB), Europe's largest satellite broadcaster. There was very vocal resistance by minority shareholders. Why was he appointed in the first place? James's father just happened to be Rupert Murdoch, who controlled 35 percent of BSkyB and chaired the board.

EXHIBIT 10-8   TRADITIONAL PRINCIPAL–AGENT CONFLICTS VERSUS PRINCIPAL–PRINCIPAL CONFLICTS: HOW THEY DIFFER ALONG DIMENSIONS

	Principal–Agent Conflicts	**Principal–Principal Conflicts**
Goal Incongruence	Between shareholders and professional managers who own a relatively small portion of the firm's equity.	Between controlling shareholders and minority shareholders.
Ownership Pattern	Dispersed—5 to 20 percent is considered "concentrated ownership."	Concentrated—Often greater than 50 percent of equity is controlled by controlling shareholders.
Manifestations	Strategies that benefit entrenched managers at the expense of shareholders in general (e.g., shirking, pet projects, excessive compensation, and empire building).	Strategies that benefit controlling shareholders at the expense of minority shareholders (e.g., minority shareholder expropriation, nepotism, and cronyism).
Institutional Protection of Minority Shareholders	Formal constraints (e.g., judicial reviews and courts) set an upper boundary on potential expropriation by majority shareholders. Informal norms generally adhere to shareholder wealth maximization.	Formal institutional protection is often lacking, corrupted, or unenforced. Informal norms typically favour the interests of controlling shareholders ahead of those of minority investors.

Source: Adapted from M. Young, M. W. Peng, D. Ahlstrom and G. Bruton, "Governing the Corporation in Emerging Economies: A Principal–Principal Perspective," *Academy of Management Best Papers Proceedings,* Denver, 2002.

Magna International is another firm that has frequently been in the news for corporate misgovernance. For example, the loans and guarantees authorized by the board toward Magna Entertainment (MEC), the thoroughbred racing, race track, and slots business, were financial arrangements that were difficult to justify or explain to shareholders.[105] The horses and their affiliated operations lost truckloads of money for years, and without the backing of Magna International they would most certainly have faced bankruptcy. Although one would be very hard pressed to find any business connections, synergistic prospects, or complementary asset allocation benefits between MEC and the global automobile parts manufacturer, MEC was very dear to Frank Stronach and, as such, it was supported by the public corporation that Mr. Stronach controlled. The board of Magna International authorized a lump-sum payment over $800 million and a series of consulting and other related contracts to companies that are controlled by Mr. Stronach and his family in exchange for his preferred shares. Analysts have argued that such arrangements, common in many countries across the world and used by public firms that are effectively controlled by a family or an individual, cause a substantial discount to the underlying value of the shares and hurt the effectiveness of the financial markets. The board at least felt (and the financial markets seemed to concur, even if holding their collective noses) that $800 million would liberate Magna from the stronghold of its founder and would finally allow it to pursue its strategic destiny unencumbered.

Another ubiquitous feature of corporate life outside of the United States and United Kingdom are *business groups,* such as the *keiretsus* of Japan and the *chaebols* of South Korea. A *business group* is "a set of firms that, though legally independent, are bound together by a constellation of formal and informal ties and are accustomed to taking coordinated action."[106] Business groups are especially common in emerging economies, and they differ from other organizational forms in that they are communities of firms without clear boundaries.

Business groups have many advantages that can enhance the value of a firm. They often facilitate technology transfer or intergroup capital allocation that otherwise might be impossible because of inadequate institutional infrastructure, such as excellent financial services firms. However, informal ties—such as cross-holdings, board interlocks, and coordinated actions—can often result in intragroup activities and transactions, often at very favourable terms to member firms. Expropriation can be legally done through *related transactions,* which can occur when controlling owners sell firm assets to another firm they own at below market prices or spin off the most profitable part of a public firm and merge it with another of their private firms.

SUMMARY

For firms to be successful, they must practise effective strategic control and corporate governance. Without such controls, the firm will not be able to achieve competitive advantages and outperform rivals in the marketplace.

We began the chapter with the key role of informational control. We contrasted two types of control systems: what we termed "traditional" and "contemporary" information control systems. Whereas traditional control systems may have their place in placid, simple competitive environments, there are fewer of those in today's economy. Instead, we advocated the contemporary approach wherein the internal and external environment are constantly monitored so that when surprises emerge, the firm can modify its strategies, goals, and objectives.

Behavioural controls are also a vital part of effective control systems. We argued that firms must develop the proper balance between culture, rewards and incentives, and boundaries and constraints. Where there are strong and positive cultures and rewards, employees tend to internalize the organization's strategies and objectives. This permits a firm to spend fewer resources on monitoring behaviour and assures the firm that the efforts and initiatives of employees are more consistent with the overall objectives of the organization.

In the final section of this chapter, we addressed corporate governance, which can be defined as the relationship among various participants in determining the direction and performance of the corporation. The primary participants include shareholders, management (led by the chief executive officer), and the board of directors. We reviewed studies that indicated a consistent relationship between effective corporate governance and financial performance. There are also several internal and external control mechanisms that can serve to align managerial interests and shareholder interests. The internal mechanisms include a committed and involved board of directors, shareholder activism, and effective managerial incentives and rewards. The external mechanisms include the market for corporate control, banks and analysts, regulators, the media, and public activists. We also addressed corporate governance both from the perspective of the United States and Canada, as well as from an international perspective.

Summary Review Questions

1. Why are effective strategic control systems so important in today's economy?

2. What are the main advantages of "contemporary" control systems over "traditional" control systems? What are the main differences between these two systems?

3. Why is it important to have a balance between the three elements of behavioural control—culture; rewards and incentives; and boundaries?

4. Discuss the relationship between types of organizations and their primary means of behavioural control.

5. Boundaries become less important as a firm develops a strong culture and reward system. Explain.

6. Why is it important to avoid a "one best way" mentality concerning control systems? What are the consequences of applying the same type of control system to all types of environments?

7. What is the role of effective corporate governance in improving a firm's performance? What are some of the key governance mechanisms that are used to ensure that managerial and shareholder interests are aligned?

8. Define *principal–principal conflicts*. What are the implications for corporate governance?

REFLECTING ON CAREER IMPLICATIONS

- *Behavioural Control:* What sources of behavioural control does your organization employ? In general, too much emphasis on rules and regulations may stifle initiative and be detrimental to your career opportunities.

- *Rewards and Incentives:* Is your organization's reward structure fair and equitable? Does it effectively reward outstanding performance? If not, there may be a long-term erosion of morale which may have long-term adverse career implications for you.

- *Culture:* Consider the type of organization culture that would provide the best work environment for your career goals. How does your organization's culture deviate from this concept? Does your organization have a strong and effective culture? If so, professionals are more likely to develop strong "firm-specific" ties, which further enhances collaboration.

- *Corporate Governance:* Does your organization practise effective corporate governance? Such practices will enhance a firm's culture, and it will be easier to attract top talent. Operating within governance guidelines is usually a strong indicator of organizational citizenship, which, in turn, should be good for your career prospects.

EXPERIENTIAL EXERCISE

Bombardier Inc, the world's third largest aerospace manufacturer, with 2016 revenues of $16 billion, has encountered declining shareholder value since 2001. Using the Internet or library sources, evaluate the quality of the corporation in terms of management, the board of directors, and shareholder activism. Are the issues you list favourable or unfavourable for sound corporate governance? Note the active role of the founding family in the affairs of the company throughout the years from inception to the recent challenges and how their involvement might have contributed to corporate governance issues.

APPLICATION QUESTIONS AND EXERCISES

1. The problems of many firms may be attributed to a "traditional" control system that failed to continuously monitor the environment and make necessary changes in their strategy and objectives. What companies are you familiar with that responded appropriately (or inappropriately) to environmental change?

2. How can a strong, positive culture enhance a firm's competitive advantage? How can a weak, negative culture erode competitive advantages? Explain and provide examples.

3. Use the Internet to research a firm that has an excellent culture and a reward and incentive system. What are this firm's main financial and non-financial benefits?

4. Go to the website of a large, publicly held corporation in which you are interested. What evidence do you see of effective (or ineffective) corporate governance?

ETHICS AND CORPORATE SOCIAL RESPONSIBILITY QUESTIONS

1. Strong cultures can have powerful effects on employee behaviour. How does this create inadvertent control mechanisms? That is, are strong cultures an ethical way to control behaviour?

2. Rules and regulations can help reduce unethical behaviour in organizations. To be effective, however, what other systems, mechanisms, and processes are necessary?

3. Some would argue that minority shareholders should not be afforded special protections; after all, they bought the shares in full knowledge of the disproportional power of the controlling shareholders or the family owners of the public corporation. Can you think of any financial and ethical implications of such a "buyer beware" attitude and why, indeed, a government might want to encourage or discourage these types of protections?

Board: © Everythingpossible/Dreamstimecom; Tablet: VICTOR DE SCHWANBERG

CHAPTER ELEVEN

STRATEGIC LEADERSHIP:
Creating a Learning, Ethical, and Socially Responsible Organization

LEARNING OBJECTIVES

After reading this chapter, you should have a good understanding of:

LO 1 The three key activities in which all successful leaders must be continually engaged.

LO 2 The three elements of effective leadership: integrative thinking, overcoming barriers to change, and the effective use of power.

LO 3 The crucial role of emotional intelligence (EI) in successful leadership, as well as its potential drawbacks.

LO 4 The value of creating and maintaining a learning organization in today's global marketplace.

LO 5 The importance of ethics in organizations and the leader's role in establishing an ethical organization.

LO 6 Why corporate social responsibility shapes, or ought to influence, managerial thinking and strategic decisions.

Valeant Pharmaceuticals, a Laval, Quebec-based specialty pharmaceutical company best known for its audacious acquisition of the eye-care company, Bausch + Lomb, was once the most valuable firm on the TSX, passing RBC for that illustrious title in July of 2015.[1] Before the year ended, though, Valeant would experience the turbulence of a number of scandals, beginning with a fraud accusation levelled in a Citron Research report. Citron Research, a notorious short-seller, in a report published in October 2015, alleged that Valeant had not fully disclosed its relationship with mail-order pharmacy company Philidor, which Valeant was using to sell its products. Combined with accusations about predatory drug price hikes and a billion-dollar bonus for Valeant's CEO, the resulting scandals followed CEO Michael Pearson to the exit door. Replacing him, though, would not necessarily solve Valeant's numerous troubles.

Shutterstock / Minerva Studio

Valeant began as a small pharmaceutical firm, investing heavily in R&D in order to develop new drugs. Pearson, upon becoming CEO in 2008, decided to rework the firm's strategy, arguing that returns on R&D were too low and too uncertain. Instead, he believed that it made more sense to buy companies which already had drugs on the market, then cut costs and raise prices in order to increase profitability. Valeant then began an aggressive acquisition strategy, completing more than a hundred acquisitions between 2008 and 2015, and hiking the prices on many of their acquired drugs. The price increases sometimes reached the extremes of price gouging. A 2015 analysis of drugs whose prices had risen between 300 and 1,200 percent in the previous two years revealed that half of those drugs belonged to Valeant.

Allegations of price gouging by U.S lawmakers continued to feed the stream of scandals for Valeant beyond the initial allegations of fraud. In 2016, lawmakers emphasized the 3,000 percent increase in price of the 30-year-old drug Syprine, acquired by Valeant in 2010. Valeant then offered rebates on several heart medications in an effort to stem off concerns of price gouging, and Pearson was swiftly replaced by Joseph Papa as CEO.

However, the scandals were not over yet. While Valeant shares increased more than 20 percent after the company announced its reorganization and the appointment of the new CEO, the positive momentum didn't last long. Two days after the announcement, the *Wall Street Journal* reported that prosecutors had opened a criminal investigation into the firm to determine the nature and extent of the fraudulent behaviour with Philidor. In late 2016, former Valeant executive Gary Tanner was arrested and charged for running a fraud-and-kickback scheme along with Andrew Davenport, former CEO of Philidor. Allegations against Tanner and Davenport claim the two set up Philidor as a market to distribute Valeant drugs.

Valeant stock price continued to fall in early 2017. On top of the various scandals and ongoing investigations, Pearson's legacy began to unravel. The Philidor and price gouging scandals were not the only concerns from his tenure as CEO. Through his aggressive acquisition strategy, he had acquired a U.S.$32-billion debt for the firm, leaving Valeant with little leeway to pay it back. Papa cut $3.6 billion from the debt in his first year as CEO, and he has committed to cutting Valeant's debt by another $5 billion through selling off non-core assets, though as of the time of this writing it is unclear if he will be able to deliver on this promise.

Papa recognizes that Valeant's issues will not disappear with the removal of Pearson and the cutting of its debt. In a shareholder meeting in early 2017, he acknowledged that he is also considering changing Valeant's name to avoid the negative image now associated with company following the accusations of fraud and price gouging. It is not clear whether this would be enough to improve the public perception of the firm and its future prospects.

Valeant's legacy is now one of fraud, price gouging, and ethical misconduct stemming from top management. Once the most highly valued company on the TSX, Valeant has lost more than 90 percent of its market share compared to its peak, delivering a sobering lesson about the financial implications of unethical leadership and misconduct. While inflating the prices of drugs may have been a successful short-term method of raising profitability, it is clear that the ramifications in the market for the unethical behaviour have far outweighed the short-term benefits of the practice. In addition, Valeant's story provides an excellent example of the need for strong leadership at the helm of a firm. Under Pearson, Valeant was led through a number of scandals, which eventually eroded its market value staggeringly. If it will ever recover, Valeant's path forward needs to be charted by strong, ethical leadership under the new CEO Joseph Papa. ■

LEADERSHIP: THREE INTERDEPENDENT ACTIVITIES

In today's chaotic world, few would argue against the need for leadership, but how do we go about encouraging it? Is it enough to merely keep an organization afloat, or is it essential to make steady progress toward some well-defined objective? We believe custodial management is not leadership. Leadership is proactive, goal-oriented, and focused on the creation and implementation of a creative vision. Leadership is the process of transforming organizations from what they are to what the leader would have them become. This definition implies a lot: dissatisfaction with the status quo, a vision of what should be, and a process for bringing about change.

There is substantial overlap between leadership and strategic management. In many respects, leadership is about managing strategically, and strategic management relies on leadership skills. Both deal with the process of guiding the organization to achieve its aspirations. Both leadership and strategic management are about identifying a vision—what the organization wants to become sometime in the future. And they both also involve the process of helping the organization to get there. We have argued in this book that strategic management is the job of every manager in an organization. That is, every manager should think and act in ways that contribute to defining and accomplishing the strategic objectives set for the organization. Similarly, even though most of our discussion revolves around the top management team (TMT) and the person in charge, leadership is not the exclusive purview of the person at the top. Every employee looks to his or her boss to set a direction and provide guidance for his or her job; an effective manager provides subordinates with a sense of purpose and an identity within the firm, creates opportunities, motivates, and makes the resources available for all employees to achieve their personal best while contributing to the success of the whole organization. In essence, every manager is, and needs to act as, a leader for the group of people that report to him or her.

W. Glen Rowe distinguishes between managerial leaders and strategic leaders.[2] The former are concerned with preserving order, applying their expertise in a functional area, ensuring compliance with rules and procedures, and creating new order, predictability, and efficiency in their area of responsibility. In contrast, strategic leaders are not only comfortable in overseeing their operating responsibilities, but they can also proactively look at situations, shape ideas, take risks, and make choices that can make a difference in their organizations. Rowe defines strategic leaders as those who are able to influence others to voluntarily make day-to-day decisions that enhance the long-term viability of their organizations; however, he suggests that managerial leaders only recognize rewards and punishments as tools to influence their subordinates' behaviours in conforming to predetermined rules. Strategic leaders make reasonable investments for the future while maintaining an appropriate level of stability in the present.

Doing the right thing is becoming more and more important. Many industries are declining; the global village is becoming increasingly complex, interconnected, and unpredictable; and product and market life cycles are getting progressively more compressed. When asked to describe the life cycle of his company's products, the chief executive officer (CEO) of a supplier of computer components replied, "Seven months from cradle to grave—and that includes three months to design the product and get it into production!" Richard D'Aveni, author of *Hypercompetition,* argued that in a world where all dimensions of competition appear to be compressed in time and heightened in complexity, sustainable competitive advantages are no longer possible.[3]

Despite the importance of doing the "right thing," leaders must also be concerned about "doing things right." Charan and Colvin strongly believe that execution, that is, the implementation of strategy, is also essential to success.

> Mastering execution turns out to be the odds-on best way for a CEO to keep his job. So, what's the right way to think about that sexier obsession, strategy? It's vitally important—obviously. The problem is that our age's fascination feeds the mistaken belief that developing exactly the right strategy will enable a company to rocket past competitors. In reality, that's less than half the battle.[4]

LO 1

Leaders are change agents whose success is measured by how effectively they formulate and implement a strategic vision and mission. Accordingly, many authors contend that successful leaders must recognize three interdependent activities that must be continually reassessed for organizations to succeed. As shown in Exhibit 11-1, these are (1) setting a direction, (2) designing the organization, and (3) nurturing a culture dedicated to excellence and ethical behaviour.[5] Strategy Spotlight 11.1 describes how some successful leaders have exhibited these attributes in their organizations.

EXHIBIT 11-1

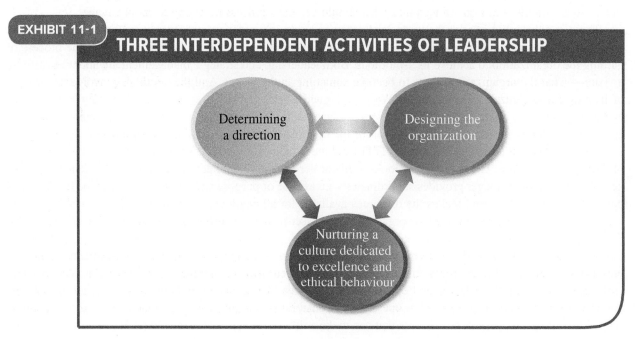

THREE INTERDEPENDENT ACTIVITIES OF LEADERSHIP

Determining a direction

Designing the organization

Nurturing a culture dedicated to excellence and ethical behaviour

11.1 STRATEGY SPOTLIGHT

How Leaders Lead in Tough Times

Dave Yost—AmerisourceBergen

AmerisourceBergen is a $66-billion drug distribution company. Unlike pharmaceutical manufacturing, drug distribution is an industry that operates on razor-thin margins—just 1 percent on average. Holding down expenses is an absolute necessity. As Amerisource CEO, Dave Yost was a model of frugality. He answered his own phone, kept plastic plants in the lobby to save on watering, and flew economy class. Sitting on a 1970s-style chair that looked like a yard sale item, Yost explained that, "The leader is very important in controlling business costs." Updating the familiar adage "Stick to the knitting," he said, "We're focused on knitting faster, better, and more creatively than anyone else." Although his tactics sound extreme, they yielded important payoffs: Under his leadership Amerisource profits were consistently above the industry average, including earnings growth of 30 percent in one quarter compared with 8 percent at McKesson and 13 percent at Cardinal Health, Amerisource's closest rivals. Specific cost-cutting initiatives created a $500-million fund for investments to improve customer service technology and upgrade operations at key distribution centres.

Herb Kelleher—Southwest Airlines

From the start, Southwest took steps to maintain its unique culture, what Herb Kelleher, its founder and legendary chairman and CEO, called "this joie de vivre, this effervescence, in our company." Fairness and a willingness to share the pain during difficult times had been an important part of Kelleher's corporate philosophy. When pilots were asked to agree to a pay freeze for five years, he also voluntarily took a five-year pay freeze "to honor what they had done. And [he had] turned down many, many millions of dollars in salary and options because it didn't set a good example." Corporate officers followed a similar practice. Kelleher noted, "Our officers have never received a salary increase that is larger on average than our noncontract employees have gotten. In other words, if they get a 3.5-percent increase, our officers get a 3.5-percent increase." Such policies contributed to Southwest's remarkable success: Within an industry notorious for red ink and a bloodbath among competitors during each economic downturn, the company has been profitable for 35 consecutive years and now carries more passengers per year than any other North American airline.

Sources: R. Charam, *Leadership in the Era of Economic Uncertainty* (New York: McGraw-Hill, 2009); A. McConnon, "Lessons from a Skinflint CEO," *BusinessWeek*, October 6, 2008, pp. 54–55; E. Smith, "Herb Kelleher," *Texas Monthly*, June 2008, pp. 78–85.

The interdependent nature of these three activities is self-evident. Consider an organization with a great mission and a superb organizational structure but that has a culture that implicitly encourages shirking and unethical behaviour, or consider another one with a strong culture but little direction or vision. Much of the failure in today's organizations can be attributed to the failure to give equal consideration to all three of these activities. The imagery of a three-legged stool is instructive: The stool will collapse if one leg is missing or broken. In the next section, we briefly look at each of these activities; we also address the important role of a leader's power in overcoming resistance to change.

Setting a Direction

Leaders need a holistic understanding of their organization and its context. This requires an ability to scan the environment to develop knowledge of all of the company's stakeholders (customers, suppliers, shareholders, community, etc.) and other salient environmental trends and events. Managers must integrate this knowledge into a vision of what the organization could become.[6] It necessitates the capacity to solve increasingly complex problems, become proactive in approach, and develop viable strategic options. A strategic vision provides many benefits: a clear future direction; a framework for the organization's mission and goals; and enhanced employee communication, participation, and commitment.

At times, the creative process involves what the CEO of Yokogawa, the Japanese partner of General Electric (GE) in the Medical Systems business, called "bullet train" thinking.[7] That is, if you want to increase the speed by 10 kilometres per hour, you look for incremental advances. However, if you want to double the speed, you have got to think "outside the box" (e.g., widen the track, change the overall suspension system). Leaders need more creative solutions than just keeping the same train with a few minor tweaks. Instead, they must come up with more revolutionary visions.

Robert Tillman, former CEO of Lowe's, dramatically revitalized his firm by setting a clear and compelling direction: He made Lowe's into a formidable competitor to Home Depot, Inc.[8] In his six years as CEO, Tillman transformed the $59-billion chain into a better alternative to its archrival. Lowe's shares more than doubled during Tillman's tenure, whereas Home Depot's practically stayed flat.

Tillman redirected Lowe's strategy by responding effectively to research showing that women initiate 80 percent of home projects. Whereas Home Depot had focused on the professionals and male customers, Tillman redesigned Lowe's stores to give them a brighter appearance, stocked them with more appliances, and focused on higher-margin goods (including everything from Laura Ashley paints to high-end bathroom fixtures). Like Walmart, Lowe's has one of the best inventory systems in retailing. In turn, Lowe's profits continued to rise faster than Home Depot's.

Mighty Home Depot has reacted swiftly. It brought into its corporate headquarters in Atlanta, Annette Verschuren, the very successful executive who led the firm's expansion in Canada from 19 outlets to 179 stores, and gave her the mandate to introduce similar changes across the corporation, as well as lead the firm's expansion into China. Verschuren's first moves included brighter-lit stores and a new concept store called Expo Design Centers emphasizing interior décor and more upscale merchandise, signalling an adjustment to the direction of the $68-billion chain and its 2,248 stores.[9] Leadership at all sides makes for a very competitive market that richly benefits consumers, customers and employees, as well as the shareholders.

Designing the Organization

At times, almost all leaders have difficulty implementing their visions and strategies. Such problems may stem from a variety of sources:

- Lack of understanding of responsibility and accountability among managers.
- Reward systems that do not motivate individuals (or collectives, such as groups and divisions) toward the desired organizational goals.
- Inadequate or inappropriate budgeting and control systems.
- Insufficient mechanisms to integrate activities across the organization.

Successful leaders are actively involved in building structures, teams, systems, and organizational processes that facilitate the implementation of their visions and strategies. We discussed the necessity for consistency between business-level and corporate-level strategies and organizational control in Chapter 10. Without appropriately structuring organizational activities, a firm would generally be unable to attain an overall low-cost advantage by closely monitoring its costs through detailed and formalized cost and financial control procedures. With regard to corporate-level strategy, a related diversification strategy would necessitate reward systems that emphasize behavioural measures, whereas an unrelated strategy should rely more on financial (or objective) indicators of performance.

These examples illustrate the important role of leadership in creating systems and structures to achieve the desired ends. As Jim Collins says about the importance of designing the organization, "Along with figuring out what the company stands for and pushing it to understand what it's really good at, building mechanisms is the CEO's role—the leader as architect."[10]

Nurturing an Excellent and Ethical Culture

As we noted in Chapter 10, organizational culture can be an effective means of organizational control. A culture is rooted in consistent, observable patterns of behaviour in organizations. It is shaped by incentives. Culture is also a process of "sense making" in organizations and a carrier of meaning. Organizational culture is shaped by and overlaps with other cultures—especially the broader culture of the societies in which it operates. The cultures of organizations are dynamic and are never monolithic.

Leaders play a key role in changing, developing, and sustaining an organization's culture. With Cirque du Soleil, Guy Laliberté has created a global sensation and a multibillion dollar enterprise from the street performances of the old city of Montreal and, in the process, has developed a strong organization dedicated to artistic excellence and social activism.[11] In 30 short years, Cirque du Soleil has transformed the seedy circus business into a high-class, distinctive brand of live performances with elements of opera and theatre, lavish costumes, stunning sets, and spectacular high-tech special effects. Laliberté has developed an almost mystical organization that still maintains a family atmosphere. At the same time, it has grown to over 5,500 employees and has evolved into a multiline company that has ventured into television, film, music, and merchandise. Still at the centre are 12 permanent and 10 touring shows in Europe, America, Asia, and Australia.

Laliberté once said, "To keep your edge, you have to feel insecure." He has been pushing himself and the artistic talents in his company to continuously experiment, innovate, and fuel the creative sparks that have brought much of their success to date. At the same time, he has shown another side of leadership with extensive philanthropic involvement and strong corporate citizenship; with a $100-million grant, he established One Drop Foundation, an initiative to bring clean water and ensure food safety across Africa and Central America; and with Cirque du Monde, he has created outlets for the artistic engagement of street children, offering circus workshops for underprivileged young people across the world, from Brazil to Mongolia. Cirque du Soleil allocates 1 percent of its gross revenue to social projects, and its philosophy of activism is shared among its performers, who are attracted to Cirque's commitment to social responsibility and to its genuine concern for its employees. Laliberté has not only been able to guide Cirque to impressive financial results but has also strengthened its valuable human capital.

Leaders can also have a highly detrimental effect on a firm's culture and ethics. Imagine the negative impact that Todd Berman's illegal activities have had on New York's private equity firm Chartwell Investments, a firm that he co-founded.[12] He pleaded guilty to fraud charges brought by the Justice Department after allegations that Berman stole more than $3.6 million from the firm and its investors. For 18 months, he misled Chartwell's investors about the financial condition of one of the firm's portfolio companies by falsely claiming that it needed to borrow funds to meet operating expenses. Instead, Berman transferred the money to his personal bank account, along with fees paid by the portfolio companies.

11.2 STRATEGY SPOTLIGHT

Strategic Leadership through Values

In 2010, Vancity (Vancouver City Savings Credit Union), Canada's largest credit union, achieved its best financial performance since its establishment 70 years ago. The results were that much more impressive considering the economic crisis that took place only two years earlier. What factors have contributed to Vancity's success? The director of the board of directors, Greg McDade, believes that Vancity's competitive advantage "results from a clear understanding of its values, the ability to think creatively, and the skills to manage flexibly." Many, including the organization itself, attribute it to a "triple bottom line" approach.

Whereas many companies incorporate a corporate social responsibility (CSR) strategy into their organizational goals, Vancity has gone so far as to include its social values in its mission statement

(Continued)

and integrate them into the core of its operations. Its mission is "to be a democratic, ethical, and innovative provider of financial services to our members." It has acted true to this pledge by not only incorporating ethical, social, and environmental practices into its operations but also by being among the first in its industry to do so. It has always sought to "do the right thing" and has taken multiple leadership roles across all dimensions of its activities; for example, Vancity was the first to explicitly provide direct loans to women, and in 2008, it became the first financial institution to become carbon neutral in all of North America.

Staying true to its values and ethics, the organization is not highly concerned about exclusivity or maintaining its competitive advantage in these areas. Instead, Vancity has opted to share its knowledge and processes. This has included providing funding for small-and medium-sized businesses to attend "Climate Smart" workshops and making the tools and processes by which it met its carbon neutrality goal available online for all organizations to access, including its competitors.

Vancity's social commitment is thought to be one of the main reasons the organization has consistently attracted young talent. Vancity was recognized as one of the Top 50 Employers for Young People in 2010 and one of B.C.'s Top Employers in 2014. However, employment at Vancity is not intended to be just a starting role for young professionals. The organization's president and CEO, Tamara Vrooman, explains that Vancity's strategy is not only to attract talent but also to provide growth opportunities to retain it. "The best way to do that," says Vrooman, "is to get those people into your organization early, understand what makes them tick, and support them in creating the kind of business values that are going to have value for your future customers." Vancity's "triple bottom line" approach has proven successful for the organization. In addition to providing new socially oriented product lines that have contributed to growth in revenue and profits, the company has shown evidence that value can be created by investing and contributing to the greater community.

Sources: 2011, "Vancity Achieves Best Financial Results in Its 64-Year History in 2010; Credit Union Will Return a Record $23.5M to Members and Their Communities," Vancity press release, March 8; French, C., 2010, September 22, "Canada's Banks See Slower Retail Revenue Growth," *Reuters,* September 22; "Royal Bank of Canada Reports 2010 and Fourth Quarter Results," RBC press release, December 10; 2010, "Top 50 Employers for Young People," *The Globe and Mail Report on Business,* June 10: 1; 2008, "Vancity Meets Its Goal to Be Carbon Neutral—A First for a North American Based Financial Institution," Vancity press release, April 9; Rockel, N., 2010, "Luring Young Talent Sets Stage for the Future," *The Globe and Mail Report on Business,* June 10: 3.

Managers and top executives must accept personal responsibility for developing and strengthening ethical behaviour throughout the organization. They must consistently demonstrate that such behaviour is central to the vision and the mission of the organization. Several elements, including role models, corporate credos and codes of conduct, reward and evaluation systems, and policies and procedures, must be present and reinforced for a firm to become highly ethical. Given the importance of these elements, we address them in detail in the last section of this chapter.

LO 2 ELEMENTS OF EFFECTIVE LEADERSHIP

The demands on leaders in today's business environment require them to perform a variety of functions. The success of their organizations often depends on how they as individuals meet challenges and deliver on promises. What practices and skills are needed to get the job done effectively? Strategy Spotlight 11.3 describes the critical issues faced by the new CEO of General Motors, Mary Barra, who was brought in to shepherd the global automobile manufacturer out of the latest financial crisis.

11.3 STRATEGY SPOTLIGHT

Mary Barra and the Need for Change at General Motors

Mary Barra was selected in 2014 as CEO by the board of General Motors (GM) after a thorough search of both internal and external candidates. The board needed to identify the right person to lead the firm out of the most recent financial crisis and into the rapidly changing environment of the industry in the 21st century. Challenges to the traditional automobile industry included electric and self-driving innovations by Tesla, as well as Chinese and Indian manufacturers asserting themselves for global dominance in shifting markets. Barra soon found herself facing an unanticipated crisis that reinforced the widely held view that GM was a company in need of major change. The obvious question then was whether Barra was up to the task.

GM had struggled for a number of decades, seeing its share of the U.S. market decline from 40 percent in 1985 to 18 percent in 2013. More recently, GM had been rocked by the financial crisis of 2008, a challenge it only survived because of a government bailout. Shortly after Barra's appointment as CEO, a new crisis arose—a problem with faulty ignition switches in GM vehicles. While the issue came to public attention in 2014, it was revealed that engineers at GM had known as early as 2001 that an ignition switch used across a wide range of GM cars could fail and cause crashes. Despite that, the firm hadn't recalled the cars to fix their switches. According to the attorney managing claims for GM, crashes caused by the faulty switches have cost at least 50 lives. Critics say the death toll is much higher.

The problems at GM run deep. Analysts have long criticized the firm for having plodding decision making, with rival departments refusing to share information and being more focused on shifting blame for failures than on working together to solve problems. Further, an internal report on GM's decision making noted that GM was hampered by a "proliferation of committees" whose conclusions were "reported to yet further committees." Analysts also accuse the company of being more cost conscious than customer-focused.

The near death of GM in 2008 could have provided the circumstances for major needed changes to the firm, but leadership turmoil has limited the degree of change that has occurred. Over the five years prior to Barra's appointment, GM had five different CEOs. None appeared to have the drive or power necessary to undertake major changes in GM's culture and operations. The prior CEO and chairman, Dan Akerson, who had no experience in the auto industry before becoming GM's leader, managed to repay the government for bailing out GM but left abruptly without undertaking a major reorganization effort at the company. He was replaced as CEO by Barra and as chairman of the board by Tim Solso.

Is Barra the right person to bring about the necessary changes at GM? Some argue she is too much of an insider. She is a second-generation GM lifetime employee. Her father was a die maker who worked at the company for 39 years. Barra has worked at GM for 33 years. She began her career while still a student, worked her way up the ladder in a variety of engineering positions, and served as a plant manager, VP of Global Manufacturing, and VP of Global Human Resources before becoming CEO. Despite being CEO, she may not have the positional power necessary to enact the necessary reforms, since she doesn't also carry the role of chairman of the board. Others argue she is the perfect candidate to take on the task. Since she knows the organization inside and out, she can act quickly and decisively where others would need to take time to develop her depth of knowledge. Her career path has taken her through various units of GM, and she has developed relationships with people throughout the firm who trust her judgment. Also, at only 52 years of age, she is likely to be at the helm for some time, making it difficult for managers to resist her change efforts in favour of trying to wait her out.

So far, Barra has taken some actions that are bold for the staid GM culture. She fired 15 employees associated with the ignition-failure debacle and moved out seven high-level GM managers in her first few months as CEO. She's also championing the use of external measures to assess the success of GM's products and financials. Up to now, GM has almost exclusively relied on internal

(Continued)

measures, such as whether projects are meeting scheduling milestones and whether new-model sales are meeting internal benchmarks. Barra wants the firm to compare itself to its competitors to become more aggressive and competitive. "I accept no excuses for why we can't be the best," Barra says.

Commentators suggest that a major restructuring and turnaround at GM is a monumental task that could take 5 to 10 years. Many have high hopes that Barra will be the leader to finally make that turnaround happen.

Sources: Levin, D. 2014. New GM: Same as it ever was? *Fortune*, April 10: 64–67; Colvin, G. 2014. Mary Barra's (unexpected) opportunity. *Fortune*, October 6: 102–108; and Anonymous. 2009. A giant falls. *economist.com*, June 9: np.

Scholars and consultants focus on three capabilities that are marks of successful leadership: (1) integrative thinking, (2) overcoming barriers to change, and (3) the effective use of power. They also stress the role of emotional intelligence in leadership. We review each one of these elements in turn.

Integrative Thinking

Today's leaders are expected to confront a host of opposing forces. As the previous section indicated, maintaining consistency across a company's culture, vision, and organizational design can be difficult, especially if the three activities are out of alignment.

How does a leader make good strategic decisions in the face of multiple contingencies and diverse opportunities? Executives who are able to think in a more integrative fashion are viewed as effective leaders. People who can consider two conflicting ideas simultaneously, without dismissing one of the ideas or becoming discouraged about reconciling them, often are the best problem solvers because of their ability to creatively synthesize the opposing thoughts. American author F. Scott Fitzgerald observed that "the test of a first-rate intelligence is the ability to hold two opposing ideas in mind at the same time and still retain the ability to function. One should, for example, be able to see that things are hopeless yet be determined to make them otherwise."[13]

In contrast to conventional thinking, which tends to focus on making choices between competing ideas from a limited set of alternatives, integrative thinking guides people to reconcile opposing thoughts and identify creative solutions that provide them with more options and new alternatives. Here are some of its elements:

- *Salience.* Take stock of what features of the decision you consider relevant and important. Do not restrict your thinking to a few major features. Consider also features that may be less important; try to think of everything that may matter.
- *Causality.* Make a mental map of the causal relationships between the features, that is, how the various features are related to one another.
- *Architecture.* Use the mental map to arrange a sequence of decisions that will lead to a specific outcome. Realize that no particular decision path is right or wrong; considering multiple options simultaneously may lead to a better decision.
- *Resolution.* Make your selection. Your final resolution is linked to how you evaluated the first three stages; if you are dissatisfied with your choices, go back through the process, and revisit your assumptions.

Applied to business, an integrative thinking approach enables decision makers to consider situations not as forced trade-offs—either decrease costs or invest more; either satisfy shareholders or please the community—but as a method for synthesizing opposing ideas into a creative solution. The key is to think in terms of "both-and" rather than "either-or." "Integrative thinking," says Roger Martin, "shows us that there's a way to integrate the advantages of one solution without cancelling out the advantages of an alternative solution." Although integrative thinking may come naturally only to some people, others can learn it if they are willing to unlearn old patterns and become aware of how they think. Strategy Spotlight 11.4 describes how Red Hat, Inc.'s co-founder, Bob Young, made his company a market leader by using integrative thinking to resolve a major problem in the domain of open-source software.

11.4 STRATEGY SPOTLIGHT

Integrative Thinking at Red Hat, Inc.

How can a software developer make money giving away free software? That was the dilemma Red Hat's founder, Bob Young, was facing during the early days of the open-source software movement. A Finnish developer named Linus Torvalds, using freely available UNIX software, had developed an operating system dubbed "Linux" that was being widely circulated in the freeware community. The software was intended specifically as an alternative to the pricey proprietary systems sold by Microsoft and Oracle. To use proprietary software, corporations had to pay hefty installation fees and were required to call Microsoft or Oracle engineers to fix things when they went wrong. In Young's view, it was a flawed and unsustainable business model.

But the free model was flawed as well. Although several companies had sprung up to help companies use Linux, there were few opportunities to profit from using it. As Young said, "You couldn't make any money selling [the Linux] operating system because all this stuff was free, and if you started to charge money for it, someone else would come in and price it lower. It was a commodity in the truest sense of the word." To complicate matters, hundreds of developers were part of the software community that was constantly modifying and debugging Linux—at a rate equivalent to three updates per day. As a result, systems administrators at corporations that tried to adopt the software spent so much time keeping track of updates that they did not enjoy the savings they expected from using free software.

Young saw the appeal of both approaches but also realized a new model was needed. While contemplating the dilemma, he realized a salient feature that others had overlooked—that most major corporations will nearly always choose to do business with the industry leader because they have to live with software decisions for at least 10 years. Young realized he had to position Red Hat as the top provider of Linux software. To do that, he proposed a radical solution: Provide the authoritative version of Linux, and deliver it in a new way—as a download rather than on CD. He hired programmers to create a downloadable version—still free—and promised, in essence, to maintain its quality (for a fee, of course) by dealing with all the open-source programmers who were continually suggesting changes. In the process, he created a product companies could trust and then profited by establishing ongoing service relationships with customers. Red Hat's version of Linux became the de facto standard. By 2000, Linux was installed in 25 percent of server operating systems worldwide, and Red Hat had captured over 50 percent of the global market for Linux systems.

By recognizing that a synthesis of two flawed business models could provide the best of both worlds, Young exhibited the traits of integrative thinking. He pinpointed the causal relationships between the salient features of the marketplace and Red Hat's path to prosperity. He then crafted an approach that integrated the aspects of the two existing approaches into a new alternative. By resolving to provide a free downloadable version, Young also took responsibility for creating his own path to success. The pay-off was substantial: When Red Hat went public in 1999, Young became a billionaire on the first day of trading. By 2008, Red Hat had over $0.5 billion in annual revenues and a market capitalization of over $3 billion.

Source: R. L. Martin, *The Opposable Mind* (Boston: Harvard Business School Press, 2007).

Overcoming Barriers to Change

What are the barriers to change that leaders often encounter, and how can they best bring about organizational change? After all, people generally have some level of choice about how strongly they support or resist a leader's change initiatives. Why is there often so much resistance? Organizations at all levels are prone to inertia and are slow to learn, adapt, and change because of the following:

1.   *Many people have vested interests in the status quo.* People tend to be risk averse and resistant to change. There is a broad stream of research on "escalation" wherein certain individuals continue to throw "good money at bad decisions" despite negative performance feedback.[14]

2. ***There are systemic barriers.*** The design of the organization's structure, information processing, reporting relationships, and so forth impede the proper flow and evaluation of information. A bureaucratic structure with multiple layers, onerous requirements for documentation, and rigid rules and procedures will often "inoculate" the organization against change.

3. ***There are behavioural barriers.*** Creating the phenomenon of tunnel vision, behavioural barriers cause managers to look at issues from a biased or limited perspective because of their education, training, work experiences, and so forth.

4. ***There are political barriers.*** Conflicts arising from power relationships can manifest in a myriad of ways, such as vested interests, refusal to share information, conflicts over resources, conflicts between departments and divisions, and petty interpersonal differences.

5. ***There are personal time constraints.*** Gresham's law of planning states that operational decisions will drive out the time necessary for strategic thinking and reflection. This tendency is accentuated in organizations experiencing severe price competition or retrenchment, wherein managers and employees are spread thin.

Leaders must draw on a range of personal skills as well as organizational mechanisms to move their organizations forward in the face of such barriers. Integrative thinking provides one avenue by equipping leaders with an ability to consider creative alternatives to the kind of resistance and doubt that cause many barriers. Two factors mentioned earlier—building a learning organization and an ethical organization—provide the kind of climate within which a leader can advance the organization's aims and make progress toward its goals. One of the most important tools a leader has for overcoming barriers to change is their personal and organizational power. On the one hand, good leaders must be on guard not to abuse power. On the other hand, successful leadership requires the measured exercise of power.

The Effective Use of Power

Successful leadership requires effective use of power in overcoming barriers to change.[15] Power refers to a leader's ability to get things done in a way he or she wants them to be done. It is the ability to influence other people's behaviour, to persuade them to do things that they otherwise would not do, and to overcome resistance and opposition to changing direction. Effective exercise of power is essential for successful leadership.[16]

A leader derives his or her power from several sources or bases. The simplest way to understand the bases of power is by classifying them as organizational and personal, as shown in Exhibit 11-2.

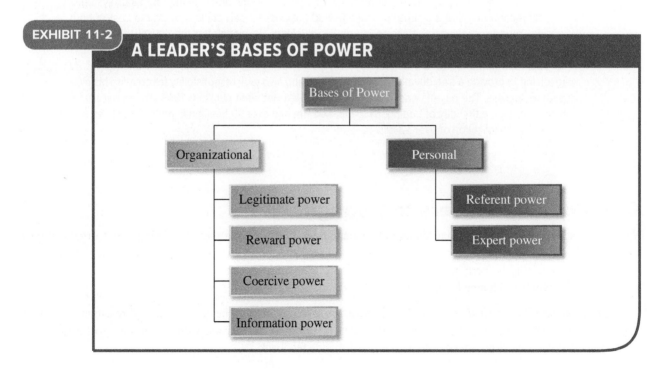

EXHIBIT 11-2

A LEADER'S BASES OF POWER

Bases of Power

Organizational
- Legitimate power
- Reward power
- Coercive power
- Information power

Personal
- Referent power
- Expert power

Organizational bases of power refer to the power that a person wields because of holding a formal management position. These include legitimate power, reward power, coercive power, and information power. Legitimate power is derived from organizationally conferred decision-making authority and is exercised by virtue of a manager's position in the organization. Reward power depends on the ability of the leader or manager to confer rewards for positive behaviours or outcomes. Coercive power is the power a manager exercises over employees using fear of punishment for errors of omission or commission. Information power arises from a manager's access, control, and distribution of information that is not freely available to everyone in an organization.

A leader might also be able to influence subordinates because of his or her personality characteristics and behaviour. These would be considered the personal bases of power, including referent power and expert power. The source of referent power is a subordinate's identification with the leader. A leader's personal attributes or charisma might influence subordinates and make them devoted to that leader. The source of expert power is the leader's expertise and knowledge in a particular field. The leader is the expert on whom subordinates depend for information that they need to do their jobs successfully.

Successful leaders use the different bases of power, and often a combination of them, as appropriate to meet the demands of a situation, such as the nature of the task, the personality characteristics of the subordinates, the urgency of the issue, and other factors. Leaders must recognize that persuasion and developing consensus are often essential, but so is pressing for action. At some point, stragglers must be prodded into line.[17]

LO 3   Emotional Intelligence

Besides the skills and activities of strategic leadership, we also need to consider the leadership traits that are the most important.[18]

There exists, as one would expect, a vast amount of literature on the successful traits of leaders.[19] These traits include integrity, maturity, energy, judgment, motivation, intelligence, expertise, and so on. For simplicity, these traits may be grouped into three broad sets of capabilities:

- Purely technical skills (e.g., accounting or operations research).
- Cognitive abilities (e.g., analytical reasoning or quantitative analysis).
- Emotional intelligence (e.g., self-management and managing relationships).

Emotional intelligence (EI) has been frequently identified as being one of the most consistent traits in successful managers.[20] Psychologist and journalist Daniel Goleman defines *emotional intelligence* as the capacity for recognizing one's own emotions and those of others.[21] Studies of successful managers have found that effective leaders consistently have a high level of EI.[22] Findings indicate that EI is a better predictor of life success (economic well-being, satisfaction with life, friendship, family life), including occupational attainments, than the intelligence quotient (IQ).

This is not to say that IQ and technical skills are irrelevant, but they become "threshold capabilities." They are the necessary requirements for attaining higher-level managerial positions. EI, however, is essential for leadership success. Without it, Goleman claims, a manager can have excellent training, an incisive analytical mind, and many smart ideas but will still not be a great leader.

Exhibit 11-3 identifies the five components of EI: (1) self-awareness, (2) self-regulation, (3) motivation, (4) empathy, and (5) social skill.

EXHIBIT 11-3   THE FIVE COMPONENTS OF EMOTIONAL INTELLIGENCE AT WORK

	Definition	Hallmarks
Self-management skills:		
Self-awareness	• The ability to recognize and understand one's moods, emotions, and drives, as well as their effect on others.	• Self-confidence • Realistic self-assessment • Self-deprecating sense of humour

(Continued)

	Definition	**Hallmarks**
Self-regulation	• The ability to control or redirect disruptive impulses and moods. • The propensity to suspend judgment—to think before acting.	• Trustworthiness and integrity • Comfort with ambiguity
Motivation	• A passion to work for reasons that go beyond money or status. • A propensity to pursue goals with energy and persistence.	• Openness to change • Strong drive to achieve • Optimism, even in the face of failure • Organizational commitment
Managing relationships:		
Empathy	• The ability to understand the emotional makeup of other people. • Skill in treating people according to their emotional reactions.	• Expertise in building and retaining talent • Cross-cultural sensitivity • Service to clients and customers
Social skill	• Proficiency in managing relationships and building networks. • An ability to find common ground and build rapport.	• Effectiveness in leading change • Persuasiveness • Expertise in building and leading teams

Source: Adapted and reprinted by permission of *Harvard Business Review.* Exhibit from "What Makes a Leader," by D. Goleman, January 2004. Copyright © 2004 by the Harvard Business School Publishing Corporation; all rights reserved.

Self-Awareness

Thousands of years ago, the Oracle of Delphi gave the advice: "Know thyself." The sentiment was echoed by Socrates, Plato, Thales and many other Greek philosophers. Self-awareness involves a person having a deep understanding of his or her emotions, strengths, weaknesses, and drives. People with strong self-awareness are neither overly critical nor unrealistically optimistic. Instead, they are honest with themselves and others.

People generally admire and respect candour. Leaders are constantly required to make judgment calls that require a candid assessment of capabilities—their own and those of others. People who assess themselves honestly (i.e., self-aware people) are well suited to do the same for the organizations they run.[23]

Self-Regulation

Biological impulses drive our emotions. Although we cannot do away with such impulses, we can strive to manage them. Self-regulation, which is akin to an ongoing inner conversation, frees us from being prisoners of our feelings.[24] People engaged in such conversation feel bad moods and emotional impulses just as everyone else does. However, they find strategies to control them and even channel them in useful ways.

People who are in control of their feelings and impulses are able to create an environment of trust and fairness, where political behaviour and infighting are sharply reduced and productivity tends to be high. People who have mastered their emotions are better able to bring about and implement changes in an organization. When a new initiative is announced, they are less likely to panic, better able to suspend judgment, to seek out information, and to listen as executives explain the new program.

Motivation

Successful executives are driven to achieve beyond expectations—their own and everyone else's. Although many people are driven by external factors, such as money and prestige, those with leadership potential are driven by a deeply embedded desire to achieve for the sake of achievement.

Motivated people show a passion for the work itself, such as by seeking out creative challenges, a love of learning, and taking pride in a job well done. They also have a high level of energy to do things better as well as a restlessness about the status quo. They are eager to explore new approaches to their work.

Empathy

Empathy is probably the most easily recognized component of EI. Empathy means thoughtfully considering an employee's feelings, along with other factors, in the process of making intelligent decisions. Empathy is particularly important in today's business environment for at least three reasons: (1) the increasing use of teams, (2) the rapid pace of globalization, and (3) the growing need to retain talent.[25]

When leading a team, a manager is often charged with arriving at a consensus—frequently in the face of high levels of emotion. Empathy enables a manager to sense and understand the viewpoints of everyone around the table.

Globalization typically involves cross-cultural dialogue that can easily lead to miscues. Empathetic people are attuned to the subtleties of body language; they can hear the message beneath the words being spoken. They have a deep understanding of the existence and importance of cultural and ethnic differences.

Empathetic leaders recognize that work is often demanding and employees can sometimes get worn down or stressed out. Empathetic leaders can appreciate, connect with, and create a work environment that high-performing knowledge workers find attractive and in which they excel.

Social Skill

Whereas the first three components of EI are all self-management skills, the last two—empathy and social skill—concern a person's ability to manage relationships with others. Social skill may be viewed as friendliness with a purpose: moving people in the direction you desire, whether that is agreement on a new marketing strategy or enthusiasm about a new product.

Socially skilled people tend to have a wide circle of acquaintances as well as a knack for finding common ground and building rapport. They recognize that nothing gets done alone, and they have a network in place when the time for action comes.

Emotional Intelligence: Some Cautionary Notes

Many great leaders have great reserves of empathy, interpersonal astuteness, awareness of their own feelings, and an awareness of their impact on others.[26] More importantly, they know how to apply these capabilities judiciously as best benefits the situation. However, sometimes, these same traits can lead to inappropriate behaviours.

Effective Leaders Have Empathy for Others

While leaders must have empathy to be effective, they also must be able to make the "tough decisions." Leaders must be able to appeal to logic and reason and acknowledge others' feelings so that people feel that the decisions made by the leader are correct and justified. However, it is easy to over-identify with others or confuse empathy with sympathy. This can make it more difficult to make the tough decisions.

Effective Leaders Are Astute Judges of People

Strong leaders are generally very perceptive about the people around them, including their motivations and abilities; however, a danger of this astuteness is that leaders may become judgmental and overly critical about the shortcomings they perceive in others. They may then become likely to dismiss other people's insights, making them feel undervalued.

Effective Leaders Are Passionate about What They Do, and They Show It

Emotionally intelligent leaders model enthusiasm for their work and the work of their subordinates. This does not mean that they are always cheerleaders. Rather, they may express their passion as persistence in pursuing an objective or a relentless focus on a valued principle. However, there is a fine line between being excited about something and letting your passion close your mind to other possibilities or cause you to ignore the realities that others may see.

Effective Leaders Create Personal Connections with Their People

Most effective leaders take time to engage employees individually and in groups, listening to their ideas, suggestions, and concerns and responding in ways that make people feel that their ideas are respected and appreciated. However, if the leader makes too many unannounced visits, it may create a culture of fear and micromanagement. Striking a correct balance is essential.

From a moral standpoint, emotional leadership is neither good nor bad. On the one hand, emotional leaders can be altruistic, focused on the general welfare of the company and its employees, and highly principled. On the other hand, they can be manipulative, selfish, and dishonest. For example, if a person is using leadership solely to gain power, that is not leadership at all.[27] Rather, he or she is using EI to grasp what people want and pander to those desires to gain authority and influence. After all, easy answers sell.

These observations suggest that EI traits need to be balanced; excessive deployment of one capability to the detriment of others is likely to lead to failure rather than success. Moreover, EI, in and of itself, is simply a set of capabilities that, to be effective, must be coupled with strong values and a moral compass to guide both the leader and the subordinates in the right direction. We will tackle the moral and ethical dimensions of leadership later in this chapter.

LO 4 DEVELOPING A LEARNING ORGANIZATION

Leading-edge organizations recognize the importance of having everyone involved in the process of actively learning and adapting. As noted by today's leading expert on learning organizations, Peter Senge of the Massachusetts Institute of Technology (MIT), the days when Henry Ford, Alfred Sloan, and Tom Watson "learned for the organization" are gone.

> In an increasingly dynamic, interdependent, and unpredictable world, it is simply no longer possible for anyone to "figure it all out at the top." The old model, "the top thinks and the local acts," must now give way to integrating thinking and acting at all levels. While the challenge is great, so is the potential payoff. "The person who figures out how to harness the collective genius of the people in his or her organization," according to former Citibank CEO Walter Wriston, "is going to blow the competition away."[28]

Learning and change typically involve the ongoing questioning of an organization's status quo or method of procedure. This means that all individuals throughout the organization must be reflective. Many organizations and their managers get so caught up in carrying out their day-to-day work that they rarely, if ever, stop to think objectively about themselves and their businesses. They often fail to ask the probing questions that might lead them to call into question their basic assumptions, to refresh their strategies, or to re-engineer their work processes. According to Michael Hammer and Steven Stanton, the pioneer consultants who touched off the re-engineering movement:

> Reflection entails awareness of self, of competitors, of customers. It means thinking without preconception. It means questioning cherished assumptions and replacing them with new approaches. It is the only way in which a winning company can maintain its leadership position, by which a company with great assets can ensure that they continue to be well deployed.[29]

To adapt to change, foster creativity, and remain competitive, leaders must build learning organizations. Exhibit 11-4 lists the five elements of a learning organization.

EXHIBIT 11-4

KEY ELEMENTS OF A LEARNING ORGANIZATION

1. Inspiring and motivating people with a mission or purpose.
2. Empowering employees at all levels.
3. Accumulating and sharing internal knowledge.
4. Gathering and integrating external information.
5. Challenging the status quo and enabling creativity.

Inspiring and Motivating People with a Mission or Purpose

Successful learning organizations create a proactive, creative approach to the unknown, actively solicit the involvement of employees at all levels, and enable all employees to use their intelligence and apply their imagination. Higher-level skills are required of everyone, not just of those at the top.[30] A learning environment involves organization-wide commitment to change, an action orientation, and applicable tools and methods.[31] It must be viewed by everyone as a guiding philosophy and not simply as another change program.

A critical requirement of all learning organizations is that everyone feels and supports a compelling purpose. In the words of the late William O'Brien, CEO of Hanover Insurance, "Before there can be meaningful participation, people must share certain values and pictures about where we are trying to go. We discovered that people have a real need to feel that they're part of an enabling mission."[32] Such a perspective is consistent with an intensive study by Kouzes and Posner, authors of *The Leadership Challenge*.[33] They analyzed data from nearly one million respondents who were leaders at various levels in many organizations throughout the world. A major finding was that what leaders struggle with most is communicating an image of the future that draws others in; that is, it speaks to what others see and feel. Employees want to feel they are part of something bigger and want to know what that bigger purpose is all about as they are asked to learn, adapt, and adjust to a rapidly changing, complex, and interconnected environment.[34]

Empowering Employees at All Levels

"The great leader is a great servant," asserted Ken Melrose, former CEO of Toro Company and author of *Making the Grass Greener on Your Side*.[35] A manager's role becomes one of creating an environment where employees can achieve their potential as they help move the organization toward its goals. Instead of viewing themselves as resource controllers and power brokers, leaders must envision themselves as flexible resources willing to assume numerous roles as coaches, information providers, teachers, decision makers, facilitators, supporters, or listeners, depending on the needs of their employees.[36]

Key to empowerment is effective leadership. Empowerment cannot occur in a leadership vacuum. According to Melrose, "You best lead by serving the needs of your people. You don't do their jobs for them; you enable them to learn and progress on the job." Robert Quinn and Gretchen Spreitzer made an interesting point about two diametrically opposite perspectives on empowerment—top-down and bottom-up.[37]

In the top-down perspective, empowerment is about delegation and accountability—senior management has developed a clear vision and has communicated specific plans to the rest of the organization.[38] This strategy for empowerment encompasses the following:

- Start at the top.
- Clarify the organization's mission, vision, and values.
- Clearly specify the tasks, roles, and rewards for employees.
- Delegate responsibility.
- Hold people accountable for results.

By contrast, the bottom-up view looks at empowerment as concerned with risk taking, growth, and change. It involves trusting people to "do the right thing" and having a tolerance for failure. It encourages employees to act with a sense of ownership and typically "ask for forgiveness rather than permission." Here, the salient elements of empowerment are as follows:

- Start at the bottom by understanding the needs of employees.
- Teach employees self-management skills, and model the desired behaviour.
- Build teams to encourage co-operative behaviour.
- Encourage intelligent risk taking.
- Trust people to perform.

These two perspectives draw a sharp contrast in assumptions that people make about trust and control. Many leading-edge organizations are moving in the direction of the second perspective—recognizing the need for trust, cultural control, and expertise at all levels instead of the extensive and cumbersome rules and regulations inherent in hierarchical control.[39] In the information economy, the strongest organizations are those that effectively use the talents of all the players on the team. Strategy Spotlight 11.5 illustrates how team training can enhance organizational learning.

11.5 STRATEGY SPOTLIGHT

Accelerating Learning by Teaching Teams

General Electric (GE) has a longstanding tradition of using training to empower its managers to improve performance. A Leadership, Innovation, and Growth (LIG) program launched by GE in 2006 revealed some important lessons: When whole teams are trained together, rather than only individual managers, the shared learning has a more profound effect. In the past, when individual managers took the lessons learned from a program back to their offices, they often had trouble persuading others to go along with what they had learned. By training all team members at once, LIG has accelerated the speed with which new learning is implemented as well as its long-term effectiveness.

The accelerated learning experience is enhanced when a few key principles are followed:

- ***Reach consensus about the barriers to change and how to address them.*** By having all team members together, the team can articulate both hard barriers (structural impediments, capabilities, and resource constraints) and soft barriers (team dynamics and competing priorities) that might affect proposed solutions.

- ***Develop a common language.*** Team members often need a new vocabulary of change—actual words that become part of the daily conversation when teams return to work. Referring to his company's new goals, GE CEO Jeffrey Immelt said the aim of the LIG program was "to embed growth into the DNA of our company."

- ***Create an action plan and a commitment to follow through.*** Focused work on an actual plan forms the basis for continued effort and ongoing learning. It also builds commitment.

By making learning team based, GE has accelerated the kinds of change processes that are needed to remain effective in a new business environment. The LIG program was developed specifically to enact Immelt's vision of a new GE—one in which expanding existing businesses and creating new ones takes priority over making acquisitions. Recognizing that such a change requires a lot of new learning, Immelt said, "A major change-management effort like this is a 10-year process. It takes a decade to build the talent, culture, and tools, and to learn from our mistakes." Creating a learning organization is a central aspect of Immelt's plan for GE.

Sources: J. R. Katzenbach and D. K. Smith, *The Wisdom of Teams* (New York: Collins Business, 2003); S. Prokesch, "How GE Teaches Teams to Lead Change," *Harvard Business Review,* 87(1), 2009, pp. 99–106; and www.ge.com.

Developing Leaders

Leadership development programs aid in the building of a learning organization in two different ways. First, programs teach participants new skills that help them be more capable in their current roles and more able to take on additional responsibility. In short, this helps enhance individual learning and, thus, increases the human capital of the firm. Second, these development programs can also train employees to be more effective at learning over time by giving them the skills to incorporate new information and better learn from their experiences.

Not all leadership development programs are equally effective, however. Research suggests that successful development programs share four common traits.[40] First, the programs are designed to fit the firm's overall strategy. For example, if a firm emphasizes organic growth, its leadership development program should emphasize building the skills to see opportunities in the firm's industry and related markets and developing internal talent. This will channel the learning capabilities of its leaders. Second, effective leadership development programs combine real-world experiences with classroom learning to build the desired skills. In line with this concept, one major engineering and construction firm emphasized developing skills in interacting with customers to build additional business. Participants were tasked to identify new business opportunities in their home units. One participant committed his team to develop a new order with a customer that spanned more than one of the group's business lines. Third, leader development programs need to have hard conversations to identify and overcome organizational biases that keep the firm from learning and being more flexible. One European industrial firm included frameworks for driving capital allocation decisions lower in the organization, but the en-trenched culture of the firm left managers reluctant to relinquish control. Once the trainers took this issue head-on, enlisting open-minded managers to take the leap first and report back to the team, and also emphasizing the learning opportunity for lower-level managers, participants more widely implemented the decentralization program. Fourth, top managers and trainers need to assess the impact of the training by following up with participants several months after the training to assess how effectively they have implemented the training, overcome the barriers to marking it work, and learned from the process.

Accumulating and Sharing Internal Knowledge

Effective organizations must also redistribute information, knowledge (skills to act on the information), and rewards.[41] A company might give front-line employees the power to act as "customer advocates," doing whatever is necessary to satisfy customers. The company needs to disseminate information by sharing customer expectations and feedback, as well as financial information. The employees must know about the goals of the business as well as how key value-creating activities in the organization are related to each other. Finally, organizations should allocate rewards based on how effectively employees use information, knowledge, and power to improve customer service quality and the company's overall performance.[42]

At Whole Foods Market, Inc., the largest natural foods grocer in North America, sharing internal information is a critical component of internal benchmarking.[43] Competition is intense within Whole Foods. Teams compete against their own goals for sales, growth, and productivity; they compete against different teams in their stores; and they compete against similar teams at different stores and regions. There is an elaborate system of peer reviews through which teams benchmark each other. The "Store Tour" is the most intense. On a periodic schedule, each Whole Foods store is toured by a group of as many as 40 visitors from another region. Lateral learning—discovering what your colleagues are doing right and carrying those practices into your organization—has become a driving force at Whole Foods. In addition to enhancing the sharing of company information both up and down as well as across the organization, leaders also need to develop means to tap into some of the more informal sources of internal information. In a recent survey of presidents, CEOs, board members, and top executives in a variety of nonprofit organizations, respondents were asked what differentiated the successful candidates for promotion. The consensus: The executive was seen as a person who listens. According to Peter Meyer, the author of the study, "The value of listening is clear: You cannot succeed in running a company if you do not hear what your people, customers, and suppliers are telling you . . . Listening and understanding well are key to making good decisions."[44]

Gathering and Integrating External Information

Recognizing opportunities, as well as threats, in the external environment is vital to a firm's success. As organizations and environments become more complex and evolve rapidly, it is far more critical for employees and managers to become more aware of environmental trends and events—both general and industry-specific ones—and more knowledgeable about their firm's competitors and customers. Information can be gathered from unlimited sources online, and everybody within the organization can actively participate in both the gathering and the integrating of such information. Much can be gleaned by reading trade and professional journals, books, and popular business magazines. Other venues for gathering external information include membership in professional or trade organizations, attendance at meetings and conventions, and networking among colleagues inside and outside of your industry. Intel's Andy Grove used to gather information from people like Dream-Works SKG's Steven Spielberg and Tele-Communications Inc.'s John Malone.[45] He famously believed that such interaction provides insights into how to make personal computers (PCs) more entertaining and better at communicating. Internally, Grove spent time with the young engineers who run Intel Architecture laboratories, an Oregon-based facility that Grove hoped would become the de facto research and development (R&D) laboratory for the entire PC industry.

Benchmarking can also be a useful structure for the gathering of external information. Here, managers seek out the best examples of a particular practice as part of an ongoing effort to improve the corresponding practice in their own organization.[46] Competitive benchmarking restricts the search for best practices to competitors, whereas functional benchmarking endeavours to determine best practices regardless of industry. Industry-specific standards (e.g., response times required to repair power outages in the electric utility industry) are typically best handled through competitive benchmarking, whereas more generic processes (e.g., answering 1-800 calls) lend themselves to functional benchmarking because the function is essentially the same in any industry.

Ford Motor Company used benchmarking to study Mazda's accounts payable operations.[47] Its initial goal of a 20-percent cut in its 500-employee accounts payable staff was ratcheted up to 75 percent and met. Ford found that staff spent most of their time trying to match conflicting data in a mass of paper, including purchase orders, invoices, and receipts. Following Mazda's example, Ford created an "invoiceless system," in which invoices no longer trigger payments to suppliers. The receipts do the job. It is often worth going directly to customers for information. For over 100 years, 3M has famously encouraged its sales force to go out and talk to the workers in the shop floors to find out what they needed, instead of calling only on procurement managers and company executives.[48] More recently, James Taylor, senior vice-president for global marketing at Gateway 2000, discussed the value of customer input in reducing response time, a critical success factor in the PC industry.

> We talk to 100,000 people a day—people calling to order a computer, shopping around, looking for tech support. Our website gets 1.1 million hits per day. The time it takes for an idea to enter this organization, get processed, and then go to customers for feedback is down to minutes. We've designed the company around speed and feedback.[49]

Challenging the Status Quo and Enabling Creativity

Earlier in this chapter, we discussed some of the barriers that leaders face when trying to bring about change in an organization. For a firm to become a learning organization, it must also overcome barriers that stifle creativity. This becomes quite a challenge if the firm is entrenched in a status quo mentality.

Perhaps the best way to challenge the status quo is for the leader to forcefully create a sense of urgency. For example, when Tom Kasten was vice president of Levi Strauss, he had a direct approach to initiating change:

> You create a compelling picture of the risks of not changing. We let our people hear directly from customers. We videotaped interviews with customers and played excerpts. One big customer said, "We trust many of your competitors implicitly. We sample their deliveries. We open all Levi's deliveries." Another said, "Your lead times are the worst. If you weren't Levi's, you'd be gone." It was powerful. I wish we had done more of it.[50]

Such initiative, if sincere and credible, establishes a shared mission and the need for major transformations. It can channel energies to bring about both change and creative endeavours.

Establishing a "culture of dissent" can be another effective means of questioning the status quo and serving as a spur toward creativity. Here, norms are established whereby dissenters can openly question a superior's perspective without fear of retaliation or retribution. Consider the perspective of Steven Ballmer, Microsoft's former CEO:

> Bill [Gates] brings to the company the idea that conflict can be a good thing. . . . . Bill knows it's important to avoid that gentle civility that keeps you from getting to the heart of an issue quickly. He likes it when anyone, even a junior employee, challenges him, and you know he respects you when he starts shouting back.[51]

Motorola has gone a step further and institutionalized its culture of dissent.[52] By filing a "minority report," an employee can go above his or her immediate supervisor's head and officially lodge a different point of view on a business decision. According to former CEO George Fisher, "I'd call it a healthy spirit of discontent and a freedom by and large to express your discontent around here or to disagree with whoever it is in the company, me or anybody else."

Closely related to the culture of dissent is the fostering of a culture that encourages risk taking. "If you're not making mistakes, you're not taking risks, and that means you're not going anywhere," claimed John Holt, co-author of *Celebrate Your Mistakes*.[53] "The key is to make errors faster than the competition, so you have more chances to learn and win."

Companies that cultivate cultures of experimentation and curiosity make sure that, in essence, *failure* is not an obscene word. They encourage mistakes as a key part of their competitive advantage. This philosophy was shared by Stan Shih, CEO of Acer, a Taiwan-based computer company. If a manager at Acer took an intelligent risk and made a mistake—even a costly one—Shih wrote off the loss as tuition payment for the manager's education. Such a culture must permeate the entire organization. As a high-tech executive told us during an interview: "Every person has the freedom to fail." Exhibit 11-5 offers insights on how organizations can both embrace risk and learn from failure.

EXHIBIT 11-5

BEST PRACTICES: LEARNING FROM FAILURES

It is innovation's great paradox: Success—that is, true breakthroughs—usually comes through failure. Here are some ideas on how to help your team get comfortable with taking risks and learning from mistakes:

- *Formalize Forums for Failure*

  To keep failures and the valuable lessons they offer from getting swept under the rug, *carve out time for reflection*. GE recently began sharing lessons from failures by bringing together managers whose "Imagination Breakthrough" efforts are put on the shelf.

(Continued)

- *Move the Goalposts*

  Innovation requires flexibility in meeting goals, since early predictions are often little more than educated guesses. Intuit's Scott Cook even suggests that teams developing new products ignore forecasts in the early days. "For every one of our failures, we had spreadsheets that looked awesome," he says.

- *Share Personal Stories*

  If employees hear leaders discussing their own failures, *they will feel more comfortable talking about their own.* But it is not just the CEO's job. "Front-line leaders are even more important," says Harvard Business School professor Amy Edmondson. "That person needs to be inviting, curious, and the first to say: 'I made a mistake'."

- *Bring in Outsiders*

  Outsiders can help neutralize the emotions and biases that prop up a flop. Customers can be most valuable. After its DNA chip failed, Corning brought pharmaceutical companies in early to test its new drug-discovery technology, Epic.

- *Prove Yourself Wrong, Not Right*

  Development teams tend to look for supporting, rather than countervailing, evidence. "You have to reframe what you're seeking in the early days," says Innosight's Scott Anthony. *"You're not really seeking proof that you have the right answer.* It is more about testing to prove yourself wrong."

- *Celebrate Smart Failures*

  Managers should design performance-management systems that reward risk taking and foster a long-term view. But they should also *celebrate failures that teach something new,* energizing people to try again and offering them closure.

LO 5 CREATING AN ETHICAL AND SOCIALLY RESPONSIBLE ORGANIZATION

Ethics may be defined as a system of right and wrong.[54] Ethics assists individuals in deciding when an act is moral or immoral, socially desirable or not. The sources for an individual's ethics include religious beliefs, national and ethnic heritage, family practices, community standards, educational experiences, and friends and neighbours. Business ethics is the application of ethical standards to commercial enterprise. Within the realm of ethical standards, today's corporations are expected to "do the right thing" for a range of stakeholders and the natural environment. Besides profit, a corporation is expected to be a good employer, a good citizen, a good partner, and an honest provider of goods and services to the markets it serves and the communities that it is a part of. Others argue that corporations have an obligation to actively advocate and address social and natural adversities, simply because they are frequently the only institution that has the wherewithal and resources to do so.[55] Tellingly, Tata, GMR, and other Indian conglomerates have undertaken such broad responsibilities in the subcontinent, in recognition of the inability of the government to adequately provide for its citizens. They regularly build houses, schools, water systems, hospitals, roads, and basic infrastructure in the communities where they operate.

Ethics and Strategy: Four Models of the Strategic Firm

Experience with a narrow economic focus on profit maximization is today leading both theorists and practitioners to challenge the utility of such an approach. Increasingly, managers are discovering the need to formulate strategies that incorporate a much broader notion of value creation. Thinking about ethics robustly has, among other things, been discovered to lead in many instances to superior outcomes, including competitive positioning and enhanced share value. Effective management requires that ethical reasoning and ethical principles and values play a central role in strategic management, but there are different degrees.

David Weitzner and James Darroch[56] argue that a gradually broadening vision of the role of ethics in strategy has led to the emergence of four models of the firm. The first is the **classic economic model** that has come to dominate strategic thinking, where strategic choice is limited to those activities that serve the core corporate objective of improving the firm's bottom line. This paradigm gives rise to strategies that provide solutions to a myriad of important problems facing a competitive firm, yet it also leaves managers with real and abiding problems labelled by economists as "externalities." As we discussed in Chapter 1, externalities are the social costs that the firm creates through its value-creating activities but does not necessarily have to pay for. Think of pollution, for example. Factories create pollution, which harms the environment and causes local communities to suffer, yet most firms do not have to pay to eliminate all of the pollution that they have caused.

The classic economic response to the issue of externalities, such as pollution and climate change, is to define rigidly the boundaries between the responsibilities of civil society and those of the firm. This position has a certain pragmatic appeal because it lets capitalists focus on what they do best and leaves the challenge of regulating the social, economic, and environmental impacts of economic activity to the government so as to achieve ethically justifiable economic outcomes.

It is worth noting, however, that even this first model with its narrow focus on maximizing the bottom line allows a role, though a very constrained role, for ethics in recognizing that the pursuit of profits should be constrained by respect for the law and local ethical custom. It follows that on this model of the firm there will be no room for strategies that involve fraud or deliberate deception or illegal behaviour. Further, employees will be expected to respect fundamental moral values, such as loyalty to the firm, honesty in their dealings with the firm, respect for and proper use of company property, and so on. These ethical constraints may or may not be explicitly articulated as ethical constraints. However, they will connect to strategy because of the negative impacts and risks which failure to respect them is likely to give rise to.

The second model is the **economic rationalist model,** where the strategic decision maker recognizes the importance of embracing multiple goals in assessing strategic choices, but the trade-offs are assessed against a standard of enlightened self-interest. This model does not construe ethics in a very narrow role and allows for the incorporation of ethics in addressing broader economic issues of identified externalities, such as social or environmental impacts. It explicitly calls on the need to consider how related decisions might advance the bottom line. Although this type of firm will still privilege economic indicators of success as the ultimate arbitrators when faced with internal conflict between ethics and profit maximization, this model recognizes that addressing ethical concerns in an interesting way may be critical to the mission of the firm. A strategist working within the framework of this model will recognize the strategic importance of crafting a value proposition that incorporates an ethical vision in order to attract like-minded customers and employees.

What distinguishes this second model from the classic model is that managers here recognize the importance of taking the time to think explicitly about ethics as a source of competitive advantage. Ethical stances can be priced, and as long as they lead to profitability, they will be embraced. An example is the active campaigning by Hewlett-Packard (HP) to encourage "taking back" old equipment and to promote recycling laws for the computer and home electronics industry. Seen from a strategic perspective, not only is HP's strategy a good thing in and of itself, it also creates competitive advantage for HP over rivals whose value and logistic chains are not as well constructed to deliver in this value dimension.

The **good citizen model** is a third approach to strategy that embraces multiple goals and rationalities. This third approach recognizes that it is not meaningful or practical to view the ethical elements of a business decision as distinct from the strategic elements. It acknowledges, as does the economic rationalist model, costs and benefits associated with acting on or ignoring ethics. But this paradigm rejects enlightened self-interest as the sole ethical criterion for determining the role of ethics in strategic management.

This third approach to strategy refuses to limit ethical choices to the pursuit of profit maximization. Strategists governed by this mode see themselves both as an agent of the firm and a responsible member of society, with moral and fiduciary obligations. On the one hand, this model poses strategic challenges not faced by the first two models, as it offers no easy prescriptions, formulas, or templates to guide strategic choice. On the other hand, its strength lies in the way in which it is able to encompass the world of visionaries and those committed to disruptive change. Think of Ballard Power Systems. Its business is creating clean-energy hydrogen-powered fuel cells. Its goal is to make money by having its product dominate the energy market. Of course, if it is successful, it will have reshaped many industries by moving them away from classic "dirty" energy sources toward a more environmentally responsible model.

The final model is the **activist strategist model,** in which the limits in a bottom line-focused economic rationality is recognized and an effort is made to reach out to embrace multiple rationalities, rejecting the notion that the corporate objective should be profit maximization. Although managing a firm with an activist stance may be profitable and may require profitability, the strategic logic of business entities adopting this model will not be driven by the maximization of profits but, rather, by some other ethically significant goal, such as sustainability.

The stance taken by managers of firms that adopt this model will require that the entire organization recognize the existence of competing rationalities and goals. This approach will generally be tied to a niche or differentiated strategy whereby the firm's values can be readily identified by prospective market segments. One could equate this position with ethical positions driven by religious or ideological concerns. For this model, while profit maximization is not the goal, the potential for significant profits cannot be ruled out. Organizations governed by this strategy model may and do find willing shareholders, as demonstrated by the field of ethical, socially responsible investment (SRI) and responsible investment (RI). However, the refusal to pursue profit maximization as the core strategic objective may mean that firms and other business entities that embrace this model will need to seek investors that share its commitment to the model.

The boundaries defining the role of ethics in strategic thinking vary with each of these four models. What the existence of four alternative approaches to strategy implies, however, is that developing an effective, well-thought-out strategy requires that decision makers determine what ethical values will guide the operations of the entity and the strategic model that will govern their strategic thinking. This will involve determining, for example, the goals and objectives of the firm or organization and developing an understanding of the entity's social, economic, and environmental responsibilities.

Individual Ethics versus Organizational Ethics

Many leaders think of ethics as a question of personal scruples, a confidential matter between employees and their consciences. Such leaders are quick to describe any wrongdoing as an isolated incident, the work of a rogue employee. They assume the company should not bear any responsibility for individual misdeeds. In their view, ethics has nothing to do with leadership.

Ethics has everything to do with leadership. Seldom does the character flaw of a lone actor completely explain corporate misconduct. Instead, unethical business practices typically involve the tacit, if not explicit, co-operation of others and reflect the values, attitudes, and behaviour patterns that define an organization's operating culture. Ethics is as much an organizational as a personal issue. Leaders who fail to provide proper leadership to institute proper systems and controls that facilitate ethical conduct share responsibility with those who conceive, execute, and knowingly benefit from corporate misdeeds.[57]

The ethical orientation of a leader is a key factor in promoting ethical behaviour. Ethical leaders must take personal, moral responsibility for their actions and decision making. Leaders who exhibit high ethical standards become role models for others and raise an organization's overall level of ethical behaviour. Ethical behaviour must start with the leader before the employees can be expected to perform accordingly.

Over the last decade, there has been a growing interest in corporate ethical performance. Some reasons for this trend may be the increasing lack of public confidence in corporate activities, the growing emphasis on quality-of-life issues, and a spate of recent corporate scandals. Without a strong ethical culture, the chances of ethical crises occurring increase. Ethical crises can be very expensive—both in terms of financial costs and in the erosion of human capital and overall reputation of the firm. Merely adhering to the minimum regulatory standards may not be enough to remain competitive in a world that is becoming more and more socially conscious.

The past several years have been characterized by numerous examples of unethical and illegal behaviour by many top-level corporate executives. These include executives of firms, such as Enron, Tyco, Worldcom, Inc., Adelphia, Hollinger, Livent, and Healthsouth Corp., who were all forced to resign and are facing (or have been convicted of) a slew of criminal and civil charges. Perhaps the most glaring example is Bernie Madoff, whose Ponzi scheme, which unravelled in 2008, defrauded investors of $50 billion in assets they had set aside for retirement and charitable donations.

The ethical organization is characterized by a conception of ethical values and integrity as a driving force of the enterprise.[58] Ethical values shape the search for opportunities, the design of organizational systems, and the decision-making process used by individuals and groups. They provide a common frame of reference that serves as a unifying force across different functions, lines of business, and employee groups. Organizational ethics helps define what a company is and what it stands for.

There are many potential benefits for an ethical organization, but they are often indirect. Research has found somewhat inconsistent results concerning the overall relationship between ethical performance and measures of financial performance.[59] However, positive relationships have generally been found between ethical performance and strong organizational culture, increased employee efforts, lower turnover, higher organizational commitment, and enhanced social responsibility.

A strong ethical orientation and a commitment to the social and natural environment can have a positive effect on employee dedication and motivation to excel. This is particularly important in today's knowledge-intensive organizations, where human capital is critical in creating value and competitive advantages. Positive, constructive relationships among individuals (i.e., social capital) are vital in leveraging human capital and other resources in an organization. Drawing on the concept of stakeholder management, an ethically sound organization can also strengthen its bonds among its suppliers, customers, and governmental agencies. Finally, research has documented that organizations with a "triple bottom line" approach (as discussed in Chapter 1, the first bottom line presents the financial measures that all leaders are familiar with, the second bottom line assesses ecological and material capitals, and the third bottom line measures human and social capitals) can better attract young talent because they can demonstrate better fit with the prospective employee's value system; the care they take of their environment signals that they would similarly take good care of their employees; and they are viewed as more prestigious to work for.[60]

Integrity-Based Approaches versus Compliance-Based Approaches to Organizational Ethics

Before discussing the key elements of an ethical organization, we must understand the links between organizational integrity and the personal integrity of an organization's members.[61] High-integrity organizations cannot exist without high-integrity individuals. However, individual integrity is rarely self-sustaining. Even good people can lose their bearings when faced with pressures, temptations, and heightened performance expectations in the absence of organizational support systems and ethical boundaries. Organizational integrity rests on a concept of purpose, responsibility, and ideals for an organization as a whole. An important responsibility of leadership is to create this ethical framework and develop the organizational capabilities to make it operational.[62]

Lynn Paine, an ethics scholar at Harvard University, identifies two approaches: (1) the compliance-based approach and (2) the integrity-based approach. Exhibit 11-6 compares compliance-based and integrity-based strategies. Faced with the prospect of litigation, several organizations reactively implement compliance-based ethics programs. Such programs are typically designed by a corporate counsel with the goal of preventing, detecting, and punishing legal violations. But being ethical is much more than being legal, and an integrity-based approach addresses the issue of ethics in a more comprehensive manner.

EXHIBIT 11-6 APPROACHES FOR ETHICS MANAGEMENT

Characteristics	Compliance-Based Approach	Integrity-Based Approach
Ethos	Conformity with externally imposed standards	Self-governance according to chosen standards
Objective	Prevent criminal misconduct	Enable responsible conduct
Leadership	Lawyer-driven	Management-driven with aid of lawyers, human resources, and others
Methods	Education, reduced discretion, auditing and controls, penalties	Education, leadership, accountability, organizational systems and decision processes, auditing and controls, penalties
Behavioural assumptions	Autonomous beings guided by material self-interest	Social beings guided by material self-interest, values, ideals, peers

Source: Reprinted by permission of *Harvard Business Review.* Exhibit from "Managing Organizational Integrity," by L. S. Paine. Copyright © 1994 by the Harvard Business School Publishing Corporation; all rights reserved.

Integrity-based ethics programs combine a concern for law with an emphasis on managerial responsibility for ethical behaviour. It is broader, deeper, and more demanding than a legal compliance initiative. It is broader in that it seeks to enable responsible conduct. It is deeper in that it cuts to the ethos and operating systems of an organization and its members, their core guiding values, thoughts, and actions. It is more demanding because it requires an active effort to define the responsibilities that constitute an organization's ethical compass. Most importantly, organizational ethics is seen as the responsibility of management.

A corporate counsel may play a role in designing and implementing integrity strategies, but it is managers at all levels and across all functions that are involved in the process. Once integrated into the day-to-day operations, such strategies can prevent damaging ethical lapses while tapping into powerful human impulses for moral thought and action. Ethics becomes the governing ethos of an organization and not a burdensome constraint. Strategy Spotlight 11.6 discusses how an organization goes beyond mere compliance to laws in building an ethical organization. By contrast, Strategy Spotlight 11.7 discusses what can happen when an organization does not deliberately build ethical values into their mission.

11.6 STRATEGY SPOTLIGHT

Instilling Ethics at Texas Instruments

In teaching ethics to its employees, Texas Instruments (TI), the $14-billion chip and electronics manufacturer, asks them to run an issue through the following steps: Is it legal? Is it consistent with the company's stated values? Will the employee feel bad doing it? What will the public think if the action is reported in the press? Does the employee think it is wrong? If the employees are not sure of the ethicality of the issue, they are encouraged to ask someone until they are clear about it. In the process, employees can approach high-level personnel and even the company's lawyers. At TI, the question of ethics goes far beyond concerns about legality. It is no surprise that this company is a benchmark for corporate ethics and has been a recipient of three ethics awards: the David C. Lincoln Award for Ethics and Excellence in Business, the American Business Ethics Award, and the Bentley College Center for Business Ethics Award.

Source: "Company Ethics: Benchmarks and Quicktest," www.ti.com. Courtesy Texas Instruments

Compliance-based approaches are externally motivated—that is, based on the fear of punishment for doing something unlawful. In contrast, integrity-based approaches are driven by a personal and organizational commitment to ethical behaviour.

To become a highly ethical and socially responsible organization, a firm must have in place several key elements:

- Role models.
- Corporate credos and codes of conduct.
- Reward and evaluation systems.
- Policies and procedures.

11.7 STRATEGY SPOTLIGHT

Tragedy and the Fallout for Joe Fresh

On April 24, 2013, an eight-storey building collapsed in the Savar district of Dhaka, Bangladesh. The building housed garment factories manufacturing clothing for many western labels, including the well-known Canadian label, Joe Fresh. Threats of boycotting Joe Fresh unless swift action was taken appeared almost immediately. This was the first bump in the road for the successful clothing line that had developed under Loblaw Companies Ltd.

With stores located within Loblaws outlets, Joe Fresh was built on the foundation of two key principles: design and value. As part of their mission to keep costs down and products affordable, consistently with almost all clothing firms, Joe Fresh had been outsourcing its manufacturing to China in order to take advantage of lower production costs. High inflation and rising labour costs in China, however, had driven them to manufacture the bulk of their products in other southeast Asian countries such as India and Bangladesh.

When the roof of a large section of the building in Dhaka collapsed, apparently due to shoddy construction and despicable labour practices, it instantly killed hundreds of workers and trapped hundreds more inside. Many of Loblaw Company's decisions were called into question. Over the days and weeks that followed, and in spite of frantic rescue efforts, the death toll climbed to over 1,120 people and more than 2,000 people were injured, making it the deadliest industrial accident in Bangladesh history.

Joe Fresh, sourcing much of the manufacturing of their clothing to Bangladesh in the interest of keeping costs low and staying competitive within the industry, had not anticipated the possibility of such a catastrophic event. The tragic collapse of the Savar building was by far the biggest ethical challenge the company had ever faced, and Joe Fresh needed to take action in order to both be socially responsible and preserve its brand image. While Loblaws had specific policies in place for supply chain ethics and vendor requirements, Joe Fresh had never marketed ethical sourcing as one of its selling points. Not only did the public need to be satisfied, but the brand also needed to be certain it was geared toward the right direction for the future. How could Joe Fresh expect its customers to keep coming back, and for the brand to continue building on past success, without taking swift action to prevent such a tragic accident from occurring again in the company's supply chain?

Source: Anonymous, Loblaw's Joe Fresh rolls out south of border, Canadian Grocer, 11 Oct 2011; Julhas, A, Joe Fresh Boycott? Bangladesh Factory Collapse Stokes Anger Among Some Consumers, Huffington Post, 26 Apr 2013; Lindsey, R, Arun, D, and Sarah, S, Joe Fresh Confirms Clothing was Produced in Bangladesh Factory that Collapsed, Toronto Star, 25 Apr 2013, Anonymous, Bangladesh Building Collapse Kills More Than 230; Joe Fresh Clothing, Other brands made at site, Toronto Star, 25 Apr 2013; the company's financial statements and website.

These elements are highly interrelated. Reward structures and policies will be useless if leaders are not sound role models. That is, leaders who implicitly say, "Do as I say, not as I do," will quickly have their credibility eroded, and such actions will sabotage other elements that are essential to building an ethical and socially responsible organization. Corporations, such as GE, IBM, Johnson & Johnson, Nestlé, and Intel, are reconsidering their social and corporate performances and introducing the concept of shared value as a new way to achieve economic success. They have adopted specific elements within their structures and systems to explicitly recognize that a corporation creating value cannot do so in isolation and without acknowledging the social implications of its actions.

Role Models

For good or for bad, leaders are role models in their organizations. Leaders must "walk the talk"; they must be consistent in their words and deeds. The values as well as the character of leaders become transparent to an organization's employees through their behaviours. When leaders do not believe in the ethical standards that they are trying to inspire, they will not be effective as good role models. Being an effective leader often includes taking responsibility for ethical lapses within the organization—even though the executives themselves are not directly involved. Consider the perspective of Dennis Bakke, former CEO of Applied Energy Services (AES), a $13-billion global electricity company based in Arlington, Virginia.

> There was a major breach (in 1992) of the AES values. Nine members of the water treatment team in Oklahoma lied to the EPA (Environmental Protection Agency) about water quality at the plant. There was no environmental damage, but they lied about the test results. A new, young chemist at the plant discovered it, told a team leader, and we then were notified. Now, you could argue that the people who lied were responsible and were accountable, but the senior management team also took responsibility by taking pay cuts. My reduction was about 30 percent.[63]

Such action enhances the loyalty and commitment of employees throughout the organization. Many would believe that it would have been much easier (and personally less expensive!) for Bakke and his management team to merely take strong punitive action against the nine individuals who were acting contrary to the behaviour expected in AES's ethical culture. However, by taking responsibility for the misdeeds, the top executives—through their highly visible action—made it clear that responsibility and penalties for ethical lapses go well beyond the "guilty" parties. Such courageous behaviour by leaders helps to strengthen an organization's ethical environment.

Increasingly, senior executives go beyond philanthropy and serve on boards of nongovernmental organizations (NGOs), actively participate in the works of not-for-profit organizations, and connect their actions to the diverse interests of their firm's stakeholders. Some individuals, such as Seymour Schulich, Guy Laliberté, and Kenneth Thomson, have served as role models for themselves and their corporations by taking an active role and contributing to the community, the arts, and education.

Corporate Credos and Codes of Conduct

Corporate credos and codes of conduct are mechanisms that provide statements of norms and beliefs as well as guidelines for decision making. They provide employees with a clear understanding of the organization's policies and ethical position. Such guidelines also provide the basis for employees to refuse to commit unethical acts and make them aware of issues before they are faced with a situation. For such codes to be truly effective, organizational members must be aware of them and know what behavioural guidelines are contained in these

11.8 STRATEGY SPOTLIGHT

Elements of a Corporate Code

Corporate codes are not only useful for conveying organizational norms and policies, but they also serve to legitimize an organization in the eyes of others. In the United States, federal guidelines advise judges, when determining how to sentence a company convicted of a crime, to consider whether the company had a written code and was out of compliance with its own ethical guidelines. The United Nations and countries around the world have endorsed codes as a way to promote corporate social responsibility. As such, a code provides an increasingly important corporate social contract that signals a company's willingness to act ethically.

For employees, codes of conduct serve four key purposes.

1. They help employees from diverse backgrounds work more effectively across cultural backgrounds.

2. They provide a reference point for decision making.

3. They help attract individuals who want to work for a business that embraces high standards.

4. They help a company to manage risk by reducing the likelihood of damaging misconduct.

With the recent scandals on Wall Street, many corporations are trying to put more teeth into their codes of conduct. NASDAQ now requires that listed companies distribute their codes to all employees. German software giant SAP's codes of conduct inform employees that violations of the codes "can result in consequences that affect employment and could possibly lead to external investigation, civil law proceedings, or criminal charges." Clearly, codes of conduct serve an important role in maintaining an ethical organization.

Sources: L. Paine, R. Deshpande, J. D. Margolis, and K. E. Bettcher, "Up to Code: Does Your Company's Conduct Meet World Class Standards?," *Harvard Business Review,* 82(12), 2005, pp. 122–126; and A. Stone, "Putting Teeth in Corporate Ethics Codes," www.businessweek.com, February 19, 2004.

codes.[64] Strategy Spotlight 11.8 identifies four key reasons why codes of conduct support organizational efforts to maintain a safe and ethical workplace.

Large corporations are not the only ones to develop and use codes of conduct. Small and privately held companies need and benefit from similarly clear statements that tell both their employees and their customers and suppliers about their commitment to honesty, ethical behaviour, and integrity.

Perhaps the best-known credo is that of Johnson & Johnson (J&J) (Exhibit 11-7). The credo stresses honesty, integrity, superior products, and putting people before profits. What distinguishes the J&J credo from others is the amount of energy the company's top managers devote to ensuring that employees live by its precepts. Over a three-year period, J&J undertook a massive effort to ensure that its original credo, already decades old, was still valid. More than 1,200 managers attended two-day seminars in groups of 25, with explicit instructions to challenge the credo. The president or CEO of the firm presided over each session. The company came out of the process believing that its original document was still valid. However, the questioning process continues. Such "challenge meetings" continue to be held every other year for all new managers. These efforts force J&J to question, internalize, and then implement its credo. Such investments have paid off handsomely many times—most notably in 1982, when eight people died from ingesting capsules of Tylenol, one of J&J's flagship products, which had been laced with cyanide. J&J's leaders, including James Burke, made an across-the-board recall of the product, even though the product tampering had affected only a limited number of untraceable units. The prompt and unequivocal action sent a strong message throughout the organization and in the community.

JOHNSON & JOHNSON'S CREDO

We believe our first responsibility is to the doctors, nurses and patients, to mothers and fathers and all others who use our products and services. In meeting their needs, everything we do must be of high quality. We must constantly strive to reduce our costs in order to maintain reasonable prices. Customers' orders must be serviced promptly and accurately. Our suppliers and distributors must have an opportunity to make a fair profit.

We are responsible to our employees, the men and women who work with us throughout the world. Everyone must be considered as an individual. We must respect their dignity and recognize their merit. They must have a sense of security in their jobs. Compensation must be fair and adequate, and working conditions clean, orderly, and safe. We must be mindful of ways to help our employees fulfill their family responsibilities. Employees must feel free to make suggestions and complaints. There must be equal opportunity for employment, development, and advancement for those qualified. We must provide competent management, and their actions must be just and ethical.

We are responsible to the communities in which we live and work and to the world community as well. We must be good citizens—support good works and charities and bear our fair share of taxes. We must encourage civic improvements and better health and education. We must maintain in good order the property we are privileged to use, protecting the environment and natural resources.

Our final responsibility is to our stockholders. Business must make a sound profit. We must experiment with new ideas. Research must be carried on, innovative programs developed, and mistakes paid for. New equipment must be purchased, new facilities provided, and new products launched. Reserves must be created to provide for adverse times. When we operate according to these principles, the stockholders should realize a fair return.

Source: Reprinted with permission of Johnson & Johnson Co.

Reward and Evaluation Systems

It is entirely possible for a highly ethical leader to preside over an organization that commits several unethical acts. How? A flaw in the organization's reward structure may inadvertently cause individuals to act in an inappropriate manner if rewards are seen as being distributed on the basis of outcomes rather than the means by which goals and objectives are achieved.[65]

Many companies have developed reward and evaluation systems that determine whether a manager is acting in an ethical manner. For example, Raytheon, a $20-billion defence contractor, incorporates the following items in its "Leadership Assessment Instrument":[66]

- Maintains unequivocal commitment to honesty, truth, and ethics in every facet of behaviour.
- Conforms to the letter and intent of company policies while working to affect any necessary policy changes.
- Actions are consistent with words; follows through on commitments; readily admits mistakes.
- Is trusted and inspires others to be trusted.

As noted by Dan Burnham, Raytheon's former CEO: "What do we look for in a leadership candidate with respect to integrity? What we're really looking for are people who have developed an inner gyroscope of ethical principles. We look for people for whom ethical thinking is part of what they do—no different from 'strategic thinking' or 'tactical thinking.'"

LO 6

Socially responsible organizations recognize that their symbiosis with the community is not a one-sided relationship, where businesses are simply called to support the community that they are a part of, necessitating trade-offs between economic performance and social good, but that businesses rely on the health of the society to drive demand and provide public assets and support. As such, the evaluation and reward systems of the businesses incorporate elements that account for shared values, social contributions, and environmental sustainability initiatives.

Policies and Procedures

Many situations that a firm faces have regular, identifiable patterns. Leaders tend to handle them by establishing a policy or procedure to be followed that can be applied uniformly to each occurrence. Such guidelines can be useful in specifying the proper relationships with a firm's customers and suppliers. For example, Levi Strauss has developed stringent global sourcing guidelines. When awarding contracts, Chemical Bank has a policy of forbidding any review that would determine if the suppliers are also customers of Chemical Bank.

Carefully developed policies and procedures guide behaviour so that all employees will be encouraged to behave in an ethical and socially responsible manner. However, the policies must be reinforced with effective communication, enforcement, and monitoring, as well as sound corporate governance practices. Some companies, such as Shell Canada, have created strong codes of ethics and introduced ombudsman offices to provide confidentiality and protection in the case of complaints.[67]

Explicit policies for sustainable behaviour; initiatives for promoting the 3Rs of "reduce, reuse, recycle"; and social contributions, such as the CIBC Run for the Cure, go beyond the explicit social standards set by legislation, rules of trade, international agreements, and the standards of a civic society. Firms that aspire to become ethical and socially responsible meet not just explicit standards but implicit societal expectations regarding all their activities.

SUMMARY

Strategic leadership is vital in ensuring that strategies are formulated and implemented in an effective manner. Leaders must play a central role in performing three critical and interdependent activities: setting the direction, designing the organization, and nurturing a culture committed to excellence and ethical behaviour. If leaders ignore or are ineffective at performing any one of the three, the organization will not be very successful. We also identified three elements of leadership that contribute to success—integrative thinking, overcoming barriers to change, and the effective use of power.

For leaders to effectively fulfil their activities, emotional intelligence (EI) is very important. Five elements that contribute to EI are self-awareness, self-regulation, motivation, empathy, and social skill. The first three elements pertain to self-management skills, whereas the last two are associated with a person's ability to manage relationships with others. We also addressed some of the potential drawbacks from the ineffective use of EI. These include the dysfunctional use of power as well as a tendency to become overly empathetic, which may result in unreasonably lowered performance expectations.

Leaders must also play a central role in creating a learning organization. Gone are the days when the top-level managers "think" and all others in the organization "do." With the rapidly changing, unpredictable, and complex competitive environments that characterize most industries, leaders must engage everyone in the ideas and energies of people throughout the organization. Great ideas can come from anywhere in the organization—from the executive suite to the factory floor. The five elements that we discussed as central to a learning organization are inspiring and motivating people with a mission or purpose, empowering people at all levels throughout the organization, accumulating and sharing internal knowledge, gathering external information, and challenging the status quo to stimulate creativity.

In the final section of the chapter, we addressed a leader's central role in instilling ethical and socially responsible behaviour in the organization. We discussed the enormous costs that firms face when ethical crises arise—costs in terms of financial and reputational loss as well as the erosion of human capital and relationships with suppliers, customers, society at large, and governmental agencies. And, as we would expect, the benefits of having a strong ethical organization are also numerous. We discussed four approaches to incorporating ethics into strategy, from the classic economic paradigm to the economic rationalist, the good citizen to the activist. We compared compliance-based approaches with integrity-based approaches to organizational ethics. Compliance-based approaches are largely externally motivated; that is, they are motivated by the fear of punishment for doing something that is unlawful. Integrity-based approaches, in contrast, are driven by a personal and organizational commitment to ethical behaviour. We also addressed the four key elements of an ethical organization: role models, corporate credos and codes of conduct, reward and evaluation systems, and policies and procedures.

Summary Review Questions

1. Three key activities—setting a direction, designing the organization, and nurturing a culture and ethics—are all part of what effective leaders do on a regular basis. Explain how these three activities are interrelated.

2. Define emotional intelligence (EI). What are the key elements of EI? Why is EI so important to successful strategic leadership? Discuss the potential "downsides" of EI.

3. The knowledge a firm possesses can be a source of competitive advantage. Describe ways that a firm can continuously learn to maintain its competitive position.

4. How can the five central elements of "learning organizations" be incorporated into global companies?

5. What are the benefits to firms and their shareholders of conducting business in an ethical manner?

6. Firms that fail to behave in an ethical manner can incur high costs. What are these costs, and what is their source?

7. What are the most important differences between an "integrity organization" and a "compliance organization" in a firm's approach to organizational ethics?

8. What are some of the important mechanisms for promoting ethics in a firm?

REFLECTING ON CAREER IMPLICATIONS

1. *Strategic Leadership:* Do the managers in your firm effectively set the direction, design the organization, and instill a culture committed to excellence and ethical behaviour? If you are in a position of leadership, do you practise all of these three elements effectively?

2. *Power:* What sources of power do managers in your organization use? For example, if there is an overemphasis on organizational sources of power (e.g., position power), there could be negative implications for creativity, morale, and turnover among professionals. How much power do you have? What is the basis of it? How might it be used to both advance your career goals and benefit the firm?

3. *Emotional Intelligence:* Do leaders of your firm have sufficient levels of EI? Alternatively, are there excessive levels of EI present that have negative implications for your organization? Is your level of EI sufficient to allow you to have effective interpersonal and judgment skills to enhance your career success?

4. *Learning Organization:* Does your firm effectively practise all of the five elements of the learning organization? If one or more elements are absent, adaptability and change will be compromised. What can you do to enhance any of the elements that might be lacking?

5. *Ethics:* Does your organization practise a compliance-based culture or integrity-based ethical culture? Integrity-based cultures can enhance your personal growth. In addition, such cultures foster greater loyalty and commitment among all employees.

EXPERIENTIAL EXERCISE

Select two well-known business leaders—one you admire and one you do not. Evaluate each of them on the five characteristics of emotional intelligence.

Emotional Intelligence Characteristics	Admired Leader	Leader Not Admired
Self-awareness		
Self-regulation		
Motivation		
Empathy		
Social skills		

APPLICATION QUESTIONS AND EXERCISES

1. Identify two CEOs whose leadership you admire. What is it about their skills, attributes, and effective use of power that causes you to admire them?

2. Founders have an important role in developing their organization's culture and values. At times, their influence persists for many years. Identify and describe two organizations in which the cultures and values established by the founder(s) continue to flourish. You may find research on the Internet helpful in completing this exercise.

3. Some leaders place a great emphasis on developing superior human capital. In what ways does this help a firm to develop and sustain competitive advantages?

4. In this chapter, we discussed the five elements of a "learning organization." Select a firm with which you are familiar, and discuss whether or not it epitomizes some (or all) of these elements.

ETHICS AND CORPORATE SOCIAL RESPONSIBILITY QUESTIONS

1. Sometimes organizations must go outside the firm to hire talent, thus bypassing employees already working for the firm. Are there conditions under which this might raise ethical considerations?

2. Ethical crises can occur in virtually any organization. Describe some of the systems, procedures, and processes that can help prevent such crises.

3. The recent failures of large financial institutions have brought to light the exorbitant compensation packages for executives who have been walking away with millions of dollars in their pockets, while the companies they led into crisis are suffering losses of billions of dollars. These executives have had legal contracts that entitle them to those payouts. Should companies or governments try to void those contracts? What may be the implications of those efforts?

Board: © Everythingpossible/Dreamstimecom; Tablet: VICTOR DE SCHWANBERG

CHAPTER TWELVE

MANAGING INNOVATION AND FOSTERING ENTREPRENEURSHIP

LEARNING OBJECTIVES

After reading this chapter, you should have a good understanding of:

LO 1 The importance of innovation in achieving an organization's mission and the role of corporate entrepreneurship in organizational renewal.

LO 2 The challenges and pitfalls of managing innovation processes.

LO 3 How an entrepreneurial orientation can enhance a firm's efforts to develop promising corporate venture initiatives.

LO 4 The role of opportunities, resources, and entrepreneurship in successfully pursuing new ventures.

LO 5 The importance of financing, as well as human capital, social capital, and government resources, in supporting new ventures.

LO 6 Three types of entry strategies—pioneering, imitative, and adaptive—commonly used to launch a new venture.

LO 7 How the generic strategies of overall cost leadership, differentiation, and focus are used by new ventures and small businesses.

CASE STUDY

JoieFarm (zh-wah farm) was established as an on-farm cooking school and European-style guesthouse in 2004 by trained chef Heidi Noble and sommelier Michael Dinn to celebrate the pleasure and joy of wine and food in the Okanagan Valley in South Central British Columbia.[1] In 2016, the winery received over 30,000 guests and had revenues in excess of $3,000,000.

Photo courtesy of JoieFarm

JoieFarm's founders did not have any formal winemaking training, but they did have experience in the wine and restaurant trade. In ten years, their tiny farm business grew from a "cute" agri-tourism attraction to a small-scale wine brand (even though they did not build their own production facility or plant their vineyard until 2007) to an ever-expanding mega-brand, selling 18,500 cases of wine in 2017.

Their growth from the early days of producing just 800 cases to the 10,000 case mark was rather unusual: JoieFarm carried no year-over-year wine inventory, but focused instead on white and rosé wines, which required no barrel aging. Specifically engineered for a turnaround within the same vintage year, their wines were considered early to bottle, and were released in the spring season into Vancouver's market. Noble and Dinn's experience in the local restaurant business informed not only the style of their wines, but also *when* to release them—they knew who bought what, when, and in what quantity. This made the growth of the brand fluid, dependable, and somewhat predictable. Over time, their focus on the vineyard gradually drew them away from the guesthouse and the agri-tourism business.

In early 2015, Noble bought out Dinn. Her intent was to stay hands-on as a winemaker while reinvigorating the brand. She embraced the changing restaurant landscape and, using the old farmhouse (once home to the guesthouse and cooking school), opened up a tasting room on the JoieFarm site, located on the beautiful Naramata Bench in the Okanagan Valley. It was a charming location to welcome the public back to the farm, which had been closed for nine years during the development of the vineyard. Returning to the culinary roots of JoieFarm, Noble added a wood-burning pizza oven and a European-style picnic area to enhance the wine-country tourism experience for her visitors.

The tasting room was a roaring success, moving almost 2,000 cases of wine through that side of the business. Almost 80 percent of the guests who visited had never heard of JoieFarm until their visit—they were new to the brand. By the time they left, many had been converted to loyal customers. Word spread quickly, gaining traction through the food and wine media. The winery's online sales tripled within the first year and their private wine store sales exploded as those who had visited the winery continued to purchase their favourite JoieFarm wines.

Noble has transformed JoieFarm from its humble beginnings to a proper winery operation, hiring a management team to help create operational and human resource systems to support businesses growth, a sales agency, and an entirely new seasonal staff to run the seasonal hospitality business. Given the B.C. liquor board's reporting system and new laws introduced in 2015, these moves were critical. JoieFarm's order taking, processing and dispatching, bookkeeping, and finance operations have all been brought in-house. Creating a strong back-end to the business provided the stability in the short-term to weather through the PR storm that blew up around the business sale and new ownership and the development of the new business arm in seasonal hospitality. It also established the long-term stability to provide contracts of employment to secure key staff members who were critical to the functioning of the business on a day-to-day level.

Looking to the future, Noble has decided to reinvest back into the business by rebuilding the treasured farmhouse. She feels that rebuilding the renowned structure only *after* establishing the brand is the right thing to do. The new farmhouse, with its purpose-built tasting room, offices for JoieFarm HQ and a small apartment residence, is a symbol of confidence that JoieFarm is here to stay as an authentic winery built for quality winemaking and wine-country tourism. However, while JoieFarm has experienced significant growth from its humble beginnings, it will need to continue to find ways to innovate within its entrepreneurial environment. As with all successful small startups, the time arrives for a serious evaluation of how entrepreneurial success can utilize strategy to attain the next level of success to ensure a viable future as a mature company. ■

The transformative activity of bringing organizations from "what they are to what their leader would have them become" requires fresh ideas and a vision of the future. Most organizations want to grow. Managing change is one of the most important functions performed by strategic leaders. There are two major avenues through which companies can expand or improve their business. The first is strategic renewal. Innovations help an organization stay fresh and reinvent itself as conditions in the business environment change, as JoieFarm has successfully done throughout its brief history. This is why managing innovation is such an important strategic implementation issue. The second avenue is the pursuit of venture opportunities. Innovative breakthroughs, as well as new product concepts, evolving technologies, and shifting demand, create opportunities for corporate venturing. In this chapter, we will explore these topics—how change and innovation can stimulate strategic renewal and foster corporate entrepreneurship.

LO 1   MANAGING INNOVATION

One of the most important sources of growth opportunities is innovation. Innovation involves using new knowledge to transform organizational processes or create commercially viable products and services. The sources of new knowledge may include the latest technology, the results of experiments, creative insights, or competitive information. However it comes about, innovation occurs when new combinations of ideas and information bring about positive change.

The emphasis on newness is a key point. The root of the word *innovation* is the Latin "novus," which means "new." Innovation involves introducing or changing to something new.[2] Among the most important sources of new ideas is new technology. Technology creates new possibilities. Technology provides the raw material that firms use to make innovative products and services. But technology is not the only source of innovations. There can be innovations in human resources, firm infrastructure, marketing, and service, or in many other value-adding areas that have little to do with anything "high-tech." Let's consider some different types of innovations and their business implications. Strategy Spotlight 12.1 discusses how a new technology, graphene, may disrupt the electronics and computer industries.

12.1 STRATEGY SPOTLIGHT

Will Graphene Radically Change the Electronics Industry?

The consumer electronics industry is generally thought of as one of the most dynamic, with new product innovations being launched on a regular basis. With this in mind, it is interesting to realize that the base technology standards of the components used to make consumer electronic products have remained largely unchanged for a number of years. For example, the semiconductor chips used in consumer electronics are made from silicon wafers, as they were 30 years ago. Today's chips are more complex, packed with more and narrower channels, but the basic technology is the same. Similarly, the screens used in electronic devices are primarily LCD panels, which have been widely used in electronic products for over 15 years.

However, a new technology, graphene, may radically change the consumer electronics industry. Graphene, which is produced in a sheet form and is a very thin layer of graphite atoms in a honeycomb lattice, is a product with amazing qualities. In the words of Jeanie Lau, professor of physics at the University of California at River-side, "Graphene is a wonderful material. It conducts heat 10 times better than copper and electricity, 100 times better than silicon, is transparent like plastic, extremely lightweight, extremely strong, yet flexible and elastic." Additionally, researchers have discovered that they can magnetize graphene. This raises the possibility of building computer systems that use spintronics—that's shorthand for "spin transport electronics." Spintronics involves processing a signal using magnetic spin rather than electric charge. It is still a number of years away, but eventual consumer and business applications for spintronics technology could include faster processors and memory with vastly higher capacities. With such amazing properties, it is not surprising that major players, such as Samsung, have invested heavily in graphene, secured patents related to its use, developed prototypes that use graphene, and plan to produce a number of graphene-based products in the coming years. Its most promising initial use may be as a transparent electrode in monitors, displays, and touch screens. It also has the potential to be used in semiconductor chips in the future, possibly replacing silicon as the primary component of the chip.

As with any radical innovation, it is not yet clear if graphene will live up to its promise. Firms have not yet figured out how to manufacture it on a large scale or at a reasonable cost. Currently, it costs around $100 to produce a 1-inch-diameter wafer. There are also questions about whether researchers will be able to figure out how to effectively turn transistors on a graphene chip on and off, an essential element if graphene is ever to be used in semiconductor chips. Michael Patterson, CEO of Graphene Frontiers, explains that researchers are "really pushing the edges of technology" with graphene, and cautions that it may take 10 years before we know if it will replace current technologies.

Sources: Noyes, K. 2014. The business potential of (amazing, wonderful, futuristic) graphene. cnnmoney. com, May 12: np; and Whitwam, R., 2015. Researchers make graphene magnetic, clearing the way for faster everything. extremetech.com, January 29: np.

While high-tech developments, such as graphene, grab a lot of headlines relating to innovation in the business and mainstream media, many successful innovations occur outside the technology industry. Often innovations happen when creative individuals rethink the way consumers use everyday items. Strategy Spotlight 12.2 describes a simple but effective innovation implemented by Target stores in America.

Finally, Strategy Spotlight 12.3 discusses a Canadian startup that is innovating by returning to old technologies. As these three Strategy Spotlight examples suggest, innovation can take many forms and follow unexpected trajectories. This was also evident in the introductory case of this chapter, where we discussed the journey of JoieFarm Winery from a small startup to a thriving business.

12.2 STRATEGY SPOTLIGHT

Target's Low-Tech, High-Value Design Innovation

Sometimes, a simple change can make a vast improvement. That is what Target discovered when it adopted a new design for the traditional amber-coloured prescription pill bottle. The new design literally flips the old bottle on its head. The base of the bottle is a large cap that uses colour-coded rings to help family members distinguish between different containers. The upper part includes a flat surface that holds wider and easier-to-read labels. "They're much easier to use, and it's a lot easier to read," says Target customer Pat Howell.

Design student Deborah Adler came up with the design of the new bottle after her grandmother Helen accidentally took her grandfather Herman's prescription. She noticed that the small lettering on the curved label of a traditional pill bottle was hard to read. Target, which commissioned a study that found that nearly 60 percent of prescription drugs are taken improperly, welcomed the design innovation. The new bottle, called the *ClearRX*, has won several design awards and improved Target's prescription drug sales by 14 percent—from $1.4 billion to $1.6 billion in a recent year.

Sources: "Target Turns Old Pill Bottle Design on its Head," *MSNBC.com*, www.msnbc.com, April 26, 2005; B. Finn, "Target ClearRX Bottle," *Business 2.0*, April 2006, p. 120; and www.target.com.

12.3 STRATEGY SPOTLIGHT

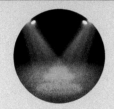

Innovative Entrepreneurship in the Toronto Publishing Scene

The publishing industry has experienced significant change in recent decades. With the rise of ebooks and streaming services coinciding with the decline in sales of physical books, publishers have had difficulties committing to physical book sales, recognizing that consumers are buying fewer and fewer books each year.

Joel William Vaughan, a PhD candidate and writer at the University of Toronto, has been working to stem this concern with his entrepreneurial startup, Nacreous March Publishing Co. Founded in 2012 in southern Ontario, Vaughan chooses to differentiate his product offering by utilizing older printing methods that privilege the quality of the printed book. "I work primarily with 19th century tools," Vaughan explains. "While I appreciate the production lines' ability to make books available to a wide audience, I worry about the quality of those books, and the way readers will interact with a low-quality book." Books manufactured on the production line are "self-destructive," he claims, as both the glue that binds them together and the paper that they're made of have a very limited lifespan. "By using 19th century tools such as a cast-iron nipping press and linen thread waxed with beeswax, we're making books that stand up to the test of time."

Innovation in the publishing industry has continually increased efficiency at the expense of quality. Ironically, the books of highest quality are some of the first texts published, Vaughan explains, because they are bound with animal skin, which is considerably more resilient to the effects of time than the paperbacks of the 20th and 21st century. By reverting to earlier technologies, Vaughan and the team at Nacreous March Publishing Co. are privileging high quality standards, and creating aesthetically pleasing, durable books that will last a lifetime, and then some.

Sources: "About us." *NacreousMarch.ca*, March 2017; M. Suttie, "Local author shortlisted for national Reader's Choice Award", *Bradford Times*, December 2014, 1; Whitehead, K., Interview with Joel William Vaughan, May 2017.

Types of Innovation

Although innovations are not always of a high-tech nature, changes in technology can be an important source of change and growth. When an innovation is based on a sweeping new technology, it often has a more far-reaching impact. Sometimes, even a small innovation can add value and create competitive advantages. Innovation can and should occur throughout an organization—in every department and all aspects of the value chain.

One distinction that is often used when discussing innovation is between process innovation and product innovation.[3] Product innovation refers to efforts to create product designs and applications of technology to develop new products for end users. Recall from Chapter 8 how generic strategies were typically different, depending on the stage of the industry life cycle. Product innovations tend to be more common during the earlier stages of an industry's life cycle. Product innovations are also commonly associated with a differentiation strategy. Firms that differentiate by providing customers with new products or services that offer unique features or quality enhancements often engage in product innovation.

Process innovation, by contrast, is typically associated with improving the efficiency of an organizational process, especially manufacturing systems and operations. By drawing on new technologies and an organization's accumulated experience (see Chapter 5), firms can often improve materials use, shorten cycle time, and increase quality. Process innovations are more likely to occur in the later stages of an industry's life cycle as companies seek ways to remain viable in markets where demand has flattened out and competition is more intense. As a result, process innovations are often associated with overall cost leader strategies because the aim of many process improvements is to lower the costs of operations.

Another way to view the impact of an innovation is in terms of its degree of innovativeness, which falls somewhere on a continuum that extends from incremental to radical.[4]

- Radical innovations produce fundamental changes by evoking major departures from existing practices. These breakthrough innovations usually occur because of technological change. They tend to be highly disruptive and can transform a company or even revolutionize a whole industry. They may lead to products or processes that can be patented, giving a firm a strong competitive advantage. Examples include electricity, the telephone, the transistor, desktop computers, fibre optics, artificial intelligence, and genetically engineered drugs.

- Incremental innovations enhance existing practices or make small improvements in products and processes. They may represent evolutionary applications within existing paradigms of earlier, more radical innovations. Because they often sustain a company by extending or expanding its product line or manufacturing skills, incremental innovations can be a source of competitive advantage by providing new capabilities that minimize expenses or speed productivity. Examples include frozen food, sports drinks, steel-belted radial tires, electronic bookkeeping, shatterproof glass, and digital telephones.

Some innovations are highly radical; others are only slightly incremental. But most innovations fall somewhere between these two extremes. Exhibit 12-1 shows where several innovations fall along the radical–incremental continuum.

Another distinction can be made between sustaining and disruptive innovations (the topic of disruptive innovation was covered extensively in Chapter 8).[5] Sustaining innovations are those that extend sales in an existing market, usually by enabling new products or services to be sold at higher margins. Such innovations may include either incremental or radical innovations. For example, the Internet was a breakthrough technology that transformed retail selling. But rather than disrupting the activities of catalogue companies, such as Lands' End and L.L. Bean, the Internet energized their existing business by extending their reach and making their operations more efficient.

By contrast, disruptive innovations are those that overturn markets by providing an altogether new approach to meeting customer needs. The features of a disruptive innovation make it somewhat counterintuitive. Disruptive innovations:

- are technologically simpler and less sophisticated than currently available products or services;
- appeal to less demanding customers who are seeking more convenient, less expensive solutions; and
- take time to take effect and only become disruptive once they have taken root in a new market or low-end part of an existing market.

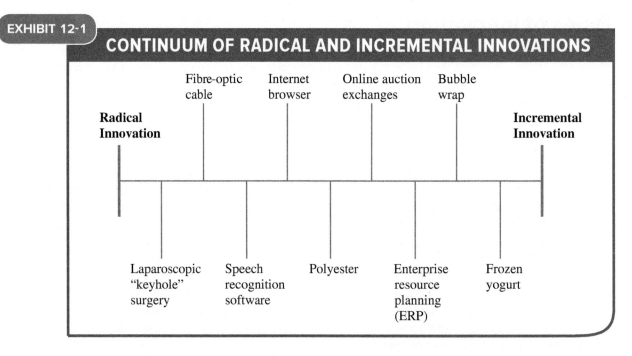

EXHIBIT 12-1

CONTINUUM OF RADICAL AND INCREMENTAL INNOVATIONS

Clayton Christensen cites Walmart and Southwest Airlines as two disruptive examples. Walmart started with a single store and Southwest with a few flights. But because they both represented major departures from existing practices and tapped into unmet needs, they steadily grew into ventures that appealed to a new category of customers and eventually overturned the status quo. "Instead of sustaining the trajectory of improvement that has been established in a market," says Christensen, a disruptive innovation "disrupts it and redefines it by bringing to the market something that is simpler."[6] Christensen argues that all disruptive innovations have led to the failure of the leading firms that dominated their markets on the basis of the older technologies. They simply could not cope with or adopt the disruptive technology.

The Linux operating system is another example. When it first became available, few systems administrators used the open-source operating system, even though it was free. Over time, though, problems with more expensive proprietary operating systems, such as Microsoft Windows, have made Linux increasingly popular. By 2008, the majority of Internet hosting companies and supercomputer operating systems were Linux based. Today, in addition to being relatively more convenient to use, it is supported by a community of developers. Desktop computers preloaded with the Linux operating system have become increasingly popular.[7]

Innovation is both a force in the external environment (technology, competition) and a factor affecting a firm's internal choices (generic strategy, value-adding activities).[8] Nevertheless, innovation can be quite difficult for some firms to manage, especially those that have become comfortable with the status quo.

Challenges of Innovation

Innovation is essential to sustaining competitive advantages. Recall from Chapter 3 that one of the four elements of the Balanced Scorecard is the innovation and learning perspective. The extent and success of a company's innovation efforts are indicators of its overall performance. As management guru Peter Drucker warned, "An established company which, in an age demanding innovation, is not capable of innovation is doomed to decline and extinction."[9] In today's competitive environment, most firms have only one choice: "Innovate or die."

LO 2

As with change, however, firms are often resistant to innovation. Only those companies that actively pursue innovation, even though it is often difficult and uncertain, will get a payoff from their innovation efforts. But managing innovation is challenging.[10] What makes innovation so difficult? The uncertainty about outcomes is one factor. Companies are often reluctant to invest time and resources into activities with an unknown future. Another factor is that the innovation process involves so many choices. These choices present five dilemmas that companies must wrestle with when pursuing innovation.[11]

- *Seeds versus Weeds.* Most companies have an abundance of innovative ideas. They must decide which of these are most likely to bear fruit—the "seeds"—and which should be cast aside—the "weeds." This is complicated by the fact that some innovation projects require a considerable level of investment before a firm can fully evaluate whether they are worth pursuing.

- *Experience versus Initiative.* Companies must decide who will lead an innovation project. Senior managers may have experience and credibility but tend to be more risk averse. Midlevel employees, who may be the innovators themselves, may have more enthusiasm because they can see first-hand how an innovation would address specific problems.

- *Internal versus External Staffing.* Innovation projects need competent staff to succeed. People drawn from inside the company may have greater social capital and know the organization's culture and routines, but this knowledge may actually inhibit them from thinking outside the box. Staffing innovation projects with external personnel requires that project managers justify the hiring and spend time recruiting, training, and relationship building.

- *Building Capabilities versus Collaborating.* Innovation projects often require new sets of skills. Firms can seek help from other departments and/or partner with other companies that bring resources and experience as well as share costs of development. However, such arrangements can create dependencies and inhibit internal skills development. Further, struggles over who contributed the most or how the benefits of the project are to be allocated may arise.

- *Incremental versus Pre-emptive Launch.* Companies must manage the timing and scale of new innovation projects. An incremental launch is less risky because it requires fewer resources and serves as a market test. But a launch that is too tentative can undermine the project's credibility. It also opens the door for a competitive response. A large-scale launch requires more resources, but it can effectively pre-empt a competitive response.

These dilemmas highlight why the innovation process can be daunting even for highly successful firms. In turn, firms can take four steps to manage the innovation process.[12]

Cultivating Innovation Skills

Some firms, such as Apple, Google, and Amazon, regularly produce innovative products and services, whereas other firms struggle to generate new, marketable products. What separates these innovative firms from the rest of the pack? Jeff Dyer, Hal Gregersen, and Clayton Christensen argue it is the Innovative DNA of the leaders of these firms.[13] Such "discovery skills" allow them to see the potential in innovations and to move the organization forward in leveraging the value of those innovations.[14] These leaders spend 50 percent more time on these discovery activities than the leaders of less innovative firms. To improve their innovative processes, firms need to cultivate the innovation skills of their managers.

The key attribute that firms need to develop in their managers in order to improve their innovative potential is creative intelligence. Creative intelligence is driven by a core skill of associating—the ability to see patterns in data and integrating different questions, information, and insights—and four patterns of action: questioning, observing, experimenting, and networking. As managers practise the four patterns of action, they will begin to develop the skill of association. Dyer and his colleagues offer the following illustration to demonstrate that individuals using these skills are going to develop more-creative, higher-potential innovations.

Imagine that you have an identical twin, endowed with the same brains and natural talents that you have. You are both given one week to come up with a creative new business-venture idea. During that week, you come up with ideas alone in your room. In contrast, your twin (1) talks with 10 people—including an engineer, a musician, a stay-at-home dad, and a designer—about the venture, (2) visits three innovative startups to observe what they do, (3) samples five "new to the market" products, (4) shows a prototype he has built to five people, and (5) asks the questions "What if I tried this?" and "Why do you do that?" at least 10 times each day during these networking, observing, and experimenting activities. Who do you bet will come up with the more innovative (and doable) ideas?

The point is that by questioning, observing, experimenting, and networking as part of the innovative process, managers will make better innovation decisions now but, more importantly, will start to build the innovative DNA needed to be more successful innovators in the future. As they get into the practice of these habits, decision makers will see opportunities and be more creative as they associate information from different parts of their life, different people they come in contact with, and different parts of their organizations. The ability to innovate is not hardwired into our brains at birth. Research suggests that only one-third of our ability to think creatively is genetic. The other two-thirds are developed over time. Neuroscience research indicates that the brain is "plastic," meaning that it changes over time due to experiences. As managers build up the ability to ask creative questions, develop a wealth of experiences from diverse settings, and link together insights from different arenas of their lives, their brains will follow suit and build the ability to easily see situations creatively and draw on a wide range of experiences and knowledge to identify creative solutions. The five traits of the effective innovator are described and examples of each trait are presented in Exhibit 12-2.

EXHIBIT 12-2 ▸ **THE INNOVATOR'S DNA**

Associating

Description:
Innovators have the ability to connect seemingly unrelated questions, problems, and ideas from different fields. This allows them to creatively see opportunities that others miss.

Example:
Pierre Omidyar saw the opportunity that led to eBay when he linked three items: (1) a personal fascination with creating more efficient markets, (2) his fiancée's desire to locate hard to find collectible Pez dispensers, and (3) the ineffectiveness of local classified ads in locating such items.

Questioning

Description:
Innovators constantly ask questions that challenge common wisdom. Rather than accept the status quo, they ask, "Why not?" or "What if?" This gets others around them to challenge the assumptions that limit the possible range of actions the firm can take.

Example:
After witnessing the emergence of eBay and Amazon, Marc Benioff questioned why computer software was still sold in boxes rather than leased with a subscription and downloaded through the Internet. This was the genesis of Salesforce.com, a firm with over $8 billion in sales in 2017.

Observing

Description:
Discovery-driven executives produce innovative business ideas by observing regular behaviour of individuals, especially customers and potential customers. Such observations often identify challenges customers face and previously unidentified opportunities.

Example:
From watching his wife struggle to keep track of the family's finances, Intuit founder Scott Cook identified the need for easy-to-use financial software that provided a single place for managing bills, bank accounts, and investments.

Experimenting

Description:
Thomas Edison once said, "I haven't failed. I've simply found 10,000 ways that do not work." Innovators regularly experiment with new possibilities, accepting that many of their ideas will fail. Experimentation can include new jobs, living in different countries, and new ideas for their businesses.

Example:
Founders Larry Page and Sergey Brin provide time and resources for Google employees to experiment. Some, such as the Android cell phone platform, have been big winners. Others, such as the Orkut and Buzz social networking systems, have failed. But Google will continue to experiment with new products and services.

Networking

Description:

Innovators develop broad personal networks. They use this diverse set of individuals to find and test radical ideas. This can be done by developing a diverse set of friends. It can also be done by attending idea conferences where individuals from a broad set of backgrounds come together to share their perspectives and ideas, such as the Technology, Entertainment, and Design (TED) Conference or the Aspen Ideas Festival.

Example:

Michael Lazaridis got the idea for a wireless email device that led him to found Research in Motion from a conference he attended. At the conference, a speaker was discussing a wireless system Coca-Cola was using that allowed vending machines to send a signal when they needed refilling. Lazaridis saw the opportunity to use the same concept with email communications, and the idea for the Blackberry was hatched.

Source: Adapted from J.H. Dyer, H.G. Gregerson and C.M. Christensen, "The Innovator's DNA," Harvard Business Review, December 2009, pp. 61–67.

Defining the Scope of Innovation

Firms must have a means to focus their innovation efforts. By defining the "strategic envelope"—the scope of a firm's innovation efforts—firms ensure that their innovation efforts are not wasted on projects that are outside the firm's domain of interest. Strategic enveloping defines the range of acceptable projects. As Alistair Corbett, an innovation expert with the global consulting firm Bain & Company, said, "One man's radical innovation is another man's incremental innovation."[15] A strategic envelope creates a firm-specific view of innovation that defines how a firm can create new knowledge and learn from an innovation initiative, even if the project fails. It also gives direction to a firm's innovation efforts, which helps separate seeds from weeds and builds internal capabilities.

One way to identify the projects to work on is to focus on a common technology. Then, innovation efforts across the firm can aim at developing skills and expertise in a given technical area. Another potential focus is on a market theme. Consider how DuPont responded to a growing concern for environmentally sensitive products:

In the early 1990s, DuPont sought to use its knowledge of plastics to identify products to meet a growing market demand for biodegradable products. It conducted numerous experiments with a biodegradable polyester resin it named *Biomax*. By trying different applications and formulations demanded by potential customers, the company was finally able to create a product that could be produced economically and had market appeal. In 2003, Biomax was certified biodegradable and compostable by the Biodegradable Products Institute, an endorsement that further boosted sales.[16]

Companies must be clear not only about the kinds of innovation they are looking for but also the expected results. Each company needs to develop a set of questions to ask itself about its innovation efforts:

- How much will the innovation initiative cost?
- How likely is it to actually become commercially viable?
- How much value will it add? That is, what will it be worth if it works?
- What will be learned if it does not pan out?

However a firm envisions its innovation goals, it needs to develop a systematic approach to evaluating its results and learning from its innovation initiatives. Viewing innovation from this perspective helps firms manage the process.[17]

Managing the Pace of Innovation

Along with clarifying the scope of an innovation by defining a strategic envelope, firms also need to regulate the pace of innovation. How long will it take for an innovation initiative to realistically come to fruition? The project time line of an incremental innovation may be six months to two years, whereas a more radical innovation is typically long term—10 years or more.[18] Radical innovations often begin with a long period of exploration in which experimentation makes strict timelines unrealistic. In contrast, firms that are innovating incrementally to exploit a window of opportunity may use a milestone approach that is more stringently driven by goals and deadlines. This kind of sensitivity to realistic time frames helps companies separate dilemmas temporally so that they are easier to manage.

Time pacing can also be a source of competitive advantage because it helps a company manage transitions and develop an internal rhythm.[19] Time pacing does not mean the company ignores the demands of market timing; instead, companies have a sense of their own internal clock in a way that allows them to thwart the efforts of competitors by controlling the innovation process.

Not all innovation lends itself to speedy development, however. Radical innovation often involves open-ended experimentation and time-consuming mistakes. The creative aspects of innovation are often difficult to time. When software maker Intuit's new CEO Steve Bennett began to turn around that troubled business, he required every department to implement Six Sigma, a quality control management technique that focuses on being responsive to customer needs—that is, everybody but the techies.

> "We're not GE, we're not a company where Jack says 'Do it,' and everyone salutes," says Bill Hensler, Intuit's vice-president for process excellence. That's because software development, according to many, is more of an art than a science. At the Six Sigma Academy, president of operations Phil Samuel says even companies that have embraced Six Sigma across every other aspect of their organization usually maintain a hands-off policy when it comes to software developers. Techies, it turns out, like to go at their own pace.[20]

Some projects cannot be rushed. Companies that hurry up their research efforts or go to market before they are ready can damage their ability to innovate—and their reputation. Thus, managing the pace of innovation can be an important factor in long-term success.

Staffing to Capture Value from Innovation

People are central to the processes of identifying, developing, and commercializing innovations effectively. They need broad sets of skills as well as experience—experience working with teams and experience working on successful innovation projects. To capture value from innovation activities, companies must provide strategic decision makers with staff members who make it possible.

This insight led strategy experts Rita Gunther McGrath and Thomas Keil to research the types of human resource management practices that effective firms use to capture value from their innovation efforts.[21] Four practices are especially important:

1. Create innovation teams with experienced players who know what it is like to deal with uncertainty and can help new staff members learn venture management skills.
2. Require that employees seeking to advance their career with the organization serve in the new venture group as part of their career climb.
3. Once people have experience with the new venture group, transfer them to mainstream management positions, where they can use their skills and knowledge to revitalize the company's core business.
4. Separate the performance of individuals from the performance of the innovation. Otherwise, strong players may feel stigmatized if the innovation effort they worked on fails.

There are other staffing practices that may sound as if they would benefit a firm's innovation activities but may, in fact, be counterproductive:

- Creating a staff that consists only of strong players whose primary experience is related to the company's core business. This provides too few people to deal with the uncertainty of innovation projects and may cause good ideas to be dismissed because they do not appear to fit with the core business.

- Creating a staff that consists only of volunteers who want to work on projects they find interesting. Such players are often overzealous about new technologies or overly attached to product concepts, which can lead to poor decisions about which projects to pursue or drop.

- Creating a climate where innovation team members are considered second-class citizens. In companies where achievements are rewarded, the brightest and most ambitious players may avoid innovation projects that have uncertain outcomes.

Unless an organization can align its key players into effective new venture teams, it is unlikely to create any differentiating advantages from its innovation efforts.[22] An enlightened approach to staffing a company's innovation efforts provides one of the best ways to ensure that the challenges of innovation will be effectively met. Strategy Spotlight 12.4 describes the approach that Air Products and Chemicals, Inc. is using to enhance its innovation efforts.

12.4 STRATEGY SPOTLIGHT

Staffing for Innovation Success at Air Products

When it comes to implementing its innovation efforts, Air Products and Chemicals, Inc. (APCI) recognizes the importance of staffing for success. APCI is a global manufacturer of industrial gases, chemicals, and related equipment. Headquartered in Allentown, Pennsylvania, APCI has annual sales of $10 billion, manufacturing facilities in over 30 countries, and 22,000 employees worldwide. The company has a strong reputation for effectively embedding innovation into its culture through its unique employee engagement processes.

Ron Pierantozzi, a 30-year veteran of the company and its director of innovation and new product development, says, "Innovation is about discipline. . . . It requires a different type of training, different tools and new approaches to experimentation." To enact this philosophy, Pierantozzi begins with his people. He recruits people with diverse backgrounds and a wide range of expertise, including engineers, entrepreneurs, and government officials. It is made clear to those on his innovation teams that they will return to mainstream operations after four years—a fact that most consider a plus, since working in the innovation unit usually provides a career boost. He also assures players that there is no stigma associated with a failed venture because experimentation is highly valued.

Innovation teams are created to manage the company's intellectual assets and determine which technologies have the most potential value. A key benefit of this approach has been to more effectively leverage its human resources to achieve innovative outcomes without increasing its research and development (R&D) expenses. These efforts resulted in an innovation award from APQC (formerly known as the American Productivity and Quality Center), which recognizes companies for exemplary practices that increase productivity.

Sources: H. Chesbrough, "Why Bad Things Happen to Good Technology," *The Wall Street Journal*, April 28–29, 2007, p. R11; P. Leavitt, "Delivering the Difference: Business Process Management at APCI," *APQC*, 2005, www.apqc.com; R. G. McGrath and T. Keil, "The Value Captor's Process: Getting the Most Out of Your New Business Ventures," *Harvard Business Review*, May 2007, pp. 128–136; and www.airproducts.ca

Collaborating with Innovation Partners

It is rare for any one organization to have all the information it needs to carry an innovation from concept to commercialization. Even a company that is highly competent with its current operations usually needs new capabilities to achieve new results. Innovation partners provide the skills and insights that are needed to make innovation projects succeed.[23]

Innovation partners may come from many sources, including research universities and the federal government. Each year the federal government issues requests for proposals (RFPs) asking private companies for assistance in improving services or finding solutions to public problems. Universities are another type of innovation partner. Chip maker Intel, for example, has benefited from underwriting substantial amounts of university research. Rather than hand universities a blank cheque, Intel bargains for rights to patents that emerge from Intel-sponsored research. The university retains ownership of the patent, but Intel gets royalty-free use of it.[24]

Strategic partnering requires firms to identify their strengths and weaknesses and make choices about which capabilities to leverage, which need further development, and which are outside the firm's current or projected scope of operations.

To choose partners, firms need to ask what competencies they are looking for and what the innovation partner will contribute.[25] These might include knowledge of markets, technology expertise, or contacts with key players in an industry. Innovation partnerships also typically need to specify how the rewards of the innovation will be shared and who will own the intellectual property that is developed.[26]

Innovation efforts that involve multiple partners and the speed and ease with which partners can network and collaborate are changing the way innovation is conducted.[27] Bombardier has asked its potential partners to actively contribute in developing the CSeries long-range jet. Different partners have taken responsibility for different components and have committed to deliver performance improvements that will make the CSeries the most efficient aircraft in its class.

The Value of Unsuccessful Innovation

Companies are often reluctant to pursue innovations due to the high uncertainty associated with innovative efforts. They are torn about whether to invest in emerging technologies, wondering which, if any, will win in the market and offer the best payoff for the firm. Conventional wisdom suggests that firms pay dearly if they bet on the wrong technology or new product direction. However, research by NYU professor J. P. Eggers suggests that betting on a losing technology and then switching to the winner can position a company to come out ahead of competitors that were on the right track all along.[28]

His research shows that firms that initially invest in an unsuccessful innovative effort often end up dominating the market in the long run. The key is that the firm remains open to change and to learning from both its mistakes and the experience of the innovators that initially chose to pursue the winning technology. Eggers offers the following insights for companies competing in a dynamic market where it is uncertain which technology will emerge triumphant:

1. *Avoid overcommitting.* This can be difficult as the firm sees the need to build specific expertise and stake out a decisive position to be seen as a leader in the market. However, managers can become entrenched as confirmation bias leads them to focus only on data that suggest they've made the right choice. Eggers suggests firms consider joint ventures and other alliances to avoid overinvestments they may come to regret.

2. *Don't let shame or despair knock you out of the game.* Shame has been shown to be a particularly destructive reaction to failure. Remember that it is very likely no one could have had complete confidence regarding which technology would win. And try to avoid seeing things as worse than they are. Some companies that bet on the wrong technology decide, unnecessarily, to get out of the market entirely, missing out on any future market opportunities.

3. *Pivot quickly.* Once they realized they made a mistake, firms that were ultimately successful changed course and moved quickly. Studies have shown that the ideal moment to enter a high-tech industry is just as the dominant design emerges. So missing the target initially doesn't have to mean that a firm is doomed to failure if the firm moves swiftly as the dominant technology becomes clear.

4. ***Transfer knowledge.*** Successful firms use the information they gathered in a losing bet to exploit other market opportunities. For example, when flat-panel computer displays were first emerging, it was unclear if plasma or LCD technology would win. IBM initially invested heavily in plasma displays, a bet that didn't pay off when LCD technology won out. But IBM took away valuable knowledge from its plasma investments. For example, the heavy glass required by plasma technology forced IBM to become skilled at glass design, which helped it push glass technology in new directions in products such as the original ThinkPad laptop.

5. ***Be aware that it can be dangerous to be right at the outset.*** Managers in firms that initially select the winning technology have a tendency to interpret their ability to choose the most promising technology as an unconditional endorsement of everything they had been doing. As a result, they fail to recognize the need to rethink some details of their product and the underlying technology. Their complacency can give firms that initially chose the wrong technology the space to catch up and then pull ahead, since the later-moving firms are more open to see the need for improvements and are hungry and aggressive in their actions. The key to who wins typically isn't who is there first. Instead, the winning firm is the one that continuously incrementally innovates on the initial bold innovation to offer the best product at the best price.

CORPORATE ENTREPRENEURSHIP

Corporate entrepreneurship (CE) has two primary aims: (1) the pursuit of new venture opportunities and (2) strategic renewal.[29] The innovation process keeps firms alert by exposing them to new technologies, making them aware of marketplace trends, and helping them evaluate new possibilities. CE uses the fruits of the innovation process to help firms build new sources of competitive advantage and renew their value propositions. Just as the innovation process helps firms to make positive improvements, corporate entrepreneurship helps firms identify opportunities and launch new ventures. Strategy Spotlight 12.5 addresses how Danish toymaker Lego effectively used entrepreneurial initiatives to strategically renew its aging business.

12.5 STRATEGY SPOTLIGHT

Entrepreneurial Initiatives Help Reinvent the Lego Group

"Toy of the Century" was the lofty label given to Lego's iconic plastic bricks by *Fortune* magazine in 1999. More recently, brand valuation and strategy consultancy named Lego the world's most powerful brand. With such impressive statistics as "seven boxes of Lego are sold every second" and "19 billion components are produced every year," the Denmark-based Lego Group would appear to be a huge success by any standards.

But 1999 was followed by a dark period for Lego, as electronic games and digital products increasingly captured children's attention. Lego took several steps to try to bolster its sinking business, including offering branded products, such as books and watches, and launching a Lego theme park. But for six years, the company continued to report heavy losses, including a $300-million loss in 2004. The founding family heir, CEO Kjeld Kirk Kristiansen, injected millions of his own money into the company to prevent bankruptcy and eventually resigned.

He was replaced by 35-year-old Jorgen Vig Knudstorp, who made drastic changes at the company, including outsourcing manufacturing of the bricks to the Czech Republic and cutting nearly 2,000 jobs. The cost savings were matched with entrepreneurial initiatives that challenged the core of the company's business culture. It launched a series of interactive games, including a highly successful Star Wars computer game. But the traditional company, whose mission had always included "nurturing the child," found it difficult to depart from its image as a producer of playful, constructive

(Continued)

toys. Referring to Star Wars creator George Lucas, play expert and 22-year Lego veteran Niels Sandal Jakobsen recalls, "Getting the license from Lucas was nothing compared to the internal struggles over having the word *war* appear under the Lego brand." Nevertheless, Knudstorp persisted, and more interactive games were introduced, including a Star Wars game for the Wii and an online Mars Mission game.

Crowdsourcing contributed to one of Lego's digital product successes: Mindstorms, a set of programmable bricks with electronic motors, sensors, and Lego Technic pieces (such as gears, axles, and beams). Within weeks of Mindstorms' release, user groups had started reverse engineering the software to make improvements. At first, Lego threatened to sue the tinkerers but quickly realized that might be a mistake. The company changed course, even including a "right to hack" as part of the Mindstorms software licensing agreement. The community of users expanded, and many of them now participate in the annual Lego World convention in the Netherlands. One of them showed up at a recent convention with a fully operational pinball machine made from 20,000 Lego bricks and 13 programmable microchips. And when Lego began design on the next version of Mindstorms, it took on a group of the most dedicated enthusiasts as de facto employees during the 11-month development cycle. Such innovations are indicative of the Lego Group's new entrepreneurial perspective.

The fusion of mass customization and peer production extended beyond the Mindstorms project. Its new Lego Factory system gave customers access to a virtual warehouse where they could design their own custom Lego sets. According to Mark Hansen, director of Lego Interactive Experiences, "With Lego Factory we can expand beyond our one hundred in-house product designers to marvel at the creativity of more than three hundred thousand designers worldwide."

The entrepreneurial spirit that animated the revitalized Lego Group paid off. Despite a downturn in toy sales worldwide, Lego reported a 32-percent increase in profits in 2008. Included in Fast Company's 2009 list of the world's 50 most innovative companies, Lego had made a remarkable rebound. CEO Knudstorp explained the reason for this, stating, "We're about many more things than just a set of bricks and a box. It's about everyday people getting incremental new ideas."

In 2012, Lego overtook Hasbro to become the world's second largest toymaker (after Mattel). Lego had managed to strike a successful balance between innovation and tradition. In 2014, Lego partnered with Warner Bros. to produce the blockbuster "The Lego Movie." The success of this partnership was noteworthy because it allowed Lego to create its own successful franchise, instead of relying on the established success of others, as it did with the Harry Potter and Star Wars product initiatives. By 2015 Lego had surpassed Mattel to become the world's largest toy company with sales of $ 2.1 billion and Knudstorp was stepping back from active operational duties.

Sources: "How Lego Became the World's Hottest Toy Company", 2014, *The Economist,* March 9. "At 50, Lego Still Going Strong," 2008, www.abc.net.au, January 29; K. Rockwood, "Fast Company 50: #41 Lego," *Fast Company,* March 2009: 93; N. D. Schwartz, "One Brick at a Time," 2006, www.cnnmoney.com, June 8; D. Tapscott and A. D. Williams, *Wikinomics* (New York: Penguin, 2006); and www.wikipedia.org.

Corporate new venture creation has been labelled "intrapreneuring" by Gifford Pinchot because it refers to building entrepreneurial businesses within existing corporations.[30] However, to engage in corporate entrepreneurship that yields above-average returns and contributes to sustainable advantages, it must be done effectively. In this section, we will examine the sources of entrepreneurial activity within established firms and the methods large corporations use to stimulate entrepreneurial behaviour.

In a typical corporation, what determines how entrepreneurial projects will be pursued? That depends on many factors, including the following:

- Corporate culture.
- Leadership.
- Structural features that guide and constrain action.
- Organizational systems that foster learning and manage rewards.

All of the factors that influence the strategy implementation process will also shape how corporations engage in internal venturing.

Other factors will also affect how entrepreneurial ventures will be pursued:

- The use of teams in strategic decision making.
- Whether the company is product or service oriented.
- Whether its innovation efforts are aimed at product or process improvements.
- The extent to which it is high-tech or low-tech.

Because these factors are different in every organization, some companies may be more involved than others in identifying and developing new venture opportunities.[31] These factors will also influence the nature of the CE process.

Successful CE typically requires firms to reach beyond their current operations and markets in the pursuit of new opportunities. It is often the breakthrough opportunities that provide the greatest returns. Such strategies are not without risks, however. In the sections that follow, we will address some of the strategic choice and implementation issues that influence the success or failure of CE activities.

Two distinct approaches to corporate venturing are found among firms that pursue entrepreneurial aims. The first is *focused corporate venturing,* in which CE activities are isolated from a firm's existing operations and worked on by independent work units. The second approach is *dispersed corporate venturing,* in which all parts of the organization and every organization member are engaged in intrapreneurial activities. Focused approaches to CE entail the creation of autonomous work groups that pursue entrepreneurial aims independent of the rest of the firm. The advantage of this approach is that it frees entrepreneurial team members to think and act without the constraints imposed by existing organizational norms and routines. This independence is often necessary for the kind of open-minded creativity that leads to strategic breakthroughs. The disadvantage is that because of their isolation from the corporate mainstream, the work groups that concentrate on internal ventures may fail to obtain the resources or support needed to carry an entrepreneurial project through to completion.

In contrast, in some firms, a dedication to the principles and practices of entrepreneurship is spread throughout the organization. The corporate culture embodies the spirit of entrepreneurship. The search for venture opportunities permeates every part of the organization, and everyone in the organization is attuned to opportunities to help create new businesses. Sony, 3M, Intel, and Cisco are among the corporations best known for their corporate venturing activities. One advantage of this approach is that organizational members do not have to be reminded to think entrepreneurially or be willing to change. The ability to change is considered a core capability. This leads to a second advantage: Because of the firm's entrepreneurial reputation, stakeholders, such as vendors, customers, or alliance partners, can bring new ideas or venture opportunities to anyone in the organization and expect them to be well received. Such opportunities make it possible for the firm to stay ahead of the competition. However, there are disadvantages as well. Firms that are overzealous about CE sometimes feel they must change for the sake of change, causing them to lose vital competencies or spend heavily on R&D and innovation to the detriment of the bottom line.

LO 3 ENTREPRENEURIAL ORIENTATION

Firms that want to engage in successful CE need to have an entrepreneurial orientation (EO).[32] EO refers to the strategy-making practices that businesses use in identifying and launching corporate ventures. It represents a frame of mind and a perspective toward entrepreneurship that is reflected in a firm's ongoing processes and corporate culture.[33]

An EO has five dimensions that permeate the decision-making styles and practices of the firm's members: (1) autonomy, (2) innovativeness, (3) proactiveness, (4) competitive aggressiveness, and (5) risk taking. These factors work together to enhance a firm's entrepreneurial performance. But even those firms that are strong in only a few aspects of EO can be quite successful.[34] Exhibit 12-3 summarizes the dimensions of entrepreneurial orientation.

Autonomy refers to willingness to act independently to carry forward an entrepreneurial vision or opportunity. It applies to both individuals and teams that operate outside an organization's existing norms and strategies. In the

> EXHIBIT 12-3   DIMENSIONS OF ENTREPRENEURIAL ORIENTATION

Autonomy
Independent action by an individual or team aimed at bringing forth a business concept or vision and carrying it through to completion.

Innovativeness
A willingness to introduce novelty through experimentation and creative processes aimed at developing new products and services as well as new processes.

Proactiveness
A forward-looking perspective characteristic of a marketplace leader that has the foresight to seize opportunities in anticipation of future demand.

Competitive aggressiveness
An intense effort to outperform industry rivals characterized by a combative posture or an aggressive response aimed at improving position or overcoming a threat in a competitive marketplace.

Risk taking
Making decisions and taking action without certain knowledge of probable outcomes; some undertakings may also involve making substantial resource commitments in the process of venturing forward.

Sources: Dess, G. G. & Lumpkin, G. T. 2005. The Role of Entrepreneurial Orientation in Stimulating Effective Corporate Entrepreneurship. *Academy of Management Executive,* 19(1): 147–156; Covin, J. G. & Slevin, D. P. 1991. A Conceptual Model of Entrepreneurship as Firm Behavior. *Entrepreneurship Theory & Practice,* Fall: 7–25; Lumpkin, G. T. and Dess, G. G. 1996. Clarifying the Entrepreneurial Orientation Construct and Linking It to Performance. *Academy of Management Review,* 21: 135–172; and Miller, D. 1983. The Correlates of Entrepreneurship in Three Types of Firms. *Management Science,* 29: 770–791.

context of corporate entrepreneurship, autonomous work units are often used to leverage existing strengths in new arenas, identify opportunities that are beyond the organization's current capabilities, and encourage development of new ventures or improved business practices.[35]

Sometimes corporations need to do more than create independent think-tanks to help stimulate new ideas. Unique organizational structures may also be necessary. Magna International is structured as a series of small autonomous units that can operate with the speed and flexibility of a startup. Virtual organizations can also help promote autonomy by allowing people to work independently and communicate via the Internet.

Creating autonomous work units and encouraging independent action may have pitfalls that can jeopardize their effectiveness, however. Autonomous teams often lack coordination. Excessive decentralization has a strong potential to create inefficiencies, such as duplication of effort and wasting resources on projects with questionable feasibility. For example, Chris Galvin, former CEO of Motorola, scrapped the skunkworks approach the company had been using to develop new wireless phones. Fifteen teams had created 128 different phones, which led to spiralling costs and overly complex operations.[36]

Innovativeness refers to a firm's attitude toward innovations and willingness to innovate. It involves creativity and experimentation that result in new products, new services, or improved technological processes.[37] Innovativeness requires that firms depart from existing technologies and practices and venture beyond the current state of the art. Inventions and new ideas need to be nurtured even when their benefits are unclear. However, in today's climate of rapid change, effectively producing, assimilating, and exploiting innovations can be an important avenue for achieving competitive advantages. Interest in global warming and other ecological concerns has led many corporations to focus their innovative efforts on solving environmental problems. Strategy Spotlight 12.6 describes an organization that uses entrepreneurial thinking and innovative practices to identify socially responsible solutions.

12.6 STRATEGY SPOTLIGHT

Socially Responsible Corporate Entrepreneurship: Best Buy Finds Social Responsibility Drives Business

In the storage areas of a Best Buy store, you might find old-style analogue TVs, desktop computers, and outmoded cell phones, and possibly an eight-track tape player or ham radio. Best Buy believes that social responsibility and good business sense meet at the recycling bin. With this perspective, Best Buy is at the forefront of a growing business trend—firms that see social responsibility as a means toward competitive success. Firms increasingly see entrepreneurial opportunities in taking a leading role on issues such as the environment, product safety, and fair trade. In focusing on Corporate Social Responsibility (CSR), they are leveraging new technologies, environmentally friendly ventures, and entrepreneurial practices to motivate workers in their firm, meet the interests and demands of their customers, and differentiate themselves from their rivals—while also meeting their societal responsibilities.

With Best Buy, we see this trend in multiple ways. The most obvious example is with their recycling program. Starting in early 2009, Best Buy began offering free recycling of a wide range of electronic products. In the first nine months of the program, Best Buy took in 25 million pounds of used electronics. To insure responsible manufacturing of new products, Best Buy instituted an auditing program of their suppliers' manufacturing facilities to ensure that workers were not exploited or the environment damaged. This was an audit with teeth. Best Buy cancelled relationships with 26 of their approximately 200 supplier factories in 2008 as a result of the audits. They also work to create a positive environment for their employees and to promote diversity by creating social networks for groups of employees. Best Buy has networks for women, Hispanic, African-American, Asian-American, and gay and lesbian employees. The firm has also targeted their charitable giving toward teens, a key customer group, and offers scholarships and grants to teenagers working for social change.

Best Buy does not take these actions simply to be a "good" company. They also see them as a means toward success. "We don't budget for corporate responsibility," said Paul Prahl, former vice president of Best Buy public affairs. "We're really trying to drive it through the business model of the company. We only feel we'll be successful in the marketplace if we are socially responsible." With the recycling program, they are driving traffic to the store. An individual dropping off an old stereo that just broke is likely shopping for a new surround sound system. For some product trade-ins, Best Buy will even give a gift card to the person bringing in the old product for recycling. This also offers a way to differentiate from more bottom-line competitors, such as Walmart. Some customers will prefer to buy from Best Buy because of their recycling program. Their auditing program is also designed to ensure they maintain a positive reputation with their customers. The worker social groups motivate workers, lower turnover, and connect with customer communities. For example, one of the groups, the women's leadership forum (WoLF), reaches out to female customers.

Best Buy's former CEO, Brian Dunn, believed that Best Buy could benefit by listening to employees and customers about socially responsible ventures. Best Buy initiated the recycling program after employees asked what the firm was doing to become more socially responsible. Dunn began posting questions to an employee website called the Water Cooler, monitoring customer comments on Facebook and Twitter, and inviting customers to leadership meetings to get stakeholder input on socially responsible actions Best Buy should take. With their success, Best Buy's experience supports the view that being a good corporate citizen does make business sense.

Sources: Gunther, M. 2009. Best Buy Wants Your Junk. *Fortune,* December 7: 96–100; Kirdahy, M. 2007. Responsibility Pays. *Forbes.com,* November 13: n.p.

Innovativeness can be a source of great progress and strong corporate growth, but there are also major pitfalls for firms that invest in innovation. Expenditures on R&D aimed at identifying new products or processes can be a waste of resources if the effort does not yield results. Another danger is related to the competitive climate. Even if a company innovates a new capability or successfully applies a technological breakthrough, another company may develop a similar innovation or find a use for it that is more profitable. Finally, R&D and other innovation efforts are among the first to be cut back during an economic downturn.

Proactiveness refers to a firm's efforts to seize new opportunities. Proactive organizations monitor trends, identify the future needs of existing customers, and anticipate changes in demand or emerging problems that can lead to new venture opportunities. Proactiveness involves not only recognizing changes but also being willing to act on those insights ahead of the competition. Strategic managers who practise proactiveness have their eye on the future in a search for new possibilities for growth and development. Proactiveness puts competitors in the position of having to respond to successful initiatives. The benefit gained by firms that are the first to enter new markets, establish brand identity, implement administrative techniques, or adopt new operating technologies in an industry is called *first mover advantage*.[38]

First movers usually have several advantages. First, industry pioneers, especially in new industries, often capture unusually high profits because there are no competitors to drive prices down. Second, first movers that establish brand recognition are usually able to retain their image and hold on to the market share gains they earned by being first. Sometimes, these benefits also accrue to other early movers in an industry, but, generally speaking, first movers have an advantage that can be sustained until firms enter the maturity phase of an industry's life cycle.[39]

Strategy Spotlight 12.7 describes the strategy of Bombardier and the proactiveness that has characterized the firm throughout its 90-year history.

12.7 STRATEGY SPOTLIGHT

Bombardier: Innovation through the Generations

From the very beginning, Bombardier, an icon of the Canadian corporate landscape, has been a leader in innovation, whether this was through new concepts, new products, new markets, new processes, or new technologies. It all started in 1924 when 15-year-old Joseph-Armand Bombardier created his first "snow vehicle" in Valcourt in rural Quebec. His company, L'Auto-Neige Bombardier Limitée, went on to produce snow vehicles for multiple functions, including ambulances, school vehicles, and mail delivery services. In 1959, he effectively created a new industry with the launch of a personal snowmobile, the "Ski-Doo." The company flourished and went on to create a strong corporate presence in the province, offering good employment opportunities for skilled workers and healthy exports.

The oil crisis of 1973 hit the recreational market hard and forced the company to halve its production; creativity and tireless innovation, under the leadership of the founder's son-in-law, Laurent Beaudoin, led Bombardier to redeploy its manufacturing know-how, and within a year, it used the excess capacity to produce its first passenger trains under a contract to provide subway cars for Montreal's transit system. The company continued to build on its initial success in railway transportation, and through the 1980s, it was able to win multiple contracts in North America, most notably its first $1-billion contract to supply New York City with subway cars and a successful expansion into Europe with rail equipment and services. By the end of the decade, Bombardier once again ventured into another new field. With the acquisition of and new investment into Learjet Corp., Bombardier entered the aerospace industry. Learjet 60 was the first midsize business jet, which soon became the top-selling aircraft in its class. Within a short period, Bombardier was recognized as the leader in business jet production and the world's third largest producer of commercial planes, behind global powerhouses Boeing and Airbus. Further innovations saw the introductions of the world's most advanced firefighting aircraft and the transcontinental super-midsize business jet, both engineering and financial successes.

When the aerospace industry took a hard hit during the 2001 recession, aircraft orders dropped precipitously, forcing the company to lay off over 5,000 staff members. At the same time, Bombardier's personal watercraft and leisure snow sport business experienced similar declines. The company turned to Bombardier Transportation, the company's rail and transportation business, to carry the firm through the rough times, and, indeed, the division delivered strong business results. By 2008, it had grown by 25 percent, becoming the largest component of the global firm and compensating for another slowdown of the aerospace business that arrived with the 2008 recession.

Sources: The discussion on Bombardier draws from http://www.bombardier.com/en/corporate/about-us/history?docID=0901260d8001dffa; Cameron, L., 2010, "Bombardier deja vu." *Canadian Business,* August 16; Layne, R., & Tomesco, F., 2010, "Bombardier First Quarter Profit Drops as Recession Curbs Demand for Jets," *Bloomberg News,* June 2; Stouffer, R., 2009, "Bombardier Inc. Pushing Boundaries to Move People from Here to There," *Tribune-Review,* May 22; http://www.aerospace.bombardier.com/en/transportation/about-transportation/awards?docID=0901260d800d8189; Rothman, A., 2009, "Bombardier Struggles in Boeing, Airbus Turbulence," *Bloomberg News,* January 21; http://www.seattlepi.com/business/396856_bombardier21.html; Shalom, F., 2011, "Sky's the Limit for CSeries," *Montreal Gazette,* February 2; Gerson Lehrman Group, March 2010, "CSeries Failure Hits Bombardier Where It Hurts," retrieved November 16, 2010, from http://www.glgroup.com/News/CSeries-Failure-Hits-Bombardier-Where-It-Hurts-47033.html.

First movers are not always successful. The customers of companies that introduce novel products or embrace breakthrough technologies may be reluctant to commit to a new way of doing things. In his book *Crossing the Chasm,* Geoffrey A. Moore notes that most firms seek evolution, not revolution, in their operations. This makes it difficult for a first mover to sell promising new technologies.[40]

Competitive aggressiveness refers to a firm's efforts to outperform its industry rivals. Companies with an aggressive orientation are willing to "do battle" with competitors. They might slash prices and sacrifice profitability to gain market share or spend aggressively to obtain manufacturing capacity. WestJet entered the Canadian airline industry with a distinct business model that was designed around drastically lower prices and a very efficient cost structure. It was able to develop a toehold in the Calgary–Edmonton and Calgary–Vancouver routes and subsequently expanded into the rest of Canada, most notably east into the Toronto and Montreal markets. In a short period, the upstart airline was able to wrestle a substantial share of the market from the dominant player, Air Canada, which was saddled with heavy debt and legacy costs from a unionized labour force.

Risk taking refers to a firm's willingness to seize a venture opportunity, even though it does not know whether the venture will be successful—to act boldly without knowing the consequences. To be successful through corporate entrepreneurship, firms usually have to take on riskier alternatives, even if it means forgoing the methods or products that have worked in the past. To obtain high financial returns, firms take such risks as assuming high levels of debt, committing large amounts of firm resources, introducing new products into new markets, and investing in unexplored technologies. Before launching their strategies, corporate entrepreneurs must know their firm's appetite for risk.[41]

Even though risk taking involves taking chances, it is not gambling. The best-run companies investigate the consequences of various opportunities and create scenarios of likely outcomes. Their objective is to reduce the riskiness of business decision making: they evaluate new venture opportunities thoroughly enough to reduce the uncertainty surrounding them. Risk taking, by its nature, involves potential dangers and pitfalls. Only carefully managed risk is likely to lead to competitive advantages. Actions that are taken without sufficient forethought, research, and planning may prove to be very costly. Strategic managers must always remain mindful of potential risks. Successful entrepreneurs are typically not risk takers; instead, they take steps to minimize risks by carefully understanding them. That is how they avoid focusing on risk and remain focused on opportunity.[42] Companies that choose to grow through internal corporate venturing must remember that entrepreneurship always involves embracing what is new and uncertain.

LO 4   LAUNCHING A NEW VENTURE

No matter what the source and type of innovation, growth and rewards come from converting innovations into successful business ventures. Large corporations pursue new business ventures through the creation of new divisions, introductions of new product lines and other activities associated with corporate entrepreneurship. Yet the majority of new business creation is the result of entrepreneurial efforts by startup firms and small businesses. Managing entrepreneurial firms can benefit greatly from applying the principles of strategic management as developed throughout this book. Although entrepreneurial ventures can vary greatly, depending on such factors as the size, age, or growth goals of the firm, entrepreneurial activities will be more successful if strategic thinking guides decision making. It is worth noting that new ventures are, indeed, risky undertakings. Even though tens of thousands of small businesses are formed each year, thousands also close. In a recent year, just over 60,000 businesses were formed in Canada. This translates into an annual business birth rate of 14 to 16 percent. But in the same year, 12 to 14 percent of existing businesses were terminated.[43]

Entrepreneurs wishing to launch a new venture must first identify a promising business opportunity. What constitutes a good opportunity? How does one know that one opportunity is better than another? A promising opportunity must be justified in terms of its attractiveness in the marketplace. But this is not all. The readiness and skills of the entrepreneurial founder and his or her team must be evaluated. Do they have the necessary knowledge, skills, experience, and drive to make the venture successful? Moreover, the availability and access to resources needed for the launch of the venture must be considered. Startup costs, operational expenses, and later-stage financing are among the requirements for a successful launch. Exhibit 12-4 identifies the three factors that are needed to successfully proceed. Both established firms and new ventures must do a good job of opportunity recognition to be successful. For the entrepreneurial startup, though, the issue of availability of resources and a qualified and motivated entrepreneurial team are especially critical. Established firms are more likely to have access to resources and may already have key personnel on board. For them, the need for corporate support and the adoption of the idea by an individual or a team who will champion the idea and push it over the various corporate hurdles is equally critical in order for the idea to take form and become a business. For new business founders, starting a new venture presents formidable challenges in securing needed resources and developing entrepreneurial talent. For corporate entrepreneurs, legitimacy and approval are equally formidable hurdles.[44] We consider each of the three factors in turn.

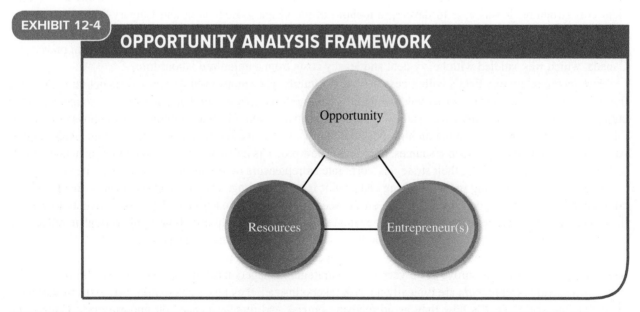

EXHIBIT 12-4

OPPORTUNITY ANALYSIS FRAMEWORK

Sources: Based on J. A. Timmons and S. Spinelli, *New Venture Creation,* 6th ed. (Burr Ridge, IL: McGraw-Hill/Irwin, 2004); and W. D. Bygrave, "The Entrepreneurial Process," in W. D. Bygrave, ed., *The Portable MBA in Entrepreneurship,* 4th ed. (New York: Wiley, 2011).

Entrepreneurial Opportunities

The starting point for any new venture is the presence of an entrepreneurial opportunity. Where do opportunities come from? For new business startups, opportunities come from many sources: current or past work experiences, hobbies that grow into businesses or lead to inventions, suggestions by friends or family, or a chance event that makes an entrepreneur aware of an unmet need. For established firms, new business opportunities come from the needs of existing customers, suggestions by suppliers, or technological developments that lead to new advances.[45] For all firms, there is a major, overarching factor behind all viable opportunities that emerge in the business landscape: change. Change creates opportunities. Entrepreneurial firms make the most of changes brought about by new technology, sociocultural trends, and shifts in consumer demand. Strategy Spotlight 12.8 highlights how the rapid pace of globalization and the advent of the Internet have changed the way new products enter a market and how one company in particular, Cove Bikes of Deep Cove, British Columbia, is capitalizing on both of these trends.

12.8 STRATEGY SPOTLIGHT

Free-Riding in British Columbia Is Becoming a Global Sport

Free-riding is a particular kind of mountain biking enjoyed on the extreme terrain of dense woods and steep pitches, such as those of the coast just north of Vancouver. The sport has quickly gained global appeal, and the North Shore has become synonymous with the genre. The highly respected British magazine *Mountain Biking* even designed a competition for its readers to build a course that would resemble the landscape around North Shore. Cove Bikes is right there, at the heart of North Shore; enthusiasts call it the "granddaddy of bike shops." It produces special bicycle frames that can take the beating that comes from travelling the steep rocky descents and traversing thick, overgrown roots. The bikes sell for a steep $1,500 to $6,000 dollars each. In the spirit of true mountain biking, Cove Bikes only produces a limited number of frames, and its store is only open a few hours each day. But once its intriguing website went online, enquiries rolled in, and sales from overseas took off. Half of the company's annual sales of $2 million come from outside North America.

Sources: M. Patriquin, "The Secret of My Address," *Report on (Small) Business*, Spring 2005, pp. 16–21; www.covebike.com; and www.mntbikehalloffame.com.

How do changes in the external environment lead to new business creation? They spark creative new ideas and innovation. For example, the increasing concern of people and businesses about the serious risks associated with global warming and our detrimental impact on the environment have spurred the creation of companies such as Zerofootprint, a renewable-energy venture based in Toronto that installs geothermal heating and cooling systems in homes, shopping malls, and complexes, with the capital investment financed by the energy savings.[46] Clean Energy Developments is a designer and installer of solar–geothermal heating and cooling systems for new homes. Enwave Energy has developed a unique deep-lake cooling system that serves the air-conditioning needs of such building complexes as the Toronto City Hall and provides alternative heating and energy management to over 100 buildings in downtown Toronto. All these companies are responding to the increasing pressure from individuals and corporate customers looking for renewable-energy options for their real estate facilities.

Each of these examples demonstrates how entrepreneurial firms respond to changes brought about by new technology, sociocultural trends, and shifts in consumer demand. Even death and tragedy stimulate business development. The Simple Alternative was set to capitalize on the frustrations and stress typically experienced by people purchasing funeral services. The company promises a simple, no-sales-pitch, low-cost alternative to high-priced traditional funerals. Chasing the same opportunity, another company is now selling factory-direct caskets at its eponymous webpage.[47]

Individuals often have ideas for entrepreneurial ventures. However, not all such ideas are good ideas—that is, viable business opportunities. To determine which ideas are strong enough to become new ventures, entrepreneurs must go through a process of identifying, selecting, and developing potential opportunities. This is the process of opportunity recognition.[48]

Opportunity recognition refers to more than just the "Eureka!" feeling that people sometimes experience at the moment they identify a new idea. Although such insights are often very important, the opportunity recognition process involves two phases of activity—discovery and evaluation—that can lead to viable new venture opportunities.[49]

The discovery phase refers to the process of becoming aware of a new business concept. Many entrepreneurs report that their idea for a new venture occurred to them in an instant, as a sort of "Aha!" experience—that is, they had some insight or epiphany, often based on their prior knowledge, that gave them an idea for a new business. The discovery of new opportunities is often spontaneous and unexpected. For example, Howard Schultz, CEO of Starbucks, was in Milan, Italy, when he suddenly realized that the coffee-and-conversation café model that was common in Europe would work in the United States as well. According to Schultz, he did not need to do research to find out if Americans would pay $3 for a cup of coffee—he just knew. Starbucks was just a small business at the time but Schultz began literally shaking with excitement about growing it into a bigger business.[50] Strategy Spotlight 12.9 tells how three Internet pioneers identified their business opportunities and grew them into billion-dollar successes.

12.9 STRATEGY SPOTLIGHT

From Pioneers to Billionaires: Internet Entrepreneurs Who Recognized Winning Opportunities

When founding a business, there is always a moment when the opportunity is first recognized. The recognition may unfold in tiny steps over time or appear suddenly as an "Aha!" experience. When pioneering entrepreneurs act on such realizations, they change the world for the rest of us. Here are three examples of pioneers who recognized how to use the transforming technology of the Internet to create new competitive advantages and make themselves billionaires.

Pierre Omidyar, Founder of eBay.com (Net Worth: $9.4 Billion)

eBay is an icon of the Internet era. The online auction model it championed made it possible for hobbyists, collectors, and seekers of highly specialized products to participate 24/7 in an enormous global "flea market." It is one of the best examples of a business that just was not possible before the Web made it so. As well known as eBay is, its origins are a bit murkier. Legend has it that founder Pierre Omidyar launched the auction site to help his fiancée sell and find pieces for her Pez-dispenser collection. These humble beginnings, however, were contrived by a public relations manager to attract media attention. In fact, the first thing sold on eBay was a broken laser pointer for $14.83. Omidyar, incredulous, asked the winning bidder if he realized it was broken. The email reply, "I collect broken laser pointers," helped Omidyar recognize he had tapped into a gold mine of business potential. By 2016, eBay had over 12,000 employees and annual revenues of $8.6 billion.

Mark Zuckerberg, Founder of Facebook.com (Net Worth: $69 Billion)

It is not clear that Mark Zuckerberg knew what he was on to when he and two friends launched Facebook in a Harvard dorm room in February 2004. But they found out pretty quickly: By the end of the month, over half of Harvard's undergraduates had registered on the service. In April, the site was opened up to another 30 universities, and by June, Zuckerberg had quit Harvard and moved to Palo Alto, California, where venture capitalist Peter Thiel recognized the potential and gave him $500,000 to take Facebook to the next level. It has been anything but level since then. In January 2014, Facebook's shares were trading at $61, making the company worth $150 billion. Facebook reached that mark faster than any company in history. Zuckerberg owns 500 million shares.

Marc Benioff, Founder of Salesforce.com (Net Worth: $4.5 Billion)

Managing customer relationships is important for all businesses, large and small. As information technology made it possible to automate thousands of customer accounts electronically, however, customer relationship management (CRM) systems became so complex that only very large companies could afford them. The typical corporate system included customized software, costly installations, and ongoing maintenance fees that shut out most small businesses. Marc Benioff, who had worked for Oracle, a major supplier of CRM systems, realized he could use the Internet to provide a simpler and substantially cheaper product online. The earliest customers for Salesforce.com, founded in 1999, were small businesses that paid as little as $50 per month. His early successes made it possible for Benioff to improve his online capabilities, and eventually he landed big customers, such as Cisco Systems and Staples. When the company went public in 2004, it was already a market leader in CRM and claimed "CRM" as its New York Stock Exchange stock symbol.

Sources: A. Farrell, "The Web Billionaires," www.forbes.com, September 8, 2008, n.p.; H. Blodget, "Mark Zuckerberg Has Made $31 Billion in the Last 10 Years", www.businessinsider.com, January 30, 2014; http://www.forbes.com/profile/marc-benioff/; www.facebook.com; www.ebay.com; www.salesforce.com; and www.wikipedia.com.

Opportunity discovery also may occur as the result of a deliberate search for new venture opportunities or creative solutions to business problems. Viable opportunities often emerge only after a concerted effort. It is very similar to a creative process, which may be unstructured and "chaotic" at first but eventually leads to a practical solution or business innovation. To stimulate the discovery of new opportunities, companies often encourage creativity, outside-the-box thinking, and brainstorming.

Opportunity evaluation occurs after an opportunity has been identified. It involves analyzing an opportunity to determine whether it is viable and strong enough to be developed into a full-fledged new venture. Ideas developed by new-product groups or in brainstorming sessions are tested by various methods, including talking to potential target customers and discussing operational requirements with production or logistics managers. Systematic analysis often leads to the decision that a new venture project should be discontinued. If the venture concept continues to seem viable, a more formal business plan may be developed.

Among the most important factors to evaluate is the market potential for the product or service. Established firms tend to operate in established markets. They have to adjust to market trends and to shifts in consumer demand, of course, but they usually have a customer base for which they are already filling a marketplace need. New ventures, in contrast, must first determine whether a market exists for the product or service they are contemplating. Thus, a critical element of opportunity recognition is assessing to what extent the opportunity is viable in the marketplace.

For an opportunity to be viable, it needs to have four qualities.[51]

1. *Attractive.* The opportunity must be attractive in the marketplace; that is, there must be market demand for the new product or service.

2. *Achievable.* The opportunity must be practical and physically possible.

3. *Durable.* The opportunity must be attractive long enough for the development and deployment to be successful; that is, the window of opportunity must be open long enough for it to be worthwhile.

4. *Value creating.* The opportunity must be potentially profitable; that is, the benefits must surpass the cost of development by a significant margin.

If a new business concept meets these criteria, two other factors must be considered before the opportunity is launched as a business: (1) the resources available to undertake it and (2) the characteristics of the entrepreneur(s) pursuing it.

LO 5 Entrepreneurial Resources

One of the major challenges that entrepreneurial firms face is a lack of resources. Young firms are confronted by the liability of newness.[52] Essentially, they are particularly vulnerable because they lack experience, are unknown in their industry, and are unfamiliar to customers. Until they have proven themselves, young firms lack credibility; banks will not lend them money, and suppliers may not extend them credit. For startups, the most important resource is usually money, because a new firm typically has to expend substantial sums just to start the business. However, financial resources are not the only kind of resource a new venture needs. Human capital and social capital are also important. Many firms also rely on government resources to help them thrive.

Financial Resources

Hand in hand with the importance of market viability to new-venture creation, entrepreneurial firms must also have financing. In fact, the level of available financing is often a strong determinant of how the business is launched and its eventual success. Cash finances are, of course, highly important. But access to capital, such as a line of credit or favourable payment terms with a supplier, can also help a new venture succeed.

The types of financial resources that may be needed depend on two factors: (1) the stage of venture development and (2) the scale of the venture.[53] Entrepreneurial firms that are starting from scratch—that is, startups—are at the earliest stage of development. Most startups also begin on a relatively small scale. The funding available to young and small firms tends to be quite limited. In fact, the majority of new firms are low-budget startups launched with personal savings and the contributions of family and friends.[54] Among firms included in the *Entrepreneur* list of the 100 fastest-growing new businesses in a recent year, 61 percent reported that their start-up funds came from personal savings.[55]

Although bank financing, public financing, and venture capital are important sources of small business finance, these types of financial support are typically available only after a company has started to conduct business and generate sales. Even "angel" investors—private individuals who provide equity investments for seed capital during the early stages of a new venture—favour companies that already have a winning business model and dominance in a market niche.[56] Says Cal Simmons, co-author of *Every Business Needs an Angel,* "I would much rather talk to an entrepreneur who has already put his money and his effort into proving the concept."[57]

Once a venture has established itself as a going concern, other sources of financing become readily available. Banks, for example, are more likely to provide later-stage financing to companies with a track record of sales or other cash-generating activity. Startups that involve large capital investments or extensive development costs—such as manufacturing or engineering firms trying to commercialize an innovative product—may have high cash requirements soon after they are founded. Others need financing only when they are on the brink of rapid growth. To obtain such funding, entrepreneurial firms often seek venture capital.

Venture capital is a form of private equity financing through which entrepreneurs raise money by selling shares in the new venture. In contrast to angel investors, who invest their own money, venture capital companies are organized to place the funds of private investors into lucrative business opportunities. Venture capitalists nearly always have high performance expectations from the companies they invest in, but they also provide important managerial advice, and links to key contacts in an industry.

Despite the importance of venture capital to many fast-growing firms, the majority of external funding for young and small firms comes from informal sources, such as family and friends. Exhibit 12-5, based on the Global Entrepreneurship Monitor survey of entrepreneurial firms, demonstrates this dramatic difference. Firms that obtain venture capital receive funding of about $2.6 million each. In contrast, companies that obtain funding from informal sources typically receive only about $10,000 each. Although relatively few companies receive venture funding, they are attractive to venture capitalists because their profit potential and impact on innovation, job growth, and wealth creation tends to be much greater.[58]

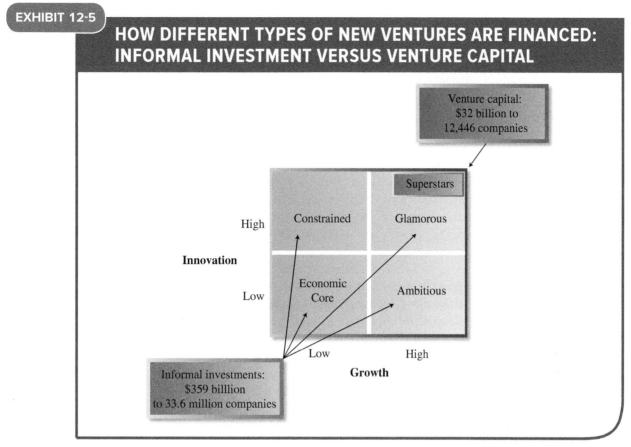

EXHIBIT 12-5

HOW DIFFERENT TYPES OF NEW VENTURES ARE FINANCED: INFORMAL INVESTMENT VERSUS VENTURE CAPITAL

Sources: P. D. Reynolds, W. D. Bygrave, and E. Autio, *Global Entrepreneurship Monitor: 2003 Executive Report* (Babson College, London Business School, and the Kauffman Foundation, 2004). The classification of the company system used by GEM is based on B. Kirchhoff, *Entrepreneurship and Dynamic Capitalism* (London: Praeger, 1994).

Human Capital

Bankers, venture capitalists, and angel investors agree that the most important asset an entrepreneurial firm can have is strong and skilled management. According to Stephen Gaal, founding member of Walnut Venture Associates, venture investors do not invest in businesses; instead, he said, "We invest in people . . . very smart people with very high integrity." Managers need to have a strong base of experience and extensive domain knowledge, as well as an ability to make rapid decisions and change direction as shifting circumstances may require. In the case of startups, more is better. New ventures that are started by teams of three, four, or five entrepreneurs are more likely to succeed in the long run than are ventures launched by "lone wolf" entrepreneurs.[59] Yet developing a strong team can be a challenge for early-stage entrepreneurial ventures. Cash-strapped founders may find it difficult to find and afford the kind of talent needed to make their startups successful.

Social Capital

New ventures founded by entrepreneurs who have extensive social contacts are more likely to succeed than are ventures started without the support of a social network.[60] Even though a venture may be new, if the founders have contacts who will vouch for them, they gain exposure and build legitimacy faster.[61] This support can come from several sources: prior jobs, industry organizations, and local business groups, such as the chamber of commerce. These contacts can all contribute to a growing network that provides support for the entrepreneurial firm. Janina Pawlowski, co-founder of the online lending company E-Loan, attributes part of her success to the strong advisors she persuaded to serve on her board of directors, including Tim Koogle, former CEO of Yahoo![62]

Strategic alliances represent a type of social capital that can be especially important to young and small firms.[63] By partnering with other companies, young firms can expand their reach into new markets, enhance their technological capabilities, enhance their reputations, and expand their revenue base. Manufacturing alliances allow them to outsource most of the physical production and grow quickly without the need for investment in capacity. Internet-enabled capabilities can be tapped to collaborate online and simplify logistics. Finally, licensing agreements can allow them to sell products and services in distant markets and take advantage of scale in spite of their small size.[64]

Government Resources

Both the federal and provincial governments, as well as governments at the regional and municipal levels, provide support for entrepreneurial firms. Federal and provincial governments especially provide critical support in two key arenas—financing and government contracting. Small business loan programs offer loan guarantees designed to support the growth and development of entrepreneurial firms. While the government itself does not typically lend money, it underwrites loans made by banks to small businesses, thus reducing the risk associated with lending to firms with unproven records. All three levels of government also offer training, counselling, and support services through local offices and Canada Business Service Centres.[65] Yet the Canadian Federation of Independent Business reports that many small businesses do not take advantage of most government programs. Reasons for this might include excessive red tape, lack of awareness, lack of trust, and, once again, delays.

Another key area of support is in government contracting. Programs sponsored by various government agencies ensure that small businesses have the opportunity to bid on contracts to provide goods and services to the government. Although working with the government sometimes has drawbacks related to issues of regulation and time-consuming decision making, programs to support small businesses and entrepreneurial activity constitute an important resource for entrepreneurial firms. Local economic development initiatives are often designed specifically to stimulate small business activity. Government-sponsored micro-enterprise funds, such as Aboriginal Business Canada, provide funding as well as training for companies established in Indigenous communities or that are to be launched by Indigenous entrepreneurs. But as a number of solar power installers and windmill farms have discovered, becoming too dependent on government subsidies can be very risky as a firm grows and as government shifts priorities.

Entrepreneurial Leadership

Whether a venture is launched by an individual entrepreneur or an entrepreneurial team, effective leadership is needed. Launching a new venture requires a special kind of leadership. It involves courage, belief in one's convictions, and the energy to work hard even in difficult circumstances. Yet these are the very challenges that motivate most business owners. Research indicates that entrepreneurs tend to have characteristics that distinguish them from corporate managers. Differences include:

- *Higher core self-evaluation.* Successful entrepreneurs evidence higher levels of self-confidence and a higher assessment of the degree to which an individual controls his or her own destiny.[66]

- *Higher conscientiousness.* Entrepreneurs tend to have a higher degree of organization, persistence, hard work, and pursuit of goal accomplishment.

- *Higher openness to experience.* Entrepreneurs also tend to score higher on openness to experience, a personality trait associated with intellectual curiosity and a desire to explore novel ideas.

- *Higher emotional stability.* Entrepreneurs exhibit a higher ability to handle ambiguity and maintain even emotions during stressful periods, and they are less likely to be overcome by anxieties.

- *Lower agreeableness.* Finally, entrepreneurs tend to score lower on agreeableness. This suggests they typically look out primarily for their own self-interest and also are willing to influence or manipulate others for their own advantage.[67]

Entrepreneurs put themselves to the test and get their satisfaction from acting independently, overcoming obstacles, and thriving financially. These personality traits are embodied in the behavioural attributes necessary for successful entrepreneurial leadership—vision, dedication and drive, and commitment to excellence:

- *Vision.* This may be an entrepreneur's most important asset. Entrepreneurs envision realities that do not yet exist. With vision, entrepreneurs are able to exercise a kind of transformational leadership that creates something new and, in some way, changes their world. Not all founders of new ventures succeed. Indeed, most of them fail. But without a vision, most entrepreneurs would never even get a new business off the ground. Just having a vision, however, is not enough. To drum up the required support from the many external stakeholders, get financial backing, and attract employees, entrepreneurial leaders must share their vision with others. They must be able to communicate their vision to a diverse collection of stakeholders, and to do so, they must understand how these constituencies differ. They must fit the vision message to address the relevant concerns and connect with the target stakeholders' aspirations. Communicating the vision effectively is just as important as crafting the vision in the first place, and both are vital elements of good leadership. At the same time, entrepreneurial leaders must be willing and able to make difficult decisions. As the new venture concept is developed, tough decisions will have to be made that define and shape the boundaries of the vision.

- *Dedication and drive.* Dedication and drive are reflected in hard work. Drive involves internal motivation; dedication calls for an intellectual commitment that keeps an entrepreneur going even in the face of bad news or misfortune. Both dedication and drive require patience, stamina, and a willingness to work long hours. However, a business built on the heroic efforts of one person may suffer in the long run. That is why the dedicated entrepreneur's enthusiasm is also important—like a magnet, it attracts others to the business to help with the work.

- *Commitment to excellence.* Excellence requires entrepreneurs to commit to knowing the customer, providing quality goods and services, paying attention to details, and continuously learning. Entrepreneurs who achieve excellence are sensitive to how these factors work together. However, entrepreneurs may flounder if they think they are the only ones who can create excellent results. The most successful, by contrast, often report that they owe their success to hiring people smarter than themselves.

In his book *Good to Great,* Jim Collins makes another important point about entrepreneurial leadership: Ventures built on the charisma of a single person may have trouble growing "from good to great" once that person leaves.[68] Thus, the leadership that is needed to build a great organization is usually exercised by a team of dedicated people working together rather than by a single leader. Such people are themselves leaders who attract other top-quality people to the organization. Another aspect of this team approach is attracting team members who fit with the company's culture, goals, and work ethic. "Those people who do not share the company's core values," Collins says, "find themselves surrounded by corporate antibodies and ejected like a virus."[69] Poor performers and laggards must be dismissed. Success requires focused and disciplined action and leaders must have the willingness and strength to get rid of people who are not working out.

ENTREPRENEURIAL STRATEGY

Once a viable opportunity, sufficient resources, and a skilled and dedicated entrepreneur or entrepreneurial team are in place, the new venture needs a strategy. Although the generic strategies introduced in Chapter 5 can be applied to entrepreneurial firms, several different strategic factors that are unique to new ventures have to also be considered.

To be successful, new ventures must evaluate industry conditions, the competitive environment, and market opportunities to position themselves strategically. However, a traditional strategic analysis may have to be altered somewhat to fit the entrepreneurial situation. For example, five-forces analysis (as discussed in Chapter 2) is typically used by established firms. It can also be applied to the analysis of new ventures to assess the impact of industry and competitive forces. But you may ask: How does a new entrant evaluate the threat of other new entrants?

First, the new entrant needs to examine barriers to entry. If the barriers are too high, the potential entrant may decide not to enter or to gather more resources before attempting to do so. Compared with an older firm with an established reputation and available resources, the barriers to entry may be insurmountable for an entrepreneurial start-up. Therefore, understanding the force of these barriers is critical in making a decision to launch.

A second factor that may be especially important to a young venture is the threat of retaliation by incumbents. In many cases, entrepreneurial ventures are the new entrants that pose a threat to incumbent firms. Therefore, in applying the five-forces model to new ventures, the threat of retaliation by established firms needs to be considered.

Part of any decision about what opportunity to pursue is a consideration of how a new entrant will actually enter a new market. The concept of entry strategies provides a useful means of addressing the types of choices that new ventures have.

LO 6 Entry Strategies

One of the most challenging aspects of launching a new venture is finding a way to begin doing business that quickly generates cash flow, builds credibility, attracts good employees, and overcomes the liability of newness. The idea of an entry strategy or "entry wedge" describes several approaches that firms may take to get a foothold in a market.[70] Several factors will affect this decision:

- Is the product or service high-tech or low-tech?
- What resources are available for the initial launch?
- What are the industry and competitive conditions?
- What is the overall market potential?
- Does the venture founder prefer to control the business or to grow it?

In some respects, any type of entry into a market for the first time may be considered entrepreneurial. But the entry strategy will vary, depending on how risky and innovative the new business concept is.[71] New-entry strategies typically fall into one of three categories: (1) pioneering new entry, (2) imitative new entry, or (3) adaptive new entry.

Pioneering New Entry

New entrants with a radical new product or highly innovative service may change the way business is conducted in an industry. This kind of breakthrough—creating new ways to solve old problems or meeting customers' needs in a unique new way—is referred to as a *pioneering new entry*. If the product or service is unique enough, a pioneering new entrant may actually have little direct competition. The first personal computer was a pioneering product; there had never been anything quite like it, and it revolutionized computing. The first Internet browser provided a type of pioneering service. These breakthroughs created whole new industries and changed the competitive landscape. And breakthrough innovations continue to inspire pioneering entrepreneurial efforts.

The pitfalls associated with a pioneering new entry are numerous. For one thing, there is a strong risk that the product or service will not be accepted by consumers. The history of entrepreneurship is littered with new ideas that never got off the launching pad. Take, for example, Smell-O-Vision, an invention designed to pump odours into movie theatres from the projection room during presribed moments in a film. It was tried only once (for the film *Scent of a Mystery*) before it was declared a major flop. Innovative? Definitely. But apparently not a very good idea for the time.[72]

A pioneering new entry is disruptive to the status quo of an industry. It is similar to a radical innovation and may actually be based on a technological breakthrough, as were the personal computer and the cellular phone, for example. If it is successful, other competitors will rush in to copy it. This can create issues of sustainability for an entrepreneurial firm, especially if a larger company with greater resources introduces a similar product. For a new entrant to sustain its pioneering advantage, it may be necessary to protect its intellectual property, advertise heavily to build brand recognition, form alliances with businesses that will adopt its products or services, and offer exceptional customer service.

Imitative New Entry

Whereas pioneers are often inventors or tinkerers with new technology, imitators usually have a strong marketing orientation. They look for opportunities to capitalize on proven market successes. An imitative new entry strategy is used by entrepreneurs who see products or business concepts that have been successful in one market niche or physical locale and introduce the same basic product or service in another segment of the market.

Sometimes, the key to success with an imitative strategy is to fill a market space where the need had previously been filled inadequately. Entrepreneurs are also prompted to be imitators when they realize that they have the resources or skills to do a job better than an existing competitor. Recall from Chapter 3 that "difficult to imitate" was viewed as one of the keys to building sustainable advantages.[73] A strategy that can be imitated, therefore, seems like a poor way to build a business. In essence, this is true. But consider the example of a franchise. Franchising is a very successful imitative new-entry strategy. Franchising provides the opportunity to own a business and work independently while benefiting from the accumulated success of others. Entrepreneurs sign up with corporations that have proven concepts and multiple successful outlets already operating in other locations. The entrepreneur imitates the existing business model in a new location and takes advantage of the corporation's reputation and size as well as brand name recognition. Competitive advantages accrue from the size of the large corporation and the individualistic dedication of the franchisee/owner/entrepreneur.

Adaptive New Entry

Most new entrants use a strategy somewhere between "pure" imitation and "pure" pioneering. That is, they offer a product or service that is somewhat new and sufficiently different to create new value for customers and capture market share. Such firms are adaptive in the sense that they are aware of marketplace conditions and conceive entry strategies to capitalize on current trends. Some would argue that "every new idea is merely a spin of an old idea." An entrepreneur does not have to be totally creative. Sometimes, a slight twist to an old idea makes all the difference.[74] An adaptive new entry approach does not involve "re-inventing the wheel," neither is it merely imitative. It involves taking an existing idea and adapting it to a particular situation. Consider the example of Green Mountain Coffee Roasters (GMCR), a Vermont-based distributor of specialty coffees and the creator of the Keurig single-cup brewer. Although the coffee business is not new and is dominated by global powerhouses, such as Starbucks, Kraft, and Procter & Gamble, GMCR has found a niche and become a tremendously successful enterprise. In the meantime, it has also become a leading advocate for fair trade practices and for providing financial support for local coffee growers. GMCR purchases coffee exclusively from small farm co-operatives in Peru, Mexico, and Sumatra. It provides micro loans to agricultural family businesses that are trying to create more diverse local economies, and it sells its roasted beans in upscale stores, side by side with Starbucks, Nabob, Maxwell House, and Folgers.[75]

There are several pitfalls that might limit the success of an adaptive new entrant. First, the value proposition must be perceived as unique. Unless potential customers believe a new product or service does a superior job of meeting their needs, they will have little motivation to try it. Second, there is nothing to prevent a close competitor from mimicking the new firm's adaptation as a way to hold on to its customers. Note how almost every coffee company today touts its own fair-trade beans. Third, once an adaptive entrant achieves initial success, the challenge is to keep the idea fresh. If the attractive features of the new business are copied, the entrepreneurial firm must find ways to adapt and improve the product or service offering.

Considering these choices, an entrepreneur or entrepreneurial team might ask: Which new entry strategy is the best? The choice depends on many competitive, financial, and marketplace considerations. Nevertheless, research indicates that the greatest opportunities may stem from being willing to enter new markets rather than seeking growth only in existing markets. A recent study found that companies that ventured into arenas that were new to the world or new to the company earned total profits of 61 percent. In contrast, companies that made only incremental improvements, such as extending an existing product line, grew total profits by only 39 percent.[76]

These findings led W. Chan Kim and Renee Mauborgne in their book *Blue Ocean Strategy* to conclude that companies that are willing to venture into market spaces where there is little or no competition—labelled "blue oceans"—will outperform those firms that limit growth to incremental improvements in competitively crowded industries—labelled "red oceans." Companies that identify and pursue blue ocean strategies follow somewhat different rules compared with those that are "bloodied" by the competitive practices in red oceans. Consider the following elements of a blue ocean strategy:

- *Create uncontested market space.* By seeking opportunities where they are not threatened by existing competitors, blue ocean firms can focus on customers rather than on the competition.
- *Make the competition irrelevant.* Rather than using the competition as a benchmark, blue ocean firms cross industry boundaries to offer new and different products and services.
- *Create and capture new demand.* Rather than fighting over existing demand, blue ocean companies seek opportunities in uncharted territory.
- *Break the value–cost trade-off.* Blue ocean firms reject the idea that a trade-off between value and cost is inevitable and, instead, seek opportunities in areas that benefit both their cost structure and their value proposition to customers.
- *Pursue differentiation and low cost simultaneously.* By integrating the range of a firm's utility, price, and cost activities, blue ocean companies align their whole system to create sustainable strategies.

The essence of blue ocean strategy is not just to find an uncontested market but to create one. Some blue oceans arise because new technologies create new possibilities, such as eBay's online auction business. Yet technological innovation is not a defining feature of a blue ocean strategy. Most blue oceans are created from within red oceans by companies that push beyond the existing industry boundaries. Any of the new entry strategies described earlier could be used to pursue a blue ocean strategy. Strategy Spotlight 12.10 considers the example of Cirque du Soleil, which created a new market for circus entertainment by making traditional circus acts more like theatrical productions.

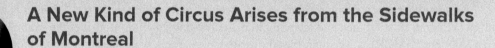

12.10 STRATEGY SPOTLIGHT

A New Kind of Circus Arises from the Sidewalks of Montreal

In the spring of 1984, funded by a Canadian government grant, a group of street performers mounted a production that would celebrate the 450th anniversary of Jacques Cartier's discovery of Canada and called it *Le Grand Tour du Cirque du Soleil.* Driven by conviction as much as limited resources, friends Guy Laliberté and Daniel Gauthier embarked on a quest to alter the industry boundaries that traditionally defined the circus concept and create a new type of circus experience. Since the days of Ringling Bros. and Barnum & Bailey, the circus had consisted of animal acts, star performers, and Bozo-like clowns. Cirque questioned this formula and researched what audiences really wanted. It found that interest in animal acts was declining, in part because of public concerns over the treatment of circus animals. Because managing animals—and the celebrity trainers who performed with them—was costly, Cirque eliminated these acts.

Instead, Cirque focused on three elements of the traditional circus tent event that still captivated audiences: acrobatic acts, clowns, and the tent itself. Elegant acrobatics became a central feature of its performances, and clown humour became more sophisticated and less slapstick. Cirque also preserved the image of the tent by creating exotic facades that captured the symbolic elements of the traditional tent. Finally, rather than displaying three different acts simultaneously, as in the classic three-ring circus, Cirque offers multiple productions with theatrical storylines, giving audiences a reason to go to the circus more often. Each production has a different theme and its own original musical score.

Cirque's efforts to redefine the circus concept have paid off. Since 1984, Cirque's productions have been seen by over 180 million people in some 400 cities around the world. Laliberté received the 2006 Ernst & Young Entrepreneur of the Year award and is considered one of Canada's richest individuals with an estimated wealth of $1.36 billion.

Sources: W. C. Kim and R. Mauborgne, "Blue Ocean Strategy," *Harvard Business Review,* October 2004, pp. 76–84; "The World's Billionaires," *Forbes,* March 10, 2010, www.forbes.com; and www.cirquedusoleil.com.

Once created, a blue ocean strategy is difficult to imitate. If customers flock to blue ocean creators, firms rapidly achieve economies of scale, learning advantages and synergies across their organizational systems. Body Shop, for example, chartered new territory by refusing to focus solely on beauty products. Traditional competitors, such as Estée Lauder and L'Oreal, whose brands are based on promises of eternal youth and beauty, found it difficult to imitate this approach without repudiating their current images.

These factors suggest that blue ocean strategies provide an avenue by which firms can pursue an entrepreneurial new entry. Such strategies are not without risks, however. A new entrant must decide not only the best way to enter into business but also what type of strategic positioning will work best as the business goes forward. Those strategic choices can be informed by the guidelines suggested for the generic strategies, although an entrepreneur may also consider some unique combination strategies that blend elements of cost leadership and differentiation.

LO 7 Generic Strategies for Entrepreneurial Firms

Overall Cost Leadership

One of the ways entrepreneurial firms achieve success is by doing more with less. By holding down costs or making more efficient use of resources than larger competitors, new ventures are often able to offer lower prices and still be profitable. Thus, under the right circumstances, a low-cost leadership strategy is a viable alternative for some new ventures. The way most companies achieve low-cost leadership, however, is typically different for young or small firms.

Recall from Chapter 5 that three of the features of a low-cost approach included operating at a large enough scale to spread costs over many units of production (economies of scale), making substantial capital investments to increase economies of scale, and using knowledge gained from experience to make cost-saving improvements. These elements of a cost-leadership strategy may be unavailable to new ventures. Because new ventures are typically small, they usually do not have high economies of scale relative to their competitors. Because they are usually cash strapped, they cannot make large capital investments to increase their scale advantages. And because many are young, they often do not have a wealth of accumulated experience to draw on to achieve cost reductions.

However, compared with large firms, new ventures often have simple organizational structures that make decision making both easier and faster. The smaller size also helps young firms change more quickly when upgrades in technology or feedback from the marketplace indicate that improvements are needed. They are also able to make decisions at the time they are founded that help them deal with the issue of controlling costs. For example, they may source materials from a supplier that provides them more cheaply or set up manufacturing facilities in another country where labour costs are especially low. Strategy Spotlight 12.11 describes how WestJet was able to find its place in the middle of a highly competitive domestic airline industry dominated by Air Canada, by offering comparable services at lower prices.

12.11 STRATEGY SPOTLIGHT

An Airline That Consistently Makes Money!

WestJet was founded in 1996 as a low-frills, service-oriented airline that initially operated on the Calgary–Edmonton and Calgary–Vancouver corridors. Its simple business formula relied on online reservations, which reduced the need for commissioned travel agents or telephone operators, as well as on the elimination of "frills" such as expensive airport lounges, frequent miles programs, and on-board free amenities, such as meals and drinks. It employed nonunion staff and operated the industry's fuel-efficient workhorse, the venerable Boeing 737, in a network of point-to-point routes that maximized the in-air time of the planes. Short domestic flights also meant quick turnaround at the airport gates to facilitate the maximum number of flights by each plane within the normal 16- to 18-hour workday.

(Continued)

Within a short period, the airline had gained the respect of travellers for its friendly and efficient service and its reliability, as well as their admiration for its low fares. Following the absorption of Canadian Airlines by Air Canada in early 2000, WestJet saw the opportunity to expand further, as the federal government was determined not to allow the dominant national carrier to harm the small upstart. Notwithstanding the government's help, WestJet's lower adjusted unit costs allowed it to undercut Air Canada's fares and gain market share while remaining profitable. Soon, WestJet was flying east, and before long, it was touching down at the country's busiest airport, Pearson International in Toronto. By 2004, WestJet controlled 28 percent of the domestic market share and had a fleet of 54 planes. The airline's next big move was to launch selected flights into the United States and the Caribbean. WestJet has carved a strong position as a low-cost competitor in the cutthroat airline industry while enjoying solid employee support (being named one of the best employers in Canada in 2015) and peer acceptance (having codeshare agreements with European, Asian, and American airlines).

Sources: K. McArthur, "Rivals Grab Bigger Piece of Air Canada's Market Share," *The Globe and Mail*, April 21, 2004, p. B1; B. Jang, "WestJet Soars on the Wings of Expansion," *The Globe and Mail*, April 7, 2005, p. B4; N. Mordant, "WestJet American Airlines Signed Code-Share Pact," *Reuters*, February 28, 2011, www.westjet.ca; various WestJet Airlines Ltd. press releases.

Differentiation

Both pioneering and adaptive entry strategies involve some degree of differentiation. That is, the success of the new entry is based on being able to offer a differentiated value proposition. In the case of pioneers, the new venture is attempting to do something strikingly different, either by using a new technology or deploying resources in a way that radically alters the way business is conducted. Often, entrepreneurs do both.

Amazon founder Jeff Bezos set out to use Internet technology to revolutionize the way books are sold. He garnered the ire of other booksellers and the attention of the public by making bold claims about being "the earth's largest bookseller." As a bookseller, Bezos was not doing anything that had not been done before. But two key differentiating features—doing it on the Internet and offering extraordinary customer service—have made Amazon a differentiated success.

There are several factors that make it more difficult for new ventures to be successful as differentiators. For one thing, the strategy is generally thought to be expensive to enact. Differentiation is often associated with strong brand identity, and establishing a brand is usually considered expensive because of the cost of advertising and promotion, paid endorsements, exceptional customer service, and so on. Differentiation successes are sometimes built on superior innovation or use of technology. These are also factors where it may be challenging for young firms to excel relative to established competitors.

Nevertheless all of these areas—innovation, technology, customer service, distinctive branding—are also arenas where new ventures have sometimes made a name for themselves, even though they must operate with limited resources and experience. To be successful, according to Garry Ridge, CEO of the WD-40 Company, "You need to have a great product, make the end user aware of it, and make it easy to buy."[77] It sounds simple, but it is a difficult challenge for new ventures with differentiation strategies.

Focus

Focus strategies are often associated with small businesses because there is a natural fit between the narrow scope of the strategy and the small size of the firm. A focus strategy may include elements of differentiation and overall cost leadership, as well as combinations of these approaches. But to be successful within a market niche, the key strategic requirement is to stay focused.

Here is why: Despite all the attention given to fast-growing new industries, most startups enter industries that are mature.[78] In mature industries, growth in demand tends to be slow, and there are often many competitors.

Therefore, if a startup wants to get a piece of the action, it often has to take business away from an existing competitor. If a startup enters a market with a broad or aggressive strategy, it is likely to evoke retaliation from a more powerful competitor. Young firms can often succeed best by finding a market niche where they can get a foothold and make small advances that erode the position of existing competitors.[79] From this position, they can build a name for themselves and grow. AbeBooks, the online bookseller from British Columbia, has set itself right in the middle, or perhaps more appropriately, in the fringe, of the multibillion dollar market dominated by the likes of Amazon and Indigo.[80] AbeBooks specializes in used and rare books, antiquarian editions, and hard-to-find titles. AbeBooks is neither Amazon nor eBay but a unique player in a narrow niche that serves book enthusiasts who do not like the auction process of eBay and are looking for titles too much on the fringe for Amazon. Similarly, Cora Tsouflidou of Montreal embarked on making one thing right in the highly competitive industry of quick restaurants.[81] Her venture focused exclusively on breakfast and giving busy and health-conscious customers heaping mounds of fresh fruit with a wholesome staple of omelettes, pancakes, and waffles. Many years later, Cora's restaurant chain of over 130 franchise stores is among the biggest players in the breakfast sector across Canada and has been approached by investors from around the world for licensing rights and a global expansion.

As the AbeBooks and Cora's successes demonstrate, many new ventures are very successful, even though their share of the market is quite small. Giant companies, such as Procter & Gamble and Ford, are often described in terms of their market share—that is, their share of sales in a whole market. But many of the industries that small firms participate in have thousands of participants that are not direct competitors. For example, auto repair shops in Nova Scotia do not compete with those in British Columbia. These industries are considered "fragmented" because no single company is strong enough to have power over other competitors. Small firms focus on the market share only in their trade area. This may be defined as a geographical area or a small segment of a larger product group.

Combination Strategies

One of the best ways for young and small businesses to achieve success is by pursuing combination strategies. By combining the best features of low-cost, differentiation, and focus strategies, new ventures can often achieve something truly distinctive.

Entrepreneurial firms are often in a strong position to offer a combination strategy because they have the flexibility to approach situations uniquely. For example, holding down expenses can be difficult for big firms because each layer of bureaucracy adds to the cost of doing business across the boundaries of a large organization.

A similar argument could be made about entrepreneurial firms that differentiate. Large firms often find it difficult to offer highly specialized products or superior customer services. Entrepreneurial firms, by contrast, can often create high-value products and services through their unique differentiating efforts.

For nearly all new entrants, one of the major dangers is that a large firm with more resources will copy what they are doing. Well-established incumbents that observe the success of a new entrant's product or service will copy it and use their market power to overwhelm the smaller firm. The threat may be lessened for firms that use combination strategies. Because of the flexibility of entrepreneurial firms, they can often enact combination strategies in ways that the large firms cannot copy. This makes the new entrant's strategies much more sustainable.

Perhaps more threatening than large competitors are close competitors because they have similar structural features that help them adjust quickly and be flexible in decision making. Here again, a carefully crafted and executed combination strategy may be the best way for an entrepreneurial firm to thrive in a competitive environment.

SUMMARY

New ventures and young businesses that capitalize on marketplace opportunities are leaders in implementing new technologies and introducing innovative products and services. This chapter has addressed how innovation and entrepreneurship can be a means of internal venture creation, strategic renewal, and new business creation, and how an entrepreneurial orientation can help corporations enhance their competitive position.

Innovation is one of the primary means by which corporations grow and strengthen their strategic position. Innovations can take several forms, ranging from radical breakthrough innovations to incremental improvement innovations. Innovations are often used to update products and services or for improving organizational processes. Managing the innovation process is often challenging because it involves a great deal of uncertainty and because there are many choices to be made about the extent and type of innovations to pursue. By defining the scope of innovation, managing the pace of innovation, staffing to capture value from innovation, and collaborating with innovation partners, firms can more effectively manage the innovation process.

We also discussed the role of corporate entrepreneurship in venture development and strategic renewal. Corporations usually take either a focused or dispersed approach to corporate venturing. Firms with a focused approach usually separate the corporate venturing activity from the ongoing operations of the firm to foster independent thinking and encourage entrepreneurial team members to think and act without the constraints imposed by the corporation. In corporations where venturing activities are dispersed, a culture of entrepreneurship permeates all parts of the company to induce strategic behaviours by all organizational members. In measuring the success of corporate venturing activities, both financial and strategic objectives should be considered.

Most entrepreneurial firms need to have an entrepreneurial orientation: the methods, practices, and decision-making styles that strategic managers use to act entrepreneurially. Five dimensions of entrepreneurial orientation—autonomy, innovativeness, proactiveness, competitive aggressiveness, and risk taking—are found in firms that pursue corporate venture strategies, and each dimension makes a unique contribution to the pursuit of new opportunities. When deployed effectively, the methods and practices of an entrepreneurial orientation can be used to engage successfully in corporate entrepreneurship and new venture creation. However, strategic managers must remain mindful of the pitfalls associated with each of these approaches.

To successfully launch new ventures or implement new technologies, three factors must be present: (1) an entrepreneurial opportunity, (2) the resources to pursue the opportunity, and (3) an entrepreneur or entrepreneurial team willing and able to undertake the venture. Firms must develop a strong ability to recognize viable opportunities. Opportunity recognition is a process of determining which venture ideas are, in fact, promising business opportunities. In addition to strong opportunities, entrepreneurial firms need resources and entrepreneurial leadership to thrive. The resources that startups need include financial resources as well as human and social capital. Many firms also benefit from government programs that support new venture development and growth. New ventures thrive best when they are led by founders or owners who have vision, drive and dedication, and a commitment to excellence.

Once the necessary opportunities, resources, and entrepreneurial skills are in place, new ventures still face numerous strategic challenges. Decisions about the strategic positioning of new entrants can benefit from conducting strategic analyses and evaluating the requirements of niche markets. Entry strategies used by new ventures take several forms, including pioneering new entry, imitative new entry, and adaptive new entry. Entrepreneurial firms can benefit from using overall low cost, differentiation, and focus strategies although each of these approaches has pitfalls that are unique to young and small firms. Entrepreneurial firms are also in a strong position to benefit from combination strategies.

Summary Review Questions

1. What is meant by the concept of a continuum of radical and incremental innovations?

2. What are the dilemmas that organizations face when deciding what innovation projects to pursue? What steps can organizations take to effectively manage the innovation process?

3. What is the difference between focused and dispersed approaches to corporate entrepreneurship?

4. Explain the difference between proactiveness and competitive aggressiveness in terms of achieving and sustaining competitive advantage.

5. Describe how the entrepreneurial orientation (EO) dimensions of innovativeness, proactiveness, and risk taking can be combined to create competitive advantages for entrepreneurial firms.

6. Explain how the combination of opportunities, resources, and entrepreneurs helps determine the character and strategic direction of an entrepreneurial firm.

7. What is the difference between discovery and evaluation in the process of opportunity recognition? Give an example of each.

8. Describe the three characteristics of entrepreneurial leadership: vision, dedication and drive, and commitment to excellence.

9. Briefly describe the three types of entrepreneurial entry strategies: pioneering, imitative, and adaptive.

10. Explain why entrepreneurial firms are often in a strong position to use combination strategies.

REFLECTING ON CAREER IMPLICATIONS

- *Innovation:* Look around at the types of innovations being pursued by your company. Do they tend to be incremental or radical? Product related or process related? What new types of innovations might benefit your organization? How can you add value to such innovations?

- *Managing Innovation:* How might your organization's chances of a successful innovation increase through collaboration with innovation partners? Your ability to collaborate with individuals from other departments and firms will make you more receptive to and capable of innovation initiatives and enhance your career opportunities.

- *Corporate Entrepreneurship:* Do you consider the company you work for to be entrepreneurial? If not, what actions might you take to enhance its entrepreneurial spirit? If so, what have been the keys to its entrepreneurial success? Can these practices be repeated to achieve future successes?

- *Entrepreneurial Orientation:* Consider the five dimensions of entrepreneurial orientation. Is your organization especially strong at any of these? Especially weak? What are the career implications of your company's entrepreneurial strengths or weaknesses?

EXPERIENTIAL EXERCISE

1. Select two different major corporations from two different industries (you might use *Report on Business 1000* companies to make your selection). Compare and contrast these organizations in terms of their entrepreneurial orientation.

Entrepreneurial Orientation	Company A	Company B
Autonomy		
Innovativeness		
Proactiveness		
Competitive aggressiveness		
Risk taking		

On the basis of your comparison, consider the following:

1. How is each entrepreneurial orientation reflected in each company's strategy?
2. Which corporation would you say has the stronger entrepreneurial orientation?
3. Is the corporation with the stronger entrepreneurial orientation also stronger in terms of financial performance?

2. Pick the most recent issue of *The Globe and Mail's Report on Small Business* magazine. Select two entrepreneurial stories, and use the information provided to evaluate the qualities of the small business opportunity identified in terms of the four characteristics. In each category, complete the following table:

Characteristics	High/Medium/Low	Rationale
1. Attractive		
2. Achievable		
3. Durable		
4. Value creating		

1. Evaluate the extent to which they met the criteria (using high, medium, or low).
2. Explain your rationale. That is, what features of the opportunity account for the score you gave them?

APPLICATION QUESTIONS AND EXERCISES

1. Select a firm known for its corporate entrepreneurship activities. Research the company, and discuss how it has positioned itself relative to its close competitors. Does it have a unique strategic advantage? Disadvantage? Explain.

2. Explain the difference between product innovations and process innovations. Provide examples of firms that have recently introduced each type of innovation. What are the types of innovations related to the strategies of each firm?

3. Using the Internet, select a company that is listed on the Toronto Stock Exchange. Research the extent to which the company has an entrepreneurial culture. What elements capture and demonstrate this culture? Do you believe its entrepreneurial efforts are sufficient to generate sustainable advantages?

4. How can an established firm use an entrepreneurial orientation to enhance its overall strategic position? Provide examples.

5. Think of an entrepreneurial firm that has been successfully launched in the last 10 years. What are the characteristics of the entrepreneur(s) who launched the firm?

6. Select a small business you are familiar with in your local community. Research the company, and discuss how it has positioned itself relative to its close competitors. Does it have a unique strategic advantage? Disadvantage? Explain.

7. Using the Internet, find an example of a young entrepreneurial firm (founded within the last five years). What kind of entry strategy did it use—pioneering, imitative, or adaptive? Since the firm's initial entry, how has it used or combined overall low-cost, differentiation, and focus strategies?

ETHICS AND CORPORATE SOCIAL RESPONSIBILITY QUESTIONS

1. Innovation activities are often aimed at making a discovery or commercializing a technology ahead of the competition. What are some of the unethical practices that companies could engage in during the innovation process? What are the potential long-term consequences of such actions?

2. Discuss the ethical implications of using entrepreneurial policies and practices to pursue corporate social responsibility goals. Are these efforts authentic and genuine or just an attempt to attract more customers?

APPENDIX

ANALYZING STRATEGIC MANAGEMENT CASES
Why Analyze Strategic Management Cases?

It is often said that the key to finding good answers is to ask good questions. Strategic managers and business leaders are required to evaluate options, make choices, and find solutions to the challenges they face every day. To do so, they must learn to ask the right questions. The process of analyzing, decision making, and implementing strategic actions raises many good questions:

- Why do some firms succeed and others fail?
- Why are some companies higher performers compared with others?
- What information is needed in the strategic planning process?
- How do competing values and beliefs affect strategic decision making?
- What skills and capabilities are needed to implement a strategy effectively?

How does a student of strategic management learn to ask the right questions? Case studies can be a tremendous tool in developing the discipline to ask good questions and in mastering the tools to answer those questions. Case analysis simulates the real-world experience that strategic managers and company leaders face as they try to determine how best to run their companies. It places students in the middle of an actual situation and challenges them to figure out what to do.[1]

Asking the right questions is just the beginning of case analysis. Throughout the chapters of the book, we discussed issues and challenges that managers face and provided analytical frameworks for understanding the situation. But once the analysis is complete, decisions have to be made. Case analysis forces us to choose among different options and set forth a plan of action based on our choices. But even then the job is not done. Strategic case analysis also requires that we address how we will implement the plan and the implications of choosing one course of action over another.

A strategic management case is a detailed description of a challenging situation faced by an organization.[2] It usually includes a chronology of events and extensive support materials, such as financial statements, product lists, and transcripts of interviews with employees. Although names or locations are sometimes disguised to provide anonymity, cases usually report the facts of a situation as authentically as possible.

One of the main reasons to analyze strategic management cases is to develop an ability to evaluate business situations critically. In case analysis, memorizing key terms and conceptual frameworks is not enough. To analyze a case, it is important that we go beyond textbook prescriptions and quick answers. It requires that we look deeply into the information provided and root out the essential issues and causes of a company's problems.

The types of skills that are required to prepare an effective strategic case analysis can benefit you in actual business situations. Case analysis adds to the overall learning experience by helping you acquire or improve skills that may not be taught in a typical lecture course. Three capabilities that can be learned by conducting case analysis are especially useful to strategic managers—the ability to differentiate, speculate, and integrate.[3] Here is how case analysis can enhance those skills.

1. ***Differentiate.*** Effective strategic management requires that many different elements of a situation be evaluated at once. This is also true in case analysis. When analyzing cases, it is important to isolate critical facts, evaluate whether assumptions are useful or faulty, and distinguish between good and bad information. Differentiating between the factors that are influencing the situation presented by a case is necessary for making a good analysis. Strategic management also involves understanding that problems are often complex and multilayered. This applies to case analysis as well. Ask whether the case deals with operational, business-level, or corporate issues. Do the problems stem from weaknesses in the internal value chain or threats in the external environment? Dig deep. Being too quick to accept the easiest or least controversial answer will usually fail to get to the heart of the problem.

2. *Speculate.* Strategic managers need to be able to use their imagination to envision an explanation or solution that might not readily be apparent. The same is true with case analysis. Being able to imagine different scenarios or contemplate the outcome of a decision can aid the analysis. Managers also have to deal with uncertainty, since most decisions are made without complete knowledge of the circumstances. This is also true in case analysis. Case materials often seem to be missing data, or the information provided is contradictory. The ability to speculate about details that are unknown or the consequences of an action can be helpful.

3. *Integrate.* Strategy involves looking at the big picture and having an organization-wide perspective. Strategic case analysis is no different. Even though the chapters in this textbook divide the material into various topics that may apply to different parts of an organization, all of this information must be integrated into one set of recommendations that will affect the whole company. A strategic manager needs to comprehend how all the factors that influence the organization will interact. This also applies to case analysis. Changes made in one part of the organization affect other parts. Thus, a holistic perspective that integrates the impact of various decisions and environmental influences on all parts of the organization is needed.

In business, these three activities sometimes "compete" with each other for a manager's attention. For example, some decision makers may have the natural ability to differentiate among elements of a problem but are not able to integrate them very well. Others have enough innate creativity to imagine solutions or fill in the blanks when information is missing. But they may have a difficult time when faced with hard numbers or cold facts. Even so, each of these skills is important. The mark of a good strategic manager is the ability to simultaneously make distinctions and envision the whole, as well as to imagine a future scenario while staying focused on the present. Thus, another reason to conduct case analysis is to practise developing and exercising the ability to differentiate, speculate, and integrate.

Case analysis takes the student through the whole cycle of activity that a manager would face. Beyond the textbook descriptions of concepts and examples, case analysis requires "walking a mile in the shoes" of the strategic decision maker and learning to evaluate situations critically. Executives and owners must make decisions every day, with limited information and a swirl of business activity going on around them. Businesses are often faced with immediate challenges that threaten their existence. Case studies illustrate how the strategic management process can help many of them survive. Students are called to put themselves in the manager's shoes and, first, realistically assess the environment, evaluate the marketplace, and analyze the company's resources. Then, they are asked to make tough decisions, which include shifting the market focus, hiring and firing, and re-deploying the company's assets.

How to Conduct a Case Analysis

The process of analyzing strategic management cases involves several steps. In this section, we will review the mechanics of preparing a case analysis. Before beginning, though, you should keep in mind two things that will help make your understanding of the process clearer and the results of the process more meaningful.

First, unless you prepare for a case discussion, there is little you can gain from the discussion and even less that you can offer. Effective strategic managers do not enter problem-solving situations without doing some homework—investigating the situation, analyzing and researching possible solutions, and sometimes gathering advice from others. Effective problem solving often requires that decision makers be immersed in the facts, options, and implications surrounding the problem. In case analysis, this means reading and thoroughly comprehending the case materials before trying to make an analysis.

The second point is related to the first. To get the most out of a case analysis, you must place yourself "inside" the case—that is, think like an actual participant in the case situation. However, there are several positions you can take. These are discussed below.

- *Strategic decision maker.* This is the position of the senior executive responsible for resolving the situation described in the case. It may be the chief executive officer (CEO), the business owner, or a strategic manager in a key executive position.

- *Board of directors.* Since the board of directors represents the owners of a corporation, it has a responsibility to step in when a management crisis threatens the company. As a board member, you may be in a unique position to solve problems.

- *Outside consultant.* Either the board or top management may decide to bring in outsiders. Consultants often have an advantage because they can look at a situation objectively. But they may also be at a disadvantage, since they have no power to enforce changes.

Before beginning the analysis, it may be helpful to envision yourself assuming one of these roles. Then, as you study and analyze the case materials, you can make a diagnosis and recommend solutions in a way that is consistent with your position. Try different perspectives. You may find that your view of the situation changes, depending on the role you play. As an outside consultant, for example, to solve a problem presented in the case, it may be easy for you to conclude that certain individuals should be replaced. However, if you take the role of the CEO who knows the individuals and the challenges they have been facing, you may be reluctant to fire them and will seek another solution instead.

The idea of assuming a particular role is similar to the real world in various ways. In your career, you may work in an organization where outside accountants, bankers, lawyers, or other professionals are advising you about how to resolve business situations or improve your practices. Their perspective will be different from yours, but it is useful to understand things from their point of view. Conversely, you may work as a member of the audit team of an accounting firm or the loan committee of a bank. In those situations, it would be helpful if you understood the situation from the perspective of the business leader who must weigh your views against all the other advice that he or she receives. Case analysis can help develop an ability to appreciate such multiple perspectives.

One of the most challenging roles to play in business is business founder or owner. In the case of small businesses or entrepreneurial startups, the founder may wear all hats at once— key decision maker, primary shareholder, and CEO. Hiring an outside consultant may not be an option. However, the issues faced by young firms and established firms are often not that different, especially when it comes to formulating a plan of action. Business plans that entrepreneurial firms use to raise money or propose a business expansion typically revolve around a few key issues that must be addressed no matter what the size or age of the business. Strategy Spotlight A.1 reviews business planning issues that are most important to consider when evaluating any case, especially from the perspective of the business founder or owner.

A.1 STRATEGY SPOTLIGHT

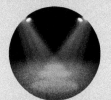

Using a Business Plan Framework to Analyze Strategic Cases

Established businesses often have to change what they are doing to improve their competitive position or sometimes simply to survive. To make the changes effectively, businesses usually need a plan. Business plans are no longer just for entrepreneurs. The kind of market analysis, decision making, and action planning that are considered standard practice among new ventures can also benefit going concerns that want to make changes, seize an opportunity, or head in a new direction.

The best business plans, however, are not those loaded with decades of month-by-month financial projections or that depend on rigid adherence to a schedule of events that is impossible to predict. The effective ones are focused on four factors that are critical to new-venture success. These factors are important in case analysis as well because they get to the heart of many of the problems found in strategic cases.

1. ***People.*** "When I receive a business plan, I always read the résumé section first," says Harvard Professor William Sahlman. The people questions that are critically important to investors include the following: What are their skills? How much experience do they have? What is their reputation? Have they worked together as a team? These same questions may also be used in case analysis to evaluate the role of individuals in the strategic case.

(Continued)

2. ***Opportunity.*** Business opportunities come in many forms. They are not limited to new ventures. The chance to enter new markets, introduce new products, or merge with a competitor provides many of the challenges that are found in strategic management cases. What are the consequences of such actions? Will the proposed changes affect the firm's business concept? What factors might stand in the way of success? The same issues are also present in most strategic cases.

3. ***Context.*** Things happen in contexts that cannot be controlled by a firm's managers. This is particularly true of the general environment where social trends, economic changes, or events, such as terrorist attacks, can change business overnight. When evaluating strategic cases, ask these questions: Is the company aware of the impact of context on the business? What will it do if the context changes? Can it influence the context in a way that favours the company?

4. ***Risk and Reward.*** With a new venture, the entrepreneurs and investors take the risks and get the rewards. In strategic cases, the risks and rewards often extend to many other stakeholders—employees, customers, suppliers, and so on. When analyzing a case, ask these questions: Are the managers making choices that will pay off in the future? Are the rewards evenly distributed? Will some stakeholders be put at risk if the situation in the case changes? What if the situation remains the same—could that be even more risky?

Whether a business is growing or shrinking, large or small, industrial or service oriented, the issues of people, opportunities, context, and risks and rewards will have a large impact on its performance. Therefore, you should always consider these four factors when evaluating strategic management cases.

Sources: Wasserman, E. 2003. A simple plan. MBA Jungle, February: 50–55; DeKluyver, C. A. 2000. Strategic thinking: An executive perspective. Upper Saddle River, NJ: Prentice Hall; and Sahlman, W. A. 1997. How to write a great business plan. Harvard Business Review, 75(4): 98–108.

Conducting a strategic management case analysis can be organized in five easy steps: (1) becoming familiar with the material, (2) identifying the problems, (3) analyzing the strategic issues using the tools and insights of strategic management, (4) proposing alternative solutions, and (5) making recommendations.[4]

Become Familiar with the Material

Written cases often include a lot of material. They may be complex and include detailed financials or long passages. Even so, to understand a case and its implications, you must become familiar with its content. Sometimes, key information is not immediately apparent. It may be contained in the footnotes to an exhibit or an interview with a lower-level employee. In other cases, the important points may be difficult to grasp because the subject matter is so unfamiliar. When you approach a strategic case, try the following technique to enhance comprehension:

- Read quickly through the case to get an overall sense of the material.
- Use the initial read-through to assess possible links to strategic concepts.
- Read through the case again, in depth. Make written notes as you read.
- Evaluate how strategic concepts might inform key decisions, or suggest alternative solutions.
- After formulating an initial recommendation, thumb through the case again quickly to assess the consequences of the actions you propose.

Identify Problems

When conducting case analysis, one of your most important tasks is to identify the problem. Earlier, we noted that one of the main reasons to conduct case analysis was to find solutions. But you cannot find a solution unless you know the problem. "A good diagnosis is half the cure" is a well-known dictum in medicine and equally applies here. In other words, once you have determined what the problem is, you are well on your way to identifying a reasonable solution.

Some cases involve more than one problem. But the problems are usually related. Consider the following case: Company A was losing customers to a new competitor. Following an analysis, it was determined that the competitor had a 50-percent faster delivery time, even though its product was of lower quality. The managers could not understand why customers would settle for an inferior product. It turned out that no marketing effort was made to convey to the company's customers that its product was superior. A second problem was that falling sales resulted in cuts in company A's sales force. Thus, there were two related problems: inferior delivery technology and insufficient sales effort.

When trying to determine the problem, avoid getting hung up on symptoms. Zero in on the problem. For example, in the situation above, losing customers was the symptom. The problems were an underfunded, understaffed sales force and an outdated delivery technology. Try to see beyond the immediate symptoms to the more fundamental problems.

Another tip when preparing a case analysis is to articulate the problem.[5] Writing down a problem statement gives you a reference point to turn to as you proceed through the case analysis. This is important because the process of formulating strategies or evaluating implementation methods may lead you away from the initial problem. Make sure your recommendation actually addresses the problem you have identified.

There is one more thing about identifying problems. Sometimes, problems are not apparent until after you have done the analysis. In some cases, the problem will be presented plainly, perhaps in the opening paragraph or on the last page of the case. But in other cases, the problem does not emerge until after the issues in the case have been analyzed.

Conduct Strategic Analyses

This textbook has presented numerous analytical tools (e.g., five-forces analysis and value-chain analysis), contingency frameworks (e.g., when to use related rather than unrelated diversification strategies), and other techniques that can be used to evaluate strategic situations. The 12 chapters have addressed practices that are common in strategic management, but only so much can be learned by studying the practices and concepts. The best way to understand these methods is to apply them by conducting analyses of specific cases.

The first step is to determine which strategic issues are involved. Is there a problem in the company's competitive environment? Or is it an internal problem? If it is internal, does it have to do with organizational structure? Strategic controls? Uses of technology? Or perhaps the company has overworked its employees or underutilized its intellectual capital. Has the company mishandled a merger? Chosen the wrong diversification strategy? Botched a new product introduction? Each of these issues is linked to one or more of the concepts discussed earlier in the text. Determine what strategic issues are associated with the problems you have identified. Remember also that most real-life case situations involve issues that are highly interrelated. Even in cases where there is only one major problem, the strategic processes required to solve it may involve several parts of the organization.

Once you have identified the issues that apply to the case, conduct the analysis. You may need to conduct a five-forces analysis or dissect the company's competitive strategy. Perhaps you need to evaluate whether its resources are rare, valuable, difficult to imitate, or difficult to substitute. Financial analysis may be needed to assess the company's economic prospects. Perhaps the international entry mode needs to be re-evaluated because of changing conditions in the host country. Employee empowerment techniques may need to be improved to enhance organizational learning. Whatever the case, all the strategic concepts introduced in the text include insights for assessing their effectiveness. Determining how well a company is doing these things is central to the case analysis process.

Financial analysis is one of the primary tools used to conduct case analyses. The second section of this Appendix, Financial Ratio Analysis, includes a discussion and examples of the financial ratios that are often used to evaluate a company's performance and financial well-being. Exhibit A-1 provides a summary of the financial ratios presented in that section.

EXHIBIT A-1 SUMMARY OF FINANCIAL RATIO ANALYSIS TECHNIQUES

Ratio	What It Measures
Short-term solvency, or liquidity, ratios:	
Current ratio	Ability to use assets to pay off liabilities
Quick ratio	Ability to use liquid assets to pay off liabilities quickly
Cash ratio	Ability to pay off liabilities with cash on hand
Long-term solvency, or financial leverage, ratios:	
Total debt ratio	How much of a company's total assets are financed by debt
Debt-equity ratio	The amount of the company financed by debt compared with the amount financed by equity
Equity multiplier	How much debt is being used to finance assets
Times interest earned ratio	How well a company has its interest obligations covered
Cash coverage ratio	A company's ability to generate cash from operations
Asset utilization, or turnover, ratios:	
Inventory turnover	How many times each year a company sells its entire inventory
Days' sales in inventory	How many days, on average, inventory is at hand before it is sold
Receivables turnover	How frequently each year a company collects on its credit sales
Days' sales in receivables	How many days on average it takes to collect on credit sales (average collection period)
Total asset turnover	How much of sales is generated for every dollar in assets
Capital intensity	The dollar investment in assets needed to generate $1 of sales
Profitability ratios:	
Profit margin	How much profit is generated by every dollar of sales
Return on assets (ROA)	How effectively assets are being used to generate a return
Return on equity (ROE)	How effectively amounts invested in the business by its owners are being used to generate a return
Market value ratios:	
Price-earnings ratio	How much investors are willing to pay per dollar of current earnings
Market-to-book ratio	Compares market value of the company's investments to the cost of those investments

In this part of the overall strategic analysis process, it is also important to test your own assumptions about the case.[6] First, what assumptions are you making about the case materials? It may be that you have interpreted the case content differently from your team members or classmates. Being clear about these assumptions will be important in determining how to analyze the case. Second, what assumptions have you made about the best way to resolve the problems? Ask yourself why you have chosen one type of analysis over another. This process of assumption checking can also help determine if you have gotten to the heart of the problem or are still just dealing with symptoms.

As mentioned earlier, sometimes the critical diagnosis in a case can only be made after the analysis has been conducted. However, by the end of this stage in the process, you should know the problems and have completed a thorough analysis of them. You can now move to the next step: finding solutions.

Propose Alternative Solutions

It is important to remember that in strategic management cases there is rarely one right answer or one best way. Even when members of a class or a team agree on what the problem is, you may not agree on how to solve the problem. Therefore, it is helpful to consider several different solutions.

After conducting strategic analysis and identifying the problem, develop a list of options. What are the possible solutions? What are the alternatives? Generate a list first, noting all of the options you can think of without prejudging any one of them. Remember that not all cases call for dramatic decisions or sweeping changes. Some companies just need to make small adjustments. In fact, "Do nothing" may be a reasonable alternative in some cases. Although that is rare, it might be useful to consider what would happen if the company did nothing. This point illustrates the purpose of developing alternatives: to evaluate what is likely to happen if a company chooses one solution over another.

Thus, during this step of a case analysis, you will evaluate choices and the implications of those choices. One aspect of any business that is likely to be highlighted in this part of the analysis is strategy implementation. Ask how the choices made will be implemented. It may be that what seems like an obvious choice for solving a problem creates an even bigger problem when implemented. Remember that no strategy or strategic "fix" is going to work if it cannot be implemented. Once a list of alternatives is generated, ask the following:

- Can the company afford it? How will it affect the bottom line?
- Is the solution likely to evoke a competitive response?
- Will employees throughout the company accept the changes? What impact will the solution have on morale?
- How will the decision affect other stakeholders? Will customers, suppliers, and others buy into it?
- How does this solution fit with the company's vision, mission, and objectives?
- Will the culture or values of the company be changed by the solution? Is it a positive change?

The point of this step in the case analysis process is to find a solution that both solves the problem and is realistic. A consideration of the implications of various alternative solutions will generally lead you to a final recommendation that is more thoughtful and complete.

Make Recommendations

The basic aim of case analysis is to find solutions. Your work is not complete until you have recommended a course of action. In this step, the task is to make a set of recommendations that your analysis supports. Describe exactly what needs to be done. Explain why this course of action will solve the problem. The recommendation should also include suggestions for how best to implement the proposed solution because the recommended actions and their implications for the performance and future of the firm are interrelated.

The solution you propose must solve the problem you identified. This point cannot be overemphasized; too often, students make recommendations that treat only symptoms or fail to tackle the central problems in the case. Make a logical argument that shows how the problem led to the analysis and how the analysis led to the recommendations you are proposing. Remember, an analysis is not an end in itself; it is useful only if it leads to a solution.

The actions you propose should describe the very next steps that the company needs to take. Do not say, for example, "If the company does more market research, then I would recommend the following course of action . . . ." Instead, make conducting the research part of your recommendation. If you also want to suggest subsequent actions that may be different, depending on the outcome of the market research, that is all right. But do not make your initial recommendation conditional on actions the company may or may not take.

In summary, case analysis can be a very rewarding process but, as you might imagine, it can also be frustrating and challenging. If you follow the steps described above, you will address the different elements of a thorough analysis. This approach can give your analysis a solid footing. Then, even if there are differences of opinion about how to interpret the facts, analyze the situation, or solve the problems, you can feel confident that you have not missed any important steps in finding the best course of action.

Oral Presentation

Students are often asked to prepare oral presentations of the information in a case and their analysis of the best remedies. This is frequently assigned as a group project. Or you may be called to present to your classmates your ideas about the circumstances or solutions for a case the class is discussing. Exhibit A-2 provides some tips for preparing an oral case presentation.

EXHIBIT A-2

PREPARING AN ORAL CASE PRESENTATION

Organize your thoughts.

Begin by becoming familiar with the material. If you are working with a team, compare notes about the key points of the case, and share insights that other team members may have gleaned from tables and exhibits. Then, make an outline. This is one of the best ways to organize the flow and content of the presentation.

Emphasize strategic analysis.

The purpose of case analysis is to diagnose problems and find solutions. In the process, you may need to unravel the case material as presented and reconfigure it in a fashion that can be more effectively analyzed. Present the material in a way that lends itself to analysis—do not simply restate what is in the case. This results in structuring the presentation along four main areas, each representing a different degree of emphasis:

> Background/Problem Statement: 10–20%
> Strategic Analysis/Insights/Conclusions/Options: 40–50%
> Recommendations/Action Plan: 20–25%
> Benefits/Results/Risks: 5–10%

As you can see, the emphasis of your presentation should be on analysis. This will probably require you to reorganize the material so that the tools of strategic analysis can be applied.

Be logical and consistent.

A presentation that is rambling and hard to follow may confuse the listener and fail to evoke a good discussion. Present your arguments and explanations in a logical sequence. Support your claims with facts. Include financial analysis, where appropriate. Be sure that the solutions you recommend address the problems you have identified.

Defend your position.

Usually an oral presentation is followed by a class discussion. Anticipate what others might disagree with, and be prepared to defend your views. This means being aware of the choices you made and the implications of your recommendations. Be clear about your assumptions. Be prepared to expand on your analysis.

Share presentation responsibilities.

Strategic management case analyses are often conducted by teams. Each member of the team should have a clear role in the oral presentation, preferably a speaking role. It is also important to coordinate the different parts of the presentation into a logical, smooth-flowing whole. How well a team works together is usually very apparent during an oral presentation.

How to Get the Most from Case Analysis

One of the reasons case analysis is so enriching as a learning tool is that it draws on many resources and skills besides what is presented in the textbook. This is especially true in the study of strategy. Strategic management itself is a highly integrative task that draws on many areas of specialization at several levels, from the individual to the whole of society. You can get the most out of case analysis if you expand your horizons beyond the concepts in this text and seek insights from your own reservoir of knowledge. Here are some tips for how to do that.[7]

- *Keep an open mind.* Like any good discussion, a case analysis discussion often evokes strong opinions and emotions. But it is the variety of perspectives that makes case analysis so valuable: Many viewpoints usually lead to a more complete analysis. Therefore, avoid letting an emotional response to another person's style or opinion keep you from hearing what he or she has to say. Once you evaluate what is said, you may disagree with it or dismiss it as faulty. But unless you keep an open mind in the first place, you may miss the importance of the other person's contribution. Also, people often place a higher value on the opinions of those they consider to be good listeners.

- *Take a stand for what you believe.* Although it is vital to keep an open mind, it is also important to state your views proactively. Do not try to figure out what your friends or the instructor wants to hear. Analyze the case from the perspective of your own background and belief system. For example, perhaps you feel that a decision is unethical or that the managers in a case have misinterpreted the facts. Do not be afraid to assert that in the discussion. For one thing, when a person takes a strong stand, it often encourages others to evaluate the issues more closely. This can lead to a more thorough investigation and a more meaningful class discussion.

- *Draw on your personal experience.* You may have experiences from work or as a customer that can shed light on some of the issues in a case. Even though one of the purposes of case analysis is to apply the analytical tools from this text, you may be able to add to the discussion by drawing on your outside experiences and background. Of course, you need to guard against carrying that to extremes. Do not think that your perspective is the only viewpoint that matters! Simply recognize that firsthand experience usually represents a welcome contribution to the overall quality of case discussions.

- *Participate and persuade.* People who are persuasive and speak their mind can often influence the views of others. But to do so, you have to be prepared and convincing. Being persuasive is more than being loud or long winded. It involves understanding all sides of an argument and being able to overcome objections to your own point of view. These efforts can make a case discussion more lively. And they parallel what happens in the real world; in business, people frequently share their opinions and attempt to persuade others to see things their way.

- *Be concise and to the point.* In addition to speaking up and "selling" your ideas to others in a case discussion, you must be clear about what you are selling. Make your arguments in a way that is explicit and direct. Zero in on the most important points. Be brief. Do not try to make a lot of points at once by jumping around between topics. Avoid trying to explain the whole case situation at once. Remember, a sure way to lose your audience is to go on and on, take up a lot of "air time," or be unnecessarily repetitive. The best way to avoid this is to stay focused and be specific.

- *Think outside of the box.* It is all right to be a little provocative; sometimes that is the consequence of taking a stand on issues. In fact, it may be equally important to be imaginative and creative when making a recommendation or determining how to implement a solution. Albert Einstein once stated, "Imagination is more important than knowledge." Managing strategically requires more than memorizing concepts. Strategic management insights must be applied to each case differently—just knowing the principles is not enough. Imagination and thinking outside the box help apply strategic knowledge in novel and unique ways.

- *Learn from the insights of others.* Before you make up your mind about a case, hear what other students have to say. Of course, in a situation where you have to put your analysis in writing, you may not be able to learn from others ahead of time. But in a case discussion, observe how various students attack the issues and engage in problem solving. Such observation skills may also be a key to finding answers within the case. For example, people tend to believe authority figures, so they would place a higher value on what a company president says. In some cases, however, the statements of middle managers may represent a point of view that is even more helpful for finding a solution to the problems presented by the case.

- *Apply insights from other case analyses.* Throughout the text, we have used examples of actual businesses to illustrate strategy concepts. The aim has been to show you how firms think about and deal with business problems. During the course, you may be asked to conduct several case analyses as part of the learning experience. Once you have performed a few case analyses, you will see how the concepts from the text apply in real-life business situations. Incorporate the insights learned from the text examples and your own previous case discussions into each new case that you analyze.

- *Critically analyze your own performance.* Performance appraisals are a standard part of many workplace situations. They are used to determine promotions, raises, and work assignments. The same can be applied to your performance in a case analysis situation. Ask yourself, were my comments insightful? Did I make a good contribution? Am I being effective? How might I improve next time? Use the same criteria on yourself that you use to evaluate others. What grade would you give yourself? This technique will not only make you more fair in your assessment of others but also indicate to you how your own performance can improve.

- *Conduct outside research.* Many times, you can enhance your understanding of a case situation by investigating sources outside the case materials. For example, you may want to study an industry more closely or research a company's close competitors. Recent moves, such as mergers and acquisitions or product introductions, may be reported in the business press. The company itself may provide useful information on its website or in its annual reports. Such information can usually spur additional discussion and enrich the case analysis. (*Caution:* It is best to check with your instructor in advance to be sure this kind of additional research is encouraged. Incorporating outside research may conflict with the instructor's learning objectives.)

Several techniques can be employed to improve case analysis; they involve the constructive discussion of a case, like that in a classroom setting. Exhibit A-3 provides some additional guidelines for preparing a written case analysis.

EXHIBIT A-3

PREPARING A WRITTEN CASE ANALYSIS

Be thorough.
Many of the ideas presented in Exhibit A-2 about oral presentations also apply to written case analysis. However, a written analysis typically has to be more complete. This means writing out the problem statement and articulating assumptions. It is also important to provide support for your arguments and reference case materials or other facts.

Coordinate team efforts.
Written cases are often prepared by small groups. Within a group, just as in a class discussion, you may disagree about the diagnosis or the recommended plan of action. This can be healthy if it leads to a richer understanding of the case material. But before committing your ideas to writing, make sure you have coordinated your responses. Do not prepare a written analysis that appears contradictory or looks like a patchwork of disconnected thoughts.

Avoid restating the obvious.
There is no reason to restate material that everyone is familiar with already—namely, the case content. It is too easy for students to use up space in a written analysis with a recapitulation of the details of the case; this accomplishes very little. Stay focused on the key points. Only restate the information that is most central to your analysis.

Present information graphically.
Tables, graphs, and other exhibits are usually one of the best ways to present factual material that supports your arguments. For example, financial calculations, such as break-even analysis, sensitivity analysis, or return on investment, are best presented graphically. Even qualitative information, such as product lists or rosters of employees, can be summarized effectively and viewed quickly by using a table or graph.

Exercise quality control.
When presenting a case analysis in writing, it is especially important to use good grammar, avoid misspelling words, and eliminate typos and other visual distractions. Mistakes that can be glossed over in an oral presentation or class discussion are often conspicuous when they appear in writing. Make your written presentation appear as professional as possible. Do not let the appearance of your written case keep the reader from recognizing the importance and quality of your analysis.

Using Conflict-Inducing Decision-Making Techniques in Case Analysis

Several techniques can be employed to improve case analyses; they involve the constructive use of conflict. In the classroom—as well as in the business world—you will frequently be analyzing cases or solving problems in groups. Although the word *conflict* often has a negative connotation, it can be very helpful in arriving at better solutions to cases. It can provide an effective means for realizing new insights as well as for rigorously questioning and analyzing assumptions and strategic alternatives. In fact, if you do not have constructive conflict, you may only get consensus. When this happens, decisions tend to be based on compromise rather than collaboration.

In your organizational behaviour classes, you probably learned the concept of "groupthink," a condition in which group members strive to reach agreement or consensus without realistically considering other viable alternatives.[8] Group norms bolster morale at the expense of critical thinking, and effective decision making processes are impaired.[9]

Many of us have probably been "victims" of groupthink at one time or another in our lives. We may be confronted with situations in which social pressure, politics, or "not wanting to stick out" may prevent us from voicing our concerns about a chosen course of action.

Let us first look at some of the symptoms of groupthink and suggest ways of preventing it. Then, we will suggest some conflict-inducing decision-making techniques—devil's advocacy and dialectical inquiry—that can help prevent groupthink and lead to better decisions.

Symptoms of Groupthink and How to Prevent It

Irving Janis identified several symptoms of groupthink. These include the following:

- *An illusion of invulnerability.* This reassures people about possible dangers and leads to over-optimism and failure to heed warnings of danger.
- *A belief in the inherent morality of the group.* Because individuals think that what they are doing is right, they tend to ignore the ethical or moral consequences of their decisions.
- *Stereotypical views of members of opposing groups.* Members of other groups are viewed as weak or not intelligent.
- *The application of pressure.* Pressure is applied on members who express doubts about the group's shared ideas or question the validity of arguments proposed.
- *The practice of self-censorship.* Members keep silent about their opposing views and downplay to themselves the value of their own perspectives.
- *An illusion of unanimity.* People assume that judgments expressed by members are shared by all.
- *The appointment of mindguards.* People sometimes appoint themselves as mindguards to protect the group from adverse information that might break the climate of consensus (or agreement).

Groupthink is an undesirable and negative phenomenon that can lead to poor decisions. Irving Janis considers it to be a key contributor to such faulty decisions as the failure to prepare for the attack on Pearl Harbor and the escalation of the Vietnam conflict. Many instances of the same type of flawed decision-making process occur in business organizations. Janis has provided several suggestions for preventing groupthink, which can be used as valuable guides in decision making and problem solving:

- Leaders must encourage group members to express their concerns and objectives.
- When higher-level managers assign to a group a problem to be solved, they should adopt an impartial stance—not mention their preferences.
- Before a group reaches its final decision, the leader should encourage the members to discuss their deliberations with trusted associates and then report the perspectives back to the group.

- The group should invite outside experts and encourage them to challenge the group's viewpoints and positions.
- The group should divide into subgroups, meet at various times under different chairpersons, and then get together to resolve differences.
- After reaching a preliminary agreement, the group should hold a "second chance" meeting that provides members a forum to express any remaining concerns and rethink the issue before making a final decision.

Using Conflict to Improve Decision Making

In addition to the above suggestions, the effective use of conflict can be a means of improving decision making. Conflict can have negative outcomes, such as ill will, anger, tension, and lowered motivation, but leaders and group members can use it in a constructive manner if they ensure that it is managed properly.

Two conflict-inducing decision-making approaches that have become quite popular are *devil's advocacy* and *dialectical inquiry*. Both approaches incorporate conflict into the decision-making process through formalized debate.

Devil's Advocacy   An individual or a small group is asked to serve as a critic to the plan. The devil's advocate tries to identify problems with the proposed alternative and suggest reasons as to why it should not be adopted. The role of the devil's advocate is to create dissonance. This ensures that the group will take a hard look at its original proposal or alternative. By having a group (or individual) assigned the role of devil's advocate, it becomes clear that such an adversarial stance is legitimate. It brings out criticisms that might otherwise not be made.

The use of a devil's advocate can be very helpful in encouraging groups, task forces, and others, such as boards of directors, to ensure that decisions are addressed comprehensively and that groupthink is avoided.[10] Charles Elson, a director of Sunbeam Corporation, made the following argument:

> Devil's advocates are terrific in any situation because they help you to figure a decision's numerous implications . . . . The better you think out the implications prior to making the decision, the better the decision ultimately turns out to be. That's why a devil's advocate is always a great person, irritating sometimes, but a great person.

As one might expect, there can be some potential problems with using the devil's advocate approach. If one's views are constantly criticized, one may become demoralized. That person may come up with "safe solutions" to minimize embarrassment or personal risk and become less subject to criticism. Additionally, even if the devil's advocate is successful with finding problems with the proposed course of action, there may be no new ideas or counterproposals to take its place. The approach frequently focuses on what is wrong without suggesting other ideas.

Dialectical Inquiry   Dialectical inquiry is a technique whereby a problem is approached from two alternative points of view. Out of a critique of the opposing perspectives—a thesis and an antithesis—a creative synthesis can occur. Dialectical inquiry involves the following steps:

1. Identify a proposal and the information that was used to derive it.
2. State the underlying assumptions of the proposal.
3. Identify a counter-plan (antithesis) that is believed to be feasible, viable, and generally credible—but rests, however, on assumptions that are opposite to the original proposal.
4. Engage in a debate in which individuals favouring each plan provide their arguments and support.
5. Identify a synthesis which, ideally, includes the best components of each alternative.

There are some potential downsides associated with dialectical inquiry. It can be quite time consuming and may require a good deal of training. Further, it may result in a series of compromises between the initial proposal and the counter-plan. In cases where the original proposal was the best approach, this would be unfortunate. People may also identify too strongly with one solution and resent their work being compromised.

Despite some possible limitations associated with these conflict-inducing decision-making techniques, they have many benefits. Both techniques force debate about underlying assumptions, data, and recommendations between subgroups. Such debate tends to prevent the uncritical acceptance of a plan that may seem to be satisfactory after a cursory analysis. They serve to tap the knowledge and perspectives of group members and continue until group members agree on both assumptions and recommended actions. Given that both approaches serve to use, rather than minimize or suppress, conflict, higher quality decisions should result. Exhibit A-4 depicts these techniques.

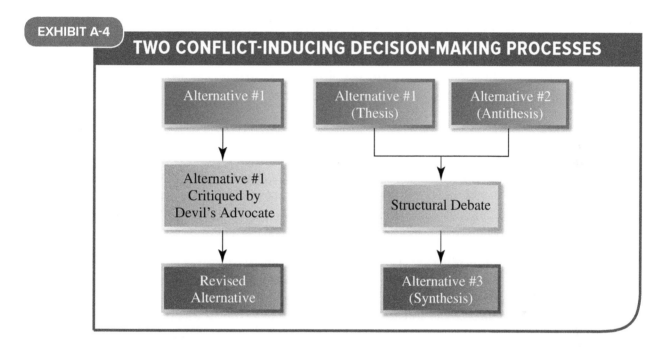

EXHIBIT A-4

TWO CONFLICT-INDUCING DECISION-MAKING PROCESSES

Following the Analysis–Decision–Action Cycle in Case Analysis

In Chapter 1, we defined strategic management as the analysis, decisions, and actions that organizations undertake to create and sustain competitive advantages. It is no accident that we chose that sequence of words because it corresponds to the sequence of events that typically occurs in the strategic management process. In case analysis, as in the real world, this cycle of events can provide a useful framework. First, an analysis of the case in terms of the business environment and current events is needed. To carry out such an analysis, the case background must be considered. Next, on the basis of that analysis, decisions must be made. This may involve formulating a strategy, choosing between difficult options, moving forward aggressively, or retreating from a bad situation. There are many possible decisions, depending on the case situation. Finally, action is required. Once decisions are made and plans are set, the action begins. The recommended action steps and understanding the consequences of implementing these actions are the final stage.

Each of the 12 chapters of this book includes techniques and information that may be useful in a case analysis. However, not all of the issues presented will be important in every case. As noted earlier, one of the challenges of case analysis is to identify the most critical points and sort through material that may be ambiguous or unimportant.

In this section, we draw on the material presented in each of the 12 chapters to show how it informs the case analysis process. The ideas are linked sequentially and in terms of an overarching strategic perspective. One of your jobs when conducting case analysis is to see how the parts of a case fit together and how the insights from the study of strategy can help you understand the case situation.

1. ***Analyzing organizational goals and objectives.*** A company's vision, mission, and objectives keep organization members focused on a common purpose. They also influence how an organization deploys its resources, relates to its stakeholders, and matches its short-term objectives with its long-term goals. The goals may even impact how a company formulates and implements strategies. When exploring issues of goals and objectives, consider the following:

   - Has the company developed short-term objectives that are inconsistent with its long-term mission? If so, how can management realign its vision, mission, and objectives?

   - Has the company considered all of its stakeholders equally in making critical decisions? If not, should the views of all stakeholders be treated the same or are some stakeholders more important than others?

   - Is the company being faced with an issue that conflicts with one of its longstanding policies? If so, how should it relate its existing policies to the potential new situation?

2. ***Analyzing the external environment.*** The business environment has two components. The general environment consists of demographic/psychographic, sociocultural, political/legal, technological, economic, and global conditions. The competitive environment includes rivals, suppliers, customers, and other factors that may directly affect a company's success. Strategic managers must monitor the external environment to identify opportunities and threats that may have an impact on performance. When investigating a firm's external environment, you might ask the following series of questions:

   - Does the company follow trends and events in the general environment? If not, how can these influences be made part of the company's strategic analysis process?

   - Is the company effectively scanning and monitoring the competitive environment? If so, how is it using the competitive intelligence it is gathering to enhance its competitive advantage?

   - Has the company correctly analyzed the impact of the competitive forces in its industry on profitability? If so, how can it improve its competitive position relative to these forces?

3. ***Analyzing the internal environment.*** A firm's internal environment consists of its resources and other value-adding capabilities. Value-chain analysis and a resource-based approach to analysis can be used to identify a company's strengths and weaknesses and determine how they are contributing to its competitive advantages. Evaluating firm performance can also help make meaningful comparisons with competitors. Consider these aspects when researching a company's internal environment:

   - Does the company know how the various components of its value chain are adding value to the firm? If not, what internal analysis is needed to determine its strengths and weaknesses?

   - Has the company accurately analyzed the sources and vitality of its resources? If so, is it deploying its resources in a way that contributes to competitive advantages?

   - Is the company's financial performance as good as or better than that of its close competitors? If so, has it balanced its financial success with the performance criteria of other stakeholders such as customers and employees?

4. ***Assessing a firm's intellectual assets.*** Human capital is a major resource in today's knowledge economy. As a result, attracting, developing, and retaining talented workers is a key strategic challenge. Other assets, such as patents and trademarks, are also critical. How companies leverage their intellectual assets through social networks and strategic alliances and how technology is used to manage knowledge may be a major influence on a firm's competitive advantage. When analyzing a firm's intellectual assets, you might ask these questions:

   - Does the company have underutilized human capital? If so, what steps are needed to develop and leverage its intellectual assets?

   - Is the company missing opportunities to forge strategic alliances? If so, how can it use its social capital to network more effectively?

   - Has the company developed knowledge-management systems that capture what it learns? If not, what technologies can it employ to retain new knowledge?

5. ***Formulating business-level strategies.*** Firms use the competitive strategies of differentiation, focus, and overall cost leadership as a basis for overcoming the five competitive forces and developing sustainable competitive advantages. Combinations of these strategies may work best in some competitive environments. Additionally, an industry's life cycle is an important contingency that may affect a company's choice of business-level strategies. There are some questions to consider when assessing business-level strategies:

   - Has the company chosen the correct competitive strategy given its industry environment and competitive situation? If not, how should it use its strengths and resources to improve its performance?

   - Does the company use combination strategies effectively? If so, what capabilities can it cultivate to further enhance profitability?

   - Is the company using a strategy that is appropriate for the industry life cycle in which it is competing? If not, how can it realign itself to match its efforts to the current stage of industry growth?

6. ***Formulating corporate-level strategies.*** Large firms often own and manage portfolios of businesses. Corporate strategies address methods for achieving synergies among these businesses. Related and unrelated diversification techniques are alternative approaches to deciding which business should be added to or removed from a portfolio. Companies can diversify by means of mergers, acquisitions, joint ventures, strategic alliances, and internal development. When analyzing corporate-level strategies, ask the following:

   - Is the company competing in the right businesses given the opportunities and threats that are present in the environment? If not, how can it realign its diversification strategy to achieve competitive advantages?

   - Is the corporation managing its portfolio of businesses in a way that creates synergies among the businesses? If so, what additional business should it consider adding to its portfolio?

   - Are the motives of the top corporate executives who are pushing diversification strategies appropriate? If not, what action can be taken to curb their activities or align them with the best interests of all stakeholders?

7. ***Formulating international-level strategies.*** Foreign markets provide both opportunities and potential dangers for companies that want to expand globally. To decide which entry strategy is most appropriate, companies have to evaluate the trade-offs between two factors that firms face when entering foreign markets: cost reduction and local adaptation. To achieve competitive advantages, firms will typically choose one of three strategies: global, multidomestic, or transnational. When evaluating international-level strategies, ask these questions:

   - Is the company's entry into an international marketplace threatened by the actions of local competitors? If so, how can cultural differences be minimized to give the firm a better chance of succeeding?

   - Has the company made the appropriate choices between cost reduction and local adaptation to foreign markets? If not, how can it adjust its strategy to achieve competitive advantages?

   - Can the company improve its effectiveness by embracing one international strategy over another? If so, how should it choose between a global, multidomestic, or transnational strategy?

8. ***Creating effective organizational designs.*** Organizational designs that align with competitive strategies can enhance performance. As companies grow and change, their structures must also evolve to meet new demands. In today's economy, boundaries of firms must be flexible and permeable to facilitate smoother interactions with external parties, such as customers, suppliers, and alliance partners. New forms of organizing are becoming more common. When evaluating the role of organizational structure on strategy implementation, consider the following:

   - Has the company implemented organizational structures that are suited to the type of business it is in? If not, how can it alter the design in ways that enhance its competitiveness?

   - Is the company employing boundaryless organizational designs where appropriate? If so, how are senior managers maintaining control of lower-level employees?

   - Does the company use outsourcing to achieve the best possible results? If not, what criteria should it use to decide which functions can be outsourced?

9. *Achieving effective strategic control.* Strategic controls enable a firm to implement strategies effectively. Informational controls involve comparing performance to stated goals and scanning, monitoring, and being responsive to the environment. Behavioural controls emerge from a company's culture, reward systems, and organizational boundaries. Consider these issues when assessing the impact of strategic controls on implementation:

   - Is the company employing the appropriate informational control systems? If not, how can it implement a more interactive approach to enhance learning and minimize response times?

   - Does the company have a strong and effective culture? If not, what steps can it take to align its values and rewards system with its goals and objectives?

   - Has the company implemented control systems that match its strategies? If so, what additional steps can be taken to improve performance?

10. *Creating a learning organization and an ethical organization.* Strong leadership is essential for achieving competitive advantages. Two leadership roles are especially important. The first is creating a learning organization by harnessing talent and encouraging the development of new knowledge. Second, leaders play a vital role in motivating employees to achieve excellence and in inspiring ethical behaviour. When exploring the impact of effective strategic leadership, you might ask the following:

    - Do company leaders promote excellence as part of the overall culture? If so, how has this influenced the performance of the firm and the individuals in it?

    - Is the company committed to being a learning organization? If not, what can it do to capitalize on the individual and collective talents of organizational members?

    - Have company leaders exhibited an ethical attitude in their own behaviour? If not, how has their behaviour influenced the actions of other employees?

11. *Fostering corporate entrepreneurship.* Many firms continually seek new growth opportunities and avenues for strategic renewal. In some corporations, autonomous work units, such as business incubators and new-venture groups, are used to focus corporate venturing activities. In other corporate settings, product champions and other firm members provide companies with the impetus to expand into new areas. When investigating the impact of entrepreneurship on strategic effectiveness, consider the following:

    - Has the company resolved the dilemmas associated with managing innovation? If so, is it effectively defining and pacing its innovation efforts?

    - Has the company developed autonomous work units that have the freedom to bring forth new product ideas? If so, has it used product champions to implement new-venture initiatives?

    - Does the company have an entrepreneurial orientation? If not, what can it do to encourage entrepreneurial attitudes in the strategic behaviour of its organizational members?

12. *Creating new ventures.* Young and small firms launch ventures that add jobs and create new wealth. In order to do so, they must identify opportunities that will be viable in the marketplace. The strategic management concepts introduced in this text can guide new ventures and small businesses in their efforts to identify markets, obtain resources, and create effective strategies. Consider these issues when examining the role of strategic thinking on the success of small business management and new-venture creation:

    - Is the company engaged in an ongoing process of opportunity recognition? If not, how can it enhance its ability to recognize opportunities?

    - Do the entrepreneurs who are launching new ventures have vision, dedication and drive, and a commitment to excellence? If so, how have these affected the performance and dedication of other employees involved in the venture?

    - Have strategic principles been used in the process of obtaining valuable resources and crafting effective entrepreneurial strategies? If not, how can the venture apply the tools of five-forces and value-chain analysis to improve its strategy making and performance?

FINANCIAL RATIO ANALYSIS

Standard Financial Statements

One obvious thing we might want to do with a company's financial statements is to compare them with those of other, similar companies. We would immediately have a problem, however. It is almost impossible to directly compare the financial statements of two companies because of differences in their sizes.

For example, Oracle and IBM are obviously serious rivals in the computer software market, but IBM is much larger (in terms of assets), so it is difficult to compare these two companies directly. For that matter, it is difficult to even compare financial statements from different points in time for the same company if the company's size has changed. The size problem is compounded if we try to compare IBM and, say, SAP (of Germany). If SAP's financial statements are denominated in euros, then we have a size difference and a currency difference.

To start making comparisons, one obvious thing we might try to do is to somehow standardize the financial statements. One very common and useful way of doing this is to work with percentages instead of total dollars. The resulting financial statements are called *common-size statements*. We consider these next.

Common-Size Balance Sheets

For easy reference, Prufrock Corporation's 2017 and 2018 balance sheets are provided in Exhibit A-5. Using these, we construct common-size balance sheets by expressing each item as a percentage of total assets. Prufrock's 2017 and 2018 common-size balance sheets are shown in Exhibit A-6.

EXHIBIT A-5 **PRUFROCK CORPORATION**
Balance Sheets as of December 31, 2017 and 2018 ($ in millions)

	2017	2018
Assets		
Current assets		
Cash	$ 84	$ 98
Accounts receivable	165	188
Inventory	393	422
Total	$ 642	$ 708
Fixed assets		
Net plant and equipment	$2,731	$2,880
Total assets	$3,373	$3,588
Liabilities and Owners' Equity		
Current liabilities		
Accounts payable	$ 312	$ 344
Notes payable	231	196
Total	$ 543	$ 540
Long-term debt	$ 531	$ 457
Owners' equity		
Common stock and paid-in surplus	$ 500	$ 550
Retained earnings	1,799	2,041
Total	$2,299	$2,591
Total liabilities and owners' equity	$3,373	$3,588

Source: Adapted from S. A. Rows, R. W. Westerfield and B. D. Jordan, *Essentials of Corporate Finance,* 2nd ed., Chapter 3. (New York: McGraw-Hill, 1999).

EXHIBIT A-6   **PRUFROCK CORPORATION**

Common-Size Balance Sheets as of December 31, 2017 and 2018 (%)

	2017	2018	Change
Assets			
Current assets			
Cash	2.5%	2.7%	+0.2%
Accounts receivable	4.9	5.2	+0.3
Inventory	11.7	11.8	+0.1
Total	19.1	19.7	+0.6
Fixed assets			
Net plant and equipment	80.9	80.3	−0.6
Total assets	100.0%	100.0%	0.0%
Liabilities and Owners' Equity			
Current liabilities			
Accounts payable	9.2%	9.6%	+0.4%
Notes payable	6.8	5.5	−1.3
Total	16.0	15.1	−0.9
Long-term debt	15.7	12.7	−3.0
Owners' equity			
Common stock and paid-in surplus	14.8	15.3	+0.5
Retained earnings	53.3	56.9	+3.6
Total	68.1	72.2	+4.1
Total liabilities and owners' equity	100.0%	100.0%	0.0%

Note: Numbers may not add up to 100.0% due to rounding.

Note that some of the totals do not check exactly because of rounding errors. Also, note that the total change has to be zero, since the beginning and ending numbers must add up to 100 percent.

In this form, financial statements are relatively easy to read and compare. For example, just looking at the two balance sheets for Prufrock, we see that current assets were 19.7 percent of total assets in 2018 up from 19.1 percent in 2017. Current liabili ties declined from 16 percent to 15.1 percent of total liabilities and equity over that same time. Similarly, total equity rose from 68.1 percent of total liabilities and equity to 72.2 percent.

Overall, Prufrock's liquidity, as measured by current assets compared with current liabilities, increased over the year. Simultaneously, Prufrock's indebtedness diminished as a percentage of total assets. We might be tempted to conclude that the balance sheet has grown "stronger."

Common-Size Income Statements

A useful way of standardizing the income statement, shown in Exhibit A-7, is to express each item as a percentage of total sales, as illustrated for Prufrock in Exhibit A-8.

EXHIBIT A-7 PRUFROCK CORPORATION
2018 Income Statement ($ in millions)

Sales		$2,311
Cost of goods sold		1,344
Depreciation		276
Earnings before interest and taxes (EBIT)		$ 691
Interest paid		141
Taxable income		$ 550
Taxes (34%)		187
Net income		$ 363
Dividends	$121	
Addition to retained earnings	242	

EXHIBIT A-8 PRUFROCK CORPORATION
2018 Common-Size Income Statement (%)

Sales		100.0%
Cost of goods sold		58.2
Depreciation		11.9
Earnings before interest and taxes (EBIT)		29.9
Interest paid		6.1
Taxable income		23.8
Taxes (34%)		8.1
Net income		15.7%
Dividends	5.2%	
Addition to retained earnings	10.5	

This income statement tells us what happens to each dollar in sales. For Prufrock, interest expense eats up $0.061 out of every sales dollar and taxes take another $0.081. When all is said and done, $0.157 of each dollar flows through to the bottom line (net income), and that amount is split into $0.105 retained in the business and $0.052 paid out in dividends.

These percentages are very useful in comparisons. For example, a relevant figure is the cost percentage. For Prufrock, $0.582 of each $1 in sales goes to pay for goods sold. It would be interesting to compute the same percentage for Prufrock's main competitors to see how Prufrock stacks up in terms of cost control.

Ratio Analysis

Another way of avoiding the problems involved in comparing companies of different sizes is to calculate and compare financial ratios. Such ratios are ways of comparing and investigating the relationships between different pieces of financial information. We cover some of the more common ratios next, but there are many others that we do not touch on.

One problem with ratios is that different people and different sources frequently do not compute them in exactly the same way, and this leads to much confusion. The specific definitions we use here may or may not be the same as others you have seen or will see elsewhere. If you ever use ratios as a tool for analysis, you should be careful to document how you calculate each one, and, if you are comparing your numbers to those of another source, be sure you know how its numbers are computed.

For each of the ratios we discuss, several questions come to mind:

1. How is it computed?
2. What is it intended to measure, and why might we be interested?
3. What is the unit of measurement?
4. What might a high or low value be telling us? How might such values be misleading?
5. How could this measure be improved?

Financial ratios are traditionally grouped into the following categories:

1. Short-term solvency, or liquidity, ratios
2. Long-term solvency, or financial leverage, ratios
3. Asset management, or turnover, ratios
4. Profitability ratios
5. Market value ratios

We will consider each of these in turn. In calculating these numbers for Prufrock, we will use the ending balance sheet (2018) figures unless we explicitly say otherwise. The numbers for the various ratios come from the income statement and the balance sheet.

Short-Term Solvency, or Liquidity, Measures

As the name suggests, short-term solvency ratios as a group are intended to provide information about a firm's liquidity, and these ratios are sometimes called *liquidity measures.* The primary concern is the firm's ability to pay its bills over the short run without undue stress. Consequently, these ratios focus on current assets and current liabilities.

For obvious reasons, liquidity ratios are particularly interesting to short-term creditors. Since financial managers are constantly working with banks and other short-term lenders, an understanding of these ratios is essential.

One advantage of looking at current assets and liabilities is that their book values and market values are likely to be similar. Often (though not always), on the one hand, these assets and liabilities just do not live long enough for the two to get seriously out of step. On the other hand, like any type of near cash, current assets and liabilities can and do change fairly rapidly, so today's amounts may not be a reliable guide to the future.

Current Ratio   One of the best-known and most widely used ratios is the current ratio. As you might guess, the current ratio is defined as:

$$\text{Current ratio} = \frac{\text{Current assets}}{\text{Current liabilities}}$$

For Prufrock, the 2018 current ratio is:

$$\text{Current ratio} = \frac{\$708}{\$540} = 1.31 \text{ times}$$

Because current assets and liabilities are, in principle, converted to cash over the following 12 months, the current ratio is a measure of short-term liquidity. The unit of measurement is either dollars or times. So, we could say Prufrock has $1.31 in current assets for every $1 in current liabilities, or we could say Prufrock has its current liabilities covered 1.31 times over.

To a creditor, particularly a short-term creditor, such as a supplier, the higher the current ratio, the better it is. To the firm, a high current ratio indicates liquidity, but it also may indicate an inefficient use of cash and other short-term assets. Absent some extraordinary circumstances, we would expect to see a current ratio of at least 1, as a current ratio of less than 1 would mean that net working capital (current assets less current liabilities) is negative. This would be unusual in a healthy firm, at least for most types of businesses.

The current ratio, like any ratio, is affected by various types of transactions. For example, suppose the firm borrows over the long term to raise money. The short-run effect would be an increase in cash from the issue proceeds and an increase in long-term debt. Current liabilities would not be affected, so the current ratio would rise.

Finally, note that an apparently low current ratio may not be a bad sign for a company with a large reserve of untapped borrowing power.

Quick (or Acid-Test) Ratio   Inventory is often the least liquid current asset. It is also the one for which the book values are least reliable as measures of market value, since the quality of the inventory is not considered. Some of the inventory may later turn out to be damaged, obsolete, or lost.

More to the point, relatively large inventories are often a sign of short-term trouble. The firm may have over-estimated sales and overbought or overproduced as a result. In this case, the firm may have a substantial portion of its liquidity tied up in slow-moving inventory.

To further evaluate liquidity, the quick, or acid-test, ratio is computed just like the current ratio except that inventory is omitted:

$$\text{Quick ratio} = \frac{\text{Current assets} - \text{Inventory}}{\text{Current liabilities}}$$

Note that using cash to buy inventory does not affect the current ratio, but it reduces the quick ratio. Again, the idea is that inventory is relatively illiquid compared with cash.

For Prufrock, this ratio in 2014 was:

$$\text{Quick ratio} = \frac{\$708 - 422}{\$540} = 0.53 \text{ times}$$

The quick ratio here tells a somewhat different story compared with the current ratio, as inventory accounts for more than half of Prufrock's current assets. To exaggerate the point, if this inventory consisted of, say, unsold nuclear power plants, then this would be a cause for concern.

Cash Ratio   A very short-term creditor might be interested in the cash ratio:

$$\text{Cash ratio} = \frac{\text{Cash}}{\text{Current liabilities}}$$

You can verify that this works out to be 0.18 times for Prufrock.

Long-Term Solvency Measures

Long-term solvency ratios are intended to address the firm's long-run ability to meet its obligations, or, more generally, its financial leverage. These ratios are sometimes called *financial leverage ratios* or just *leverage ratios.* We consider three commonly used measures and some variations.

Total Debt Ratio   The total debt ratio takes into account all debts of all maturities to all creditors. It can be defined in several ways, the easiest of which is:

$$\text{Total debt ratio} = \frac{\text{Total assets} - \text{Total equity}}{\text{Total assets}}$$

$$= \frac{\$3,588 - 2,591}{\$3,588} = 0.28 \text{ times}$$

In this case, an analyst might say that Prufrock uses 28 percent debt.* Whether this is high or low or whether it even makes any difference depends on whether or not capital structure matters.

Prufrock has $0.28 in debt for every $1 in assets. Therefore, there is $0.72 in equity ($1 − 0.28) for every $0.28 in debt. With this in mind, we can define two useful variations on the total debt ratio, the debt-equity ratio and the equity multiplier:

$$\text{Debt-equity ratio} = \text{Total debt/Total equity}$$
$$= \$0.28/\$0.72 = 0.39 \text{ times}$$
$$\text{Equity multiplier} = \text{Total assets/Total equity}$$
$$= \$1/\$0.72 = 1.39 \text{ times}$$

The fact that the equity multiplier is 1 plus the debt-equity ratio is not a coincidence:

$$\text{Equity multiplier} = \text{Total assets/Total equity} = \$1/\$0.72 = 1.39$$
$$= (\text{Total equity} + \text{Total ebt}) \text{ Total equity}$$
$$= (1 + \text{Debt-equity ratio} = 1.39 \text{ times})$$

The point to note here is that given any one of these three ratios, you can immediately calculate the other two, so they all say exactly the same thing.

Times Interest Earned   Another common measure of long-term solvency is the times interest earned (TIE) ratio. Once again, there are several possible (and common) definitions, but we will stick with the most traditional:

$$\text{Times interest earned ratio} = \frac{\text{EBIT}}{\text{Interest}}$$
$$= \frac{\$691}{\$141} = 4.9 \text{ times}$$

As the name suggests, this ratio measures how well a company has its interest obligations covered, and it is often called the *interest coverage ratio*. For Prufrock, the interest bill is covered 4.9 times over.

Cash Coverage   A problem with the TIE ratio is that it is based on EBIT, which is not really a measure of cash available to pay interest. The reason is that depreciation, a noncash expense, has been deducted. Since interest is most definitely a cash outflow (to creditors), one way to define the cash coverage ratio is:

$$\text{Cash coverage ratio} = \frac{\text{EBIT} + \text{Depreciation}}{\text{Interest}}$$
$$= \frac{\$691 + 276}{\$141} = \frac{\$967}{\$141} = 6.9 \text{ times}$$

The numerator here, EBIT plus depreciation, is often abbreviated EBDIT (earnings before depreciation, interest, and taxes). It is a basic measure of the firm's ability to generate cash from operations, and it is frequently used as a measure of cash flow available to meet financial obligations.

Asset Management, or Turnover, Measures

We next turn our attention to the efficiency with which Prufrock uses its assets. The measures in this section are sometimes called *asset utilization ratios*. The specific ratios we discuss can all be interpreted as measures of turnover. What they are intended to describe is how efficiently, or intensively, a firm uses its assets to generate sales. We first look at two important current assets: inventory and receivables.

Inventory Turnover and Days' Sales in Inventory   During the year, Prufrock had a cost of goods sold of $1344. Inventory at the end of the year was $422. With these numbers, inventory turnover can be calculated as:

$$\text{Inventory turnover} = \frac{\text{Cost of goods sold}}{\text{Inventory}}$$
$$= \frac{\$1,344}{\$422} = 3.2 \text{ times}$$

In a sense, we sold off, or turned over, the entire inventory 3.2 times. As long as we are not running out of stock and thereby forgoing sales, the higher this ratio is, the more efficiently we are managing inventory.

   If we know that we turned our inventory over 3.2 times during the year, then we can immediately figure out how long it took us to turn it over on average. The result is the average days' sales in inventory:

$$\text{Days' sales in inventory} = \frac{365 \text{ days}}{\text{Inventory turnover}}$$
$$= \frac{365}{3.2} = 114 \text{ times}$$

This tells us that, on average, inventory sits 114 days before it is sold. Alternatively, assuming we used the most recent inventory and cost figures, it will take about 114 days to work off our current inventory.

For example, we frequently hear things like "Majestic Motors has a 60 days' supply of cars." This means that, at current daily sales, it would take 60 days to deplete the available inventory. We could also say that Majestic has 60 days of sales in inventory.

Receivables Turnover and Days' Sales in Receivables   Our inventory measures give some indication of how fast we can sell products. We now look at how fast we collect on those sales. The receivables turnover is defined in the same way as inventory turnover:

$$\text{Receivables turnover} = \frac{\text{Sales}}{\text{Accounts receivable}}$$

$$= \frac{\$2,311}{\$188} = 12.3 \text{ times}$$

In some sense, receivables turnover suggests that the company could collect its outstanding credit accounts and reloan the money 12.3 times during the year.[*]

This ratio makes more sense if we convert it to days, so the days' sales in receivables is:

$$\text{Days' sales in receivables} = \frac{365 \text{ days}}{\text{Receivables turnover}}$$

$$= \frac{365}{12.3} = 30 \text{ days}$$

Therefore, on average, we collect on our credit sales in 30 days. For obvious reasons, this ratio is very frequently called the *average collection period (ACP)*.

Also, note that if we are using the most recent figures, we can also say that we have 30 days' worth of sales currently uncollected.

Total Asset Turnover   Moving away from specific accounts, such as inventory or receivables, we can consider an important "big picture" ratio, the total asset turnover ratio. As the name suggests, total asset turnover is:

$$\text{Total asset turnover} = \frac{\text{Sales}}{\text{Total assets}}$$

$$= \frac{\$2,311}{\$3,588} = 0.64 \text{ times}$$

In other words, for every dollar in assets, we generated $0.64 in sales.

A closely related ratio, the capital intensity ratio, is simply the reciprocal of (i.e., 1 divided by) total asset turnover. It can be interpreted as the dollar investment in assets needed to generate $1 in sales. High values correspond to capital intensive industries (e.g., public utilities). For Prufrock, total asset turnover is 0.64, so, if we flip this over, we get that capital intensity is $1 ÷ 0.64 = $1.56. That is, it takes Prufrock $1.56 in assets to create $1 in sales.

Profitability Measures

The three measures we discuss in this section are probably the best known and most widely used of all financial ratios. In one form or another, they are intended to measure how efficiently the firm uses its assets and how efficiently the firm manages its operations. The focus in this group is on the bottom line, net income.

Profit Margin   Companies pay a great deal of attention to their profit margin:

$$\text{Profit margin} = \frac{\text{Net income}}{\text{Sales}}$$

$$= \frac{\$363}{\$2,311} = 15.7 \%$$

This tells us that Prufrock, in an accounting sense, generates a little less than 16 cents in profit for every dollar in sales.

All other things being equal, a relatively high profit margin is obviously desirable. This situation corresponds to low expense ratios relative to sales. However, we hasten to add that other things are often not equal.

For example, lowering our sales price will usually increase unit volume but will normally cause profit margins to shrink. Total profit (or, more importantly, operating cash flow) may go up or down; the fact that margins are smaller does not necessarily lead to lower overall profits. Still, margins have to be positive in order to have any profits.

Return on Assets   Return on assets (ROA) is a measure of profit per dollar of assets. It can be defined several ways, but the most common is:

$$\text{Return on assets} = \frac{\text{Net income}}{\text{Total assets}}$$

$$= \frac{\$363}{\$3,588} = 10.12\%$$

Return on Equity   Return on equity (ROE) is a measure of how the shareholders fared during the year. Since benefiting shareholders is our goal, ROE is, in an accounting sense, the true bottom-line measure of performance. ROE is usually measured as:

$$\text{Return on equity} = \frac{\text{Net income}}{\text{Total equity}}$$

$$= \frac{\$363}{\$2,591} = 14\%$$

For every dollar in equity, therefore, Prufrock generated 14 cents in profit, but, again, this is only correct in accounting terms.

Because return on assets (ROA) and ROE are such commonly cited numbers, we stress that it is important to remember they are accounting rates of return. For this reason, these measures should properly be called return on book assets and return on book equity. In addition, ROE is sometimes called *return on net worth*. Whatever it is called, it would be inappropriate to compare the results with, for example, an interest rate observed in the financial markets.

The fact that ROE exceeds ROA reflects Prufrock's use of financial leverage. We will examine the relationship between these two measures in more detail below.

Market Value Measures

Our final group of measures is based, in part, on information not necessarily contained in financial statements—the market price per share of the stock. Obviously, these measures can only be calculated directly for publicly traded companies.

We assume that Prufrock has 33 million shares outstanding and the stock sold for $88 per share at the end of the year. If we recall that Prufrock's net income was $363 million, then we can calculate that its earnings per share were:

$$\text{EPS} = \frac{\text{Net income}}{\text{Shares outstanding}} = \frac{\$363}{33} = \$11$$

Price-Earnings Ratio The first of our market value measures, the price-earnings, or PE, ratio (or multiple), is defined as:

$$\text{PE ratio} = \frac{\text{Price per share}}{\text{Earnings per share}}$$

$$= \frac{\$85}{\$11} = 8 \text{ times}$$

Commonly, we would say that Prufrock shares sell for eight times earnings, or we might say that Prufrock shares have, or "carry," a PE multiple of 8.

Since the PE ratio measures how much investors are willing to pay per dollar of current earnings, higher PEs are often taken to mean that the firm has significant prospects for future growth. Of course, if a firm had no or almost no earnings, its PE would probably be quite large; so, as always, be careful when interpreting this ratio.

Market-to-Book Ratio   A second commonly quoted measure is the market-to-book ratio:

$$\text{Market-to-book ratio} = \frac{\text{Market value per share}}{\text{Book value per share}}$$

$$= \frac{\$88}{(\$2,591/33)} = \frac{\$88}{\$78.5} = 1.12 \text{ times}$$

Note that book value per share is total equity (not just common shares) divided by the number of shares outstanding.

Since book value per share is an accounting number, it reflects historical costs. In a loose sense, the market-to-book ratio therefore, compares the market value of the firm's investments to their cost. A value less than 1 could mean that the firm has not been successful overall in creating value for its shareholders.

Exhibit A-9 summarizes the five types of ratios we have discussed.

EXHIBIT A-9   **A SUMMARY OF FIVE TYPES OF FINANCIAL RATIOS**

I. Short-term solvency, or liquidity, ratios

$$\text{Current ratio} = \frac{\text{Current assets}}{\text{Current liabilities}}$$

$$\text{Quick ratio} = \frac{\text{Current assets} - \text{Inventory}}{\text{Current liabilities}}$$

$$\text{Cash ratio} = \frac{\text{Cash}}{\text{Current liabilities}}$$

II. Long-term solvency, or financial leverage, ratios

$$\text{Total debt ratio} = \frac{\text{Total assets} - \text{Total equity}}{\text{Total assets}}$$

$$\text{Debt-equity ratio} = \text{Total debt/Total equity}$$

$$\text{Equity multiplier} = \text{Total assets/Total equity}$$

$$\text{Times interest earned ratio} = \frac{\text{EBIT}}{\text{Interest}}$$

$$\text{Cash coverage ratio} = \frac{\text{EBIT} + \text{Depreciation}}{\text{Interest}}$$

III. Asset utilization, or turnover, ratios

$$\text{Inventory turnover} = \frac{\text{Cost of goods sold}}{\text{Inventory}}$$

$$\text{Days' sales in inventory} = \frac{365 \text{ days}}{\text{Inventory turnover}}$$

$$\text{Receivables turnover} = \frac{\text{Sales}}{\text{Accounts receivable}}$$

$$\text{Days' sales in receivables} = \frac{365 \text{ days}}{\text{Receivables turnover}}$$

$$\text{Total asset turnover} = \frac{\text{Sales}}{\text{Total assets}}$$

$$\text{Capital intensity} = \frac{\text{Total assets}}{\text{Sales}}$$

IV. Profitability ratios

$$\text{Profit margin} = \frac{\text{Net income}}{\text{Sales}}$$

$$\text{ROA} = \frac{\text{Net income}}{\text{Total assets}}$$

$$\text{ROE} = \frac{\text{Net income}}{\text{Sales}} \times \frac{\text{Sales}}{\text{Assets}} \times \frac{\text{Assets}}{\text{Equity}}$$

V. Market value ratios

$$\text{Price-earnings ratio} = \frac{\text{Price per share}}{\text{Earnings per share}}$$

$$\text{Market-to-book ratio} = \frac{\text{Market value per share}}{\text{Book value per share}}$$

SOURCES OF COMPANY AND INDUSTRY INFORMATION*

For business executives to make the best decisions when developing strategy, it is critical for them to be knowledgeable about their competitors and about the industries in which they compete. We offer below an overview of important sources of information that may be useful in conducting company and industry analysis. Much information of this nature is available in libraries, article databases, business reference books, and on websites. This list recommends a variety of them. Ask a librarian for assistance because library collections and resources vary.

The information sources are organized into 11 categories: (1) Competitive Intelligence, (2) Company Directories, (3) Company Research Databases, (4) North America: Corporate Disclosure Reports, Filings and Submissions, (5) International Corporate Annual Reports & Filings Collections, (6) Library Guides to Conducting Company & Industry Research, (7) Company Rankings, (8) Business Metasites and Portals, (9) Strategic and Competitive Analysis—Information Sources, (10) Sources for Industry Research and Analysis, and (11) Search Engines.

Competitive Intelligence

Students and other researchers who want to learn more about the value and process of competitive intelligence should see five recent books on this subject.

- Biere, M. *The New Era of Enterprise Business Intelligence: Using Analytics to Achieve a Global Competitive Advantage* (Upper Saddle River, NJ: IBM Press, 2011).
- Hakansson, C. & Nelke, N. *Competitive Intelligence for Information Professionals* (Waltham, MA: Chandos Publishing, 2015).
- Horwath, R. *Elevate: The Three Disciplines of Advanced Strategic Thinking* (Hoboken, NJ: John Wiley & Sons Inc., 2014).
- Sharp, S. *Competitive Intelligence Advantage: How to Minimize Risk, Avoid Surprises, and Grow Your Business in a Changing World* (Hoboken, NJ: Wiley, 2009).
- Fleisher, C.R. & Bensousssan, E. B. *Business and Competitive Analysis: Effective Applications of New and Classic Methods,* 2nd edition. (Upper Saddle River, New Jersey: Pearson Education, 2015).

Public or Private, Subsidiary or Division, Domestic or Foreign?

Companies traded on stock exchanges are required to file a variety of reports that disclose company information. This begins a process that produces a wealth of data on public companies and, at the same time, distinguishes them from private companies, which often lack available data. Similarly, the financial data of subsidiaries and divisions are typically filed in a consolidated financial statement by the parent company, rather than treated independently, thus limiting the kind of data available on them. Additional filing requirements provide useful sources of information. For example, foreign companies that trade on U.S. stock exchanges are required to file 20F reports, similar to the 10-K reports required of U.S. companies, the most comprehensive of the required reports. Company websites often provide access to annual reports, corporate governance materials, and so on. See the section on "Corporate Disclosure Reports" for more information.

Company Directories

The following directories are available online via a subscription or are reputable directories available in the public domain:

- ***Corporate Affiliations.*** New Providence, NJ: National Register Publishing, A Lexis-Nexis Group Company. This directory is an authoritative source of company and executive information featuring brief profiles of over 2 million global public and private companies, identifying major U.S. and foreign corporations as well as their subsidiaries, divisions, and affiliates. The directory also indicates hierarchies of corporate affiliation for each firm, as well as the latest mergers and acquisitions data via MergerTrak.
- ***Ward's Directories of Public and Private Companies.*** Detroit, MI: Gale Group. Published by Gale, one directory is available with coverage of U.S. companies only, while a second directory provides coverage for Canada and Mexico. These directories are designed to profile data on privately-held companies and

hard-to-find information on small and mid-sized companies. *Ward's Directories* lists brief company profiles and indicates whether each company is public or private, a subsidiary or a division. *Ward's* lists the Standard Industrial Classification (SIC) and the newer North American Industry Classification System (NAICS) and features company rankings within industries.

- *Scott's Directories.* Toronto, ON: Business Information Group. *Scott's* contains a directory for each region of Canada and this resource also offers coverage of the Greater Toronto Area. A brief profile of both public and private companies is provided, along with contact information.

- *Canadian Company Capabilities.* Produced by the Government of Canada, this database contains extensive information on over 60,000 Canadian businesses, including both private and publicly-traded companies at www.ic.gc.ca/eic/site/ccc-rec.nsf/eng/home

- *Crunchbase.* A database available free on the web, featuring data on innovative companies worldwide, including industry trends, investments, and news about global companies, at www.crunchbase.com

- *Opencorporates.* With coverage of over 100 million companies globally, this is the largest open database of companies and company data available in the public domain. It is a useful starting place when engaging in company research. See www.opencorporates.com

Company Research Databases

- *Hoovers database.* New York: Mergent Inc. This database was acquired by Mergent which has distribution rights for the academic market. It contains both public and private company information based on Dun & Bradstreet data for thousands of U.S., Canadian, and international firms. Data includes overviews, key people and contacts, history, competitors, news, basic financials, subsidiaries information, and more. The Build a List function is very useful for creating competitor lists that match stipulated criteria.

- *Mergent Online.* New York: Mergent, Inc. Provides corporate and financial data for publicly traded companies worldwide, including detailed business descriptions, competitors, corporate histories, annual reports, up to 15 years of financial statements, information on subsidiaries, ownership, and more.

- *Bloomberg.* New York: Bloomberg L.P. Bloomberg is a real-time financial service that provides current and historical data, news, and financial analysis of companies, stocks, bonds, and indices data. Economic statistics are also available. Academic licences mean that academic libraries can only provide access on campus.

- *Lexis Nexis Academic.* Dayton, Ohio: Lexis Nexis Inc. Includes information on public and private companies in Canada, the U.S., and globally. Coverage includes company descriptions, key financials, SEC filings, competitors, news, stock information, SWOT analyses, mergers and acquisitions, analyst reports, parent and subsidiary information, and more.

- *PrivCo.* New York: PrivCo Media LLC. Provides business and financial data on major, non-publicly traded corporations, including family-owned, private equity-owned, venture-backed, and international unlisted companies. Also offers information on private investors, private M&A deals, and venture capital funding rounds.

- *Orbis.* Bureau van Dijk. Provides descriptions and financials, as well as news, ratings, ownership, and M&A data for millions of public and private companies globally.

- *S&P Capital IQ.* New York: Standard & Poor's. Provides detailed coverage of public and private companies, investment firms and executives. It serves as a powerful data and analysis tool featuring coverage of financial statements, M&A activity, debt, equity offerings and IPOs, compensation, corporate news, financial modeling, comparable companies, and much more.

- *Investext Plus via Thomson One.* New York: Thomson Research. A database providing global company and industry analyst reports from key brokerage firms and consultants. To search for industry reports, click on "Screening & Analysis," then on the sub-menu item, "Research." You may search by SIC, NAICS, or text. *N.B. Be sure to change the report date to a longer period than the 90-day default range in order to retrieve a good selection of reports. Use Internet Explorer browser for full functionality.

- *Thomson One Banker.* Database provides access to current and historical data, including financial statements, filings, stock prices, earnings estimates, deals, analyst reports, and more.

- *Sustainalytics.* This database covers leading publicly traded companies globally with a focus on ESG and corporate governance research and ratings.

North America: Corporate Disclosure Reports, Filings and Submissions

Securities and Exchange Commission (SEC) filings are the various reports that publicly traded companies must file with the SEC to disclose information about themselves. These are often referred to as "EDGAR" filings, the acronym for the Electronic Data Gathering, Analysis and Retrieval System. Some websites and commercial databases improve access to these reports by offering additional retrieval features not available on the official (www.sec.gov) website. Although SEC filings pertain exclusively to public corporations listed in U.S. stock exchanges, much of the information below is relevant to anyone conducting research on companies.

Companies traded on Canadian stock exchanges are required to file all public documents, such as annual reports, financial statements, prospectuses, and so on, with SEDAR (System for Electronic Document Analysis and Retrieval), a subsidiary of The Canadian Depository for Securities Limited. www.sedar.com

- *EDGAR Database—Securities Exchange Commission.* Company 10-K reports and other corporate documents are made available in the EDGAR database within 24 hours after being filed. Annual reports, on the other hand, are sent to shareholders and are not required as part of EDGAR by the SEC, although some companies voluntarily provide them. Both 10-Ks and shareholders' annual reports are considered basic sources of company research. www.sec.gov/edgar.shtml

- *SEDAR.* Provides access to electronic filings submitted by public companies and mutual funds to the Canadian Securities Administrators from January 1997 to the present. Contains all Canadian regulatory submissions such as annual reports, IPOs filings, and management discussion documents. www.sedar.com

- *Lexis Nexis Securities Mosaic.* A comprehensive collection of United States and Canadian corporate public disclosure documents. For example, view filings associated with IPOs, such as prospectus and pricing supplements. Examine 10-K and 8-K items with regard to executive compensation, MD&A, financial statements, and much more.

- *Mergent Online—EDGAR and SEDAR*. New York: Mergent, Inc. From the "Government Filings" tab within Mergent Online, EDGAR SEC or SEDAR filings and reports can be searched by company name or ticker symbol, filing date range, and file type (e.g., 10-K, 8-K, ARS). It is also possible to conduct a text search of EDGAR documents. The reports are available in HTML, PDF, Excel, or MS Word format. Using the "Find in Page" option from the browser provides the capability of jumping to specific sections of an SEC report.

- *Lexis-Nexis Academic.* Dayton, Ohio: Lexis Nexis Inc. EDGAR filings and reports are available at this site. Select the "Search by Subject or Topic" option offered just above the red search box. Select "SEC Filings" under the main heading "Companies" from the list of menu options provided. Various options are provided in advanced search mode including the ability to limit to specific filing types, (i.e., annual reports, proxy statements, registration statements, and more). It is also possible to search by specific date.

- *The Public Register Online.* Woodstock Valley, CT: Baytact Corp. Provides free annual reports of public companies trading on the NYSE, NASDAQ, AMEX, OTC, and TSX exchanges. Visitors to this website may choose from more than 5,000 company annual reports and 10-K filings to view online or order a paper copy. www.annualreportservice.com

International Corporate Annual Report & Filings Collections

Many companies make their annual report to shareholders and other financial and corporate governance reports available on corporate websites. A number of databases (some free and some fee-based) allow searching for annual reports and provide global coverage. A few of these e-resources also offer historical coverage.

- *Mergent WebReport.* Full-text annual reports are available for companies globally back to the late 1990s in most cases. Select the "Annual Report Search" tab. Historic company information extracted from corporate reports is available for U.S. and Canadian companies dating back to the early 1900s. Select "Corporate Manual Search" to retrieve historic company information and financials. Also provides the option to search current and historical North American, European, and Asia-Pacific industry reports.

- *Mergent Archives.* Provides annual reports and other filings information back to the early 1900s. This includes over 108,000 Canadian documents, over 228,000 U.S. documents, and over 370,000 international documents. Also includes Mergent's full collection of digitized manuals dating back to the first manual, published in 1909, which includes information extracted from annual reports.

- *AnnualReports.com.* Weston, FL: IR Solutions. Provides access to annual reports for companies globally. Usually most recent year only available in PDF format. Possible to browse reports by exchange, industry, sector or alphabetically by company name. Also includes investor fact sheets plus a link to Responsibility Reports.com a free service providing access to corporations' responsibility reports available online.www.annualreports.com
- *Companies House.* Allows searching and viewing of official filings with the government by U.K. companies. Service made available by Companies House, the official U.K. agency (and a division of the Department for Business, Energy & Industrial Strategy) that incorporates and dissolves companies and collects and makes available data that companies are legally required to provide to the public. This site is currently in beta mode and allows free searching of filings, though archival reports are available on a paid subscription basis only. beta.companieshouse.gov.uk

Library Guides to Conducting Company & Industry Research

- *Business Research at York Toolkit (BRYT).* This resource provides instructional videos, real-time database walkthroughs, and step-by-step PDF tip sheets on a wide range of databases supporting both company and industry research. While it is geared to students at York University, it is available in the public domain, and features databases commonly held at leading academic business libraries. bryt.library.yorku.ca
- *Company Research.* A Bronfman Business Library, York University Web-based guide highlights key print and electronic resources for finding company and competitive information. rsearchguides.library.yorku.ca/companyresearch
- *Finance Research.* Also from the Bronfman Business Library, this York University Web-based guide highlights key print and electronic resources for finding finance information. researchguides.library.yorku.ca/finance
- *Industry Research.* This Bronfman Business Library, York University Web-based guide highlights key print and electronic resources for finding industry information. researchguides.library.yorku.ca/industryresearch
- *Company Research.* A David Lam Management Research Library, University of British Columbia Web-based guide to finding resources for company research. guides.library.ubc.ca/company
- *Industry/Market Research.* A David Lam Management Research Library, University of British Columbia Web-based guide to finding resources for industry/market research. guides.library.ubc.ca/industry
- *The Toronto Public Libraries' Virtual Reference Library.* A compiled list of online resources to help with business and career research. Any member of the public entitled to membership at TPL can access these online resources at the library or remotely. www.torontopubliclibrary.ca/books-video-music/articles-online-research/business-careers/

Company Rankings

Top Rankings Sites

- *Fortune 500.* Time Warner, New York. The Fortune 500 list and other company rankings are available at the *Fortune* magazine website. www.fortune.com/fortune500/
- *Global 500.* Time Warner, New York. The Global 500 list and other company rankings are available at the *Fortune* magazine website. www.fortune.com/global500/
- *Report on Business 1000.* Toronto, ON: *The Globe and Mail.* This special issue of *The Globe and Mail* ranks the top 1,000 Canadian companies and also provides industry sector rankings. www.theglobeandmail.com/report-on-business/rob-magazine/top-1000/
- *FP500.* Toronto, ON: *National Post Business.* This supplement of the *National Post* ranks the top 500 Canadian companies. www.financialpost.com/news/fp500/index.html

Other Recommended Guides & Resources for Company Rankings

- *Market Share Reporter.* A subscription resource which provides information and rankings of companies, with a focus on the U.S. Can be searched by brand, product, or company name.

- *Ward's Directories of Public and Private Companies.* Detroit, MI: Gale Group. Published by Gale, one directory is available with coverage of U.S. companies only, while a second directory provides coverage for Canada and Mexico. These directories are designed to profile data on privately-held companies and hard-to-find information on small and mid-sized companies. *Ward's Directories* lists brief company information and indicates whether companies are public or private, a subsidiary or a division. *Ward's* also lists the Standard Industrial Classification (SIC) and the newer North American Industry Classification System (NAICS) and features company rankings within industries.

- *Company Rankings – Company Research Guide.* A Bronfman Business Library, York University Web-based guide that features an aggregated list of rankings of various types including top company rankings available online, as well as sustainability, small business, non-profit, technology/R&D, brand, employer, and people rankings. researchguides.library.yorku.ca/c.php?g=679633&p=4793661

Business Metasites and Portals

- *Innovation, Science and Economic Development Canada.* Government of Canada. This website provides access to a wide range of business information for consumers and businesses but is useful in an academic context also. This includes Canadian industry data and research reports as well as company directories, patent and trademark databases, an importers database and export/import data (Trade Data Online), along with guides to starting and incorporating a business. www.ic.gc.ca

- *Google Finance.* In addition to news, this website provides a broad range of information about stocks, mutual funds, and public and private companies, including quotes and charts. www.google.com/finance

- *Yahoo Finance.* Sunnyvale, CA: Yahoo! Inc. This metasite links to information on U.S. markets, world markets, data sources, finance references, investment editorials, financial news, and other helpful websites. http://finance.yahoo.com/ There is also a Canadian site: ca.finance.yahoo.com/

Strategic and Competitive Analysis—Information Sources

Analyzing a company can take the form of examining its internal and external environment. In the process, it is useful to identify the company's strengths, weaknesses, opportunities, and threats (SWOT). Sources for this kind of analysis are varied. There are several commercial databases which provide SWOT analyses for large publicly-traded companies including *Marketline Advantage* and *Lexis Nexis Academic* (see information below)Another approach would be to start by locating articles from the leading financial newspapers, the *Globe and Mail*, the *Wall Street Journal*, and the *Financial Times*. In addition, search for articles in business magazines and industry trade publications. Such publications can be found in the following databases available at many public and academic libraries. Try searching the company name combined with one or more key words, such as "Air Canada and competition" or "Hollinger and courts" or "Microsoft and growth" to retrieve articles relating to the external environment. There are also many excellent subscription databases.

A guide to searching business article databases and constructing effective search strategies is available via the Finding Business Articles section of the Business Research at York Toolkit (BRYT), a resource available in the public domain (bryt.library.yorku.ca/find-business-articles/). BRYT also offers videos and step-by-step guides on databases that can be used to find company SWOT analyses: bryt.library.yorku.ca/locate-company-swot-strengths-weaknesses-opportunities-threats-analyses/

- *Business Source Complete.* Ipswich, MA: EBSCO Publishing. A database featuring the full text for more than 2,200 journals, including scholarly, trade, and popular titles covering management, economics, finance, accounting, international business, and more. Also includes company profiles, industry reports, and SWOT analyses.

- *Proquest Business.* Ann Arbor, MI: ProQuest Information & Learning. Nearly every Canadian academic library subscribes to *Proquest Business* either in whole or in part, as it comprises a range of constituent databases, e.g., *ABI/ Inform Global, ABI/Inform Trade and Industry, CBCA Business.* Such ProQuest databases provide full-text articles (scholarly, trade, popular, and news) covering a wide range of business topics, including management, marketing, law, taxation, human resources, and company and industry information from thousands of business and management journals. Also includes company profiles, industry and market reports.

- *Lexis Nexis Academic.* Dayton Ohio, Lexis Nexis Inc. Includes information on public and private companies in Canada, U.S. and globally. Coverage includes company descriptions, key financials, competitors, news, stock information, SWOT analyses, mergers and acquisitions, analyst reports, parent and subsidiary information, and more. Timely business articles can be retrieved from newspapers, magazines, journals, wires, and broadcast transcripts.

- *Factiva.* Ann Arbor, MI: ProQuest Information & Learning. A reputable news source, offering full-text coverage of over 3,000 national, international, and regional newspapers, including major titles such as the *Wall Street Journal*, the *Financial Times*, the *New York Times*, and the *Guardian.* Also includes the full text of the *Globe & Mail, Toronto Star* and *National Post.* Other resources in Factiva include newswires, news websites, blogs and podcasts, and many trade and popular magazines. May also be used as a company research tool with extensive coverage of public and private companies worldwide, including corporate overviews, key executives, financial data, press releases, current news, and a list of competitors.

- *MarketLine Advantage.* London, U.K., Marketline. Includes industry reports, country information, company analysis, case studies, and financial deals. It provides SWOT analyses for over 2,500 public and private enterprises worldwide, and offers fast and reliable insights on thousands of industry sectors including market value, volume and segmentation data, and Porter's Five Forces analysis, as well as offering PESTLE analyses for some 150 countries. Recent additions include the company financial analysis tools (financial deals tracker, company report generator, company prospector, and investment and advisory prospector), in addition to the market data analytics database.

- *Mergent Online.* Provides company information and annual reports for Canadian, international, and U.S. companies. Also includes industry reports covering current environment, sector performance, market trends, outlook, etc. for some 24 industries globally. Earnings estimates and long-term debt data included. In addition, the Horizon tab provides data on the relationships between a company's major customers and suppliers and partners.

- *Investext Plus via Thomson One.* Detroit, MI: Thomson Research. A database providing global company and industry analyst reports from key brokerage firms and consultants, as well as SWOT analyses for companies. To search for industry reports, click on "Screening & Analysis," then on the sub-menu item "Research." You may search by SIC, NAICS or text. *N.B. Be sure to change the report date to a longer period than the 90-day default range in order to retrieve a good selection of reports. Use Internet Explorer browser for full functionality.

- *Capital IQ.* Standard and Poor's. This is a research and data analysis tool used to retrieve information on public and private companies, including financial statements, M&A activity, corporate executives, compensation, debt, equity offerings and IPOs, news, macroeconomic data, and more.

Sources for Industry Research and Analysis

A guide to conducting industry research using key databases is available via the Industries section of the Business Research at York Toolkit (BRYT), a resource available in the public domain: bryt.library.yorku.ca/industries/ This is supplemented by an Industry Research Guide, also available from the Bronfman Library at the Schulich School of Business: researchguides.library.yorku.ca/industryresearch

- *Mergent Online.* New York: Mergent, Inc. Search by company name and use the competitors link, and/or click on "Industry Analysis" to find industry reports. Use the advanced search to create custom company analysis reports to compare companies in the same industry using various criteria.

- *BMI Research (formerly Business Monitor Online).* London, U.K.: BMI Research. In addition to some company intelligence, this resource provides in-depth analysis and data on almost 25 industries with current and archived industry reports for countries all over the world, including Asia, Latin America, Europe, the Middle East, and Africa. Additionally, this resource provides country risk intelligence and forecast data.

- *MarketLine Advantage.* London, U.K., Marketline. Includes industry reports, country information, company analysis, case studies, and financial deals. It provides SWOT analyses for over 2,500 public and private enterprises worldwide, and offers fast and reliable insights of thousands of industry sectors including market value, volume and segmentation data, and Porter's Five Forces analysis, as well as offering PESTLE analyses for some 150 countries. Recent additions include the company financial analysis tools (financial deals tracker, company report generator, company prospector, and investment and advisory prospector), in addition to the market data analytics database.

- *Passport.* London, U.K.: Euromonitor International. This database provides statistics, analysis, reports, surveys, and breaking news on industries, countries, and consumers worldwide. Especially useful for researching consumer goods and services industries. Industry analysis includes market performance, market size, company and brand shares, and profiles of leading companies and brands.

- *IBISWorld.* Los Angeles, CA: IBISWorld. This database includes Canadian, U.S., Chinese, and global industry reports and a business environment database. Many of the reports are on niche industries and include the NAICS industry report collection and the specialized industry report collection.

- *IBISWorld Procurement.* Los Angeles, CA: IBISWorld. Covers a multitude of indirect purchasing lines for over 1,000 business-to-business product and service markets in the U.S. These reports will assist students and researchers by facilitating industry research, especially in areas such as purchasing, supply chain management, and strategic sourcing. These detailed reports cover price environment, product characteristics, supply chain and vendors (including supplier benchmarking and supply chain risk), elements of the purchasing process, and negotiation questions and tactics.

- *Investext Plus via Thomson One.* New York: Thomson Research. A database providing global company and industry analyst reports from key brokerage firms and consultants. To search for industry reports, click on "Screening & Analysis," then on the sub-menu item, "Research." You may search by SIC, NAICS, or text. *N.B. Be sure to change the report date to a longer period than the 90-day default range in order to retrieve a good selection of reports. Use Internet Explorer browser for full functionality.

- *Innovation, Science and Economic Development.* Government of Canada. This website provides access to a wide range of business information for consumers and businesses but is useful in an academic context also. This includes Canadian industry data and research reports as well as company directories, patent and trademark databases, an importers database and export/import data (Trade Data Online), along with guides to starting and incorporating a business. www.ic.gc.ca

- *Factiva.* Ann Arbor, MI: ProQuest Information & Learning. The Factiva database has several options for researching an industry. One is to search the database for articles in the business magazines and industry trade publications. A second option in Factiva is to search the "Companies/Markets" category to find industry snapshots including targeted news, industry averages and ratios, trade association websites, and top participants by sales.

- *Standard & Poor's NetAdvantage database—Industry Surveys.* New York: Standard & Poor's This database provides an overview of over 50 U.S. industries. Each industry report includes a table of contents, narrative description, history, trends, financial and company information, glossary of terms, and a section on how to perform an analysis of the industry. Industry References (associations, periodicals, and websites), Composite Industry Data (industry norms and ratios), and Comparative Company Analysis (comparison of 50 major companies, their operating ratios, P/E, revenue, and so forth) complete the industry report section.

- *Bloomberg.* New York: Bloomberg. A real-time financial service that provides current and historical data, news, and financial analysis of companies and industries, in addition to stocks, bonds, and indices data. Economic statistics are also available. Academic licences mean that academic libraries can only provide access on campus.

Search Engines

- *Google.* Mountain View, CA: Google, Inc. Recognized for its advanced technology, quality of results, and simplicity, the search engine Google is highly recommended by librarians and other expert Web "surfers." www.google.com or www.google.ca

- *Google Scholar.* Mountain View, CA: Google, Inc. Allows you to search for scholarly literature across many disciplines. scholar.google.ca

Endnotes

Chapter 1

1. The case material draws on De Montigny, Philippe. "Holt Renfrew closing stores in Quebec City and Ottawa to focus on flagship locations," *Financial Post,* Aug 28, 2014; Gollom, Mark. "Saks, Nordstrom seek to compete in 'crowded' Canadian luxury market," *CBC News,* Feb 19, 2016; Kopun, Francine. "Nordstrom countdown to opening begins," *The Toronto Star,* Sept 10, 2016; Shaw, Hollie. "With Saks on cusp of Canadian debut and a flagship renovation, Liz Rodbell brings buzz to HBC," *Financial Post,* May 25, 2015; Strauss, Marina. "Sakes braces for battle in Canada's crowded luxury fashion market," *The Globe and Mail,* Feb 16, 2016; Strauss, Marina. "HBC cuts outlook for 2015 and 2016 ahead of Saks Canadian launch," *The Globe and Mail,* Dec 11, 2015; *The Canadian Press.* "HBC to buy online shopping business Gilt for $250-million," *The Globe and Mail,* Jan 7, 2016; Toller, Carol. "Nordstrom: The Luxury Chain That Does Everything Right," *Marketing Mag,* March 6, 2015; Wahba, Phil. "Take off, eh: Nordstrom, Saks in race to win Canadian luxury shoppers," Fortune.com, Sept 19, 2014; the company's financial statements and website.
2. For a discussion of the "romantic" perspective versus "external control" perspective, refer to Meindl, J. R., 1987, "The romance of leadership and the evaluation of organizational performance," *Academy of Management Journal,* 30: 92–109; and Pfeffer, J., & Salancik, G. R., 1978, *The External Control of Organizations: A Resource Dependence Perspective* (New York: Harper & Row).
3. This example draws on 2000, "Time names Nortel Networks CEO John Roth Canadian newsmaker of the year," *Canada NewsWire,* December 17: 1; Kari, S., 2001, "An unapologetic John Roth," *CanWest News,* February 18: 1; Macklem, K., 2001, "Plunge from grace," *Maclean's,* March 5: 41; Wahl, A., 2001, "Warning? What Warning?" *Canadian Business,* March 19: 46; Macklem, K., 2001, "The trials of John Roth: Nortel's chief, like his stock, fights an image problem," *Maclean's,* April 9: 24; Avery, S., Perkins, T., & Blackwell, R., 2008, "White-collar crime: Arrests made nearly five years after tech firm's bubble burst," *The Globe and Mail,* June 20, B1.
4. For an interesting perspective on the need for strategists to maintain a global mind-set, refer to Begley, T. M., & Boyd, D. P., 2003, The need for a global mind-set, *MIT Sloan Management Review,* 44(2): 25–32.
5. Porter, M. E., 1996, What is strategy?, *Harvard Business Review,* 74(6): 61–78.
6. See, for example, Barney, J. B., & Arikan, A. M., 2001, The resource-based view: Origins and implications, in Hitt, M. A., Freeman, R. E., & Harrison, J. S., eds., *Handbook of Strategic Management* (Malden, MA: Blackwell Business), 124–89.
7. Barney, J., 1991, Firm resources and sustained competitive advantage, *Journal of Management,* 17(1): 99–120.
8. Much of Gary Hamel's work advocates the importance of not focusing on incremental change. For example, refer to Hamel, G., & Prahalad, C. K., 1994, *Competing for the Future* (Boston: Harvard Business School Press); see also Christensen, C. M., 2001, The past and future of competitive advantage, *Sloan Management Review,* 42(3): 105–9.
9. Porter, M. E., 1996, What is strategy?, *Harvard Business Review,* 74(6): 61–78; and Hammonds, K. H., 2001, Michael Porter's big ideas, *Fast Company,* March: 55–56.
10. This section draws on Dess, G. G., & Miller, A., 1993, *Strategic Management* (New York: McGraw-Hill).
11. See, for example, Hrebiniak, L. G., & Joyce, W. F., 1986, The strategic importance of managing myopia, *Sloan Management Review,* 28(1): 5–14.
12. For an insightful discussion on how to manage diverse stakeholder groups, refer to Rondinelli, D. A., & London, T., 2003, How Corporations And Environmental Groups Cooperate: Assessing Cross-Sector Alliances And Collaborations, *Academy of Management Executive,* 17(1): 61–76.
13. Senge, P., 1996, Leading Learning Organizations: The Bold, The Powerful, And The Invisible, in Hesselbein, F., Goldsmith, M., & Beckhard, R., eds., *The Leader of the Future* (San Francisco: Jossey Bass), 41–58.
14. For another interesting perspective on this issue, refer to Abell, D. F., 1999, Competing Today While Preparing For Tomorrow, *Sloan Management Review,* 40(3): 73–81.
15. Loeb, M., 1994, Where Leaders Come From, *Fortune,* September 19: 241 (quoting Warren Bennis).
16. Address by Norman R. Augustine at the Crummer Business School, Rollins College, Winter Park, FL, October 20, 1989.
17. Hemp, P. 2004. An Interview with CEO Kevin Sharer. *Harvard Business Review,* 82(7/8): 66–74.
18. New perspectives on "management models" are addressed in: Birkinshaw, J. & Goddard, J. 2009. What Is Your Management Model? *MIT Sloan Management Review,* 50(2): 81–90.
19. Mintzberg, H., 1985, Of strategies: Deliberate and emergent, *Strategic Management Journal,* 6: 257–72.
20. Monks, A. G., & Minow, N., 2001, *Corporate Governance,* 2nd ed. (Malden, MA: Blackwell).
21. Intel Corp., www.intel.com/intel/finance/corp_gov.html.
22. Baer, D. A. 2014. The West's bruised confidence in capitalism. *The Wall Street Journal,* September 22: A17; and Miller, D. 2014. Greatness is gone. *Dallas Morning News,* October 26: 1 D.
23. Hessel, E. & Woolley, S. 2008. Your money or your life. *Forbes,* October 27: 52.
24. Task, A. 2012. Finance CEO pay rose 20% in 2011, even as stocks stumbled. *www.finance.yahoo.com,* June 5: np.
25. Matthews, C. 2014. 5 companies that pay CEOs big for a job poorly done.*fortune.com,* June 17: np.
26. For a definitive, recent discussion of the stakeholder concept, refer to Freeman, R. E., & McVae, J., 2001, A stakeholder approach to strategic management, in Hitt, M. A., Freeman, R. E., & Harrison, J. S., eds., *Handbook of Strategic Management* (Malden, MA: Blackwell), 189–207.
27. Atkinson, A. A., Waterhouse, J. H., & Wells, R. B., 1997, A stakeholder approach to strategic performance measurement, *Sloan Management Review,* 39(3): 25–38.
28. For an insightful discussion on the role of business in society, refer to Handy, op. cit.
29. Campbell, A. & Alexander, M., 1997, What is wrong with strategy? *Harvard Business Review,* 75(4): 42–51.
30. Stakeholder symbiosis. op. cit., p. S3.
31. Rucci, A. J., Kirn, S. P., & Quinn, R. T., 1998, The employee-customer-profit chain at Sears, *Harvard Business Review,* 76(1): 82–97.
32. The discussion on crowdsourcing draws from Libert, B. & Spector, J., 2008, *We are smarter than me* (Philadelphia: Wharton School Publishing); and Howe, J., 2008, *Crowd sourcing* (New York: Crown Business).
33. An excellent theoretical discussion on stakeholder activity is provided by Rowley, T. J., & Moldoveanu, M., 2003, When will

stakeholder groups act? An interest- and identity-based model of stakeholder group mobilization, *Academy of Management Review,* 28(2): 204–19; a comprehensive work on current debates in CSR can be found in, Crane, A., McWilliams, A., Matten, D., Moon, J., & Siegel, D.S., eds., 2008, *The Oxford Handbook of Corporate Social Responsibility* (Oxford, UK: Oxford University Press).

34. Thomas, J. G., 2000, Macroenvironmental forces. In Helms, M. M., ed., *Encyclopedia of Management,* 4th ed. (Farmington Hills, MI: Gale Group), 516–20.

35. Trudel, R., & Cotte, J., 2009, *MIT Sloan Management Review,* 50(2): 61–68; Waddock, S., and Bodwell, C., 2004, Managing responsibility: What can be learned from the quality movement? *California Management Review,* 47(1): 25–37.

36. This section draws on: Porter, M. E. & Kramer, M. R., 2011, Creating shared value, *Harvard Business Review,* 89 (1/2): 62–77.

37. This discussion draws on Austin, J. E., 2000, Measuring a triple bottom line, *Leader to Leader,* Fall: 51.

38. Funk, K., 2003, Sustainability and performance, *MIT Sloan Management Review,* 44(2): 65–70.

39. The company's website www.suncor.ca reports on a range of social and environmental initiatives.

40. McKinsey & Company, 1991, *The corporate response to the environmental challenge* (Amsterdam, McKinsey & Company).

41. Vogel, D.J., 2005, Is there a market for virtue? The business case for corporate social responsibility, *California Management Review,* 47(4): 19–36; KPMG, 2006, *KPMG International survey of environmental reporting* (The Netherlands).

42. Chamberlain, M. 2013. Socially responsible investing: What you need to know. *Forbes.com,* April 24: np.

43. Kaahwarski, T. 2010. It pays to be good. Bloomberg Businessweek, February 1 to February 8: 69.

44. Andrew S. Winston, *The Big Pivot: Radically Practical Strategies for a Hotter, Scarcer, and More Open World.* (Massachusetts: Harvard Business Review Press: 2014): p. 170.

45. Senge, P. M., 1990, The leader's new work: Building learning organizations, *Sloan Management Review,* 32(1): 7–23.

46. Barkema, G. G., Baum, A. C., & Mannix, E. A., 2002, Management challenges in a new time, *Academy of Management Journal,* 45(5): 916–30.

47. This section draws on a variety of sources, including Tetenbaum, T. J., 1998, Shifting paradigms: From Newton to chaos, *Organizational Dynamics,* 26(4): 21–33; Ulrich, D., 1998, A new mandate for human resources, *Harvard Business Review,* 76(1): 125–35; and Hitt, M. A., 2000, The new frontier: Transformation of management for the new millennium, *Organizational Dynamics,* 28(2): 7–17.

48. An interesting discussion on the impact of acquired immune deficiency syndrome (AIDS) on the global economy is found in Rosen, S., 2003, AIDS is your business, *Harvard Business Review,* 81(2): 80–87.

49. Ulrich, D., 1998, Intellectual capital: Competence=commitment, *Strategic Management Journal,* 39(2): 15–26.

50. Rivette, K. G., & Kline, D., 2000, Discovering new value in intellectual property, *Harvard Business Review,* 78(1): 54–66.

51. For an interesting perspective on the role of middle managers in the strategic management process, refer to Huy, Q. H., 2001, In praise of middle managers, *Harvard Business Review,* 79(8): 72–81.

52. Senge, 1996, op. cit., pp. 41–58.

53. Helgesen, S., 1996, Leading from the grass roots. In Hesselbein, F., Goldsmith, M., & Beckhard, R., eds., *The Leader of the Future* (San Francisco: Jossey-Bass), 19–24.

54. Wetlaufer, S., 1999, Organizing for empowerment: An interview with AES's Roger Sant and Dennis Blake, *Harvard Business Review,* 77(1): 110–26.

55. Kets de Vries, M. F. R., 1998, Charisma in action: The transformational abilities of Virgin's Richard Branson and ABB's Percy Barnevik, *Organizational Dynamics,* 26(3): 7–21.

56. Hammonds, K. H., 2000, The next agenda, *Fast Company,* April: 140.

57. Hamel, G., 2006, The why, what and how of management innovation, *Harvard Business Review,* 84(2): 72–87; Salter, C., 2005, Whirlpool finds its cool, *Fast Company,* June: 73.

58. Our discussion draws on a variety of sources. These include Lipton, M., 1996, Demystifying the development of an organizational vision, *Sloan Management Review,* 37(4): 83–92; Bart, C. K., 2000, Lasting inspiration, *CA Magazine,* May: 49–50; and Quigley, J. V., 1994, Vision: How leaders develop it, share it, and sustain it, *Business Horizons,* September–October: 37–40.

59. Lipton, op. cit.

60. Quigley, op. cit.

61. Ibid.

62. Lipton, op. cit. Additional pitfalls are addressed in this article.

63. Brinker International homepage. www.brinker.com. Accessed August 11, 2017.

64. Lipton, op. cit.

65. Sexton, D. A., & Van Aukun, P. M., 1985, A longitudinal study of small business strategic planning, *Journal of Small Business Management,* January: 8–15, cited in Lipton, op. cit.

66. Ibid.

Chapter 2

1. This case draws on De Vynck, G., 2016, Netflix Dominating in Canada as Rogers, Shaw Shut Down Shomi, *Bloomberg Technology,* Sept 26:1; Jackson, E., 2016, Why Shomi's demise doesn't mean the end for Canadian video streaming companies, *Financial Post,* Sept 27:1; Mudhar, R, and Hudes, S., 2016, Canadian Streaming service Shomi shutting down, *The Toronto Star,* Sept 26:1; Nowak, P., 2016, Why Shomi failed and why CraveTV is next, *Alphabeatic,* Sept 27:1.

2. Hamel, G., & Prahalad, C. K., 1994, *Competing for the Future* (Boston: HBS Press).

3. Drucker, P. F., 1994, Theory of the business, *Harvard Business Review,* 72: 95–104.

4. Merino, M. 2013. You can't be a wimp: Making the tough calls. Harvard Business Review, 91(11): 73–78 2

5. For an insightful discussion on managers' assessment of the external environment, refer to Sutcliffe, K. M., & Weber, K., 2003, The high cost of accurate knowledge, *Harvard Business Review,* 81(5): 74–86.

6. Charitou, C. D., & Markides, C. C., 2003, Responses to disruptive strategic innovation, *MIT Sloan Management Review,* 44(2): 55–64.

7. Our discussion of scanning, monitoring, competitive intelligence, and forecasting concepts draws on several sources. These include Fahey, L., & Narayanan, V. K., 1983, *Macroenvironmental Analysis for Strategic Management* (St. Paul, MN: West); Lorange, P., Scott, F. S., & Ghoshal, S., 1986, *Strategic Control* (St. Paul, MN: West); Ansoff, H. I., 1984, *Implementing Strategic Management* (Englewood Cliffs, NJ: Prentice Hall); and Schreyogg, G., & Stienmann, H., 1987, Strategic control: A new perspective, *Academy of Management Review,* 12: 91–103.

8. Elenkov, D. S., 1997, Strategic uncertainty and environmental scanning: The case for institutional influences on scanning behavior, *Strategic Management Journal,* 18: 287–302.

9. For an interesting perspective on environmental scanning in emerging economies, see May, R. C., Stewart, W. H., & Sweo, R., 2000, Environmental scanning behavior in a transitional economy: Evidence from Russia, *Academy of Management Journal,* 43(3): 403–27.

10. "Automobile Dealers—Industry Overview," "Automobile Manufacturing—Industry Overview," "Automobile Parts Manufacturing—Industry Overview," *Hoover's Online.* Hoover's Inc. n. pag. Web., 15 March 2014; "Global Automobiles: Industry Profile," July 2011, *Marketline Advantage.* Datamonitor USA. n. pag. Web., 15 March 2014.

11. Walters, B. A., & Priem, R. L., 1999, Business strategy and CEO intelligence acquisition, *Competitive Intelligence Review,* 10(2): 15–22.

12. Prior, V., 1999, The language of competitive intelligence, Part 4, *Competitive Intelligence Review,* 10(1): 84–87.

13. Zahra, S. A., & Charples, S. S., 1993, Blind spots in competitive analysis, *Academy of Management Executive,* 7(2): 7–27.

14. Wolfenson, J., 1999, The world in 1999: A battle for corporate honesty, *The Economist Publications,* 38: 13–30.

15. Drucker, P. F., 1997, The future that has already happened, *Harvard Business Review,* 75(6): 22.

16. Evans, P. B., & Wurster, T. S., 1997, Strategy and the new economics of information, *Harvard Business Review,* 75(5): 71–82.

17. Fahey & Narayanan, op. cit., p. 41.

18. Courtney, H., Kirkland, J., & Viguerie, P., 1997, Strategy under uncertainty, *Harvard Business Review,* 75(6): 66–79.

19. Odlyzko, A., 2003, False hopes, *Red Herring,* March: 31.

25. Walgreen's, Inc., 2000, annual report, 20.

21. For an interesting perspective on how Accenture, the leading consulting firm has developed its approach to scenario planning, refer to Feguson, G., Mathur, S., & Shah, B, 2005. Evolving from information to insight, *MIT Sloan Management Review,* 46(2): 51–58.

22. Martin, R., 2002, The oracles of oil, *Business 2.0,* January: 35–39; and Epstein, J., 1998, Scenario planning: An Introduction, *The Futurist,* September: 50–52.

23. Colvin, G., 1997, How to beat the boomer rush, *Fortune,* August 18: 59–63.

24. Grant, P., 2000, Developing plans to serve a graying population, *The Wall Street Journal,* October 18: B12; and Rostoks, L., 2003, The changing profile of the consumer, *Canadian Grocer,* March: 32.

25. Walgreen's, Inc., 2000, annual report, 20.

26. Peterson, R., 1999, *Global Entrepreneurship Monitor,* Canadian National Executive Report.

27. Challenger, J., 2000, Women's corporate rise has reduced relocations, *Lexington (KY) Herald-Leader,* October 29: D1.

28. Peterson, op. cit.; Challenger, op. cit.; and OECD Conference on Women Entrepreneurs in SMEs: A Major Force in Innovation and Job Creation, Paris, 1998. figures updated in August 2017.

29. Watkins, M. D., 2003, Government games, *MIT Sloan Management Review,* 44(2): 91–95.

30. Gillies, J., 2001, Globalization and Canadian economic and industrial strategy in the twenty-first century, in Wesson, T., ed., *Canada and the New World Economic Order* (Toronto: Captus Press), 178–201.

31. Business ready for Internet revolution, 1999, *Financial Times,* May 21: 17.

32. The Internet example draws on Bernasek, A., 2000, How the broadband adds up, *Fortune,* October 9: 28, 30; and Kromer, E., B2B or not B2B? *UW Alumni Magazine,* 10–19.

33. Ginsburg, J., 2000, Letting the free market clear the air, *BusinessWeek,* November 6: 200, 204.

34. Smith, G., Wheatley, J., & Green, J., 2000, Car power, *BusinessWeek,* October 23: 72–80.

35. Mellgren, D., 2000, Norwegian ships relied on in global disasters, *Lexington (KY) Herald-Leader,* November 6: A8.

36. Goll, I., & Rasheed, M. A., 1997, Rational decision-making and firm performance: The moderating role of environment, *Strategic Management Journal,* 18: 583–91.

37. Our discussion of crowdsourcing draws on the first two books that have addressed the concept: Libert, B. & Spector, J. 2008. We are smarter than me. Philadelphia: Wharton; and Howe, J. 2008. Crowdsourcing. New York: Crown Business. Eric von Hippel addressed similar issues in his 2005 book, Democraticizing innovation, Cambridge, MA.: MIT Press.

38. This discussion draws heavily on Porter, M. E., 1980, *Competitive Strategy* (chap. 1) (New York: Free Press).

39. Ibid.

40. Fryer, B., 2001, Leading through rough times: An Interview with Novell's Eric Schmidt, *Harvard Business Review,* 78(5): 117–23.

41. Wise, R., & Baumgarter, P., 1999, Go downstream: The new profit imperative in manufacturing, *Harvard Business Review,* 77(5): 133–41.

42. Salman, W. A., 2000, The new economy is stronger than you think, *Harvard Business Review* 77(6): 99–106; The B2B Tool That Really Is Changing the World, *Time Inc.*

43. Mudambi, R., & Helper, S., 1998, The "close but adversarial" model of supplier relations in the U.S. auto industry, *Strategic Management Journal,* 19: 775–92.

44. HP Company: 2010, Annual Report and various press releases; Rollins, M., 2008, HP upgrades teleconference technology developed in Corvallis, *Corvallis Gazette-Times,* March 18.

45. Foust, D. 2007. The best performers. *Business Week,* March 26: 58–95; Rosenblum, D., Tomlinson, D., & Scott, L. 2003. Bottom-feeding for blockbuster businesses. *Harvard Business Review,* 81(3): 52–59; Paychex 2006 Annual Report; and, WellPoint Health Network 2005 Annual Report.

46. Kumar, N., 1996, The power of trust in manufacturer-retailer relationship, *Harvard Business Review,* 74(6): 92–110.

47. The discussion draws heavily on McGahan, A., 2004. How industries change, *Harvard Business Review,* 82(10): 87–94.

48. Brandenburger, A., & Nalebuff, B. J., 1995, The right game: Use game theory to shape strategy, *Harvard Business Review,* 73(4): 57–71.

49. Peteraf, M., & Shanly, M., 1997, Getting to know you: A theory of strategic group identity, *Strategic Management Journal,* 18 (Special Issue): 165–86.

50. An interesting scholarly perspective on strategic groups may be found in Dranove, D., Perteraf, M., & Shanly, M., 1998, Do strategic groups exist? An economic framework for analysis, *Strategic Management Journal,* 19(11): 1029–44.

51. This section draws on several sources, including Kerwin, K. R., & Haughton, K., 1997, Can Detroit make cars that baby boomers like? *BusinessWeek,* December 1: 134–48; and Taylor, A., III, 1994, The new golden age of autos, *Fortune,* April 4: 50–66.

52. Csere, C., 2001, Supercar supermarket, *Car and Driver,* January, 2001: 118–27.

53. Healey, J. R., 1999, Groomed so as not to marry, *USA Today,* August 6: B1 and www.digitaltrends.com/cars/most-expensive-cars-in-the-world/ updated August 2017.

Chapter 3

1. This examples draws on 2017, Our History, *CBC Radio Canada:* 1; Décoste, R., 2015, With So Many Scandals, Why Should We Save the CBC?, *Huffington Post,* Oct 6:1; Donovan, K., 2015, CBC Host Evan Solomon fired after Star investigation finds he took secret cut of art deals, *The Star,* June 9:1; Libin, K., 2016, The CBC screwed up big on Jian Ghomeshi – and it still doesn't realize it, *Financial Post,* May 12:1; Niazi, A., 2016, How the CBC Let Us Down in the Wake of Jian Ghomeshi Scandal, *Vice,* May 11:1; Roumeliotis, I., 2015, CBC Inquiry concludes management mishandled Ghomeshi, *CBC,* Apr 16:1; Szklarski, C., 2015, 2015 a scandal-plagued year for CBC, *Toronto Sun,* Dec 7:1.

2. Our discussion of the value chain will draw on Porter, M. E., 1985, *Competitive Advantage* (New York: Free Press), Chapter 2.

3. Dyer, J. H., 1996, Specialized Supplier Networks as a Source of Competitive Advantage: Evidence from the Auto Industry, *Strategic Management Journal* 17: 271–91.

4. For an insightful perspective on value-chain analysis, refer to Stabell, C. B., & Fjeldstad, O. D., 1998, Configuring Value for Competitive Advantage: On Chains, Shops, and Networks, *Strategic Management Journal,* 19: 413–37. The authors develop concepts of value chains, value shops, and value networks to extend the value-creation logic across a broad range of industries. Their work builds on the seminal contributions of Porter, 1985, op. cit. and others who have addressed how firms create value through key interrelationships among value-creating activities.

5. Ibid.

6. Maynard, M., 1999, Toyota Promises Custom Order in 5 Days, *USA Today,* August 6: B1.

7. Shaw Industries, 1999, annual report, 14–15.

8. Fisher, M. L., 1997, What Is the Right Supply Chain for Your Product? *Harvard Business Review* 75(2): 105–16.

9. Jackson, M., 2001, Bringing a Dying Brand Back to Life, *Harvard Business Review* 79(5): 53–61.

10. Anderson, J. C., & Nmarus, J. A., 2003, Selectively Pursuing More of Your Customer's Business, *MIT Sloan Management Review* 44(3): 42–50.

11. Insights on advertising are addressed in: Rayport, J. F. 2008. Where Is Advertising? Into 'stitials. *Harvard Business Review* 66(5): 18–20.

12. An insightful discussion of the role of identity marketing—that is, the myriad labels that people use to express who they are—in successful marketing activities is found in Reed, A., II & Bolton, L. E. 2005. The Complexity of Identity. *MIT Sloan Management Review,* 46(3): 18–22.

13. Insights on the usefulness of off-line ads are the focus of: Abraham, M. 2008. The Off-Line Impact of Online Ads. *Harvard Business Review* 66(4): 28.

14. Berggren, E., & Nacher, T., 2000, Why Good Ideas Go Bust, *Management Review,* February: 32–36.

15. Brown, J., 2000, Service, Please, *BusinessWeek E. Biz,* October 23: EB 48–50.

16. For a cautionary note on the use of IT, refer to McAfee, A., 2003, When Too Much IT Knowledge Is a Dangerous Thing, *MIT Sloan Management Review* 44(2): 83–90.

17. Rivette, K. G., & Kline, D., 2000, Discovering New Value in Intellectual Property, *Harvard Business Review* 78(1): 54–66.

18. Ulrich, D., 1998, A New Mandate for Human Resources, *Harvard Business Review* 96(1): 124–34.

19. Wood, J., 2003, Sharing Jobs and Working from Home: The New Face of the Airline Industry, *AviationCareer.net.* February 21.

20. Follow AT&T's Lead in This Tactic to Retain "Plateaued" Employees, n.d., *Recruitment & Retention:* 1.

21. Green, S., Hasan, F., Immelt, J., Marks, M., & Meiland, D., 2003, In Search of Global Leaders, *Harvard Business Review* 81(8): 38–45.

22. Bensaou, B. M., & Earl, M., 1998, The Right Mindset for Managing Information Technology, *Harvard Business Review* 96(5): 118–28.

23. Williams, D.H., 2004, The Strategic Implication of Wal-Mart's RFID Mandate, *Directions Magazine,* July 29; Wal-Mart RFID Plans Change, *RFid Gazette,* February 27, 2007.

24. Imperato, G., 1998, How to Give Good Feedback, *Fast Company,* September: 144–56.

25. This section draws on Andersen, M. M., Froholdt, M. & Poulfelt, F., 2010., *Return on strategy,* New York: Routledge: 96–100.

26. Quote from Hartmut Jenner, CEO, Alfred Karcher GmbH, IBM Global CEO Study, P. 27.

27. Verhoef, P. C., Beckers, S. F. M., & van Doorn, J. 2013. Understand the perils of co-creation. Harvard Business Review, 91(9): 28; and Winston, A. S. 2014. The big pivot. Harvard Business Review

28. Barney, 1991, op. cit.; Collis, D. J., & Montgomery, C. A., 2005, *Corporate Strategy* (Boston: McGraw-Hill); and Grant, R., 1991, *Contemporary Strategy Analysis* (Cambridge: Blackwell Business).

29. Barney, J. B., 1986, Types of Competition and the Theory of Strategy: Towards an Integrative Framework, *Academy of Management Review* 11(4): 791–800.

30. Harley-Davidson, 1993, annual report.

31. Dutta, S., Narasimhan, O., & Rajiv, S., 2005, Conceptualizing and Measuring Capabilities: Methodology and Empirical Application, *Strategic Management Journal* 26(3): 277–286; Lorenzoni, G., & Lipparini, A., 1999, The Leveraging of Interfirm Relationships as a Distinctive Organizational Capability: A Longitudinal Study, *Strategic Management Journal* 20: 317–38.

32. Collins, J., 1997, The Most Creative Product Ever, *Inc.,* May: 75–78.

33. Barney, 1991, op. cit.

34. Barney, 1986, op. cit. Our discussion on inimitability and substitution draws on this source.

35. Deephouse, D. L., 1999, To Be Different, or To Be the Same? It's a Question (and Theory) of Strategic Balance, *Strategic Management Journal,* 20: 147–66.

36. Yeoh, P. L., & Roth, K., 1999, An Empirical Analysis of Sustained Advantage in the U.S. Pharmaceutical Industry: Impact of Firm Resources and Capabilities, *Strategic Management Journal,* 20: 637–53.

37. Barreto, I., 2010, Dynamic Capabilities: A Review of Past Research and an Agenda for the Future, *Journal of Management,* 36: 256–280; Eisenhardt, K.M. & Martin, J.A., 2000, Dynamic Capabilities: What Are They? *Strategic Management Journal,* 22: 1105–1121; Teece, D.J., 2007, Explicating dynamic Capabilities: The Nature and Microfoundations of (Sustainable) Enterprise Performance, *Strategic Management Journal,* 28: 1319–1350; Teece, D.J., Pisano, G. & Shuen, A., 1997, Dynamic Capabilities and Strategic Management, *Strategic Management Journal,* 18: 509–533.

38. Robins, J. A., & Wiersema, M. F., 2000, Strategies for Unstructured Competitive Environments: Using Scarce Resources to Create New Markets, in Bresser, R. F., et al., eds., *Winning Strategies in a Deconstructing World* (New York: John Wiley), 201–20.

39. For an insightful account on how Dell was able to build its sustainable competitive advantage in the marketplace, refer to J.W. Rivkin and M.E. Porter, Matching Dell, *Harvard Business School case 9: 799–158* (June 1999); for a discussion on Dell's eroding advantage and HP's strategy in the personal computer business, refer to Byrnes, N. & Burrows, P. 2007, Where Dell Went Wrong, *BusinessWeek,* February 18: 62–63; Smith, A. D., 2007, Dell's Moves Create Buzz, *Dallas Morning News,* February 21: D1; and Edwards, C., 2008, How HP Got the Wow! Back, *BusinessWeek,* December 22: 60–61.

40. Amit, R., & Schoemaker, J. H., 1993, Strategic Assets and Organizational Rent, *Strategic Management Journal* 14(1): 33–46; Collis & Montgomery, op. cit.; 1995, Coff, R. W., 1999, When competitive Advantage Doesn't Lead to Performance: The Resource-Based View and Stakeholder Bargaining Power, *Organization Science,* 10(2): 119–33; and Blyler, M., & Coff, R. W., in press, Dynamic Capabilities, Social Capital, and Rent Appropriation: Ties That Split Pies, *Strategic Management Journal.*

41. Munk, N., 1998, The New Organization Man, *Fortune,* March 16: 62–74.

42. Coff, R. W., op. cit.

43. We have focused our discussion on how internal stakeholders (e.g., employees, managers, and top executives) may appropriate a firm's profits (or rents). For an interesting discussion of how a firm's innovations may be appropriated by external stakeholders (e.g., customers, suppliers) as well as competitors, refer to Grant, R. M., 2002, *Contemporary Strategy Analysis,* 4th ed. (Malden, MA: Blackwell Business), 335–40.

44. Luehrman, T. A., 1997, What's It Worth? A General Manager's Guide to Valuation, *Harvard Business Review* 45(3): 132–42.

45. See, for example, Kaplan, R. S., & Norton, D. P., 1992, The Balanced Scorecard—Measures That Drive Performance, *Harvard Business Review* 69(1): 71–79.

46. Hitt, M. A., Ireland, R. D., & Stadter, G., 1982, Functional importance of Company Performance: Moderating Effects of Grand Strategy and Industry Type, *Strategic Management Journal* 3: 315–30.

47. Home Depot, 2007, annual report.

48. Berner, R., 2000, Procter & Gamble: Just Say No to Drugs, *BusinessWeek,* October 9: 128.

49. Kaplan & Norton, op. cit.

50. Ibid.

51. Rucci, A. J., Kirn, S. P., & Quinn, R. T., 1998, The Employee-Customer-Profit Chain at Sears, *Harvard Business Review* 76(1): 82–97.

52. Angel, R & Rampersad, H., 2005, Do Scorecards Add Up? *Camemagazine.com,* May, n.p.; and Niven, P., 2002, *Balanced Scorecard Step by Step; Maximizing Performance and Maintaining Results* (New York: John Wiley & Sons).

53. Our discussion on strategy maps draws from Kaplan, R.S., & Norton, D.P., 1996, Linking the balanced Scorecard to Strategy, *California Management Review,* 39(1); and Olve, N, Roy, J., &Wetter, M., 1999, *Performance Drivers: A Practical Guide to Using the Balanced Scorecard* (New York: John Wiley & Sons).

54. Eckerson, W.W., 2006, *Performance Dashboards: Measuring, Monitoring, and Managing Your Business* (New York: John Wiley & Sons).

Chapter 4

1. This example draws on Decker, S., 2015, Blackberry's Patent Portfolio is Wireless Trove for Acquirer, Bloomberg, Jan 14: 1; Jain, A., 2016, Blackberry Makes Headway in Monetizing Patent Portfolio, Value Walk, Feb 16: 1; Lonkevich, D., 2017, Blackberry May Have a Brighter Future Monetizing Patents Than as a Software Developer, PatentVue, Feb 27:1; Rocha, E., 2015, Blackberry Ltd CEO John Chen sees patents as key to turnaround strategy, Financial Post, Sept 17:1; Silcoff, S., Mcnish, J., and Ladurantaye, S., 2013, Inside the Fall of Blackberry: How the smartphone inventor failed to adapt, The Globe and Mail, Sept 27:1.

2. Drucker, P., 1992, The new society of organizations, *Harvard Business Review,* 70(4): 44–52.

3. Swap, W., & Leonard, D., 2000, Gurus in the garage, *Harvard Business Review,* 78(6): 71–82; Hamel, G., 1999, Bringing Silicon Valley inside, *Harvard Business Review,* 77(5): 71–84; and Alley, J., 1997, Silicon Valley is the intellectual incubator of the digital age, *Fortune,* July 7: 67–74.

4. Keenan, G., Pitts, G., & Scoffield, H., 2006, A place that does not hold back its best, *The Globe and Mail,* April 25, B10.

5. An acknowledged trend: The world economic survey, 1996, *The Economist,* September 28: 25–28.

6. Quinn, J. B., Anderson, P., & Finkelstein, S., 1996, Leveraging intellect, *Academy of Management Executive,* 10(3): 7–27.

7. Hamel, G., & Prahalad, C. K., 1996, Competing in the new economy: Managing out of bounds, *Strategic Management Journal,* 17: 238.

8. Stewart, T. A., 1997, *Intellectual Capital: The New Wealth of Organizations* (New York: Doubleday/Currency); and Conley, J. G., & Szobocsan, J., 2001, Snow White shows the way, *Managing Intellectual Property,* June: 15–25.

9. Conley, J. G., 2005, *Intellectual capital management,* Kellogg School of Management and Schulich School of Business, York University, Toronto, KS '03.

10. Thomas Stewart has suggested this formula in his book *Intellectual capital.* He provides an insightful discussion on pages 224–225, including some of the limitations of this approach to measuring intellectual capital. We recognize, of course, that during the late 1990s and in early 2000, there were some excessive market valuations of high-technology and Internet firms. For an interesting discussion of the extraordinary market valuation of Yahoo!, an Internet company, refer to Perkins, A. B. 2001. The Internet bubble encapsulated: Yahoo! *Red Herring,* April 15: 17–18.

11. One of the seminal contributions on knowledge management is Becker, G. S., 1993, *Human Capital: A Theoretical and Empirical Analysis with Special Reference to Education,* 3rd ed. (Chicago: University of Chicago Press).

12. For an excellent discussion of social capital and its impact on organizational performance, refer to Nahapiet, J., & Ghoshal, S., 1998, Social capital, intellectual capital, and the organizational advantage, *Academy of Management Review,* 23: 242–66.

13. Polanyi, M., 1967, *The Tacit Dimension* (Garden City, NY: Anchor Publishing).

14. Conley & Szobocsan, op. cit.

15. Barney, J. B., 1991, Firm resources and sustained competitive advantage, *Journal of Management,* 17: 99–120.

16. Some of the notable books on this topic include Edvisson, L., & Malone, M. S., 1997, *Intellectual Capital: Realizing Your Company's True Value by Finding Its Hidden Brainpower* (New York: Harper Business); Stewart, op. cit.; and Nonaka, I., & Takeuchi, I., 1995, *The Knowledge Creating Company* (New York: Oxford University Press).

17. Stewart, T. A., 2000, Taking risk to the marketplace, *Fortune,* March 6: 424.

18. Dutton, G., 1997, Are you technologically competent? *Management Review,* November: 54–58.

19. Dess, G. G., & Picken, J. C., 1999, *Beyond Productivity* (New York: AMACOM).

20. Webber, A. M., 1998, Danger: Toxic company, *Fast Company,* November: 152–61.

21. Key to success: People, people, people, 1997, *Fortune,* October 27: 232.

22. Martin, J., 1998, So, you want to work for the best. . . , *Fortune,* January 12: 77.

23. Carbonara, P., 1997, Hire for attitude, train for skill, *Fast Company,* August–September: 66–67.

24. Stewart, T. A., 1996, Why value statements don't work, *Fortune,* June 10: 138.

25. Carbonara, op. cit.

26. Martin, op. cit.; Henkoff, R., 1993, Companies that train best, *Fortune,* March 22: 53–60.

27. Bartlett, C. A., & Ghoshal, S., 2002, Building competitive advantage through people, *MIT Sloan Management Review,* 43(2): 34–41.

28. Stewart, T. A., 1998, Gray flannel suit? moi? *Fortune,* March 18: 80–82.

29. Key to success: People, people, people, 1997, *Fortune,* October 27: 232.

30. The discussion of the 360-degree feedback system draws on UPS, 1997, *360-Degree Feedback: Coming from All Sides, Vision* (a UPS Corporation internal company publication), March: 3; Slater, R., 1994, *Get Better or Get Beaten: Thirty-one Leadership Secrets from Jack Welch* (Burr Ridge, IL: Irwin); Nexon, M., 1997, General Electric: The secrets of the finest company in the world, *L'Expansion,* July 23: 18–30; and Smith, D., 1996, Bold new directions for human resources, *Merck World* (internal company publication), October: 8.

31. Kets de Vries, M. F. R., 1998, Charisma in action: The transformational abilities of Virgin's Richard Branson and ABB's Percy Barnevik, *Organizational Dynamics,* Winter: 20.

32. One has only to consider Air Canada's pending lawsuit against WestJet or the most celebrated case of industrial espionage in recent years, wherein José Ignacio Lopez was indicted in a German court for stealing sensitive product planning documents from his former employer General Motors and sharing them with his executive colleagues at Volkswagen. The lawsuit was dismissed by the German courts, but Lopez and his colleagues were investigated by the U.S. Justice Department. Also, consider the recent litigation involving non-compete employment contracts and confidentiality clauses of *International Paper v. Louisiana-Pacific, Campbell Soup v. H. J. Heinz Co.,* and *PepsiCo v. Quaker Oats's Gatorade.* In addition to retaining valuable human resources and often their valuable network of customers, firms must also protect proprietary information and knowledge. For interesting insights, refer to Carley, W. M., 1998, CEO gets hard lesson in how not to keep his lieutenants, *Wall Street Journal,* February 11: A1, A10; and Lenzner, R., & Shhok, C., 1998, Whose Rolodex is it, anyway? *Forbes,* February 23: 100–103.

33. DesMarteau, K., 1999, Magna: Master of automotive innovation, *Columbia,* April: 58–60.

34. Sutherland, J., 2005, Unbeatable, *Report on Business,* January: 47.

35. The examples in this section draw on a variety of sources, including Lubove, S., 1998, New age capitalist, *Forbes,* April 6: 42–43; Kets de Vries, op. cit.; Pfeffer, J., 1995, Producing sustainable competitive advantage through the effective management of people, *Academy of Management Executive,* 9(1): 55–69. Vlasic, B., 2008, Honda stays true to efficient driving, *The New York Times,* August 26, C1. The concept of strategic intent is generally credited to Hamel, G., & Prahalad, C. K., 1989, Strategic intent, *Harvard Business Review,* 67: 63–76.

36. Kets de Vries, op. cit., pp. 73–92.

37. Amabile, T. M., 1997, Motivating creativity in organizations: On doing what you love and loving what you do, *California Management Review,* Fall: 39–58.

38. The discussion of internal markets for human capital draws on Hamel, op. cit.

39. Pfeffer, J., 2001, Fighting the war for talent is hazardous to your organization's health, *Organizational Dynamics,* 29(4): 248–59.

40. For an insightful discussion on strategies for retaining and developing human capital, refer to Coff, R. W., 1997, Human assets and management dilemmas: Coping with hazards on the road to resource-based theory, *Academy of Management Review,* 22(2): 374–402.

41. Reguly, E., 2005, David versus the Goliaths, *Report on Business,* January: 19.

42. Galt, V., 2005, Babysitting service pays off for CIBC, *The Globe and Mail,* February 16: B10. The statistics on child care trends are drawn from Bubbar, S. E., & Aspelin, D. J., 1998, The overtime rebellion: Symptom of a bigger problem? *Academy of Management Executive,* 12: 68–76. The other examples in this section are drawn from various sources, including Munk, N., 1998, The new organization man, *Fortune,* March 16: 68–72;

and Hammonds, K. H., Furchgott, R., Hamm, S., & Judge, P. C., 1997, Work and family, *BusinessWeek,* September 15: 96–104.

43. Dess, G. G., & Lumpkin, G. T., 2001. Emerging issues in strategy process research, in Hitt, M. A., Freeman, R. E., & Harrison, J. S., eds., *Handbook of Strategic Management* (Malden, MA: Blackwell), 3–34; Complin, M., 2002, Now it's getting personal, *BusinessWeek,* December 16: 90–93; and Pfau, B., & Kay, I., 2002, The hidden human resources: Shareholder value, *Optimize,* June: 50–54.

44. This section draws on Dewhurst, M., Hancock, B., & Ellsworth, D. 2013. Redesigning knowledge work. Harvard Business Review, 91 (1/2): 58–64.

45. Cox, T. L. 1991. The multinational organization. Academy of Management Executive, 5(2): 34–47. Without doubt, a great deal has been written on the topic of creating and maintaining an effective diverse workforce. Some excellent, recent books include Harvey, C. P. & Allard, M. J. 2005. Understanding and managing diversity: Readings, cases, and exercises (3rd ed.). Upper Saddle River, NJ: Pearson Prentice-Hall; Miller, F. A. & Katz, J. H. 2002. The inclusion breakthrough: Unleashing the real power of diversity. San Francisco: Berrett Koehler; and Williams, M. A. 2001. The 10 lenses: Your guide to living and working in a multicultural world. Sterling, VA: Capital Books.

46. Day, J. C. Undated. National population projections. cps.ipums.org: np

47. Hewlett, S. A. & Rashid, R. 2010. The battle for female talent in emerging markets. Harvard Business Review, 88(5): 101–107.

48. This section, including the six potential benefits of a diverse workforce, draws on Cox, T. H. & Blake, S. 1991. Managing cultural diversity: Implications for organizational competitiveness. Academy of Management Executive, 5(3): 45–56.

49. www.pwcglobal.com/us/eng/careers/diversity/index.html.

50. Hewlett, S. A., Marshall, M., & Sherbin, L. 2013. How diversity can drive innovation. Harvard Business Review, 91(12): 30.

51. The discussion draws on Adler, P. S., & Kwon, S.-W., 2002, Social capital: Prospects for a new concept, *Academy of Management Review,* 27(1): 17–40.

52. Capelli, P., 2000, A market-driven approach to retaining talent, *Harvard Business Review,* 78(1): 103–13.

53. This hypothetical example draws on Peteraf, M., 1993, The cornerstones of competitive advantage, *Strategic Management Journal,* 14: 179–91.

54. Wernerfelt, B., 1984, A resource-based view of the firm, *Strategic Management Journal,* 5:171–80.

55. Wysocki, B., Jr., 2000, Yet another hazard of the new economy: The Pied Piper effect, *Wall Street Journal,* March 20: A1–A16.

56. McMillan, C. J., & Jasson, E. M. V., 2001, Technology and the new economy: A Canadian strategy, in Wesson, T., ed., *Canada and the New World Economic Order* (Toronto: Captus Press).

57. Buckman, R. C., 2000, Tech defectors from Microsoft resettle together, *Wall Street Journal,* October: B1–B6.

58. For an insightful discussion on the creation of social capital, see Bolino, M. C., Turnley, W. H., & Bloodgood, J. M., 2002, Citizenship behavior and the creation of social capital in organizations, *Academy of Management Review,* 27(4): 505–22.

59. An insightful discussion of the interorganizational aspects of social capital can be found in Dyer, J. H., & Singh, H., 1998, The relational view: Cooperative strategy and sources of interorganizational competitive advantage, *Academy of Management Review,* 23: 66–79.

60. Aime, F., Johnson, S., Ridge, J. W. & Hill, A. D. 2010. The routine may be stable but the advantage is not: Competitive implications of key employee mobility. *Strategic Management Journal,* 31(1): 75–87.

61. Hoppe, B. 2005. Structural holes, Part one. *connectedness. blogspot.com.* January 18: np.

62. There has been a tremendous amount of theory building and empirical research in recent years in the area of social network analysis. Unquestionably, two of the major contributors to this domain have been Ronald Burt and J. S. Coleman. For excellent background discussions, refer to: Burt, R. S. 1992. *Structural holes: The social structure of competition.* Cambridge, MA: Harvard University Press; Coleman, J. S. 1990. *Foundations of social theory.* Cambridge, MA: Harvard University Press; and Coleman, J. S. 1988. Social capital in the creation of human capital. *American Journal of Sociology.* 94: S95–S120. For a more recent review and integration of current thought on social network theory, consider: Burt, R. S. 2005. *Brokerage & closure: An introduction to social capital.* Oxford Press: New York.

63. Our discussion draws on the concepts developed by Burt, 1992, op. cit.; Coleman, 1990, op. cit.; Coleman, 1988, op. cit.; and Oh, H., Chung, M. & Labianca, G. 2004. Group social capital and group effectiveness: The role of informal socializing ties. *Academy of Management Journal,* 47(6): 860–875. We would like to thank Joe Labianca (University of Kentucky) for his helpful feedback and ideas in our discussion of social networks.

64. Arregle, J. L., Hitt, M. A., Sirmon, D. G., & Very, P. 2007. The development of organizational social capital: Attributes of family firms. *Journal of Management Studies,* 44(1): 73–95.

65. Oh et al., op. cit.

66. Hoppe, op. cit.

67. The discussion of these two contingent factors draws on Dess, G. G. & Shaw, J. D. 2001. Voluntary turnover, social capital, and organizational performance. *Academy of Management Review,* 26(3): 446–456.

68. The business-level strategies of overall low cost and differentiation draws upon Michael E. Porter's classic work and will be discussed in more detail in Chapter 5. Source: Porter, M. E. 1985. *Competitive advantage* (New York: Free Press).

69. Prusak & Cohen, op. cit., pp. 86–93.

70. This section draws on Hansen, M. T. 2009. Collaboration: How leaders avoid the traps, create unity, and reap big results. Boston: Harvard Business Press.

71. Prusak, L. & Cohen, D. 2001. How to invest in social capital. Harvard Business Review, 79(6): 86–93.

72. Lei, D., Slocum, J., & Pitts, R. A., 1999, Designing organizations for competitive advantage: The power of unlearning and learning, *Organizational Dynamics,* Winter: 24–38.

73. For an innovative study on how firms share knowledge with competitors and the performance implications, read Spencer, J. W., 2003, Firms' knowledge sharing strategies in the global innovation system: Empirical evidence from the flat panel display industry, *Strategic Management Journal,* 24(3): 217–35.

74. The examples of Accenture and Access Health draw on Hansen, M. T., Nohria, N., & Tierney, T., 1999, What's your strategy for managing knowledge? *Harvard Business Review,* 77(2): 106–18.

75. Ibid.; and Magretta, J., 1998, The power of virtual integration: An interview with Dell Computer's Michael Dell, *Harvard Business Review,* 76(3): 73–84.

76. Capelli, op. cit.

77. The ensuing discussion draws on Conley, 2005, op. cit.; Conley & Szobocsan, 2001, op. cit.; Greenspan, A., 2004, Intellectual property rights, The Federal Reserve Board, Remarks by the chairman, February 27; and Teece, D. J., 1998, Capturing value from knowledge assets, *California Management Review,* 40 (3): 54–79.

Chapter 5

1. This case draws on McMahon, T., 2015, Missing the mark: Five reasons why Target failed in Canada, Jan 15: 1; Northrup, L., 2016, 15 Things We Learned About the Downfall of Target Canada, Consumerist, Jan 22:1; Peterson, H., 2015, 5 Reasons Target Failed in Canada, Business Insider, Jan 15: 1; Wahba, P., 2015, Why Target failed in Canada, Fortune, Jan 15: 1.

2. An excellent overview of the various schools of strategic management is provided in Mintzberg, H., Ahlstrand, B., & Lampel, J., 1998, *Strategy Safari: A Guided Tour through the Wilds of Strategic Management* (New York: The Free Press).

3. Porter, M.E., 1980, *Competitive Strategy* (New York: McGraw-Hill). For a more recent perspective by Porter on competitive strategy, refer to Porter, M.E., 1996, What is strategy? *Harvard Business Review,* 74(6): 61–78.

4. For a scholarly discussion and analysis of the concept of competitive parity, refer to Powell, T. C., 2003, Varieties of competitive parity, *Strategic Management Journal,* 24(1): 61–86.

5. Rao, A.R., Bergen, M.E., & Davis, S., 2000, How to fight a price war, *Harvard Business Review,* 78(2): 107–20.

6. For a perspective on the sustainability of competitive advantages, refer to Barney, J., 1995, Looking inside for competitive advantage, *Academy of Management Executive,* 9(4): 49–61.

7. Thornton, E., 2001, Why e-brokers are broker and broker, *BusinessWeek,* January 22: 94.

8. Koretz, G., 2001, E-commerce: The buyer wins, *BusinessWeek,* January 8: 30.

9. MacMillan, I., & McGrath, R., 1997, Discovering new points of differentiation, *Harvard Business Review,* 75(4): 133–45; Wise, R., & Baumgarter, P., 1999, Beating the clock: Corporate responses to rapid change in the PC industry, *California Management Review,* 42(1): 8–36; Austin, R.D., 2008, High margins and the quest for aesthetic coherence, *Harvard Business Review,* 86(1): 18–19.

10. For a discussion on quality in terms of a company's software and information systems, refer to Prahalad, C. K., & Krishnan, M. S., 1999, The new meaning of quality in the information age, *Harvard Business Review,* 77(5): 109–18.

11. Taylor, A., III, 2001, Can you believe Porsche is putting its badge on this car? *Fortune,* February 19: 168–72.

12. Ward, S., Light, L., & Goldstine, J., 1999, What high-tech managers need to know about brands, *Harvard Business Review,* 77(4): 85–95.

13. Zesiger, S., 1999, Silicon speed, *Fortune,* September 13: 120. www.caranddriver.com; www.cnbc.com/two-year-waiting-list-for-ferrari-488.gtb

14. Bonnabeau, E., Bodick, N., & Armstrong, R.W., 2008, A more rational approach to new-product development, *Harvard Business Review,* 66(3): 96–102.

15. See http://yourquestions.mcdonalds.ca/

16. The authors would like to thank Scott Droege, a faculty member at Mississippi State University, for providing this example.

17. Symonds, W.C., 2000, Can Gillette regain its voltage? *BusinessWeek,* October 16: 102–4.

18. Gadiesh, O., & Gilbert, J. L., 1998, Profit pools: A fresh look at strategy, *Harvard Business Review,* 76 (3): 139–58.

19. Colvin, G., 2000, Beware: You could soon be selling soybeans, *Fortune,* November 13: 80.

20. Straus, M., 2005, Staples courts small business with more value, less Britney, *The Globe and Mail,* February 7: B6.

21. Whalen, C.J., Pascual, A. M., Lowery, T., & Mueller J., 2001, The top 25 managers, *BusinessWeek,* January 8: 63.

22. Bloom, R., 2005, Keg chews up competition even as industry sales drop, *The Globe and Mail,* February 7: B5.

23. Hall, W. K., 1980, Survival strategies in a hostile environment, *Harvard Business Review* 58: 75–87; on the paint and allied products industry, see Dess, G. G., & Davis, P. S., 1984, Porter's (1980) generic strategies as determinants of strategic group membership and organizational performance, *Academy of Management Journal,* 27: 467–88; for the Korean electronics

industry, see Kim., L., & Lim, Y., 1988, Environment, generic strategies, and performance in a rapidly developing country: A taxonomic approach, *Academy of Management Journal,* 31: 802–27; Wright, P., Hotard, D., Kroll, M., Chan, P., & Tanner, J., 1990, Performance and multiple strategies in a firm: Evidence from the apparel industry, in Dean, B. V., & Cassidy, J. C., eds., *Strategic Management: Methods and Studies* (Amsterdam: Elsevier-North Holland), 93–110; and Wright, P., Kroll, M., Tu, H., & Helms, M., 1991, Generic strategies and business performance: An empirical study of the screw machine products industry, *British Journal of Management,* 2: 1–9.

24. Gilmore, J. H., & Pine, B. J., II, 1997, The four faces of customization, *Harvard Business Review,* 75(1): 91–101.

25. Ibid.

26. Goodstein, L. D., & Butz, H. E., 1998, Customer value: The linchpin of organizational change, *Organizational Dynamics,* Summer: 21–34.

27. Randal, T, Terwiesch, C, & Ulrich, K.T., 2005, Principles for user design of custom products, *California Management Review,* 47(4) 68–85.

28. Kiron, D. 2013. From value to vision: Reimagining the possible with data analytics. MIT Sloan Management Review Research Report, Spring: 1–19.

29. Gadiesh, O., & Gilbert, J.L., 1998, Profit pools: A fresh look at strategy, *Harvard Business Review,* 76 (3): 139–58.

30. This example draws on Dess, G. G., & Picken, J. C., 1999, Creating competitive (dis)advantage: Learning from Food Lion's freefall, *Academy of Management Executive,* 13(3): 97–111.

31. Mintzberg et al., op. cit.

32. Rumelt, R., 1980, The evaluation of business strategy, in Glueck, W.F., *Strategic Management and Business Policy,* New York: McGraw-Hill; Hambrick, D.C. & J.W. Fredrickson, 2001, Are you sure you have a strategy? *Academy of Management Executive,* 15(4): 48–59.

33. For an insightful, recent discussion on the difficulties and challenges associated with creating advantages that are sustainable for any reasonable period of time and suggested strategies, refer to: D'Aveni, R. A., Dagnino, G. B. & Smith, K. G. 2010. The age of temporary advantage. *Strategic Management Journal,* 31(13): 1371–1385. This is the lead article in a special issue of this journal that provides many ideas that are useful to both academics and practicing managers. For an additional examination of declining advantage in technologically intensive industries, see: Vaaler, P. M. & McNamara, G. 2010. Are technology-intensive industries more dynamically competitive? No and yes. *Organization Science,* 21: 271–289.

34. Rita McGrath provides some interesting ideas on possible strategies for firms facing highly uncertain competitive environments: McGrath, R. G. 2011. When your business model is in trouble. *Harvard Business Review,* 89(1/2); 96–98.

35. The Atlas Door example draws on: Stalk, G., Jr. 1988. Time—the next source of competitive advantage. *Harvard Business Review,* 66(4): 41–51.

Chapter 6

1. This case draws on 2016, Stantec to Acquire MWH, a Global Professional Services Firm with Leading Expertise in Water Resources Infrastructure,*Stantec Company Webpage,* Mar 29: 1; 2017, Acquisition History, *Stantec Company Webpage:* 1; McCullough, M., 2016, Stantec CEO Bob Gomes on how to merge corporate cultures, *Canadian Business,* Aug 11:1; Morgan, G., 2015, Stantec continues to buy up engineering firms in fractured U.S. market with acquisition of Massachusetts company, *Financial Post,* Aug 27:1.

2. The relationship and divergence of interests between individual shareholders and managers have attracted significant attention

and have yielded many powerful insights through what has been called "agency theory." (Jensen, M., & Meckling, W., 1976, Theory of the firm: Managerial behaviour, agency costs, and ownership structure, *Journal of Financial Economics,* 3: 305–60; Fama, E., 1980, Agency problems and the theory of the firm, *Journal of Political Economy,* 88: 288–307.) Briefly, agency theory considers the reality that frequently, if not always, the interests of managers (i.e., agents) deviate from those of owners/shareholders (i.e., principals). Diversification serves those interests differently. Growth, expansion, and diversification create a larger firm (whether more or less profitable), higher salaries and other forms of compensation, more prestige, more perks, and even less probability of loss of employment for its managers. Whether the owners/shareholders would undertake many of those ventures, given their risk profiles, is questionable; typically, the shareholders do not possess the means or the information to properly assess the merits of each proposed venture nor the time to closely monitor managers, who are better informed about the affairs of the business. Diversification can provide managers with substantial personal benefits while causing declines in shareholders' wealth.

3. Our discussion draws on a variety of sources, including Goold, M., & Campbell, A., 1998, Desperately seeking synergy, *Harvard Business Review,* 76(5): 131–43; Porter, M. E., 1987, From competitive advantage to corporate strategy, *Harvard Business Review,* 65(3): 43–59; and Hitt, M. A., Ireland, R. D., & Hoskission, R. E., 2001, *Strategic Management: Competitiveness and Globalization,* 4th ed. (Cincinnati, OH: South-Western).

4. www.Onex.com; Anonymous, 2011, Onex sells US$66.1 million worth of its shares in Spirit AeroSystems, *The Canadian Press,* April 13; Freeman, S., 2010, Onex Corp. sees investment opportunities in continued bleak economic times, *The Canadian Press,* August 11.

5. Collis, D. J., & Montgomery, C. A., 1987, *Corporate Strategy: Resources and the Scope of the Firm* (New York: McGraw-Hill).

6. This imagery of the corporation as a tree and related discussion draws on Prahalad, C. K., & Hamel, G., 1990, The core competence of the corporation, *Harvard Business Review,* 68(3): 79–91. Parts of this section also draw on Picken, J. C., & Dess, G. G., 1997, *Mission Critical* (Burr Ridge, IL: Irwin Professional Publishing), chap. 5.

7. This section draws on Prahalad & Hamel, op. cit.; and Porter, op. cit.

8. Harley-Davidson, 1993, annual report.

9. Collis, D. J., & Montgomery, C. A., 1998, Creating corporate advantage, *Harvard Business Review,* 76 (3): 70–83.

10. Chesbrough, H. 2011. Bringing open innovation to services. MIT Sloan Management Review, 52(2): 85–90.

11. Henricks, M., 1994, VF seeks global brand dominance, *Apparel Industry Magazine,* August: 21–40; VF Corporation, 1993, 1st quarter, corporate summary report, 1993 VF Annual Report.

12. Lowry, T., 2001, Media, *BusinessWeek,* January 8: 100–1.

13. The Tribune Company, 1999, annual report.

14. Hill, A., & Hargreaves, D., 2001, Turbulent times for GE-Honeywell deal, *Financial Times,* February 28: 26.

15. This discussion draws on Hrebiniak, L. G., & Joyce, W. F., 1984, *Implementing Strategy* (New York: MacMillan); Oster, S. M., 1994, *Modern Competitive Analysis* (New York: Oxford University Press); and Hax, A. C., & Majluf, N. S., 1991, *The Strategy Concept and Process: A Pragmatic Approach* (Englewood Cliffs, NJ: Prentice Hall), 139.

16. Anwar, H., 2005, Diamond firm's results shine with newly acquired retailer, *The Globe and Mail,* March 10: B5.

17. This discussion draws on Oster, S. M., 1994, *Modern Competitive Analysis,* 2nd ed. (New York: Oxford University

Press); and Harrigan, K., 1986, Matching vertical integration strategies to competitive conditions, *Strategic Management Journal,* 7(6): 535–56.

18. Bettis, R. A., Bradley, S. P., & Hamel, G., 1992, Outsourcing and industrial decline, *Academy of Management Executive,* 6(1): 7–22.

19. For a scholarly explanation on how transaction costs determine the boundaries of a firm, see Oliver E. Williamson's pioneering books *Markets and Hierarchies: Analysis and Antitrust Implications* (New York: Free Press, 1975) and *The Economic Institutions of Capitalism* (New York: Free Press, 1985).

20. Campbell, A., Goold, M., & Alexander, M., 1995, Corporate strategy: The quest for parenting advantage, *Harvard Business Review,* 73(2): 120–32; and Picken & Dess, op. cit.

21. Anslinger, P. A., & Copeland, T. E., 1996, Growth through acquisition: A fresh look, *Harvard Business Review,* 74(1): 126–35.

22. Willis, A., 2005, Boeing play will follow Onex's familiar script, *The Globe and Mail,* February 24: B15; and Kalawsky, K., & Kirby, J., 2005, Onex buys Boeing plants for $1.5B, *National Post,* February 23: FP1–FP16; 2011, Onex sells partial stake in Sprit AeroSystems for 7 times cost, April 13, Onex Corp; News Release.

23. This section draws on Porter, op. cit.; and Hambrick, D. C., 1985, Turnaround strategies, in Guth, W. D., ed. *Handbook of Business Strategy* (Boston: Warren, Gorham & Lamont), 10-1–10-32.

24. There is an important difference between companies that are operated for a long-term profit and those that are bought and sold for short-term gains. The latter are sometimes referred to as "holding companies" and are generally more concerned about financial issues than strategic issues.

25. Casico, W. F., 2002, Strategies for responsible restructuring, *Academy of Management Executive,* 16(3): 80–91; and Singh, H., 1993, Challenges in researching corporate restructuring, *Journal of Management Studies,* 30(1): 147–72.

26. Strauss, M., 2008, Shoppers shrugs off recession worries; Drugstore chain posts record profit gains, issues bullish forecast for 2008, *The Globe and Mail,* February 6: B6; Reguly, E., 2007, A peek into the pages of KKR's playbook, *The Globe and Mail,* April 27, B8; www.kkr.com; www.shoppersdrugmart.ca.

27. Hax & Majluf, op. cit. By 1979, 45 percent of Fortune 500 companies employed some form of portfolio analysis, according to Haspelagh, P., 1982, Portfolio planning: Uses and limits, *Harvard Business Review,* 60: 58–73. A later study conducted in 1993 found that over 40 percent of the respondents used portfolio analysis techniques, but the level of usage was expected to increase to more than 60 percent in the near future, according to, Rigby, D. K., 1994, Managing the management tools, *Planning Review,* September–October: 20–24.

28. Goold, M., & Luchs, K., 1993, Why diversify? Four decades of management thinking, *Academy of Management Executive,* 7(3): 7–25.

29. Other approaches include the industry attractiveness–business strength matrix developed jointly by General Electric and McKinsey and Company, the life-cycle matrix developed by Arthur D. Little, and the profitability matrix proposed by Marakon. For an extensive review, refer to Hax & Majluf, op. cit., pp. 182–94.

30. Porter, op. cit., pp. 49–52.

31. Collins, D. J., 1995, Portfolio planning at Ciba-Geigy and the Newport investment proposal, Harvard Business School Case No. 9-795-040. Novartis AG was created in 1996 by the merger of Ciba-Geigy and Sandoz.

32. Buzzell, R. D., & Gale, B. T., 1987, *The PIMS Principles: Linking Strategy to Performance* (New York: Free Press); and

Miller, A., & Dess, G. G., 1996, *Strategic Management,* 2nd ed. (New York: McGraw-Hill).

33. Seeger, J., 1984, Reversing the images of BCG's growth share matrix, *Strategic Management Journal,* 5(1): 93–97.

34. Perkins, T., 2007, CEO urges action on takeover frenzy, *The Globe and Mail,* May 4: B5; Martin, R., & Nixon, G., 2007, Whoa, Canada: More must be done to protect companies from foreign takeovers. The country's place in the word depends on it, *The Globe and Mail,* July 2: B1.

35. Carey, D., moderator, 2000, A CEO roundtable on making mergers succeed, *Harvard Business Review,* 78(3): 146.

36. Shinal, J., 2001, Can Mike Volpi make Cisco sizzle again?, *BusinessWeek,* February 26: 102–4; Kambil, A., Eselius, E. D., & Monteiro, K. A., 2000, Fast venturing: The quick way to start web businesses, *Sloan Management Review,* 41(4): 55–67; and Elstrom, P., 2001, Sorry, Cisco: The old answers won't work, *BusinessWeek,* April 30: 39. https://www.cisco.com/c/en/us/about/corporate-strategy-office/acquisitions/acquisitions-list-years.html and multiple company announcements from www.cisco.com

37. Like many high-tech firms during the economic slump that began in mid-2000, Cisco Systems has experienced declining performance. On April 16, 2001, it announced that its revenues for the quarter closing April 30 would drop 5 percent from a year earlier—and a stunning 30 percent from the previous three months—to about $4.7 billion. Furthermore, Cisco announced that it would lay off 8,500 employees and take an enormous $2.5 billion charge to write down inventory. By late October 2002, its stock was trading at around $10, down significantly from its 52-week high of $70. Elstrom, op. cit., p. 39.

38. Sisario, B. 2014. Jimmy Iovine, a master of Beats, lends Apple a skilled ear. nytimes.com, May 28: np; and Dickey, M. 2014. Meet the executives Apple is paying $3 billion to get. businessinsider.com, May 28: np.

39. Barrett, A., 2001, Drugs, *BusinessWeek,* January 8: 112–13.

40. McArthur, K., 2005, Coors' toughest tasks are only just beginning, *The Globe and Mail,* February 2: B4.

41. Coy, P., Thornton, E., Arndt, M. & Grow, B. 2005, Shake, rattle, and merge. *BusinessWeek,* January 10: 32–35; and, Anonymous, 2005, The rise of the superbrands. *Economist,* February 5: 63–65; and, Sellers, P., 2005, It was a no-brainer. *Fortune,* February 21: 96–102.

42. Muoio, A., ed., 1998, Unit of one, *Fast Company,* September: 82.

43. The discussion draws on Porter, M. E., 1987, From competitive advantage to corporate strategy, *Harvard Business Review* 65(3): 43; Hitt, M.A., Harrison, J. S. & Ireland, R. D., 2001, *Mergers, Acquisitions: A guide to Creating Value for Stakeholders* (New York: Oxford Press); Mankins, M.C., Harding, D., & Weddigne, R-M., 2008, How to best divest, *Harvard Business Review,* 86(1): 92–99.

44. Porter, M. E., 1987, From competitive advantage to corporate strategy. *Harvard Business Review,* 65(3): 43.

45. This section draws on Anard, B. N., & Khanna, T., 2000, Do firms learn to create value?, *Strategic Management Journal,* 12(3): 295–317; Vermeulen, F., & Barkema, H. P., 2001, Learning through acquisitions, *Academy of Management Journal,* 44(3): 457–76; Hutt, M. D., Stafford, E. R., Walker, B. A., & Reingen, P. H., 2000, Case study: Defining the strategic alliance, *Sloan Management Review,* 41(2): 51–62; and Walters, B. A., Peters, S., & Dess, G. G., 1994, Strategic alliances and joint ventures: Making them work, *Business Horizons,* 4: 5–10.

46. Leitch, C., 2005, Master of the impulse-buy attacks investors with strategic purchases, *The Globe and Mail,* February 10: B16.

47. Edmondson, G., & Reinhardt, A., 2001, From niche player to Goliath, *BusinessWeek,* March 12: 94–96.

48. Anonymous, 2006, Magna to work with IBM to create really smart cars, *Toronto Star,* September 14: C2.

49. Anonymous, 2006, Tim Hortons raises C783 million in initial offering, *Bloomberg News,* March 23; company annual reports and www.timhortons.ca.

50. Waldie, P. & Straus, M., 2007, Lululemon supplier navigates rocky shoals, *The Globe and Mail,* November 16: B3.

51. Hoskin, R. E., 1994, *Financial Accounting* (New York: Wiley).

52. We know stock options as derivative assets, i.e., "an asset whose value depends on or is derived from the value of another, the underlying asset." (Amram, M., & Kulatilaka, N., 1999, *Real Options: Managing Strategic Investment in an Uncertain World* [Boston: Harvard Business School Press], 34).

53. de Neufville, R., 2001, Real options: Dealing with uncertainty in systems planning and design, paper presented to the Fifth International Conference on Technology Policy and Innovation at the Technical University of Delft, Delft, Netherlands, June 29.

54. For an interesting discussion on why it is difficult to "kill options," refer to Royer, I., 2003, Why bad projects are so hard to kill, *Harvard Business Review,* 81(2): 48–57.

55. Triantis, A., et al., 2003, University of Maryland roundtable on real options and corporate practice, *Journal of Applied Corporate Finance,* 15(2): 8–23.

56. For a more in-depth discussion of ROA, refer to Copeland, T. E., & Keenan, P. T., 1998, Making real options real, *McKinsey Quarterly,* 3; and Luehrman, T. A., 1998, Strategy as a portfolio of real options, *Harvard Business Review,* September–October.

57. Janney, J. J., Dess, G. G., 2004, Can real options analysis improve decision making? Promises and pitfalls, *Academy of Management Executive,* 18(4): 60–75.

58. Porter, op. cit., pp. 43–59.

59. Editors, 2003, The fallen, *BusinessWeek,* January 13: 80–82.

60. The Jack Welch example draws on Sellers, P., 2001, Get over yourself, *Fortune,* April 30: 76–88.

61. Polek, D., 2002, The rise and fall of Dennis Kozlowski, *BusinessWeek,* December 23: 64–77.

62. DeCloet, D., 2008, The cost of playing backup to Stronach, *The Globe and Mail,* August 12: B1.

63. This section draws on Weston, J. F., Besley, S., & Brigham, E. F., 1996, *Essentials of Managerial Finance,* 11th ed. (Fort Worth, TX: Dryden Press, Harcourt Brace), 18–20; Chakraborty, A., & Baum, C. F., 1998, Poison pills, optimal contracting and the market for corporate control: Evidence from Fortune 500 firms, *International Journal of Finance,* 10(3): 1120–38; Sundramurthy, C., 1996, Corporate governance within the context of antitakeover provisions, *Strategic Management Journal,* 17: 377–94; and Vicente, J. P., 2001, Toxic treatment: Poison pills proliferate as internet firms worry they've become easy marks, *Red Herring,* May 1–15: 195.

64. DeCloet, D., 2005, Ottawa urged to tie Bombardier aid, *The Globe and Mail,* March 18: B1.

65. Porter, M.E.,2008, *On Competition,* Boston: Harvard Business School Press.

Chapter 7

1. This case draws on 2016, Canadian marijuana company Canopy Growth forms Brazilian Partnership, *The Star,* Jun 28:1; 2016, Canopy Growth Brazil Cannabis Venture Progresses, *New Cannabis Ventures,* Nov 23:1; 2016, Canopy Growth Establishes Germany Based Operations Through Acquisition of Licensed Distributor, MedCann GmbH, *Newswire,* Nov 28:1; Freeman, S., 2016, Canopy Growth enters German marijuana market by buying distribution network MedCann, *Financial Post,* Nov 28:1.

2. Our discussion of globalization draws on Engardio, P., & Belton, C., 2000, Global capitalism: Can it be made to work better? *BusinessWeek,* November 6: 72–98.

3. Sellers, P. 2005. Blowing in the wind. *Fortune,* July 25: 63.

4. Ibid.

5. The above discussion was initially based on Clifford, M. L., Engardio, P., Malkin, E., Roberts, D., & Echikson, W., 2000, Up the ladder, *BusinessWeek,* November 6: 78–84; and Unicef's Guatemala at a Glance, retrieved from https://www.unicef.org/infobycountry/guatemala_statistics; www.worldbank.org; and www.hdr.undp.org with updates on population and economic statistics from OECD, World Bank and Unicef.

6. The following discussion draws heavily on Porter, M. E., 1990, The competitive advantage of nations, *Harvard Business Review,* March–April: 73–93.

7. For another interesting discussion on a country perspective, refer to Makino, S., 1999, MITI Minister Kaora Yosano on reviving Japan's competitive advantages, *Academy of Management Executive,* 13(4): 8–28.

8. Landes, D. S., 1998, *The Wealth and Poverty of Nations* (New York: W. W. Norton).

9. Part of our discussion of the motivations and risks of international expansion draws on Gregg, F. M., 1999, International strategy, in Helms, M. M., ed., *Encyclopedia of Management* (Detroit: Gale Group), 434–38.

10. These two examples are discussed, respectively, in Dawar, N., & Frost, T., 1999, Competing with giants: Survival strategies for local companies in emerging markets, *Harvard Business Review,* 77(2): 119–29; and Prahalad, C. K., & Lieberthal, K., 1998, The end of corporate imperialism, *Harvard Business Review,* 76(4): 68–79.

11. This discussion draws on Gupta, A. K., & Govindarajan, V., 2001, Converting global presence into global competitive advantage, *Academy of Management Executive,* 15(2): 45–56.

12. Stross, R. E., 1997, Mr. Gates builds his brain trust, *Fortune,* December 8: 84–98.

13. For a useful summary of the benefits and risks of international expansion, refer to Bartlett, C. A., & Ghoshal, S., 1987, Managing across borders: New strategic responses, *Sloan Management Review* 28(5): 45–53; and Brown, R. H., 1994, *Competing to Win in a Global Economy* (Washington, DC: U.S. Department of Commerce).

14. Capron, L. & Bertrand, O. 2014. Going abroad in search of higher productivity at home. *Harvard Business Review,* 92(6): 26.

15. For an interesting insight into rivalry in global markets, refer to MacMillan, I. C., van Putten, A. B., & McGrath, R. G., 2003, Global gamesmanship, *Harvard Business Review,* 81(5): 62–73.

16. For a discussion of the political risks in China for U.S. companies, refer to Garten, J. E., 1998, Opening the doors for business in China, *Harvard Business Review,* 76(3): 167–75.

17. Shari, M., 2001, Is a holy war brewing in Indonesia?, *BusinessWeek,* October 15: 62.

18. Iosebashvili, I. 2012. Renault-Nissan buy into Russia's aged auto giant. wsj.com, May 3: np.

19. Ferguson, N. 2013. Is the business of America still business? *Harvard Business Review,* 91(6): 40.

20. Gikkas, N. S., 1996, International licensing of intellectual property: The promise and the peril, *Journal of Technology Law & Policy,* 1(1): 1–26.

21. For an excellent theoretical discussion of how cultural factors can affect knowledge transfer across national boundaries, refer to Bhagat, R. S., Kedia, B. L., Harveston, P. D., & Triandis, H. C., 2002, Cultural variations in the cross-border transfer of organizational knowledge: An integrative framework, *Academy of Management Review,* 27(2): 204–21.

22. Berkowitz, E. N., 2000, *Marketing,* 6th ed. (Burr Ridge, IL: McGraw-Hill).

23. Levitt, T., 1983, The globalization of markets, *Harvard Business Review,* 61(3): 92–102.

24. Our discussion of these assumptions draws on Douglas, S. P., & Wind, Y., 1987, The myth of globalization, *Columbia Journal of World Business,* Winter 19–29.

25. Ghoshal, S., 1987, Global strategy: An organizing framework, *Strategic Management Journal,* 8: 425–40.

26. Bartlett, C. A., & Ghoshal, S., 1989, *Managing across Borders: The Transnational Solution* (Boston: Harvard Business School Press).

27. Bartlett, C. A., ibid.; for insights on global branding, refer to Aaker, D. A. & Joachimsthaler, E., 1999, The lure of global branding, *Harvard Business Review,* 77(6): 137–46.

28. For an interesting perspective on how small firms can compete in their home markets, refer to Dawar & Frost, op. cit., pp. 119–29.

29. Hout, T., Porter, M. E., & Rudden, E., 1982, How global companies win out, *Harvard Business Review,* 60(5): 98–107.

30. Fryer, B., 2001, Tom Siebel of Siebel Systems: High tech the old-fashioned way, *Harvard Business Review,* 79(3): 118–30.

31. The risks that are discussed for the global, multidomestic, and transnational strategies draw on Gupta & Govindarajan, op. cit.

32. Sigiura, H., 1990, How Honda localizes its global strategy, *Sloan Management Review,* 31: 77–82.

33. Prahalad & Lieberthal, op. cit., pp. 68–79. Their article also discusses how firms may have to reconsider their brand management, costs of market building, product design, and approaches to capital efficiency when entering foreign markets.

34. Hofstede, G., 1980, *Culture's Consequences: International Differences in Work-Related Values* (Beverly Hills, CA: Sage); Hofstede, G., 1993, Cultural constraints in management theories, *Academy of Management Executive,* 7(1): 81–94; Kogut, B., & Singh, H., 1988, The effect of national culture on the choice of entry mode, *Journal of International Business Studies,* 19: 411–32; and Usinier, J. C., 1996, *Marketing across Cultures* (London: Prentice Hall).

35. This discussion draws on Bartlett, C. A., & Ghoshal, S., 1991, *Managing across Borders: The Transnational Solution* (Boston: Harvard Business School Press); and Raisinghani, M., 2000, Transnational organization, in Helms, M. M., ed., *Encyclopedia of Management,* 4th ed. (Detroit: Gale Group), 968–69.

36. Prahalad, C. K., & Doz, Y. L., 1987, *The Multinational Mission: Balancing Local Demands and Global Vision* (New York: Free Press).

37. Kidd, J. B., & Teramoto, Y., 1995, The learning organization: The case of Japanese RHQs in Europe, *Management International Review,* 35 (Special Issue): 39–56.

38. Gupta, A. K., & Govindarajan, V., 2000, Knowledge flows within multinational corporations, *Strategic Management Journal,* 21(4): 473–96.

39. Wetlaufer, S., 2001, The business case against revolution: An interview with Nestlé 's Peter Brabeck, *Harvard Business Review,* 79(2): 112–21.

40. Nobel, R., & Birkinshaw, J., 1998, Innovation in multinational corporations: Control and communication patterns in international R&D operations, *Strategic Management Journal,* 19(5): 461–78.

41. Chan, C. M., Makino, S., & Isobe, T., 2010, Does subnational region matter? Foreign affiliate performance in the United States and China, *Strategic Management Journal,* 31 (11): 1226–1243.

42. This section draws upon Ghemawat, P., 2005, Regional strategies for global leadership, *Harvard Business Review,* 84(12): 98–108; Ghemawat, P., 2006, Apocalypse now? *Harvard Business Review,* 84 (12): 32; Ghemawat, P., 2001, Distance still matters: The hard reality of global expansion. *Harvard Business Review,* 79(8): 137–147; Peng, M.W., 2006,Global strategy: 387. (Mason, OH: Thomson Southwestern); and Rugman, A. M. & Verbeke, A., 2004, A perspective on regional and global strategies of multinational enterprises, *Journal of International Business Studies,* 35: 3–18.

43. For a rigorous analysis of performance implications of entry strategies, refer to Zahra, S. A., Ireland, R. D., & Hitt, M. A., 2000, International expansion by new venture firms: International diversity, modes of entry, technological learning, and performance, *Academy of Management Journal,* 43(6): 925–50.

44. Li, J. T., 1995, Foreign entry and survival: The effects of strategic choices on performance in international markets, *Strategic Management Journal,* 16: 333–51.

45. For a discussion of how home-country environments can affect diversification strategies, refer to Wan, W. P., & Hoskisson, R. E., 2003, Home country environments, corporate diversification strategies, and firm performance, *Academy of Management Journal,* 46(1): 27–45. For further discussion on entry mode, refer to Sharma, A., 1998, Mode of entry and ex-post performance, *Strategic Management Journal,* 19(9): 879–900.

46. Arnold, D., 2000, Seven rules of international distribution, *Harvard Business Review,* 78(6): 131–37.

47. This section draws on Arnold, op. cit., pp. 131–37; and Berkowitz, op. cit.

48. Kline, D., 2003, Strategic licensing, *MIT Sloan Management Review,* 44(3): 89–93.

49. Arnold, op. cit.; and Berkowitz, op. cit.

50. Martin, J., 1999, Franchising in the Middle East, *Management Review,* June: 38–42. www.franchise.org and www.franchise.org/annualreport2016

51. Manufacturer–supplier relationships can be very effective in global industries, such as automobile manufacturing. Refer to Kotabe, M., Martin, X., & Domoto, H., 2003, Gaining from vertical partnerships: Knowledge transfer, relationship duration, and supplier performance improvement in the U.S. and Japanese automotive industries, *Strategic Management Journal,* 24(4): 293–316.

52. For a useful discussion, refer to Merchant, H., & Schendel, D., 2000, How do international joint ventures create shareholder value?, *Strategic Management Journal,* 21(7): 723–38.

53. This discussion draws on Walters, B. A., Peters, S., & Dess, G. G., 1994, Strategic alliances and joint ventures: Making them work, *Business Horizons,* 37(4): 5–11.

54. For a rigorous discussion of the importance of information access in international joint ventures, refer to Reuer, J. J., & Koza, M. P., 2000, Asymmetric information and joint venture performance: Theory and evidence for domestic and international joint ventures, *Strategic Management Journal,* 21(1): 81–88.

55. Dyer, J. H., Kale, P., & Singh, H., 2001, How to make strategic alliances work, *MIT Sloan Management Review,* 42(4): 37–43.

56. For a discussion of some of the challenges in managing subsidiaries, refer to O'Donnell, S. W., 2000, Managing foreign subsidiaries: Agents of headquarters, or an independent network?, *Strategic Management Journal,* 21(5): 525–48.

57. Won, S., 2005, Edmonton design firm targets spot in global top 10, *The Globe and Mail,* January 8: B4.

58. Lei, D., 2005, Outsourcing, in Hitt, M. A. & Ireland, R. D. (Eds.), *The Blackwell Encyclopedia of Management,* Entrepreneurship: 196–199. (Malden, MA: Blackwell).

59. Future trends in offshoring are addressed in: Manning, S., Massini, S., & Lewin, A. Y, 2008, A dynamic perspective on next-generation offshoring: The global sourcing of science

and engineering talent. *Academy of Management Perspectives,* 22(3): 35–54.

60. An interesting perspective on the controversial issue regarding the offshoring of airplane maintenance is in: Smith, G. & Bachman, J., 2008, Flying in for a tune-up overseas. *BusinessWeek,* April 21: 26–27.

61. Dolan, K.A., 2006. Offshoring the offshorers, *Forbes,* April 17: 74–78.

62. The discussion above draws from Colvin, J., 2004, Think your job can't be sent to India? Just watch. *Fortune,* December 13: 80; Schwartz, N. D., 2004, Down and out in white collar America. *Fortune,* June 23: 321–325; Hagel, J. 2004. Outsourcing is not just about cost cutting. *The Wall Street Journal,* March 18: A3.

63. Insightful perspectives on the outsourcing of decision making are addressed in: Davenport, T. H. & Iyer, B., 2009, Should you outsource your brain? *Harvard Business Review,* 87(2): 38.

Chapter 8

1. This example draws on 2015, Anti-Uber protests around the world, in pictures, *The Telegraph,* 1; Cheney, P., 2016, Why Uber is the best thing to happen to Toronto's taxi industry, *The Globe and Mail,* May 2: 1; Chittley, J., 2015, Taxi industry losing war to Uber because of customer service, not technology, *The Globe and Mail,* Dec 9:1; Husser, A., 2015, Taxis likely hurting themselves, helping Uber with protests: experts, *CBC,* Dec 13:1; Kay, J., 2015, Uber v. Taxi: One must die for the other to live, *The Walrus,* Sept 24:1; Owram, K., 2015, New e-hail app The Ride aims to help cab drivers fight back against Uber, *Financial Post,* Dec 14:1; Rieti, J., 2016, Toronto taxi cab drivers stage morning protest, *CBC,* Aug 17:1; Wutke, S., 2016, Isn't It Time You Got The Ride App?, *Life Safer,* Mar 30:1;

2. For an interesting perspective on the influence of the product life cycle and rate of technological change on competitive strategy, refer to Lei, D. & Slocum, J. W., Jr., 2005, Strategic and organizational requirements for competitive advantage, *Academy of Management Executive,* 19(1): 31–45.

3. Dickson, P. R., 1994, *Marketing Management* (Fort Worth, TX: Dryden Press); Day, G. S., 1981, The product life cycle: Analysis and application, *Journal of Marketing Research,* 45: 60–7.

4. Bearden, W. O., Ingram, T. N., & LaForge, R. W., 1995, *Marketing Principles and Practices* (Burr Ridge, IL: Irwin).

5. MacMillan, I. C., 1985, Preemptive strategies, in Guth, W. D. (Ed.), *Handbook of Business Strategy* (Boston: Warren, Gorham & Lamont), pages 9-1–9-22; Pearce, J. A. & Robinson, R. B., 2000, *Strategic Management* (7th ed.) (New York: McGraw-Hill); Dickson, op. cit.: 295–96.

6. Christensen, C.M., 1997, *The innovator's dilemma: when new technologies cause great firms to fail* (Boston, MA: Harvard Business School Press).

7. Christensen, C.M., Hatkoff, C. & Kula, I., 2013, *Disruptive Innovation Theory Revisited: Toward Quantum Innovation!* Blog post on http://www.innovationexcellence.com/ July 31, 2013.

8. Ibid.

9. Bartlett, C. A. & Ghoshal, S., 2000, Going global: Lessons for late movers, *Harvard Business Review,* 78(2): 132–42.

10. Neuborne, E., 2000, E-tailers hit the relaunch key, *BusinessWeek,* October 17: 62.

11. Berkowitz, E. N., Kerin, R. A., & Hartley, S. W., 2000, *Marketing* (6th ed.) (New York: McGraw-Hill).

12. MacMillan, op. cit.

13. Brooker, K., 2001, A game of inches, *Fortune,* February 5: 98–100.

14. Our discussion of reverse and breakaway positioning draws on Moon, Y., 2005, Break free from the product life cycle, *Harvard*

Business Review, 83(5): 87–94. This article also discusses stealth positioning as a means of overcoming consumer resistance and advancing a product from the introduction to the growth phase.

15. MacMillan, op. cit.

16. Berkowitz et al., op. cit.

17. Bearden et al., op. cit.

18. The discussion of these four strategies draws on MacMillan, op. cit.; Berkowitz et al., op. cit.; and Bearden et al., op. cit.

19. Augustine, N. R., 1997, Reshaping an industry: Lockheed Martin's survival story, *Harvard Business Review,* 75(3): 83–94.

20. Snow, D. C., 2008, Beware of old technologies' last gasps, *Harvard Business Review,* January: 17–18. Lohr, S., 2008, Why old technologies are still kicking, *New York Times,* March 23: n.p.; and McGrath, R. G., 2008, Innovation and the last gaps of dying technologies, ritamcgrath.com, March 18: n.p.

21. A study that draws on the resource-based view of the firm to investigate successful turnaround strategies is: Morrow, J. S., Sirmon, D. G., Hitt, M. A., & Holcomb, T. R., 2007, Creating value in the face of declining performance: firm strategies and organizational recovery. *Strategic Management Journal,* 28(3): 271–84.

22. For a study investigating the relationship between organizational restructuring and acquisition performance, refer to: Barkema, H. G. & Schijven, M., Toward unlocking the full potential of acquisitions: The role of organizational restructuring, *Academy of Management Journal,* 51(4): 696–722.

23. For some useful ideas on effective turnarounds and handling downsizing, refer to Marks, M. S. & De Meuse, K. P., 2005, Resizing the organization: Maximizing the gain while minimizing the pain of layoffs, divestitures and closings, *Organizational Dynamics,* 34(1): 19–36.

24. Hambrick, D. C. & Schecter, S. M., 1983, Turnaround strategies for mature industrial product business units, *Academy of Management Journal,* 26(2): 231–48.

25. Mullaney, T. J., 2002, The wizard of Intuit, *BusinessWeek,* October 28: 60–3.

26. Ghemawat, P., 2001, *Strategy and the Business Landscape* (Upper Saddle River, NJ: Prentice-Hall).

27. Smith, K. G, Ferrier, W.J., & Grimm, C.M., 2001, King of the hill: Dethroning the industry leader, *Academy of Management Executive,* 15(2): 59–70.

28. Kumar, N., 2006, Strategies to fight low-cost rivals, *Harvard Business Review,* December: 104–12.

29. Grove, A., 1999, *Only the paranoid survive: How to Exploit the Crises Points that Challenge Every Company* (New York: Random House).

30. Stalk, Jr., G. & Lachenauer, R., 2004, *Hardball: Are You Playing to Play or Playing to Win?* (Cambridge, MA: Harvard Business School Press).

31. Peteraf, M. A. & Bergen, M. A., 2003, Scanning competitive landscapes: A market-based and resource-based framework, *Strategic Management Journal,* 24: 1027–45.

32. Wingfield, N., 2007, Boss Talk: Netflix vs. Naysayers — CEO Hastings Keeps Growth Strong; Plans for Future after Death of DVDs, *The Wall Street Journal,* http://www.classroomedition.com/monday/mx_07apr02%.pdf.

33. Chen, M. J., 1996, Competitor analysis and interfirm rivalry: Toward a theoretical integration, *Academy of Management Review,* 21(1): 100–34.

34. Chen, 1996, op.cit.

35. Chen, M. J., Su, K. H, & Tsai, W., 2007, Competitive tension: The awareness-motivation-capability perspective, *Academy of Management Journal,* 50(1): 101–18.

36. St. John, W., 1999, Barnes & Noble's Epiphany, *Wired,* www.wired.com, June.

37. Kumar, 2006, op. cit.

38. Chen, M. J. & Hambrick, D., 1995, Speed, stealth, and selective attack: How small firms differ from large firms in competitive behavior, *Academy of Management Journal,* 38: 453–82.

39. Lyons, D., 2006, The cheap revolution, *Forbes,* September 18: 102–11.

40. For a discussion of how the strategic actions of Apple Computer contribute to changes in the competitive dynamics in both the cellular phone and music industries, see Burgelman, R. A. & Grove, A. S., 2008, Cross-boundary disruptors: Powerful interindustry entrepreneurial change agents, *Strategic Entrepreneurship Journal,* 1(1): 315–27.

41. Smith, K. G., Ferrier, W. J., & Ndofor, H., 2001, Competitive dynamics research: Critique and future directions, in M. A. Hitt, R. E. Freeman, & J. S. Harrison (Eds.), *The Blackwell Handbook of Strategic Management* (Oxford, UK: Blackwell), pp. 315–61.

42. Gee, P., 2000, Co-opetition: The new market milieu, *Journal of Healthcare Management,* 45: 359–63.

43. Ketchen, D. J., Snow, C. C., & Hoover, V. L., 2004, Research on competitive dynamics: Recent accomplishments and future challenges, *Journal of Management,* 30(6): 779–804.

44. Khanna, T., Gulati, R., & Nohria, N., 2000, The economic modeling of strategy process: Clean models and dirty hands, *Strategic Management Journal,* 21: 781–90.

Chapter 9

1. This case draws from 2016, Netflix how has more than 5.2 million customers in Canada, report suggests, *CBC,* Jun 15:1; Friend, D., 2015, Bell Media's plans to cut 380 jobs in Toronto, Montreal will hit local news hard: union, *Financial Post,* Nov 6:1; Jackson, E., 2017, Bell Media cites CRTC Super Bowl ad policy as a factor in latest round of layoffs, *Financial Post,* Jan 31:1; Krashinsky Robertson, S., 2017, Bell will fight CRTC ad policy after Super Bowl ratings drop, *The Globe and Mail,* Feb 6:1; O'Brien, G., 2017, Update #4: Bell Media restructuring again, cutting local TV, radio positions, *Cartt,* Jan 30:1.

2. This introductory discussion draws upon Hall, R. H., 2002, *Organizations: Structures, processes, and outcomes* (8th ed.). (Upper Saddle River, NJ: Prentice Hall); and Duncan, R. E., 1979, What is the right organization structure? Decision-tree analysis provides the right answer, *Organizational Dynamics,* 7(3): 59–80. For an insightful discussion of strategy-structure relationships in the organization theory and strategic management literatures, refer to Keats, B. & O'Neill, H. M., 2001, Organization structure: Looking through a strategy lens, in Hitt, M. A., Freeman, R. E., & Harrison, J. S., 2001, *The Blackwell Handbook of Strategic Management,* (Malden, MA: Blackwell), 520–42.

3. An interesting discussion on the role of organizational design in strategy execution is in: Neilson, G. L., Martin, K. L., & Powers, E., 2009, The secrets to successful strategy execution, *Harvard Business Review,* 87(2): 60–70.

4. This discussion draws upon Chandler, A. D., 1962, *Strategy and Structure* (Cambridge, MA: MIT Press); Galbraith J. R. & Kazanjian, R. K., 1986, *Strategy Implementation: The Role of Structure and Process* (St. Paul, MN: West Publishing); and Scott, B. R., 1971, *Stages of Corporate Development,* Intercollegiate Case Clearing House, 9-371-294, BP 998, Harvard Business School.

5. Our discussion of the different types of organizational structures draws on a variety of sources, including Galbraith & Kazanjian, op. cit.; Hrebiniak, L. G. & Joyce, W. F., 1984, *Implementing Strategy* (New York: Macmillan); Distelzweig, H., 2000, Organizational structure, in Helms, M. M. (Ed.). *Encyclopedia of Management* (Farmington Hills, MI: Gale), 692–699; and

Dess, G. G. & Miller, A., 1993, *Strategic Management* (New York: McGraw-Hill).

6. A discussion of an innovative organizational design is in: Garvin, D. A. & Levesque, L. C., 2009, The multiunit enterprise, *Harvard Business Review,* 87(2): 106–17.

7. Schein, E. H., 1996, Three cultures of management: The key to organizational learning, *Sloan Management Review,* 38(1): 9–20.

8. Insights on governance implications for multidivisional forms are in: Verbeke, A. & Kenworthy, T. P., 2008, Multidivisional vs. metanational governance, *Journal of International Business,* 39(6): 940–56.

9. For a discussion of performance implications, refer to Hoskisson, R. E., 1987, Multidivisional structure and performance: The contingency of diversification strategy, *Academy of Management Journal,* 29: 625–44.

10. For a thorough and seminal discussion of the evolution toward the divisional form of organizational structure in the United States, refer to Chandler, op. cit. A rigorous empirical study of the strategy and structure relationship is found in Rumelt, R. P., 1974, *Strategy, Structure, and Economic Performance* (Cambridge, MA: Harvard Business School Press).

11. Ghoshal, S. & Bartlett, C. A., 1995, Changing the role of management: Beyond structure to processes, *Harvard Business Review,* 73(1): 88.

12. Koppel, B., 2000, Synergy in ketchup?, *Forbes,* February 7: 68–69; and Hitt, M. A., Ireland, R. D., & Hoskisson, R. E., 2001, *Strategic Management: Competitiveness and Globalization* (4th ed.) (Cincinnati, OH: Southwestern Publishing).

13. Pitts, R. A., 1977, Strategies and structures for diversification, *Academy of Management Journal,* 20(2): 197–208.

14. Dell, M. & Rollins, K., 2005, Execution without excuses, *Harvard Business Review,* 83(3): 102–11.

15. Daniels, J. D., Pitts, R. A., & Tretter, M. J., 1984, Strategy and structure of U.S. multinationals: An exploratory study, *Academy of Management Journal,* 27(2): 292–307.

16. Habib, M. M. & Victor, B., 1991, Strategy, structure, and performance of U.S. manufacturing and service MNCs: A comparative analysis. *Strategic Management Journal,* 12(8): 589–606.

17. Our discussion of global start-ups draws from Oviatt, B. M. & McDougall, P. P., 2005, The internationalization of entrepreneurship. *Journal of International Business Studies,* 36(1): 2–8; Oviatt, B. M. & McDougall, P. P., 1994, Toward a theory of international new ventures. *Journal of International Business Studies,* 25(1): 45–64; and Oviatt, B. M. & McDougall, P. P., 1995, Global start-ups: Entrepreneurs on a worldwide stage, *Academy of Management Executive,* 9(2): 30–43.

18. Some useful guidelines for global start-ups are provided in Kuemmerle, W., 2005, The entrepreneur's path for global expansion, *MIT Sloan Management Review,* 46(2): 42–50.

19. See, for example, Miller, D. & Friesen, P. H., 1980, Momentum and revolution in organizational structure, *Administrative Science Quarterly,* 13: 65–91.

20. Many authors have argued that a firm's structure can influence its strategy and performance. These include Amburgey, T. L. & Dacin, T., 1995, As the left foot follows the right? The dynamics of strategic and structural change, *Academy of Management Journal,* 37: 1427–52; Dawn, K. & Amburgey, T. L., 1991, Organizational inertia and momentum: A dynamic model of strategic change. *Academy of Management Journal,* 34: 591–612; Fredrickson, J. W., 1986, The strategic decision process and organization structure, *Academy of Management Review* 11: 280–97; Hall, D. J. & Saias, M. A., 1980, Strategy follows structure!, *Strategic Management Journal,* 1: 149–64; and Burgelman, R. A., 1983, A model of the interaction of strategic behavior, corporate context, and

the concept of strategy, *Academy of Management Review,* 8: 61–70.

21. This discussion of generic strategies and their relationship to organizational control draws upon Porter, M. E.1980. *Competitive strategy* (New York: Free Press); and Miller, D., 1988, Relating Porter's business strategies to environment and structure: Analysis and performance implications. *Academy of Management Journal,* 31(2): 280–308.

22. Rodengen, J. L., 1997, *The Legend of Nucor Corporation* (Fort Lauderdale, FL: Write Stuff Enterprises).

23. The 3M example draws upon: Blueprints for service quality, 1994, New York: American Management Association; personal communication with Katerine Hagmeier, program manager, external communications, 3M Corporation, March 26, 1998; Lei, D., Slocum, J. W., & Pitts, R. A., 1999, Designing organizations for competitive advantage: The power of unlearning and learning. *Organizational Dynamics,* 27(3): 24–38; and Graham, A. B. & Pizzo, V. G., 1996, A question of balance: Case studies in strategic knowledge management. *European Management Journal,* 14(4): 338–46.

24. The Sharp Corporation and Hanson plc examples are based on Collis, D. J. & Montgomery, C. A., 1998, Creating corporate advantage, *Harvard Business Review,* 76(3): 70–83.

25. Kunii, I., 2002, Japanese companies' survival skills, *BusinessWeek,* November 18: 18.

26. White, G., 1988, How I turned $3,000 into $10 billion, *Fortune,* November 7: 80–9. After the death of the founders, the Hanson plc conglomerate was found to be too unwieldy and was broken up into several separate, publicly traded corporations. For more on its more limited current scope of operations, see www.hansonplc.com.

27. An interesting discussion on how the Internet has affected the boundaries of firms can be found in Afuah, A., 2003, Redefining firm boundaries in the face of the Internet: Are firms really shrinking?, *Academy of Management Review,* 28(1): 34–53.

28. Collis & Montgomery, op. cit.

29. For a discussion of the role of coaching on developing high performance teams, refer to Kets de Vries, M. F. R., 2005, Leadership group coaching in action: The zen of creating high performance teams, *Academy of Management Executive,* 19(1): 77–89.

30. Pfeffer, J., 1998, *The Human Equation: Building Profits by Putting People First* (Cambridge, MA: Harvard Business School Press).

31. For a discussion on how functional area diversity affects performance, see Bunderson, J. S. & Sutcliffe, K. M., 2002, *Academy of Management Journal,* 45(5): 875–93.

32. Groth, A. 2015. Holacracy at Zappos: It's either the future of management or a social experiment gone awry. qz.com, January 14: np; Anonymous. 2014. The holes in holacracy. economist.com, July 5: np; and Van De Kamp, P. 2014. Holacracy—A radical approach to organizational design. medium.com, August 2: np.

33. See, for example, Hoskisson, R. E., Hill, C. W. L., & Kim, H., 1993, The multidivisional structure: Organizational fossil or source of value?, *Journal of Management,* 19(2): 269–98.

34. Pottruck, D. A., 1997, Speech delivered by the co-CEO of Charles Schwab Co., Inc., to the Retail Leadership Meeting, San Francisco, CA, January 30; and Miller, W., 1999, Building the ultimate resource, *Management Review,* January: 42–5.

35. Public-private partnerships are addressed in: Engardio, P., 2009, State capitalism, *BusinessWeek,* February 9: 38–43.

36. Magretta, J., 1998, The power of virtual integration: An interview with Dell Computer's Michael Dell, *Harvard Business Review,* 76(2): 75.

37. Forster, J., 2001, Networking for cash, *BusinessWeek,* January 8: 129.

38. Dess, G. G., Rasheed, A. M. A., McLaughlin, K. J., & Priem, R., 1995, The new corporate architecture. *Academy of Management Executive,* 9(3): 7–20.

39. Barnes, C., 1998, A fatal case. *Fast Company,* February–March: 173.

40. Handy, C., 1989, *The Age of Unreason* (Boston: Harvard Business School Press); Ramstead, E., 1997, APC maker's low-tech formula: Start with the box. *The Wall Street Journal,* December 29: B1; Mussberg, W., 1997, Thin screen PCs are looking good but still fall flat. *The Wall Street Journal,* January 2: 9; Brown, E., 1997, Monorail: Low cost PCs. *Fortune,* July 7: 106–08; and Young, M., 1996, Ex-Compaq executives start new company. *Computer Reseller News,* November 11: 181.

41. An original discussion on how open-sourcing could help the Big 3 automobile companies is in: Jarvis, J., 2009, How the Google model could help Detroit, *BusinessWeek,* February 9: 32–6.

42. For a discussion of some of the downsides of outsourcing, refer to Rossetti, C. & Choi, T. Y., 2005, On the dark side of strategic sourcing: Experiences from the aerospace industry, *Academy of Management Executive,* 19(1): 46–60.

43. Tully, S., 1993, The modular corporation, *Fortune,* February 8: 196.

44. Offshoring in manufacturing firms is addressed in: Coucke, K., & Sleuwaegen, L., 2008, Offshoring as a survival strategy: Evidence from manufacturing firms in Belgium, *Journal of International Business Studies,* 39(8): 1261–77.

45. Quinn, J. B., 1992, *Intelligent Enterprise: A Knowledge and Service Based Paradigm for Industry* (New York: Free Press).

46. For an insightful perspective on outsourcing and its role in developing capabilities, read Gottfredson, M., Puryear, R., & Phillips, C., 2005, Strategic sourcing: From periphery to the core, *Harvard Business Review,* 83(4): 132–9.

47. This discussion draws upon Quinn, J. B., & Hilmer, F. C., 1994, Strategic outsourcing, *Sloan Management Review,* 35(4): 43–55.

48. Insights on outsourcing and private branding can be found in: Cehn, S-F. S., 2009, A transaction cost rationale for private branding and its implications for the choice of domestic vs. offshore outsourcing, *Journal of International Business Strategy,* 40(1): 156–75.

49. For an insightful perspective on the use of outsourcing for decision analysis, read: Davenport, T. H. & Iyer, B., 2009, Should you outsource your brain?, *Harvard Business Review,* 87(2): 38.

50. See also Stuckey, J. & White, D., 1993, When and when not to vertically integrate, *Sloan Management Review,* Spring: 71–81; Harrar, G., 1993, Outsource tales, *Forbes ASAP,* June 7: 37–39, 42; and Davis, E. W., 1992, Global outsourcing: Have U.S. managers thrown the baby out with the bath water?, *Business Horizons,* July–August: 58–64.

51. For a discussion of knowledge creation through alliances, refer to Inkpen, A. C., 1996, Creating knowledge through collaboration, *California Management Review,* 39(1): 123–40; and Mowery, D. C., Oxley, J. E., & Silverman, B. S., 1996, Strategic alliances and interfirm knowledge transfer. *Strategic Management Journal,* 17 (Special Issue, Winter): 77–92.

52. Doz, Y. & Hamel, G., 1998, *Alliance Advantage: The Art of Creating Value through Partnering* (Boston: Harvard Business School Press).

53. DeSanctis, G., Glass, J. T., & Ensing, I. M., 2002, Organizational designs for R&D, *Academy of Management Executive,* 16(3): 55–66.

54. Barringer, B. R., & Harrison, J. S., 2000, Walking a tightrope: Creating value through interorganizational alliances, *Journal of Management,* 26: 367–403.

55. Davis, E., 1997, Interview: Norman Augustine, *Management Review,* November: 14.

56. One contemporary example of virtual organizations is R&D consortia. For an insightful discussion, refer to Sakaibara, M., 2002, Formation of R&D consortia: Industry and company effects, *Strategic Management Journal*, 23(11): 1033–50.

57. Bartness, A. & Cerny, K., 1993, Building competitive advantage through a global network of capabilities, *California Management Review*, Winter: 78–103. For an insightful historical discussion of the usefulness of alliances in the computer industry, see Moore, J. F., 1993, Predators and prey: A new ecology of competition, *Harvard Business Review*, 71(3): 75–86.

58. See Lorange, P. & Roos, J., 1991, Why some strategic alliances succeed and others fail, *Journal of Business Strategy*, January–February: 25–30; and Slowinski, G., 1992., The human touch in strategic alliances, *Mergers and Acquisitions*, July–August: 44–47. A compelling argument for strategic alliances is provided by Ohmae, K., 1989, The global logic of strategic alliances, *Harvard Business Review*, 67(2): 143–154.

59. Some of the downsides of alliances are discussed in Das, T. K., & Teng, B. S., 2000, Instabilities of strategic alliances: An internal tensions perspective, *Organization Science*, 11: 77–106.

60. This section draws upon Dess, G. G. & Picken, J. C., 1997, *Mission Critical* (Burr Ridge, IL: Irwin Professional Publishing).

61. Katzenbach, J. R. & Smith, D. K., 1994, *The Wisdom of Teams: Creating the High Performance Organization* (New York: Harper Business).

62. Hammer, M. & Champy, J., 1993, *Reengineering the Corporation: A Manifesto for Business Revolution* (New York: HarperCollins).

63. This section draws on Birkinshaw, J. & Gibson, C., 2004, Building ambidexterity into an organization. *MIT Sloan Management Review*, 45(4): 47–55; and Gibson, C. B. & Birkinshaw, J., 2004, The antecedents, consequences, and mediating role of organizational ambidexterity. *Academy of Management Journal*, 47(2): 209–26. Robert Duncan is generally credited with being the first to coin the term "ambidextrous organizations" in his article entitled: Designing dual structures for innovation. In Kilmann, R. H., Pondy, L. R., & Slevin, D. (Eds.), 1976, *The Management of Organizations*, vol. 1: 167–88. For a seminal academic discussion of the concept of exploration and exploitation, which parallels adaptation and alignment, refer to: March, J. G., 1991, Exploration and exploitation in organizational learning. *Organization Science*, 2: 71–86.

64. This section is based on O'Reilly, C. A. & Tushman, M. L., 2004, The ambidextrous organization, *Harvard Business Review*, 82(4): 74–81.

Chapter 10

1. This case draws on 2017, TD Bank reviewing sales practices, CEO Bharat Masrani tells AGM, *CBC*, Mar 30:1; Israel, S., 2017, Controversial TD tactics show need for consumer code, says advocacy group, *CBC*, Mar 14:1; Johnson, E., 2017, 'I will do anything I can to make my goal': TD teller says customers pay price for 'unrealistic' sales targets, *CBC*, Mar 6:1; Johnson, E., 2017, 'We do it because our jobs are at stake': TD Bank employees admit to breaking the law for fear of being fired, *CBC*, Mar 10:1.

2. This chapter draws upon Picken, J. C. & Dess, G. G., 1997, *Mission Critical* (Burr Ridge, IL: Irwin Professional Publishing); Simons, R., 1994, How new top managers use control systems as levers of strategic renewal, *Strategic Management Journal*, 15: 169–89; and Simons, R., 1995, Control in an age of empowerment, *Harvard Business Review*, 73: 80–88.

3. Argyris, C., 1977, Double-loop learning in organizations, *Harvard Business Review*, 55: 115–25.

4. Good, M., & Quinn, J. B., 1990, The paradox of strategic controls, *Strategic Management Journal*, 11 (1): 43–57.

5. Mintzberg, H., 1987, Crafting strategy, *Harvard Business Review*, 65(4): 66–75.

6. Quinn, J. B., 1980, *Strategies for Change* (Homewood, IL: Richard D. Irwin).

7. Weston, J. S., 1992, Soft stuff matters, *Financial Executive*, July–August: 52–3.

8. Argyris, C., 1977, Double-loop learning in organizations, *Harvard Business Review*, 55: 115–25.

9. This discussion of control systems draws upon Simons, op. cit.

10. For an interesting perspective on this issue and how a downturn in the economy can reduce the tendency toward "free agency" by managers and professionals, refer to Morris, B., 2001, White collar blues, *Fortune*, July 23: 98–110.

11. For a colourful example of behavioural control in an organization, see: Beller, P. C., 2009, Activision's unlikely hero, *Forbes*, February 2: 52–8.

12. Ouchi, W., 1981, *Theory Z* (Reading, MA: Addison-Wesley); Deal, T. E. & Kennedy, A. A., 1982, *Corporate Cultures* (Reading, MA: Addison-Wesley); Peters, T. J. & Waterman, R. H., 1982, *In Search of Excellence* (New York: Random House); Collins, J., 2001, *Good to Great* (New York: HarperCollins).

13. Collins, J. C. & Porras, J. I., 1994, *Built to Last: Successful Habits of Visionary Companies* (New York: Harper Business).

14. Lee, J. & Miller, D., 1999, People matter: Commitment to employees, strategy, and performance in Korean firms, *Strategic Management Journal*, 6: 579–94.

15. For an insightful discussion of IKEA's unique culture, see Kling, K. & Goteman, I., 2003, IKEA CEO Anders Dahlvig on international growth and IKEA's unique corporate culture and brand identity, *Academy of Management Executive*, 17(1): 31–7.

16. Watkins, M. 2013. What Is Organizational Culture? And Why Should We Care? *Harvard Business Review Blog Network*, posted on May 15.

17. For a discussion of how professionals inculcate values, refer to Uhl-Bien, M. & Graen, G. B., 1998, Individual self-management: Analysis of professionals' self-managing activities in functional and cross-functional work teams, *Academy of Management Journal*, 41(3): 340–50.

18. A perspective on how antisocial behaviour can erode a firm's culture can be found in Robinson, S. L. & O'Leary-Kelly, A. M. 1998. Monkey see, monkey do: The influence of work groups on the antisocial behavior of employees. *Academy of Management Journal*, 41(6): 658–72.

19. An interesting perspective on organization culture is in: Mehta, S. N., 2009, Under Armour reboots, *Fortune*, February 2: 29–33.

20. For insights on social pressure as a means for control, refer to: Goldstein, N. J., 2009, Harnessing social pressure, *Harvard Business Review*, 87(2): 25.

21. Mitchell, R., 1989, Masters of innovation, *BusinessWeek*, April 10: 58–63.

22. Sellers, P., 1993, Companies that serve you best, *Fortune*, May 31: 88.

23. Southwest Airlines Culture Committee, 1993, *Luv Lines* (company publication), March–April: 17–8; for an interesting perspective on the "downside" of strong "cultlike" organizational cultures, refer to Arnott, D. A., 2000, *Corporate Cults*, New York: AMACOM.

24. Kerr, J. & Slocum, J. W., Jr., 1987, Managing corporate culture through reward systems, *Academy of Management Executive*, 1(2): 99–107.

25. For a unique perspective on leader challenges in managing wealthy professionals, refer to Wetlaufer, S., 2000, Who wants to manage a millionaire?, *Harvard Business Review*, 78(4): 53–60.

26. These next two subsections draw upon Dess, G. G. & Picken, J. C., 1997, *Beyond Productivity* (New York: AMACOM).

27. For a discussion of the benefits of stock options as executive compensation, refer to Hall, B. J., 2000, What you need to know about stock options, *Harvard Business Review,* 78(2): 121–9.

28. Tully, S., 1993, Your paycheck gets exciting, *Fortune,* November 13: 89.

29. Zellner, W., Hof, R. D., Brandt, R., Baker, S., & Greising, D., 1995, Go-go goliaths. *BusinessWeek,* February 13: 64–70.

30. Sirota, D., Mischkind, L. & Meltzer, I. 2008. Stop demotivating your employees! Harvard Management Update, July: 3–5; Nelson, B. 2003. Five questions about employee recognition and reward. Harvard Management Update; Birkinshaw, J., Bouquet, C., & Barsaoux, J. 2011. The 5 myths of innovation. MIT Sloan Management Review. Winter, 43–50; and Dewhurst, M. Guthridge, M., & Mohr, E. 2009. Motivating people: Getting beyond money. mckinsey.com. November: np

31. This section draws on Ho, V. T., Wong, S. S., & Lee, C. H. 2011. A tale of passion: Linking job passion and cognitive engagement to employee work performance. Journal of Management Studies, 48(1): 26–47

32. This section draws on Dess & Picken, op. cit.: chap. 5.

33. Simons, op. cit.

34. Davis, E., 1997, Interview: Norman Augustine, *Management Review,* November: 11.

35. This section draws upon Dess, G. G. & Miller, A., 1993, *Strategic Management* (New York: McGraw-Hill).

36. For a useful review of the goal-setting literature, refer to Locke, E. A. & Latham, G. P., 1990, *A Theory of Goal Setting and Task Performance* (Englewood Cliffs, NJ: Prentice Hall).

37. For an interesting perspective on the use of rules and regulations that is counter to this industry's (software) norms, refer to Fryer, B., 2001, Tom Siebel of Siebel Systems: High tech the old fashioned way, *Harvard Business Review,* 79(3): 118–30.

38. Thompson, A. A., Jr. & Strickland, A. J., III., 1998, *Strategic Management: Concepts and Cases,* 10th ed. (New York: McGraw-Hill), p. 313.

39. Ibid.

40. Teitelbaum, R., 1997, Tough guys finish first, *Fortune,* July 21: 82–4.

41. Weaver, G. R., Trevino, L. K., & Cochran, P. L., 1999, Corporate ethics programs as control systems: Influences of executive commitment and environmental factors, *Academy of Management Journal,* 42 (1): 41–57.

42. Cadbury, S. A., 1987, Ethical managers make their own rules, *Harvard Business Review,* 65: 3, 69–73.

43. William Ouchi has written extensively about the use of clan control (which is viewed as an alternate to bureaucratic or market control). Here, a powerful culture results in people aligning their individual interests with those of the firm. Refer to Ouchi, op. cit. This section also draws on Hall, R. H., 2002, *Organizations: Structures, Processes, and Outcomes,* 8th ed. (Upper Saddle River, NJ: Prentice Hall).

44. Lieber, R., 1996, "Wired for Hiring: Microsoft's Slick Recruiting Machine," *Fortune,* http://money.cnn.com/magazines/fortune/fortune_archive/1996/02/05/207333/index.htm.

45. Interesting insights on corporate governance are in: Kroll, M., Walters, B. A., & Wright, P., 2008, Board vigilance, director experience, and corporate outcomes, *Strategic Management Journal,* 29(4): 363–82.

46. Management cannot ignore the demands of other important firm stakeholders, such as creditors, suppliers, customers, employees, and government regulators. At times of financial duress, powerful creditors can exert strong and legitimate pressures on managerial decisions. In general, however, the attention to stakeholders other than the owners of the corporation must be addressed in a manner that is still consistent with maximizing long-term shareholder returns. For a seminal discussion on stakeholder management, refer to Freeman, R. E. 1984. *Strategic Management: A Stakeholder Approach* (Boston: Pitman). For a brief review of some central issues in corporate governance research, see: Hambrick, D. C., Werder, A. V., & Zajac, E. J., 2008, New directions in corporate governance research, *Organization Science,* 19(3): 381–5.

47. Monks, R. & Minow, N., 2001, *Corporate Governance,* 2nd ed. (Malden, MA: Blackwell).

48. Pound, J. 1995, The promise of the governed corporation, *Harvard Business Review,* 73(2): 89–98.

49. Maurer, H. & Linblad, C., 2009, Scandal at Satyam, *BusinessWeek,* January 19: 8; Scheck, J. & Stecklow, S., 2008, Brocade ex-CEO gets 21 months in prison, *The Wall Street Journal,* January 17: A3; Heinzl, M., 2004, Nortel's directors and investors discuss changes to the board, *The Wall Street Journal,* September 30: B4; Editorial, 2003, Pulling Boeing out of a tailspin, *BusinessWeek,* December 15: 136; and Zimmerman, A., Ball, D., & Veen, M., 2003, A global journal report: Supermarket giant Ahoud ousts CEO in big accounting scandal, *The Wall Street Journal,* February 25: A1; Ibid; and Maurer, H., 2006, Is this "the HP way"?, *BusinessWeek,* September 25: 34.

50. Corporate governance and social networks are discussed in: McDonald, M.L., Khanna, P., & Westphal, J.D., 2008, *Academy of Management Journal,* 51(3): 453–75.

51. This discussion draws on Monks & Minow, op. cit.

52. For an interesting perspective on the politicization of the corporation, read: Palazzo, G. & Scherer, A. G., 2008, Corporate social responsibility, democracy, and the politicization of the corporation, *Academy of Management Review,* 33(3): 773–4.

53. Eisenhardt, K. M., 1989, Agency theory: An assessment and review, *Academy of Management Review,* 14(1): 57–74. Some of the seminal contributions to agency theory include Jensen, M. & Meckling, W., 1976, Theory of the firm: Managerial behavior, agency costs, and ownership structure, *Journal of Financial Economics,* 3: 305–60; Fama, E. & Jensen, M., 1983, Separation of ownership and control, *Journal of Law and Economics,* 26: 301, 325; and Fama, E., 1980, Agency problems and the theory of the firm, *Journal of Political Economy,* 88: 288–307.

54. Managers may also engage in "shirking"—that is, reducing or withholding their efforts. See, for example, Kidwell, R. E., Jr. & Bennett, N., 1993, Employee propensity to withhold effort: A conceptual model to intersect three avenues of research, *Academy of Management Review,* 18(3): 429–56.

55. For an interesting perspective on agency and clarification of many related concepts and terms, visit the following website: www.encycogov.com.

56. The relationship between corporate ownership structure and export intensity in Chinese firms is discussed in: Filatotchev, I., Stephan, J., & Jindra, B., 2008, Ownership structure, strategic controls and export intensity of foreign-invested firms in transition economies, *Journal of International Business,* 39 (7): 1133–48.

57. Argawal, A. & Mandelker, G., 1987, Managerial incentives and corporate investment and financing decisions, *Journal of Finance,* 42: 823–37.

58. For an insightful, recent discussion of the academic research on corporate governance, and in particular the role of boards of directors, refer to Chatterjee, S. & Harrison, J. S., 2001, Corporate governance, in Hitt, M. A., Freeman, R. E., & Harrison, J. S. (Eds.), *Handbook of Strategic Management* (Malden, MA: Blackwell), pp. 543–63.

59. For an interesting theoretical discussion on corporate governance in Russia, see: McCarthy, D. J. & Puffer, S. M.,

2008, Interpreting the ethicality of corporate governance decisions in Russia: Utilizing integrative social contracts theory to evaluate the relevance of agency theory norms, *Academy of Management Review,* 33(1): 11–31.

60. This opening discussion draws on Monks & Minow, op. cit. 164, 169; see also Pound, op. cit.

61. Business Roundtable, 1990, *Corporate governance and American competitiveness,* March: 7.

62. The director role in acquisition performance is addressed in: Westphal, J. D. & Graebner, M. E., 2008, What do they know? The effects of outside director acquisition experience on firm acquisition performance, *Strategic Management Journal,* 29(11): 1155–78.

63. Byrne, J. A., Grover, R., & Melcher, R. A., 1997, The best and worst boards, *BusinessWeek,* November 26: 35–47. The three key roles of boards of directors are monitoring the actions of executives, providing advice, and providing links to the external environment to provide resources. See Johnson, J. L., Daily, C. M., & Ellstrand, A. E., 1996, Boards of directors: A review and research agenda, *Academy of Management Review,* 37: 409–38.

64. The role of outside directors is discussed in: Lester, R. H., Hillman, A., Zardkoohi, A., & Cannella, A. A., Jr., 2008, Former government officials as outside directors: The role of human and social capital, *Academy of Management Journa,* 51(5): 999–1013.

65. McGeehan, P., 2003, More chief executives shown the door, study says, *New York Times,* May 12: C2.

66. Gerdes, L., 2007, Hello, goodbye, *BusinessWeek,* January 22: 16.

67. For an analysis of the effects of outside directors' compensation on acquisition decisions, refer to Deutsch, T., Keil, T., & Laamanen, T., 2007, Decision making in acquisitions: The effect of outside directors' compensation on acquisition patterns, *Journal of Management,* 33(1): 30–56.

68. Director interlocks are addressed in: Kang, E., 2008, Director interlocks and spillover effects of reputational penalties from financial reporting fraud, *Academy of Management Journal,* 51(3): 537–56.

69. There are benefits, of course, to having some insiders on the board of directors. Inside directors would be more aware of the firm's strategies. Additionally, outsiders may rely too often on financial performance indicators because of information asymmetries. For an interesting discussion, see Baysinger, B. D. & Hoskisson, R. E., 1990, The composition of boards of directors and strategic control: Effects on corporate strategy, *Academy of Management Review,* 15: 72–87.

70. Hambrick, D. C. & Jackson, E. M., 2000, Outside directors with a stake: The linchpin in improving governance. *California Management Review,* 42(4): 108–27.

71. Ibid.

72. Disney has begun to make many changes to improve its corporate governance, such as assigning only independent directors to important board committees, restricting directors from serving on more than three boards, and appointing a lead director who can convene the board without approval by the CEO. In recent years, the Disney Co. has shown up on some "best" board lists. In addition Eisner has recently relinquished the chairman position.

73. Talk show, 2002, *BusinessWeek,* September 30: 14.

74. Ward, R. D., 2000, *Improving Corporate Boards* (New York: Wiley).

75. A discussion on the shareholder approval process in executive compensation is presented in: Brandes, P., Goranova, M., & Hall, S., 2008, Navigating shareholder influence: Compensation plans and the shareholder approval process, *Academy of Management Perspectives,* 22(1): 41–57.

76. Monks and Minow, op. cit.: 93.

77. A discussion of the factors that lead to shareholder activism is found in Ryan, L. V. & Schneider, M., 2002, The antecedents of institutional investor activism, *Academy of Management Review,* 27(4): 554–73.

78. For an insightful discussion of investor activism, refer to David, P., Bloom, M., & Hillman, A., 2007, Investor activism, managerial responsiveness, and corporate social performance, *Strategic Management Journal,* 28(1): 91–100.

79. There is strong research support for the idea that the presence of large block shareholders is associated with value-maximizing decisions. For example, refer to Johnson, R. A., Hoskisson, R. E., & Hitt, M. A., 1993, Board of director involvement in restructuring: The effects of board versus managerial controls and characteristics, *Strategic Management Journal,* 14: 33–50.

80. For an interesting perspective on the impact of institutional ownership on a firm's innovation strategies, see Hoskisson, R. E., Hitt, M. A., Johnson, R. A., & Grossman, W., 2002, *Academy of Management Journal,* 45(4): 697–716.

81. For a study of the relationship between ownership and diversification, refer to Goranova, M., Alessandri, T. M., Brandes, P., & Dharwadkar, R., 2007, Managerial ownership and corporate diversification: A longitudinal view, *Strategic Management Journal,* 28(3): 211–26.

82. Jensen, M. C. & Murphy, K. J., 1990, CEO incentives—It's not how much you pay, but how, *Harvard Business Review* 68(3): 138–49.

83. For a perspective on the relative advantages and disadvantages of "duality"—that is, one individual serving as both Chief Executive Office and Chairman of the Board, see Lorsch, J. W. & Zelleke, A., 2005, Should the CEO be the chairman?, *MIT Sloan Management Review,* 46(2): 71–4.

84. A discussion of knowledge sharing is addressed in: Fey, C. F. & Furu, P., 2008, Top management incentive compensation and knowledge sharing in multinational corporations. *Strategic Management Journal,* 29(12): 1301–24.

85. http://www.huffingtonpost.ca/2016/09/16/canadian-ceo-pay-average-worker_n_12051316.html.

86. Byrnes, N. & Sasseen, J., 2007, Board of hard knocks, *BusinessWeek,* January 22: 36–39.

87. A perspective on whether or not CEOs are overpaid is provided in: Kaplan, S. N., 2008, Are U.S. CEOs overpaid: A response to Bogle and Walsh, J. P. *Academy of Management Perspectives,* 22(3): 28–34.

88. www.tiaa-cref.org/pubs.

89. Some insights on CEO compensation—and the importance of ethics—are addressed in: Heineman, B. W., Jr., 2008, The fatal flaw in pay for performance, *Harvard Business Review,* 86(6): 31, 34.

90. Chahine, S. & Tohme, N. S., 2009, Is CEO duality always negative? An exploration of CEO duality and ownership structure in the Arab IPO context, *Corporate Governance: An International Review,* 17(2): 123–141; and McGrath, J., 2009, How CEOs work. *HowStuffWorks.com.* January 28: n.p.

91. Tuggle, C. S., Sirmon, D. G., Reutzel, C. R. & Bierman, L., 2010, Commanding board of director attention: Investigating how organizational performance and CEO duality affect board members' attention to monitoring, *Strategic Management Journal,* 31: 946–968; Weinberg, N., 2010, No more lapdogs, *Forbes,* May 10: 34–36; and Anonymous, 2010, Corporate constitutions, *The Economist,* October 30: 74.

92. Weitzner, D. & Peridis, T., 2011, *Corporate Governance as Part of the Strategic Process: Rethinking the Role of the Board, Journal of Business Ethics,* 102: 33–42.

93. Such opportunistic behaviour is common in all principal–agent relationships. For a description of agency problems, especially in the context of the relationship between shareholders and

managers, see Jensen, M. C. & Meckling, W. H., 1976, Theory of the firm: Managerial behavior, agency costs, and ownership structure, *Journal of Financial Economics*, 3: 305–60.

94. Hoskisson, R. E. & Turk, T. A., 1990, Corporate restructuring: Governance and control limits of the internal market, *Academy of Management Review*, 15: 459–77.

95. For an insightful perspective on the market for corporate control and how it is influenced by knowledge intensity, see Coff, R., 2003, Bidding wars over R&D-intensive firms: Knowledge, opportunism, and the market for corporate control, *Academy of Management Journal*, 46(1): 74–85.

96. Walsh, J. P. & Kosnik, R. D., 1993, Corporate raiders and their disciplinary role in the market for corporate control, *Academy of Management Journal*, 36: 671–700.

97. Gunning for KPMG, 2003, *Economist*, February 1: 63.

98. Timmons, H., 2003, Investment banks: Who will foot their bill?, *BusinessWeek*, March 3: 116.

99. The role of regulatory bodies in the banking industry is addressed in: Bhide, A., 2009, Why bankers got so reckless, *BusinessWeek*, February 9: 30–1.

100. Wishy-washy: The SEC pulls its punches on corporate-governance rules, 2003, *Economist*, February 1: 60.

101. Lavelle, L, & McNamee, M., 2002, Will overseas boards play by America's rules?, *BusinessWeek*, December 16: 35; and Kemp, S., 2002, U.S. laws to hinder SA companies, *CFO web*, November.

102. McLean, B., 2001, Is Enron overpriced?, *Fortune*, March 5: 122–5.

103. Bernstein, A., 2000, Too much corporate power, *BusinessWeek*, September 11: 35–7.

104. This section draws upon Young, M. N., Peng, M. W., Ahlstrom, D., Bruton, G. D., & Jiang, Y., 2005, Principal–principal conflicts in corporate governance (unpublished manuscript); and, Peng, M. W., 2006, *Global strategy* (Cincinnati: Thomson South-Western). We are very appreciative of the helpful comments of Mike Young of Hong Kong Baptist University and Mike Peng of the University of Texas at Dallas.

105. DeCloet, D., 2008, The cost of playing back up to Stronach, *The Globe and Mail*, August 12: B1.

106. Khanna, T. & Rivkin, J. 2001. Estimating the performance effects of business groups in emerging markets. *Strategic Management Journal*, 22: 45–74.

Chapter 11

1. This case draws on 2017, The rise and fall of Valeant Pharmaceuticals, *CBC*, Mar 14:1; 2017, Valeant shareholders pressure company at annual meeting, *CBC*, May 2: 1; Bloomfield, D., 2017, Valeant Pharmaceuticals International Inc. tumbles to $9.52 today for first time since 2009, two years ago it peaked at $262.52 a share, *Financial Post*, Apr 5:1; Gara, A., 2016, Two Are Charged in Fraud and Kickback Scheme Against Valeant Pharmaceuticals, *Forbes*, Nov 17:1; Neate, R., 2016, Valeant CEO resigns over drug company's 'improper' financial conduct, *The Guardian*, Mar 21:1; Surowiecki, J., 2016, Inside the Valeant Scandal: The Roll-Up Racket, *The New Yorker*, Apr 4:1.

2. Rowe, W. G., 2001, Creating wealth in organizations: The role of strategic leadership, *Academy of Management Executive*, 15(1): 81–94.

3. D'Aveni, R., 1994, *Hyper competition* (New York: Free Press).

4. Charan, R. & Colvin, G., 1999, Why CEOs fail, *Fortune*, June 21: 68–78; Yukl, G., 2008, How leaders influence organizational effectiveness, *Leadership Quarterly*, 19(6): 708–722.

5. These three activities and our discussion draw from Kotter, J. P., 1990, What leaders really do, *Harvard Business Review*, 68(3): 103–11; Pearson, A. E., 1990, Six basics for general managers, *Harvard Business Review*, 67(4): 94–101; and Covey, S. R., 1996, Three roles of the leader in the new paradigm, in *The Leader of the Future*, Hesselbein, F., Goldsmith, M., & Beckhard, R. (Eds.). (San Francisco: Jossey-Bass), pp. 149–160. Some of the discussion of each of the three leadership activity concepts draws on Dess, G. G. & Miller, A., 1993, *Strategic Management* (New York: McGraw-Hill), pp. 320–325.

6. Garcí a-Morales, V. J., Lloré ns-Montes, F. J., & Verdú -Jover, A. J., 2008, The effects of transformational leadership on organizational performance through knowledge and innovation, *British Journal of Management*, 19(4): 299–319.

7. Day, C., Jr. & LaBarre, P., 1994, GE: Just your average everyday $60 billion family grocery store, *Industry Week*, May 2: 13–8.

8. The best (& worst) managers of the year, 2003, *BusinessWeek*, January 13: 63.

9. Nuttall-Smith, C., &York, G., 2007, Orange China, Report on Business, March: 24-www.homedepot.com; Flavelle, D., 2006, I've won the lottery, says Home Depot's Vershuren, *Toronto Star*, December 14: C1.

10. Collins, J., 1997, What comes next?, *Inc. Magazine*, October: 34–45.

11. Face value: Lord of the rings, 2005, *The Economist*, February 5: 61.

12. Anonymous, 2006, Looking out for number one, *BusinessWeek*, October 30: 66.

13. Evans, R., 2007, The either/or dilemma, www.ft.com, December 19; and Martin, R. L., 2007, *The Opposable Mind* (Boston: Harvard Business School Press).

14. For insightful perspectives on escalation, refer to Brockner, J., 1992, The escalation of commitment to a failing course of action, *Academy of Management Review*, 17(1): 39–61; and Staw, B. M., 1976, Knee-deep in the big muddy: A study of commitment to a chosen course of action, *Organizational Behavior and Human Decision Processes*, 16: 27–44. The discussion of systemic, behavioural, and political barriers draws on Lorange, P. & Murphy, D., 1984, Considerations in implementing strategic control, *Journal of Business Strategy* 5: 27–35. In a similar vein, Noel M. Tichy has addressed three types of resistance to change in the context of General Electric: technical resistance, political resistance, and cultural resistance. See Tichy, N. M., 1993, Revolutionalize your company, *Fortune*, December 13: 114–8. Examples draw from O'Reilly, B., 1997, The secrets of America's most admired corporations: Newideas and new products, *Fortune*, March 3: 60–4.

15. This section draws on Champoux, J. E., 2000, *Organizational Behavior: Essential Tenets for a New Millennium* (London: South-Western); and The mature use of power in organizations, 2003, RHR International-Executive Insights, May 29, 12.19.168.197/execinsights/8-3%. htm.

16. An insightful perspective on the role of power and politics in organizations is provided in Ciampa, K., 2005, Almost ready: How leaders move up, *Harvard Business Review*, 83(1): 46–53.

17. A discussion of the importance of persuasion in bringing about change can be found in Garvin, D. A. & Roberto, M. A., 2005, Change through persuasion, *Harvard Business Review*, 83(4): 104–13.

18. Some consider EI to be a "trait," that is, an attribute that is stable over time. However, many authors, including Daniel Goleman, have argued that it can be developed through motivation, extended practice, and feedback. For example, in D. Goleman, 1998, What makes a leader?, *Harvard Business Review*, 76 (5): 97, Goleman addresses this issue in a sidebar: "Can emotional intelligence be learned?"

19. For a review of this literature, see Daft, R., 1999, *Leadership: Theory and Practice* (Fort Worth, TX: Dryden Press).

20. This section draws on Luthans, F., 2002, Positive organizational behavior: Developing and managing psychological strengths, *Academy of Management Executive,* 16(1): 57–72; and Goleman, D., 1998, What makes a leader?, *Harvard Business Review,* 76(6): 92–105.

21. EI has its roots in the concept of "social intelligence" that was first identified by E. L. Thorndike in 1920 (Intelligence and its uses. *Harper's Magazine,* 140: 227–35). Psychologists have been uncovering other intelligences for some time now and have grouped them into such clusters as abstract intelligence (the ability to understand and manipulate verbal and mathematical symbols), concrete intelligence (the ability to understand and manipulate objects), and social intelligence (the ability to understand and relate to people). See Ruisel, I., 1992, Social intelligence: Conception and methodological problems, *Studia Psychologica,* 34(4–5): 281–96. Refer to trochim.human.cornell.edu/gallery.

22. See, for example, Luthans, op. cit.; Mayer, J. D., Salvoney, P., & Caruso, D., 2000, Models of emotional intelligence, in Sternberg, R. J. (Ed.), *Handbook of Intelligence* (Cambridge, UK: Cambridge University Press); and Cameron, K., 1999, Developing emotional intelligence at the Weatherhead School of Management, Strategy, *The Magazine of the Weatherhead School of Management,* Winter: 2–3.

23. Tate, B., 2008, A longitudinal study of the relationships among self-monitoring, authentic leadership, and perceptions of leadership, *Journal of Leadership & Organizational Studies,* 15(1): 16–29.

24. Moss, S. A., Dowling, N., & Callanan, J., 2009, Towards an integrated model of leadership and self-regulation, *Leadership Quarterly,* 20(2): 162–76.

25. An insightful perspective on leadership, which involves discovering, developing and celebrating what is unique about each individual, is found in Buckingham, M., 2005, What great managers do, *Harvard Business Review,* 83(3): 70–9.

26. This section draws upon Klemp. G., 2005, Emotional intelligence and leadership: What really matters, Cambria Consulting, Inc., www.cambriaconsulting.com.

27. Heifetz, R., 2004, Question authority, *Harvard Business Review,* 82(1): 37.

28. Senge, P. M., 1990, The leader's new work: Building learning organizations, *Sloan Management Review,* 32(1): 7–23.

29. Hammer, M. & Stanton, S. A., 1997, The power of reflection, *Fortune,* November 24: 291–6.

30. Hannah, S. T. & Lester, P. B., 2009, A multilevel approach to building and leading learning organizations, *Leadership Quarterly,* 20(1): 34–48.

31. For some guidance on how to effectively bring about change in organizations, refer to Wall, S. J., 2005, The protean organization: Learning to love change, *Organizational Dynamics,* 34(1): 37–46.

32. Covey, S. R., 1989, *The Seven Habits of Highly Effective People: Powerful Lessons in Personal Change* (New York: Simon & Schuster).

33. Kouzes, J. M. & Posner, B. Z., 2009, To lead, create a shared vision, *Harvard Business Review,* 87(1): 20–21.

34. Kouzes and Posner, op. cit.

35. Melrose, K., 1995, *Making the grass greener on your side: A CEO's journey to leading by servicing* (San Francisco: Barrett-Koehler).

36. Tekleab, A. G., Sims, H. P., Jr., Yun, S., Tesluk, P. E., & Cox, J., 2008, Are we on the same page? Effects of self-awareness of empowering and transformational leadership. *Journal of Leadership & Organizational Studies,* 14(3): 185–201.

37. Quinn, R. C. & Spreitzer, G. M., 1997, The road to empowerment: Seven questions every leader should consider, *Organizational Dynamics,* 25: 37–49.

38. For an interesting perspective on top-down approaches to leadership, see Pellegrini, E. K. & Scandura, T. A., 2008, Paternalistic leadership: A review and agenda for future research, *Journal of Management,* 34 (3): 566–93.

39. Helgesen, S., 1996, Leading from the grass roots, in Hesselbein et al., *Leader of the Future* (San Francisco: Jossey Bass), pp. 19–24.

40. Gurdjian, P. & Halbeisen, T. 2014. Why leadership-development programs fail. mckinsey.com, January: np

41. Bowen, D. E. & Lawler, E. E., III, 1995, Empowering service employees, *Sloan Management Review,* 37: 73–84.

42. Easterby-Smith, M. & Prieto, I. M., 2008, Dynamic capabilities and knowledge management: An integrative role for learning?, *British Journal of Management,* 19(3): 235–49.

43. Schafer, S., 1997, Battling a labor shortage? It's all in your imagination, *Inc. Magazine,* August: 24.

44. Meyer, P., 1998, So you want the president's job. . . , *Business Horizons,* January–February: 2–8.

45. Novicki, C., 1998, The best brains in business, *Fast Company,* April: 125.

46. The introductory discussion of benchmarking draws on Miller, A., 1998, *Strategic Management* (New York: McGraw-Hill), pp. 142–3.

47. Port, O. & Smith, G., 1992, Beg, borrow—and benchmark, *BusinessWeek,* November 30: 74–5.

48. Main, J., 1992, How to steal the best ideas around, *Fortune,* October 19: 102–6.

49. Taylor, J. T., 1997, What happens after what comes next?, *Fast Company,* December–January: 84–5.

50. Sheff, D., 1996, Levi's changes everything, *Fast Company,* June–July: 65–74.

51. Isaacson, W., 1997, In search of the real Bill Gates, *Time,* January 13: 44–57.

52. Baatz, E. B., 1993, Motorola's secret weapon, *Electronic Business,* April: 51–3.

53. Holt, J. W., 1996, *Celebrate Your Mistakes* (New York: McGraw-Hill).

54. This opening discussion draws upon Conley, J. H., 2000, Ethics in business, in Helms, M. M. (Ed.). *Encyclopedia of Management,* 4th ed. (Farmington Hills, MI: Gale Group), pp. 281–5; Paine, L. S., 1994, Managing for organizational integrity, *Harvard Business Review* 72(2): 106–117; and Carlson, D. S. & Perrewe, P. L., 1995, Institutionalization of organizational ethics through transformational leadership, *Journal of Business Ethics,* 14: 829–38.

55. The discussion on CSR draws on Porter, M.E. & Kramer M.R., 2006, Strategy and society: the link between competitive advantage and corporate social responsibility, *Harvard Business Review,* December, 84: 78–92; and Porter, M.E., & Kramer, M.R., 2011, The big idea: Creating shared value. *Harvard Business Review,* February: 89.

56. The discussion in this section is based on Weitzner, D. & Darroch, J., 2010, The limits of strategic rationality: Ethics, enterprise risk management and governance, *Journal of Business Ethics,* 92: 361–372.

57. Pinto, J., Leana, C. R., & Pil, F. K., 2008, Corrupt organizations or organizations of corrupt individuals? Two types of organization-level corruption. *Academy of Management Review,* 33(3): 685–709.

58. Soule, E. 2002, Managerial moral strategies—in search of a few good principles, *Academy of Management Review,* 27(1): 114–24.

59. Carlson & Perrewe, op. cit.

60. Willness, C., 2010, Three reasons why job seekers find your organization's CSR attractive, *The National Post,* October 30: FP6.

61. This discussion is based on Paine: Managing for organizational integrity; Paine, L. S., 1997, *Cases in leadership, ethics, and*

organizational integrity: A Strategic approach (Burr Ridge, IL: Irwin); and Fontrodona, J., 2002, Business ethics across the Atlantic. Business Ethics Direct, www.ethicsa.org/BED_art_fontrodone.html.

62. For more on operationalizing capabilities to sustain an ethical framework, see Largay, III, J. A. & Zhang, R. 2008, Do CEOs worry about being fired when making investment decisions, *Academy of Management Perspectives,* 22(1): 60–1.

63. Wetlaufer, S., 1999, Organizing for empowerment: An interview with AES's Roger Sant and Dennis Bakke. *Harvard Business Review* 77(1): 110–26.

64. For an insightful, academic perspective on the impact of ethics codes on executive decision making, refer to Stevens, J. M., Steensma, H. K., Harrison, D. A., & Cochran, P. S., 2005, Symbolic or substantive document? The influence of ethics code on financial executives' decisions, *Strategic Management Journal,* 26(2): 181–95.

65. For a recent study on the effects of goal setting on unethical behaviour, read Schweitzer, M. E., Ordonez, L., & Douma, B., 2004, Goal setting as a motivator of unethical behavior, *Academy of Management Journal,* 47(3): 422–32.

66. Fulmer, R. M., 2004, The challenge of ethical leadership, *Organizational Dynamics,* 33(3): 307–17.

67. McClearn, M., 2004, A snitch in time, *Canadian Business,* January: 61 and Bogomolny, L, 2004, Good housekeeping, *Canadian Business,* March 1: 87.

Chapter 12

1. This case draws on Crosariol, B., 2016, The Okanagan's JoieFarm incorporates all that is great about wine from British Columbia, The Globe and Mail, May 24; McLennan, N., 2014, Inside JoieFarm's Rustic Modern Winery Home in Naramata, Western Living Magazine May 30 as well as first-person interviews with Heidi Noble.

2. For an interesting discussion, see Johannessen, J. A., Olsen, B., & Lumpkin, G. T., 2001, Innovation as newness: What is new, how new, and new to whom?, *European Journal of Innovation Management,* 4 (1): 20–31.

3. The discussion of product and process innovation is based on Roberts, E. B. (Ed.), 2002, *Innovation: Driving product, process, and market change* (San Francisco: Jossey-Bass); Hayes, R. & Wheelwright, S., 1985, Competing through manufacturing, *Harvard Business Review,* 63(1): 99–109; and Hayes, R. & Wheelwright, S., 1979, Dynamics of product–process life cycles, *Harvard Business Review,* 57(2): 127–36.

4. The discussion of radical and incremental innovations draws from Leifer, R., McDermott, C. M., Colarelli, G., O'Connor, G. C., Peters, L. S., Rice, M. P., & Veryzer, R. W., 2000, *Radical Innovation: How Mature Companies Can Outsmart Upstarts* (Boston: Harvard Business School Press); Damanpour, F., 1996, Organizational complexity and innovation: Developing and testing multiple contingency models, *Management Science* 42(5): 693–716; and Hage, J., 1980, *Theories of Organizations* (New York: Wiley).

5. Christensen, C. M. & Raynor, M. E., 2003, *The Innovator's Solution* (Boston: Harvard Business School Press).

6. Dressner, H., 2004, The Gartner Fellows interview: Clayton M. Christensen, www.gartner.com, April 26.

7. Christensen et al., op. cit.; and www.wikipedia.org.

8. For another perspective on how different types of innovation affect organizational choices, see Wolter, C. & Veloso, F. M., 2008, The effects of innovation on vertical structure: Perspectives on transactions costs and competences, *Academy of Management Review,* 33(3): 586–605.

9. Drucker, P. F., 1985, *Innovation and Entrepreneurship: 2000* (New York: Harper & Row).

10. Birkinshaw, J., Hamel, G., & Mol, M. J., 2008, Management innovation, *Academy of Management Review,* 33(4): 825–45.

11. Morrissey, C. A., 2000, Managing innovation through corporate venturing, *Graziadio Business Report,* Spring, gbr.pepperdine.edu; and Sharma, A., 1999, Central dilemmas of managing innovation in large firms, *California Management Review,* 41(3): 147–64.

12. Sharma, op. cit.

13. Dyer, J. H., Gregerson, H. B., & Christensen, C. M. 2009. The innovator's DNA. *Harvard Business Review,* 13: 61–67.

14. Eggers, J. P., & Kaplan, S. 2009. Cognition and renewal: Comparing CEO and organizational effects on incumbent adaptation to technical change. *Organization Science,* 20: 461–477.

15. Canabou, C., 2003, Fast ideas for slow times, *Fast Company,* May: 52.

16. Biodegradable Products Institute, 2003, "Compostable Logo" of the Biodegradable Products Institute gains momentum with approval of DuPont™ Biomax® resin, www.bpiworld.org, June 12; Leifer et al., op. cit.

17. For more on defining the scope of innovation, see Valikangas, L. & Gibbert, M., 2005, Boundary–setting strategies for escaping innovation traps, *MIT Sloan Management Review,* 46(3): 58–65.

18. Leifer et al., op. cit.

19. Bhide, A. V., 2000, *The Origin and Evolution of New Businesses* (New York: Oxford University Press); Brown, S. L. & Eisenhardt, K. M., 1998, *Competing on the Edge: Strategy as Structured Chaos* (Cambridge, MA: Harvard Business School Press).

20. Caulfield, B. 2003. Why techies don't get Six Sigma. *Business 2.0,* June: 90.

21. McGrath, R. G. & Keil, T. 2007. The value captor's process: Getting the most out of your new business ventures. *Harvard Business Review,* May: 128–36.

22. For an interesting discussion of how sharing technology knowledge with different divisions in an organization can contribute to innovation processes, see Miller, D. J., Fern, M. J., & Cardinal, L. B., 2007, The use of knowledge for technological innovation within diversified firms, *Academy of Management Journal,* 50(2): 308–26.

23. Ketchen, D. J., Jr., Ireland, R. D., & Snow, C. C., 2007, Strategic entrepreneurship, collaborative innovation, and wealth creation, *Strategic Entrepreneurship Journal,* 1(3–4): 371–85.

24. Chesbrough, H., 2003, *Open Innovation: The New Imperative for Creating and Profiting from Technology* (Boston: Harvard Business School Press).

25. For a recent study of what makes alliance partnerships successful, see Sampson, R. C., 2007, R&D alliances and firm performance: The impact of technological diversity and alliance organization on innovation, *Academy of Management Journal,* 50(2): 364–86.

26. For an interesting perspective on the role of collaboration among multinational corporations see Hansen, M. T. & Nohria, N., 2004, How to build collaborative advantage, *MIT Sloan Management Review,* 46(1): 22–30.

27. Wells, R. M. J., 2008, The product innovation process: Are managing information flows and cross-functional collaboration key?, *Academy of Management Perspectives,* 22(1): 58–60.

28. Eggers, J. P. 2014. Get ahead by betting wrong. Harvard Business Review, 92(7/8): 26; and Lepore, J. 2014. The disruption machine. newyorker.com, June 23: np.

29. Guth, W. D. & Ginsberg, A., 1990, Guest editor's introduction: Corporate entrepreneurship, *Strategic Management Journal,* 11: 5–15.

30. Pinchot, G. 1985. *Intrapreneuring* (New York: Harper & Row).

31. For an interesting perspective on the role of context on the discovery and creation of opportunities, see Zahra, S. A., 2008, The virtuous cycle of discovery and creation of entrepreneurial opportunities, *Strategic Entrepreneurship Journal,* 2(3): 243–57.

32. For more on how entrepreneurial orientation influences organizational performance, see Wang, L., 2008, Entrepreneurial orientation, learning orientation, and firm performance, *Entrepreneurship Theory & Practice* 32(4): 635–57; and Runyan, R., Droge, C., & Swinney, J., 2008, Entrepreneurial orientation versus small business orientation: What are their relationships to firm performance?, *Journal of Small Business Management,* 46(4): 567–88.

33. Covin, J. G. & Slevin, D. P., 1991, A conceptual model of entrepreneurship as firm behaviour, *Entrepreneurship Theory and Practice,* 16(1): 7–24; Lumpkin, G. T. & Dess, G. G., 1996, Clarifying the entrepreneurial orientation construct and linking it to performance, *Academy of Management Review,* 21 (1): 135–72; and McGrath, R. G. & MacMillan, I. C., 2000, *The Entrepreneurial Mindset* (Cambridge, MA: Harvard Business School Press).

34. Lumpkin, G. T. & Dess, G. G., 2001, Linking two dimensions of entrepreneurial orientation to firm performance: The moderating role of environment and life cycle, *Journal of Business Venturing,* 16: 429–51.

35. For an interesting discussion, see Day, J. D., Mang, P. Y., Richter, A., & Roberts, J., 2001, The innovative organization: Why new ventures need more than a room of their own, *McKinsey Quarterly,* 2: 21–31.

36. Crockett, R. O., 2001, Chris Galvin shakes things up—again, *BusinessWeek,* May 28: 38–9.

37. For insights into the role of information technology in innovativeness, see Dibrell, C., Davis, P. S., & Craig, J., 2008, Fueling innovation through information technology in SMEs, *Journal of Small Business Management,* 46(2): 203–18.

38. Lieberman, M. B. & Montgomery, D. B., 1988, First mover advantages, *Strategic Management Journal,* 9 (Special Issue): 41–58.

39. The discussion of first mover advantages is based on several articles, including Lambkin, M., 1988, Order of entry and performance in new markets, *Strategic Management Journal* 9: 127–40; Lieberman & Montgomery, op. cit.: 41–58; and Miller, A. & Camp, B., 1985, Exploring determinants of success in corporate ventures, *Journal of Business Venturing,* 1(2): 87–105.

40. Moore, G. A., 1999, *Crossing the Chasm,* 2nd ed. (New York: HarperBusiness).

41. Miller, K. D., 2007, Risk and rationality in entrepreneurial processes, *Strategic Entrepreneurship Journal,* 1(1–2): 57–74.

42. Drucker, op. cit., pp. 109–10.

43. .*Report on Trade* (Toronto, ON: Canadian Federation of Independent Business, 2004); and The importance of small business in Canada, Industry Canada, http://strategis.ic.gc.ca.

44. Timmons, J. A., & Spinelli, S., 2004, *New Venture Creation,* 6th ed. (Burr Ridge, IL: McGraw-Hill/Irwin); and Bygrave, W. D., 1997, The entrepreneurial process, in W. D. Bygrave, ed., *The Portable MBA in Entrepreneurship,* 2nd ed. (New York: Wiley), 1–26.

45. Fromartz, S., 1998, How to get your first great idea, *Inc. Magazine,* April 1: 91–4; and Vesper, K. H., 1990, *New Venture Strategies,* 2nd ed. (Englewood Cliffs, NJ: Prentice Hall).

46. Hamilton, T., 2006, Greening the machine, *Toronto Star,* August 21: D1; www.enwave.com; www.toronto.ca/ewmo.

47. www.casketxpress.com.

48. For an interesting perspective on the nature of the opportunity recognition process, see Baron, R. A. 2006, Opportunity recognition as pattern recognition: How entrepreneurs 'connect the dots' to identify new business opportunities, *Academy of Management Perspectives,* February: 104–19.

49. Gaglio, C. M., 1997, Opportunity identification: Review, critique and suggested research directions, in J. A. Katz, ed., *Advances in Entrepreneurship, Firm Emergence and Growth,* vol. 3 (Greenwich, CT: JAI Press), 139–202; Hills, G. E., Shrader, R. C., & Lumpkin, G. T., 1999, Opportunity recognition as a creative process, in *Frontiers of Entrepreneurship Research, 1999.* (Wellesley, MA: Babson College), 216–27; and Long, W., & McMullan, W. E., 1984, Mapping the new venture opportunity identification process, in *Frontiers of Entrepreneurship Research,1984* (Wellesley, MA: Babson College), 567–90.

50. Stewart, T. A., 2002, How to think with your gut, *Business 2.0,* November: 99–104.

51. Timmons, J. A., 1997, Opportunity recognition, in W. D. Bygrave, ed., *The Portable MBA in Entrepreneurship,* 2nd ed. (New York: Wiley), 26–54.

52. Stinchcombe, A. L., 1965, Social structure in organizations, in J. G. March, ed., *Handbook of Organizations* (Chicago: Rand McNally), 142–93.

53. Bhide, A. V., 2000, *The Origin and Evolution of New Businesses* (New York: Oxford University Press).

54. Small business 2001: Where are we now? 2001, *Inc. Magazine,* May 29: 18–19; and Zacharakis, A. L., Bygrave, W. D., & Shepherd, D. A., 2000, *Global Entrepreneurship Monitor— National Entrepreneurship Assessment: United States of America 2000 Executive Report* (Kansas City, MO: Kauffman Center for Entrepreneurial Leadership).

55. Cooper, S., 2003, Cash cows, *Entrepreneur,* June: 36.

56. Seglin, J. L., 1998, What angels want, *Inc. Magazine,* 20(7): 43–4.

57. Torres, N. L., 2002, Playing an angel, *Entrepreneur,* May: 130–38.

58. For more on how different forms of organizing entrepreneurial firms as well as different stages of new firm growth and development affect financing, see Cassar, G., 2004, The financing of business start-ups. *Journal of Business Venturing,* 19(2): 261–83.

59. Eisenhardt, K. M. & Schoonhoven, C. B., 1990, Organizational growth: Linking founding team, strategy, environment, and growth among U.S. semiconductor ventures, 1978–1988, *Administrative Science Quarterly,* 35: 504–29.

60. Dubini, P. & Aldrich, H., 1991, Personal and extended networks are central to the entrepreneurship process, *Journal of Business Venturing* 6(5): 305–33.

61. For more on the role of social contacts in helping young firms build legitimacy, see Chrisman, J. J., & McMullan, W. E., 2004, Outside assistance as a knowledge resource for new venture survival, *Journal of Small Business Management,* 42(3): 229–44.

62. Vogel, C., 2000, Janina Pawlowski, *Working Woman,* June: 70.

63. For a recent perspective on entrepreneurship and strategic alliances, see Rothaermel, F. T., & Deeds, D. L., 2006, Alliance types, alliance experience and alliance management capability in high-technology ventures, *Journal of Business Venturing* 21(4): 429–60; and Lu, J. W., & Beamish, P. W., 2006, Partnering strategies and performance of SMEs' international joint ventures *Journal of Business Venturing,* 21(4): 461–86.

64. Peridis, T., 1992, Strategic alliances for smaller firms, *Research in Global Strategic Management,* JAI Press, Vol 3, pp. 129–142; Misner, I., 2008, Use small actions to get big results, *Entrepreneur,* www.entrepreneur.com, December 3.

65. For more information, go to the Canada Business Service Centres website at www.bsa.cbsc.org.

66. Simsek, Z., Heavey, C., & Veiga, J. 2009. The impact of CEO core self-evaluation on entrepreneurial orientation. Strategic Management Journal, 31: 110–119.

67. Zhao, H. & Seibert, S. 2006. The big five personality dimensions and entrepreneurial status: A meta-analytic review. Journal of Applied Psychology, 91: 259–271.

68. Collins, J., 2001, *Good to Great* (New York: Harper-Collins).

69. Collins, op. cit.

70. The idea of entry wedges was discussed by Vesper, K., 1990, *New Venture Strategies,* 2nd ed. (Englewood Cliffs, NJ: Prentice-Hall); and Drucker, P. F., 1985, *Innovation and Entrepreneurship* (New York: Harper-Business).

71. See Dowell, G., & Swaminathan, A., 2006, Entry timing, exploration, and firm survival in the early U.S. bicycle industry, *Strategic Management Journal,* 27: 1159–82, for a recent study of the timing of entrepreneurial new entry.

72. Maiello, M., 2002, They almost changed the world, *Forbes,* December 22: 217–20.

73. More on the role of imitation strategies is addressed in a recent article: Lieberman, M. B., & Asaba, S., 2006, Why do firms imitate each other?, *Academy of Management Review,* 31(2): 366–85.

74. Williams, G., 2002, Looks like rain, *Entrepreneur,* September 104–11.

75. Asmus, P., 2005, 100 best corporate citizens for 2005, *Business Ethics,* www.business-ethics.com.

76. Pedroza, G. M., 2002, Tech tutors, *Entrepreneur,* September: 120.

77. Barret, A., 2003, Hot growth companies, *BusinessWeek,* June 9: 74–77.

78. Dennis, W. J., Jr., 2000, *NFIB Small Business Policy Guide* (Washington, DC: National Federation of Independent Business); *The State of Small Business: A Report of the President, 1992.* (Washington, DC: U.S. Government Printing Office), 65–90.

79. Romanelli, E., 1989, Environments and strategies of organization start-up: Effects on early survival. *Administrative Science Quarterly,* 34(3): 369–87.

80. Lorinc, J., 2004, The niche play, *Report on (Small) Business,* Fall: 28–33.

81. Shaw, H., 2008, Diner eats into breakfast market. *National Post,* June 16: FP4.

Appendix

1. The material in this appendix is based on several sources, including Barnes, L. A., Nelson, A. J., & Christensen, C. R., 1994, *Teaching and the Case Method: Text, Cases, and Readings* (Boston: Harvard Business School Press); Guth, W. D., 1985, Central concepts of business unit and corporate strategy, in W. D., Guth, ed., *Handbook of Business Strategy* (Boston: Warren, Gorham & Lamont), 1–9; Lundberg, C. C., & Enz, C., 1993, A framework for student case preparation, *Case Research Journal* 13 (Summer): 129–140; and Ronstadt, R., 1980, *The Art of Case Analysis: A Guide to the Diagnosis of Business Situations* (Dover, MA: Lord Publishing).

2. Edge, A. G., & Coleman, D. R., 1986, *The Guide to Case Analysis and Reporting,* 3rd ed. (Honolulu, HI: System Logistics).

3. Morris, E., 1987, Vision and strategy: A focus for the future, *Journal of Business Strategy* 8: 51–58.

4. This section is based on Lundberg & Enz, op. cit.; and Ronstadt, op. cit.

5. The importance of problem definition was emphasized in Mintzberg, H., Raisinghani, D., & Theoret, A., 1976, The structure of "unstructured" decision processes, Administrative Science Quarterly 21(2): 246–275.

6. Drucker, P. F., 1994, The theory of the business, *Harvard Business Review* 72(5): 95–104.

7. This section draws on Edge & Coleman, op. cit.

8. Irving Janis is credited with coining the term groupthink, and he applied it primarily to fiascos in government (such as the Bay of Pigs incident in 1961). Refer to Janis, I. L., 1982, *Victims of Groupthink,* 2nd ed. (Boston: Houghton Mifflin).

9. Much of our discussion is based on Finkelstein, S., & Mooney, A. C., 2003, Not the usual suspects: How to use board process to make boards better, *Academy of Management Journal* 17(2): 101–113; Schweiger, D. M., Sand-berg, W. R., & Rechner, P. L., 1989, Experiential effects of dialectical inquiry, devil's advocacy, and consensus approaches to strategic decision making, *Academy of Management Journal* 32(4): 745–772; and Aldag, R. J., & Stearns, T. M., 1987, *Management* (Cincinnati: South-Western Publishing).

10. Finkelstein and Mooney, op. cit.

INDEX